ACCA

Strategic Business Leader
Workbook

For exams in September 2020,
December 2020, March 2021
and June 2021

Third edition 2020

ISBN 9781 5097 8489 9
Internal 9781 5097 8289 5
Previous ISBN: 9781 5097 2344 7
e-ISBN 9781 5097 2877 0

British Library Cataloguing-in-Publication Data
A catalogue record for this book is available from the British Library

Published by

BPP Learning Media Ltd
BPP House, Aldine Place
142–144 Uxbridge Road
London W12 8AA

www.bpp.com/learningmedia

Printed in the United Kingdom

Your learning materials, published by BPP Learning Media Ltd, are printed on paper obtained from traceable sustainable sources.

We are grateful to the Association of Chartered Certified Accountants for permission to reproduce past examination questions and extracts from the syllabus. The suggested solutions in the practice answer bank have been prepared by BPP Learning Media Ltd, except where otherwise stated.

Contents

*Note. Sections marked with an asterisk are available in the digital eBook version of the Workbook, accessed via the Exam Success Site (see inside cover for details).

Helping you to pass

BPP Learning Media – ACCA Approved Content Provider

As an ACCA Approved Content Provider, BPP Learning Media gives you the opportunity to use study materials reviewed by the ACCA examining team. By incorporating the examining team's comments and suggestions regarding the depth and breadth of syllabus coverage, the BPP Learning Media Workbook provides excellent, ACCA-approved support for your studies.

These materials are reviewed by the ACCA examining team. The objective of the review is to ensure that the material properly covers the syllabus and study guide outcomes, used by the examining team in setting the exams, in the appropriate breadth and depth. The review does not ensure that every eventuality, combination or application of examinable topics is addressed by the ACCA Approved Content. Nor does the review comprise a detailed technical check of the content as the Approved Content Provider has its own quality assurance processes in place in this respect.

BPP Learning Media do everything possible to ensure the material is accurate and up to date when sending to print. In the event that any errors are found after the print date, they are uploaded to the following website: www.bpp.com/learningmedia/Errata.

The PER alert

Before you can qualify as an ACCA member, you not only have to pass all your exams but also fulfil a three-year practical experience requirement (PER). To help you to recognise areas of the syllabus that you might be able to apply in the workplace to achieve different performance objectives, we have introduced the 'PER alert' feature (see the next section). You will find this feature throughout the Workbook to remind you that what you are learning to pass your ACCA exams is equally useful to the fulfilment of the PER requirement. Your achievement of the PER should be recorded in your online My Experience record.

Chapter features

Studying can be a daunting prospect, particularly when you have lots of other commitments. This Workbook is full of useful features, explained in the key below, designed to help you to get the most out of your studies and maximise your chances of exam success.

Key to icons

Key term

Central concepts are highlighted and clearly defined in the Key terms feature. Key terms are also listed in bold in the Index, for quick and easy reference.

Key term

Formula to learn

This boxed feature will highlight important formulae which you need to be aware of in the lead up to your exam.

PER alert

This feature identifies when something you are reading will also be useful for your PER requirement (see 'The PER alert' section above for more details).

PER alert

Exam success skills

Exam success skills are the six key skill areas which BPP considers vital for success in the Strategic Business Leader exam.

ACCA Professional skills focus

The ACCA Professional skills focus on the five professional skills which will be assessed in the Strategic Business Leader exam.

Real world examples

These will give real examples to help demonstrate the concepts you are reading about.

Illustration

Illustrations walk through how to apply key knowledge and techniques step by step.

Activity

Activities give you essential practice of techniques covered in the chapter.

Exercise

Exercises suggest tasks which can be done to further your understanding.

Essential reading

Links to the Essential reading are given throughout the chapter. The Essential reading is included in the free eBook, accessed via the Exam Success Site (see inside cover for details on how to access this).

Knowledge diagnostic

Summary of the key learning points from the chapter.

 BPP LEARNING MEDIA

At the end of each chapter you will find a Further study guidance section. This contains suggestions for ways in which you can continue your learning and enhance your understanding. This can include: recommendations for question practice from the Further question practice and solutions, to test your understanding of the topics in the chapter; suggestions for further reading which can be done, such as technical articles and ideas for your own research.

Introduction to the Essential reading

The digital eBook version of the Workbook contains additional content, selected to enhance your studies. Consisting of revision materials, activities (including practice questions and solutions) and background reading, it is designed to aid your understanding of key topics which are covered in the main printed chapters of the Workbook.

To access the digital eBook version of the BPP Workbook, follow the instructions which can be found on the inside cover; you'll be able to access your eBook, plus download the BPP eBook mobile app on multiple devices, including smartphones and tablets.

A summary of the content of the Essential reading is given below.

Chapter		Summary of Essential reading content
1	Strategy, leadership and culture	• Leadership theories. This section explores in greater detail trait, behavioural, and contingency theories of leadership. • The role of culture. This section discusses the factors that influence organisational culture and introduces the organisational iceberg.
2	Stakeholders and social responsibility	• Agency problem. This section discusses the issues caused by the agency problem. • The emergence of ecosystems. This section discusses the emergence of ecosystem environments and how organisations interact with stakeholders. • Purpose and advantages of environmental reporting.
3	Impact of corporate governance on strategy	• Institutional investors. This section focuses on institutional investors and considers how they exercise their influence and how they might intervene in the affairs of a company.
4	The external environment	• Porter's Five Forces. This section provides more detailed coverage of the Five Forces model. • Market attractiveness. This section considers the factors a firm should consider before deciding whether to enter a market.
5	Strategic capability	• Managing strategic capability. This section focuses on how strategic capability can be improved. • Staff development. This section focuses on the role that staff development plays in relation to strategic capability. • Knowledge work. This section considers the increasing importance of knowledge in organisations, and introduces the 'knowledge worker' concept. • Data, information and knowledge. This section explores the key differences between the three terms. • TOWS Matrix. This section explores the use of the TOWS Matrix, which is a variant of a SWOT analysis.

Chapter		Summary of Essential reading content
6	Competitive advantage and strategic choice	• Conceptual difficulties with generic strategy. This section considers some of the main difficulties of applying generic strategies. • The seven Ps. This section provides greater coverage of the seven Ps framework.
7	Assessing and managing risk	• COSO's Enterprise Risk Management - Integrating with Strategy and Performance (2017). This section explores how five connected components can assist in managing risks across a whole enterprise. • Significant rapid changes in risk. This section considers the changes in risk that may affect an organisation.
8	Internal control systems	• Controls. This section considers the different types of control that may be used by organisations. • Reviewing internal control reports. This section outlines the types of information that the board need to consider to carry out an effective review of internal controls. • The internal audit team. This section explores the types of work that may be undertaken by the internal audit team.
9	Applying ethical principles	• Possible fraud risks. This section highlights a number of possible indicators of potential fraud. • Bribery and corruption. This section highlights why bribery and corruption can be particularly problematic for organisations. • Combating bribery and corruption. This section explores some of ways that organisations can look to address bribery and corruption.
10	Financial analysis	• Investment appraisal techniques. This section highlights the key features of the ROCE, payback period, NPV and IRR methods of investment appraisal. • Key financial ratios. This section should serve as a reminder of the key financial ratios that exist. • Variances. This section provides an overview of the types of variances that exist and outlines their meaning.
11	Applications of IT	• Computerised accounting process controls. This section explores the types of controls used by organisations when operating computerised accounting software.
12	E-business	• Benefits and risks of e-procurement. This section explores a number of benefits and risks associated with adopting e-procurement. • Ecosystems and digital business platforms. This section explores concepts of mutuality and orchestration in ecosystem environments, and also gives consideration to the role of digital business platforms.

Chapter		Summary of Essential reading content
13	Enabling success and strategic change	• Team-based and project-based structures. This section builds upon the discussion of matrix structures. • Collaborative working practices between organisations and their customers. This section introduces the concepts of crowdsourcing and user contribution systems. • Succession planning. This section focuses on the topic of succession planning which is closely linked to talent management. • Creating a digital workforce. This section focuses on the steps that an organisation can take to develop the skills of its workforce in the digital age.
14	Process redesign	• Business process re-engineering (BPR). This section explores the key features of BPR. • Lean production. This section explores the key features of lean production. Parallels exist between the principles of lean production and value-added analysis. • Workflow systems. This section explores the rise of workflow systems. • Process diagram. This section considers how the use of process diagrams can be used when undertaking process redesign.
15	Project management	• Building the business case. This section highlights the purpose of the business case and explores the key features. • Project benefits. This section provides greater coverage of the different types of project benefit that exist. • Critical path analysis (CPA). This section provides greater coverage of CPA. • Data visualisation. This section considers the important role that data visualisation plays in project work.

Introduction to Strategic Business Leader (SBL)

Overall aim of the syllabus

Strategic Business Leader is ACCA's case study examination. It requires students to demonstrate organisational leadership and senior consultancy or advisory capabilities and relevant professional skills, through the context of an integrated case study.

Brought forward knowledge

The Strategic Business Leader syllabus assumes knowledge acquired in the ACCA exam Accountant in Business, the Ethics and Professional Skills Module (EPSM), and the Applied Skills exams.

This knowledge is developed and applied in Strategic Business Leader and is therefore vitally important.

If it has been some time since you studied Accountant in Business or if you were exempted from the Accountant in Business exam as a result of having a relevant degree, then we recommend that you revise the following topics before you begin your SBL studies:

- Business organisations and their stakeholders
- The business environment
- Business organisation, structure and strategy
- Organisational culture and committees
- Corporate governance and social responsibility
- Control, security and audit
- Identifying and preventing fraud
- Leading and managing people
- Recruitment and selection
- Diversity and equal opportunities
- Individuals, groups and teams
- Motivating individuals and groups

The syllabus

The broad syllabus headings are:

A	Leadership
B	Governance
C	Strategy
D	Risk
E	Technology and data analytics
F	Organisational control and audit
G	Finance in planning and decision-making
H	Innovation, performance excellence and change management
I	Professional skills

Main capabilities

On successful completion of this exam, you should be able to:

A   Apply excellent leadership and ethical skills to set the 'tone from the top' and promote a positive culture within the organisation, adopting a whole organisation perspective in managing performance and value creation

B   Evaluate the effectiveness of the governance and agency system of an organisation and recognise the responsibility of the board or other agents towards their stakeholders, including the organisation's social responsibilities and the reporting implications

C   Evaluate the strategic position of the organisation against the external environment and the availability of internal resources, to identify feasible strategic options

D   Analyse the risk profile of the organisation and of any strategic options identified, within a culture of responsible risk management

E   Select and apply appropriate information technologies and data analytics, to analyse factors affecting the organisation's value chain to identify strategic opportunities and implement strategic options within a framework of robust IT security controls

F   Evaluate management reporting and internal control and audit systems to ensure compliance and the achievement of organisation's objectives and the safeguarding of organisational assets

G   Apply high level financial techniques from the Applied Skills exams in the planning, implementation and evaluation of strategic options and actions

H   Enable success through innovative thinking, applying best in class strategies and disruptive technologies in the management of change; initiating, leading and organising projects, while effectively managing talent and other business resources

I   Apply a range of Professional Skills in addressing requirements within the Strategic Business Leader examination and in preparation for, or to support, current work experience

Links with other exams

Achieving ACCA's Study Guide Learning Outcomes

This BPP Workbook covers all the SBL syllabus learning outcomes. The tables below show in which chapter(s) each area of the syllabus is covered.

A Leadership

A1	Qualities of leadership	**Chapter 1**
A2	Leadership and organisational culture	**Chapter 1**
A3	Professionalism, ethical codes and the public interest	**Chapter 9**

B Governance

B1	Agency	**Chapter 2**
B2	Stakeholder analysis and social responsibility	**Chapter 2**
B3	Governance scope and approaches	**Chapter 3**
B4	Reporting to stakeholders	**Chapter 2**
B5	The board of directors	**Chapter 3**
B6	Public sector governance	**Chapter 3**

C Strategy

C1	Concepts of strategy	**Chapter 1**
C2	Environmental issues	**Chapter 4**
C3	Competitive forces	**Chapters 4 and 5**
C4	The internal resources, capabilities and competences of an organisation	**Chapter 5**
C5	Strategic choices	**Chapter 6**

D Risk

D1	Identification, assessment and measurement of risk	**Chapter 7**
D2	Managing, monitoring and mitigating risk	**Chapter 7**

E Technology and data analytics

E1	Cloud and mobile technology	**Chapter 11**
E2	Big data and data analytics	**Chapter 11**
E3	E-business: value chain	**Chapter 12**
E4	IT systems security and control	**Chapter 11**

F   Organisational control and audit

F1	Management and internal control systems	**Chapter 8**
F2	Audit and compliance	**Chapter 8**
F3	Internal control and management reporting	**Chapter 8**

G   Finance in planning and decision-making

G1	Finance function	**Chapter 10**
G2	Financial analysis and decision-making techniques	**Chapter 10**
G3	Cost and management accounting	**Chapter 10**

H   Innovation, performance excellence and change management

H1	Enabling success: organising	**Chapter 13**
H2	Enabling success: disruptive technology	**Chapter 12**
H3	Enabling success: talent management	**Chapter 13**
H4	Enabling success: performance excellence	**Chapter 13**
H5	Managing strategic change	**Chapter 13**
H6	Managing Innovation and change management	**Chapter 14**
H7	Leading and managing projects	**Chapter 15**

I   Professional skills

I1	Communication	**Throughout the workbook**
I2	Commercial acumen	**Throughout the workbook**
I3	Analysis	**Throughout the workbook**
I4	Scepticism	**Throughout the workbook**
I5	Evaluation	**Throughout the workbook**

The complete syllabus and study guide can be found by visiting the exam resource finder on the ACCA website: www.accaglobal.com/gb/en.html.

The exam

Computer-based exams

With effect from the March 2020 sitting, ACCA have commenced the launch of computer-based exams (CBEs) for this exam with the aim of rolling out into all markets internationally over a short period. Paper-based examinations (PBE) will be run in parallel while the CBEs are phased in. BPP materials have been designed to support you, whichever exam option you choose. For more information on these changes, when they will be implemented and to access Specimen Exams in the Strategic Professional CBE software, please visit the ACCA website. Please note that the Strategic Professional CBE software has more functionality than you will have seen in the Applied Skills exams.

www.accaglobal.com/gb/en/student/exam-support-resources/strategic-professional-specimen-exams-cbe.html

Approach to examining the syllabus

Strategic Business Leader is ACCA's **case study examination** and is examined as a **closed book exam** of four hours, including reading, planning and reflection time which can be used flexibly within the examination. There is no pre-seen information and all exam-related materials, including case information, exhibits and questions, are available within the examination. The pass mark is **50%**.

Strategic Business Leader is an exam based on one main business scenario which involves candidates completing a **series of tasks** many of which will integrate syllabus areas in a single requirement.

All questions are compulsory and each examination will contain a total of **80 technical marks** and **20 professional skills** marks. Each exam will therefore assess both technical skills and the professional skills. Whilst marks will be awarded for the relevant technical points that candidates make, up to 20% of the total marks within each exam will be allocated to these professional skills, as determined by the task requirements.

The broad structure of each case will give candidates information about an organisation from a range of sources, such as the following:

- Interviews with staff
- Survey results
- Board or organisation reports
- Press articles/website extracts
- Organisation reports and <IR> extracts
- Emails
- Memos
- Spreadsheets
- Pictures
- Figures
- Tables

The Strategic Business Leader exam will **contain several task requirements** relating to the same scenario information. The number of task requirements can vary in each exam. The questions will usually assess and link a range of subject areas across the syllabus. The exam will require students to demonstrate high-level capabilities to understand the complexities of the case and evaluate, relate and apply the information in the case study to the task requirements. The examining team have stressed the importance of reading the case in detail, taking notes as appropriate and getting a feel for what the issues are. The exam will have a **global focus**.

Format of the exam	Marks
One compulsory case scenario, containing a number of task requirements	
Application of syllabus (technical) knowledge marks	80
ACCA professional skills marks	20
	100

Time allowed: 4 hours. The **pass mark** is 50%.

Analysis of past exams

The table below provides details of when each element of the syllabus has been examined in respect of the most recent sittings.

Covered in Workbook chapter		Specimen exam 2	Sept 2018	Dec 2018	Mar/Jun 2019	Sept/Dec 2019
1	Agency (agency relationships)	Q1(a)				
12	Big data and data analytics		Q4		Q4(a)	
3	Board structures	Q1(b)				
15	Business cases	Q5(a)				
3	Corporate governance		Q3(c)			
11	Cybersecurity			Q3(b)		
12	Disruptive technology			Q3(a)		
4	Environmental analysis (PEST analysis)				Q1(a)	
9	Ethics		Q3(a)		Q2(b)	
10	Financial analysis		Q1		Q5(a)(b)	Q1(b)
10	Financial decision making				Q4(b)	
2	Integrated reporting			Q2(b)		
8	Internal control problems and deficiencies	Q2(b)	Q3(b)		Q3	Q2
4	National competitive advantage (Porter's diamond)			Q1(a)	Q2(a)	
13	Performance excellence					Q3
10	Performance management	Q2(a)				
15	Project management	Q5(b)	Q2			
7	Risk assessment and risk management	Q4			Q1(b)	Q2
2	Stakeholder analysis and stakeholder management			Q2(a)		

Covered in Workbook chapter		Specimen exam 2	Sept 2018	Dec 2018	Mar/Jun 2019	Sept/Dec 2019
6	Strategic options			Q1(b)	Q2(b)	Q1(a)
13	Talent management	Q3				

IMPORTANT! The table above gives a broad idea of how frequently major topics in the syllabus are examined. It should **not** be used to question spot and predict, for example, that a topic will not be examined because it came up two sittings ago. The examining team's reports indicate that they are well aware that some students try to question spot. They avoid predictable patterns and may, for example, examine the same topic two sittings in a row, particularly if there has been a recent change in legislation.

Essential skills areas to be successful in Strategic Business Leader

There are three essential skills areas which students must develop to be successful in the ACCA Strategic Business Leader exam. ACCA is clear that students cannot expect to be successful in this exam without demonstrating competence in **all** three areas.

Technical knowledge

The syllabus for Strategic Business Leader is extensive and provides a vital foundation for students to demonstrate their abilities as accountants, strategic advisers and business leaders. Eighty marks are assigned to application of syllabus knowledge to specific business scenarios. Knowledge is developed through reading or listening to your tutor, reading the business press and, importantly, by practising new cases and completing tasks as a principal focus of your studies.

Use of theories of models in the Strategic Business Leader Exam

Strategic Business Leader exam set by the ACCA Examining Team is a practical exam and unlike other exams will not test individual theories or models in isolation or require for the these theories or models to be quoted in answers to exam questions. However, understanding the technical theories, models and knowledge is essential as these provide a framework for students to help them approach the practical tasks that they will need to complete in the Strategic Business Leader exam.

The use of models in the exam will be a judgement made by students and is part of the ACCA Professional Skills for analysis and evaluation. Students are advised to use models which they judge to be relevant for a particular task or scenario to generate the scope of their answer. There is not a prescriptive list of theories and models, however, the BPP Workbook focuses on the most relevant models which it considers to be most relevant to the syllabus and to aid students in being successful in Strategic Business Leader.

BPP
LEARNING
MEDIA

ACCA professional skills

Following consultation with employers, ACCA has identified that qualified accountants need to possess a range of key professional skills. In the Strategic Business Leader exam, 20 marks are assigned to the demonstration of ACCA professional skills. ACCA has defined five main 'professional' skills which will be assessed in the Strategic Business Leader exam and all five will be assessed at each exam sitting. Each ACCA professional skill has been clearly defined by ACCA, along with three further defined aspects, as follows:

ACCA professional skill: Definition	Three aspects of each ACCA professional skill
1. Communication To express yourself clearly and convincingly through an appropriate medium, while being sensitive to the needs of the intended audience.	Inform Persuade Clarify
2. Commercial acumen To show awareness of the wider business and external factors affecting business, and use commercially sound judgement and insight to resolve issues and exploit opportunities.	Demonstrate awareness Use judgement Show insight
3. Analysis To thoroughly investigate and research information from a variety of sources, and logically process it with a view to considering it for recommending appropriate action.	Investigate Enquire Consider
4. Scepticism To probe, question and challenge information and views presented to you, to fully understand business issues and to establish facts objectively, based on ethical and professional values.	Probe Question Challenge
5. Evaluation To assess situations, proposals and arguments in a balanced way, using professional and ethical judgement to predict future outcomes and consequences as a basis for sound decision making.	Assess Estimate Appraise

Throughout the BPP Practice & Revision Kit for the Strategic Business Leader exam, you will find a range of activities and questions which will help to develop your ACCA professional skills alongside your technical knowledge.

But what do the skills mean, and what do you have to do to demonstrate them?

The following section includes the defined aspects of each of the five ACCA professional skills and then makes suggestions to help you demonstrate them in your Strategic Business Leader studies.

Communication

Communication means to express yourself clearly and convincingly through the appropriate medium while being sensitive to the needs of the intended audience and also understanding both the context and situation. In the exam, this means to present written and numerical work in the required format with a professional tone and use of language and avoiding ambiguity, unnecessary explanations and repetition. **Communication** is assessed over three aspects: inform, persuade and clarify.

> **Inform** concisely, objectively and unambiguously, while being sensitive to cultural differences, using appropriate media and technology.

Advice on demonstrating 'inform':

- Think about who you are addressing in your answer: eg if you are writing an extract for a board report, you need to focus on strategic issues, without going into lots of operational details

- Adopt an appropriate tone to suit your audience: eg formal vs informal; use language they will understand; will they understand jargon and technical terms, or should you avoid them?

- Use an appropriate style of communication: eg written vs graphic; slides; diagrams

- If the task requirement asks you to use a specific format, eg bullet point slides, you **must** present your answer in that format

> **Persuade** using compelling and logical arguments demonstrating the ability to counter-argue when appropriate.

Advice on demonstrating 'persuade':

- Support your arguments with facts
- Explain why you think a course of action is suitable/unsuitable
- Use 'justifying' words, such as 'because': 'I recommend you do this **because**...'

> **Clarify** and simplify complex issues to convey relevant information in a way that adopts an appropriate tone and is easily understood by the intended audience.

Advice on demonstrating 'clarify':

- Focus on key points, and avoid unnecessary detail
- Use succinct sentences
- Use headings to break down information into clearly identifiable sections
- Present your arguments in a logical order

Commercial acumen

Commercial acumen means showing awareness of the wider business and external factors affecting business, using commercially sound judgement and insight to resolve issues and exploit opportunities. In the exam, this includes considering the change in revenue, cost or profit as an important driver in decision making and avoid suggesting solutions which will have a negative financial impact, unless it is to address a wider sustainability issue, such as ethics and governance. **Commercial acumen** is assessed over three aspects: demonstrate awareness, use judgement and show insight, as follows.

> **Demonstrate awareness** of organisational and wider external factors affecting the work of an individual or a team in contributing to the wider organisational objectives.

BPP LEARNING MEDIA

Advice on demonstrating awareness:

- Think about the specific context of a scenario and identify how this affects a decision
- Make sure recommendations are appropriate – and practical – to the context of the scenario

Use judgement to identify key issues in determining how to address or resolve problems and in proposing and recommending the solutions to be implemented.

Advice on demonstrating judgement:

- Prioritise key points

- Only make points which are relevant to the scenario and which help to address/resolve the issue at hand

- Make sure recommendations resolve issues and/or exploit opportunities

- Avoid making points which are not supported by facts; recommendations need to be justified

Show insight and perception in understanding work-related and organisational issues, including the management of conflict, demonstrating acumen in arriving at appropriate solutions or outcomes.

Advice on demonstrating insight:

- Make sure recommendations are appropriate and practical in the context of the scenario, eg are they feasible? Will they be acceptable to key stakeholders?

- Make sure recommendations address key issues identified in the scenario

- Make sure decisions and strategies are appropriate for an organisation, rather than just making generic points

- Ask yourself: will the points you are making help the organisation make a decision which successfully addresses the issues it is facing?

Analysis

Analysis means to thoroughly investigate and research information from a variety of sources and logically process it with a view to considering it for recommending appropriate action. In the exam, this means to produce relevant analysis from the information provided in the case overview and exhibits which creates new evidence in response to the task requirement and a basis for action you are recommending an organisation should take. **Analysis** is assessed over three aspects: investigate, enquire and consider, as follows.

Investigate relevant information from a wide range of sources, using a variety of analytical techniques to establish the reasons and causes of problems, or to identify opportunities or solutions.

Advice on demonstrating 'investigation':

- Don't simply repeat points from the scenario; explain why they are significant and/or what their implications are

- Identify relevant data from different places within a scenario, rather than only including the most obvious (or most easily accessible) points

- Give reasons **why** a problem has happened, rather than simply stating the problem

Enquire of individuals or analyse appropriate data sources to obtain suitable evidence to corroborate or dispute existing beliefs or opinions and come to appropriate conclusions.

Advice on demonstrating 'enquire':

- The reference to suitable evidence is key here: data and evidence must be relevant to the points you are making

- Does data in the scenario support arguments made elsewhere; for example, are revenue figures or profit margins consistent with how well someone says an organisation is performing?

> **Consider** information, evidence and findings carefully, reflecting on their implications and how they can be used in the interests of the department and wider organisational goals.

Advice on demonstrating 'consider':

- Make use of the information in the scenario in order to recommend appropriate actions
- How does the evidence in the scenario affect the suitability of a potential course of action?

Scepticism

Scepticism means to probe, question and challenge information and views presented, to fully understand business issues and to establish facts objectively, based on ethical and professional values. In the exam this means to be aware of the quality, scope, source and age of the information provided, as well as the purpose for which the information was produced and by whom; where necessary suggest information used for analysis, evaluation and decision making is updated, improved or extended through questioning or appropriate challenge. This is so the best possible information is applied before a final decision is made. **Scepticism** is assessed over three aspects: probe, question and challenge, as follows.

> **Probe** deeply into the underlying reasons for issues and problems, beyond what is immediately apparent from the usual sources and opinions available.

Advice on demonstrating 'probe':

- Don't automatically accept that the initial reason given to explain an issue is correct. (Is the explanation somebody gives you consistent with other evidence? Does the explanation properly explain the issue or problem you are addressing?) For example, if a management accountant is offering an explanation of a variance between actual figures and budget, are you satisfied their explanation properly explains the variance?

- Draw together information from different sources, rather than just including the most obvious (or most easily accessible) points. Does information from one source support, or contradict information from another source?

> **Question** facts, opinions and assertions, by seeking justifications and obtaining sufficient evidence for their support and acceptance.

Advice on demonstrating 'question':

- Scrutinise any assumptions being made: are they reasonable; can they be supported by the evidence available? (Don't simply accept everything you are told.)

- Question the motive or rationale behind facts or statements. For example, does the person making a statement have a vested interest in one decision being taken in preference to another? If so, how reliable, or objective, is their evidence likely to be?

- Identify additional information or evidence which may be required to corroborate facts or assertions being made

> **Challenge** information presented or decisions made, where this is clearly justified, in a professional and courteous manner; in the wider professional, ethical, organisational, or public interest.

Advice on demonstrating 'challenge':

- Highlight the weaknesses of, or problems with, information presented or potential decisions

- Use evidence to support your challenge, and justify challenges you make, perhaps by demonstrating evidence of wider reading

- Identify potential alternative interpretations of information or alternative courses of action, to reinforce your challenge

- Your 'challenge' should focus specifically on the problems with a decision, rather than trying to evaluate problems against benefits

Evaluation

Evaluation means to carefully assess situations, proposals and arguments in a balanced way, using professional and ethical judgement to predict future outcomes and consequences as a basis for sound decision making. In the exam this means ensuring possible courses of action are examined from different perspectives and, where relevant, clearly stating reasonable assumptions and including points both for and against. Conclusions and recommendations made should be consistent with the most persuasive factors presented which provide logical argument for the course of action suggested. **Evaluation** is assessed over three aspects: assess, estimate and appraise, as follows.

> **Assess** and use professional judgement when considering organisational issues, problems, or when making decisions, taking into account the implications of such decisions on the organisation and those affected.

Advice on demonstrating 'assessment':

- Consider the potential importance and urgency of a problem when deciding a suitable response to the problem

- Determine the potential advantages and disadvantages associated with a decision

- Determine the potential impact of a decision on key stakeholders, and how they are likely to react to it

> **Estimate** trends or make reasoned forecasts of the implications of external and internal factors on the organisation, or of the outcomes of decisions available to the organisation.

Advice on demonstrating 'estimate':

- Present sensible, justified estimates and forecasts; for example, in assessing the impact which a change in the business environment could have on an organisation's performance

- Identify the possible impact that different decisions could have on an organisation's performance

> **Appraise** facts, opinions and findings objectively, with a view to balancing the costs, risks, benefits and opportunities, before making or recommending solutions or decisions.

Advice on demonstrating 'appraise':

- Present the arguments for and against a proposed strategy, so that an informed decision can be made about whether or not to pursue that strategy

- Make decisions, or recommend solutions, which are appropriate to the circumstances, on the basis of a balanced appraisal of advantages and disadvantages. For example, do the potential benefits from a strategy justify the costs involved?

In summary

Overall, remember that technical knowledge is not intended to be learned for the purpose of being either described or explained as part of these skills – it is designed to be demonstrated appropriately as part of these skills through synthesis and application.

Exam success skills

Passing the SBL exam requires more than applying syllabus knowledge and demonstrating the specific SBL skills; it also requires the development of excellent exam technique through question practice.

We consider the following six skills to be vital for exam success. The Skills Checkpoints show how each of these skills can be applied in the exam.

Exam success skill 1

Case scenario: Managing information

This requires swift understanding of the case overview and exhibits, as well as the identification, prioritisation and assimilation of key facts, events, information and data (which is both unstructured and non-sequential) and to comprehend its usefulness, relevance and importance in responding to question requirements.

Advice on demonstrating case scenario: Managing Information

Using the scenario is essential to answer the task requirement and to pass the question. Most of what you write should relate directly to the scenario provided and be guided by the information given, with the remainder being based on the skills and experience you bring into the exam. The skill is using your judgement to determine what information is important to best answer each task requirement. If there is a lot of information and detail given on a specific issue then it is likely to play a big part in at least one of the tasks.

The ACCA Strategic Business Leader examining team advise that at least 40 minutes is spent during the exam on reading and interpreting the information provided in the case overview and exhibits and considering each task requirement. The advised 40-minute reading time is a useful benchmark to check you are committing sufficient time to managing the information provided.

Correct interpretation of the requirements

The active verb used often dictates the approach that written answers should take (eg 'explain', 'discuss', 'evaluate'). It is important you identify and use the verb to define your approach. The **Correct Interpretation of the Requirements** skill is correctly producing only what is being asked for by a task requirement. Anything not required will not earn marks.

Advice on demonstrating Correct Interpretation of the Requirements

There is a real skill to understanding very quickly exactly what the ACCA examining team expect you to deliver in an answer and within the time frame indicated by the mark allocation. This skill can be developed by analysing task requirements and applying this process:

Step 1 **Read the requirement**

Firstly, read the task requirement a couple of times slowly and carefully and highlight the active verbs. Use the active verbs to define what you plan to do. For example, **discuss** means consider and debate or argue about the pros and cons of an issue (remember also that **critically discuss** requires you to focus on the key points that you need to criticise).

Step 2 **Read the scenario**

By reading the task requirement first, you will have an idea of what you are looking out for as you read through the case overview and exhibits. This is a great time saver and means you don't end up having to read the whole question in full twice – it also allows you to identify which elements of the exhibit materials are most relevant for each task. As you go through the scenario you should be annotating key information which you think will play a key role in answering the specific task requirements.

Step 3 **Read the requirement again**

Read the task requirement again to remind yourself of the exact wording before starting your written answer. This will capture any misinterpretation of the task requirements or any missed tasks entirely. This should become a habit in your approach and, with repeated practice, you will find the focus, relevance and depth of your answer plan will improve.

Exam success skill 3

Answer planning: Priorities, structure and logic

This skill requires the drafting of the key aspects of an answer which accurately and completely responds to the task requirement in the format specified **before** calculations and a written answer are attempted. A good answer plan is one which prioritises what can be covered in the time available, is in a logical order and focuses on points that are likely to score the best marks in the exam.

Advice on developing Answer planning: Priorities, structure and logic

This skill can be developed by applying the following process:

Step 1   **Identify key words and mark allocation**

The answer plan should directly relate to the key words in the task requirement and the mark allocation. Use the active verb to start your answer plan and use the mark allocation to determine the time available to complete the answer and guide the number of points to discuss.

Step 2   **Plan any calculations**

The creation of numerical analysis must be essential to completing the task requirement, otherwise it should not be included. Plan the scope of numerical work to avoid unnecessary complexity and to ensure analysis is relevant to the question.

Step 3   **Take time to plan in sufficient detail**

The plan should go into sufficient detail to enable you to move smoothly into writing out a good answer without having to stop too often and rethink. To do this requires creative thinking up front, but beware of writing too much at the planning stage; the plan is essential for a good answer, but is not an answer in itself.

Good answer planning has been shown as a valuable contributor to good time management and efficient answer writing – using the marks on offer can help with this time allocation as well.

Efficient numerical analysis

This skill is to maximise the marks awarded by making the process of arriving at the answer clear to the marker. This is achieved by laying out an answer in such a way that still scores well, even if a few errors occur along the way, with explanations of key figures or assumptions. It is vital that you do not lose marks purely because the marker cannot follow what you have done.

Advice on developing Efficient numerical analysis

This skill can be developed by applying the following process:

Step 1   **Use a standard proforma working where relevant**

If answers can be laid out in a standard proforma or table then always plan to do so. This will help the marker to understand your working and locate the marks easily. It will also help you to work through the figures in a methodical and time-efficient way.

Step 2   **Show your workings**

Keep your workings as clear and simple as possible and ensure they are cross-referenced to the main part of your answer. Where it helps, provide brief narrative explanations to help the marker understand the steps in the calculation. This means that if a mistake is made then you do not lose any subsequent marks for follow-on calculations.

Step 3   **Keep moving!**

It is important to remember that, in an exam situation, it is difficult to get every number 100% correct. The key is therefore ensuring you do not spend too long on any single calculation. If you are struggling with a solution then make a sensible assumption, state it and move on.

Efficient numerical analysis means providing sufficient numerical evidence to support your written arguments, evaluations, conclusions and recommendations, so the creation of numerical work must not replace effective writing and presentation.

Exam success skill 5

Effective writing and presentation

Written answers should be presented so that the marker can clearly see the different points you are making, presented in the format specified by the task requirement. The skill is to provide efficient written answers with sufficient breadth of points that actually answer the task set and provide necessary depth of explanation in the time available.

Advice on developing Effective writing and presentation

This skill can be developed by applying the following features to your written work.

| Step 1 | **Use subheadings** |

Using the subheadings taken from your answer plan will give you structure, order and logic. This will ensure your answer links back to the task requirement and is clearly signposted, making it easier for the marker to understand the different points you are making and award marks accordingly.

| Step 2 | **Write your answer in short, punchy sentences** |

Use short, punchy sentences when presenting written answers with the aim that every written sentence should say something different and generate marks.

| Step 3 | **Extend your points with depth** |

You should not leave the marker in a position asking why, or so what. A useful technique is to use short sentences to explain what you mean in one sentence and then to explain why it matters in the next. If further depth is required, consider how the consequences of inaction or making a decision will impact on the organisation in the future.

Good time management

This skill means planning your time across all the task requirements so that all tasks have been attempted at the end of the four hours available and actively checking on time during your progress through the exam. This is so that, if necessary, you can flex your approach and prioritise tasks which, in your judgement, will generate the maximum marks in the available time remaining.

Advice on developing Good time management

This skill can be developed by applying the following process:

Step 1   **Stick to mark and time allocations**

At the beginning of a question, work out the amount of time you should be spending on each task requirement. The ACCA examining team advise spending at least 40 minutes on reading, which leaves 200 minutes to complete your answer planning and calculations and write up your answer.

Step 2   **Follow your answer plan**

It is not uncommon to spend five minutes creating a good plan then not use it when writing up the answer. This means explanations of good points which had been identified are missed or the time allocation is ignored. The key is using the answer plan to limit how much is written and how much time is used.

Step 3   **Keep an eye on the clock**

Aim to attempt all tasks, but be ready to be ruthless and move on if your answer is not going as planned. The challenge for many is sticking to planned timings. Be aware this is difficult to achieve in the early stages of your studies and be ready to let this skill develop over time.

The good time management skill means actively planning for exam success as your written answers cover more of the available marks.

If you find yourself running short on time and know that a full answer is not possible in the time you have, consider recreating your plan in overview form and then add key terms and details as time allows. Remember, some key marks may still be available, for example, simply stating a conclusion which you don't have time to justify in full.

The importance of question practice in your studies

The best study approach to improve your knowledge of the ACCA professional skills and exam success skills is to focus on question practice as a core part of learning new topic areas, ensuring you focus on improving the Exam Success Skills – personal to your needs – by obtaining feedback or through a process of self-assessment.

INTRODUCTION TO STAGE 1:
Effective Leadership

Effective Leadership

Mark Constantine and a small group of colleagues founded Lush in 1995, selling natural hair and beauty products at a shop in the British seaside town of Poole. Constantine had started out as a hairdresser, then set up a company manufacturing hair care products that became the biggest supplier to the ethical brand The Body Shop. He subsequently sold his business to The Body Shop in order to found a mail order company Cosmetics-To-Go with his wife Mo. This venture failed, but its successor Lush has been a great success. In 2019 the company had 928 stores worldwide, as well as extensive online sales. It remains privately owned by the Constantines and close associates.

The Constantines have an unconventional approach to leadership and ethics. Their personal values are fundamental to the way they run the company and the values that the brand represents. A section of their website sets out the company's approach to issues ranging from animal testing to tax and air travel. They are not frightened of controversy, and past campaigns have included opposition to fox hunting and fracking, as well as support for refugees and Guantanamo Bay detainees. However, Lush resist being described as an 'ethical company'. Their website states:

'All business should be ethical and all trade should be fair. Individual companies should not stand out simply by not being damaging or unfair. No company should be trading from an unethical position and society has a right to expect as the norm fairness and resource stewardship from the companies that supply them' (Lush, 2019).

The Constantines' approach is extreme, but it does illustrate the responsibility that leaders should now see as necessary for setting the right culture and values in an organisation, which are key influences on the way people behave. In this section, we look at what these concepts mean, and the way in which leaders must identify key stakeholders, managing relationships with them. These may include shareholders, customers, suppliers and the media, and increasingly society as a whole which is seen as a stakeholder for large and high-profile organisations. The process by which organisations are run is known as corporate governance. Good governance aims to support organisational success, as well as providing mechanisms to deal with problems. Good governance is aimed at promoting effective, ethical leadership, which is ultimately reflected in the culture, values and performance of the organisation. Effective Leadership, the theme of this stage, therefore has consequences for everything else we cover in the course.

Strategy, leadership and culture

1

Learning objectives

On completion of this chapter, you should be able to:

	Syllabus reference no.
Recognise the fundamental nature of strategy and strategic decisions within different organisational contexts	C1(a)
Explore the Johnson, Scholes and Whittington model for defining elements of strategic management – the strategic position, strategic choices and strategy into action	C1(b)
Explain the role of effective leadership and identify the key leadership traits effective in the successful formulation and implementation of strategy and change management	A1(a)
Apply the concepts of entrepreneurship and 'intrapreneurship' to exploit strategic opportunities and to innovate successfully	A1(b)
Apply in the context of organisation governance and leadership qualities, the key ethical and professional values underpinning governance	A1(c)
Discuss the importance of leadership in defining and managing organisational culture	A2(a)
Advise on the style of leadership appropriate to manage strategic change	A2(b)
Analyse the culture of an organisation using the cultural web, to recommend suitable changes	A2(c)
Assess the impact of culture and ethics on organisational purpose and strategy	A2(d)

Business and exam context

As we start our journey through Strategic Business Leader, it is important that you remember throughout each chapter the importance of ethical leadership as a concept underpinning everything that an organisation is and does. The formal roles of leaders include setting mission, objectives and strategy, governance of the organisation and making key operational decisions, but more informally they set a 'tone from the top' which has a significant influence on the culture of an organisation and the ethics within it.

In this first chapter, we will look at how leadership is defined, who makes a good leader and what skills they need to lead effectively, regardless of the challenges they face. The roles played by both strategy and culture are also explored and framed in the context of bigger organisational issues such as ethics, governance and corporate social responsibility, all of which you will meet later on in your studies.

Chapter overview

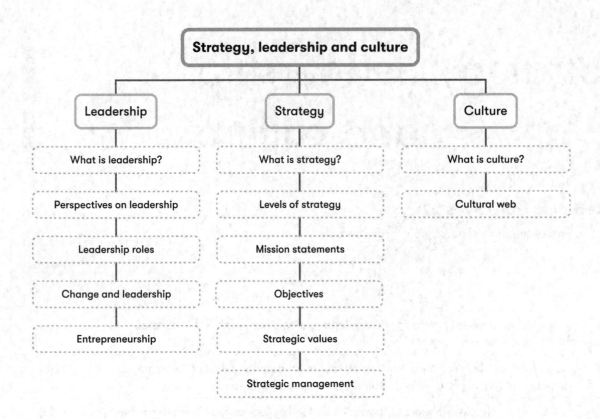

Strategy, leadership and culture

Leadership
- What is leadership?
- Perspectives on leadership
- Leadership roles
- Change and leadership
- Entrepreneurship

Strategy
- What is strategy?
- Levels of strategy
- Mission statements
- Objectives
- Strategic values
- Strategic management

Culture
- What is culture?
- Cultural web

BPP
LEARNING
MEDIA

1 Leadership

1.1 What is leadership?

Key term

> **Leadership:** Is the process of influencing an organisation (or group within an organisation) in its efforts towards achieving an aim or goal (Johnson *et al*, 2017: p.470).

Good leadership is often considered to be a key factor in organisational success. In particular, **visionary leaders** are expected to have a clear vision for where the organisation needs to go and communicate this vision to inspire others.

Ethics are fundamental to good leadership. Leaders have a particular responsibility to ensure that their behaviour and decision-making reflect a high standard of ethics, which will then have an impact through the whole organisation. We will examine ethics in more detail later in this Chapter and in Chapter 9.

Exercise 1: Qualities of effective leaders

Required

Think of three people you consider effective leaders, past or present. What qualities do they have in common?

Solution

1.2 Perspectives on leadership

Yukl (2013) identifies the following main approaches to studying leadership:

1.2.1 Trait approach

Key term

> **Trait theories:** The qualities possessed by good leaders.

Research in the first part of the 20th century tended to assume that 'natural leaders' possessed traits that others did not, such as energy, intuition and persuasiveness. However, this research failed to identify a set of traits that would guarantee success in leadership. More recent research tends to focus on how certain attributes can relate to leadership behaviour and effectiveness. Some research emphasises **values** that are important in displaying **ethical leadership**.

1.2.2 Behaviour approach

This focuses on what managers actually do in their jobs and relates leadership effectiveness to how well managers cope with the demands and constraints of their job.

BPP
LEARNING
MEDIA

1.2.3 Power-Influence approach

This explains leadership effectiveness in terms of the amount and type of power possessed by a leader, and how it is exercised. This is not just power in relation to subordinates, but peers, superiors and external stakeholders. Leadership can be exercised in a way that is autocratic (leaders exercise significant power) or participative (power is limited and subordinates exercise more decision-making and autonomy).

1.2.4 Situational approach

This emphasises that different leadership traits, skills and behaviours will be effective in different situations. The effectiveness of a certain style of leadership may depend on the characteristics of followers, nature of the work performed, type of organisation and the external environment. This can also be referred to as **contingency theory**.

1.2.5 Integrative approach

This means considering more than one type of the leadership variables described above.

> **Essential reading**
>
> See Chapter 1 section 1 of the Essential Reading, available in Appendix 2 of the digital edition of the Workbook, for more detail on the theory of leadership.

1.3 Leadership roles

Johnson *et al* (2017) identify a number of key roles in strategic leadership.

1.3.1 Top managers

The following roles are carried out by the CEO and other senior managers.

- **Envisioning future strategy** means communicating a clear vision of the future and strategy to internal and external stakeholders.
- **Aligning** the organisation to deliver the strategy, building relationships of trust and ensuring that people are committed to the strategy and empowered to deliver it.
- **Embodying change** is being a symbol and role model for the organisation.

1.3.2 Middle managers

The role of middle managers is not just to implement top-down strategic plans but has multiple other aspects.

- **Advisers** to senior management, as they are often closest to day-to-day operations.
- **'Sense making'** of strategy, means translating the strategy into specific contexts.
- **Reinterpretation and adjustment** of strategy as circumstances change internally and externally.
- **Local leadership of change** mirrors the senior management role of aligning and embodying change, but at a more local level, particularly in large organisations.

1.4 Change and leadership

> **Change agent:** 'Is an individual or group that helps to effect strategic change in an organisation.' (Johnson *et al*, 2017)

Key term

Change is unavoidable as organisations and individuals do not operate in a vacuum. As a leader, how do you make sure that your organisation is able to cope with change?

Change agency (everything associated with making change happen) is an activity that might be concentrated in one person, but which is just as likely to be spread among the members of a group, such as a project team or management staff generally. Outsiders, such as consultants, may share in change agency.

1.4.1 Charismatic and transactional leadership

Johnson *et al* (2017) note that leadership styles may be fitted into a general model of leadership that recognises two general types.

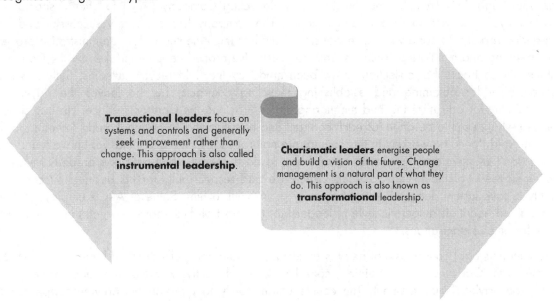

Transactional leaders focus on systems and controls and generally seek improvement rather than change. This approach is also called **instrumental leadership**.

Charismatic leaders energise people and build a vision of the future. Change management is a natural part of what they do. This approach is also known as **transformational** leadership.

Key terms

Instrumental leadership: Leadership based on systems and controls (also called transactional leadership).

Transformational leadership: Leadership that energises people and builds a clear vision of the future (also called charismatic leadership).

In practice, these are two extremes and there are a number of points in between. This fits with the **situational approach** described earlier, which suggests leadership style needs to be adjusted to specific circumstances.

1.4.2 Change management styles

Balogun and Hope Hailey (2008) identify five styles of change management which may be appropriate in a given context.

Education and communication – explaining in detail why change is necessary, to win people round

Collaboration and participation – bringing people affected by change into the process of managing it

Intervention – change is led by a change agent who will delegate some tasks to project teams; the idea is that involvement of those teams will lead to greater commitment from them

Direction – management use their authority to establish their strategy and how change will occur in a top-down fashion

Coercion – an extreme form of direction – change is simply imposed by management

Activity 1: Academic Recycling Company

You work as a consultant specialising in the area of personnel and management development. You have been approached by Sully Truin who is keen for some advice about how he should be leading his organisation.

Ten years ago Sully Truin formed the Academic Recycling Company (ARC) to offer a specialised waste recycling service to schools and colleges. The company has been very successful and has expanded rapidly. To cope with this expansion, Sully has implemented a tight administrative process for operating and monitoring contracts. This administrative procedure is undertaken by the Contracts Office, which tracks that collections have been made by the field recycling teams. Sully has sole responsibility for obtaining and establishing recycling contracts, but he leaves the day-to-day responsibility for administering and monitoring the contracts to the Contracts Office. He has closely defined what needs to be done for each contract and how this should be monitored. 'I needed to do this,' he said, 'because workers in this country are naturally lazy and lack initiative. I have found that if you don't tell them exactly what to do and how to do it, then it won't get done properly.' Most of the employees working in the Contracts Office like and respect Sully for his business success and ability to take instant decisions when they refer a problem to him. Some of ARC's employees have complained about his autocratic style of leadership, but most of these have now left the company to work for other organisations.

A few months ago, conscious that he was a self-taught manager, Sully enrolled himself on a week's course with Gapminding, a training consultancy which actively advocates and promotes a democratic style of management. The course caused Sully to question his previous approach to leadership. It was also the first time, for three years, that Sully had been out of the office during working hours for a prolonged period of time. However, each night, while he was attending the course, he had to deal with emails from the Contracts Office listing problems with contracts and asking him what action they should take. He became exasperated by his employees' inability to take actions to resolve these issues. He discussed this problem with his course tutors. They suggested that his employees would be more effective and motivated if their jobs were enriched and that they were empowered to make decisions themselves.

On his return from the course, Sully called a staff meeting with the Contracts Office where he announced that, from now on, employees would have responsibility for taking control actions themselves, rather than referring the problem to him. Sully, in turn, was to focus on gaining more contracts and setting them up. However, problems with the new arrangements arose very quickly. Fearful of making mistakes and unsure about what they were doing led to employees discussing issues amongst themselves at length before coming to a tentative decision. The operational (field) recycling teams were particularly critical of the new approach. One commented that 'before, we got a clear decision very quickly. Now decisions can take several days and appear to lack authority.' The new approach also caused tensions and stress within the Contracts Office and absenteeism increased.

At the next staff meeting, employees in the Contracts Office asked Sully to return to his old management style and job responsibilities. 'We prefer the old Sully Truin,' they said, 'the training course has spoilt you.' Reluctantly, Sully agreed to their requests and so all problems are again referred up to him. However, he is unhappy with this return to the previous way of working. He is working long hours and is concerned about his health. Also, he realises that he has little time for obtaining and planning contracts and this is severely restricting the capacity of the company to expand.

Required

Analyse Sully Truin's leadership style before and immediately after the training course and explain why the change of leadership style at ARC was unsuccessful. **(12 marks)**

Professional skills marks are available for demonstrating **analysis** skills as part of your diagnosis of the leadership styles on display here. **(2 marks)**

(Total = 14 marks)

Solution

1.5 Entrepreneurship

Role of leadership can also include entrepreneurship. We can contrast this with intrapreneurship

Key terms

Entrepreneurship: Is a process by which individuals, teams or organisations identify and exploit opportunities for new **products** or services that satisfy a need in a market.

Intrapreneurship: Means applying entrepreneurial principles within organisations.

Entrepreneurship involves recognising opportunities and responding by choosing and implementing an appropriate business model and strategy. **Social entrepreneurship** is applying similar principles to addressing social problems and needs, not necessarily for profit, although clearly some kind of funding model is needed. This is examined in more detail in Chapter 12.

Some companies encourage intrapreneurship to support innovation, for example by giving employees more autonomy, encouraging a culture of risk-taking, rewarding intrapreneurial behaviour and allocating resource to new, speculative ventures. However, conflict with corporate management may sometimes be necessary to get ideas and innovations accepted

2 Strategy

As noted above, one of the key roles of leadership to develop and communicate the organisation's strategy.

2.1 What is strategy?

According to Johnson *et al* (2017):

Key term

Strategy: 'Is the long-term direction of an organisation.' (Johnson *et al*, 2017).

So strategy is concerned with the following.

The **long term:** this will mean a number of years, which can be thought of as 'three horizons'. Horizon 1 means defending and extending the current business. Horizon 2 businesses are emerging activities that should provide new sources of profit. Horizon 3 ventures are new and risky, and might provide returns in several years' time. Managers need to consider all three in formulating strategy.

Strategic direction: organisations will generally have objectives and then organise themselves to meet those objectives.

Organisation: organisations generally contain people with differing views and interests, which are relevant in setting strategy. It will also have to consider its internal and external **stakeholders** and its **boundaries** – what it decides to include or exclude in its activities.

2.2 Levels of strategy

Strategy may be developed at three levels in an organisation.

Corporate strategy deals with the overall purpose and scope of an organisation and how to add value to the different parts (business units) of an organisation (for example, the decision to expand into a new geographical location or market)

Business-level strategy is about how to compete successfully in particular markets (continuing with the expansion analogy, the head of a business unit must decide where to be based, what products to sell and the markets to target etc)

Operational strategies are about how parts of an organisation such as marketing, finance or IT support the overall strategy (the heads of IT, HR, finance, marketing etc need to develop a plan to support the overall strategy in terms of recruitment, appraisal and agreeing terms and conditions)

2.3 Mission statements

Key term

Mission statements: Are formal documents that state the organisation's mission. They are published within organisations to promote desired behaviour: support for strategy and purpose, adherence to core values and adoption of policies and standards of behaviour.

Real-world example

Famous organisations may not always have famous mission statements.

Nike   'To bring inspiration and innovation to every athlete* in the world.' (Nike, 2019)

Facebook   'Facebook's mission is to give people the power to build community and bring the world closer together. People use Facebook to stay connected with friends and family, to discover what's going on in the world, and to share and express what matters to them. ' (Facebook, 2019)

Airbnb   'Airbnb's mission is to create a world where people can belong through healthy travel that is local, authentic, diverse, inclusive and sustainable. (Airbnb, 2019)

These are different from their more familiar advertising slogans or brands:

Similar to a mission statement, a **vision statement** can be used to express the future an organisation is trying to create. For example, Henry Ford's aim was to create a car that everyone could afford.

The **Ashridge College model of mission** created by Campbell and Yeung (1991) links business strategy to culture and ethics by including four separate elements in an expanded definition of mission.

Purpose. Why does the organisation exist? Who does it exist for? (i) To create wealth for owners? (ii) To satisfy the needs of all stakeholders? (iii) To reach some higher goal such as the advancement of society?	Values are the beliefs and moral principles that underlie the organisation's culture
Policies and standards of behaviour provide guidance on how the organisation's business should be conducted. For example, a service company that wishes to be the best in its market must aim for standards of service, in all its operations, which are at least as good as those found at its competitors	Strategy provides the commercial logic for the company, and so addresses the following questions: 'What is our business? What should it be?'

Stakeholder views will be important in determining an organisation's mission, its fundamental purpose and values. This may be written down in the form of a mission statement which may help to guide the organisation, although in reality many people consider that mission statements are meaningless, ignored in practice or both. Some are suspicious of mission statements for the following reasons.

They can sometimes be **public relations** exercises rather than an accurate portrayal of the firm's actual values.

They can often be full of **generalisations** which are impossible to tie down to specific strategic implications.

They may be ignored by the people responsible for formulating or implementing strategy.

2.4 Objectives

A mission needs to be supported by more detailed **objectives**.

PER alert

Performance Objective 13 'Plan and Control Performance' of the Practical Experience Requirement requires you to 'contribute to setting objectives to plan and control business activities' (ACCA, 2019b). As you will need to display how you have contributed to setting objectives in the workplace you are strongly advised to take your time as you go through the following section which considers the role that goals, objectives and targets play in organisations.

A simple model of the relationship between the various goals, objectives and targets is a **pyramid** analogous to the traditional organisational hierarchy.

Overall mission (supported by a small number of wide-ranging goals: profit; growth; innovation etc)

Each of the high-level goals is supported in turn by more detailed, **subordinate goals**. These may correspond, perhaps, to the responsibilities of the senior managers in the function concerned. A more modern pattern is for the hierarchy (and indeed many other aspects of the organisation) to be based on major **value-creating processes** rather than on functional departments

In any event, the pattern is continued downwards until we reach the **work targets** of individual members of the organisation

Drucker (1989) was the first to suggest that objectives should be SMART:

Specific   **M**easurable   **A**chievable   **R**ealistic   **T**ime-related

Today, **realistic** is often replaced with **results-focused**, to emphasise that managerial attention needs to be directed towards **achieving results** rather than just **administering established processes**.

2.5 Strategic Values

2.5.1 Ethics in business

> **Ethics:** The study of right and wrong.

Key term

Ethics are the rules and principles of behaviour which help us decide between right and wrong. Organisations can seek to safeguard their ethical standards by publishing a formal code of ethics. However, this can backfire if companies are not seen to be adhering to their codes.

It is a key responsibility of leaders to role model high ethical standards for the organisation and set an appropriate 'tone from the top'.

Ethics and leadership

Ethics is fundamental to good leadership. Leaders have a particular responsibility to ensure that their behaviour and decision-making reflects a high standard of ethics, which will then have an impact throughout the whole organisation.

Business life is a fruitful source of ethical dilemmas because its whole purpose is material gain, the making of profit. All too often, success in business requires a constant, avid search for potential advantage over others, so business leaders are under pressure to do whatever yields such advantage. It is often these pressures which lead otherwise good people to make poor business decisions and to act unethically.

BPP
LEARNING
MEDIA

The ethical values of leaders

The ethical values held by leaders will be shaped by a variety of factors including their own experiences and beliefs. The ethical views of leaders are often based on values including:

- Accountability
- Integrity
- Honesty
- Objectivity
- Fairness
- Transparency
- Openness
- Responsibility
- Loyalty

The leaders view of the values and principles listed above will ultimately drive how they interact with stakeholders, view CSR and corporate governance. The role of ethical leadership is discussed in more detail in the context of stakeholders, CSR and corporate governance in the sections which follow.

Ethical leadership and the fair treatment of stakeholders

Acting ethically requires leaders to treat stakeholders fairly by recognising the fact that they have rights of their own. This includes respecting workers' dignity and the obligations that exist in terms of equality, diversity and health and safety.

The need for the ethical treatment of staff is particularly important during times of redundancy. Here it is important that leaders select workers for redundancy following a fair and legal process.

The fair treatment of stakeholders also covers the need to respect the rights of customers in terms of not deliberately taking advantage of them by, for example, knowingly charging inflated prices for goods or services. This logic also applies to protecting the interests of shareholders by avoiding unnecessarily risky or reckless strategies which may jeopardise their investment. This requires leaders to conduct the affairs of the business in such a way that it is commercially viable but remains sensitive to the interests of its stakeholders.

Exam Focus Point

The March/June 2019 exam released by ACCA featured a clothing retailer called SmartWear. Task 2(b) asked candidates to evaluate the strategic and ethical implications of a proposal for the company to close a number of loss-making shops in Noria (SmartWear's home market) and the withdrawal from Centrum (another country in which SmartWear had a presence). Professional skills marks were on offer for applying scepticism to the underlying issues and problems which may arise from the decision to close the shops. The examining team noted that 'on the whole this question was answered well, with most candidates identifying that it was good to stop the ongoing losses from the stores/market to be closed, and also identifying the ethical issues of jobs being lost. Many candidates went further to identify the redundancy costs incurred and the increased level of unemployment. The best candidates showed scepticism and questioned the likelihood of the possible turnaround in Noria, the loss of presence/market share, damage to reputation and SmartWear brand, and aligned these issues to SmartWear's strategy.' (ACCA, 2019a).

To earn the 2 professional skills marks candidates needed to identify and explain the key strategic and ethical issues in respect of the proposed closure decision. This required the creation of an answer which focused on the implications of this course of action for SmartWear, and which also explored the positive and negative impacts that the decision would have on the company's stakeholders.

2.5.2 Corporate social responsibility

Corporate social responsibility (CSR) centres on the approach taken by organisations to provide **benefit to society in general** rather than specific stakeholders.

Corporate social responsibility (CSR): The approach taken by organisations to provide benefit to society in general rather than specific stakeholders.

Key term

Ethical leadership and CSR

Growing demand around the world for organisations to act in an ethical manner that acknowledges the impact that their activities have on the natural world have led many leading organisations to embrace the concept of corporate social responsibility (CSR).

Corporate social responsibility (CSR) is a concept whereby organisations consider the interests of society by taking responsibility for the impact of their activities. This obligation extends beyond statutory obligations to comply with legislation.

The planting of trees to replenish those used in production or the establishment of a charitable foundation to help support local communities living near to an organisation's factory are common examples of CSR activities.

The establishment of CSR programmes requires ethical leadership at the top of organisations to ensure that they are taken seriously and to avoid accusations that they are merely window dressing that enables organisations to appear superficially concerned about ethical matters. For such programmes to have real meaning leaders need to make ethics part of the organisation's culture. The important role that culture plays in organisations is discussed in greater detail in Section 3 of this Chapter.

2.5.3 Corporate governance

Corporate governance: Concerns the conduct of senior officers in an organisation. It also relates to the way organisations are directed and controlled.

Key term

Corporate governance can be defined as the conduct of senior officers in an organisation. The **governance framework** describes who the organisation serves and how priorities are decided.

Corporate governance issues may arise from the **agency problem** – the separation in many cases between **ownership** (shareholders) and day-to-day **control** (managers). Managers are required to act in the best interests of shareholders but may in fact act in their own best interests if they can.

Corporate governance issues are not confined to commercial companies. A public sector hospital, for example, is there to benefit patients but decisions may in practice be taken to benefit staff and management.

Ethical values and corporate governance

The following section illustrates how the ethical values held by leaders supports and underpins corporate governance.

Fairness

The leaders' deliberations and values (and those of the board) that underlie the company must be **balanced** by taking into account everyone who has a legitimate interest in the company and respecting their rights and views. In many jurisdictions, corporate governance guidelines reinforce legal protection for certain groups; for example, minority shareholders.

Openness/transparency

Transparency means **open and clear disclosure** of relevant information to shareholders and other stakeholders, also not concealing information when it may affect decisions. It means open discussions and a default position of information provision, rather than concealment.

Honesty and loyalty

Honesty relates not only to telling the truth but also not misleading shareholders and other stakeholders. Lack of honesty includes not only obvious examples of dishonesty such as taking bribes but also presenting information in a slanted way that is designed to give an unfair impression.

Responsibility

Responsibility requires that leaders' need to be willing to accept the credit when things go well and be just as willing to accept the blame for governance failings in the event they occur.

Accountability

Accountability requires organisational leaders' to be answerable for the consequences of their actions. Accountability is closely linked to the issue of judgement. Leaders' need to exercise sound judgement when making decisions. Leaders' need to make decisions which **enhance the prosperity** of the organisation. Leaders' must acquire a broad enough knowledge of the **business and its environment** to be able to provide meaningful direction to it.

Integrity

Integrity can be taken as meaning someone of **high moral character**, who sticks to principles no matter the pressure to do otherwise. In working life this requires leaders to adhere to the principles of professionalism and probity. **Straightforward dealing in relationships** with the different groups is particularly important as this creates trust between parties with different interests in the organisation. Integrity is an essential principle of the **corporate governance relationship**, particularly when representing shareholder interests and exercising agency.

Syllabus link

We will return to all of these issues in later chapters of the workbook – however, you can already see the importance of leadership in all of these elements.

2.6 Strategic management

Johnson *et al* (2017) highlight the main elements of strategic management as consisting of the following:

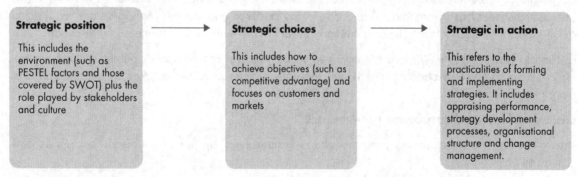

Strategic position

This includes the environment (such as PESTEL factors and those covered by SWOT) plus the role played by stakeholders and culture

Strategic choices

This includes how to achieve objectives (such as competitive advantage) and focuses on customers and markets

Strategic in action

This refers to the practicalities of forming and implementing strategies. It includes appraising performance, strategy development processes, organisational structure and change management.

(Adapted from: Johnson *et al*, 2017: p.12)

These elements are explored in later chapters.

Strategic decisions are likely to lead to **change** within the organisation as resource capacity is adjusted to permit new courses of action. Changes with implications for **organisational culture** are particularly complex and difficult to manage.

3 Culture

3.1 What is culture?

Key term

> **Organisational culture:** 'A pattern of shared basic assumptions...considered valid and transmitted to new members' (Schein, 1985). It has also been described as 'the way we do things round here'.

Culture will have formal or visible aspects, such as goals, policies and terminology as well as informal or less visible aspects such as beliefs, values and norms.

Exercise 2: Culture

Required

Consider your employer, or an organisation with which you are familiar. If you were trying to work out what the culture was like in that organisation, how would you go about doing it and what do you think you would find?

Solution

An organisation's culture may be influenced by a number of factors:

- The **national culture** where the organisation is located, or even the prevailing culture in its home region.

- The **founders** of the organisation – particularly if it is fairly new, the values and approach of the founders may still be pervasive.

- The **history** of the organisation. For example, one which has grown organically, using its own resources, is more likely to have a distinctive culture than one which has grown by acquisition and has had to absorb other cultures.

- The **style** of current leaders will have an impact, for example an autocratic style may encourage a 'compliance culture'.

- Organisational **structure** can affect culture – organisations sometimes restructure as a way of trying to change their culture.

There is no 'best culture' for organisations. However, successful organisations generally align their culture with their strategy as closely as possible. The connections between culture, leadership and strategy are therefore evident.

> ### Essential reading
>
> See Chapter 1 section 2 of the Essential Reading, available in Appendix 2 of the digital edition of the Workbook, for more detail about the role of culture in organisations.

BPP
LEARNING
MEDIA

3.2 The cultural web

3.2.1 Theory

Cultural web: An analysis that compares the paradigm (assumptions) in an organisation's culture with the physical manifestations of that culture.

Culture is, by definition, hard to evaluate, manage or change. To assist with this, Johnson (1992) developed the term **cultural web** to mean a combination of the assumptions that make up the **paradigm**, together with the **physical manifestations** of culture.

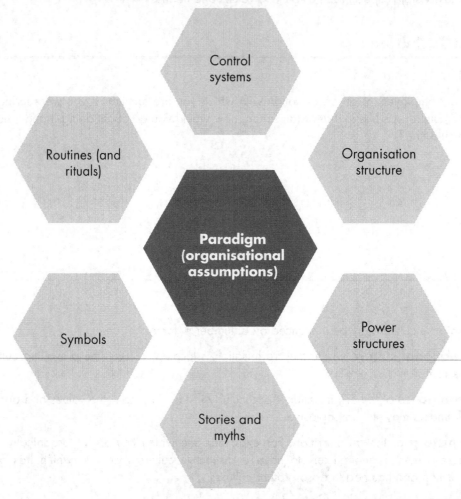

(Adapted from: Johnson *et al*, 2017: p.175)

These are defined as follows.

- **Control systems** – what is measured and rewarded in the organisation, eg people may be rewarded based on volume of sales rather than customer service

- **Routines** – the way members of an organisation behave to each other and to those outside the organisation and **Rituals** – events that are important to the organisation, whether formal (eg recruitment and induction processes) or informal (eg drinks after work)

- **Organisation structure** – this will determine formal and informal relationships and what is important, for example a hierarchical structure suggest a 'top-down' approach

- **Paradigm** – the shared assumptions of the organisation, including beliefs, that are taken for granted and represent a collective experience

- **Symbols** – this can include logos, office layouts, titles and uniforms, often in the form of 'status symbols'

- **Power structures** – people holding power in the organisation. This may not just be based on seniority, eg in professional firms' technical experts may hold significant power

- **Stories and myths** – stories told to each other, outsiders and new recruits such as the organisation's foundation or key decisions

You can remember these terms if you need to analyse an organisation's culture using the cultural web by the mnemonic 'CROPS PS'.

Illustration 1

Example of the cultural web

The following table illustrates some of the questions which the cultural web prompts us to ask about an organisation. It also gives some examples of the expressions of culture that could be generated by the web. The example below is based on the cultural web for a car repair workshop.

Cultural web	Examples
Control systems	
Which process has the strongest controls?	Costs are very tightly controlled. Customers are billed for all parts used.
Which process has the weakest controls?	Quality is not seen as important. Getting work done as cheaply as possible is emphasised ahead of quality.
Is the emphasis on rewarding good work or penalising poor work?	In their pay review, employees are judged on the actual costs of their jobs compared to their job quotes. Staff whose actual costs exceed quotes tend to get smaller pay rises than those whose job costs are lower than their quotes.
Rituals and routines	
What do employees expect when they come to work?	Employees have to sign in, and are then given a job sheet by the boss showing their jobs for the day.
What do customers expect when they walk in?	Customers expect to hear the radio playing and to be given a mug of coffee while they wait to collect cars.
What would be immediately obvious if it changed?	Workshop repainted and new machinery installed
What behaviour do the routines encourage?	Lots of talk about money-saving, and especially how to cut costs
Organisational structure	
Is the structure formal or informal? Flat or hierarchical?	Flat structure: Owner, Mechanics, Receptionist
What are the formal lines of authority?	The mechanics report to the owner (who is also a mechanic by trade).
Are there any informal lines of authority?	The receptionist is the owner's wife so she discusses customer complaints directly with him.
Do structures encourage co-operation and collaboration?	Each mechanic works by themselves. There is no sharing of tools or jobs.
Paradigm	

What are the shared assumptions?

What common experiences exist?

What do people take for granted?

Cultural web	Examples
Symbols	
What language and jargon is used? Is it well known and usable by all?	Mechanics use jargon which customers don't understand to describe parts and problems.
What aspects of strategy are highlighted in publicity?	Adverts and leaflets say they won't be beaten on price.
Are there any status symbols?	No, the boss wears an overall, like the staff.
Power structures	
Who has the real power in the organisation?	The owner
How strongly held are the beliefs of the people with power?	The owner believes strongly in a low-cost model, and is prepared to lose repeat customers in order to keep costs down.
How is power used or abused?	Knowing that their pay reviews are dependent on cost control keeps mechanics working to this low-cost model.
What are the main blockages to change?	The owner insists that his low-cost model is the best way to run the business and won't invest in any new equipment if it will cost lots of money to do so.
Stories	
What stories do people tell about the organisation?	They're always the cheapest on the market; they do things the cheapest way they can.
What do these stories say about the values of the organisation?	They are known for having high numbers of customer complaints, and for low-quality workmanship.
What reputation is communicated among customers and other stakeholders?	
What do employees talk about when they think of the history of the organisation?	The founder started the company himself with a loan from a friend.

PER alert

Performance Objective 2 'Stakeholder Relationship Management' of the Practical Experience Requirement requires you to 'display sensitivity, empathy and cultural awareness in all your communications'. (ACCA, 2019b). As you will need to display cultural awareness in the work environment you are strongly advised to take your time as you go through the following sections which explore the important role that culture plays in organisations.

3.2.2 The cultural web and organisation strategy

The importance of the cultural web for business strategy is that it provides a means of looking at cultural assumptions and practices, to make sure that organisational elements are aligned with one another, and with an organisation's strategy.

If an organisation is not delivering the results its management wants, management can use the web to help diagnose whether the organisation's culture is contributing to the underperformance.

There are three phases to such analysis. First, management can look at organisational culture as it is now. Second, they can look at how they want the culture to be, and third, they can identify the

BPP
LEARNING
MEDIA

differences between the two. These differences indicate the changes which will need to be made to achieve the high-performance culture that they are seeking.

In this way, the cultural web can play a significant role in change management, and changing organisational culture.

Activity 2: iCompute

| **ACCA Professional skills focus** |
| Analysis: Investigate |

You are working as a consultant specialising in organisational culture. You have been handed some client notes by a colleague and asked to comment on the culture in place and how it might affect the organisation's prospects.

iCompute was founded 20 years ago by the entrepreneur, Ron Yeates. It initially specialised in building bespoke computer software for the financial services industry. However, it has expanded into other specialised areas and it is currently the third largest software house in the country, employing 400 people. It still specialises in bespoke software, although 20% of its income now comes from the sales of a software package designed specifically for car insurance.

The company has grown based on a 'work hard, play hard' work ethic and this still remains. Employees are expected to work long hours and to take part in social activities after work. Revenues have continued to increase over the last few years, but the firm has had difficulty in recruiting and retaining staff. Approximately one-third of all employees leave within their first year of employment at the company. The company appears to experience particular difficulty in recruiting and retaining female staff, with 50% of female staff leaving within 12 months of joining the company. Only about 20% of the employees are female and they work mainly in marketing and human resources.

The company is currently in dispute with two of its customers who claim that its bespoke software did not fit the agreed requirements. iCompute currently outsources all its legal advice problems to a law firm that specialises in computer contracts and legislation. However, the importance of legal advice has led to iCompute considering the establishment of an internal legal team, responsible for advising on contracts, disputes and employment legislation.

The support of bespoke solutions and the car insurance software package was also outsourced a year ago to a third party. Although support had been traditionally handled in-house, it was unpopular with staff. One of the senior managers responsible for the outsourcing decision claimed that support calls were 'increasingly varied and complex, reflecting incompetent end users, too lazy to read user guides.' However, the outsourcing of support has not proved popular with iCompute's customers and a number of significant complaints have been made about the service given to end users. The company is currently reviewing whether the software support process should be brought back in-house.

The company is still regarded as a technology leader in the market place, although the presence of so many technically gifted employees within the company often creates uncertainty about the most appropriate technology to adopt for a solution. One manager commented that 'we have often adopted, or are about to adopt, a technology or solution when one of our software developers will ask if we have considered some newly released technology. We usually admit we haven't and so we re-open the adoption process. We seem to be in a state of constant technical paralysis.'

Although Ron Yeates retired five years ago, many of the software developers recruited by him are still with the company. Some of these have become operational managers, employed to manage teams of software developers on internal and external projects. Subba Kendo is one of the managers who originally joined the company as a trainee programmer. 'I moved into management because I needed to earn more money. There is a limit to what you can earn here as a software developer.

I still keep up to date with programming though, and I am a goalkeeper for one of the company's five-a-side football teams. I am still one of the boys.'

However, many of the software developers are sceptical about their managers. One commented that 'they are technologically years out of date. Some will insist on writing programs and producing code, but we take it out again as soon as we can and replace it with something we have written. Not only are they poor programmers, they are poor managers and don't really know how to motivate us.' Although revenues have increased, profits have fallen. This is also blamed on the managers. 'There is always an element of ambiguity in specifying customers' requirements. In the past, Ron Yeates would debate responsibility for the requirement changes with the customer. However, we now seem to do all amendments for free. The customer is right even when we know he isn't. No wonder margins are falling. The managers are not firm enough with their customers.'

The software developers are also angry that an in-house project has been initiated to produce a system for recording the time spent on tasks and projects. Some of the justification for this is that a few of the projects are on a 'time and materials' basis and a time recording system would permit accurate and prompt invoicing. However, the other justification for the project is that it will improve the estimation of 'fixed-price' contracts. It will provide statistical information derived from previous projects to assist account managers preparing estimates to produce quotes for bidding for new bespoke development contracts.

Vikram Soleski, one of the current software developers, commented that 'managers do not even have up-to-date mobile phones, probably because they don't know how to use them. We (software developers) always have the latest gadgets long before they are acquired by managers. But I like working here, we have a good social scene and after working long hours we socialise together, often playing computer games well into the early hours of the morning. It's a great life if you don't weaken!'

Required

Analyse the culture of iCompute and assess the implications of your analysis for the company's future performance. **(13 marks)**

Professional skills marks are available for demonstrating **analysis** skills as part of your analysis of the culture of iCompute. **(2 marks)**

(Total = 15 marks)

Solution

Chapter summary

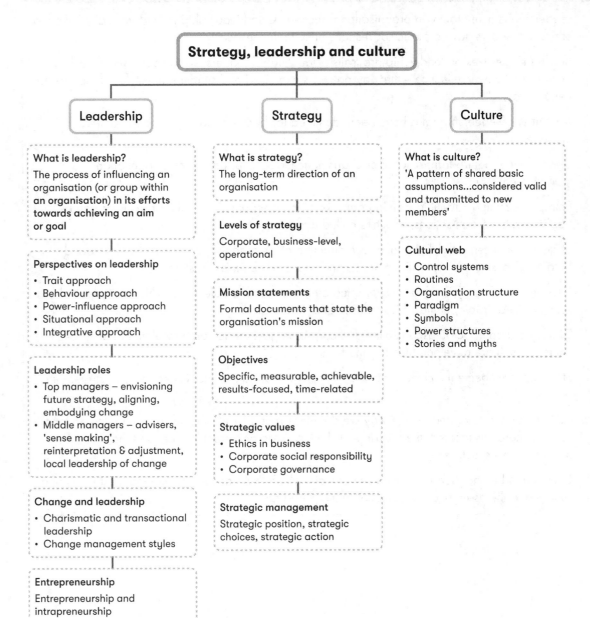

Strategy, leadership and culture

Leadership

What is leadership?
The process of influencing an organisation (or group within an organisation) in its efforts towards achieving an aim or goal

Perspectives on leadership
- Trait approach
- Behaviour approach
- Power-influence approach
- Situational approach
- Integrative approach

Leadership roles
- Top managers – envisioning future strategy, aligning, embodying change
- Middle managers – advisers, 'sense making', reinterpretation & adjustment, local leadership of change

Change and leadership
- Charismatic and transactional leadership
- Change management styles

Entrepreneurship
Entrepreneurship and intrapreneurship

Strategy

What is strategy?
The long-term direction of an organisation

Levels of strategy
Corporate, business-level, operational

Mission statements
Formal documents that state the organisation's mission

Objectives
Specific, measurable, achievable, results-focused, time-related

Strategic values
- Ethics in business
- Corporate social responsibility
- Corporate governance

Strategic management
Strategic position, strategic choices, strategic action

Culture

What is culture?
'A pattern of shared basic assumptions...considered valid and transmitted to new members'

Cultural web
- Control systems
- Routines
- Organisation structure
- Paradigm
- Symbols
- Power structures
- Stories and myths

BPP
LEARNING
MEDIA

1. Leadership is a key factor in organisational success. Good leadership is fundamentally linked to ethics, as leaders have a particular responsibility in this respect.

2. Broad perspectives on leadership are traits or qualities of leaders, behaviour – what leaders actually do, power-influence – the way power is exercised and situational – styles of leadership need to vary.

3. A number of leadership roles have been identified for both top managers and middle managers.

4. Change may require transactional or charismatic leadership, and a range of change management styles.

5. Entrepreneurship is about identifying and exploiting opportunities. Similar principles can be applied within organisations, which is called intrapreneurship.

6. Strategy is concerned with the long-term direction of an organisation. It may be developed at corporate, business or operational level, and supported by mission statements.

7. Mission and strategy need to be supported by more detailed objectives, which will ideally be specific, measurable, achievable, realistic and time-related.

8. Ethics, corporate social responsibility and corporate governance are key elements of strategic values, which are developed later in the text.

9. Strategic management includes analysis of strategic position, strategic choices and strategy in action.

10. Culture can be described as 'the way we do things round here'. It is influenced by the national culture where it is located, the founders, its history, style of current leaders and the organisation's structure.

11. Culture can be analysed using the cultural web, which looks at the physical manifestations of a culture and the assumptions that make up the paradigm.

Further study guidance

Question practice

Now try the question below from the Further question practice bank (available in the digital edition of the Workbook):

Q1 *Bonar Paint*

Further reading

There are articles on the ACCA website written by members of the SBL examining team which are relevant to your studies and which would be useful to read:

Culture and configuration

This article gives further consideration to the cultural web and explores the importance of organisational structure and configuration.

Performance indicators

This article focuses on the interaction between objectives, critical success factors, and key performance indicators.

Approaching SBL overview

This article provides a one-page summary of the key features of the SBL exam.

Approaching SBL reading and planning

This article provides a one-page summary of how best to approach the SBL exam.

SBL – 10 things to learn from the September 2018 sitting

This article highlights some of the issues that ACCA identified in candidates' answers during the September 2018 SBL exam sitting. The article provides some useful advice for improving your chances of passing the SBL exam.

Strategic Business Leader – The importance of effective communication for SBL

This article provides some useful insights into the different formats which you will be expected to use when answering SBL exam tasks.

Own research

It is critical that you start practicing application of this knowledge as early as possible. Using web searches, the business press, your own experience and your personal network, look for examples of leaders or organisations where you can consider application of these concepts. For example:

- Leadership: who do you consider to be a good leader? Why is this? Who do you consider to be a bad leader? Again, why is this? Are there any common themes you can think of that connect leaders – where do they get this from?

- Strategy: research an organisation you either work for or are familiar with in some way – what do you think this organisation's strategy is? How does it determine this strategy? How does it respond to change?

- Culture: what form of culture are you part of, either at your place of work or another organisation you are familiar with? Why does this culture exist – is it due to individuals, history, technology or something else? Does the culture change (and does it need to change)?

Exercise 1

Here are some suggestions that you may have considered.

- Charisma – 'star quality'
- Good communication skills, whether written and/or spoken
- Seen to live in line with their message – 'walk the talk'
- Expertise in their field
- Willingness to take risk, including the risk of unpopularity

Exercise 2

This could range from formal aspects such as procedures manuals, contracts and codes of conduct to things like looking at how people deal with each other, what they wear, their hours of work etc.

The findings of your research would be dependent on the organisation that you investigated.

Stakeholders and social responsibility

2

Learning objectives

On completion of this chapter, you should be able to:

	Syllabus reference no.
Discuss the nature of the principal-agent relationship in the context of governance	B1(a)
Analyse the issues connected with the separation of ownership and control over organisation activity	B1(b)
Discuss and critically assess the concept of stakeholder power and interest using the Mendelow model and apply this to strategy and governance	B2(a)
Evaluate the stakeholders' roles, claims and interests in an organisation and how they may conflict	B2(b)
Explain social responsibility and viewing the organisation as 'corporate citizen' in the context of governance	B2(c)
Discuss the factors that determine organisational policies on reporting to stakeholders, including stakeholder power and interests	B4(a)
Assess the role and value of integrated reporting and evaluate the issues concerning accounting for sustainability	B4(b)
Advise on the guiding principles, the typical content elements and the six capitals of an integrated report, and discuss the usefulness of this information to stakeholders	B4(c)
Describe and assess the social and environmental impacts that economic activity can have (in terms of social and environmental 'footprints' and environmental reporting)	B4(d)
Describe the main features of internal management systems for underpinning environmental and sustainability accounting including EMAS and ISO 14000	B4(e)
Examine how the audit of integrated reports can provide adequate assurance of the relevance and reliability of organisation reports to stakeholders	B4(f)

Business and exam context

We are going to learn more about governance throughout this book, but here we are looking at how important it is to be aware of the world around us as leaders and consider how we can demonstrate that we have taken our responsibilities seriously.

We will explore the dynamic that exists between the owners and managers of an entity and consider who else we need to consider and how to prioritise them. We will also look at the duty of care that an organisation owes to the society in which it exists and consider the various approaches that could be taken.

Finally, we will consider both the social and environmental impacts that an organisation can have on society, how they can be communicated and the benefits from disclosing this information in a way that can be trusted.

Chapter overview

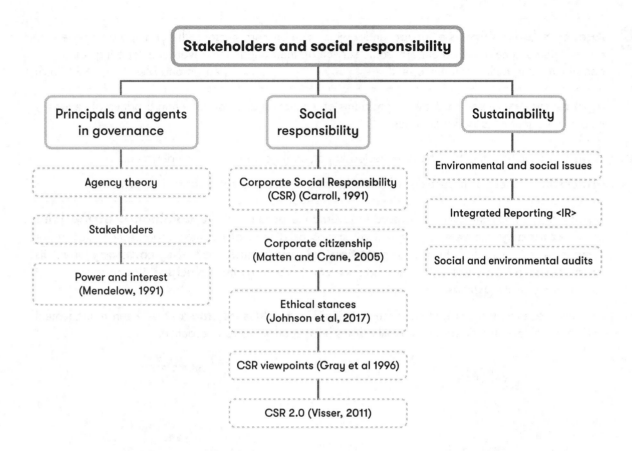

1 Principals and agents in governance

1.1 Agency theory

Agency relationship: 'Is a contract under which one or more persons (the principals) engage another person (the agent) to perform some service on their behalf that involves delegating some decision-making authority to the agent'. (Jensen and Meckling, 1976: p.5)

Agency theory is used to study the problems of motivation and control when a principal needs the help of an agent to carry out activities.

Agent: Is usually a director who is interested in personal gain from their employment.

Principal: Is usually a shareholder who is interested in wealth creation from their investment.

Agency is a significant issue in corporate governance because of the **dominance of the joint stock company**, the company limited by shares as a form of business organisation. For larger companies this has led to the **separation of ownership of the company** from its **management**. The owners (the shareholders) can be seen as the **principal**, the management of the company as the **agents**.

For these reasons, therefore, there is the potential for **conflicts of interest** between management and shareholders. The diagram below illustrates how agency works in practice:

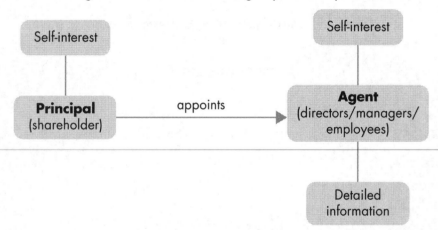

Exam Focus Point

The Strategic Business Leader specimen 2 exam featured a public sector rail company, Rail Co, which was responsible for providing rail services within the country of Beeland. The first question required candidates to act in the capacity of a non-executive member of the Rail Co nominations and corporate governance committee. Part (a) of question 1 asked candidates to prepare a briefing paper which identified and explained 'the agency relationship of the parties involved in Rail Co' and discussed 'the rights and responsibilities of those parties' (ACCA, 2017a). This task was worth 8 technical marks and tested the ACCA Professional Skill of Communication. To produce a good answer candidates needed to use their knowledge of agency theory applied in relation to Rail Co. To earn the two professional skills marks candidates needed set their answer out using the specified briefing paper format.

BPP LEARNING MEDIA

1.1.1 The agency problem

In an ideal world, agents would simply act on behalf of their principals. However, agency theory assumes that agent and principal will act in their own self-interest which may not be aligned and may even be in conflict with each other. The **agency problem** in joint stock companies derives from the principals (shareholders) not being able to run the business themselves and therefore having to rely on agents (directors) to do so for them, despite the fact that they cannot always trust their agents to do everything they would want them to.

For example, shareholders (principals) would rather be paid the maximum amount of earnings via dividends each year, but in doing so, may not pay directors (agents) enough to motivate them to maximise these earnings (or may pay them to take inappropriate levels of risk). Leaving directors to manage the company as they see fit may lead to strategies that shareholders perceive as either too risky or too safe, but in either event, without being involved in the day-to-day running of the company, shareholders may be powerless to stop directors from pursuing these strategies in time.

Addressing the agency problem appears to be a complex balancing act which is seldom perfected and underpins many of the controls in place as part of sound systems of corporate governance.

Essential reading

See Chapter 2 section 1 of the Essential Reading, available in Appendix 2 of the digital edition of the Workbook, for more detail about the agency problem.

1.1.2 Agency monitoring systems

Principals can take a number of steps to monitor their agents when they perceive the agency problem to be present (or at risk of materialising):

- Request formation of committees
- Employ consultants
- Increase numbers of Non-Executive Directors (NEDs)
- Attend AGM and question board

1.1.3 The agency solution

The power that shareholders possess is the right to remove the directors from office. But shareholders have to take the initiative to do this, and in many companies the shareholders lack the energy and organisation to take such a step. Ultimately, they can vote in favour of a takeover or removal of individual directors or entire boards, but this may be undesirable.

Shareholders can take steps to exercise control, but such action will be expensive, time-consuming and difficult to manage because it is difficult to:

(a) Verify what the board is doing, partly because the board has access to more information about its activities than the principal does; and

(b) Introduce mechanisms to control the activities of the board, without preventing it from functioning effectively.

Any steps taken by shareholders are likely to incur '**agency costs**' (Jensen and Meckling, 1976: p5). Common agency costs include:

- Costs of studying company data and results (either in-house or externally)

- Purchase of expert analysis (such as consultants)

- External auditors' fees

- Costs of devising and enforcing directors' contracts (see later content on remuneration)

- Time spent attending company meetings (such as the annual general meeting or AGM)

- Costs of direct intervention in the company's affairs (including legal fees)

- Transaction costs of shareholding (such as brokers' fees and any tax implications for dividends)

Overall, the agency problem is usually addressed by aligning the interests of both agents and principals – how can this be done?

Exercise 1: Agency issues

Required

(a) Identify some reasons why shareholders might become concerned about the management of an organisation in which they hold an investment.

(b) Suggest some ways in which principals can align their interests with those of their agents in order to address the problems identified.

Solution

1.2 Stakeholders

Key term

Stakeholder: Is someone who affects or is affected by an entity and who has a corresponding claim (usually this is what they want).

Stakeholders are people, groups or organisations that can affect or be affected by the actions or policies of an organisation. Each stakeholder group has different expectations about what it wants, and therefore different **claims** upon the organisation.

A useful distinction is between direct and indirect stakeholder claims.

(a) Stakeholders who make **direct claims** do so with their own voice and generally do so clearly. Normally stakeholders with direct claims themselves communicate with the company.

(b) Stakeholders who have **indirect claims** are generally unable to make the claims themselves because they are for some reason inarticulate or voiceless. Although they cannot express their claim directly to the organisation, this does not necessarily invalidate their claim. Stakeholders may lack power because they have no significance for the organisation, have no physical voice (animals and plants), are remote from the organisation (suppliers based in other countries) or are future generations.

1.2.1 Who are stakeholders?

Activity 1: Stakeholders

ACCA Professional skills focus

Commercial acumen: Demonstrate awareness

You work as a senior advisor to the board of a large listed organisation that operates in the construction industry. The services offered range from homebuilding to large civil engineering projects, such as bridges and dams, and can be undertaken for central and local government bodies as well as other profit-making companies. All projects are carried out by staff who require formal accreditation by their professional body.

As part of your work, you have been asked to brief the board about its stakeholders.

Required

Draft a list of stakeholders for the board; briefly explain the nature of each stakeholder's claim.

(6 marks)

Professional skills marks are available for demonstrating **commercial acumen** skills in demonstrating awareness of stakeholders and their claims.

(2 marks)

(Total = 8 marks)

Solution

1.2.2 Classifying stakeholders

Stakeholders can be classified by their proximity to the organisation.

Stakeholder group	Members
Internal	Employees, management, the board
Connected	Shareholders, customers, suppliers, lenders
External	The government, local government, the public, pressure groups, the media, competition, trade unions

Another way of viewing stakeholders is as follows:

Stakeholder group	Members
Active	Those who seek to participate in the organisation's activities. This includes managers and some shareholders but may also include other groups such as regulators and pressure groups.
Passive	Those who do not seek to participate in policy making, such as most shareholders, local communities and government.

Passive stakeholders may still be interested and powerful. If corporate governance arrangements are to develop still further, there may be a need for powerful, passive stakeholders (eg **institutional investors**) to take a more active role.

Illustration 1

Why might an organisation need to recognise its stakeholders when making significant strategic decisions? Here are some suggestions:

To identify ways of communicating with and managing stakeholders

To pre-empt negative reactions and manage stakeholder conflicts

To assess level of interest and power

To establish support for strategic goals

Each of these is a valid reason for focusing on stakeholders and their claims – however, the most important one is likely to be to ensure that various inevitable stakeholder conflicts can be managed.

Performance Objective 2 'Stakeholder Relationship Management' of the Practical Experience Requirement requires you to 'gain commitment from stakeholders by consulting and influencing them to solve problems, meet objectives and maximise mutually beneficial opportunities' (ACCA, 2019b). To help improve your effectiveness in managing and influencing stakeholders you are strongly advised to take your time as you go through the following section which explores the different approaches that can be taken when managing different stakeholder groups.

PER alert

BPP
LEARNING
MEDIA

1.3 Power and interest

One way of assessing stakeholders is to look at the **power** they exert and the **level of interest** they have about its activities.

Mendelow (1991) classifies stakeholders on a matrix whose axes are **power** held and likelihood of showing an **interest** in the organisation's activities. These factors will help define the type of relationship the organisation should seek with its stakeholders and how it should view their concerns. Mendelow's matrix represents a continuum, a map for plotting the relative influence of stakeholders. Stakeholders in the bottom right of the continuum are more significant because they combine the highest power and influence.

Level of interest

		Low	High
Power	**Low**	A	B
	High	C	D

(Adapted from: Mendelow, 1991)

- **Key players** are found in Segment D. The organisation's strategy must be **acceptable** to them, at least. An example would be a major customer.

- Stakeholders in Segment C must be treated with care. They are capable of moving to Segment D. They should therefore be **kept satisfied**. Large institutional shareholders might fall into Segment C.

- Stakeholders in Segment B do not have great ability to influence strategy, but their views can be important in influencing more powerful stakeholders, perhaps by lobbying. They should therefore be **kept informed**. Community representatives and charities might fall into Segment B.

- Minimal effort is expended on Segment A.

1.3.1 Using Mendelow's approach to analyse stakeholders

Stakeholder mapping is used to assess the significance of stakeholders. This in turn has implications for the organisation. The framework of corporate governance and the direction and control of the business should recognise **stakeholders' levels** of **interest** and **power**.

Power means who can exercise **most influence** over a particular decision (though the power may not be used). These include those who **actively participate** in decision making (normally directors, senior managers) or those whose views are **regularly consulted** on important decisions (major shareholders). It can also in a negative sense mean those who have the right of veto over major decisions (creditors with a charge on major business assets can prevent those assets being sold to raise money). Stakeholders may be more influential if their power is combined with:

- **Legitimacy**: the company perceives the stakeholders' claims to be valid
- **Urgency**: whether the stakeholder claim requires immediate action

Level of interest reflects the **effort** stakeholders put in to attempting to participate in the organisation's activities, whether they succeed or not. It also reflects the amount of knowledge stakeholders have about what the organisation is doing.

Companies may try to **reposition** certain stakeholders and discourage others from repositioning themselves, depending on their attitudes. Key **blockers** and **facilitators** of change must be identified. Stakeholder mapping can also be used to establish **future priorities**.

1.3.2 Stakeholder power and interest in reporting

The more influential a stakeholder group is in terms of their level of power and interest the better placed they are to influence the approach the organisation takes when reporting its performance. Stakeholders classified as key players (per Mendelow) are able to influence the issues they would like the organisation to report on in its annual report. This is evident given that most annual reports produced by listed entities focus upon the financial performance and position of the entity. Such reporting aims to meet the needs of influential groups, each of which has its own distinct interest in the financial affairs of the organisation, for example:

- Shareholders want to gain a better understanding of how their investment is performing and whether or not to continue their support

- Regulators want to ensure compliance with relevant laws, e.g. including provisions to cover environmental pollution obligations

- Tax authorities want to assess the profitability of the organisation for the purpose of ensuring the correct amount of tax is paid

Despite this, organisations are increasingly changing the approach that they adopt when reporting on performance with many now reporting on a far broader range of issues. Many organisations focus on providing information to stakeholders that are more likely to be classified as 'keep informed' and 'keep satisfied 'groups per Mendelow. Later in this Chapter consideration is given to sustainability and Integrated Reporting which view performance reporting in a broader sense.

Activity 2: Goaway Hotels

ACCA Professional skills focus

Evaluation: Assess

Goaway Hotels is a chain of hotels based in one country. Ninety per cent of its shares are held by members of the family of the founder of the Goaway group. None of the family members is a director of the organisation. Over the last few years, the family has been quite happy with the steady level of dividends that their investment has generated. Directors are encouraged to achieve high profits by means of a remuneration package with potentially very large profit-related bonuses.

The directors of Goaway Hotels currently wish to take significant steps to increase profits. The area they are focusing on at present is labour costs. Over the last couple of years, many of the workers they have recruited have been economic migrants from another country, the East Asian People's Republic (EAPR). The EAPR workers are paid around 30% of the salary of indigenous workers, and receive fewer benefits. However, these employment terms are considerably better than those that the workers would receive in the EAPR. Goaway Hotels has been able to fill its vacancies easily from this source, and the workers from the EAPR that Goaway has recruited have mostly stayed with the company. The board has been considering imposing tougher employment contracts on home country workers, perhaps letting the number of dismissals and staff turnover of home country workers increase significantly.

In Goaway Hotels' home country, there has been a long period of rule by a government that wished to boost business and thus relaxed labour laws to encourage more flexible working. However, a year ago the opposition party finally won power, having pledged in their manifesto to tighten labour laws to give more rights to home country employees. Since their election the new government has brought in the promised labour legislation, and there have already been successful injunctions obtained, preventing companies from imposing less-favourable employment terms on their employees.

An international chain of hotels has recently approached various members of the founding family with an offer for their shares. The international chain is well known for its aggressive approach to employee relations and the high demands it makes on its managers. Local employment laws allow some renegotiation of employment terms if companies are taken over.

Required

You are acting as an advisor to the board, specialising in negotiating changes to employment conditions. Using Mendelow's matrix, evaluate the importance of the following stakeholders to the decision to change the employment terms of home country's workers in Goaway Hotels.

(a) The board of directors
(b) The founding family shareholders
(c) The trade unions to which the home country workers belong
(d) Migrant workers   **(8 marks)**

Professional skills marks are available for demonstrating **evaluation** skills in assessing the importance of the different stakeholders.   **(2 marks)**

(Total = 10 marks)

Solution

1.3.2 Problems with stakeholder mapping

However, there are a number of issues with Mendelow's (1991) approach:

(a) It can be **very difficult to measure each stakeholder's power and influence**.

(b) The map is **not static**. Changing circumstances may mean stakeholders' positions move around the map. For example, stakeholders with a lot of interest but not much power may improve their position by combining with other stakeholders with similar views.

(c) The map is based on the idea that **strategic positioning**, rather than moral or ethical concerns, should govern an organisation's attitude to its stakeholders.

(d) If there are a number of key players, and their views are in conflict, it can be very difficult to resolve the situation, hence there may be **uncertainties** over the organisation's future direction.

(e) Mendelow's matrix considers power and influence but fails to take **legitimacy** into account.

Legitimacy is a distinct concept from power. For example, minority shareholders in a company controlled by a strong majority may not have much power, but law in most countries recognises that they have legitimate rights which the company must respect. Mitchell *et al* (1997) argue that legitimacy is a desirable social goal, dependent on more than the perception of individual stakeholders.

1.3.3 Problems with stakeholder theory

We saw in Illustration 1 that an organisation's stakeholders can be a diverse and lengthy list of parties, often with conflicting claims. One reason for analysing stakeholder claims is therefore to ensure that each of these can be managed in some way. However, keeping all parties satisfied is far from straightforward.

Key term

Fiduciary duty: Is a duty of care and trust which one person or entity owes to another. It can be a legal or ethical obligation.

One such conflict comes from the general principle of fiduciary duty that expects managers to maximise shareholder wealth. This can create significant problems, especially if managers are also expected to satisfy other stakeholder claims which conflict with the stated aim of long-term profitability.

There are two fundamentally different motivations for considering stakeholders which may be used by managers to define their actions.

The **instrumental** view justifies considering stakeholders purely because of the economic benefits to the company – everything else is of secondary importance	The **normative** view is based on the idea that the company has moral obligations towards all its stakeholders, including those whose main aim is not profit-driven

Essential reading

See Chapter 2 section 2 of the Essential Reading, available in Appendix 2 of the digital edition of the Workbook, for a discussion about the emergence of ecosystem environments in business. Although the concept of ecosystems is a relatively new one and is not covered by the Strategic Business Leader syllabus, it is worth taking the time to read this additional material as it considers how organisational interactions with stakeholders are starting to evolve.

2 Social responsibility

Corporate social responsibility (CSR) is a concept whereby organisations consider the interests of society by taking responsibility for the impact of their activities on wider stakeholder groups. This obligation can be seen to extend beyond statutory obligations to comply with legislation. Let's have a look at some examples of how such responsibilities could be categorised and described.

2.1 Corporate social responsibility (CSR) (Carroll, 1991)

This approach is modelled on the idea of a hierarchy of needs that an organisation should be aiming to fulfil, starting at the most basic level (**economic**) which expects some form of profitability for investors. However, it will be seen as more socially responsible if such profits are earned **legally**, as opposed to aiming simply to maximise the proceeds of crime! Many organisations aspire to legal profits, but beyond that there is no obligation. Consequently, acting in an **ethical** manner (such as adopting a code of conduct or extended paid maternity leave for staff) is a choice that is made for a variety of reasons that goes beyond the bare minimum of what the law demands. To be classed as **philanthropic**, an organisation's behaviour needs to include activities that go far beyond the law – establishing a charitable foundation that supports the local community, for example.

Philanthropic
Charitable donations, contributions to local communities, and providing employees with the chances to improve their own lives

Ethical
Organisations are required to act in a fair and just way even if the law does not compel them to do so

Legal
Obeying the law is a requirement in all societies, though legal compliance imposes greater burdens in some societies than others

Economic
To shareholders wanting dividends/capital gains, to employees wanting fair employment, to customers wanting good quality products

(Adapted from: Carroll, 1991)

2.2 Corporate citizenship (Matten and Crane, 2005)

> Limited view consists of limited projects undertaken in the business' self-interest

- The main stakeholder groups that the corporation engages with are local communities and employees

> Equivalent view (similar to Carroll's view of CSR having four key elements)

- Based on a wider general definition of corporate social responsibility that is partly voluntary and partly imposed

> Extended view organisations will promote:

- Social rights of citizens by provision of, for example, decent working conditions
- Civil rights, by intervening to promote citizens' individual rights themselves or to pressurise governments to promote citizens' rights
- Political rights by allowing individuals to promote their causes by using corporate power
- Reinforces the idea of a company being part of a community and meeting the citizenship needs that government does not currently fulfil

2.3 Ethical stances (Johnson *et al*, 2017)

Short-term shareholder interest	Long-term shareholder interest
It is up to governments to impose constraints on governance (ie laws) but beyond that, there is no obligation to go any further. Companies are there to make profits, pay taxes and provide jobs but only in order to comply with the law – no more! Relies on strong controls and objectives being set to achieve this main aim and is unlikely to respond to outside pressures. Examples include large multinational corporations quoted on many different stock exchanges.	Corporate image may be enhanced by an assumption of wider responsibilities. The responsible exercise of corporate power may prevent a build-up of social and political pressure for legal regulation. This approach is quite pragmatic and acknowledges that the pursuit of profit alone will not maintain shareholder wealth over the long term. Such organisations are led by supportive individuals who encourage best practice to engage with stakeholders and respond to outside pressures. Examples include groceries stores and other retailers with a strong consumer focus.

Which one is right?

Multiple stakeholder obligations	Shaper of society
Accept the legitimacy of stakeholders and their claims because without recognising groups such as suppliers, employers and customers, the organisation would not be able to function. Interested in operating in partnership with stakeholders and being proactive in championing many of their claims. Stakeholders' views are used by the board to pursue strategies that go beyond pure profit generation. Examples include public sector organisations, educational establishments and those operating in the arts.	Although it is accepted that this role is largely the preserve of public sector organisations, it is aspirational enough for all organisations to at least attempt to emulate (whether they achieve it or not). Requires visionary leadership to pursue an agenda of social and market change in conjunction with other organisations. Supports individual responsibility being taken across the organisation to achieve this. In its purest form, it is debatable whether such organisations truly exist, although some of these traits may be present (such as visionary leadership, supportive management styles and a desire for social change) in isolation.

2.4 CSR viewpoints (Gray *et al*, 1996)

Pristine capitalist

Business has no moral responsibilities beyond its obligations to shareholders and creditors. Profit is the only aim for such organisations – everything else is irrelevant. Could include any organisation where profit maximisation is the only objective.

Expedient

Social responsibility may be appropriate, but usually only if it is in the business's economic interests. Such a pragmatic approach to social responsibility could simply be seen to be a cynical response to maintain profits, not to benefit stakeholders' interests. Includes organisations with a strong consumer focus (eg retailers marketing themselves as being on the same side as the consumer).

Proponent of the social contract

There is effectively a contract or agreement between these organisations and those who are affected by their decisions (for example, such as between UK state broadcaster the BBC, the UK Government and licence fee payers who receive ther content). Change is usually not allowed unless it can be accommodated by all parties involved.

Social ecologist

Traditional business activities result in natural resources being used up in the pursuit of profits. Social ecologists believe that strategies leading to waste and pollution must be modified and organisations must become more socially responsible in their resource usage (for example, cosmetics being sourced from natural products and sold in recyclable packaging).

Socialist

Business decision-making should no longer be determined by the requirements of capitalism and materialism alone, but should promote equality and treat all parties' interests equally. This is equivalent to the political definition of socialism in many respects and aims to reduce the abuse of workers by the ruling classes.

Radical feminist

Can include a variety of approaches, but in general terms, such organisations aim to promote feminine values (such as co-operation and empathy) over typically masculine values (such as aggression and conflict) in order to achieve more socially desirable objectives, and not just profit.

Deep ecologist ('Deep Green')

Suggests that humans have no greater right to resources or life than any other species on the planet. Organisations therefore should not destroy animal habitats (using techniques such as deforestation or greenfield development) or pursue animals (such as commercial whaling) at all, let alone for profit. Environmental pressure groups are examples of organisations that take such a stance.

BPP
LEARNING
MEDIA

2.5 CSR 2.0 (Visser, 2011)

In his book **The Age of Responsibility – CSR 2.0 and the New DNA of Business** (Visser, 2011), Visser takes stock of the current state of corporate social responsibility across the globe, charting its history and development over time using the following 'ages' (some of which imply that current views on CSR may be in need of some radical overhaul):

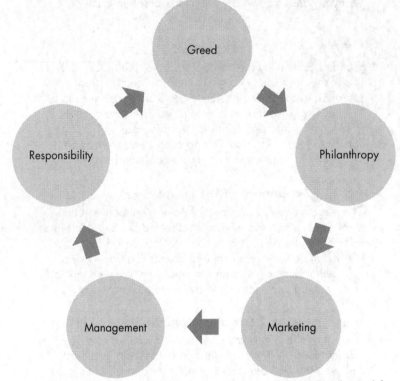

(Adapted from: Visser, 2011)

Consequently, Visser suggests that we need 'CSR 2.0' to take CSR to the next level, identifying five principles that should be adopted in order to achieve this:

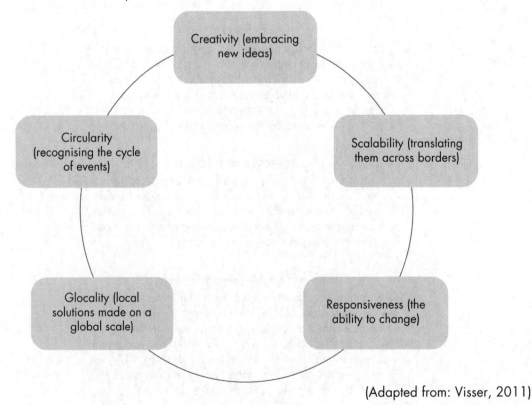

(Adapted from: Visser, 2011)

In conclusion, he discusses barriers to achieving CSR 2.0 which question as a society both our ability and our desire to change, suggesting that good CSR may still only be a choice, not an imperative.

Activity 3: Corporate social responsibility

ACCA Professional skills focus

Communication: Inform

You work as a senior advisor to the board of a large listed organisation that operates in the construction industry. The services offered range from homebuilding to large civil engineering projects, such as bridges and dams, and can be undertaken for central and local government bodies as well as other profit-making companies. All projects are carried out by staff who require formal accreditation by their professional body.

As part of your work, you have been asked to brief the board about its corporate social responsibility (CSR) position. Proponents of CSR argue that there is a strong business case for considering stakeholders, whereas critics argue that CSR distracts from the fundamental economic role of businesses.

Required

Draft one presentation slide with presenter's notes showing arguments supporting both the case for and against CSR.

(6 marks)

Professional skills marks are available for demonstrating **communication** skills in informing the audience of the arguments for and against CSR. **(2 marks)**

(Total = 8 marks)

Solution

Activity 4: CSR and tax

ACCA Professional skills focus

Commercial acumen: Demonstrate awareness

GSA is a listed pharmaceutical manufacturer that operates across different countries but has its headquarters in a European country. In general terms it always complies with the law – financial statements are filed on time, employee and sales taxes are paid over to the local tax authority – but despite the parent company recording high operating profits, it recently paid a very low level of corporate tax due to apparent loopholes in the legislation (sometimes referred to as 'legal tax avoidance'). This became a controversial news story and led to calls for a boycott of the company's products unless they voluntarily paid more corporate tax. GSA's Chief Executive Martyn Rice agreed to respond to the media on behalf of the board.

Required

You are a senior manager working in the strategy function of GSA.

Recommend a series of responses for the Chief Executive to make based on current CSR theory. You should aim to include at least four different points of view. **(8 marks)**

Professional skills marks are available for demonstrating **commercial acumen** skills in demonstrating awareness of the factors influencing this decision. **(2 marks)**

(Total = 6 marks)

Solution

3 Sustainability

3.1 Environmental and social issues

3.1.1 Environmental and social footprint

Sustainability: Means limiting the use of depleting resources to a level that can be replenished.

Sustainable development: Is development that meets the needs of the present without compromising the ability of future generations to meet their own needs.

Key terms

When considering sustainability, a number of questions need to be considered:

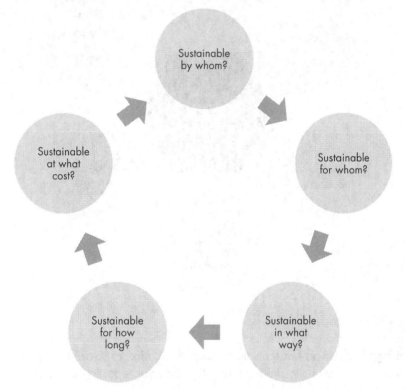

A key issue is **generational equity**, ensuring that future generations are able to enjoy the same environmental conditions, and in social terms per capita welfare is maintained or increased.

The two approaches to sustainability are:	
Weak sustainability believes that the focus should be on sustaining the human species and the natural environment can be regarded as a resource. The weak sustainability viewpoint tends to dominate discussion within the Western economic viewpoint.	**Strong sustainability** stresses the need for harmony with the natural world; it is important to sustain all species, not just the human race. There is a requirement for fundamental change, including a change in how man perceives economic growth (and whether or not it is pursued at all).

Environmental footprint: Is a measure of the impact that a particular business's activities have upon the environment including its resource, environment and pollution emissions.

Social footprint: Is a measure of the impact or effect that an entity can have on a given set of concerns or stakeholder interests.

Key terms

It is the impact on people, society and the wellbeing of communities. Impacts can be positive (such as job creation and community benefits) or negative, such as when a plant closure increases unemployment and the local community suffers.

Examples of factors that could be used to determine a firm's environmental footprint include the following items (note that many of them could be assessed using metrics that may be measured and reported as part of assessing an organisation's environmental footprint):

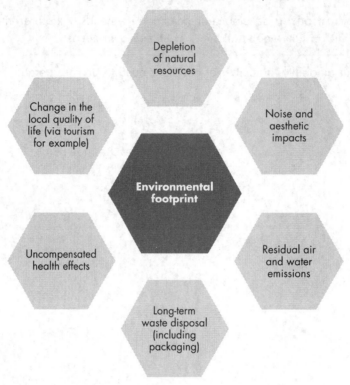

3.1.2 Social and environmental reporting

Social accounting: Is a concept describing the communication of social and environmental effects of a company's economic actions to stakeholders. A number of reporting guidelines have been developed to serve as frameworks.

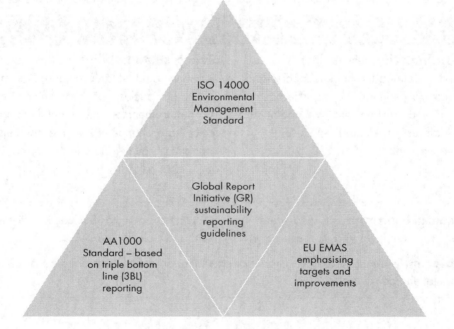

AA1000 standard

The AA1000 standard is produced by AccountAbility.

'AccountAbility is a global consulting and sustainability standards firm that works with businesses, governments and multilateral organisations to advance responsible business practices and improve long-term performance.' (AccountAbility, 2019).

The AA1000 (2008) standard was based on the concept of triple bottom line accounting which encourages organisational activities to be accounted for in less obvious ways than just financial reporting terms:

People – the equivalent of social accounting (for example, the amount of charitable donations made)
Planet – a focus on environment performance such as waste management and recycling targets
Profit – a measure of the success of the business, but considering the redistribution of wealth which brings benefits to the local community (for example, education schemes and community projects)

The AA1000 standard was updated in 2018, and is based on the following principles:

- 'Inclusivity – People should have a say in the decisions that impact them.

- Materiality – Decision makers should identify and be clear about the sustainability topics that matter.

- Responsiveness – Organisations should act transparently on material sustainability topics and their related impacts.

- Impact – Organisations should monitor, measure and be accountable for how their actions affect their broader ecosystems.' (AccountAbility, 2018).

The AA1000 standard provides organisations with guidance on how to respond to the challenges presented by sustainability issues.

Global Reporting Initiative (GR)

The **Global Reporting Initiative (GR)** (2016) is a reporting framework and arose from the need to address the failure of the current governance structures to respond to changes in the global economy. The GR aims to develop transparency, accountability, reporting and sustainable development. Its vision is that reporting on **economic**, **environmental** and **social** importance should become as routine and comparable as financial reporting.

Essential reading

See Chapter 2 section 3 of the Essential Reading, available in Appendix 2 of the digital edition of the Workbook, for more detail about the purpose and advantages of environmental reporting.

Eco-Management and Audit Scheme (EMAS)

EMAS (EU, 2019) is a voluntary scheme that emphasises targets and improvements, on-site inspections and requirements for disclosure and verification.

Requirements for EMAS registration
An environmental policy containing commitments to comply with legislation and achieve continuous environmental performance improvement
An on-site environmental review

Requirements for EMAS registration
An environmental management system that is based on the review and the company's environmental policy
Environmental audits at sites
Audit results to form the basis of setting environmental objectives and the revision of the environmental policy to achieve those objectives
A public environmental statement validated by accredited environmental verifiers containing detailed disclosures about policy, management systems and performance in areas such as pollution, waste, raw material usage, energy, water and noise

ISO 14000

ISO 14000 (ISO, 2015) provides a general framework on which a number of specific standards have been based (the ISO family of standards).

ISO 14001 (ISO, 2015) prescribes that an environmental management system must comprise:

An environmental policy statement, which should be the basis for future action; it needs therefore to be based on reliable data, and allow for the development of specific targets	Assessment of environmental aspects and legal and voluntary obligations	A management system ensuring effective monitoring and reporting on environmental compliance
Internal audits and reports to senior management	A public declaration that ISO 14001 is being complied with	

ISO 14005 (ISO, 2019) was published in 2019. ISO 14005 aims to encourage and support organisations to develop and implement their own environmental management system based on a phased approach which meets the requirements set out by ISO 14001.

3.2 Integrated Reporting <IR>

The aim of integrated reporting (sometimes referred to by this symbol: <IR>) is to **demonstrate the linkage between strategy, governance and financial performance and the social, environmental and economic context within which the business operates**. <IR> is based on the concept of integrated thinking.

Key term

Integrated thinking: 'Is the **active consideration** by the organization of the **relationships between its various operating** and **functional units** and **the capitals** that the organization uses or affects.' (International Integrated Reporting Council, 2019)

Adopting integrated thinking helps organisations to improve their approach to decision-making, as decisions and actions are not made or undertaken in isolation from the wider situation facing the entity. Integrated thinking, in essence ensures that managers and organisational leaders make decisions and undertake actions that consider value creation not in just the short-term but in the medium to longer term. The International Integrated Reporting Council (2019) note that this requires 'thinking holistically about the resources and relationships the organization uses or affects, and the dependencies and trade-offs between them as value is created. In applying this mindset, the organization views itself as part of a greater system, one shaped by the quality, availability and cost of resources, as well as evolving regulations, norms and stakeholder expectations.'

Exercise 2: Integrated thinking

Required

Identify how the adoption of integrated thinking might benefit a clothing retailer, listed on a national stock exchange, which operates 100 stores and sells all of its products at low prices.

Solution

By making these connections, businesses should be able to take more sustainable decisions, helping to ensure the effective allocation of scarce resources. Investors and other stakeholders should better understand how an organisation is really performing. In particular, they should make a meaningful assessment of the long-term viability of the organisation's business model and its strategy.

<IR> should also achieve the simplification of accounts, with excessive detail being removed and critical information being highlighted.

Key term

'**<IR>:** Is a **process** founded on integrated thinking that results in a **periodic integrated report** by an organization about **value creation** over time and related **communications** regarding aspects of **value creation**. An **integrated report** is a concise communication about how an organization's strategy, governance, performance and prospects, in the context of its external environment, lead to the **creation** of **value** in the **short**, **medium** and **long term**.' (International Integrated Reporting Council, 2018)

Where <IR> differs from other forms of reporting is that it focuses on the **process** not the **product**, using a series of capitals to illustrate how an organisation **creates value** for all stakeholders, not just shareholders. The International Integrated Reporting Council (2018) have identified the following six capitals:

Category of capital	Characteristic elements of the category of capital
Financial	**Funds** available for use in production or service provision, **obtained** through **financing** or **generated** through **operations**
Manufactured	Manufactured physical objects **used in production** or **service provision**; including buildings, equipment and infrastructure

Category of capital	Characteristic elements of the category of capital
Human	**Skills**, **experience** and **motivation** to innovate: • Alignment and support for an organisation's governance framework and ethical values • Ability to understand and implement organisation's strategies • Loyalties and motivations for improvements
Intellectual	**Intangible assets**, providing competitive advantage: • Patents, copyrights, software and organisation systems • Brand and reputation
Natural	**Inputs** to goods and services, and natural environment on which an organisation's activities have an impact: • Water, land, minerals and forests • Biodiversity and health of eco-systems
Social	The **institutions** and **relationships** established within and between each community, stakeholder group and network to enhance individual and collective wellbeing. Includes an organisation's **social licence** to operate.

There are seven guiding principles or characteristics that <IR> requires an organisation's reporting to display in some way in order to be seen as **meaningful**:

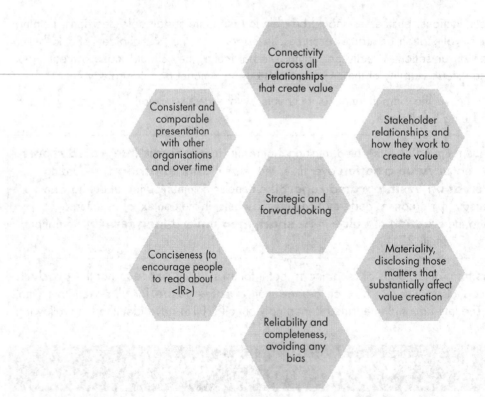

3.2.1 Auditing Integrated Reports

The audit of an organisation's Integrated Report by an independent assurance provider allows the users of such reports to place greater levels of reliance on their content. Enhanced reliance helps organisations to build trust among investors and other stakeholder groups. This is evident as it shows that the organisation is open to reporting (and having its performance verified by an independent party) from a number of perspectives beyond the traditional financial viewpoint.

Enhanced transparency and the improved levels of accountability that audited Integrated Reports bring heighten the likelihood for the company to attract new investors to purchase shares. This is supported by the fact that investors are becoming increasingly interested in understanding how the organisations they own have performed from an environmental and social perspective. The audit of Integrated Reports helps to ensure that management avoid the temptation of simply paying 'lip service' to recent developments in performance reporting. Instead of viewing the production of an Integrated Report as a PR exercise in which the production of the report is viewed as the final output, managers are instead forced to commit, in the longer term, to the concept of integrated reporting by permitting regular outside scrutiny.

Nonetheless, it is not straightforward for organisations who are interested in having their Integrated Report audited. A significant issue for such organisations concerns the reluctance, among many audit firms, to provide the same level of assurance over the content of Integrated Reports that they give when conducting a statutory financial audit. A significant issue for auditors concerns the high costs incurred in being able to provide even limited assurance. This situation has been driven in part by the fact that often the performance objectives and measures used in reporting the six capitals are qualitative in nature. This increases the subjectivity of measuring performance. The lack of mandatory assurance over integrated reporting in many jurisdictions around the world has hindered the process of auditing integrated reports.

Exam Focus Point

The March/June 2019 exam released by ACCA featured a clothing retailer called SmartWear. Task 5(a) required the preparation of one slide with notes for a presentation to be given by the CFO at SmartWear to the rest of the board. The slide and notes needed to describe the benefits of integrated thinking within SmartWear to all stakeholders. The examining team commented that 'most, but not all, candidates included a presentation slide, and most had accompanying notes. However, the quality of these varied considerably, with some slides containing masses of text, and others one or two basic bullet points. Candidates should be able to communicate this way with ease, so it is suspected that many answers were rushed due to poor time management'. (ACCA, 2019a).

Task 5(b) followed on from part (a) and required the creation of a briefing paper for SmartWear's CFO. The briefing paper would allow the CFO to address the wider finance team, explaining how corporate reporting, using the <IR> framework, would provide better information for SmartWear's shareholders about the creation of sustainable long-term value. The examining team noted that many candidates seemed to understand the theory of integrated reporting but struggled to apply it to the case. 'The weakest candidates only listed the 6 Integrated Reporting Capitals, with only the best candidates able to show how these are clearly linked to how sustainable long-term value can be created for the SmartWear shareholders.' (ACCA, 2019a). Professional skills marks were available for parts (a) and (b) of the task by demonstrating appropriate communication skills to the different audiences.

To earn the 2 professional skills marks on offer candidates needed to produce a slide and notes which communicated the main elements about integrated thinking in respect of part (a). The briefing paper in part (b) needed to be structured in such a way that it was informative and convincing to the shareholders about introducing integrated reporting.

3.3 Social and environmental audits

3.3.1 Social audits

Social audit is the process of checking whether an organisation has achieved set targets.

Generally, social audits will involve a process that focuses on reviewing the following (note that no one area is given any overall priority as they are all expected to interact):

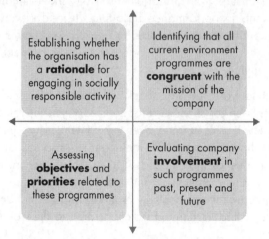

Universities and public sector organisations are examples of the type of organisation that might be expected to use social audits (usually due to their interaction with a range of individuals across the various stakeholder groups they engage with, such as students, hospital patients and vulnerable members of society).

3.3.2 Environmental audits

An **environmental audit** is a systematic, documented, periodic and objective evaluation of how well an entity, its management and equipment are performing, with the aim of helping to safeguard the environment by facilitating management control of environmental practices and assessing compliance with entity policies and external regulations.

Environmental audits help organisations to identify **possible liabilities** from their ongoing activities, assess the threat of **unethical behaviour** and even act as a form of marketing for **investors** especially sensitive to having environmentally and socially questionable representation in their portfolios.

The process of completing environmental audits requires three stages:

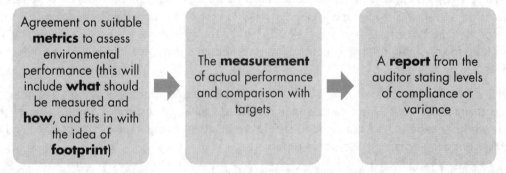

Examples of organisations that make use of environmental audits will obviously include those whose environmental footprint is either significant or high-profile (or in the case of petrochemical and pharmaceutical companies, both).

Chapter summary

```
                    ┌─────────────────────────────────────────┐
                    │   Stakeholders and social responsibility  │
                    └─────────────────────────────────────────┘
```

Principals and agents in governance

Agency theory
- Principals (shareholders) vs agents (directors)
- Agency problems
- Agency monitoring
- Agency solutions

Stakeholders
- Who are stakeholders? What do they want (claims)?
- Classifying stakeholders

Power and interest (Mendelow, 1991)
- Low power, low interest = minimal effort
- Low power, high interest = keep informed
- High power, low interest = keep satisfied
- High power, high interest = key player

Social responsibility

Corporate Social Responsibility (CSR) (Carroll, 1991)
- Economic (basic requirement)
- Legal (and comply with laws)
- Ethical (go beyond the law)
- Philanthropic (help others)

Corporate citizenship (Matten and Crane, 2005)
- Limited view = self-interest only
  - Equivalent view = CSR
- Extended view = going above and beyond

Ethical stances (Johnson et al, 2017)
- Short-term stakeholder interest
- Long-term stakeholder interest
- Multiple stakeholders
- Shaper of society

CSR viewpoints (Gray et al 1996)
- Pristine capitalist
- Expedient
- Social contractarian
- Social ecologist
- Socialist
- Radical feminist
- Deep ecologist

CSR 2.0 (Visser, 2011)
- Responding to change: greed; philanthropy; marketing; management; responsibility
- CSR 2.0: creativity; scalability; responsiveness; glocality; circularity
- Our ability to change

Sustainability

Environmental and social issues
- Environmental and social footprint
- Social and environmental reporting

Integrated Reporting <IR>
- Founded on integrated thinking
- Financial capital
- Manufactured capital
- Human capital
- Intellectual capital
- Natural capital
- Social capital
- Auditing Integrated Reports

Social and environmental audits
- Social audits – engaging in socially responsible activity; goal congruence with this; assess objectives and priorities
- Environmental audits – agree on suitable metrics; measure performance and compare with targets; report from auditor on compliance (or otherwise)

BPP
LEARNING
MEDIA

Knowledge diagnostic

1. Principals and agents often have different goals that can be in conflict with each other, but organisational success comes from finding ways of aligning these interests

2. Stakeholders are not just people who are affected by an entity; they can also affect the entity, so knowing their claims and assessing their power and interest is essential in managing them

3. There are many stances that could be taken to explain how a corporate entity displays its responsibility to society (CSR) – this ranges from pure economic gain for all parties to putting the needs of the environment first and foremost, with plenty of grey in the middle!

4. Social and environmental footprints need to be understood, assessed and communicated and this can be done in a variety of ways using techniques such as the GR and 3BL

5. Integrated reports are fast becoming the preferred method of communicating value for organisations who wish to inform their stakeholders, so an awareness of the various capitals used and created is essential for this to be effective

6. Social and environmental audits are fast becoming a way of holding organisations to account for their impact on society and the environment they operate in, usually via an assessment of a series of metrics or other deliverables

Further study guidance

Question practice

Now try the question below from the Further question practice bank (available in the digital edition of the Workbook):

Q2 *ZK*

Further reading

There are articles on the ACCA website written by members of the SBL examining team which are relevant to your studies and which would be useful to read:

All about stakeholders (Part 1)

This article considers the nature of stakeholder claims and explores Mendelow's matrix in the context of stakeholder influence.

All about stakeholders (Part 2)

This article considers different stakeholder groups and further explores the work of Gray et al.

The integrated report framework

This article explores the main principles of integrated reporting.

Approaching SBL overview

This article provides a one-page summary of the key features of the SBL exam.

Approaching SBL reading and planning

This article provides a one-page summary of how best to approach the SBL exam.

SBL – 10 things to learn from the September 2018 sitting

This article highlights some of the issues that ACCA identified in candidates' answers during the September 2018 SBL exam sitting. The article provides some useful advice for improving your chances of passing the SBL exam.

Strategic Business Leader – The importance of effective communication for SBL

This article provides some useful insights into the different formats which you will be expected to use when answering SBL exam tasks.

Own research

Consider your own organisation, or one with which you are very familiar – let's see if you can find out more about the topics considered in this chapter:

- How does the organisation aim to control its agents and who are the principals?

- What stakeholders does your organisation have? What are their claims?

- In terms of its CSR position or stance, what kind of entity is your organisation?

- What information does your organisation publish about its social and environmental footprint?

- Does your organisation publish an integrated report? If so, try and get access to it to see how it works in practice. If not, use the ACCA integrated report as an illustration available on the ACCA website.

Exercise 1

The following could be reasons for a principal becoming concerned about their agent(s):

- Decline in profitability
- Lack of disclosures in annual accounts
- Fall in share price
- Adverse commentary by analysts
- Change in business environment
- Change in key personnel

The alignment of interests between principal and agent can be achieved by the following:

- Performance-related pay
- Bonuses
- Share options

Exercise 2

The benefits of adopting integrated thinking:

- Helps the retailer to ensure that its approach to business considers inter-related factors when developing strategies. This helps to ensure sustainable value creation. For example, the adoption of integrated thinking should help to ensure that the retailer's low-priced strategy aligns to the underlying opportunities for market growth, such as developing new product ranges or selling through new mediums, for example through social media platforms.

- Integrated thinking should force the board to not only consider those strategies that will result in short-term gains, such as increased profits, but to devise and implement strategies which focus on key business areas which will enhance performance in the long-term. For example, pursuing strategies which build brand awareness or improve the customer experience so that shoppers return in the future.

- Enhanced reputation among key stakeholders, for example, among investors and providers of finance. Integrated thinking should help to ensure that the retailer's decisions are joined up and consistent with previous decisions made. This should result in better performance. Integrated thinking should help to prove to the retailer's shareholders that the decisions taken by the board are made in their best interests. This in turn may also help improve the retailer's approach to risk management.

- Integrated thinking increases employee engagement. Employee knowledge about the issues affecting the retailer's operations can be fed into the process of setting strategy. This should enhance the selected strategies by making use of operational-level employee knowledge to improve operational efficiency, which, in turn, should improve overall performance. Integrated thinking should help to break-down organisational silos and improve the flow of knowledge and data between departments and stores.

Impact of corporate governance on strategy

3

Learning objectives

On completion of this chapter, you should be able to:

	Syllabus reference no.
Analyse and discuss the role and influence of institutional investors in governance systems and structures, including the roles and influences of pension funds, insurance companies and mutual funds	B3(a)
Compare rules versus principles-based approaches to governance and when they may be appropriate	B3(b)
Discuss different models of organisational ownership that influence different governance regimes (family firms vs joint stock company-based models) and how they work in practice	B3(c)
Describe the objectives, content and limitations of governance codes intended to apply to multiple national jurisdictions: (i) Organisation for Economic Co-operation and Development (OECD) Report (ii) International Corporate Governance Network (ICGN) Global Governance Principles	B3(d)
Assess the major areas of organisational life affected by issues in governance: (i) Duties of directors and functions of the board (including setting a responsible 'tone' from the top and being accountable for the performance and impacts of the organisation) (ii) The composition and balance of the board (and board committees) (iii) Relevance and reliability of organisation reporting and external auditing (iv) Directors' remuneration and rewards (v) Responsibility of the board for risk management systems and internal control (vi) Organisation social responsibility and ethics	B5(a)
Evaluate the cases for and against unitary and two-tier board structures	B5(b)

	Syllabus reference no.
Describe and assess the purposes, roles, responsibilities and performance of Non-Executive Directors (NEDs)	B5(c)
Describe and assess the importance and execution of induction and continuing professional development of directors on boards of directors	B5(d)
Explain the meanings of 'diversity' and critically evaluate issues of diversity on boards of directors	B5(e)
Assess the importance, roles, purposes and accountabilities of the main committees within the effective governance of organisations	B5(f)
Describe and assess the general principles of remunerating directors and how to modify directors' behaviour to align with stakeholder interests	B5(g)
Explain and analyse the regulatory, strategic and labour market issues associated with determining directors' remuneration	B5(h)
Compare and contrast public sector, private sector, charitable status and non-governmental (NGO and quasi-NGO) forms of organisation, including agency relationships, stakeholders' aims and objectives and performance criteria	B6(a)
Assess and evaluate the strategic objectives, leadership and governance arrangements specific to public sector organisations as contrasted with private sector	B6(b)
Explain democratic control, political influence and policy implementation in public sector organisations	B6(c)
Discuss obligations of the public sector organisations to meet the economy, effectiveness, efficiency (3 Es) criteria and promote public value	B6(d)

Business and exam context

You have already learned about stakeholders and social responsibility, plus the role that agency plays in the relationships that leaders develop with their various stakeholders.

Now we are going to examine how leaders use corporate governance as part of their 'strategic tool kit' when considering how stakeholders and their claims can be satisfied, especially with the various forms of ownership that an organisation might have.

In this chapter, we will explore corporate governance using three broad questions:

- What is corporate governance?
- How is corporate governance achieved across the world?
- What impact does ownership have on corporate governance?

In your exam, you will be expected to operate according to the type of organisation featured in the case study, considering current governance arrangements and possibly recommending suitable improvements in line with the various requirements.

Chapter overview

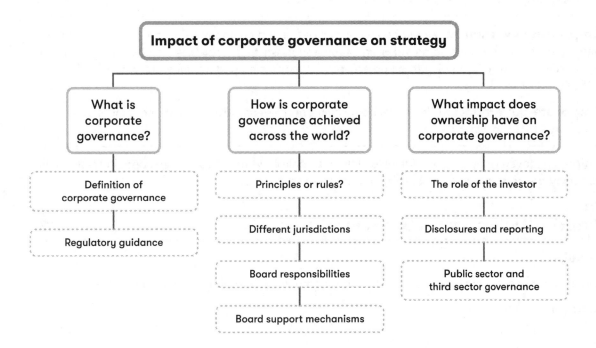

1 What is corporate governance?

1.1 Definition of corporate governance

Key terms

Corporate governance: 'A set of relationships between a company's directors, its shareholders and other stakeholders. It also provides structure through which the objectives of the company are set, and the means of obtaining these objectives and monitoring performance are determined.' (OECD, 2004: p.4)

Corporate governance: Is the system by which organisations are directed and controlled. (Cadbury, 1992: p.15)

Corporate governance is a fundamental internal control system ensuring the best interests of the company are serviced in the most efficient and effective manner.

Exercise 1: Corporate governance

Required

Identify the benefits to any business of applying a corporate governance framework.

Solution

For corporate governance to be effective it must be embedded as a feature of the inherent business culture, ie the way business is conducted.

In the exam you may also need to ascertain whether or not the governance procedures in use in a particular company are in line with best practice (covered later).

PER alert

Performance Objective 4 'Governance Risk and Control' of the Practical Experience Requirement requires you to 'operate according to the governance standards, policies and controls of your organisation'. (ACCA, 2019b). You are strongly advised to take your time as you go through the following sections as they explore the important role that corporate governance plays in organisations.

The following diagram illustrates the **11 core principles** that underlie most good corporate governance systems across the world.

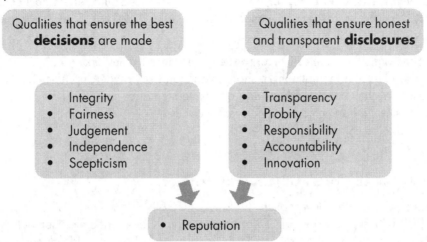

Definitions of each of these:

Key terms

Integrity: Is concerned with straightforward dealing and completeness; high moral character; honesty.

Fairness: Is concerned with balance; respecting the rights and views of any group with a legitimate interest.

Judgement: Making complex decisions that enhance the organisation's prosperity.

Independence: Means being free from bias or undue influence; independence of mind and in appearance.

Scepticism: Means considering all parts of a business with an open mind; no preconceptions.

Transparency: Providing open and clear disclosure, including voluntary disclosure of reliable information.

Probity: Means being truthful and not misleading; avoiding disingenuous behaviour.

Responsibility: Acknowledgement of praise or blame; open management of errors and failures.

Accountability: Having to answer for the consequences of actions and knowing who that relates to.

Innovation: Change happens and governance must stay fit for purpose regardless.

Reputation: Other people's perceptions or expectations: a valuable asset of any organisation.

1.2 Regulatory guidance

1.2.1 Organisation for Economic Co-operation and Development

The Organisation for Economic Co-operation and Development (OECD) developed its **Principles of Corporate Governance** in 1998 and issued revised versions in 2004 and 2015. They are non-binding principles, intended to assist governments in their efforts to evaluate and improve the legal, institutional and regulatory framework for corporate governance in their countries.

They are also intended to provide guidance for stock exchanges, investors and companies. The focus is on stock exchange listed companies, but many of the principles can also apply to private companies and state-owned organisations. The OECD principles deal mainly with governance problems that result from the **separation of ownership and management** of a company. Issues of ethical concern and environmental issues are also relevant, although not central to the problems of governance.

BPP
LEARNING
MEDIA

1.2.2 The OECD principles

In conjunction with the G20 (a group of the 20 largest advanced and emerging economies in the world) the OECD issued its revised principles in 2015 (OECD, 2015). They are grouped into six broad areas.

(a) Ensuring the basis for an effective corporate governance framework
(b) The rights and equitable treatment of shareholders and key ownership functions
(c) Institutional investors, stock markets, and other intermediaries
(d) The role of stakeholders in corporate governance
(e) Disclosure and transparency
(f) The responsibilities of the board

1.2.3 International Corporate Governance Network

The International Corporate Governance Network (ICGN) first issued its Global Governance Principles in 2005 to support the OECD principles. The ICGN principles set out the corporate governance responsibilities that boards and institutional shareholders should adhere to. The purpose was to provide practical guidance for corporate boards to use when attempting to meet the expectations of investors.

The ICGN believes that companies will only achieve value in the longer term if they effectively manage their relationships with stakeholders such as employees, customers, local communities and the environment as a whole. The most recent version of this guidance (ICGN, 2017) uses the following Global Governance Principles:

(a) **Board role and responsibilities** – be informed and support long-term shareholder benefit

(b) **Leadership and independence** – clarity and integrity for the board in order to be successful

(c) **Composition and appointment** – balance of skills, experience and objectivity for decisions

(d) **Corporate culture** – blend of corporate objectives, values and business ethics as part of strategy

(e) **Risk oversight** – proactive approach to managing risks as part of a changing world

(f) **Remuneration** – alignment of board, shareholders and strategy to create sustainable value for all

(g) **Reporting and audit** – internal and external reporting to maintain corporate accountability

(h) **Shareholder rights** – protecting equal rights and ensuring that all shareholders, including minority shareholders, can vote on major decisions affecting the company

1.2.4 Limitations of international codes

Corporate governance codes such as those issued by the OECD and ICGN (discussed in the sections above) have their limitations:

- They assume a 'one size fits all' approach which is not necessarily appropriate for organisations operating in different parts of the world

- As they are non-binding it reduces their relevance

- Different countries and regions have their own legislative approaches which may undermine some of the provisions set out in international codes

- They ignore the fact that countries have different preferences in respect of corporate governance. This is evident as some countries prefer 'rules' and others prefer 'principles-based' approaches to governance

- The pursuit of international consensus in respect of international corporate governance leads to a lowest common denominator mentality which heightens the scope for poor quality governance

2 How is corporate governance achieved across the world?

2.1 Principles or rules?

Key terms

Principles-based governance: Uses a broad series of ideas to set corporate governance behaviour, usually requiring 'comply or explain' disclosure (eg UK Corporate Governance Code).

Rules-based governance: A system based on inflexible rules that must be complied with, or else face sanctions from a regulator (eg Sarbanes-Oxley in the USA).

The big debate about corporate governance globally is whether the guidance should be in the form of principles or detailed rules and regulations.

	Principles-based approach	Rules-based approach
Features	Sets out broad principles (eg 'The Board should be effective') supported by guidance. Works on a **comply or explain** basis, with any departure from the specific provisions of codes requiring an explanation. Allows investors to decide if they agree that departure from the code is appropriate.	Organisations are required to comply with a detailed and rigid code. Non-compliance cannot be justified. A company has either succeeded or failed in complying. Investors tend to rely on a third party (eg SEC) to penalise the company for non-compliance.
Benefits	Allows for greater flexibility and potential cost savings. Applies across different legal jurisdictions, which makes the governance of a multi-national business more effective. Forces both boards and shareholders to think about the consequence of governance arrangements.	Easier compliance with the rules, as they are unambiguous, and can be evidenced. Provides a consistent minimum standard of governance for investors' confidence.
Disadvantages	The principles are so broad that they are of very little use as a guide to best corporate governance practice. Investors cannot be confident of consistency in approach. Incorrectly viewed as voluntary.	Allows no leeway or deviation, irrespective of how illogical the situation is. Enforcement can be difficult for situations that are not covered explicitly in the rules.
Where you find them	Favoured in legal jurisdictions where the governing bodies of stock markets have had the prime role in setting standards for companies to follow.	Favoured in legal jurisdictions (and cultures) that lay great emphasis on obeying the letter of the law rather than the spirit of it.

	Principles-based approach	Rules-based approach
Examples	UK Corporate Governance Code 2018	USA Sarbanes-Oxley Act (2002) (SOx)

2.2 Different jurisdictions

2.2.1 Corporate governance in the UK

Cadbury Report 1992
- Voluntary code of best practice
- Defined roles for all involved with financial statements
- Clear division of responsibilities
- Non-executive directors
- Audit committee

Greenbury Report 1995
- Determination of directors' pay
- Disclosure of directors' pay
- Remuneration committee

Hampel Report 1998
- Reduce regulatory burden
- Principles-based approach

Combined Code 1998
- Code of best practice derived from
  - Cadbury
  - Greenbury
  - Hampel

Turnbull Report 1998
- Risk management
- Internal control

Smith Report 2003
- Role of audit committees

Higgs Report 2003
- Role of non-executive directors

Combined Code 2006 and 2008
- 2006 updated for Turnbull, Smith & Higgs
- 2008 revision 2 minor restrictions removed
- 2010 onwards saw the introduction of the UK Corporate Governance Code

UK Corporate Governance Code
- The UK Corporate Governance Code was last updated in 2018
- 2018 Code emphasises improving the quality of the board's relationships with a wider range of stakeholders
- Greater focus on board engagement with the workforce

2.2.2 The Sarbanes-Oxley Act 2002 (USA)

Sarbanes-Oxley (SOx) (2002) arose from the inadequacies in US corporate governance arrangements, shown by the Enron scandal.

SOx adopts a **rules-based approach** to governance.

Specific provisions of SOx legislation include:

The establishment of the Public Company Accounting Oversight Board (PCAOB).
Auditors should review internal control systems.
There should be rotation of lead or reviewing audit partners every five years.
Auditors are expressly prohibited from carrying out most non-audit services.
Audit committees should be responsible for the appointment, compensation and oversight of auditors.
All members of audit committees should be independent, and at least one member should be a financial expert.
Annual reports should contain internal control reports (s404 reports) that state the responsibility of management for establishing and maintaining an adequate internal control structure and procedures for financial reporting and assess their effectiveness.
The chief executive officer and chief finance officer should certify the appropriateness of the financial statements.

The impact of SOx is widespread, illustrated in the table below:

US domestic impact	International impact
For **listed companies**, fulfilling the requirement to ensure their internal controls are properly documented and tested	Around **1,500 non-US companies list** their shares in the US. They are covered by the provisions of SOx
For **accountancy firms**, SOx has formally stripped them of almost all non-audit revenue streams that they used to derive from their audit clients	The US being such a **significant influence worldwide**, SOx is likely to persuade other countries to adopt a rules-based approach to corporate governance
For **lawyers**, SOx requires them to whistle blow on any wrongdoing they uncover at client companies, right up to board level	

There are a number of criticisms of SOx, including:

(a)   It is not strong enough on some issues, and at the same time over-rigid on others.

(b)   Directors may avoid consulting lawyers if they believe that SOx could override lawyer-client privilege.

(c)   A SOx compliance industry has sprung up.

(d)   Companies are turning away from the US stock markets and towards other markets.

2.2.3 South Africa

South Africa's major contribution to the corporate governance debate has been the **King Report**, first published in 1994 and updated in 2002, 2009 and 2016 to take account of developments in South Africa and elsewhere in the world.

BPP
LEARNING
MEDIA

The 2016 King Report (IV) advocates an integrated approach to corporate governance in the interest of a wide range of stakeholders – embracing the social, environmental and economic aspects of a company's activities. The King Report (IV) highlights that good corporate governance requires organisations to avoid thinking that they operate in isolation and requires an acknowledgement of the important role that they play in society. The nature of this relationship in turn makes organisations accountable towards existing and future stakeholders. (PWC, 2019). Although, the King Report is voluntary (unless prescribed by law or stock exchange Listings Requirement, KPMG, 2016) it aims to apply to all organisations, regardless of their form of incorporation, with the aim that the concept of corporate governance gains broader acceptance across different industries and sectors.

The King Report (IV) notes that the exercise of ethical and effective leadership by the organisations governing body should link to the achievement of four outcomes:

- Ethical culture
- Good performance
- Effective control
- Legitimacy

The King Report (IV) requires organisations to follow an 'apply and explain' approach in the achievement of the four outcomes specified above. This requires organisations to apply 17 principles which should help lead to the achievement of good corporate governance outcomes. Organisations are then required to explain the practices that they have undertaken to demonstrate application of those principles. (IoDSA, 2016).

2.2.4 Singapore Code of Corporate Governance

The Code of Corporate Governance in Singapore (first published in 2001, revised in 2005 and 2012, most recently issued in 2018) takes a similar approach to the UK Corporate Governance Code ('comply or explain') with the emphasis being on companies giving a detailed description of their governance practices and explaining any deviation from the Code.

However, the Singapore Code (Monetary Authority of Singapore, 2018) does deviate subtly from the UK Code (Financial Reporting Council, 2018) – some examples follow.

UK	Area	Singapore
At least half (Provision 11)	**The typical proportion of independent (non-executive) directors on the board**	At least one third but should be half if the Chair is not considered independent
Should not be the same person (Provision 9)	**Separate Chair and Chief Executive roles**	Should be separate persons but if not, can be allowed along with suitable safeguards (such as a lead independent director)
For FTSE 350 companies, after one year (Provision 18)	**Re-election periods for directors**	All directors should submit themselves to re-appointment every three years
Full-time executive directors should not take on more than one non-executive or chair role for a FTSE 100 company (Provision 15)	**Directors serving simultaneously on more than one board**	Guidelines should be adopted by the board to ensure sufficient time and attention is devoted

UK	Area	Singapore
Should not include share-options or performance-related elements (Provision 34)	**Remuneration for independent or non-executive directors**	Remuneration for non-executive directors needs to be appropriate to their contribution based on their effort, time and responsibilities
Entirely made up of independent non-executive directors with at least one possessing recent financial expertise (Provision 24)	**Composition of the Audit Committee**	Consist of at least three non-executive directors with at least two members, including the Chair, having recent and relevant financial experience

An overview of four jurisdictions clearly cannot illustrate the whole world, but this small cross-section does show that while there are many areas of common ground, local variations in governance best practice do still exist, leading us to consider whether this is acceptable or not.

Activity 1: Rules for corporate governance

ACCA Professional skills focus

Communication: Clarify

You work within the Executive Support function of your organisation and are preparing some briefing notes for a member of the board who has been asked to participate in a meeting with other business leaders. The agenda for this meeting includes a focus group which will be commenting on the current state of corporate governance across the world. The board member has asked that you prepare a balanced view of whether or not global rules for corporate governance should be adopted so that she can contribute fully in the discussions.

Required

Prepare briefing notes that consider whether a universal set of corporate governance rules should be adopted or whether the existing localised approach is better. **(6 marks)**

Professional skills marks are available for demonstrating **communication** skills in clarifying the arguments for and against having global governance rules. **(2 marks)**

(Total = 8 marks)

Solution

2.3 Board responsibilities

The board is collectively responsible for promoting the success of the company by directing and supervising the company's affairs.

The board provides entrepreneurial leadership of the company, within a framework of prudent and effective controls, which enable risk to be assessed and managed. The board should also set the company's strategic aims, ensuring that the necessary financial and human resources are in place for the company to meet its objectives and review management performance.

2.3.1 Effectiveness of boards

Responsibilities

In order to be effective, boards should have a formal schedule of tasks – the following shows what this could include:

Monitoring the chief executive officer
Overseeing strategy
Monitoring risks, control systems and governance
Monitoring the human capital aspects of the company, eg succession, morale, training, remuneration, etc
Managing potential conflicts of interest
Ensuring that there is effective communication of its strategic plans, both internally and externally

Focus

Boards should meet regularly and frequently in order to be effective and need to take sufficient time to fulfil these and other responsibilities.

Real world example

The phrase 'going plural' was coined by former Royal Mail Chair and Asda Chief Executive Allan Leighton to describe the amalgamation of several part-time non-executive roles to constitute a full-time non-executive role, thus allowing his business experience to be shared simultaneously across many organisations. While not a new phenomenon, it does illustrate the role of the 21st century director but also highlights the risks of spreading yourself too thinly across each role to the extent that you may become less effective due to not devoting sufficient time and attention to each role.

(Management Today, 2013)

Syllabus link

Board members need to be effectively briefed to be able to fulfil their duties – consequently, they need information from a variety of sources to support this responsibility. We shall cover this in a later chapter.

Membership

Key issues for consideration regarding **board membership** are shown below.

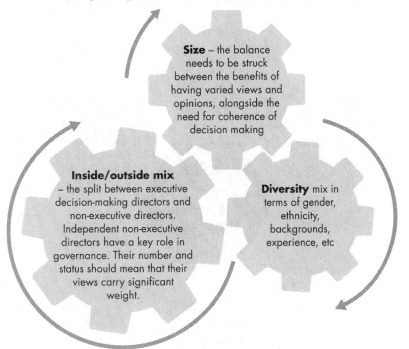

Diversity issues are becoming increasingly important to consider when resourcing a board.

Boards need to ensure that they are accessing the talent pool to ensure they have the best calibre of candidate. However, taking gender as an example, around 60% of European and US graduates are women yet board room representation in these places is far lower – why?

Boards also need to reflect the market in which they operate: considering who makes purchasing decisions in households, should boards reflect this demographic more readily in order to get closer to their customers?

Various academic studies have shown that better corporate governance practices (such as succession planning, training and induction) and hence better financial results come from more diverse companies.

Should diversity by addressed by quotas – for example, having a legally enforced minimum percentage of women on boards? This does at least guarantee representation but creates a stigma if board members are only there because of the quota and not their contribution to the board.

Knowledge, skills and appraisal

To remain effective, directors should extend their knowledge and skills continuously, starting with their first day in office. Once recruited, a director will then require induction training which should help them to understand the organisation's business and markets, its staff and its stakeholders.

During their tenure, continuing professional development (CPD) should cover a number of issues on a regular basis – for example, the diagram below shows some of the areas that ongoing CPD could cover to ensure that directors continue to be adequately prepared for their roles.

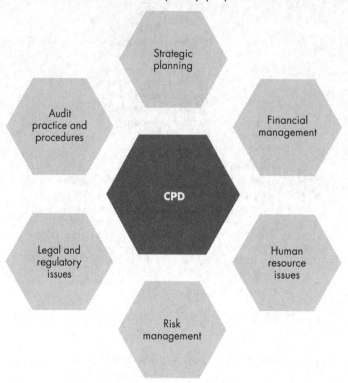

An appraisal of the **board's performance** is an important control over its effectiveness, aimed at maximising strengths and tackling weaknesses. It should be seen as an essential part of the feedback process within the company and may prompt the board to change its methods and/or objectives.

All directors should also be **individually appraised**. The following diagram shows criteria that could include the following:

2.3.2 Board leadership

The division of responsibilities at the head of an organisation is most simply achieved by separating the roles of chair and chief executive.

Responsibilities of the chair of the board	Responsibilities of the chief executive officer
Provide leadership to the board, ensuring its effectiveness and setting its agenda	**Provide leadership to the business**, ensuring the effectiveness of business operations and setting strategy
Ensuring the board receives accurate and timely information	Providing accurate and timely information
Ensuring effective communication with shareholders and that their views are communicated to the board as a whole	Communicating effectively with significant stakeholders
Facilitate effective contribution from NEDS, ensure constructive relations between execs and NEDs	Facilitate the effective implementation of board decisions
Take the lead in providing an induction programme for new directors and in board development	Co-operate in induction and development
Meet with the NEDs without the executives present	Co-operate by providing any necessary resources
Facilitating board appraisal	Co-operate in board appraisal
Encouraging active engagement by all the members of the board	Co-operate with all the members of the board

Key terms

Chair: Is employed to run the board of directors, usually non-executive.

Chief Executive Officer (CEO): Is employed to manage the company through its executive directors.

Non-executive director: Is employed to support the board in the areas of strategy, scrutiny, people and risk but not employed in an executive position (so can be independent of the main board).

Activity 2: Chair and chief executive

 ACCA Professional skills focus

Commercial acumen: Use judgement

You work within the Executive Support function of your organisation and are preparing some materials for the induction training programme that your organisation runs when it recruits new senior management positions. Part of these materials require an overview of the reasons for having a separate chair and chief executive in post.

BPP
LEARNING
MEDIA

Required

Prepare part of the frequently asked questions (FAQs) for these training materials by providing answers to the following questions:

Why should the roles of chair and chief executive be separate?
How does separating these roles create more accountability? **(6 marks)**

Professional skills marks are available for demonstrating **commercial acumen** skills in using judgement to identify the key issues and arguments. **(2 marks)**

(Total = 8 marks)

Solution

Exam Focus Point

The Strategic Business Leader specimen 2 exam featured a public sector rail company, Rail Co, which was responsible for providing rail services within the country of Beeland. The third question required candidates to act in the capacity of the non-executive chairperson of a sub-committee. Following the removal of the previous chief executive the role had been advertised and two individuals had been shortlisted for a final interview. In the exam candidates were provided with a summary of the CV's of the two shortlisted individuals. Part (a) of question 3 asked candidates to prepare a report for the chair of Rail Co's nomination and corporate governance committee which evaluated 'the suitability of the shortlisted candidates for the position of chief executive of Rail Co' and recommended 'with justification, which candidate [was...] most suitable for the position' (ACCA, 2017a).

This task was worth 8 technical marks and tested the ACCA Professional Skill of Commercial Acumen. To produce a good answer, candidates needed to make use of the specified exhibit information, and address the two distinct parts of the task ie the suitability of the individuals and to provide a recommendation. To earn the two professional skills marks candidates were expected to use the 'person specification [CVs] to form a clear judgement of the task requirements of the role' [and to demonstrate a] 'strong awareness of the factors impacting on the successful contribution of the new [chief executive]' (ACCA, 2017a).

2.3.3 Unitary and multi-tier boards

Key terms

Unitary boards: A board structure with only one board of directors.

Multi-tier board structure: This could be two or three-tiered and have a variety of representation.

The single board structure with sub-committees is known as a **unitary** structure

Advantages of unitary structure	Disadvantages of a unitary structure
All participants have equal legal responsibility for management of the company and strategic performance	An NED or independent director cannot be expected to both manage and monitor
A single board promotes easier co-operation and co-ordination	The time requirements on non-executive directors may be onerous
The presence of NEDs should lead to better decisions being made	There is no specific provision for employees to be represented on the management board
Independent NEDs are less likely to be excluded from decision making and given restricted access to information	Emphasises the divide between the shareholders and the directors

In some countries (eg Germany) the board is split into **multi-tiers**, separating the executive from other directors (and senior management). This structure is also common in not-for-profit organisations.

This multi-tier approach can take the form of a:

(a) **Supervisory board** with no executive function. It reviews the company's direction and strategy, and is responsible for safeguarding stakeholders' interests.

(b) **Management or executive board** composed entirely of executive directors/managers. It is responsible for the running of the business. The supervisory board appoints the management board.

Japanese companies have three tiers:

- **Policy boards** – concerned with long-term strategic issues
- **Functional boards** – made up of the main senior executives with a functional role
- **Monocratic boards** – with few responsibilities and having a more symbolic role

Advantages of a two-tier board structure	Disadvantages of a two-tier board structure
The clear and formal separation of duties between the monitors and those being monitored.	Confusion over authority and therefore a lack of accountability can arise with multi-tier boards. This criticism has been particularly levelled at Japanese companies where the consequence is allegedly often over-secretive procedures.

Advantages of a two-tier board structure	Disadvantages of a two-tier board structure
The supervisory/policy board has the capacity to be an effective guard against management inefficiency or worse. Its existence may act as a deterrent to fraud or irregularity in a similar way to the independent audit.	The management board may restrict the information passed on to the supervisory board and the boards may only liaise infrequently.
The supervisory board system should take account of the needs of stakeholders other than shareholders, specifically employees, who are clearly important stakeholders in practice.	The supervisory board may not be as independent as would be wished, depending on how rigorous the appointment procedures are.
The system actively encourages transparency within the company, between the boards and, through the supervisory board, to the employees and the shareholders. It also involves the shareholders and employees in the supervision and appointment of directors.	In addition, members of the supervisory board can be, indeed are likely to be, shareholder representatives; this could detract from legal requirements that shareholders don't instruct directors how to manage if the supervisory board was particularly strong.

2.3.4 Leaving the board

A director may leave office in a number of ways.

Resignation (written notice may be required)

Not **offering themselves for re-election** when their term of office ends

Failing to be re-elected

Death in service

Reaching retirement age

Being **removed** from office

Dissolution of the company

Prolonged absence meaning that director cannot fulfil duties

Being **disqualified** (by virtue of the constitution or by the court)

Agreed departure, possibly with compensation for loss of office

PER alert Performance Objective 20 'Review and report on the findings of an audit or assurance engagement' of the Practical Experience Requirement requires you to 'discuss the findings and implications of an audit or assurance engagement with management and governance teams' (ACCA, 2019b). You are strongly advised to take your time as you go through the following sections which discuss the role and remit of the different committees which play an important role in the governance of organisations.

2.4 Board support mechanisms

2.4.1 Committees

Many companies operate a series of board **sub-committees** responsible for supervising specific aspects of governance. The main board committees are:

Audit Committee is responsible for liaising with external audit, supervising internal audit and reviewing the annual accounts and internal controls.

Remuneration Committee is responsible for advising on executive director remuneration policy and the specific package for each director.

Nominations Committee is responsible for recommending the appointments of new directors to the board.

Risk Committee is responsible for overseeing risk management.

Syllabus links

We will focus on the audit committee and risk committee later on in this workbook.

2.4.2 Non-executive directors

Non-executive directors (NEDs) have no executive, or managerial, responsibilities or power. Their primary function is to consider and safeguard the interests of shareholders.

NEDs have a key role in reducing conflicts of interest between management (including executive directors) and shareholders by providing balance to the board. They bring an independent viewpoint as they are not full-time employees.

The role of non-executive directors includes:

Strategy. Contributing to, and challenging the direction of, strategy.	**Risk**. NEDs should satisfy themselves that financial information is accurate and that financial controls and systems of risk management are robust.
Scrutiny. NEDs should scrutinise the performance of management in meeting goals and objectives, monitor the reporting of performance. They should represent the shareholders' interests to ensure agency issues don't arise to reduce shareholder value.	**People**. NEDs are responsible for determining appropriate levels of remuneration for executives, and are key figures in the appointment and removal of senior managers and in succession planning.

Syllabus link

You will have already met the term 'non-executive director' (NED) in Audit and Assurance and other parts of your study.

 BPP LEARNING MEDIA

Activity 3: Non-executive directors

ACCA Professional skills focus

Commercial acumen: Use judgement

You work within the Executive Support function of your organisation and are preparing some materials for the induction training programme that your organisation runs when it recruits new senior management positions. Part of these materials require an overview of the advantages and disadvantages of non-executive directors (NEDs) and how these disadvantages can be addressed.

Required

Prepare a section of these training materials by providing answers to the following questions, using what you know about corporate governance from your studies and workplace experience:

What are the advantages to an organisation of having NEDs?
What are the disadvantages to an organisation of having NEDs?
What can our organisation do to overcome these disadvantages? **(8 marks)**

Professional skills marks are available for demonstrating **commercial acumen** skills in using judgement as to the appropriate ways of overcoming the disadvantages of NEDs. **(2 marks)**

(Total = 10 marks)

Solution

Exam Focus Point

The Strategic Business Leader specimen 2 exam featured a public sector rail company, Rail Co, which was responsible for providing rail services within the country of Beeland. The first question required candidates to act in the capacity of a non-executive member of the Rail Co nominations and corporate governance committee. Part (b) of question 1 asked candidates to prepare a briefing paper which assessed 'the role and value of non-executive directors on the board of Rail Co, as a public sector company' (ACCA, 2017a). This task was worth 6 technical marks and tested the ACCA Professional Skill of Evaluation. To produce a good answer candidates needed to use their knowledge of non-executive directors applied in the context of a public sector organisation. Corporate governance in the public sector is covered later in this chapter. Candidates needed to identify the fact that the task consisted of two parts ie the role and value of non-executive directors. Failing to pick up on this would restrict the number of marks that could be earned. To earn the two professional skills marks candidates needed ensure that their evaluation addressed the two parts of the task and focused on the public sector environment.

2.4.3 Directors' remuneration

The purpose of directors' remuneration is to be sufficient to:

(a) **Attract** and **retain** individuals of sufficient calibre; and

(b) **Motivate** them to achieve performance levels that are in the shareholders' best interests as well as their own personal interests.

Factors to consider when agreeing remuneration packages:

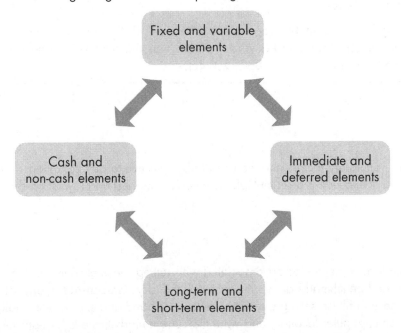

The **Remuneration Committee** usually determines the organisation's general policy on the remuneration of executive directors. This should be both independently agreed and transparently disclosed to maximise its chances of being accepted by stakeholders. As an illustration, the UK Corporate Governance Code (2018) recommends that remuneration committees should comprise NEDs only and should also consider the following:

- **Support strategy:** Remuneration needs to support the organisation's strategy and promote the long-term success of the entity. Executive director remuneration should be aligned to the company's purpose and values.

- **Need for transparency:** Organisations should have in place transparent procedures for determining the remuneration of executive directors. Directors should not be involved in setting their own remuneration.

- **Need for judgement:** When determining remuneration packages directors need to make use of their judgement and discretion to take account of organisational and individual performance, and the wider context facing the entity.

Other factors relevant when determining director's remuneration include:

Connected to performance

A significant proportion of rewards should be related to measurable business performance or enhanced shareholder value, and the Remuneration Committee should be alert to the risk of remuneration levels rising with no corresponding improvement in the organisation's performance.

 Real world example

The following real-world example illustrates the interaction between poor performance in delivering organisational strategy and director remuneration.

In December 2014 in the UK, Mark Carne, the Chief Executive of Network Rail, was in line for a bonus of up to £135,000 on top of his £675,000 salary. Following severe rail disruption due to over-running engineering works at King's Cross, with tens of thousands of passengers stranded and badly delayed, Mr Carne said:

'I've decided that I'm accountable for the performance of the railway and in my view the performance over the Christmas and New Year period was not acceptable and I've decided that I should not take the bonus for this year.' (BBC, 2014c).

Best practice

Needs to consider regulatory factors and the need to be sensitive to pay conditions within the company (such as not exceeding a set multiple between the highest and lowest paid in an organisation).

Market factors

Needs to consider labour market factors associated with setting remuneration – this may require the use of consultants and benchmarks across the sector or industry and consider if any roles being recruited for are hard to fill (so setting a rate that reflects demand and supply, especially for a role that is offered in an unpopular location) and what the current market rate is for equivalent roles in other similar companies

Service contracts and termination payments

Length of service contracts can be a particular problem. If service contracts are too long, and then have to be terminated prematurely, the perception often arises that the amounts paying off directors for the remainder of the contract are essentially rewards for failure. Most corporate governance guidance suggests that service contracts greater than 12 months need to be carefully considered and should ideally be avoided. A few are stricter.

Some companies have cut the notice period for dismissing directors who fail to meet performance targets from one year to six months. Other solutions include continuing to pay a director to the end of their contract, but ceasing payment if the director finds **fresh employment**, or paying the director for **loss of office** in the form of **shares**.

Activity 4: Remuneration packages

ACCA Professional skills focus

Commercial acumen: Show insight

You work within the Executive Support function of your organisation and are preparing some guidance notes for a new member of the Remuneration Committee who has just been recruited to the post of non-executive director (NED). The guidance is designed to explain the various components of an executive director's remuneration package and assess the effect that each element would have on a director's behaviour.

Required

Prepare the guidance notes required for the newly appointed NED using the following categories, explaining in each case what each element includes and its effect on a director's behaviour:

(a) Basic salary
(b) Performance-related pay
(c) Benefits
(d) Pensions
(e) Shares
(f) Share options **(9 marks)**

Professional skills marks are available for demonstrating **commercial acumen** in showing insight to each of the remuneration package components. **(2 marks)**

(Total = 11 marks)

Solution

Remuneration disclosures

In order for the financial statements to present an accurate picture of remuneration arrangements, the annual report would need to disclose:

Remuneration policy
Detailed arrangements for individual directors
Performance conditions attached to remuneration packages
The duration of contracts with directors, and notice periods and termination payments under such contracts

Does all this mean that shareholders are going to be happy with the amounts paid to directors?

Not necessarily! Recent research has highlighted the fact that executive remuneration has risen but returns to investors (both in terms of share prices and dividend policies) have fallen. This has led to an increase in shareholder activism, such as voting against remuneration reports (but not against the re-election of directors) which can be legally binding. Pressure groups representing investors (such as PIRC in the UK) can often be seen objecting to unpopular packages. Regulations to address clawing back directors' bonuses have been discussed in the UK and may be written into the terms and conditions of directors' contracts at some stage.

Real-world examples

Wednesday 4 January 2017 was labelled 'Fat Cat Wednesday' by the UK media to draw attention to a calculation which showed the average Chief Executive's pay for the year to date (four days) matching the average annual UK salary of £28,200 per annum. (BBC, 2017)

3 What impact does ownership have on corporate governance?

3.1 The role of the investor

A key distinction that has been drawn between the corporate governance systems worldwide in different regimes has been between the **insider** and **outsider** models of ownership described below. In practice, most regimes fall somewhere between the two.

3.1.1 Insider systems

Key term

> **Insider system:** Occurs when most companies listed on the local stock exchange are owned by a small number of dominant investors (eg family-owned).

Insider (or relationship-based) systems are where most companies listed on the local stock exchange are owned and controlled by a small number of major shareholders – often family owned and run organisations are seen in this category. The other shareholders could be banks, other companies or even the government.

The reason for the concentration of share ownership is the legal system.

Advantages	Disadvantages
It is easier to establish ties between owners and managers, therefore the agency problem is reduced.	There may be discrimination against minority shareholders, especially if they are not part of the family for example.
It is easier to influence management, policy and strategy through dialogue.	Insider systems tend not to develop more formal governance structures until they are forced to.
A smaller base of shareholders may be more willing to take a long-term strategic view of their investment.	May be reluctant to employ outsiders in influential positions or recruit independent non-executive directors.
Owner-managed organisations (often family owned and run) develop systems that have grown over time and are cultural, as opposed to companies where there is no continuity.	More prone to opaque financial transactions and misuse of funds.
	Many large shareholders (particularly institutional investors – see below) tend to avoid shares like this that are seen as speculative and invest only in 'blue chip' shares (forcing up their price).

3.1.2 Outsider systems

Key term

> **Outsider system:** Occurs where shareholding is more widely dispersed by large numbers of investors (eg stock market shareholders).

Outsider systems are ones where shareholding is more widely dispersed, and there is the **manager-ownership separation**. Such shareholders can be drawn from varied and disparate sources and can have both small and large holdings.

There tends to be more diverse shareholder ownership in jurisdictions such as the UK that have strong protection for non-controlling (minority) interests.

Advantages	Disadvantages
The separation of ownership and management has provided an impetus for the development of more robust legal and governance regimes to protect shareholders.	Companies are more likely to have an agency problem and significant agency costs.
Shareholders have voting rights that they can use to exercise control.	The larger shareholders in these regimes tend to have short-term priorities and prefer to sell their shares.

BPP LEARNING MEDIA

Advantages	Disadvantages
Hostile takeovers are far more frequent, and the threat of these acts as a disciplining mechanism on company management.	

British and American systems can both be classified as outsider systems.

3.1.3 Institutional investors

Key term

> **Institutional investors:** Include investors such as pension funds that make up a sizeable proportion of shareholders in any one company, usually for the purpose of holding a portfolio of shares.

Institutional investors have large amounts of money to invest. They are covered by fewer protective regulations, on the grounds that they are knowledgeable and able to protect themselves. They include investors managing funds invested by individuals. The term also includes agents employed on the investors' behalf.

Institutional investors are now the biggest investors in many stock markets but they might also invest venture capital, or lend directly to companies. UK trends show that institutional investors can wield great powers over the companies in which they invest. The major institutional investors in the UK are:

- **Pension funds**
- **Insurance companies**
- **Investment and unit trusts** (set up to invest in portfolios of shares)
- **Venture capital organisations** (investors particularly interested in companies that are seeking to expand)

Their funds will be managed by a fund manager who aims to benefit investors in the funds or pension or policy holders. Although fund managers will use lots of different sources of information, their agency costs will be high in total because they have to track the performance of all the investments that the fund makes.

Advantages	Disadvantages
Makes investments such as pensions available that are separate to an employer (less risky) Access to big markets for smaller investors	Their dominance can influence the economy unduly and lead to anti-competitive behaviour
	Play too safe, avoiding risky speculative shares, making them more expensive
	Can be too short-termist
	Investors cannot influence the companies in which their fund managers have invested their money – but institutional investors are encouraged to engage with directors if they believe poor governance practices are present

> **Essential reading**
>
> See Chapter 3 section 1 of the Essential Reading, available in Appendix 2 of the digital edition of the Workbook, for more detail about institutional investors (including how they exercise their influence and when they might intervene in the affairs of a company in which they have invested).

Illustration 1

How is corporate governance evolving?

Increasing internationalisation and globalisation has meant that investors, and institutional investors in particular, have begun to invest outside their home countries.

The **differential treatment of domestic and foreign investors**, both in terms of reporting and associated rights and dividends (and also the excessive influence of majority shareholders in insider jurisdictions) has caused many investors to call for parity of treatment.

Issues concerning **financial reporting** have been raised by many investors and are the focus of much debate and litigation. Shareholder confidence in what has been reported in many instances is being eroded, especially in cases where financial statements have been deliberately misstated.

The characteristics of individual countries may have a **significant influence** on the way corporate governance has developed.

The number of **high profile corporate scandals** and collapses (including Polly Peck International, BCCI and Maxwell Communications Corporation) prompted the development of governance codes in the early 1990s. However, scandals since then (Enron, RBS and Lehman Brothers) have raised questions about further measures that may still be necessary. The story goes on!

3.2 Disclosures and reporting

3.2.1 Organisational reporting and external auditing

Issues concerning **financial reporting and auditing** are seen by many investors as crucial because of their central importance in ensuring management accountability.

They have been the focus of much debate and litigation. While focusing the corporate governance debate solely on accounting and reporting issues is inadequate, the greater regulation of practices such as off-balance sheet financing has led to **greater transparency** and a **reduction in risks** faced by investors.

External auditors may not carry out the necessary questioning of senior management because of fears of **losing their audit**, and internal auditors do not ask awkward questions because the chief financial officer **determines their employment prospects**.

3.2.2 Corporate social responsibility (CSR) and business ethics

The lack of consensus about the issues for which businesses are responsible and the stakeholders to whom they are responsible has inevitably made corporate social responsibility and business ethics an important part of the corporate governance debate.

Syllabus links

The relevant topics in reporting CSR and ethics (governance requirements, meeting stakeholder expectations and loss of corporate reputation) are all covered elsewhere in this workbook.

3.2.3 Annual reports

Annual reports should disclose whether the organisation has complied with governance regulations and codes. In the UK, for example, this can be a statement explaining how a company has either complied or not complied with the UK Code.

Governance disclosures can vary across jurisdictions, but as rule usually include the following information.

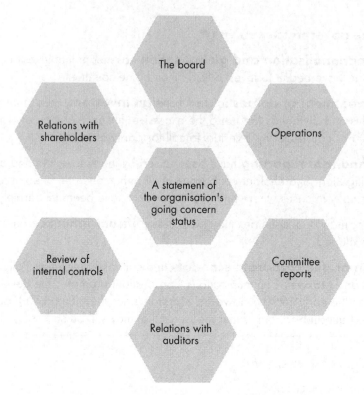

3.3 Public sector and third sector governance

In addition to the governance of private companies, you need to be able to **describe**, **compare** and **contrast** the following types of organisation in the following ways:

	Private sector	Public sector	Charitable	NGO/QuANGO*
Purposes and objectives (what are they for?)	Profit Market	Public goods or services not delivered by the private sector	Meeting a need not provided by either public or private sectors (the so-called 'third sector') such as health, relief, education and support	
Performance (how is success measured?)	Agency-driven, but usually profit and market share	Value for money (3 Es) Meeting social needs	Value for money (3 Es) Meeting own needs	More tailored results than charities or the public sector could deliver
		Economy – obtaining inputs of the appropriate quality at the lowest price available Efficiency – delivering the service to the appropriate standard at minimum cost, time and effort Effectiveness – achieving the desired objectives as stated in the entity's performance plan		

	Private sector	Public sector	Charitable	NGO/QuANGO*
Ownership (who owns them?)	Partners, shareholders and lenders	Taxpayer	Independent (with some philanthropic influence)	Can be state or government owned
Stakeholders (including lobby groups) (who also holds an interest in them?)	Lobby groups may influence government policy to support their own aims (both for and against)	Population (local and national) Taxpayers may lobby for better use of their taxes	Trustees Population (local and national) Pressure groups to stop action that may have initially led to the creation of the charity/NGO	

*NGO = non-government organisation; QuANGO = Quasi-autonomous non-government organisation

Key term

QuANGO: Is a quasi-autonomous non-governmental organisation (supporting government even if not a government department).

3.3.1 Agency and public sector organisations

Public sector organisations also incorporate an agency relationship between the principals (the political leaders and ultimately the taxpayers/electors) and agents (the elected and executive officers and departmental managers). Because the taxpayers and electors have differing interests and objectives, establishing and monitoring the achievement of strategic objectives, and interpreting what is best for the principals, can be very difficult.

The agency problem in public services is also enhanced by limitations on the audit of public service organisations. In many jurisdictions the audit only covers the integrity and transparency of financial transactions and does not include an audit of performance or fitness for purpose.

3.3.2 Levels of public sector organisations

The term 'public sector' can be used to describe entities at a variety of **levels**:

Sub-national	**Regional assemblies, local authorities, states or cantons with a variety of responsibilities and devolved political powers.**
National	Based upon the four organs of state: **executive** (responsible for running the state); **legislature** (responsible for the legal framework); **judiciary** (responsible for enforcing that legal framework) and **secretariat** (the administration function charged with delivering executive policy). The **executive** (or **government**) is made up of many departments and setting strategy based on policy. In the case of a democracy, the governing party (or a coalition if no one party has overall control) sets this strategy in line with its **elected mandate** from the **population**.
Supra-national	Governments form bodies for shared purposes – examples are the **European Union**, **United Nations** and the **World Trade Organization**.

3.3.3 Strategic objectives, leadership and governance arrangements

When contrasted with private sector organisations, **governance** in the public sector can vary quite significantly, although it ultimately depends on **objectives** and **leadership**:

	Private sector	**Public sector**
Strategic objectives	**Profit** and/or **market share** Anything else in their incorporation documents	Achievement of state-defined **service delivery** to meet social need Securing **value for money** with taxpayers' funds
Leadership	Board of directors (influenced by shareholders)	Delegated authority from state (based on principles of public life)
Governance	Principles or rules-based in order to satisfy **shareholders** **External audit** (for entities above certain thresholds)	Reporting to an **oversight body** (such as a board of governors) **External audit** and political (as well as media) **scrutiny** Demonstration of good use of public funds in meeting social need (controlled by budgets and KPIs)

3.3.4 Democratic control, political influence and public sector policy implementation

Democratically elected executives (governments) are voted in after an election with a mandate to set public sector policy. What factors will influence that policy?

Illustration 2

When considering public sector policy provision, there are no right and wrong answers (unless based on factual inaccuracies) so the debate should attempt to consider all possible viewpoints and attempt to find a way to accommodate as many of them as possible (in keeping with the process of democracy).

Consider the following questions when considering factors that could influence public sector policy, as well as some points that could be considered for each question.

Should there be a public sector?

*   Do companies provide society with everything they need?
*   What if people face hardship – should they get any help?
*   Can we afford a public sector? Can we afford not to have one?

What are the priorities?

*   Health, education and welfare ('from the cradle to the grave') – are these key?

*   What about defence, business, foreign policy (including overseas aid), the environment, agriculture, the arts, energy, transport etc?

*   To what extent is the public sector obliged to secure public value (economy of inputs, efficiency of processes and effectiveness of outputs) when resources are limited but social need is most acute (for example, in the case of emergency aid to those suffering from natural disaster and warfare) and should it be any different for those whose lifestyles have led to this social need emerging (for example paying for healthcare to treat those suffering from problems associated with obesity or smoking)?

What about the influence of taxpayers who do not use services they still have to pay for?

- Receiving free healthcare, education and social care at point of service happens in many states (eg the UK) but in others (eg the USA) such services are paid for to some extent by those that use them.

- If you pay your taxes and they go towards funding services that you prefer to pay for yourself (eg private education or private medical care via health insurance) should you be able to opt out of paying taxes?

- Should people pay more or less tax in this way? Should people pay taxes at all?

Does privatisation play a positive role in helping economies to deliver public sector provision?

- Should public utilities such as water, gas, electricity and railways ever be privatised? Can markets ever deliver the efficiencies required to benefit consumers if profit gets in the way? Are regulators strong enough to make such markets fair to consumers and companies alike?

- Short-term cash boost, reckless sale of 'family silver' or wise decision to limit future liabilities (eg in the UK in 2013, the Royal Mail was floated via IPO but six months later allegations were made by politicians that it had been undervalued by £1bn in the UK Government's haste to make the sale a success. While the Royal Mail presented a potentially significant liability on public sector finances due to pension and operating deficits, it had started to show signs of recovery, prompting calls that it was only sold to benefit investors and not the UK in general. Time will tell on this, although in an industry where physical deliveries are being phased out in favour of digital products – books, music and other entertainments – maybe this was a good deal after all. (BBC, 2014a).

- Outside the UK in many parts of the World privatisation remains a divisive issue.

Impact of corporate governance on strategy

What is corporate governance?

How is corporate governance achieved across the world?

What impact does ownership have on corporate governance?

Definition of corporate governance

- 'The system by which organisations are directed and controlled'
- 11 Core principles:
  - Integrity
  - Fairness
  - Judgement
  - Independence
  - Scepticism
  - Transparency
  - Probity
  - Responsibility
  - Accountability
  - Innovation
  - Reputation

Regulatory guidance

- OECD (governments)
- OECD principles:
  - Ensuring the basis for an effective corporate governance framework
  - The rights and equitable treatment of shareholders and key ownership functions
  - Institutional investors, stock markets, and other intermediaries
  - The role of stakeholders in corporate governance
  - Disclosure and transparency
  - The responsibilities of the board
- ICGN (companies):
  - Board role and responsibilities
  - Leadership and independence
  - Composition and appointment
  - Corporate culture
  - Risk oversight
  - Remuneration
  - Reporting and audit
  - Shareholder rights
- Limitations of international codes

Principles or rules?

- Principles:
  - Broad principles
  - Comply or explain
  - Deviations require disclosure and explanation
  - Requires investors to make an informed decision
- Rules:
  - Compliance is required
  - Pass or fail – no middle ground
  - Requires a third party or regulator to enforce the rules

Different jurisdictions

- Corporate governance in the UK (principles-based)
- USA Sarbanes- Oxley Act (rules-based)
- South Africa – King Report
- Singapore Code

Board responsibilities

- Effectiveness of boards:
  - Entrepreneurial leadership
  - Strategy
  - Briefing, training and appraisals
  - Membership: size and diversity
- Leadership CEO vs chair
- Unitary and multi-tier boards
- Leaving the board

Board support mechanisms

- Committees: Audit; Nomination; Remuneration; Risk
- NEDs: Strategy; scrutiny; risk; people
- Remuneration: balance across package; accountability for results; market factors

The role of the investor

- Insider systems: small numbers of large shareholders; family ownership; more expensive
- Outsider systems: eg stock market; strong systems to counter the agency problem
- Institutional investors: strategic focus; possible short-term interest; can influence strategy of their investment by close involvement

Disclosures and reporting

- Organisational
- CSR and business ethics
- Annual reports

Public sector and third sector governance

- Purposes and objectives of private sector, public sector; charitable institutions; QuANGOs Performance and ownership
- Agency and public sector organisations
- Levels of public sector organisation
- Strategy, objectives, leadership and governance
- Democratic control, political influence and public sector policy implementation

Knowledge diagnostic

1. Governance does not happen by accident – it is the outcome of a series of processes with a number of key goals related to how organisations are directed and controlled. However, underpinning all of this should be transparency (all actions are visible) and accountability (both success and failure should be attributable to someone).

2. Shareholders and stakeholders all have very different needs but still need to be considered as part of sound governance.

3. Most jurisdictions choose either a principles-based or rules-based system – the levels of disclosure necessary tend to illustrate how each one works in practice in conjunction with ensuring stakeholders can make an educated guess about the governance in place in their investment.

4. Boards of directors require many factors to be considered to ensure their effectiveness – education, diversity and assessment are three key areas

5. Central to the success of most systems of governance is the role of NEDs, committees and remuneration policies as a form of control.

6. The role of institutional investors is key in determining levels of disclosure.

7. If your organisation is in the public sector, there are a number of factors that need to be considered when adopting best practice governance, such as their objectives, the influence of stakeholders and how to measure performance.

Independent study

Question practice

Now try the question below from the Further question practice bank (available in the digital edition of the Workbook):

Q3 Caius

Further reading

There are articles on the ACCA website written by members of the SBL examining team which are relevant to your studies and which would be useful to read:

Public sector governance

This article explores the concept of governance in public sector organisations.

Corporate governance from the inside out

This article explores the internal and external drivers behind effective corporate governance.

Diversifying the board – a step towards better governance

This article considers the important role that the board of directors play in ensuring good governance and highlights the need for board diversity.

Independence as a concept in corporate governance

This article explores the importance of independence in relation to corporate governance and professional behaviour.

Approaching SBL overview

This article provides a one-page summary of the key features of the SBL exam.

Approaching SBL reading and planning

This article provides a one-page summary of how best to approach the SBL exam.

SBL – 10 things to learn from the September 2018 sitting

This article highlights some of the issues that ACCA identified in candidates' answers during the September 2018 SBL exam sitting. The article provides some useful advice for improving your chances of passing the SBL exam.

Strategic Business Leader – The importance of effective communication for SBL

This article provides some useful insights into the different formats which you will be expected to use when answering SBL exam tasks.

Own research

Consider your own organisation, or one with which you are very familiar – let's see if you can find out more about the topics considered in this chapter:

- How much of what you have read in this chapter can you find?

- What's been added that is different and what do you think is missing?

- In each case, why do you think the organisation you have selected has reported its corporate governance in this way?

- If possible, perform the same analysis for a public sector organisation (this could be a charity or QuANGO instead of a local council or a hospital) – what's different about this organisation's governance reporting and why do you think this is?

- Finally, how do you think you could be tested on this content in the SBL exam?

Exercise 1

- Improved risk management. The reduction of downside risk will reduce business losses.

- Overall business performance is enhanced by focusing attention on areas of critical importance.

- Defines clear accountability for executive decision making.

- It provides both an appropriate and adequate system of internal control, which permeates the organisation from top to bottom.

- Best practice guidelines are applied by management, who therefore strive to improve their performance.

- Encourages ethical behaviour and corporate social responsibility.

- Safeguards the firm from misuse of business assets, both tangible and intangible.

- Can attract new investment, particularly in developing countries.

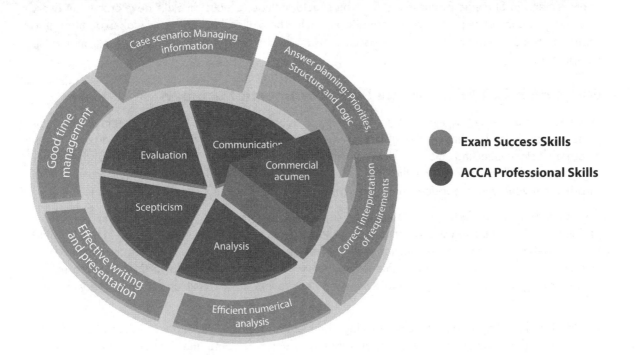

Exam Success Skills

ACCA Professional Skills

Introduction

In Stage 1 you have learned about effective leadership.

However, only 80% of marks are awarded for the application of knowledge. The remaining marks are awarded for good demonstration of the specific ACCA Professional Skills outlined in the task requirement.

You need to able to:

1. Identify the ACCA Professional Skill in the task requirement. Remember the five: Analysis, Communication, Commercial Acumen, Evaluation and Scepticism

2. Understand what the skill requires in the context of the question

3. Consider how to demonstrate the skill(s) as part of your answer planning

The ACCA Professional Skills are assessing your ability to present your answers to a standard which would be expected in the workplace. However, in order to do this effectively in the Strategic Business Leader Exam, you must develop a further series of Exam Success Skills, so you are able to produce your very best solution in the four-hour timeframe.

Therefore, success in Strategic Business Leader requires the simultaneous demonstration of syllabus knowledge, ACCA Professional Skills and Exam Success Skills. This Skills Checkpoint specifically targets the development of your skills as you progress through the syllabus. This should provide you with all of the tools that you will need during the Learning phase, so you can focus on improving these at the Revision Stage.

The five Skills Checkpoints focus each on one of the five ACCA Professional Skills and provide further guidance on how to develop certain Exam Success Skills, so you can effectively manage questions and meet the expected standard for both knowledge and skills.

Your role

Developing skills requires more than listening and reading, it requires you to try for yourself, use guidance and feedback to consider whether you have met the skills objective, then plan for further improvement. In Strategic Business Leader, you should include a focus on skills development in every question you attempt as part of your normal approach. The Skills Checkpoints will take you through a series of **steps** where you will attempt aspects of a question and review your progress from a skills perspective.

Focus on ACCA Professional Skill: Commercial acumen

There are three essential elements to commercial acumen that ACCA have identified for their professional skills. The first is the ability to demonstrate awareness of organisational and wider external factors affecting the work of an individual or a team in contributing to the wider organisational objectives. Given that this is a strategic professional exam, it should come as no surprise that you need to consider the 'bigger picture' when producing answers to questions.

The second is to use judgement to identify key issues in determining how to address or resolve problems and in proposing and recommending the solutions to be implemented. Again, demonstrating higher level skills (often in conjunction with higher level question verbs such as 'recommend' or 'evaluate') is crucial for success at this level. Professional marks will be awarded in this area for demonstrating sensible and appropriate solutions that reflect the context of the case overview and exhibits.

The third and final approach to demonstrating commercial acumen is to show insight and perception in understanding work-related and organisational issues, including the management of conflict, demonstrating acumen in arriving at appropriate solutions or outcomes. This suggests the role played by emotional intelligence in formulating plans, considering the 'human' element when making recommendations and judgements.

Demonstrating Exam Success Skills

For this question, we will focus on the following exam success skills:

- **Case scenario: Managing information**. In the exam, you will be presented with both structured and unstructured information which could be non-sequential and include data and other material, which may not all be relevant to every task requirement. Your ability to identify the key parts of the case overview and supporting exhibits (and by implication, knowing which parts you do not need to worry about) is a key skill that we will start to consider in this checkpoint.

- **Correct interpretation of requirements**. Task requirements can sometimes be presented in a complicated manner that does not read well. This is most likely deliberate, although it is not done just to try and deliberately confuse you: the complexity of a task requirement is designed to test how you can cope with specific instructions that may just be complex. The example we have for this checkpoint is deliberately challenging to illustrate the approach that you will need to be successful.

- **Answer planning: Priorities, Structure and Logic**. It seems logical that, following the analysis of a scenario and the interpretation of task requirements, a plan should emerge, and so this is what we are also going to look at in this checkpoint. Extracting the key parts of the case scenario that meet the task requirement should give you a series of points, but these must be organised so you have the best chance of scoring as many marks as possible. The next question will help show you how this can be done.

Skills Activity

 STEP 1 Read the following task requirement for the question 'Conference', identifying the verbs and the professional skills being examined, and start to set up your answer plan. Remember your skills of 'Correct interpretation of the requirements' as there are two task requirements here and they are not immediately straightforward to interpret!

Required

Assess the benefits of the separation of the roles of chief executive and chair that Alliya Yongvanich argued for and explain her belief that 'accountability to shareholders' is increased by the separation of these roles. **(12 marks)**

Professional skills marks are available for demonstrating **commercial acumen** skills in relation to your assessment and explanation. **(2 marks)**

(Total = 14 marks)

- There are two verbs here – 'assess' and 'explain' but only one mark score (12 marks) so until I find out more from the case information I probably need to treat them both equally.

- I need to list the benefits of separating the chief executive and chair role, and put some sort of score on each benefit to see how significant these benefits are.

- I also need to understand why Alliya believes that having two separate roles increases accountability to shareholders.

- I need to make sure I can define 'accountability' in my answer to set it in context.

 STEP 2 You should now read the scenario, considering how you can isolate the key parts that relate to the task requirement. The scenario has been annotated to show what sort of things you should be looking for when performing this kind of 'active' reading.

> Is this it? I need to read this scenario carefully to make sure I extract everything I need to answer the question.

> This is evidently a reason for not splitting these roles – how does this impact on my answer?

> While it is important to understand that there is no one perfect form of governance, we are being asked to consider things from one perspective (separating the two roles) so this part may not be that relevant to my answer.

Question – Conference   (14 marks)

At a recent international meeting of business leaders, Seamus O'Brien said that multi-jurisdictional attempts to regulate corporate governance were futile because of differences in national culture. He drew particular attention to the Organisation for Economic Co-operation and Development (OECD) and International Corporate Governance Network (ICGN) codes, saying that they were 'silly attempts to harmonise practice'. He said that in some countries, for example, there were 'family reasons' for making the chair and chief executive the same person. In other countries, he said, the separation of these roles seemed to work. Another delegate, Alliya Yongvanich, said that the roles of chief executive and chair should always be separated because of what she called 'accountability to shareholders'.

> These are the 'bigger picture' than for any one place, so what do I need to remember about general guidance in this area?

> Why would this be and where might we see this?

One delegate, Vincent Viola, said that the right approach was to allow each country to set up its own corporate governance provisions. He said that it was suitable for some countries to produce and abide by their own 'very structured' corporate governance provisions, but in some other parts of the world, the local culture was to allow what he called 'local interpretation of the rules'. He said that some cultures valued highly structured governance systems while others do not care as much.

STEP 3 You are now in a position to create an answer plan.

Guidance in helping you develop your answer plan

As the question is worth 14 marks, using two minutes per mark as a guide equates to a total of 28 minutes to attempt the requirement. Working on the basis that you will spend at least five minutes creating your answer plan, this leaves no more than 23 minutes to write up your answer.

Each point you make could score up to two marks, so you are looking at six separate points overall – assuming an even split, that's at least three benefits that need to be assessed and three points that need to be explained. Accountability needs to be defined as part of your answer so that should be at least another mark.

Demonstrating commercial acumen is necessary to earn the two professional marks and these seem to relate in the first instance to showing an understanding of the wider cultural and legal factors that have led to Alliya taking one view on the separation of the roles of chief executive and chair. The professional marks would also be awarded for demonstrating awareness of the wider work-related and organisational issues that make the separation of these two roles more likely to lead to greater accountability to shareholders.

Having already annotated the scenario with the task requirements in mind, you will have probably concluded that there is very little in the scenario that you can use to populate your answer. Consequently, technical knowledge will be necessary, but must still be applied in the context of your awareness of the commercial acumen skills discussed above.

Taking all this into account, your plan may start to look something like this.

- 'Separating the roles of chief executive and chair is a good idea because....'

    - Avoids having too much power in one person's hands (key issue)
    - Complex, time-consuming role needs two people
    - Avoids conflicts of interest between non-executive role and executive remuneration
    - Family reasons per Seamus?

- Accountability = facing the consequences of your actions

- 'Accountability to shareholders is increased by the separation of these roles because....'

    - If something goes wrong, it can be diagnosed and rectified (policy = chair; execution = chief executive)

    - Supports non-executives in their role overseeing the executives

    - Shareholders know who is responsible

STEP 4 **Check the task requirements**

Before you start writing up your answer it is worthwhile reviewing the task requirement again to ensure that there is nothing that you have overlooked.

- Have you assessed the idea that the two roles should be separate?

- Have you defined accountability?

- Have you said why accountability to shareholders is increased by separating the roles?

STEP (5) **Complete your written answer**

You can now bring your workings together to create a solution, making sure that you use logical headings and short punchy sentences. Drawing together the key points from the scenario with your assessments and explanations will show the marker that you have dealt with both task requirements. A model answer is given below, with comment boxes illustrating where the answer is demonstrating good commercial acumen skills.

Suggested solution

Benefits of splitting the roles

Authority

There is an important difference between the authority of the chair and the authority of the chief executive, which having the roles taken by different people will clarify. The chair **carries the authority of the board** whereas the chief executive has the authority that is **delegated by the board**. Having the roles separate emphasises that the chair is acting on behalf of the board, whereas the chief executive has the authority given in his **terms of appointment**. Having the same person in both roles means that **unfettered power** is concentrated into one pair of hands; the board may be ineffective in controlling the chief executive if it is led by the chief executive. The chair provides a second **effective viewpoint** and also contributes their own **experience**, augmenting the board.

> This is demonstrating commercial acumen, specifically by understanding the cultural factors associated with separating this role in certain jurisdictions

Time considerations

An argument in favour of splitting the roles of chair and chief executive is that both are very demanding functions. In large, complex organisations no one individual will have the time to do both jobs effectively, although this is not the case in US companies, where the role of executive chair is common. Splitting the roles does mean that the chair is responsible for the functions of **leading and running the board**, with the chief executive **running the organisation and developing its strategy**.

> Again, good awareness of cultural and legal factors shows commercial acumen skills

Leadership of non-executive directors

Governance reports emphasise the importance of a strong, influential presence of **independent non-executive directors**. A **non-executive chair** can provide effective leadership for the non-executive directors which an executive chair might struggle to maintain.

> Again, good awareness of cultural and legal factors shows commercial acumen skills

Information for non-executive directors

The chair is responsible for obtaining the information that other directors require to **exercise proper oversight**. If the chair is also chief executive, then directors may not be sure that the information they are getting is sufficient and objective enough to support their supervision (due to the chief executive frequently being remunerated on the basis of business results). The chair should ensure that the board is receiving sufficient information to make **informed decisions**, and should put pressure on the chief executive if the chair believes that the chief executive is not providing adequate information.

> Again, good awareness of cultural and legal factors shows commercial acumen skills

Information for markets

Having a separate chair means that there is a division of roles between the person **responsible for communicating business performance to markets** (the chair), and the person **responsible for that performance** (the chief executive).

Protection of minority shareholders

A separate chair can also ensure that executive management pays **sufficient attention to the interests of minority shareholders** and protects their interests. Seamus O'Brien's comment about family reasons highlights a situation where a separate chair is particularly important; in companies where a founding family dominates executive management, shareholders who are not family members often feel that their interests are neglected.

> Some further awareness and understanding of the cultural and legal factors that you could display in your answer

Accountability

Definition

Accountability means ensuring that the chief executive is **answerable for the consequences** of their actions (technically this is both positive and negative, rewarding and sanctioning in cases of good and bad behaviour respectively).

Role in appraising chief executive

A separate chair can take responsibility for regularly appraising the chief executive's performance. The chair may also be responsible for advising the remuneration committee on the chief executive's remuneration, having taken **account of shareholder views**.

Focal point for non-executive directors

If the non-executive directors or shareholders have **concerns about the way executive management** is running the company, a chair not involved in executive management can offer an effective point for reporting these concerns. If, however, the chief executive is also the chair, the non-executive directors may doubt their objectivity, as they are ultimately responsible for managing the company.

> You can demonstrate commercial acumen skills here by displaying good awareness of wider work-related and organisational matters

> Again, good awareness of cultural and legal factors shows commercial acumen skills

Ensuring accountability to shareholders

The UK Corporate Governance Code (2018) and other reports stress the role of the chair in seeking the **views of shareholders** and ensuring **effective communication with them**. This provides a means for shareholders to raise concerns about the chief executive, and the chair, as board representative, can **ultimately be held to account for this**.

Ensuring legal accountability

As representative of the board, the chair can be **held responsible in law** for its activities including the supervision exercised over the chief executive.

 Complete the exam success skills diagnostic

Finally, use the diagnostic below to assess how effectively you demonstrated the exam success skills in answering the question.

Exam Success Skills	Your reflections/observations
Case scenario: Managing information	Notice that in this case, there was very little in the scenario for you to work with, so applying technical knowledge and professional skills will have been crucial in understanding the case scenario.
Correct interpretation of requirements	Did you notice that although there was only one task requirement, it still contained two verbs, 'assess' and 'explain'? A key word to look out for in such cases is the word 'and' in the middle of a task requirement as it is frequently followed by a verb and unless this is spotted, an entire section of the requirement may go unanswered. Did you appreciate the importance of displaying your commercial acumen skills?
Answer planning: Priorities, Structure and Logic	Did you adopt a systematic approach to planning, understanding the task requirements first, then working through the scenario to extract relevant information?
Efficient numerical analysis	Not applicable in this question.
Effective writing and presentation	Have you used headings to structure your answer, with short sentences and paragraphs? Are your points made clearly and succinctly?
Time management	Did you allocate sufficient time to attempt both parts of the task requirement?
Most important action points to apply to your next question	

Summary

Answering exam questions is like any other skill – the more you practise, the better you will get! But, after attempting a question, make sure you take time to reflect and debrief how well you managed it, whether you followed the key steps and whether you demonstrated professional skills. Carry forward your learning points to the next question you attempt, and over the course of your studies you will see significant improvements.

BPP LEARNING MEDIA

INTRODUCTION TO STAGE 2:
Optimising Strategic Decisions

Optimising Strategic Decisions

Founded in 1985, US-based company Blockbuster rode the growth in video rentals to become a major global success story. Using the latest technology to monitor inventory levels and developing an innovative business model, at its peak in 2004 the company had over 9,000 stores worldwide. In 2000, it turned down the opportunity to buy a small start-up called Netflix for $50m, believing it was operating in a niche market and its losses were too great to take on board. In the same year, the company partnered with Enron to create a video-on-demand service, a deal soon after terminated by Enron.

However, overall the company was too slow to respond to the DVD-by-post services being offered by some providers, and online streaming pioneered by Netflix. Gradually its operations were sold off or shut down. Blockbuster is one of many companies that have failed to respond to what was happening in their environment, and failed to choose the strategies that may have led to their continued survival. In this section, we cover the tools that can be used to analyse an organisation's environment – the things happening externally that will or may have an impact on it. We also look at how an organisation can understand its own resources, capabilities and competences, which can be exploited to achieve success. We also consider the tools that can help leaders make strategic choices about the long-term direction and scope of their organisations. Success is never guaranteed, but understanding the influences on an organisation and choices that can be made may help future organisations avoid the fate of Blockbuster.

The external
environment

4

Learning objectives

On completion of this chapter, you should be able to:

	Syllabus reference no.
Assess the macro-environment of an organisation using PESTEL	C2(a)
Assess the implications of strategic drift	C2(b)
Evaluate the external key drivers of change likely to affect the structure of a sector or market	C2(c)
Explore, using Porter's Diamond, the influence of national competitiveness on the strategic position of an organisation	C2(d)
Prepare scenarios reflecting different assumptions about the future environment of an organisation	C2(e)
Evaluate the source of competition in an industry or sector using Porter's five forces framework	C3(a)
Analyse customers and markets including market segmentation	C3(b)
Evaluate the opportunities and threats posed by the environment of an organisation	C3(e)

Business and exam context

An organisation needs to analyse the environment in which it operates in order understanding its current strategic position, and to develop future strategies.

The external environment is a source of opportunities and threats to an organisation, which can influence an organisation's ability to survive and grow. Changes in the environment may mean that the organisation needs to change its strategy in response: either to take advantage of opportunities, or to protect itself from potential threats.

In this chapter we will look at the different models and frameworks an organisation can use to analyse its environment, and how the choice of model depends on the level at which the environment is being analysed.

Chapter overview

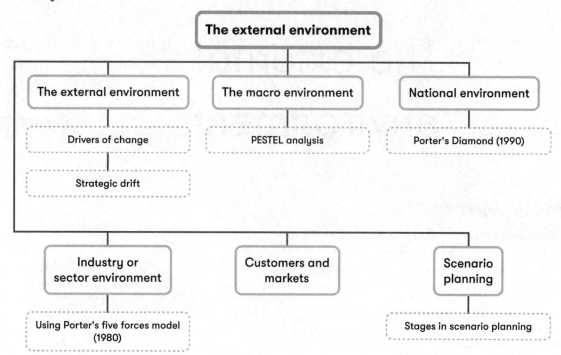

The external environment

- The external environment
  - Drivers of change
  - Strategic drift
- The macro environment
  - PESTEL analysis
- National environment
  - Porter's Diamond (1990)
- Industry or sector environment
  - Using Porter's five forces model (1980)
- Customers and markets
- Scenario planning
  - Stages in scenario planning

1 The external environment

The external environment can be analysed in terms of the broad factors which affect all businesses (**macro-environment**) or those relevant to a specific industry or market (**micro-environment**).

The **macro-environment** includes broad factors which could affect all businesses; for example, political or economic factors, or technological change. These can be assessed using **PESTEL analysis**.

The **micro-environment** relates to the factors which affect an organisation's ability to operate effectively in its chosen industry or market sector. Key factors here are: customers, competitors, distributors and suppliers. These can be assessed using **Porter's five forces** analysis.

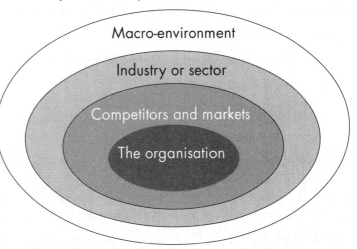

Levels of the external environment

(Adapted from: Johnson, *et al* 2017:p.33)

The external environment is a source of **threats** (external changes which could damage a business) and also **opportunities** (external changes which a business could exploit to its advantage).

PER alert

> Performance Objective 3 'Strategy and Innovation' of the Practical Experience Requirement requires you to 'research and be familiar with your employer's business, the sector it operates within and the wider business environment' (ACCA, 2019b). It is particularly important that you take the time to read through the sections in this chapter carefully as a number of important theoretical models are discussed which may help you to better analyse the wider business environment in which your employer operates.

1.1 Drivers of change

Organisations, or industries more generally, need to take advantage of opportunities which arise in the external environment and respond to the threats it poses.

As such, changes in the external environment can act as drivers for change; for example, car manufacturers moving towards producing more environmentally friendly cars in response to customer concerns about carbon emissions and pollution.

The stimulus for organisational change can be driven by both internal or external events. Events are sometimes referred to as '**triggers**'. External triggers (change drivers) may include the following:

- Increasing competition
- Changes in customer tastes and buying behaviour
- Social changes, eg demographics (age, income and gender)
- Changes in the economic cycle (recession)
- Political and legal pressures (new laws, regulations and tax rules)
- Increasing use of new technologies (internet and mobile
- technologies)

Exam Focus Point

As the focus of this Chapter is upon the external environment the 'triggers' discussed above specifically relate to external events. It is important to note that internal events can also act as triggers for change within organisations. Internal triggers can include:

- Out of date working practices/processes

- Changes in organisational performance, eg reducing profitability

- Introduction of new technologies

- Changes in senior management

- High staff turnover

Internal triggers for change are closely linked to the themes considered in Chapter 5 which focuses on Strategic Capability.

1.1.1 Determining how to respond to external change events

Organisations' are continually faced with external change events, and as such need to determine which events they will respond to and those they will not. This process will be influenced by a range of factors but might include:

- **The objectives of the organisation**. For example, an organisation which has an objective of becoming the market leader in its industry would need to proactively respond to opposing moves by a competitor to ensure that its objective is achieved. This might involve undertaking a new promotional campaign or changing the prices it charges for its products/services.

- **Stakeholders.** An external change event which threatens the interest of those groups identified as 'key players' (per Mendelow in Chapter 2), or heightens the scope for 'keep satisfied' stakeholders to exert their power, increases the likelihood of a speedy management response. For example, changes in customer tastes may reduce demand for the organisation's products which is reflected in falling profits. This situation heightens the scope for large institutional shareholders to express concern or sell their shares. Such a situation will require management to introduce strategies to address the situation.

- **Time.** Some external events may be known about some time in advance of them coming into effect. For example, new legislation might be announced that will come into effect in 12 months' time which will restrict the sale of some of the organisation's products or services. In cases such as this, management should be able to plan for the change in an orderly fashion. By contrast, a problem with one of the organisation's products may need to be prioritised as it requires urgent action, for example, issuing a product recall to protect the safety of customers.

- **Severity.** The severity of the external event will drive the speed and the priority with which it is managed.

Ultimately, the process of deciding which external events the organisation will respond to and how this will be achieved will be determined by the skill and experience of the organisation's leadership.

Syllabus links

Opportunities and threats from the external environment are discussed in greater detail in Chapter 5. The section covering the use of SWOT analysis in business provides organisations with a useful tool in understanding its internal strengths and weaknesses and its external opportunities and threats. SWOT analysis provides a helpful start point for determining the organisation's future strategic options.

1.2 Strategic drift

Environmental change is inevitable. To survive, companies need to respond effectively to opportunities and threats, and to avoid strategic drift.

Strategic drift: An organisation's strategies fail to address its strategic position, particularly in response to environmental change, leading to a deterioration in the organisation's performance.

Key term

Real world examples

Marks and Spencer in the UK clothes retail market is an example of a company that has not adapted to changing customer demands and has lost customers as a result.

Nokia. For a short time, Nokia was the largest mobile phone supplier in the world, but its smartphone operating system was inferior to competitors' systems, and by 2014 Nokia had sold its mobile phone business to Microsoft.

Toys R Us in 2018 announced that it was closing all of its UK stores having failed to recognise the growth in demand for increasingly technologically advanced devices such as virtual reality (VR) headsets, drones and go-pro cameras which were being targeted at younger buyers. This shift in consumer buying resulted in less demand for conventional children's toys available for purchase from large out-of-town stores such as those operated by Toys R Us.

2 The macro environment

2.1 PESTEL analysis

Organisations can use PESTEL analysis as a framework for analysing the general business environment (macro-environmental), and the opportunities and threats present in the environment.

Political	Economic	Social
eg government decisions and policies, such as changes in competition policy or consumer policies	eg impact of the economic cycle (recession or economic growth); inflation; interest rates; tax rates; foreign exchange rates	eg demographics; changes in tastes or culture (demographic changes can affect workforces as well as consumers)

Organisation – opportunities
and threats

Technological	Environmental (or Ecological)	Legal
Changes in technology that affect ways of working, or the types of products and services demanded	'Green' issues, such as pollution, climate change, environmental regulation, consumer attitudes to products (environmentally friendly; sustainable etc)	Laws and regulation, including any changes to them (eg employment law; health and safety; data protection)

Demographics: Is the study of the human population and particular groups within it; analysis of data relating to the population.

Key term

Activity 1: Organic fruit farm

ACCA Professional skills focus

Analysis: Consider

Discussion:

You are a management accountant for an organic fruit farm in Teeland. The farm grows apples and produces apple juice, both of which it sells at local markets and to retail companies.

The farm's management team are considering its future strategy, and have asked for your help in assessing its macro-environment.

Required

Using the information below, **analyse** the THREE key factors in the environment which are likely to have most impact on the farm.   **(6 marks)**

Professional skills marks are available for demonstrating **analysis skills** in considering how the environmental factors affect the farm.   **(2 marks)**

(Total = 8 marks)

Organic farming and the food industry in Teeland

Organic food must be produced using environmentally friendly farming methods, so no genetically modified (GM) crops, growth enhancers or artificial pesticides and fertilisers may be used. Any farmer claiming to be organic must be certified by a government-approved body, such as the Teeland Soil Association. Food producers must also comply with government-approved regulations regarding the production, packaging and labelling of food.

Regulatory bodies have the authority to forbid the use of misleading labels and product descriptions, and can issue fines for inappropriate production. In extreme cases, regulatory bodies can close down operations which regularly fail to comply with regulations for production, packaging and labelling of their products.

Consumers increasingly want food that is healthy and is sourced both ethically and locally. Consequently, although organic food was initially perceived as a luxury niche product, it is now increasingly seen as a lifestyle choice by those consumers who regard non-organic products as more harmful to health and the environment. Major supermarkets in Teeland have started to stock more organic and locally grown food.

A key issue for all farmers is the weather, which significantly affects the volume (yield) and quality of a crop and hence the market price. Organic farmers are unable to use artificial fertilisers or pesticides, so have developed alternative high-tech farming methods to improve profitability and cash flow. Weather information systems help plan planting, harvesting and irrigation. Climate-controlled growing tunnels and stores provide a pest-free environment with temperature, light and humidity control. These methods increase yields, extend the possible growing season and allow crops to be stored for longer before usage or sale, with no loss of flavour or quality.

Solution

Environmental factor	Impact of the factors

Exam Focus Point

Although PESTEL can be a useful checklist, in practice many of the factors can be interlinked. The value of PESTEL analysis comes from identifying factors which could affect an organisation, and what the impact of those factors might be. Whether or not a factor has been classified in the correct category is far less important to a strategic business leader.

3 National environment

Assessing the opportunities and threats which are present in different countries can be particularly important for multinational companies which are thinking about investing in a new country.

However, another key consideration in the investment decision could be how competitive the country is.

3.1 Porter's Diamond

Michael Porter (1990) observed that some nations' industries are more successful than others', and he identified four key factors which collectively determine a country's attractiveness for a given industry:

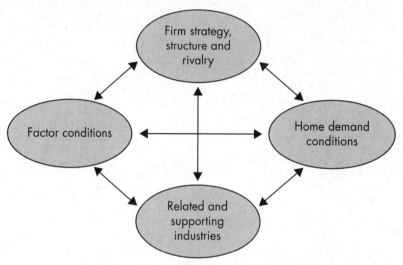

(Source: Porter, 1990)

3.2 Components of the diamond

The inter-related elements that can be used to assess a nation's competitive advantage are:

- **Factor conditions** – relates to a country's resources, (so in effect are 'supply side' factors). These can be categorised as:

    - **Basic factors** – for example, natural resources, climate, semi-skilled or unskilled labour. These are basic pre-conditions which are needed for an industry to be successful, but, by themselves, they do not provide any sustainable competitive advantage

    - **Advanced factors** – for example, infrastructure and communications, higher education, and skilled employees (eg skilled scientists or engineers to support high-tech industries. In contrast to basic factors, the presence of advanced factors can help to promote competitive advantage.

- **Demand conditions** – A tough domestic market is likely to encourage competitiveness, as firms have to produce cost-efficient, high-quality goods to satisfy the requirements of their domestic customers. The experience a firm gains from meeting domestic customers' needs will then allow it to compete successfully on an international scale.

- **Related and supporting industries** – Industries need to be supported by a good local supply chain, which contributes to quality and cost advantages

- **Firm strategy, structure and rivalry** – Cultural factors, social attitudes and management styles can all lead to competitive advantage in certain industries. Intense domestic rivalry among firms means they need to perform well to survive (eg through cost reduction or quality improvement and innovation). Intense domestic rivalry may also encourage firms to look for export markets.

3.3 Clustering

The combination of these elements can create a 'cluster' of extremely competitive firms that are well-placed to compete internationally.

Clustering helps to reinforce the factors in the diamond – for example, by providing a concentration of advanced factor conditions, and related/supporting industries (as with the high-tech electronics industry in Silicon Valley, California).

3.4 Government policy

Government policy can also be important in nurturing the elements of the diamond, for example, by investing in infrastructure and higher education.

The tax regime and government's attitudes to foreign investors could also affect a multinational company's decision about whether or not to invest in a country.

Exam Focus Point

The March/June 2019 exam released by ACCA featured a clothing retailer called SmartWear. Task 2(a) required candidates to prepare a report for the board which analysed SmartWear's strategic position in the Southland market (one of the countries that SmartWear operated in) and to determine why the company appeared to be performing well in this country compared to the country of Noria (SmartWear's home country). Professional skills marks were awarded for demonstrating analysis skills in determining SmartWear's strategic position in Southland.

The examining team noted that task 2(a) was 'fairly well answered, although few candidates picked up on all the contributing factors. Some answers recognised the benefit of using Porter's Diamond model, whereas others were presented without any structure. The factors behind the relative success of SmartWear in Southland were largely identified, although in a reflection of not reading the question carefully, often far too much emphasis was based on the problems in Noria. Better candidates provided more detail on their interpretation of these comparisons and why it meant the Southland market was performing better'. (ACCA, 2019a).

The examining team highlighted that some candidates provided answers which were too detailed, and failed to effectively apply the key elements of Porter's Diamond model to the case material. To earn the 2 professional skills marks candidates needed to prepare a report which identified and used the most important, relevant data to analyse SmartWear's strategic position. The report needed to be structured and presented in a way that was sufficiently user-friendly that it could be used by the board.

Real world example – Silicon Valley

Silicon Valley in San Francisco is one of the world's most famous clusters of companies. It is home to high-tech innovators including Apple, Cisco Systems, Google, Facebook and eBay.

Setting up operations close to firms operating in similar industries allows new firms to achieve economies of scale which may not have been available to them elsewhere. New start-ups benefit from the Valley's pool of highly skilled workers with expertise in innovation. Companies in Silicon Valley are able to capitalise on their close proximity to Stanford University, which provides a readily available source of new graduates in high-tech specialisms. A number of the graduates from Stanford University have gone on to start up their own businesses in Silicon Valley, such as Hewlett-Packard.

Exercise 1: Silicon Valley

Required

Using Porter's Diamond, analyse why the US, and Silicon Valley in particular, has a competitive advantage as a location for technology companies.

Solution

Diamond factor	How factor contributes to competitive advantage
Factor conditions	
Demand conditions	
Related and supporting industries	
Firm structure, strategy and rivalry	

4 Industry or sector environment

An organisation's strategic position and performance is affected not only by the macro-environment (PESTEL factors) but also by factors specific to its industry or market sector.

Porter (1980) argues that the level of profit which can be sustained in an industry is influenced by the state of competition in that industry ('Porter's five forces'). The stronger the five forces, the lower the level of profit which can be sustained in the industry.

4.1 Using Porter's five forces model

The five forces model has three main uses:

- Analysing the inherent profitability (and therefore attractiveness) of a particular industry or market segment. If possible, companies should aim to invest in industries where the five forces are in their favour and high returns can be made.

- Identifying actions relating to the different competitive forces on an organisation that:
    - Mitigate their damaging effects (**threats**); and/or
    - Promote the beneficial effects (**opportunities**).

- Considering whether all competitors are affected equally by the forces. For example, higher buyer power may mean that small competitors cannot raise prices, giving an advantage to large ones who can, or who can afford to operate on lower margins.

4.1.1 Porter's five forces model

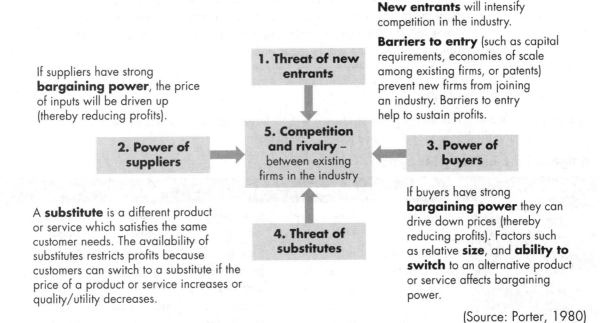

New entrants will intensify competition in the industry.

Barriers to entry (such as capital requirements, economies of scale among existing firms, or patents) prevent new firms from joining an industry. Barriers to entry help to sustain profits.

If suppliers have strong **bargaining power**, the price of inputs will be driven up (thereby reducing profits).

A **substitute** is a different product or service which satisfies the same customer needs. The availability of substitutes restricts profits because customers can switch to a substitute if the price of a product or service increases or quality/utility decreases.

If buyers have strong **bargaining power** they can drive down prices (thereby reducing profits). Factors such as relative **size**, and **ability to switch** to an alternative product or service affects bargaining power.

(Source: Porter, 1980)

Competition and rivalry – intense competition in an industry will reduce profits. This may result from slow-growing or declining markets, excess capacity, or barriers to exit.

In some industries, it is relevant to consider a 'sixth force', organisations that are **complementors**. This means an organisation that 'enhances your business attractiveness to customers or suppliers' (Johnson *et al*, 2017). For example, app developers are complementors to smartphone and tablet providers because apps make the devices more useful. These organisations need to be taken into account in assessing the environment.

Essential reading

See Chapter 4 section 1 of the Essential Reading, available in Appendix 2 of the digital edition of the Workbook, for more detail about Porter's five forces.

Exam Focus Point

Task 1(a) in the March/June 2019 exam released by ACCA asked candidates to prepare a briefing paper for the board at SmartWear, a clothing retailer. Candidates were required to analyse the environment in which the company was operating and to consider how this might impact the company's business model, mission and strategic goals.

The examining team commented that 'on the whole this question was reasonably well answered with many candidates scoring highly, and some achieving full marks. Most answers used the PESTEL model, some Porter's Five Forces, and a few SWOT. With the minority of candidates using all three but by doing so the answers were very long and repetitive. This approach took a disproportionate amount of time to complete, with the result that their answers to Task 5 were often rushed and incomplete'. (ACCA, 2019a).

The examining team noted that some candidates tried to apply all elements of the PESTEL model, even though there was no information in the case material relating to environmental and legal matters. In essence, candidates attempted to fit their answer around the model, as opposed to only using relevant bits of the model to help structure their answer. The examining team also highlighted that a number of candidates failed to tie their observations back SmartWear's business model, mission and strategic goals, which was the whole focus of the task.

4.2 Industry life cycle

The stage an industry has reached in its life cycle can have important implications for the level of competition, and the basis on which firms look to compete.

Stages of the industry life cycle

	Development	Growth	Shakeout	Maturity	Decline
Typical five forces	Low rivalry: High differentiation, innovation key	Low rivalry: High growth and weak buyers, but low entry barriers, growth ability key	Increasing rivalry: Slower growth and some exits, managerial and financial strength key	Stronger buyers: Low growth and standard products, but higher entry barriers, market share and cost key	Extreme rivalry: Typically many exits and price competition, cost and commitment key

(Adapted from: Johnson *et al*, 2017)

Activity 2: Happy Day theme parks

ACCA Professional skills focus

Analysis: Investigate

Happy Day Company ('Happy Day') operates a chain of 15 theme parks across Western Europe.

Happy Day's parks are family oriented, and are intended to provide 'a great day out for all the family'. Each Happy Day park offers roller coasters and other thrill rides, live entertainment and exhibits (such as animals and sea-life). Each park also offers a range of food outlets and gift shops.

You are a management consultant, and your consultancy firm has been asked to advise Happy Day on some strategic issues, including an analysis of their industry environment.

Required

Using the information provided in Exhibit 1, **analyse** the theme park industry in Western Europe.

(8 marks)

Professional skills marks are available for demonstrating **analysis skills** in investigating the likely impact of environmental factors on the profitability of the industry. **(2 marks)**

(Total = 10 marks)

Exhibit 1 – The theme park industry in Western Europe

The leisure and entertainment industry in Western Europe is a mature market. In addition to an increasing number of theme parks, there is also a wide range of alternative forms of entertainment available to tourists and domestic customers – for example, cinemas, sport events and cultural attractions.

There are three types of theme parks and park operators:

* Major complexes, operated worldwide by large multinational entertainment corporations
* Regional chains, such as Happy Day
* Smaller, simpler local parks

The multinational entertainment corporations gain marketing benefits from linking rides with film and television characters. They also have access to the significant capital and technology required to develop exciting new rides. Most multinational and regional theme park chains add at least one new ride per park per year to attract visitors. Operators spend, on average, 20% of annual revenue on building new rides and attractions.

Competition in the industry is fierce. To increase profits, parks need to attract more visitors, and increase the amount they spend during a visit. The key factors for a successful theme park are:

* Convenience of location
* Popularity of rides
* Health and safety
* Price
* Availability and quality of wider amenities (eg food, merchandise)

The difficult economic climate in Western Europe has led to a fall in consumer spending across leisure activities in general. However, this has also resulted in theme parks suffering declining attendance and falling profitability.

In view of increasing competition in the established park locations in North America and Western Europe, and the fact that possible land for expansion is expensive and restricted, a number of the multinational operators have started to look at other markets in Asia and South America.

Solution

4.3 Triggers for change

Changes in the industry environment can change the strength of the competitive forces; for example:

- Arrival of new entrants into the market; or mergers/acquisitions between existing competitors

- Slowdown in the market growth rate

- Innovations or technological developments leading to the emergence of new substitutes

- Consolidation in supply chain or distribution networks (eg mergers/acquisitions between suppliers)

Changes like these could affect the profitability of the industry, and therefore prompt an organisation to reconsider its strategic position (in relation to opportunities and threats) and its future strategy.

If the organisation doesn't respond effectively to the changes though, it could be vulnerable to strategic drift.

5 Customers and markets

To be successful, a company needs to satisfy its customers better, and respond to market opportunities more effectively, than its competitors. To be able to do this, a company first needs to understand its customers and the markets in which it is competing, in order to develop appropriate strategies.

5.1 Customers

Customers buy a product and service because it satisfies a need or provides them with some value. To deliver value, an organisation must understand its customers (or its stakeholders for not-for-profit organisations) and what they consider to be important.

Aspects of a product or service that are particularly valued by customers are known as **critical success factors** (CSFs). An organisation must excel at CSFs in order to gain a competitive advantage (Johnson *et al*, 2017).

Key term

> **Critical success factors:** The aspects of a product or service that are particularly valued by customers and therefore those at which a business must excel in order to outperform its competitors.

5.2 Markets

In order to trade effectively in a market, a company needs to understand the composition and behaviour of the market.

5.2.1 Market attractiveness

The attractiveness of a market is determined by factors such as: the size of the market; profit margins; market growth (and growth expectations); existing suppliers; and intensity of competition.

Essential reading

See Chapter 4 section 2 of the Essential Reading, available in Appendix 2 of the digital edition of the Workbook, for more detail about the factors a firm should consider before deciding whether to enter a market.

5.2.2 Business attractiveness

As well as considering the characteristics of the market, a company also needs to consider whether its products or services will be attractive to the customers in that market.

5.3 Market segmentation

Very few products can satisfy all the customers in a market, because customers have different requirements from the products they buy.

To satisfy customer needs successfully, different products or services need to be offered to the different customer groups that comprise a market.

Key term

> **Market segmentation:** The division of a market into homogeneous groups of potential customers who may be treated similarly for marketing purposes.

An organisation's marketing activity is more likely to be effective if it targets particular market segments – which can be reached with a **distinct marketing mix** (product, price, place, promotion) – rather than trying to sell to the total market as a whole. The marketing mix concept is explored in greater detail in Chapter 6.

Segmentation enables an organisation to get a better understanding of customer requirements in a segment, so that the organisation can tailor its product to meet the needs of those customers as effectively as possible.

Market segmentation can also be useful when attempting to spot opportunities and threats. As customers' requirements change, new segments emerge. If a company can identify a 'new' segment before its competitors, it could be a source of growth.

BPP LEARNING MEDIA

Real world example

Intercontinental Hotels Group (IHG) Plc owns a number of different hotel brands – for example, Hotel Indigo, Crowne Plaza, Holiday Inn and Staybridge Suites – which target different sectors of the overall hotel market.

6 Scenario planning

The complexity of the external environment makes it difficult for firms to predict the future.

However, to help them plan and assess potential opportunities and threats, firms can develop scenarios based on the key influences and change drivers in the environment.

Key term

> **Scenario planning:** Involves constructing plausible views of how the business environment of an organisation might develop in the future, based on sets of key drivers for change.

Scenarios are **not** forecasts and predictions, but are plausible views of possible future conditions. The aim of scenario planning is to learn rather than predict the future, so organisations are often advised to produce multiple scenarios, to maximise the learning and contingency planning if necessary.

Scenarios can be developed at a **macro-environmental** level (ie relating to changes in PESTEL factors) or an **industry** level (ie relating to Porter's five forces).

6.1 Stages in scenario planning

1	Identify the scope (eg time frame involved; products considered; markets considered) and major stakeholders
2	Identify key trends and areas of uncercertainy (eg based on PESTEL factors)
3	Construct initial scenarios based on the key areas of uncertainty
4	Check scenario for consistency and plausibility
5	Expand initial scenarios into full descriptions as if the scenario was actually occurring – in order for management to assess the implications each scenario could have on the organisation
6	Develop quantitative models of the effect of different scenarios on the organisation's activities and profitability or cash flow
7	Develop strategies or courses of action which could be adopted in different scenarios if they actually happen

 BPP LEARNING MEDIA

Activity 3: Scenario plans

ACCA Professional skills focus

Commercial acumen: Demonstrate awareness

Required

Based on the information in Exhibit 1 below, **discuss** the potential use of scenarios by NESTA's managers as part of their analysis of NESTA's possible entry into the discount fixed-price retail market in Eurobia. **(8 marks)**

Professional skills marks are available for demonstrating **commercial acumen** in identifying key areas of uncertainty which could be included in NESTA's scenario plans. **(2 marks)**

(Total = 10 marks)

Exhibit 1

NESTA is a large chain of fixed-price discount stores based in the country of Eyanke. Its stores offer ambient goods (goods that require no cold storage and can be kept at room temperature, such as cleaning products, stationery, biscuits and plastic storage units) at a fixed price of one dollar.

NESTA has observed the long-term economic decline in the neighbouring country of Eurobia, where a prolonged economic recession has led to the growth of so-called 'dollar shops'. Three significant dollar shop chains have already developed: ItzaDollar, DAIAD and DollaFellas. The shops of these three chains are particularly found on the high streets of towns and cities where there is significant financial hardship.

Many of these towns and cities have empty stores which are relatively cheap to rent. Furthermore, landlords who once required high rents and long leases are increasingly willing to allow/offer these stores a relatively short fixed-term lease. The fixed-price dollar shop chains in Eurobia advertise extensively and continually stress their expansion plans. Few weeks go by without one of the chains announcing plans for a significant number of new shops throughout the country.

NESTA has recognised the growth of fixed-price discount retailers in Eurobia and is considering entering this market.

Alongside the discount retailers, there are also many conventional supermarket chains operating in Eurobia. Supermarkets in Eurobia tend to increasingly favour out-of-town sites which allow the stores to stock a wide range and quantity of products. Customer car parking is plentiful and it is relatively easy for supplying vehicles to access such sites. As well as stocking non-ambient goods, most supermarkets also stock a very wide range of ambient goods, often with competing brands on offer. However, prices for such goods vary and no supermarkets have yet adopted the discount fixed-price sales approach. In general, the large supermarket chains largely compete with each other and pay little attention to the fixed-price dollar shop discounters.

Many supermarkets also have internet-based home ordering systems, offering (usually for a fee of $10) deliveries to customers who are unable or unwilling to visit the supermarket.

Solution

Chapter summary

The external environment

The external environment

Drivers of change
Assessing opportunities and threats

Strategic drift
Failing to respond to change can cause strategic drift

The macro environment

- Broad factors affecting all businesses
- **Analyse the overall business environment using PESTEL**

PESTEL analysis
Framework for analysing sources of opportunities and threats:
- Political
- Economic
- Social
- Technological
- Environmental
- Legal

National environment

- Factors influencing a country's attractiveness for different industries or types of organisation
- **Analyse national competitive environment using Porter's Diamond**

Porter's Diamond (1990)
- Components of the diamond (influences on national competitiveness):
  – Factor conditions
  – Demand conditions
  – Related and supporting industries
  – Firm strategy, structure and rivalry
- Clustering
- Government policy

Industry or sector environment

- (Micro-environment)
- Factors affecting the profitability, and attractiveness, of different industries or markets
- **Analyse using Porter's five forces**

Using Porter's five forces model (1980)
- Attractiveness of an industry
- Five forces:
  – Threat of new entrants
  – Substitutes
  – Bargaining power of customers
  – Bargaining power of suppliers
  – Competition and rivalry
- Industry life cycle
- Triggers for change

Customers and markets

- Key issue: offering an attractive product to an attractive market
- Customers
- Markets
  – Market attractiveness
  – Business attractiveness
- Market segmentation

Scenario planning

- View of how the environment could develop in future
- Consider these when setting strategy

Stages in scenario planning
- Identify key areas of uncertainty
- Construct scenarios based on those key areas
- Assess potential impact of different scenarios on the organisation
- Develop strategies to adopt in different strategies

Knowledge diagnostic

1. The external environment can be in terms of the broad factors which affect all businesses (macro-environment) or those relevant to a specific industry or market (micro-environment).

2. The external environment is a source of threats (external changes which could damage a business) and also opportunities (external changes which a business could exploit to its advantage).

3. Changes in the external environment can act as drivers for change.

4. Environmental change is inevitable. To survive, companies need to respond effectively to opportunities and threats, and to avoid strategic drift.

5. Organisations can use PESTEL analysis as a framework for analysing the general business environment (macro-environmental), and the opportunities and threats present in the environment.

6. Michael Porter (1990) observed that some nations' industries are more successful than others', and he identified four key factors which collectively determine a country's attractiveness for a given industry: firm, strategy, structure and rivalry; home demand conditions; related and supporting industries; factor conditions. These four elements make up Porter's Diamond.

7. The combination of these elements can create a 'cluster' of extremely competitive firms that are well-placed to compete internationally.

8. Government policy can also be important in nurturing the elements of the diamond, for example, by investing in infrastructure and higher education.

9. Porter (1980) argues that the level of profit which can be sustained in an industry is influenced by the state of competition in that industry ('Porter's five forces').

10. Porter's five forces model consists of: the threat of new entrants; the threat of substitutes; power of buyers; power of suppliers; and competition and rivalry. Complementors may also be considered.

11. The stage an industry has reached in its life cycle can have important implications for the level of competition in an industry, and the basis on which firms look to compete.

12. To be successful, a company needs to satisfy its customers better, and respond to market opportunities more effectively, than its competitors. To be able to do this, a company first needs to understand its customers and the markets in which it is competing, in order to develop appropriate strategies.

13. Aspects of a product or service that are particularly valued by customers are known as critical success factors (CSFs). An organisation must excel at CSFs in order to outperform its competitors.

14. In order to trade effectively in a market, a company needs to understand the composition and behaviour of the market.

15. To satisfy customer needs successfully, different products or services need to be offered to the different customer groups that comprise a market. This is the basis of market segmentation.

16. The complexity of the external environment makes it difficult for firms to predict the future. However, to help them plan and assess potential opportunities and threats, firms can develop scenarios based on the key influences and change drivers in the environment.

Further study guidance

Question practice

Now try the question below from the Further question practice bank (available in the digital edition of the Workbook):

Q4 *Joe Swift Transport*

Further reading

There are articles on the ACCA website written by members of the SBL examining team which are relevant to your studies and which would be useful to read:

The strategic planning process – part 1

This article considers the complexities of strategic planning and discusses Porter's five forces and PESTEL in further detail.

Approaching SBL overview

This article provides a one-page summary of the key features of the SBL exam.

Approaching SBL reading and planning

This article provides a one-page summary of how best to approach the SBL exam.

SBL – 10 things to learn from the September 2018 sitting

This article highlights some of the issues that ACCA identified in candidates' answers during the September 2018 SBL exam sitting. The article provides some useful advice for improving your chances of passing the SBL exam.

Strategic Business Leader – The importance of effective communication for SBL

This article provides some useful insights into the different formats which you will be expected to use when answering SBL exam tasks.

Own research

It is important to link the topics covered in this chapter to a practical, real-world context. As such, we have suggested some areas for you to investigate further:

- Research an organisation whose performance has suffered due to strategic drift. What factors have led to the strategic drift? What could the organisation have done differently?

- Use the PESTEL framework to assess the potential opportunities or threats the business environment presents to different organisations.

- Identify the ways an organisation has segmented its market. What factors has it used to distinguish different groups of customers? How does the organisation's strategy, and marketing mix, vary for different segments?

Exercise 1

Diamond factor	How factor contributes to competitive advantage
Factor conditions	Stanford University has always had a strong focus on technology and research, and so provides a good supply of highly skilled workers.
Demand conditions	As the world's richest and most sophisticated economy, the US is the largest market for high-technology products.
Related and supporting industries	External economies of scale due to the presence of similar firms – eg local support firms, such as lawyers, used to dealing with high-tech firms and start-ups. Silicon Valley has a strong network of venture capitalists who are used to investing in promising technology companies.
Firm structure, strategy and rivalry	The direct competition between so many successful companies encourages high standards. Firms are constantly competing for the best IT staff, which leads to excellent pay and conditions, and attracts skilled staff from all over the world to move there. (Some people also argue, more generally, that the creative Californian culture encourages innovation and new ideas.)

Strategic capability

5

Learning objectives

On completion of this chapter, you should be able to:

	Syllabus reference no.
Identify and evaluate an organisation's strategic capability, threshold resources, threshold competences, unique resources and core competences	C4(a)
Discuss the capabilities required to sustain competitive advantage	C4(b)
Discuss the contribution of organisational knowledge to the strategic capability of an organisation	C4(c)
Apply Porter's value chain to assist organisations to identify value-adding activities in order to create and sustain competitive advantage	C3(c)
Advise on the role and influence of value networks	C3(d)
Identify and evaluate the strengths and weaknesses of an organisation and formulate an appropriate SWOT analysis	C4(d)

Business and exam context

In the previous chapter we explored the important role that the external environment has on the ability of an organisation to achieve its strategic aims. The external environment presents organisations with both opportunities and threats.

The focus of this chapter is upon the concept of strategic capability being those internal resources and competences which impact on the ultimate success, or not, of an organisation. Managers responsible for an organisation's strategy need a clear and detailed knowledge of its strategic capability.

In this chapter we introduce Porter's value chain model which can be used to assess the strengths and weaknesses of an organisation's internal activities. We conclude the chapter by introducing SWOT analysis, which draws together the strengths and weaknesses discussed in this chapter with the opportunities and threats which we explored in Chapter 4.

Chapter overview

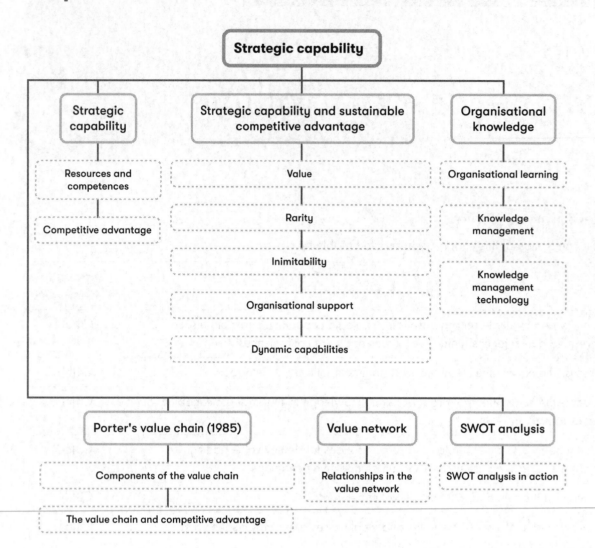

Strategic capability

- Strategic capability
  - Resources and competences
  - Competitive advantage

- Strategic capability and sustainable competitive advantage
  - Value
  - Rarity
  - Inimitability
  - Organisational support
  - Dynamic capabilities

- Organisational knowledge
  - Organisational learning
  - Knowledge management
  - Knowledge management technology

- Porter's value chain (1985)
  - Components of the value chain
  - The value chain and competitive advantage

- Value network
  - Relationships in the value network

- SWOT analysis
  - SWOT analysis in action

1 Strategic capability

Strategic capability is the term used to describe the strengths and weaknesses of an organisation.

Strategic capability: An organisation's ability to survive and prosper depends on its strategic capability; this can be defined as the adequacy and suitability of its resources and competences.

1.1 Resources and competences

As the key term above illustrates, capability is assessed in terms of competences and resources. Competences and resources can be classified as either threshold (ie those regarded as the minimum to compete) or unique (ie those which provide a competitive advantage).

Threshold competences: Those activities and processes needed to meet the customer's minimum requirements.

Threshold resources: Those resources needed to meet the customer's minimum requirements. Resources can be tangible or intangible.

Core competences: The activities and processes through which resources are deployed in such a way as to achieve competitive advantage in ways that others cannot imitate or obtain.

Unique resources: Those resources that critically underpin competitive advantage and that others cannot easily imitate or obtain. Resources can be tangible or intangible.

1.2 Competitive advantage

Competitive advantage: The ability of an organisation to generate greater returns than those of competitors over the long term, as opposed to short-term tactics which provide a temporary advantage.

Competitive advantage is the term used to describe the ability of an organisation to generate greater returns than those of competitors over the long term, as opposed to short-term tactics which provide a temporary advantage.

Illustration 1

An industry-standard piece of machinery used by a manufacturing company represents a **tangible threshold resource**. The right of an airline to use the landing slots at an airport, when all competitors have the same right, represents an **intangible threshold resource**. In this example as competitors have access to the same resources no lasting competitive advantage can be gained from possessing them alone.

A patent for a new medicine belonging to an international pharmaceutical company is an **intangible unique resource**. A diamond mine owned by a mining firm is a **tangible unique resource**. In both cases it is the exclusivity of each resource which stops competitors from being able to benefit from using the same resource.

Operating an automated production facility to produce simple mobile phones means that the manufacturer can sell phones to customers at the lowest possible prices (meeting the customers' minimum requirements). This is a **threshold competence**. A mobile phone manufacturer renowned for producing innovative phones employs a dedicated R&D team of engineers which constantly develop phones which feature the latest technologies. The specialist skills in the R&D team are not available elsewhere in the industry. The R&D team represents a **core competence**.

Exercise 1: Upmarket restaurant

Required

What unique resources and core competences might give an upmarket restaurant a competitive advantage?

Solution

Unique resources	Core competences

2 Strategic capability and sustainable competitive advantage

2.1 Four qualities

It is clear that unique resources and core competences are of great importance in creating a sustainable competitive advantage. Johnson *et al* (2017) suggest that if competitive advantage is to be achieved resources and competences must have four qualities:

- **Value**
- **Rarity**
- **Inimitability**
- **Organisational support**

2.2 Value

Value is concerned with the value placed on resources and competences by a customer or organisation. It is the extent to which resources or competences allow a customer or organisation to take advantage of opportunities, and/or neutralise threats. No matter how rare a resource or how well-developed a competence is, it cannot create competitive advantage if customers do not value it or the things it enables the organisation to do.

2.3 Rarity

A single **unique resource or core competence may** have the potential to create competitive advantage by itself. The importance of rarity is that if a resource or competence is generally available (ie not rare) then an organisation's competitors will have access to it in the same way as the organisation does. In which case, the resource or competence does not confer any advantage to the organisation compared to its rivals.

2.4 Inimitability

Inimitability is the term Johnson *et al* (2017) use to mean that a resource is difficult for competitors to imitate. They point out that, generally, it is difficult to base competitive advantage simply on possession of tangible resources, since they can often be imitated or simply bought in. Inimitability most frequently resides in the **competences** involved in linking activities and processes in ways that both satisfy customer priorities, and which are difficult for competitors to imitate.

2.5 Organisational support

Organisational support focuses upon whether or not an organisation is able to support its capabilities, including its processes and systems. For example, an organisation may have a unique and valuable patent, but is not able to exploit it because it does not have the sales force to sell the resulting product.

2.6 Dynamic capabilities

Strategic capabilities are generally regarded as being more valuable if they can be counted on to last a long time. As we explored in the previous chapter, constant change from the external environment puts organisations under increasing pressure. In order to deal with rapid market changes, firms must possess **dynamic capabilities**.

Key term

> **Dynamic capabilities:** 'Are an organisation's abilities to develop and change competences to meet the needs of rapidly changing environments.' (Johnson *et al*, 2017)

Such capabilities demand the ability to change, to innovate and to learn. They can take many forms and may include such things as systems for new product development or the acquisition of market intelligence and the absorption of new skills and products acquired by merger or acquisition. Indeed, we might regard the ability to 'develop and change competences' as a competence in its own right: a higher-order competence, perhaps.

> **Essential reading**
>
> See Chapter 5 section 1 of the Essential Reading, available in Appendix 2 of the digital edition of the Workbook, for more detail regarding how organisations can manage strategic capability.

3 Organisational knowledge

Knowledge management is connected with the theory of the **learning organisation** and founded on the idea that knowledge can be a major factor in creating a sustainable competitive advantage and should form part of an organisation's strategic capability. Knowledge is thus seen as an important **resource** and may in itself constitute a **competence**: it can certainly **underpin** many competences.

> **Essential reading**
>
> See Chapter 5 section 2 of the Essential Reading, available in Appendix 2 of the digital edition of the Workbook, for detail about the important role that staff development plays in strategic capability. Section 3 gives consideration to the concept of knowledge work.

3.1 Organisational learning

Organisational learning has become particularly important as business environments becomes increasingly complex and dynamic. It becomes necessary for strategic managers to promote and foster a **culture that values intuition**, discussion of **conflicting views** and **experimentation**. A willingness to back ideas that are not guaranteed to succeed is another aspect of this culture: there must be freedom to make mistakes.

3.2 Knowledge management

Knowledge management is becoming increasingly important in helping organisations sustain competitive advantage. The aim of **knowledge management** is to exploit existing knowledge and to create new knowledge so that it may be exploited in turn. **Tacit knowledge** is the term used by Nonaka and Takeuchi (1995) to describe the knowledge locked in the minds of individuals. Even when it is made **explicit**, by being recorded in some way, it may be difficult and time consuming to get at, as is the case with most paper archives.

Essential reading

See Chapter 5 section 4 of the Essential Reading, available in Appendix 2 of the digital edition of the Workbook, for detail relating to the differences between data, information and knowledge.

3.3 Knowledge management technology

In order for knowledge to provide a source of sustainable competitive advantage it is important that any insights gleaned from it are regularly explored and exploited. Recognition of this has led to the need to organise data in such a way as to make it more accessible, this in turn has facilitated the development of sophisticated IT systems, including:

- **Office automation systems** are IT applications that improve productivity in an office. These include word processing and voice messaging systems.

- **Groupware**, such as **IBM Notes** provides functions for collaborative work groups. In a sales context, for instance, it would provide a facility for recording and retrieving all the information relevant to individual customers. This detail could then be updated and made available to anyone working in the sales department.

- An **intranet** is an internal network used to share information using internet technology and protocols.

- An **expert system** is a computer program that captures **human expertise** in a limited domain of knowledge. For example, many financial institutions now use expert systems to process straightforward loan applications by applying judgements based on the details input.

- **Data warehouses** can be used to store vast amounts of operational data in accessible form. Analytical and query software can then be used so that reports can be produced at any level of summarisation and incorporate any comparisons or relationships desired.

- The value of a data warehouse is enhanced when **data mining** software is used. True data mining software **discovers previously unknown relationships** and provides insights that cannot be obtained through ordinary summary reports.

4 Porter's value chain

Porter's (1985) **value chain** model is a useful framework for assessing the strategic capabilities of an organisation as it offers a bird's eye view of the firm and what it does and how its activities (processes) add value to the end customer:

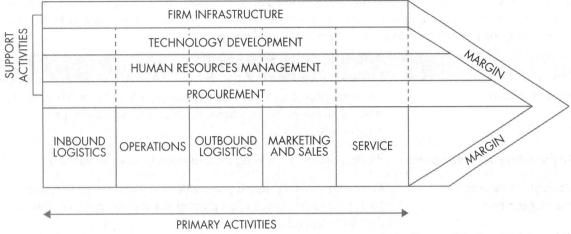

(Source: Porter, 1985: p.46)

4.1 Components of the value chain

The **margin** is the excess the customer is prepared to **pay** over the **cost** to the firm of obtaining resource inputs and providing value activities. It represents the **value created** by the **value activities** themselves and by the **management of the linkages** between them.

Key term

> **Value activities:** Are the means by which a firm creates value in its products.

The primary activities are predominately involved in the production of goods, and support activities provide necessary assistance. Linkages are the relationships between activities.

Primary activities are directly related to production, sales, marketing, delivery and service.

	Comment
Inbound logistics	Receiving, handling and storing inputs to the production system: warehousing, transport, inventory control and so on
Operations	Converting resource inputs into a final product: resource inputs are not only materials. People are a resource, especially in service industries.
Outbound logistics	Storing the product and its distribution to customers: packaging, testing, delivery and so on. For service industries, this activity may be more concerned with bringing customers to the place where the service is available; an example would be front of house management in a theatre.
Marketing and sales	Informing customers about the product, persuading them to buy it, and enabling them to do so: advertising, promotion and so on
After-sales service	Installing products, repairing them, upgrading them, providing spare parts and so forth

Support activities provide purchased inputs, human resources, technology and infrastructural functions **to support the primary activities**. It may seem an obvious point that support activities need to support the primary activities, but do not overlook it. For example, staff recruitment and training need to be appropriate for the item being produced in the operations. Support activities can also play a crucial role in helping organisations to meet their obligations in respect of corporate social responsibility and sustainability. For example, an organisation which claims that the packaging used in its products is recyclable needs to ensure that its procurement activities are geared towards purchasing environmentally friendly packaging.

Activity	Comment
Procurement	All of the processes involved in acquiring the resource inputs to the primary activities (eg purchase of materials, subcomponents equipment)
Technology development	Product design, improving processes and resource utilisation
Human resource management	Recruiting, training, managing, developing and rewarding people; this activity takes place in all parts of the organisation, not just in the HRM department
Firm infrastructure	Planning, finance, quality control, the structures and routines that make up the organisation's culture

Linkages connect the activities of the value chain:

(a) **Activities in the value chain affect one another**. For example, more costly product design or better quality production might reduce the need for after-sales service.

(b) **Linkages require co-ordination**. For example, Just In Time requires smooth functioning of operations, outbound logistics and service activities such as installation.

Activity 1: Carriages

> **ACCA Professional skills focus**
>
> Communication: Inform

You are a management consultant currently undertaking an assignment at Carriages, a world renowned, high quality restaurant which is located in the capital city of a developed European country. The owner of the restaurant is keen to gain understanding of how the restaurant's activities have contributed to its success. You are due to give a presentation to the owner and his senior management team, and are currently working on a slide and supporting notes which will illustrate Carriages' value-adding activities. As this is your firm's first assignment for Carriages you are keen to impress the client's management team and want to make your slide interesting and attention-grabbing. To assist you in your work your colleague has conducted a brief analysis (Exhibit 1) of Carriages' current activities.

Required

Using the information outlined in Exhibit 1, prepare ONE presentation slide and supporting notes which show the key value-adding activities of Carriages restaurant.   **(6 marks)**

Professional skills marks are available for demonstrating **communication skills** when informing Carriages' owner of the restaurant's value-adding activities.   **(2 marks)**

(Total = 8 marks)

Exhibit 1 – Carriages' current activities

Carriages is currently ranked as one of the top restaurants in the world. It has won many awards for culinary excellence and often appears in the 'best restaurant' guides. Carriages has appeared in every edition of the annual Michelin guide for the last 20 years. The majority of its chefs have experience of working in Michelin star restaurants. A large team of waiting staff report to five highly trained maître d's. Carriages prides itself on only employing waiting staff who have three or more years' experience of working in 5-star hotels or restaurants.

All hiring decisions go through the owner who also acts as the restaurant's senior manager. The Head Chef however has complete autonomy over the running of the kitchen and food-related decisions. The current Head Chef insists on only purchasing the very finest ingredients, as this allows her team to cook the most creative and exciting dishes. The kitchen staff maintain very tight control over the food preparation and food storage facilities. They always check the freshness of the ingredients taken from storage before they are used for cooking. The kitchen facilities are at the cutting edge of food preparation and use the very best utensils, ovens and refrigeration units.

Carriages regularly advertises in quality newspapers which are aimed at customers in its target market. This is the only type of direct advertising undertaken. Diners are able to make dinner reservations using the automated, online booking system. To ensure the reliability of the booking system the software used is reviewed every two years and, if needed, upgraded. To enhance the dining experience soft, classical music is played into the restaurant to improve the ambience. The tables and chairs used in the dining area were made especially for the restaurant by a world-famous designer and as such are made of highest quality wood and fabric. Carriages' owner prides himself on the car parking service the restaurant offers diners when they arrive, as this is a feature other local restaurants are currently unable to provide.

Solution

4.2 The value chain and competitive advantage

The value chain concept is an important tool in analysing the organisation's strategic capability, since it focuses on the overall means by which value is created, rather than on structural functions or departments. There are two important, connected aspects to this analysis:

(a)   It enables managers to establish the **activities** that are particularly important in **providing customers with the value they want**. Such an understanding assists managers in building a sustainable competitive advantage as consideration can be given to where management attention and other resources are best applied, either to improve weaknesses or to further exploit strengths.

(b)   Value chain analysis can be extended to include an assessment of the **costs and benefits** associated with the various value activities.

Activity 2: DRB Electronic Services

> **ACCA Professional skills focus**
>
> Analysis: Investigate

DRB Electronic Services (DRB) is based in Western Europe and imports electronic products from SK Co, a supplier based in a highly developed Asian country. These products are then sold to business and domestic customers in DRB's home market.

You are a management consultant, and the consultancy firm for which you work has been approached by Dilip Masood the owner of DRB, who has requested some assistance in analysing DRB's strategic capabilities.

Required

Using the information provided in Exhibit 1, ANALYSE the activities of DRB and comment on the significance of each of these.   **(10 marks)**

Professional skills marks are available for demonstrating **analysis skills** in investigating the significance of these activities and the value that they offer to DRB's customers.   **(2 marks)**

(Total = 12 marks)

Exhibit 1 – DRB's activities

DRB Electronic Services (DRB) operates in a high labour cost environment; a key part of its operations involve importing electronic products from a highly developed Asian country. It re-brands and re-packages them as DRB products and then sells them to business and domestic customers in the local geographical region. Its only current source of supply is SK Co (SK) which is based in a factory on the outskirts of a major city in an Asian country. DRB regularly places orders for products through the SK website and pays for them by credit card. As soon as the payment is confirmed SK automatically emails DRB a confirmation of order, an order reference number and likely shipping date. When the order is actually despatched, SK send DRB a notice of despatch email and a container reference number. SK currently organises all the shipping of the products. The products are sent in containers and then trans-shipped to EIF, the logistics company used by SK to distribute its products. EIF then delivers the products to the DRB factory. Once they arrive, they are quality inspected and products that pass the inspection are re-branded as DRB products (by adding appropriate logos) and packaged in specially fabricated DRB boxes. These products are then stored ready for sale. All customer sales are from stock. Products that fail the inspection are returned to SK.

Currently 60% of sales are made to domestic customers and 40% to business customers. Domestic customers pick up their products from DRB and set them up themselves. In contrast, most business customers ask DRB to set up the electronic equipment at their offices, for which DRB makes a small charge. DRB currently advertises its products in local and regional newspapers. DRB also has a website which provides product details. Potential customers can enquire about the specification and availability of products through an email facility in the website. DRB then emails an appropriate response directly to the person making the enquiry. Payment for products cannot currently be made through the website.

Feedback from existing business customers suggests that they particularly value the installation and support offered by the company. The company employs specialist technicians who (for a fee) will install equipment in both the homes and offices of its business customers. They will also come out and troubleshoot problems with equipment that is still under warranty for both domestic and business customers. DRB also offer a helpline and a back-to-base facility for customers whose products are out of warranty. Feedback from current customers suggests that this support is highly valued. One commented that 'it contrasts favourably with your large competitors who offer support through impersonal off-shore call centres and a time-consuming returns policy'. Customers can also pay for technicians to come on-site to sort out problems with out-of-warranty equipment.

DRB now plans to increase its product range and market share. It plans to grow from its current turnover of $5m per annum to $12m per annum in two years' time. Dilip recognises that growth will mean that the company has to sell more products outside its region and the technical installation and support so valued by local customers will be difficult to maintain.

Solution

5 Value network

As well as managing its own value chain, a firm can secure competitive advantage by managing the linkages (ie relationships) with the value chains of its suppliers and customers. An organisation's value chain is not bounded by an organisation's borders, it is connected to what Johnson *et al* (2017) call a value network:

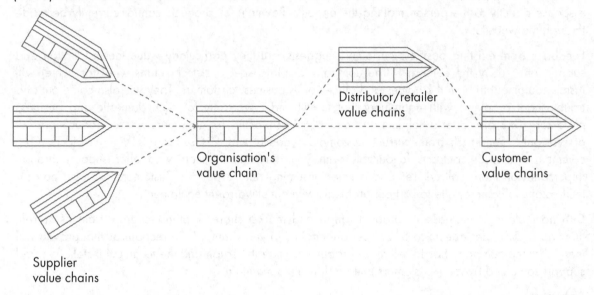

(Adapted from: Porter, 1985: p.35)

Key term

The **value network:** 'Is the set of inter-organisational links and relationships that are necessary to create a product or service.' (Johnson *et al*, 2017)

The diagram illustrates the similarities between the value network and a supply chain. However, whereas a supply chain shows the system of organisations, people, technology or activities involved in transforming a product or service from its raw materials to a finished product to be delivered to the end user customer, the value network places an emphasis on the value-creating capability within the supply chain processes.

5.1 Relationships in the value network

It is possible for large organisations to exercise power over suppliers and customers in the value network by using their **bargaining power** to achieve preferential purchase and selling prices. Nonetheless careful management of the relationships in the value network can promote **innovation** and the **creation of knowledge between organisations**.

Illustration 2

The following provides an illustration of an everyday value network.

When a restaurant serves a meal, the quality of the ingredients – although they are chosen by the chef – is determined by the grower. The grower has added value, and the grower's success in growing produce of good quality is as important to the customer's ultimate satisfaction as the skills of the chef.

6 SWOT analysis

SWOT analysis: Summarises the key issues from the business environment and the strategic capability of an organisation that are most likely to impact on strategy development.

Performance Objective 3 'Strategy and Innovation' of the Practical Experience Requirement requires you to 'develop financial acumen and commercial awareness. This will allow you to adopt and apply innovative methods and technologies to identify business problems and evaluate strategic options and manage solutions. ' (ACCA, 2019b). Developing the ability to identify business problems and weaknesses in organisational strategies and to then be able to recommend appropriate solutions makes the following section on SWOT analysis particularly important. You are strongly advised to take the time to read through this section carefully.

We examined the way in which **opportunities and threats** in the environment are detected and analysed in the previous chapter. In this chapter, we have discussed the analysis of the organisation's strategic capability; that is to say, its **strengths and weaknesses**. A complete awareness of the organisation's environment and its internal capacities is **necessary** for a rational consideration of future strategy, but it is not **sufficient**. The threads must be drawn together so that potential strategies may be developed and assessed. This is done by combining the internal and external analyses into a **SWOT analysis** or **corporate appraisal**:

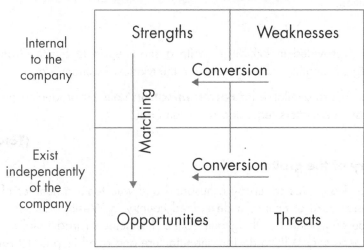

(Diagram: SWOT analysis model)

6.1 SWOT analysis in action

When conducting a SWOT analysis it is important to remember that the organisation's strengths and weaknesses relate to its strategic capabilities whereas opportunities and threats come from the external environment. By conducting a SWOT analysis an organisation is aiming to match its strengths with the available market opportunities that it can exploit. Strengths that do not match any available opportunity are of limited use, while opportunities which do not have any matching strengths are of little immediate value.

Once conducted SWOT analysis should form the starting point from which future strategic options can be assessed. Strategies need to be developed that convert weaknesses into strengths to take advantage of some particular opportunity, or to convert a threat into an opportunity which can then be matched by existing strengths.

Essential reading

See Chapter 5 section 5 of the Essential Reading, available in Appendix 2 of the digital edition of the Workbook, for detail about using a TOWS matrix. The TOWS matrix is a variant of the traditional SWOT analysis and is particularly useful when evaluating strategies.

Syllabus links

In Chapter 7 we move on to explore the strategic options available to organisations. The results from the SWOT analysis ultimately drive the viability of the strategic options available to an organisation.

Activity 3: The Marlow Fashion Group

ACCA Professional skills focus

Communication: Inform

Susan Grant is in something of a dilemma. She has been invited to join the board of the troubled Marlow Fashion Group as a non-executive director but is uncertain as to the level and nature of her contribution to the strategic thinking of the Group. Susan has approached the consultancy firm for which you work and has requested a short report to help her better understand the Marlow Fashion Group's current position.

Required

Using the information provided in Exhibit 1, write a short report to Susan Grant identifying and explaining the strategic strengths and weaknesses in the Marlow Fashion Group. **(10 marks)**

Professional skills marks are available for **communication** skills by producing a concise, informed report which addresses the matters requested by Susan Grant. **(2 marks)**

(Total = 12 marks)

Exhibit 1 – History of the group

The Marlow Fashion Group was set up by a husband and wife team a number of years ago in an economically depressed part of Ecuria, a developed country in Western Europe. They produced a comprehensive range of women's clothing built round the theme of traditional style and elegance. The Group had the necessary skills to design, manufacture and retail its product range. The Marlow brand was quickly established, and the company built up a loyal network of suppliers, workers in the company factory and franchised retailers spread around the world.

Marlow Fashion Group's products were able to command premium prices in the world of fashion. Rodney and Betty Marlow ensured that their commitment to traditional values created a strong family atmosphere in its network of partners and were reluctant to change this.

Unfortunately, changes in the market for women's wear presented a major threat to Marlow Fashion. First, women had become a much more active part of the workforce and demanded smarter, more functional outfits to wear at work. Marlow Fashion's emphasis on soft, feminine styles became increasingly dated. Second, the tight control exercised by Betty and Rodney Marlow and their commitment to control of design, manufacturing and retailing left them vulnerable to competitors who focused on just one of these core activities.

Third, there was a reluctance by the Marlows and their management team to acknowledge that a significant fall in sales and profits were as a result of a fundamental shift in demand for women's clothing. Finally, the share price of the company fell dramatically. Betty and Rodney Marlow retained a significant minority ownership stake, but the company has had a new Chief Executive Officer every year since.

Solution

Strategic capability

Strategic capability

Resources and competences

Threshold resources and competences/unique resources and core competences

Competitive advantage

Competitive advantage is the term used to describe the ability of an organisation to generate greater returns than those of competitors over the long term

Strategic capability and sustainable competitive advantage

Four qualities

Value

Need to be valued by the customer and/or organisation

Rarity

Competitors cannot obtain same resource/competence

Inimitability

Competitors cannot copy the resource/competence

Organisational support

The organisation must be able to support its capabilities, including its processes and systems

Dynamic capabilities

The ability to develop and change competences in response to changing environments

Organisational knowledge

Knowledge is a major source of competitive advantage

Organisational learning

Culture that values intuition, argument from conflicting views and experimentation

Knowledge management

Exploit existing knowledge and to create new knowledge so that it may be exploited in turn

Knowledge management technology

Sophisticated IT systems to facilitate knowledge management

Porter's value chain (1985)

Framework for assessing the strategic capabilities (activities) of an organisation

Components of the value chain
- Margin is the excess the customer is prepared to pay over the cost to the firm
- Activities can be primary or supporting

The value chain and competitive advantage

Managers can focus on those activities that give customers what they want/assess costs and benefits of certain activities

Value network

Set of inter-organisational links and relationships

Relationships in the value network

Bargaining power/promote innovation

SWOT analysis

Strengths, weaknesses, opportunities and threats

SWOT analysis in action
- Strengths and weaknesses are internal
- Opportunities and threats are external
- Lead to strategic options

Knowledge diagnostic

1. Strategic capability is fundamentally concerned with the internal strengths and weaknesses of an organisation.

2. Strategic capability consists of resources and competences. Threshold resources and competences are those needed to meet the customer's minimum requirements. Unique resources and core competences underpin competitive advantages and cannot be easily imitated or obtained.

3. Competitive advantage describes the ability of an organisation to generate greater returns than its competitors.

4. Resources and competences can provide a sustainable competitive advantage. They must possess four qualities: value, rarity, inimitability, and provide organisational support.

5. Constant environmental change makes possessing dynamic capabilities strategically important. Dynamic capabilities concern the ability to develop and change competences quickly.

6. Organisational knowledge can be a major factor in creating sustainable competitive advantage. Knowledge management is aimed at exploiting existing knowledge with a view to creating new knowledge.

7. Knowledge management technology including office automation systems, groupware, and intranets are increasingly being used to capture and disseminate knowledge.

8. Porter's value chain is used to assess the strategic capabilities of an organisation, what it does and how it does it. It focuses on primary and support activities.

9. The value network concerns the linkages with the value chains of an organisation's suppliers and customers.

10. SWOT analysis draws together the internal strengths and weaknesses in an organisation's strategic capabilities, and the external opportunities and threats which exist. The results from the analysis are then used to assess future strategic options.

BPP
LEARNING
MEDIA

Question practice

Now try the question below from the Further question practice bank (available in the digital edition of the Workbook):

Q5 *Chelsea Co*

Further reading

There are articles on the ACCA website written by members of the SBL examining team which are relevant to your studies and which would be useful to read:

The strategic planning process – part 1

If you have not already reviewed this article, then you are strongly advised to do so. The article considers the impact of the strategic planning process in relation to organisational resources.

Approaching SBL overview

This article provides a one-page summary of the key features of the SBL exam.

Approaching SBL reading and planning

This article provides a one-page summary of how best to approach the SBL exam.

SBL – 10 things to learn from the September 2018 sitting

This article highlights some of the issues that ACCA identified in candidates' answers during the September 2018 SBL exam sitting. The article provides some useful advice for improving your chances of passing the SBL exam.

Strategic Business Leader – The importance of effective communication for SBL

This article provides some useful insights into the different formats which you will be expected to use when answering SBL exam tasks.

Own research

It is important to link the topics covered in this chapter to a practical, real-world context. As such, we have suggested some areas for you to investigate further:

- Research an organisation with which you are familiar such as a well-known retailer or airline and identify those threshold resources and competences which allow it to meet its customer's minimum requirements. If you are struggling to find an organisation to consider you may find it helpful to choose a well-known business listed on a recognised stock exchange such as the FTSE 100.

- Identify the organisation's unique resources and core competences. Have these unique resources and core competences given the organisation a sustainable competitive advantage?

- Use the value chain model as a framework to assess the strengths and weaknesses in the organisation's primary and secondary activities. How can the organisation address the weaknesses that you identify?

- What opportunities and threats does the organisation face?

Exercise answer

Exercise 1

Unique resources	Core competences
• Presence of a celebrity chef to improve brand awareness • Unique location, eg in a castle • Ownership of secret recipes	• Skilled cooking processes • Creativity in creating dishes • Delivering good customer service

BPP
LEARNING
MEDIA

Competitive advantage and strategic choice

6

Learning objectives

On completion of this chapter, you should be able to:

	Syllabus reference no.
Assess the opportunities and potential problems of pursuing different organisation strategies of product/market diversification from a national, multinational and global perspective	C5(b)
Advise on how the 7 Ps, including price-based strategies, differentiation and lock-in can help an organisation sustain its competitive advantage	C5(c)
Apply the Boston Consulting Group (BCG) and public sector matrix portfolio models to assist organisations in managing their organisational portfolios	C5(d)
Recommend generic development directions using the Ansoff matrix	C5(e)
Assess how internal development, or business combinations, strategic alliances and partnering can be used to achieve business growth	C5(f)
Assess the suitability, feasibility and acceptability of different strategic options to an organisation	C5(a)

Business and exam context

At the end of Chapter 5 we explored the important role that SWOT analysis plays in the process of setting strategy. Having considered the organisation's internal strengths and weaknesses, and having matched these to the external opportunities and threats we now move on to consider the strategic choices available. As would be expected the strategic options available will vary from organisation to organisation and will be driven by a range of factors. The aim for the organisation is to undertake those strategies which help it to create a sustainable competitive advantage.

This is an important chapter as it introduces a number of very important models and frameworks which senior management can use as they formulate the future direction of the organisation. We begin the chapter by exploring the work of Porter's generic strategies as the decisions made here form the basis of future strategic choices.

Chapter overview

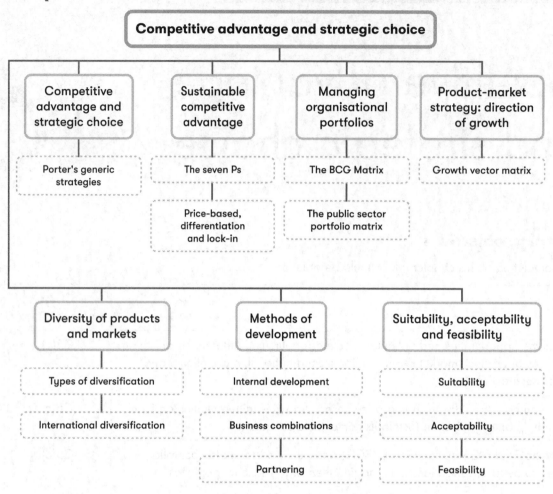

Competitive advantage and strategic choice

- Competitive advantage and strategic choice
  - Porter's generic strategies

- Sustainable competitive advantage
  - The seven Ps
  - Price-based, differentiation and lock-in

- Managing organisational portfolios
  - The BCG Matrix
  - The public sector portfolio matrix

- Product-market strategy: direction of growth
  - Growth vector matrix

- Diversity of products and markets
  - Types of diversification
  - International diversification

- Methods of development
  - Internal development
  - Business combinations
  - Partnering

- Suitability, acceptability and feasibility
  - Suitability
  - Acceptability
  - Feasibility

1 Competitive advantage and strategic choice

1.1 Porter's generic strategies

We begin our consideration of strategic choice by exploring the work of Michael Porter (1980). You should recall from the previous chapter that the concept of competitive advantage is concerned with anything which gives one organisation an edge over its rivals. Porter (1980) argued that organisations need to adopt an appropriate competitive strategy (Porter referred to them as generic strategies) which will help them to achieve a competitive advantage. Porter (1980) suggested that organisations must first decide upon its **competitive basis**, being either to compete on the basis of lowest cost, or to differentiate. Porter argued that to do neither and be 'stuck in the middle' would lead to an inability to compete over the long term, as illustrated below.

Cost leader	**Stuck in the middle**	**Differentiator**
Potentially higher profit	Low Profit	Potentially higher profit
Low Costs ✓	High Costs ✗	High Costs ✓

Once the competitive basis has been decided Porter (1980) argues that organisations need to determine their **competitive scope**:

- Narrow target (focus) – aimed at a defined market group only
- Broad target – available to the market as a whole

		Competitive basis	
		Cost drive	Differentiation driven
Competitive scope	Broad	Cost leadership	Differentiation
	Narrow	Cost focus	Differentiated focus

(Source: Porter, 1980)

Key terms

Cost leadership: Means being the lowest cost producer in the industry as a whole.

Differentiation: Is the exploitation of a product or service which the industry as a whole believes to be unique.

Focus: Involves a restriction of activities to only part of the market (a segment).

- Providing goods and/or services at lower cost (cost focus)
- Providing a differentiated product or service (differentiation focus)

1.1.1 Cost leadership

Porter (1980) suggests that a cost leadership strategy seeks to achieve the position of lowest-cost producer in the **industry as a whole**. By producing at the lowest cost, the manufacturer can compete on price with every other producer in the industry, and earn the higher unit profits, if the manufacturer so chooses.

How to achieve overall cost leadership

(a)   Set up production facilities to obtain **economies of scale**

(b)   Use the **latest technology** to reduce costs and/or enhance productivity (or use cheap labour if available)

(c)   In high technology industries, and in industries depending on labour skills for product design and production methods, exploit the **learning curve effect**. By producing more items than any other competitor, an organisation can benefit more from the learning curve, and achieve lower average costs.

(d)   Concentrate on **improving productivity**

(e)   **Minimise overhead costs**

(f)   **Get favourable access to sources of supply**

1.1.2 Differentiation

Porter (1980) suggests that a differentiation strategy assumes that competitive advantage can be gained through **particular characteristics** of an organisation's products.

Products may be divided into three categories.

(a)   **Breakthrough products** offer a radical performance advantage over the competition, perhaps at a drastically lower price. Innovation in product design and performance is often central to breakthrough products, for example, the Powermat which can charge mobile devices without the need for conventional wired power charging.

(b)   **Improved products** are not radically different from their competition but are obviously superior in terms of better performance at a competitive price (eg microchips).

(c)   **Competitive products** derive their appeal from a particular compromise of cost and performance. For example, cars are not all sold at rock-bottom prices, nor do they all provide immaculate comfort and performance. They compete with each other by trying to offer a more attractive compromise than rival models.

How to differentiate

(a)   **Build up a brand image**

(b)   **Give the product special features** to make it stand out

(c)   **Exploit other activities of the value chain** (for example, quality of after-sales service or speed of delivery)

(d)   **Use IT and innovation** to create new services or product features

(e)   **Build customer relationships** through effective branding and marketing

(f)   **Create complementary products and/or services**, for example Apple's app store allows the users of its phones and tablets to download apps

1.1.3 Focus (or niche) strategy

Porter (1980) notes that a focus strategy requires an organisation to concentrate its attention on one or more particular segments or niches of the market, and does not try to serve the entire market with a single product.

(a)   A **cost focus strategy**: aim to be a cost leader for a particular segment. This type of strategy is often found in the printing, clothes manufacture and car repair industries.

(b)   A **differentiation focus strategy**: pursue differentiation for a chosen segment. Luxury goods suppliers are the prime exponents of such a strategy.

Porter (1980) suggests that a focus strategy can achieve competitive advantage when '**broad-scope**' businesses succumb to one of two errors.

(a)   **Underperformance** occurs when a product does not fully meet the needs of a segment and offers the opportunity for a **differentiation focus** player.

(b)   **Overperformance** gives a segment more than it really wants and provides an opportunity for a **cost focus** player.

Advantages

(a)   A niche is more secure and an organisation can insulate itself from competition.

(b)   The organisation does not spread itself too thinly.

(c)   Both cost leadership and differentiation require **superior performance** – life is easier in a niche, where there may be little or no competition.

Drawbacks of a focus strategy

(a)   The organisation sacrifices economies of scale which would be gained by serving a wider market.

(b)   Competitors can move into the segment, with increased resources (eg the Japanese moved into the US luxury car market, to compete with German car makers).

(c)   The segment's needs may eventually become less distinct from the main market.

1.1.4 Which generic strategy?

Although there is a risk with any of the generic strategies, Porter (1980) argues that an organisation must pursue one of them. A **stuck-in-the-middle** strategy is almost certain to make only low profits. 'This firm lacks the market share, capital investment and resolve to play the low-cost game, the industry-wide differentiation necessary to obviate the need for a low-cost position, or the focus to create differentiation or a low-cost position in a more limited sphere.'

Essential reading

See Chapter 6 section 1 of the Essential Reading, available in Appendix 2 of the digital edition of the Workbook, for detail relating to the conceptual difficulties of using generic strategies.

2 Sustainable competitive advantage

Creating a sustainable competitive advantage requires organisations to make important decisions about the strategic options available to them.

2.1 The seven Ps

The strategic choices an organisation makes regarding its marketing strategy will be driven by its choice of generic strategy. Creating a marketing strategy involves developing and tailoring elements of the so-called marketing mix.

BPP
LEARNING
MEDIA

Key term

> **Marketing mix:** Is the set of controllable variables and their levels that the organisation uses to influence the target market.

The concept of the marketing mix consisting of the so-called 4Ps was devised by McCarthy (1960); this was extended to 7Ps by Booms and Bitner (1981).

The extended marketing mix consists of seven Ps:

(a) **Product** – the item/good purchased by the customer. From a customer's point of view, this will be a solution to a problem or package of benefits.

(b) **Place** – how the product is delivered to customers. For example, sold in shops or online.

(c) **Promotion** – the activities involved in telling the customer or potential customer(s) about the product. For example, advertising, sales promotions, public relations

(d) **Price** – setting an appropriate price with reference to factors such as cost, competitors' prices, perceived quality, firm strategy etc.

(e) **People** – the interaction between customers and the organisation's staff.

(f) **Processes** – fast and efficient processes (eg booking a service) may bring significant marketing advantages

(g) **Physical evidence** – as services are intangible, it is sometimes important to provide evidence of ownership, eg a ticket to travel or certificate of attainment for training

The final three elements listed above (people, processes, physical evidence) are also known as the service marketing mix as they related specifically to the marketing of services, rather than physical products. The intangible nature of services makes these extra three Ps particularly important.

Exercise 1: Marketing mix

Required

Consider how you would market Product Princess, a new cosmetic, to the teenage market. How would you use the traditional 4Ps (product, place, promotion, price) of the marketing mix to go after that market and successfully sell this new product?

Solution

Essential reading

See Chapter 6 section 2 of the Essential Reading, available in Appendix 2 of the digital edition of the Workbook, for more detail relating to the seven Ps.

2.2 Price-based, differentiation and lock-in

To generate long-term value, any advantage based on price or differentiation must be sustainable, meaning it is hard for others to copy or obtain.

2.2.1 Sustaining price-based strategies

Johnson *et al* (2017) note a number of ways in which a price-based strategy can be sustained:

(a) **Low margins** can be sustained, either by increased volumes or by cross-subsidisation from another business unit.

(b) A **cost leader** can operate at a price advantage, but to be sustainable, cost leaders must constantly and aggressively drive down all of their costs.

(c) A cost leader or an organisation with extensive financial resources can win a **price war**.

(d) A **no-frills strategy** can succeed in the long term if it is aimed at a segment that particularly appreciates low price.

2.2.2 Sustaining differentiation

Sustaining differentiation is difficult. To begin with, it is more than just being different: the difference must be **valued by customers**. Secondly, a difference that a competitor can easily imitate gives no sustainable advantage. Johnson *et al* (2017) note the following:

(a) **Attempts at imitation can be obstructed** by, for example, securing preferred access to customers or suppliers through bidding or licensing procedures.

(b) Some resources are **inherently immobile**. This can be the result of **intangibility**, as in the case of brands; high customer switching costs, as with proprietary technology; or **co-specialisation**, which occurs when organisations' value chains are intimately linked.

(c) **Cost advantage** can be used to sustain differentiation, rather than price advantage, by investing in innovation, brand management or quality improvement.

2.2.3 Lock-in

Key term

Lock-in: Is achieved in a market when an organisation's product becomes the industry standard.

Hax and Wilde (1999) proposed the concept of lock-in in relation to creating a sustainable competitive advantage. **Lock-in** is achieved in a market when an organisation's product becomes the **industry standard** (Johnson *et al*, 2017). Direct competitors are reduced to minor niches and **compatibility** with the industry standard becomes a prerequisite for complementary products.

3 Managing organisational portfolios

Matrix-based models such as the BCG matrix and the public sector portfolio matrix can be used by organisations to manage their activities. They can also be used by an organisation's management as a tool in making decisions about the future direction of the organisation.

3.1 The BCG matrix

Many profit-making organisations consist, essentially, of a number of strategic business units (SBUs) and a **corporate parent**. The term conglomerate is sometimes used to describe large organisations which consist of many diversified strategic business units (individual businesses).

Perhaps one of the most well-known conglomerates is South Korea's Samsung which operates in a range of diverse markets from pharmaceuticals to electronics. Each SBU has its own products, with which it serves its own market sector, and its managers are, to a greater or lesser extent, responsible for its overall success (or failure). Corporate parents can use a number of models to help them make strategic choices regarding the management of their collection of SBUs for maximum advantage.

The BCG matrix devised by Henderson (1970) categorises SBUs in terms of **market growth rate** and **relative market share**. It assesses SBUs based on financial performance only.

Assessing rate of **market growth** (eg sales growth in the industry as a whole) as high or low depends on the conditions in the market. No single percentage rate can be set, since new markets may grow explosively while mature ones grow hardly at all. High market growth rate can indicate good opportunities for profitable operations. However, intense competition in a high growth market can erode profit, while a slowly growing market with high barriers to entry can be very profitable.

Relative market share is assessed as a ratio: it is market share (eg sales turnover of own organisation) compared with the market share (sales turnover) of the **largest competitor**. Thus, a relative market share greater than unity indicates that the SBU is the market leader. Henderson (1970) settled on market share as a way of **estimating costs** and thus **profit potential**, because both costs and market share are connected with **production experience**: as experience in satisfying a particular market demand for value increases, market share can be expected to increase also, and costs to fall.

BCG matrix

Relative market share

		High	Low
Market growth	High	Stars	Question marks
	Low	Cash cows	Dogs

(Adapted from: Henderson, 1970)

According to their position on the matrix, SBUs will be categorised as follows:

- **Stars** offer good future returns so the parent needs to invest in and develop them. Due to the industry life cycle, stars will become cash cows in time.

- **Cash cows** do not need much investment so will generate cash income. Parents can use this cash to invest in stars or simply provide a return to shareholders.

- **Question marks** should be assessed to see whether they have the potential to become stars. If so, the parent should invest in them; if not, they should be sold or run down.

- **Dogs** can tie up funds and provide a poor return. In general, they should be sold off although may be retained if they are a useful niche business.

Ideally the portfolio should be balanced, with cash cows providing finance for stars and question marks; and a minimum of dogs.

Activity 1: Shoal plc

ACCA Professional skills focus

Commercial acumen: Use judgement

The date is early 20X3.

You work for Consult-Us, a well-known consultancy firm. You are currently undertaking an assignment on behalf of Shoal plc. Shoal plc owns three companies which are concerned with fishing and related industries. Your assignment requires you to give a presentation to the board of directors. Part of your presentation is to focus on the balance of Shoal plc's portfolio of companies. The board want to find out what future actions they should take in respect of Shoal plc's current business units. Certain members of the board believe that some of the SBUs would benefit from further investment, while others believe that it may be time to divest certain activities. It is your understanding that the board's request for help is being driven by a recent announcement that Shoal plc is to purchase the Captain Haddock chain of fish restaurants. Your colleague has prepared some notes (Exhibit 1) for you on the three Shoal plc companies.

Required

Prepare information for ONE presentation slide to be presented to the Shoal plc board of directors, including relevant points and brief supporting notes which analyse the position of the three companies in Shoal plc's portfolio. Recommend the actions that Shoal plc should take in respect of the three companies. **(15 marks)**

Professional skills marks are available for demonstrating **commercial acumen** by displaying judgement when analysing the position and contribution of the three companies to Shoal plc.

(2 marks)

(Total = 17 marks)

Exhibit 1: Shoal plc's three companies

ShoalFish Ltd (ShoalFish) – a fishing fleet operating in the western oceans

Shoal plc formed ShoalFish many years ago when it bought three small fishing fleets and consolidated them into one fleet. The primary objective of the acquisition was to secure supplies for ShoalPro. Forty per cent of the fish caught by ShoalFish are currently processed in the ShoalPro factories. The rest are sold in wholesale fish markets. ShoalFish has recorded modest profits since its formation but it is operating in a challenging market. The western oceans where it operates have suffered from many years of over-fishing and the government has recently introduced quotas in an attempt to conserve fish stocks. Today ShoalFish has 35 boats and this makes it the sixth largest fleet in the western oceans. Almost half of the total number of boats operating in the western oceans are individually owned and independently operated by the boat's captain. Financial information for ShoalFish:

	20X0 $m	20X1 $m	20X2 $m
ShoalFish			
Turnover of market sector	200.00	198.50	190.00
Turnover of ShoalFish	24.00	23.50	21.50

ShoalPro Ltd (ShoalPro) – a company concerned with processing and canning fish

ShoalPro was acquired nearly 20 years ago when Shoal plc bought the assets of the Trevarez Canning and Processing Company. Just after the acquisition of the company, the government declared the area around Trevarez a 'zone of industrial assistance'. Grants were made available to develop industry in an attempt to address the economic decline and high unemployment of the area. ShoalPro benefited from these grants, developing a major fish processing and canning capability in the area. However, despite this initiative and investment, unemployment in the area still remains above the average for the country as a whole. ShoalPro's modern facilities and relatively low costs have made it attractive to many fishing companies. The fish received from ShoalFish now accounts for a declining percentage of the total amount of fish processed and canned in its factories in the Trevarez area. Financial information for ShoalPro:

	20X0 $m	20X1 $m	20X2 $m
ShoalPro			
Turnover of market sector	40.00	40.10	40.80
Turnover of ShoalPro	16.00	16.20	16.50

ShoalFarm Ltd (ShoalFarm) – a company with saltwater fish farms

ShoalFarm was acquired five years ago as a response by Shoal plc to the declining fish stocks in the western oceans. It owns and operates saltwater fish farms. These are in areas of the ocean close to land where fish are protected from both fishermen and natural prey, such as sea birds. Fish stocks can be built up quickly and then harvested by the fish farm owner. Shoal plc originally saw this acquisition as a way of maintaining supply to ShoalPro. Operating costs at ShoalFarm have been higher than expected and securing areas for new fish farms has been difficult and has required greater investment than expected. Financial information for ShoalFarm is as follows:

	20X0 $m	20X1 $m	20X2 $m
ShoalFarm			
Turnover of market sector	10.00	11.00	12.00
Turnover of ShoalFarm	1.00	1.10	1.12

Solution

3.2 The public sector portfolio matrix

The **public sector portfolio matrix** (Montanari and Bracker, 1986) classifies activities in terms of their popularity and the resources available for them. The matrix provides for an analysis of services provided by public sector bodies, which can prove useful particularly when making strategic decisions about public sector activities.

This might be applied at the level of local or national government, or an executive agency with a portfolio of services. The axes are an assessment of service efficiency and public attractiveness: naturally, political support for a service or organisation depends to a great extent on the degree to which the public need and appreciate it.

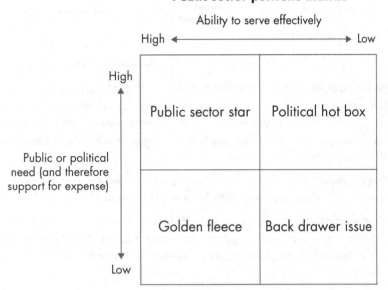

Public sector portfolio matrix

(Adapted from: Montanari and Bracker, 1986)

Montanari and Bracker (1986) classify public sector organisations as follows:

- A **public sector star** is something that the system is doing well and should not change. They are essential to the viability of the system.

- **Political hot boxes** are services that the public wants, or which are mandated, but for which there are not adequate resources or competences.

- **Golden fleeces** are services that are done well but for which there is low demand. They may therefore be perceived to be undesirable uses for limited resources. They are potential targets for cost cutting.

- **Back drawer issues** are unappreciated and have low priority for funding. They are obvious candidates for cuts, but if managers perceive them as essential, they should attempt to increase support for them and move them into the **political hot box** category.

4 Product-market strategy: direction of growth

We now move on to consider the strategic choices facing organisations in respect of their product-market strategies.

Product-market strategies involve determining which products should be sold in which markets, by market penetration, market development, product development and diversification. Diversification is assumed to be risky, especially diversification that is entirely unrelated to current products and markets.

Key term

Product-market mix: Is a shorthand term for the products and services a firm sells (or a service which a public sector organisation provides) and the markets it sells them to.

BPP LEARNING MEDIA

4.1 Growth vector matrix

Ansoff (1987) drew up a **growth vector matrix**, describing how a combination of a firm's activities in current and new markets, with existing and new products, can lead to **growth**.

	Products	
	Existing	New
Markets Existing	Market Penetration	Product Development
New	Market Development	Diversification

Diagram: Growth vector matrix (Ansoff, 1987)

- **Market penetration** means increasing market share of existing products via promotions, price reductions, increasing usage etc. It represents a relatively low-risk strategy since it requires no capital investment. As such, it is attractive to the unadventurous type of organisation. This approach can also apply to an organisation which simply wants to maintain or even reduce its position in a market.

- **Market development** means seeking new customers for existing products, eg exporting or selling via new distribution channels. Risk here is still reasonably low.

- **Product development** is selling new products to existing customers ('cross-selling'). This strategy is riskier than both market penetration and market development since it is likely to require major investment in the new product development process and, for physical products, in suitable production facilities.

- **Diversification**, selling new products to new customers, may offer significant growth potential but it is risky as it may require significant investment and new competences.

5 Diversity of products and markets

In the previous section we introduced diversification as a strategy that organisations can pursue. In this section we consider the advantages and potential issues associated with diversification, the different types of diversification strategy which exist, before moving on to consider international diversification. In the past it was not uncommon for organisations to produce and sell one type of product to customers operating in the organisation's home market. In recent decades it has become increasingly common for larger organisations to modify the types of products they sell and the markets in which they operate; this is known as diversification.

5.1 The need for diversification

Johnson *et al* (2017) highlight a number of advantages of diversification. They also give three questionable reasons often used by management to justify a policy of diversification:

Advantages:	Questionable reasons for diversification:
Economies of scope (as opposed to economies of scale) may result from the **greater use of under-utilised resources**. These benefits are often referred to as **synergy**.	To respond to **environmental change** in order to protect shareholder value by, for example, responding to the emergence of new and threatening technology developments. This can, however, be used as a cover to protect the interests of top management; typically, this will lead to ill-considered acquisitions that destroy value.

Advantages:	Questionable reasons for diversification:
Corporate management skills may be extendible across a range of unrelated businesses. Richard Branson's Virgin Group is a good example.	**Risk spreading** can be a valid reason for an owner-managed business to diversify, but modern financial theory suggests that shareholders in large corporations can manage their risk exposure better themselves by diversifying their own share portfolios.
Diversification can increase **market power** via cross-subsidisation. A high-margin business unit can subsidise a low-margin one, enabling it to create a price advantage over its rivals and build market share.	The **expectations of powerful stakeholders** can lead to inappropriate strategies generally.
Diversification in some cases allows organisations to **exploit existing superior internal processes** to seize opportunities to establish new businesses. This often happens when external processes, such as those relating to capital and labour markets are deemed to be inefficient.	

5.2 Types of diversification

Diversification can take the form of related or unrelated diversification.

5.2.1 Related diversification

Key term

Related diversification: Is strategy development beyond current products and markets but within the capabilities or value network of the organisation (Johnson *et al* 2017).

Related diversification can be achieved through either **horizontal** or **vertical** integration:

Horizontal integration makes use of current capabilities by development into activities that are competitive with, or directly **complementary** to, an organisation's present activities. An example would be a TV company that moved into film production.	**Vertical integration** occurs when an organisation expands **backwards** or **forwards** within its existing value network and thus becomes its own supplier or distributor. For example, **backward integration** would occur if a milk processing business acquired its own dairy farms, rather than buying raw milk from independent farmers. If a cloth manufacturer began to produce shirts instead of selling all of its cloth to other shirt manufacturers that would be **forward integration**.

Key terms

Horizontal integration: Makes use of current capabilities by development into activities that are competitive with, or directly complementary to, an organisation's present activities.

Vertical integration: Occurs when an organisation expands backwards or forwards within its existing value network and thus becomes its own supplier or distributor.

BPP
LEARNING
MEDIA

Real world examples

- **Horizontal integration**. In August 2014 Bradshaw and Mishkin (2014) noted that online retailer, Amazon, had paid $970m to buy video-gaming service Twitch. Formerly known as Twitch.tv, Twitch enables users to watch other people play video games online. Amazon's acquisition of Twitch was in response to the emergence of YouTube and Netflix. The purchase of Twitch enabled Amazon to reach committed gamers, and was seen by many as a natural extension of Amazon's existing offering. Amazon's Prime service already allows subscribers to stream television shows and movies. In August 2016 Hsu (2016) highlighted that since the acquisition 'Twitch had come close to doubling its monthly visitors and had greatly expanded its base of streamers, with more than 100 million visitors watching more than 1.7 million streamers each month.'

- **Vertical integration**. In July 2014 Anzolin (2014) reported that Italy's Ferrero – maker of Nutella chocolate spread and Ferrero Rocher chocolates – had purchased Turkey's largest hazelnut company, Oltan Gida. Ferrero's acquisition of Oltan Gida was viewed as an attempt to secure the company's supply of hazelnuts for use in its products. Subsequently, in July 2015, Ferrero acquired UK company Thorntons, gaining access to retail outlets in an example of forward vertical integration.

5.2.2 Advantages and disadvantages of vertical integration

The following table outlines the key advantages and disadvantages of vertical integration:

Advantages	Disadvantages
Secure supply of components or **materials**, hence lower supplier bargaining power	**Overconcentration**. Such a policy is fairly inflexible, more sensitive to instabilities and increases the firm's dependence on a particular aspect of economic demand.
Stronger relationships with the final consumer of the product	The firm **fails to benefit from any economies of scale or technical advances** in the industry into which it has diversified. This is why, in the publishing industry, most printing is subcontracted to specialist printing firms, who can work machinery to capacity by doing work for many firms.
A share of the **profits** at all stages of the value network	
More effective pursuit of a **differentiation strategy**	
Creation of **barriers to entry**	

Activity 2: Elite Fabrics

ACCA Professional skills focus

Evaluation: Assess

Your firm has recently been appointed to provide management consultancy services to Elite Fabrics (EF), a medium-sized manufacturer of clothing fabrics and clothes. The board at EF are considering integrating the company even further forward into retailing. They would like your help so that they can gain a better understanding of the implications of this proposal. They have provided you with some background information (Exhibit 1) on EF to assist you with your work.

Required

EF's potential expansion into retailing presents both advantages and disadvantages to the company. Using the information provided (Exhibit 1) evaluate the consequences of such a move for the business and assess the change in competences which would be required by the newly expanded business.

(10 marks)

Professional skills marks are available for demonstrating **evaluation** skills in assessing the consequences of EF's move into retailing.

(2 marks)

(Total = 12 marks)

Exhibit 1 – Background information on EF

Historically, EF has built up a strong reputation as a quality fabric manufacturer with appealing designs and has concentrated mainly on the women's market, producing fabrics to be made up into dresses and suits. The designs of the fabric are mainly of a traditional nature but the fabrics, almost all woven from synthetic yarns, include all the novel features which the large yarn producers are developing.

Three years ago EF decided that more profit and improved control could be obtained by diversifying through forward integration into designing and manufacturing the end products (ie clothes) in-house rather than by selling its fabrics directly to clothing manufacturing companies.

EF's intention had been to complement its fabric design skills with the skills of both dress design and production. This had been achieved by buying a small but well-known dress design and manufacturing company specialising in traditional products, targeted mainly at the middle-aged and middle-income markets. This acquisition appears to have been successful, with combined sales turnover during the first two years increasing to $100m (+ 34%) with a pre-tax profit of $14m (+ 42%). This increased turnover and profit could be attributed to two main factors: firstly, the added value generated by designing and manufacturing end-products and secondly, the increased demand for fabrics as EF was more able to influence its end-users more directly.

In the last financial year, however, EF had experienced a slowdown in its level of growth and profitability. EF's penetration of its chosen retail segment – the independent stores specialising in sales to the middle-class market – may well have reached saturation point. The business had also attempted to continue expansion by targeting the large multiple stores which currently dominate the retail fashion sector. Unfortunately, the buying power of such stores has forced EF to accept significantly lower, and potentially unacceptable, profit margins. The management team at EF believes that the solution is to integrate even further forward by moving into retailing itself. EF is now considering the purchase of a chain of small, but geographically dispersed, retail fashion stores. At the selling price of $35m, EF would have to borrow substantially to finance the acquisition.

Solution

5.2.3 Unrelated diversification

Key term

> **Unrelated diversification:** Is the development of products or services beyond the current capabilities or value network (Johnson *et al*, 2017).

Unrelated diversification produces the type of organisation known as a **conglomerate**. Conglomerate diversification involves the development of a portfolio of businesses with no similarities between them.

5.2.4 Advantages and disadvantages of conglomerate diversification

The following table outlines the key advantages and disadvantages of conglomerate diversification:

Advantages	Disadvantages
Risk-spreading. Entering new products into new markets can compensate for the failure of current products and markets.	The **dilution of shareholders' earnings** if diversification is into growth industries with high P/E ratios.
Improved profit opportunities. An improvement of the **overall profitability and flexibility** of the firm may arise through acquisition in industries with better prospects than those of the acquiring firms.	**Lack of a common identity and purpose** in a conglomerate organisation. A conglomerate will only be successful if it has a high quality of management and financial ability at central headquarters, where the diverse operations are brought together.

Advantages	Disadvantages
Escape from a declining market.	**Failure in one of the businesses may drag down the rest**, as it will eat up resources.
Use an organisation's image and reputation in one market to develop into another where corporate image and reputation could be vital ingredients for success.	**Lack of management experience**. Japanese steel companies diversified into areas completely unrelated to steel, such as personal computers, with limited success.

5.2.5 Diversity and strategic success

Johnson *et al* (2017) highlight that organisations undertaking a **limited degree of related diversification are likely to perform better** than those that remain undiversified. However, as the degree of diversification **increases**, the rate of performance improvement is likely to reduce and may then become negative as the organisation becomes extensively diversified into unrelated fields.

5.3 International diversification

The growth in the number of organisations diversifying their operations internationally has been driven by globalisation.

> **Globalisation:** Refers to the growing interdependence of countries worldwide through increased trade, increased capital flows and the rapid diffusion of technology.

The rise of globalisation has meant a growth in the number of suppliers exporting to, or trading in, a wider variety of places. In many domestic markets, it is now likely that the same international companies will be competing with one another.

5.3.1 Management orientation

International product/market diversification requires organisations to adopt an appropriate management orientation. Perlmutter (1969) identified three orientations for use in the management of international business: ethnocentrism, polycentrism and geocentrism. Regiocentrism was later added by Wind *et al* (1973).

Ethnocentrism

> **Ethnocentrism:** Is a home country orientation. The organisation focuses on its domestic market and sees exports as secondary to domestic marketing.

This approach simply ignores any inter-country differences which exist. Ethnocentric companies will tend to market the same products with the same marketing programmes in foreign countries as at home. Marketing management is centralised in the home country and the marketing mix is standardised. There is no local market research or adaptation of promotion. As a result, market opportunities may not be fully exploited and foreign customers may be alienated by the approach.

Polycentrism

> **Polycentrism:** Involves the formulation of objectives on the assumption that it is necessary to adapt almost totally the product and the marketing programme to each local environment. Thus, the various country subsidiaries (SBUs) of a multinational corporation are free to formulate their own objectives and plans.

The polycentric organisation believes that each country is unique. It therefore establishes largely independent local subsidiaries (SBUs) and decentralises its marketing management. This can produce major increases in turnover but the loss of economies of scale can seriously damage profitability. Such companies tend to think of themselves as **multinationals**.

Geocentrism and regiocentrism

Key terms

> **Geocentrism** and **regiocentrism:** Are based on the assumption that there are both similarities and differences between countries that can be incorporated into regional or world objectives and strategies.

Geocentrism and **regiocentrism** differ only in geographical terms: the first deals with the world as a unity, while the second considers that there are differences between regions.

Geocentrism treats the issues of standardisation and adaptation on their merits so as to formulate objectives and strategies that exploit markets fully while minimising costs. The aim is to create a global strategy that is fully responsive to local market differences. This has been summed up as: 'think globally, act locally'. **Geocentric** companies use an integrated approach to marketing management. Each country's conditions are given due consideration, but no one country dominates. A great deal of experience and commitment are required to make this approach work. A strong, globally recognised brand is a major aspect of the marketing approach. Geocentrically oriented companies both promote and benefit from **market convergence**.

6 Methods of development

Once management have determined which products they want to sell and the markets they want to operate in, decisions must then be made regarding how best to go about achieving these objectives. This brings us on to methods of development. A range of methods are available to organisations.

6.1 Internal development

Key term

> **Internal development (sometimes referred to as organic growth):** Is the primary method of growth for many organisations, for a number of reasons.

Internal development is achieved through the development of internal resources.

Reasons for pursuing internal development	Problems with internal development
Learning. The process of developing a new product gives the firm the best understanding of the market and the product.	**Time** – sometimes it takes a long time to descend a learning **curve**.
Innovation. It might be the only sensible way to pursue genuine technological innovations, and exploit them.	**Barriers to entry** (eg distribution networks) are harder to overcome: for example, a brand image
Internal development can be **planned more meticulously** and offers little disruption.	The firm will have to **acquire the resources independently**.
The **same style of management and corporate culture** can be maintained.	Internal development may be **too slow for the dynamics of the market**.
There is **no suitable target for acquisition**.	

Internal development is probably ideal for market penetration, and suitable for product or market development, but it might be a problem with extensive diversification projects.

6.2 Business combinations

Key term

Business combination: Occurs where an entity enters into formal, legal relationships with another entity through some form of joint ownership. Acquisitions and mergers are common types of business combination.

A key feature of a business combination is that it involves bringing together two (or more) entities that were previously independent of one another, and combining them for a common purpose. The associate relationship that is created when one entity purchases less than 50% of the shares in another entity is also a type of business combination. You may recall from your Financial Reporting studies that an associate relationship is formed when one party is able to exert significant influence over the other without having full control as would be the case with a subsidiary.

Key terms

Acquisition: Involves the purchase of one entity by another.

Merger: Involves two separate organisations joining together to form a single entity.

An acquisition involves the purchase of one entity by another, whereas a merger involves two separate organisations joining together to form a single entity. The rationale often given by management for acquisitions and mergers is that it provides greater opportunities for business growth, than if both entities remained independent of one another. Other explanations given for acquisitions and mergers are provided below:

Reasons for acquisitions and mergers	Problems with acquisitions and mergers
Buy in a new product range	**Cost**. They might be too expensive, especially if resisted by the directors of the target organisation
Buy a market presence (especially true if acquiring a foreign organisation)	**Customers** of the target organisation might resent a sudden takeover and consider going to other suppliers for their goods
Buy in technology, intellectual property and skills	**Incompatibility**. Problems of assimilating new products, customers, suppliers, markets, employees and different systems of operating might create 'indigestion' and management overload in the acquiring organisation. A proposed merger between two financial institutions was called off because of incompatible information systems
Obtain greater production capacity	**Asymmetric information**. The existing management know more about the organisation than the purchaser. This can lead the purchaser to pay more than the real value of the organisation to acquire it
Safeguard future supplies of raw materials	**Driven by the personal goals** of the acquiring organisation's managers, as a form of sport, perhaps

Reasons for acquisitions and mergers	Problems with acquisitions and mergers
Gain undervalued assets or surplus assets that can be sold off	**Firms rarely take into account non-financial factors**. Purchasers often fail to carry out a full management audit of the acquisition target, and fail to consider the human resource issues which impact on the ultimate success of the acquisition
Spread risk	**Poor success record of acquisitions**. Takeovers benefit the shareholders of the acquired organisation often more than the acquirer
Buy a high quality management team, which exists in the acquired organisation	**Corporate financiers and banks** have a stake in the acquisitions process as they can charge fees for advice
Many acquisitions **do** have a logic, and the **acquired organisation can be improved** with the extra resources	

6.3 Partnering

Key term

Partnering: Is the term used to describe the types of arrangements which fall short of formal business combinations.

6.3.1 External partnering

Key term

External partnering: Joint ventures, franchising and strategic alliances are all forms of partnering in which arrangements are established with external third parties with a view to achieving a common purpose. External partnering usually restricts formal legal arrangements between entities to specific operations.

6.3.2 Joint ventures

Key term

Joint venture: Is an arrangement when two (or more) entities join forces to create a separate entity which has a purpose which is distinct from the business operations of the two entities that established it.

Joint ventures are usually set up to facilitate a project which is of mutual interest to the founding entities, for example, two firms may wish to bring together their respective technical expertise to undertake joint product development. The two entities which established the joint venture will each have a share in the equity and management of the business. Arrangements such as this enable the founding entities to share the costs of setting up the venture, which can be significant especially when the purpose of the joint venture is to develop new technologies. The establishment of a joint venture may also enable synergies to be realised as one entity's production expertise can be supplemented by the other's knowledge of marketing and distribution.

Joint venture arrangements are however prone to conflicts of interest between the interested parties. Disagreements commonly arise in relation to matters of sharing profits and the management of the joint venture.

6.3.3 Franchising

Key term

> **Franchising:** Is a method of expanding the business on less capital than would otherwise be possible, because franchisees not only pay a capital lump sum to the franchiser to enter the franchise but they also bear some of the running costs of the new outlets/operations.

Franchising is another form of partnering. Franchising is commonly used by entities that are keen to achieve rapid growth. For suitable businesses, it is an **alternative business strategy to raising extra capital** for growth. Franchising is particularly common in the restaurant sector, with McDonald's probably the most well-known fast food franchiser. As is the case with partnering arrangements is important to remember that a franchising agreement will be confined to specific operations. This is best illustrated by considering the table below which outlines the main inputs that the franchiser and franchisee provide under a franchising agreement.

The franchiser	The franchisee
Name, and any goodwill associated with it	Capital, personal involvement and local market knowledge
Systems and business methods, business strategy and managerial know-how	Payment to the franchiser for rights and for support services
Support services, such as advertising, training, research and development, and help with site decoration	Responsibility for the day-to-day running, and the ultimate profitability of the franchise

Advantages of franchising

Franchising offers the following main advantages:

- **Reduces capital requirements**. Organisations (franchisers) often franchise because they cannot readily raise the capital required to set up company-owned stores or operations.

- **Reduces managerial resources required**. An organisation (franchiser) may be able to raise the capital required for growth, but it may lack the managerial resources required to set up a network of company-owned stores. Under a franchise agreement, the franchisees supply the staff required for the day-to-day running of the operation.

- **Improves return on promotional expenditure through speed of growth**. A retail firm's brand and brand image are crucial to the success of its stores. Companies often develop their brand through extensive advertising and promotion, but this only translates into sales if they have a number of stores that customers can visit after seeing their advertisements. To reap the benefits of its national or regional advertising efforts, the company needs to attain the minimum efficient scale, in terms of number of stores, as quickly as possible.

- **Risk management**. When opening new stores, an organisation does not know with certainty the business potential and the chances of success of different locations. Under a franchising arrangement, the franchiser can judge the profitability potential of different sites without incurring a significant business risk. If a particular store fails, the franchisee bears the brunt of the failure.

Disadvantages of franchising

- **Profits are shared**. The franchisee receives the revenue from the customer at the point of sale and then pays the franchiser a share of the profits.

- The **search for competent candidates** is both costly and time-consuming where the franchiser requires many outlets (eg McDonald's).

- **Control** over franchisees. For example, a franchisee could refuse to co-operate in a marketing campaign.

- **Risk to reputation**. A franchisee can damage the public perception of a brand by providing inferior goods or services.

6.3.4 Strategic alliances

Key term

> A **strategic alliance:** Is a type of external partnering that involves some form of co-operation between two or more organisations. Strategic alliances often involve the sharing of resources and activities to pursue a given strategy.

Strategic alliances range from formal joint ventures or licensing agreements, through to looser alliance collaboration. Reasons for entering into strategic alliances include:

(a) **Share development costs** of a particular technology.

(b) The **regulatory environment prohibits take-overs** (eg most major airlines are in strategic alliances because in most countries there are limits to the level of control an 'outsider' can have over an airline).

(c) **Complementary markets or technology**.

(d) **Learning**. Alliances can also be a 'learning' exercise in which each partner tries to learn as much as possible from the other.

(e) **Technology**. New technology offers many uncertainties and many opportunities. Such alliances provide funds for expensive research projects, spreading risk.

(f) **The alliance itself can generate innovations**.

(g) The alliance can involve **'testing' the firm's core competence** in different conditions, which can suggest ways to improve it.

It is important however, to recognise that strategic alliances can only go so far, as there may be disputes over control of strategic assets. Alliances do also have some limitations, namely that each organisation should be able to focus on its core competence. Most types of alliance do not enable organisations to create new competences or develop their own expertise. Furthermore, if a key aspect of strategic delivery is handed over to a partner, the organisation loses flexibility.

6.3.5 Internal partnering

Partnering is not only restricted to the relationships that organisations may create with external third parties, but can also be applied to the internal business functions that exist within organisations. Internal partnering involves active collaboration between different departments with the aim of successfully completing business tasks. For example, members of the sales department may need to partner directly with the finance team to establish the organisations new pricing policy, or may involve members of the marketing department working with the R&D team to undertake new product development. It is believed that a greater focus on building internal relationships between departments should help organisations to realise their strategies and support their prospects for future growth.

Syllabus link

In Chapter 10 we explore the concept of internal partnering in relation to the role of the finance function. As we shall see later on organisations are increasingly adopting a business partner model when structuring their finance functions. In Chapter 13 we give consideration to the implications of introducing a partnering approach.

7 Suitability, acceptability and feasibility

Having explored a number of the strategic choices facing most types of organisation it is important that we give consideration to the criteria which management may use to select the strategies that they identify. Johnson *et al* (2017) highlight that strategies can be evaluated according to their suitability to the organisation's strategic situation, their acceptability to key stakeholder groups (eg shareholders) and their feasibility in terms of resources and competences.

7.1 Suitability

Suitability relates to the **strategic logic** of the strategy. The strategy should fit the organisation's current strategic position and should satisfy a range of requirements:

- **Exploit** strengths: that is, **unique** resources and **core competences**
- **Rectify** an organisation's **weaknesses**, or deal with problems identified in it
- **Neutralise** or deflect environmental **threats**
- Help the firm to **seize opportunities**
- **Satisfy the goals** of the organisation
- Generate/maintain **competitive advantage**
- Involve an acceptable level of **risk**
- Suit the **politics** and corporate **culture**

7.2 Acceptability

The acceptability of a strategy depends on expected performance outcomes and the extent to which these are acceptable to stakeholders. Typical stakeholder interests may include:

- **Shareholders** will generally be interested in generating a good **financial return** (using measures such as return on investment, earnings per share, payback period etc) while keeping **risk** to an acceptable level (which may be measured via sensitivity analysis, scenario analysis and financial ratios).

- **Management and staff** may object to changes if they believe that a new strategy will not suit their skillset, or if they will be personally worse off.

- **Customers** may be unhappy with changes that involve higher prices or poorer services.

- **Banks** will want to see good future cashflows to repay debt.

- **Government** might block certain strategies, such as an acquisition not being allowed because it reduces competition.

- The **media and public** may protest if they believe a strategy will be detrimental, such as opening an out-of-town superstore which will damage small shops.

7.3 Feasibility

Feasibility asks whether the strategy can be implemented and, in particular, if the organisation has adequate **strategic capability**. Feasibility can be considered against the organisation's:

- Financial resources
- Management skills
- Skilled staff
- Required competences

If the organisation does not possess these, it may be possible to acquire them, but this is likely to require time and money.

Competitive advantage and strategic choice

Competitive advantage and strategic choice

Porter's generic strategies

- Cost leadership means being the lowest-cost producer in the industry as a whole
- Differentiation is the exploitation of a product or service which the industry as a whole believes to be unique
- Focus (or niche) strategy involves a restriction of activities to only part of the market (a segment)
- Which generic strategy? Need to avoid being stuck in the middle

Sustainable competitive advantage

The seven Ps

- Product
- Place
- Promotion
- Price
- People
- Processes
- Physical evidence

Price-based, differentiation and lock-in

- Sustaining price-based strategies
- Sustaining differentiation
- Lock-in is achieved in a market when a product becomes the industry standard

Managing organisational portfolios

The BCG Matrix

Consists of:

- Stars
- Cash Cows
- Question Marks
- Dogs

The public sector portfolio matrix

Consists of:

- Public Sector Stars
- Political Hot Boxes
- Golden Fleeces
- Back Drawer Issues

Product-market strategy: direction of growth

Growth vector matrix

Consists of:

- Market Penetration
- Product Development
- Market Development
- Diversification

Diversity of products and markets

The need for diversification

Types of diversification
- Related diversification (horizontal and vertical integration)
- Advantages and disadvantages of vertical integration
- Unrelated diversification
- Advantages and disadvantages of conglomerate diversification
- Diversity and strategic success

International diversification
Management orientation (ethnocentrism, polycentrism, geocentrism and regiocentrism)

Methods of development

Internal development
Uses internal resources

Business combinations
Acquisitions (buy another) and mergers (two entities join)

Partnering
- External partnering (restricts formal legal arrangements between entities to specific operations)
- Joint ventures (two (or more) entities join forces to create a separate entity which has a common purpose)
- Franchising (franchiser and franchisee)
- Strategic alliances (involves some form of co-operation between two or more organisations)
- Internal partnering (involves active collaboration between different departments)

Suitability, acceptability and feasibility

Suitability
Relates to strategic logic

Acceptability
To stakeholders?

Feasibility
Concerns whether a strategy can be implemented

BPP
LEARNING
MEDIA

1. Porter (1980) suggests that organisations need to adopt an appropriate competitive strategy. Porter referred to them as generic strategies. An organisation must first decide its competitive basis, being either to compete on the basis of lowest cost, or to differentiate.

2. Porter (1980) argued that to do neither and be 'stuck in the middle' would lead to an inability to compete over the long term.

3. Once an organisation's competitive basis has been determined Porter (1980) argues that competitive scope must be decided. This might take a narrow (focus) or broad form (available to the market as a whole).

4. The strategic choices an organisation makes regarding its marketing strategy will be driven by its choice of generic strategy. Creating a marketing strategy involves developing and tailoring elements of the so-called marketing mix. The seven Ps consist of product, place, promotion, price, people, processes and physical evidence.

5. Johnson *et al* (2017) suggest that a price-based strategy can be sustained by maintaining low margins, being a cost leader, using financial resources to win price wars, adopting a no-frills strategy.

6. Sustaining differentiation can be difficult as this involves more than just being different: the difference must be valued by customers.

7. Hax and Wilde (1999) proposed the concept of lock-in in relation to strategic sustainability. Lock-in is achieved in a market when an organisation's product becomes the industry standard.

8. The BCG matrix devised by Henderson (1970) categorises SBUs in terms of market growth rate and relative market share. SBUs can be classified as Stars, Cash Cows, Question Marks and Dogs.

9. The public sector portfolio matrix (Montanari and Bracker, 1986) classifies activities in terms of their popularity and the resources available for them. Activities are classified as being Public Sector Stars, Political Hot Boxes, Golden Fleeces, Back Drawer Issues.

10. Product-market strategies involve determining which products should be sold in which markets, by market penetration, market development, product development and diversification. These terms make up the quadrants in Ansoff's (1987) growth vector matrix.

11. Diversification can take the form of related or unrelated diversification.

12. Related diversification is strategy development beyond current products and markets but within the capabilities or value network of the organisation. Related diversification can be achieved through either horizontal or vertical integration.

13. Unrelated diversification is the development of products or services beyond the current capabilities or value network.

14. The growth in the number of organisations diversifying their operations internationally has been driven by globalisation.

15. International product/market diversification requires organisations to adopt an appropriate management orientation. Perlmutter (1969) identified three orientations for use in the management of international business: ethnocentrism, polycentrism and geocentrism. Regiocentrism was later added by Wind *et al* (1973).

16. A range of methods are available to organisations looking to grow, including: internal development, business combinations, and partnering.

17. Johnson *et al* (2017) highlight that strategies can be evaluated according to their suitability to the organisation's strategic situation, their acceptability to key stakeholder groups (eg shareholders) and their feasibility in terms of resources and competences.

Further study guidance

Question practice

Now try the question below from the Further question practice bank (available in the digital edition of the Workbook):

Q6 *Environment Management Society*

Further reading

There are articles on the ACCA website written by members of the SBL examining team which are relevant to your studies and which would be useful to read:

The strategic planning process – part 2

This article discusses Porter's generic strategies and explores the work of Ansoff in the context of strategic choice.

Approaching SBL overview

This article provides a one-page summary of the key features of the SBL exam.

Approaching SBL reading and planning

This article provides a one-page summary of how best to approach the SBL exam.

SBL – 10 things to learn from the September 2018 sitting

This article highlights some of the issues that ACCA identified in candidates' answers during the September 2018 SBL exam sitting. The article provides some useful advice for improving your chances of passing the SBL exam.

Strategic Business Leader – The importance of effective communication for SBL

This article provides some useful insights into the different formats which you will be expected to use when answering SBL exam tasks.

Own research

It is important to link the topics covered in this chapter to a practical, real-world context. As such, we have suggested some areas for you to investigate further:

- Research an organisation with which you are familiar (this could include your current or past employer), and consider which competitive basis the organisation is pursuing (cost leadership or differentiation). If you are struggling to find an organisation to consider you may find it helpful to choose a well-known business listed on a recognised stock exchange such as the FTSE 100.

- Is this organisation pursuing a wide or narrow competitive scope?

- Go online and find the annual report of a large, diversified conglomerate. Review the SBUs which make up the business activities of the conglomerate. Using the BCG matrix as a guide, do you think the organisation has a well-balanced portfolio?

- Which method(s) of development has the organisation used in the past to expand its operations?

- Did the method(s) of development used by the organisation prove successful or not?

Exercise 1

Product

- Natural ingredients
- Colourful packaging
- Brand clearly displayed (teenagers tend to be brand sensitive)

Price

- Dependent on brand although premium brand may not mean premium price as teenagers cannot afford
- Would not be cheap product as again teenagers tend not to want cheap products

Place

- High Street stores to attract the teenagers to buy
- Supermarkets so that parents can purchase for their teenage children
- Internet would depend on a variety of factors, one key issue is would it be environmentally and economically viable

Promotion

- Facebook groups, interactive website attached to the parent company's site
- Promoted by famous celebrities known to the teenage population
- BOGOF/vouchers for discounts

This question requirement focused on the traditional 4Ps as these are most relevant to the marketing of tangible products. The final 3Ps which make up the fuller version of the marketing mix (sometimes referred to as the service marketing mix) relate to the marketing of services and cover: people, processes and physical evidence. As such they have not been applied in the answer to this question.

SKILLS CHECKPOINT 2

Optimising strategic decisions

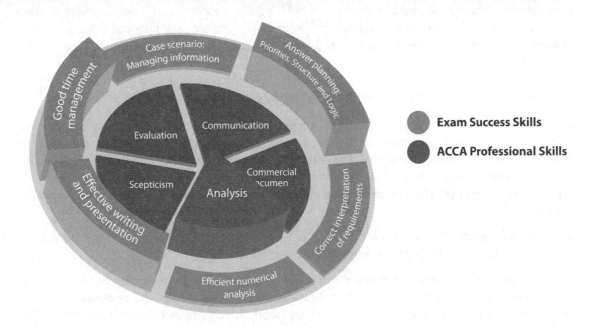

Exam Success Skills

ACCA Professional Skills

Introduction

In Stage 2 you have learned about Optimising Strategic Decisions.

However, only 80% of marks are awarded for the application of knowledge. The remaining marks are awarded for good demonstration of the specific ACCA Professional Skills outlined in the task requirement. You need to able to:

1. Identify the ACCA Professional Skill in the task requirement. Remember the five: Analysis, Communication, Commercial Acumen, Evaluation and Scepticism

2. Understand what the skill requires in the context of the question

3. Consider how to demonstrate the skill(s) as part of your answer planning

The ACCA Professional Skills are assessing your ability to present your answers to a standard which would be expected in the workplace. However, in order to do this effectively in the Strategic Leader Exam, you must develop a further series of Exam Success Skills, so you are able to produce your very best solution in the four-hour timeframe.

Therefore, success in Strategic Business Leader requires the simultaneous demonstration of syllabus knowledge, ACCA Professional Skills and Exam Success Skills. This is the second in a series of Skills Checkpoints which specifically target skills development as you progress through the syllabus, so you are equipped with all the tools you need during the Learning phase, so you can focus on improving at the Revision Stage.

In each of the five Skills Checkpoints we will focus on one of the five ACCA Professional Skills and provide further guidance on how to develop certain Exam Success Skills, so you can effectively manage questions and meet the expected standard for both knowledge and skills.

Your role

Developing skills requires more than listening and reading; it requires you to try for yourself, use guidance and feedback to consider whether you have met the skills objective, then plan for further improvement. In Strategic Business Leader, you should include a focus on skills development in every question you attempt as your normal approach. The Skills Checkpoints will take you through a series of **steps** where you will attempt aspects of a question and review your progress from a skills perspective.

Focus on ACCA Professional Skill: Analysis

You will find the ACCA definition of Analysis under 'ACCA Professional Skills in the introduction. Analysis means logically investigating and processing information to respond to a question or request, or meet a stated objective. For example, you might gather information about an organisation from a range of sources, including financial and non-financial data, to establish the reasons for its current performance, and then make recommendations which follow logically from this evidence.

Analysis includes explaining why a certain piece of data is important, marshalling relevant evidence and explaining how your findings can help the organisation.

In this question, ensure that you demonstrate analysis skills by not simply repeating the scenario but adding value in some way to the information it contains. For example, can you prioritise the factors affecting the museum in the question below, showing clearly which you feel are most important? Can you draw out the implications of at least some of the factors – having answered the 'what', have you answered the 'so what'?

Demonstrating Exam Success Skills

For this question, we will focus on the following exam success skills and in particular:

- **Answer planning: Priorities, Structure and Logic**. This type of question relies heavily on you picking up relevant clues in the scenario, so a good approach to planning is firstly to read the task requirement, then read the scenario carefully, annotating where you find information that is useful for your answer. We advise annotating rather than simply highlighting, firstly so that you remember why you picked out this information and secondly because it forces you to think about the significance of the information.

- **Effective writing and presentation**. You should always use sub-headings in your answer and sometimes, as in this case, using relevant theory will give you a ready-made set of headings to use. Using headings will give your answer logic and structure, and make it easier for the marker to follow.

- **Good time management**. The exam will be time-pressured and you will need to manage it carefully to ensure that you can make a good attempt at every part of every task. As the task is worth 17 marks, using two minutes per mark as a guide equates to a total of 34 minutes to attempt the task requirement. Working on the basis that you will spend at least five minutes creating your answer plan, this leaves no more than 29 minutes to write up your answer. Remember time spent planning will generally improve your answer.

Skill Activity

 STEP 1 Read the task requirement for the following question, interpret the active verb, identify the skill and set up your answer plan

Your verb is 'analyse'. This is defined by the ACCA as 'Break into separate parts and discuss, examine, or interpret each part. Key tips: Give reasons for the current situation or what has happened.' You are asked to analyse the macro-environment so you are looking at factors outside the organisation, breaking them down in some way and bringing in some interpretation – what are the implications for the organisation of what is going on in the environment? It is helpful to consider whether some theory would give you ideas and structure – a common tool for analysing the macro-environment is PESTEL and, while not a task requirement, using this as a framework would improve your answer.

The skill is 'analysis', which breaks down as 'investigate', 'enquire' and 'consider'. To earn these professional marks you will have to ensure you are not just repeating points from the scenario, but explaining their significance and using them to draw conclusions, for example about appropriate actions for the organisations.

 STEP 2 Now briefly read the scenario and use your 'Case Scenario: Managing information' skills to pick out important facts and data which are relevant to the task requirement identified in Step 1

Question – National Museum (17 marks)

The National Museum (NM) was established over 150 years ago to house collections of art, textiles and metalware for the nation. It remains in its original building which is itself of architectural importance. Unfortunately, the passage of time has meant that the condition of the building has deteriorated and so it requires continual repair and maintenance. Alterations have also been made to ensure that the building complies with the disability access and health and safety laws of the country. However, these alterations have been criticised as being unsympathetic and out of character with the rest of the building. The building is in a previously affluent area of the capital city. However, what were once large middle-class family houses have now become multi-occupied apartments and the socio-economic structure of the area has radically changed. The area also suffers from an increasing crime rate. A visitor to the museum was recently assaulted while waiting for a bus to take her home. The assault was reported in both local and national newspapers.

Thirty years ago, the government identified museums that held significant Heritage Collections. These are collections that are deemed to be very significant to the country. Three Heritage Collections were identified at the NM, a figure that has risen to seven in the intervening years as the museum has acquired new items.

The NM is currently 90% funded by direct grants from government. The rest of its income comes from a nominal admission charge and from private sponsorship of exhibitions. The direct funding from the government is based on a number of factors, but the number of Heritage Collections held by the museum is a significant funding influence. The Board of Trustees of the NM divide the museum's income between departments roughly on the basis of the previous year's budget plus an inflation percentage. The division of money between departments is heavily influenced by the Heritage Collections. Departments with Heritage Collections tend to be allocated a larger budget.

One year ago, a new national government was elected. The newly appointed Minister for Culture implemented the government's election manifesto commitment to make museums more self-funding. The minister has declared that in five years' time the museum must cover 60% of its own costs and only 40% will be directly funded by government. This change in funding will gradually be phased in over the next five years. The 40% government grant will be linked to the museum achieving specified targets for disability access, social inclusion and electronic commerce and access. The government is

committed to increasing museum attendance by lower socio-economic classes and younger people so that they are more aware of their heritage. Furthermore, it also wishes to give increasing access to museum exhibits to disabled people who cannot physically visit the museum site. The government has asked all museums to produce a strategy document showing how they intend to meet these financial, accessibility and technological objectives. The government's opposition has, since the election, also agreed that the reliance of museums on government funding should be reduced.

Required

Note the key verb

Note the professional skill to be demonstrated

Analyse the macro-environment of the National Museum   **(15 marks)**

Professional skills marks are available for demonstrating **analysis** skills in relation to the macro-environment.   **(2 marks)**

(Total = 17 marks)

A brief review of the scenario will show you that:

- The organisation is a public museum. You will therefore not think in terms of making profit or shareholder wealth, but achieving its goals in terms of public service, while being financially sustainable.

- There are many clues in the scenario about environmental factors – you will need to identify them and explain their implications.

- There is a significant change going on in the environment, driven by political factors. This will be a key point to bring out in your solution.

STEP 3 Now create an answer plan. Use the mark allocation to determine how many factors to explain, also think about the logical flow of your point before you start writing. Finally, as you create your plan, think about how you will demonstrate 'analysis' in your answer; for example, does it require numbers and if so, how will these be clearly presented or do we need to interpret information from the scenario to evidence a view or argument.

Guidance to help you develop your answer plan

The use of the term 'macro-environment' should suggest to you the use of PESTEL analysis in your answer. This was not essential as you would still get marks for points relevant to the environment (anything external to the museum) but would help greatly in generating ideas and structuring your answer. The most efficient way to plan an answer to this type of question is to annotate the scenario, underlining key points and making very brief notes about their significance and potential actions resulting from your analysis. Your plan could look something like this:

The National Museum (NM) was established over 150 years ago to house collections of art, textiles and metalware for the nation. It remains in its original building which is itself of architectural importance. Unfortunately, the passage of time has meant that the condition of the building has deteriorated and so it **requires continual repair and maintenance**. Alterations have also been made to ensure that the building complies with the disability access and health and safety laws of the country. However, these alterations have been criticised as being unsympathetic and **out of character with the rest of the building**. The building is in a previously affluent area of the capital city. However, what were once large middle-class family houses have now become multi-occupied apartments and the socio-economic structure of the area has radically changed. The area also suffers from an increasing crime rate. A visitor to the museum was recently assaulted while waiting for a bus to take her home. **The assault was reported in both local and national newspapers**.

> Environmental factor – higher costs

> Legal factor – difficult to comply with laws

> Social factors – location a problem

Thirty years ago, the government identified museums that held significant Heritage Collections. These are collections that are deemed to be very significant to the country. Three Heritage Collections were identified at the NM, a figure that has risen to seven in the intervening years as the museum has acquired new items.

> Big political factor – funding depends on govt

> Political factor – govt defines these

The NM is currently 90% funded by direct grants from government. The rest of its income comes from a nominal admission charge and from private sponsorship of exhibitions. The direct funding from the government is based on a number of factors, but the **number of Heritage Collections held by the museum is a significant funding influence.** The Board of Trustees of the NM divide the museum's income between departments roughly on the basis of the previous year's budget plus an inflation percentage. The division of money between departments is heavily influenced by the Heritage Collections. Departments with Heritage Collections tend to be allocated a larger budget.

> Economic factor – now exposed to economy

> Social factor – need to appeal to these groups

> Political factor – need to work to govt performance measures

> Political factor – change in funding

> Political driver to increase attendance

> Technology factor – new ways of displaying exhibits

One year ago, a new national government was elected. The newly appointed Minister for Culture implemented the government's election manifesto commitment to make **museums more self-funding.** The minister has declared that in five years' time the **museum must cover 60% of its own costs and only 40% will be directly funded by government.** This change in funding will gradually be phased in over the next five years. The 40% government grant will be linked to the museum achieving specified targets for **disability access, social inclusion** and electronic commerce and access. **The government is committed to increasing museum attendance by lower socio-economic classes and younger people** so that they are more aware of their heritage. Furthermore, it also wishes to give increasing access to museum exhibits to disabled people who **cannot physically visit the museum site.** The government has asked all museums to produce a strategy document showing how **they intend to meet these financial, accessibility and technological objectives.** The government's opposition has, since the election, also agreed that the reliance of museums on government funding should be reduced.

If you wish, you can note these points under relevant headings, also starting to demonstrate your analysis skills by drawing out the implications of the information. Your notes may look like this:

Political

Govt funding reduced

Govt performance measures – need to meet targets

Economic

Now exposed as need to generate income

Setting appropriate ticket price

Social

Govt wants social inclusion

Location may mean visitors don't feel safe

Links to community to meet inclusion targets?

Consider relocating if a problem for visitors?

Technological

Virtual museum = better accessibility

Also helps with safety concerns

Use e-marketing to increase appeal?

Revenue from e-commerce?

Environmental

Upkeep of old building an issue

Dilemma re alterations to comply with laws

Consider moving to new purpose-built site?

Legal

Need to comply with H&S, access legislation. Consider how to do this?

 Check the task requirements

Before you start writing it is good practice to check the task requirement once again, to make sure your answer directly addresses it. In this case, the key questions are:

- Have you focused on the museum's environment, ie matters external to it? Do not get side-tracked by discussing or speculating on their internal issues.

- Have you demonstrated analysis skills by 'adding value' to the information? Make sure you have not just collated points from the scenario.

 Complete your written answer

You can now bring these together into a solution, making sure that you use logical headings and short, clear sentences. These are key factors in Effective Writing & Presentation – one of your Exam Success Skills. Make sure you are making connections and drawing conclusions to signal to the marker that you are demonstrating analysis skills. A model answer is given below, with comment boxes to show where the answer is demonstrating good analysis skills.

Suggested Solution

Political

Funding and funding changes – The museum is currently 90% funded by direct grants from government, meaning that the government's decision to gradually reduce that funding over five years will have a **major impact on the National Museum**.

> Identifying the scale of the impact of this factor

The government and the opposition party have both agreed that museums' reliance on government funding should be reduced, and so it appears that these funding reductions are unlikely to be reversed in the near future.

Performance measures – Going forward, the museum's government funding will be linked to certain performance measures – such as disability access. These measures will have a **major impact on the museum's outlook**. The museum will have to meet a number of targets if it wishes to retain any government funding.

> Again, identifying a change as particularly significant and explaining why

Economic

Economic exposure – When the museum was substantially government funded, it has been largely sheltered from any changes in the economic environment. Funding appears to have been stable, increasing to reflect inflation each year, and based on the Heritage Collections held by the museum.

> This is drawing out a very significant point implied, but not stated in the scenario.

However, the reduction in the level of government funding will mean that **the museum will be increasingly exposed to commercial pressures**. For example, it will have to generate revenues through admissions, and this revenue will be affected by the relationship between price and visitor numbers.

Ticket pricing – One of the key issues the museum will have to address is the price it charges visitors. Historically, visitors have been used to paying only a nominal entry charge. **If prices are set too high, people will not visit the museum, particularly the lower social classes which the government is keen to include. However, if prices are set too low, they may not generate enough revenue to make good the shortfall in government funding**.

> Going beyond identifying factors to explore their implications

Social

Social inclusion – The government is keen that museum attendance increases among the lower social classes and among younger people. The museum needs to identify ways it can become more attractive to younger people or lower social classes.

Urban decline and local geographical context – The decline of the local neighbourhood around the museum may deter fee-paying visitors. Therefore the museum will need to ensure that visitors feel safe on their way to and from the museum, for example, **improving security around the museum if necessary**.

> Practical suggestions coming out of the analysis

Location and visitors – It is likely that the museum's visitors are mainly middle class people, but the decline in the local neighbourhood means these are the people who will be moving away from the area. However, while this is a problem for the museum on one hand, on the other hand it means that the neighbourhood around the museum is increasingly housing more of the people the government wants it to encourage as visitors. **Therefore, if the museum can create linkages with its local community this could help it to achieve the social inclusion the government wants to promote**.

> Thinking beyond the obvious to how a difficult situation could be turned to advantage

Conversely, if the problem of middle class visitors not wanting to visit the area becomes too bad, and therefore visitor numbers drop still further, **the museum may ultimately have to consider relocating from its current site to one in an area which is perceived to be safer to visit**.

> Alternative recommendation

Technological

Increased visitor accessibility – A virtual museum would also reduce problems with the physical accessibility of the museum. People from all round the country, and internationally, could read about the collections and view the online displays through a virtual museum. **The virtual museum could also benefit some disabled people who cannot physically visit the site**.

> Linking two types of external factors – technological and social

A virtual museum also allows people to view the museum's collections from the comfort of their own homes, if they have concerns about the safety and security of the neighbourhood around the museum.

E-marketing – The museum could also use technology to increase the scope of its marketing activity. **For example, if it collects a list of email addresses of regular visitors, it could notify them of special exhibitions which may be of interest to them – either in the virtual museum or the physical museum. As an initiative to attract younger visitors, the collections could also publish blogs, highlighting some of their more interesting features, and illustrating their relevance to younger people**.

> Developing the point about technology to make further suggestions

Electronic commerce – One of the government's targets for the museum is to increase its level of electronic commerce. On the one hand, this could be achieved if online visitors pay a subscription fee to view the virtual museum; on the other hand, the museum could have an online shop where visitors can buy replica items and souvenirs through a secure payment facility.

Environmental

Upkeep of building – The museum building is over 150 years old, and requires continual repair and maintenance. It is likely that an old building is less energy-efficient than a modern, purpose-built one would be, and therefore the museum's heating costs may be higher than they could be.

Alterations to building – The museum has had to make alterations to its building to comply with disability and health and safety legislation. It is likely that these alterations were relatively expensive. However, they have been criticised as being out of character with the rest of the building. **The museum faces a dilemma here – it has to make its building compliant with the legislation, while trying to preserve the fabric of the existing building**.

> Highlighting key issue being faced by senior management which does not have an obvious solution

The criticisms about these alterations to the building, **plus its energy inefficiency may encourage the museum's Board to consider moving to a modern, purpose-built site; particularly in conjunction with concerns about the decline of the museum's neighbourhood**.

> Building additional evidence for the recommendation

Legal

Access requirements and safety legislation – We have already noted that the museum has had to make alterations to its building to comply with legal requirements for disability access and health and safety legislation. If the government is keen to encourage social inclusion, further changes may be required – **for example, including all public notices in a variety of languages or in Braille**.

> Going beyond what is in the scenario and showing evidence of creative thinking

 Complete the exam success skills diagnostic

Finally, use the diagnostic below to assess how effectively you demonstrated the exam success skills in answering this question.

Exam Success Skills	Your reflections/observations
Case scenario: Managing information	Did you extract the key points from the scenario? In this case, you should have seen that the organisation was a not-for-profit and therefore reference to shareholder wealth and similar concepts would be inappropriate. A key 'big picture' point was that political change was driving the situation.
Correct interpretation of requirements	Did you understand that the question focused on the environment, and therefore you should only have dealt with matters external to the museum? Did you appreciate the importance of analysis skills?
Answer planning: Priorities, Structure and Logic	Did you adopt a systematic approach to planning, understanding the task requirements first, then working through the scenario to extract relevant information? Did you stop to consider key points and connections before starting to write?
Efficient numerical analysis	Not applicable in this question.
Effective writing and presentation	Have you used headings to structure your answer, with short sentences and paragraphs? Are your points made clearly and succinctly?

Most important action points to apply to your next question

Summary

Answering exam questions is like any other skill – the more you practise the better you will get! But, after attempting a question, make sure you take time to reflect and debrief how well you managed it, whether you followed the key steps and whether you demonstrated professional skills. Carry forward your learning points to the next question you attempt, and over the course of your studies you will see significant improvements.

INTRODUCTION TO STAGE 3:
Assessing and Managing Risk and Ethical Issues

Assessing and Managing Risk and Ethical Issues

Olympus is a well-established Japanese manufacturer of optical imaging, laboratory and medical equipment. In 2011 it appointed its first-ever non-Japanese president, a 30-year company veteran from the UK called Michael Woodford. A few months later, Mr Woodford was also appointed Chief Executive. In July of that year, his attention was drawn to an article alleging that Olympus had made substantial and secret payments relating to a series of acquisitions. He attempted to find out the truth behind these allegations but all his enquiries were blocked by staff and fellow directors. In October, at an emergency board meeting at which Mr Woodford was not allowed to speak or vote, the board unanimously fired him as Chief Executive. In a press release, the company explained Mr Woodford's removal as being due to the fact that he had 'largely diverted from the rest of the management team in regard to the management direction and method...'

Mr Woodford turned 'whistle-blower', telling the media about the issue and calling for the resignation of the entire board. The company denied any problems but, after extensive investigations and involvement of law enforcement authorities around the world, it was discovered that secret payments had been made to cover up losses on investments going back to the 1980s and 1990s. There were many arrests and resignations. Mr Woodford received a substantial settlement from Olympus, and went on to work as a speaker and consultant.

Olympus represented a spectacular failure of internal controls and ethical standards, with senior management colluding in accounting fraud. In this situation, it was only the ethical principles of a new CEO that brought the issue to light. Most situations are not so extreme, but all organisations face risks and therefore need to have in place internal controls to deal with them as far as possible. As this section will show, leaders of an organisation need to be personally confident that controls are effective, and one of the tools they often use is an internal audit function, exercising independent oversight of the control systems.

The Olympus scandal cut its stock market valuation by 75–80%. The penalty for poor ethics and controls can be severe.

Assessing and
managing risk

7

Learning objectives

On completion of this chapter, you should be able to:

	Syllabus reference no.
Discuss the relationship between organisational strategy and risk management strategy	D1(a)
Develop a framework for risk management and establish risk management systems	D1(b)
Identify and evaluate the key risks and their impact on organisations and projects	D1(c)
Distinguish between strategic and operational risks	D1(d)
Assess attitudes towards risk and risk appetite and how this can affect risk policy	D1(e)
Discuss the dynamic nature of risk and the ways in which risk varies in relation to the size, structure and development of an organisation	D1(f)
Recognise and analyse the sector or industry-specific nature of many organisation risks	D1(g)
Assess the severity and probability of risk events using suitable models	D1(h)
Explain and assess the ALARP ('as low as reasonably practicable') principle in risk assessment and how this relates to severity and probability	D1(i)
Explain and evaluate the concepts of related and correlated risk factors	D1(j)
Explain and assess the role of a risk manager	D2(a)
Evaluate a risk register and use heat maps when identifying or monitoring risks	D2(b)
Describe and evaluate the concept of embedding risk in an organisation's culture and values	D2(c)
Explain and analyse the concepts of spreading and diversifying risk and when this would be appropriate	D2(d)
Explain, and assess the importance of, risk transfer, avoidance, reduction and acceptance (TARA)	D2(e)
Explain and assess the benefits of incurring or accepting some risk as part of competitively managing an organisation	D2(f)

Business and exam context

Risk is everywhere you look – from the risk of oversleeping in the morning all the way through to a corporate failure that threatens to bring down a government and beyond. Organisations need to find ways of understanding the risks they face and how to deal with them effectively as part of their normal operations.

In this chapter you will learn about how risk is not always a bad thing and how it can actually have a positive impact on a company. You will also learn more about the various types of risk that an organisation needs to consider in order to achieve its objectives and how to decide on the best way to manage these risks.

Chapter overview

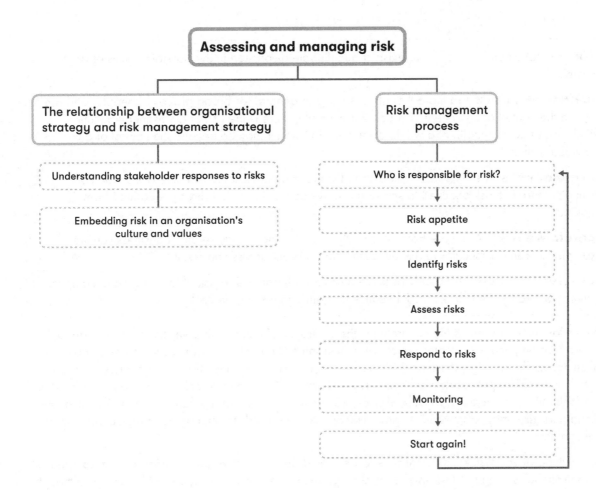

1 The relationship between organisational strategy and risk management strategy

1.1 Understanding stakeholder responses to risk

Key terms

Risk: Is a condition in which there exists a quantifiable dispersion in the possible results of an activity.

Fundamental risks: Are those that affect society in general, or broad groups of people, and are beyond the control of any one individual. For example, there is the risk of atmospheric pollution which can affect the health of a whole community but which may be beyond the control of an individual within it.

Particular risks: Are risks over which an individual may have some measure of control. For example, there is a risk attached to smoking and we can mitigate that risk by refraining from smoking.

Speculative risks: Are those from which either good or harm may result. A business venture, for example, presents a speculative risk because either a profit or loss can result.

Pure risks: Are those whose only possible outcome is harmful. The risk of loss of data in computer systems caused by fire is a pure risk because no gain can result from it.

When formulating organisational strategy, the board of directors will give careful consideration to ensure that only those strategies which fall within the bounds of the organisation's risk appetite are taken forward. Although the term 'risk' tends to indicate something that we should be concerned about, stakeholder groups do not necessarily always want to eliminate risk for an organisation. They are only likely to react adversely if the organisation does not conform to their expectations. Managing risk may also require organisations to get used to managing expectations among stakeholders.

The attitude of some stakeholder groups to risk could therefore have an influence on the company's organisational strategy. These **stakeholder groups** are likely to include the following (although others could also be present):

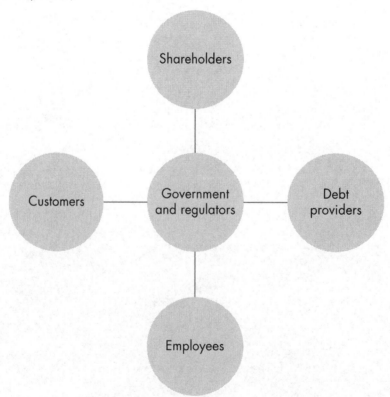

Exercise 1: Stakeholders and risk

Required

For each of the stakeholder groups in the diagram above, evaluate their attitude towards risk-taking by the organisation they are linked to. You can consider this in the context of any organisation you are familiar with.

Solution

1.2 Embedding risk in an organisation's culture and values

Key term

Embedding risk: Ensuring that the approach to managing risks is considered at all times and in all roles by making it a part of the culture and values of an organisation.

Risk should be embedded in the company's systems and procedures, and also its culture and values, because the alignment of strategy and operational activities (which will support the achievement of shareholder value) can only happen if all levels of the organisation embrace the risks faced by that organisation.

Essential reading

See Chapter 7 section 1 of the Essential Reading, available in Appendix 2 of the digital edition of the Workbook, for detail on COSO's Enterprise Risk Management – Integrating with Strategy and Performance (2017). This content complements the discussion of the COSO cube which is discussed in Chapter 8. This content focuses on how five connected components can assist in managing risks across a whole enterprise.

Activity 1: Risk awareness

ACCA Professional skills focus

Communication: Inform

You work as a consultant for a board member who sits on the board of a large listed manufacturing organisation. You have just received an instant message (IM) from the board member asking for your help: the director is currently in a meeting with institutional shareholders and is concerned the organisation's health and safety record is going to be questioned following a series of 'near misses' at its biggest manufacturing site. The director would like you to inform him about how the organisation takes risk seriously at all levels of the organisation.

BPP
LEARNING
MEDIA

Required

Recommend practical ways in which risk awareness can be embedded in this organisation at different levels. **(5 marks)**

Professional skills marks are available for demonstrating **communication** skills in informing your readers using appropriate style for an IM response. **(2 marks)**

(Total = 7 marks)

Solution

2 Risk management process

We now know what risk is and why it needs to be managed to support the strategy of an organisation. How can risk be managed though? There are many different approaches that you can look at, but for the purposes of this Workbook, we have chosen to present the following approach as it includes the most common recurring elements:

1.   Set responsibilities
2.   Set risk appetite
3.   Identify risks
4.   Assess risks
5.   Respond to risks
6.   Monitor and review the process and adapt if necessary
7.   Start again!

2.1 Who is responsible for risk?

The board has overall accountability for risk management as part of its corporate governance responsibilities. However, the board may choose to delegate responsibility to line management or a separate risk management function instead of managing risk through the board. Let's have a look at who could be involved in this.

2.1.1 Risk committee

A **risk committee** could be set up by the board. The tasks that this committee should fulfil will depend on the organisation, their industry and their size and complexity but, in general, they could include the following.

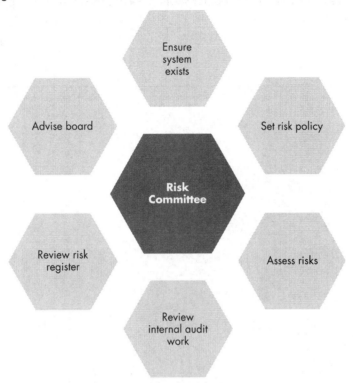

The risk committee will probably consist of board members, but who should that be?

Exam Focus Point

Question 3 of the Strategic Business Leader exam in September 2018 featured a task which asked candidates to prepare a briefing paper which advised the board at the featured entity of the advantages of establishing a risk committee.

Activity 2: Risk committee

ACCA Professional skills focus

Evaluation: Appraise

You work as a consultant for the board of a medium-sized online retailing organisation which has only been trading for three years, having previously operated from a network of five independent retail outlets across one country. The prime business of the organisation is the sale of leisure equipment for outdoor activities such as rock climbing, hang gliding and archery. Since incorporation, the organisation has grown rapidly and the need for sound risk management has become one of its key priorities as it attempts to secure additional funding for further expansion. It currently has a board which consists of a Managing Director, Finance Director and Retail Director, plus two non-executive directors (a lawyer and a retired bank manager) who have recently been recruited to operate an audit committee in advance of becoming a listed entity.

The board is currently considering having a specific risk committee to address the specific risks that the organisation faces, from both existing and proposed products and services. You have been asked to advise the board by producing a slide for the next board meeting which explains who should be on this risk committee.

BPP
LEARNING
MEDIA

Required

Draft the presentation slide, explaining the benefits of having a risk committee that is staffed by (i) executive directors only and (ii) non-executive directors only. **(6 marks)**

Professional skills marks are available for demonstrating **evaluation** skills in appraising the benefits of each approach. **(2 marks)**

(Total = 8 marks)

Solution

PER alert

Performance Objective 20 'Review and report on the findings of an audit or assurance engagement' of the Practical Experience Requirement requires you to 'discuss the findings and implications of an audit or assurance engagement with management and governance teams'. (ACCA, 2019b). To achieve this performance objective, you could draw upon your experience of reporting to those charged with governance the risks identified during audit work that you have undertaken.

If there is no risk committee, the **audit committee** may take responsibility for risk management instead. They may however need the support of a dedicated **risk manager**.

2.1.2 Risk manager

Key term

Risk manager: A role that supports the board by taking the lead on risk and developing policy and practice on managing risks.

This role may be set up to support the board's risk responsibilities. A risk manager needs to combine technical skills in managing various risks (such as compliance, legal and industry-specific risks) with leadership and persuasive skills.

A risk manager's responsibilities can be listed as:

Leadership of enterprise risk management (essentially the process of risk management across the entire organisation)
Establishing and promoting enterprise risk management
Developing common risk management policies
Establishing a common risk language
Dealing with insurance companies
Implementing risk indicators, (such as designing early warning systems)
Allocation of resources based on risk
Reporting to the CEO/board/risk committee as appropriate

2.2 Risk appetite

Risk appetite: Describes the nature and strength of risks that an organisation is prepared to bear.

Risk attitude: Is the directors' views on the level of risk that they consider desirable.

Risk averse: Accepting risks up to a certain point as long as they represent an acceptable return.

Risk seeker: Pursuing the highest returns regardless of risks (within reason).

Risk capacity: Describes the nature and strength of risks that an organisation is able to bear.

Different businesses will have different attitudes towards taking risk. This appetite for risk is likely to be considered as part of an organisation's **control environment** (covered in Chapter 8).

Risk-averse businesses may be willing to **tolerate risks up to a point** provided they receive **acceptable return** or, if risk is 'two-way' or symmetrical, that it has both positive and negative outcomes. Some risks may be an unavoidable consequence of operating in their business sector. However, there will be upper limits to the risks they are prepared to take, whatever the level of returns they could earn.

Risk-seeking businesses are likely to focus on maximising returns and may not be worried about the level of risks that have to be taken to maximise returns (indeed their managers may thrive on taking risks).

Activity 3: Risk appetite

 ACCA Professional skills focus

Commercial acumen: show insight

You work as a consultant for the board of a medium-sized online retailing organisation which has only been trading for three years having previously operated from a network of five independent retail outlets across one country. The prime business of the organisation is the sale of leisure equipment for outdoor activities such as rock climbing, hang gliding and archery. Since incorporation, the organisation has grown rapidly and the need for sound risk management has become one of its key priorities as it attempts to secure additional funding for further expansion. It currently has a board which consists of a Managing Director, Finance Director and Retail Director, plus two non-executive directors (a lawyer and a retired bank manager) who have recently been recruited to operate an audit committee in advance of becoming a listed entity.

The board has been in discussions with a number of financial institutions about possible future investment and the subject of the organisation's risk appetite has come up. Some board members have previously ignored the idea of considering risks as they have always operated in this industry and feel they know the business well enough without having to justify their approach to anyone else.

You have been asked by one of the non-executives to draft a short briefing note explaining why risk is always present and why the organisation may actually seek to embrace more risk.

Required

Draft the briefing note, explaining why risk is always going to be present for this organisation and why more risk may actually be worth seeking. **(5 marks)**

Professional skills marks are available for demonstrating **commercial acumen** skills in showing insight into why risk may be worth seeking. **(2 marks)**

(Total = 7 marks)

Solution

2.3 Identify risks

You will be expected to be able to identify and evaluate the key risks and their impact on organisations and projects. Risk identification is a continuous, iterative process. Consequently, organisations need to consider how best to identify risks before they can evaluate them and eventually respond appropriately. Methods for identifying risk include:

(a)   Brainstorming and workshops
(b)   Stakeholder consultation
(c)   Benchmarking
(d)   Scenario analysis
(e)   Results of audits and inspections
(f)   Use of standard checklists

Activity 4: Airline risks

ACCA Professional skills focus

Commercial acumen: Demonstrate awareness

You are a senior manager working in the risk management department of British Airways (BA), which is described on its website as a 'full service global airline, offering year-round low fares with an extensive global route network flying to and from centrally-located airports' (British Airways, 2019).

The activities undertaken by BA in addition to offering flights include:

- Fleet
- Engineering
- Ground handling services
- Corporate entertainment
- Listed company information
- Corporate responsibility

You have been asked to draft a list of key risks faced by BA as part of the board's induction process.

Required

Draft these training resources by identifying at least five key risks faced by BA (if you feel unfamiliar with BA, you could select a different airline organisation on which to base your analysis). **(5 marks)**

Professional skills marks are available for demonstrating **commercial acumen** in demonstrating awareness of the wider factors affecting BA's risks. **(2 marks)**

(Total = 7 marks)

Solution

Performance Objective 4 'Governance risk and control' of the Practical Experience Requirement requires you to 'evaluate and identify areas of risk including data and cyber security risks – assessing the probability of fraud, error and other hazards in your area of responsibility, and the impact they would have' (ACCA, 2019b). The following section focuses on the different types of risk factors that could affect an organisation. You are strongly advised to take the time to read through this content carefully prior to attempting PER Performance Objective 4.

2.3.1 Risk factors

A key aspect at this stage is the identification of **risk factors** that could impact upon the successful implementation of strategy or the achievement of a firm's objectives.

Typical risk factors could include the following.

External events such as economic changes, political developments or technological advances

Internal events such as equipment problems, human error or difficulties with products

Leading event indicators – conditions that could give rise to an event such as overdue customer balances which may lead to default.

Escalation triggers are events happening or levels being reached that require immediate action, such as making changes after a deadline has passed or an effective response following product failure

Related risks are risks that are connected because the causes of the risk are the same (such as risks brought about by economic uncertainty) or because one risk links to another (increasing sales volatility can lead to risks over the price of raw materials)

Correlated risks are two risks that vary together. If **positive correlation** exists, the risks will increase or decrease together (such as legal risks from being sued and the associated reputation risk). If **negative correlation** exists, one risk will increase as the other decreases and vice versa (for example, the risk of stock out reduces as the risk of over-supply of production increases). The **correlation coefficient** measures the extent of any correlation.

2.3.2 Strategic and operational risks

Strategic risk: The risk that arises from longer-term decisions or events.

Operational risk: Risk that arises from the normal day-to-day activity of a company.

The main differences between strategic and operational risks relate to:

(a) Scope of impact
(b) Source of risk
(c) Duration of impact
(d) Scale of financial and resource consequences

Strategic risks are those risks that relate to the fundamental long-term decisions that directors take about the future of an organisation. The most significant risks are focused on the impact they would have on the company's ability to survive in the **long term**, such as:

Changes in technology
Market or industry sector changes
Product or competitor issues
The failure to innovate

| Macro-economic factors |
| Issues with commodities |
| Capital availability |

Operational risk is the risk of loss from a failure of internal business and control processes and will affect **day-to-day operations**. Operational risk includes losses arising from:

| Internal control deficiencies |
| Human error |
| Fraud |
| Business interruption |
| Loss of key personnel |

2.3.3 Categories of risk

We have already seen a number of different types of **risk factor** and considered some of the **causes** of risks, as well as their strategic and/or operational impact. How can we start to make sense of all this? There is **no standard method for categorising risks** – however, one possible method of categorisation is as follows:

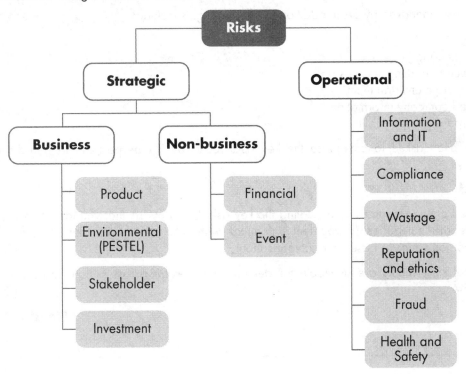

Exam Focus Point

Task 1(b) in the March/ June 2019 exam released by ACCA required an assessment of the major risks facing the featured entity, a clothing retailer called SmartWear, and its current business model. Candidates were expected to suggest appropriate actions to mitigate the risks identified. Professional skills marks were on offer for evaluation skills in assessing the risks identified at SmartWear in an objective manner.

The examining team noted that task 1(b) was generally answered well with the majority of candidates able to identify several of the key risks and to provide practical actions. 'Many candidates adopted a tabular format to answer this question which allowed for more focused answers. The table reduced the temptation to include unnecessary material and deterred unnecessary repetition and could be produced relatively quickly so was a good use of limited answering time'. (ACCA, 2019a). To earn the 4 professional skills marks on offer candidates needed to assess the most significant risks facing SmartWear, and to recommend mitigation actions which were both proportionate and would be effective at addressing the major risks identified. The answer needed to be presented in the specified format of a briefing paper.

Activity 5: Categorising airline risks

ACCA Professional skills focus

Evaluation: Assess

You are a senior manager working in the risk management department of British Airways (BA), which is described on its website as a 'full service global airline, offering year-round low fares with an extensive global route network flying to and from centrally-located airports' (British Airlines, 2019).

The activities undertaken by BA in addition to offering flights include:

- Fleet
- Engineering
- Ground handling services
- Corporate entertainment
- Listed company information
- Corporate responsibility

You have been asked to categorise the key risks faced by BA as part of the board's induction process.

Required

Draft these training resources by allocating the key risks faced by BA that you identified in Activity 4 to suitable risk categories (if you feel unfamiliar with BA, you could select a different airline organisation on which to base your categorisation).   **(5 marks)**

Professional skills marks are available for demonstrating **evaluation** skills in assessing the risks faced by BA.   **(2 marks)**

(Total = 7 marks)

Solution

2.3.4 Risk register

Organisations should have formal methods of collecting information on risks and responses. A risk register **lists and prioritises the main risks** an organisation faces and is used as the basis for decision making on how to deal with risks. The register also details **who is responsible for dealing** with risks and the **actions taken**. The register should show the risk levels **before** and **after** control action is taken, to facilitate a cost-benefit analysis of controls. Once identified and categorised, risks can be included within the firm's **risk register** and kept under review.

An advantage of separating risks into **strategic** and **operational** is to ensure they are considered by the most appropriate level of management. Some organisations choose to maintain separate risk registers for strategic and operational risks.

2.4 Assess risks

2.4.1 Techniques

How are risks assessed? This may involve **quantifying** risks and what would happen if they were to materialise. There are different ways to do this, including **statistical** techniques (such as **value at risk**, **regression analysis** and **simulation**). Other techniques for carrying out risk quantification include **sensitivity analysis** and calculating **accounting ratios** (such as margins, gearing, days, interest cover and current ratio). Another way of quantifying risk is by using **expected values (EV)**:

> **Formula to learn**
>
> **Expected value of loss = Probability of loss × Impact or size of potential loss**

Where there is uncertainty and a range of possible future outcomes has been quantified (often best, worst and most likely) probabilities can be assigned to these outcomes and a weighted average (expected value) of those outcomes calculated:

> **Formula to learn**
>
> $EV = \Sigma px$

where **p** is the **probability** of the outcome occurring and **x** is the **value of the outcome** (profit or cost). When faced with a number of alternative decisions, the one with the highest EV may be selected.

BPP
LEARNING
MEDIA

2.4.2 Risk maps

Key term

> **Risk maps (sometimes called heat maps):** These show risks in a visual way by plotting them on a chart according to their impact and likelihood.

Quantifying risks can bring problems, for example, giving a false impression of accuracy, so **qualitative techniques** are often used as well, such as visual techniques like **risk mapping**.

A risk map or **heat map** can be drawn, as a chart or graph, using risks from a risk register and each series of risks can be plotted on this map in order to decide on the best way to manage them. A typical risk map is a chart with one scale for **severity** or **impact** of loss and the other scale for **frequency** or **likelihood** of loss. The approach to managing the risks should vary according to their position on the risk map.

The **solid line** in the diagram below is known as the **risk tolerance boundary** and reflects the company's **risk appetite**. This allows the company to **prioritise** its treatment of different risks. It may choose to spend less on managing one risk in order to release funds to manage another more effectively.

An example of a Heat Map

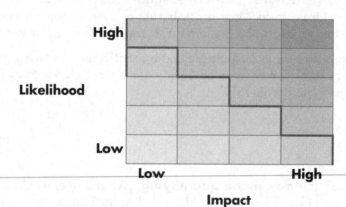

Diagram: Heat Map

2.4.3 Subjectivity

One problem with risk assessment is the problem of **subjectivity** – something like assessing the risk of getting a head when tossing a coin can be assessed objectively but estimating the risk of an accident occurring or its impact could still be heavily influenced by subjectivity.

Real world example

The 2009 Turner report highlighted faulty measurement techniques as a reason why many UK financial institutions underestimated their risk position. The required capital for their trading activities was excessively light. Turner also highlighted the rapid growth of off-balance sheet vehicles that were highly leveraged but were not included in standard risk measures. However, the crisis demonstrated the economic risks of these vehicles, with liquidity commitments and reputational concerns requiring banks to take the assets back onto their balance sheets, increasing measured leverage significantly.

Turner also saw the complexity of the techniques as being a problem in itself. 'The very complexity of the mathematics used to measure and manage risk made it increasingly difficult for top management and boards to assess and exercise judgements over risks being taken. Mathematical sophistication ended up not containing risk but providing false assurance that other *prima facie* indicators of increasing risk (eg rapid credit extension and balance sheet growth) could be safely ignored.' (Turner, 2009)

2.5 Respond to risks

2.5.1 TARA

Key term

TARA: The model referred to when considering responses to risks – **T**ransfer, **A**void, **R**educe and **A**ccept.

In order to respond to risk, organisations tend to consider the following approaches for the following combinations of likelihood and impact:

- Risk **T**ransfer – low likelihood but high impact
- Risk **A**voidance – high likelihood and high impact
- Risk **R**eduction – high likelihood and low impact
- Risk **A**cceptance – low likelihood and low impact

Plotting them on a chart showing likelihood and impact would look like this:

		Impact	
		Low	**High**
High		**R**educe	**A**void
Likelihood			
Low		**A**ccept	**T**ransfer

Diagram: TARA risk management matrix

You should remember this as the **TARA** model. This is a means of matching a suitable strategy to a given risk, although it may not always deliver perfect results every time as the following activity will show.

Activity 6: TARA

ACCA Professional skills focus

Analysis: Consider

You work as a freelance risk consultant supporting organisations who are interested in setting up their own risk management functions. You have been approached by a company that is keen to follow best practice and has heard of the 'TARA' model but is unclear about how the model works.

You have agreed to produce some training materials that illustrate how the TARA model works using the following four scenarios:

- Shoplifting in a supermarket: this happens quite often but items stolen tend to be of low value
- A courier company experiencing minor, infrequent delays due to 'rush hour' traffic
- Repairing significant property damage arising from unexpected flooding
- Loss of human life as part of drilling for oil on an oil rig

Required

Create the training materials, suggesting a suitable risk response for each of the four scenarios listed above by plotting them on the TARA model shown below. **(6 marks)**

Professional skills marks are available for demonstrating **analysis** skills in considering how the risks identified fit into the TARA model. **(2 marks)**

(Total = 8 marks)

BPP LEARNING MEDIA

Solution

	Impact	
	Low	**High**
High		
Likelihood		
Low		

Syllabus link

Risk and risk management form a key part of the Strategic Business Leader syllabus, and link closely to the Ethics and Professional Skills Module (EPSM) that you are required to complete on your journey towards full ACCA membership. Part of the EPSM requires you to make recommendations in light of having analysed different situations facing an organisation, part of which may involve considering organisational risk. You are therefore strongly advised to complete the EPSM before sitting your Strategic Business Leader exam as this will assist with your exam preparations.

The risk management process helps organisations to **prioritise** their risks but cannot **eliminate** them altogether: usually **gross risks** (risks without any mitigation) and **residual risks** (risks that remain once management action has been taken to address them) are compared to assess how **effective** such **risk response** action has been. Taking the example of oil exploration above – clearly, the **gross risks** are significant and without the ability to deploy suitable controls (such as protective clothing, heavy machinery and training) such activity would probably be **avoided**. However, once these steps have been taken, the **residual risk** is low enough to be considered **acceptable** (clearly, the risk appetite of such an organisation would come into play here as well).

2.5.2 ALARP

Key term

ALARP: Refers to 'as low as reasonably practicable' – a pragmatic approach to managing risks that seeks the most appropriate response to any risk by balancing cost and benefit.

Some businesses face risks which are high likelihood and high consequence. If they occur as part of their core business (for example, oil exploration or providing fire and rescue services) they are unlikely to avoid such risks, so adopt a pragmatic approach, trading off **cost** and **benefit** by implementing controls appropriate to the level of risk faced. This approach is sometimes referred to as **ALARP** – **'as low as reasonably practicable'** and is illustrated by the diagram below.

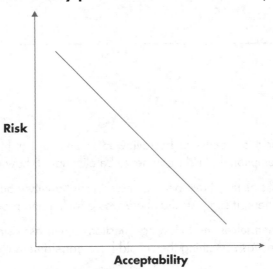

2.5.3 Diversification of risks

Imagine a company that has identified a series of risks and identified them as being **positively correlated** (for example, manufacturing products that are only in demand during warm, dry and sunny weather). What happens when the weather is no longer sunny? There is a risk that demand will fall and you will not achieve your targets. One response to this is also having a series of **negatively correlated** risks to balance these out (also manufacturing products that are popular in cold, wet and windy weather). This approach to spreading risks is often referred to as a **portfolio** and can be observed in many organisations.

Key terms

Correlated risks: Two risks that vary together. If positive correlation exists, the risks will increase or decrease together. If negative correlation exists, one risk will increase as the other decreases and vice versa.

Related risks: Risks that are connected because the causes of the risk are the same.

Diversification: Offsetting risks that are negatively correlated to balance their impact and likelihood regardless of the circumstances (sometimes called a 'portfolio' approach).

Exercise 2: Diversifying risks

Required

List **THREE** examples of organisations that have diversified their risks using a portfolio approach.

How have they diversified their risks?

LEARNING
MEDIA

Solution

2.6 Monitoring

2.6.1 Review the process

Clearly, it makes sense for this process to be reviewed to ensure it is fit for purpose and actually manages risks. On the assumption that risks can never be eliminated, how can you assess this?

One way is to compare risks as they have been assessed with how they actually materialise – if there is any significant variance here, it suggests that there was a fault in the process somewhere.

Organisations might ask themselves the following questions when assessing whether they managed risks well enough or if there was something they could have done differently:

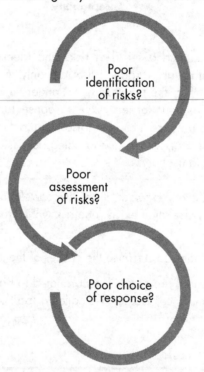

Fundamentally, whatever the reason, the process requires some form of review to ensure each of the stages is operating as expected (and suitable remedial action taken as a result).

2.6.2 Dynamic nature of risks

How often should this process be assessed? It depends! Best practice in corporate governance recommends an **annual review** of risk management processes and controls to ensure effectiveness.

However, if you consider the **dynamic nature** of risks (for example, during a terrorist attack or a period of economic uncertainty) such a review may occur far more frequently and in the case of an ongoing situation, this may be reviewed constantly.

Similarly, if you consider the ways in which risk varies in relation to the **size**, **structure** and **development** of an organisation, this adds more weight to the argument that risks should be managed as frequently as is appropriate to the circumstances in any situation.

Essential reading

See Chapter 7 section 2 of the Essential Reading, available in Appendix 2 of the digital edition of the Workbook, for more detail on the types of situation that could lead to significant rapid changes in an organisation's risks.

2.6.3 Adapt if necessary

It seems logical that if any improvements are identified during this review process, the system of risk management should be updated as soon as possible to take such feedback into account.

2.7 Start again!

As you might expect, the **cycle** has come **full circle** and any issues identified with the risks identified, the quality of their assessment and the suitability of any responses have all been addressed. The process of risk management can **begin again** and will continue to run its course until the **next iteration** is complete. Risks don't tend to go away, so neither should the system for managing them!

Assessing and managing risk

The relationship between organisational strategy and risk management strategy

Understanding stakeholder responses to risks
Link to organisational strategy Stakeholder view

Embedding risk in an organisation's culture and values
- Why?
- How?

Risk management process

Who is responsible for risk?
- Risk committee
- Risk manager

Risk appetite
- Risk averse vs risk seeker
- Risk capacity

Identify risks
- Risk factors
- Strategic and operational
- Categories of risk
- Risk registers

Assess risks
- Techniques
- Risk maps
- Subjectivity, including frequency vs severity

Respond to risks
- TARA
- ALARP – as low as reasonably practicable
- Diversification of risks

Monitoring
- Review the process
- Dynamic nature of risks
- Adapt if necessary

Start again!

Knowledge diagnostic

1. Different stakeholder groups have different views of risk (not all of them bad) which can influence the way an organisation responds to and interacts with risk

2. Risks can be managed by a variety of different people and approaches within an organisation

3. Risk can be categorised in a number of different ways but always requires visibility for effective management

4. Risk assessment can be carried out in a number of different ways – however, most tend to focus on assessing risks for impact and likelihood

5. Risk never goes away – just like the weather, it is dynamic and does not stand still – so you have to find a way of keeping on top of it!

Question practice

Now try the question below from the Further question practice bank (available in the digital edition of the Workbook):

Q7 *Azure Airline*

Further reading

There are articles on the ACCA website written by members of the SBL examining team which are relevant to your studies and which would be useful to read:

Strategic and operational risks

This article explores the difference between strategic and operational risks.

COSO enterprise risk management framework

This article explores the key features of the COSO framework:

Approaching SBL overview

This article provides a one-page summary of the key features of the SBL exam.

Approaching SBL reading and planning

This article provides a one-page summary of how best to approach the SBL exam.

SBL – 10 things to learn from the September 2018 sitting

This article highlights some of the issues that ACCA identified in candidates' answers during the September 2018 SBL exam sitting. The article provides some useful advice for improving your chances of passing the SBL exam.

Strategic Business Leader – The importance of effective communication for SBL

This article provides some useful insights into the different formats which you will be expected to use when answering SBL exam tasks.

Own research

- Consider other examples of risk management models that can be seen to support the approach we have discussed:

    - COSO ERM cube
    - CIMA Risk Management Cycle model
    - Deal and Kennedy: risk, feedback and reward
    - Institute of Risk Management – a risk management standard
    - COCO standard (Canadian Institute of Chartered Accountants)

- From your analysis of all the various models of risk management that exist, how many of them can you see working in real life? Would any of these approaches to risk management be appropriate for your own organisation?

- Below is a link to a news article relating to the problems that TSB encountered in 2018 when the company undertook a planned upgrade of its customer online banking services. Read the article and consider what sort of risk management TSB would have needed to operate to have reduced its exposure to the risks that it encountered.

    https://www.theguardian.com/business/2018/jun/06/timeline-of-trouble-how-the-tsb-it-meltdown-unfolded

Exercise answers

Exercise 1

(a) **Shareholders** are not necessarily risk averse, but they will expect higher returns from high risk companies. They may well have acquired their shares to fit into a balanced portfolio. They will be concerned if there is an unexpected change in the company's risk appetite and may choose to invest elsewhere.

(b) **Debt providers** are most concerned about the risk of non-payment and they can take various actions with potentially serious consequences such as:

- Denial of credit
- Higher interest charges
- Applying restrictive covenants
- Requiring security (eg mortgage)
- Putting the company into liquidation

(c) **Employees** will be concerned about threats to their job prospects (money, promotion, benefits and satisfaction) and ultimately threats to the jobs themselves. The variety of actions employees can take include:

- Pursuing of their own goals rather than shareholder interests
- Industrial action
- Refusal to co-operate
- Resignation

(d) **Customers** will be concerned with threats to their getting the goods or services that they have been promised, or not getting the value from the goods or services that they expect. The risk to the firm is that they could take their business elsewhere. Perhaps the organisation has a reputation based on quality, value or customer service – these can be eroded if risks are taken to compromise the achievement of these.

(e) **Governments and regulators** will be particularly concerned with risks that the organisation does not act as a good corporate citizen, implementing, for example, poor employment or environmental policies. A number of the variety of actions that can be taken could have serious consequences. Government can impose tax increases or further regulation or take legal action. Pressure groups' tactics can include publicity, direct action, sabotage or pressure on government, regulators or other stakeholders.

Exercise 2

Some examples of types of organisation that have diversified their risks using a portfolio approach (clearly there are many others that you could have considered):

- **Supermarkets** – value brands, named brands and highest quality (not to mention diversifying into books, games, multimedia, banking, insurance, home goods...)

- **Clothing retailers** – again, ranges to suit different budgets for men, women and children plus changing styles and fashions on a regular basis

- **Professional firms** that cater for all stages of a client's life cycle: start-up and advisory; accounting and tax; acquisitions; mergers; disposals; insolvency...

- **Motor manufacturers** who offer a range of vehicles to suit people's tastes and needs (usually under different brands, such as Jaguar Land Rover or BMW Mini)

BPP
LEARNING
MEDIA

Internal control systems

8

Learning objectives

On completion of this chapter, you should be able to:

	Syllabus reference no.
Evaluate the key components or features of effective internal control systems	F1(a)
Assess the need for adequate information flows to management for the purposes of the management of internal control and risk	F1(b)
Evaluate the effectiveness and potential weaknesses of internal control systems	F1(c)
Discuss and advise on the importance of sound internal control and compliance with legal and regulatory requirements and the consequences to an organisation of poor control and non-compliance	F1(d)
Recommend new internal control systems or changes to the components of existing systems to help prevent fraud, error or waste	F1(e)
Examine the need for an internal audit function in the light of regulatory and organisational requirements	F2(a)
Justify the importance of auditor independence in all client-auditor situations (including internal audit) and the role of internal audit in compliance	F2(b)
Respond credibly to requests and enquiries from internal or external auditors	F2(c)
Justify the importance of having an effective internal audit committee overseeing the internal audit function	F2(d)
Assess the appropriate responses to auditors' recommendations	F2(e)
Justify the need for reports on internal controls to shareholders	F3(a)
Discuss the typical contents of a report on internal control and audit	F3(b)
Assess how internal controls underpin and provide information for reliable financial reporting	F3(c)

Business and exam context

Just as we saw with risk management, there are many different approaches to setting up a system of internal control. In this chapter we will be looking at the main components that you would expect to be considered best practice when it comes to internal control systems.

We will also look at how the audit committee, assisted by an internal audit function, manages this system and the type of information created in various reports that can be used to support an organisation's goals and objectives.

Chapter overview

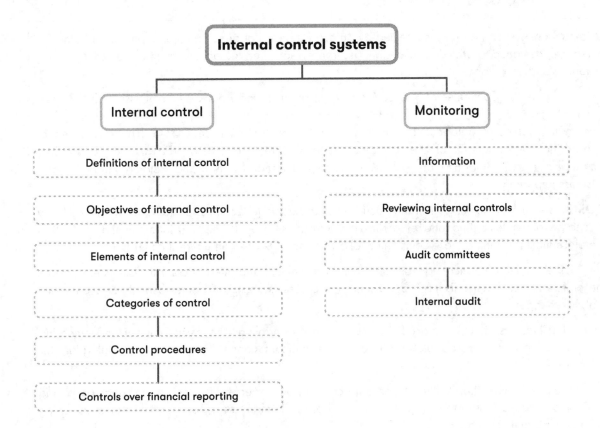

1 Internal control

1.1 Definitions of internal control

Key term

> **Internal control:** 'Is a process affected by an entity's board of directors, management and other personnel, designed to provide reasonable assurance regarding the achievement of objectives, reporting and compliance.'
>
> (Committee of Sponsoring Organisations of the Treadway Commission, 2013: p.3)

Two main sources of guidance on internal controls are contained in **COSO** (The Committee of Sponsoring Organisations of the Treadway Commission) and the UK **Financial Reporting Council's (FRC)** Guidance on Risk Management, Internal Control and Related Financial and Business Reporting.

COSO (2013) has the support of the Securities and Exchange Commission (SEC) which is the body in charge of implementing and enforcing the Sarbanes-Oxley (SOx) legislation in the USA. It is therefore most relevant to those companies following the SOx rules on internal controls.

The **FRC's** (2014) guidance highlights that risk management and internal control systems encompass the policies, culture, organisation, behaviours, processes, systems and other aspects of a company that, taken together:

- 'Facilitate its effective and efficient operation by enabling it to assess current and emerging risks, respond appropriately to risks and significant control failures, and to safeguard its assets;

- Help to reduce the likelihood and impact of: poor judgement in decision making; risk-taking that exceeds the levels agreed by the board; human error; or control processes being deliberately circumvented;

- Help ensure the quality of internal and external reporting; and

- Help ensure compliance with applicable laws and regulations, and also with internal policies with respect to the conduct of business.' (FRC, 2014).

According to the FRC (2014), the board also needs to consider the following factors:

- 'The operation of the relevant controls and control processes

- The effectiveness and relative costs and benefits of particular controls

- The impact of the values and culture of the company, and the way that teams and individuals are incentivised, on the effectiveness of the systems.' (FRC, 2014).

Key terms

> **COSO:** The US standard approach to internal controls which supports 'RORCS'.
>
> **RORCS:** The objectives of any system of internal control: **r**isk management; **o**perations; **r**eporting; **c**ompliance; **s**afeguarding assets.
>
> **Sarbanes-Oxley (sometimes referred to as either SarbOx or just SOx):** Is the US corporate governance legislation (of greatest relevance here is the section that relates to the need for a management review of the effectiveness of internal controls).
>
> **FRC guidance:** UK guidance relating to risk management and internal controls.

Performance Objective 4 'Governance risk and control' of the Practical Experience Requirement requires you to 'operate according to the governance standards, policies and controls of your organisation' (ACCA, 2019b). To help you identify examples from your own work experience of applying internal controls it is important that you take the time to go through the contents of this chapter carefully. The focus of Chapter 8 is dedicated to internal control systems.

PER alert

1.2 Objectives of internal control

The objectives of internal control systems generally include:

- A focus on managing the **risks** facing the entity.
- Maintaining the effectiveness and efficiency of **operations**.
- Ensuring the reliability of both internal and external **reporting**.
- Supporting **compliance** with relevant laws and regulations.
- **Safeguarding** shareholder's investments and protecting the entity's assets.

This can be remembered using the mnemonic '**RORCS**'.

More practically, internal controls should help organisations to counter risk, maintain the quality of financial reporting and ensure compliance.

1.2.1 Inherent limitations of internal control

They provide **reasonable assurance** that organisations will achieve their objectives – however, there can never be more than **reasonable assurance** that their objectives are reached, because of **inherent limitations**, including:

The **costs of control** not **outweighing** their **benefits**	**Poor judgement** in decision making	The potential for **human error** or **fraud**
Collusion between employees	The **possibility of controls being bypassed** or overridden by management or employees	Controls only being designed to cope with **routine and not non-routine transactions**
Controls being unable to cope with **unforeseen circumstances**	Controls depending on the **method of data processing**	Controls not being **updated** over time

Illustration 1

The Swiss Cheese model is used to show the continual variability of the risks organisations face and how control systems interact to counter risks – and on occasions fail to interact, leading to accidents happening and losses being incurred.

The psychologist James Reason (1990), the creator of this model, hypothesised that most accidents are due to one or more of the four levels of failure.

- Organisational influences
- Unsafe supervision
- Preconditions for unsafe acts
- Unsafe acts

BPP
LEARNING
MEDIA

The first three elements in the list can be classified as 'latent failures', contributory factors that may have lain dormant for some time. Unsafe acts can be classified as active errors, human actions in the form of careless behaviour or errors.

Organisations can have control systems in place to counter all of these, but they can be seen as a series of slices of Swiss cheese. Slices of Swiss cheese have holes in them, and seeing control systems in these terms emphasises the weaknesses inherent in them. Reason went on to say that the holes in the systems are continually varying in size and position. Systems failure occurs and accidents happen when the holes in each system align.

Reason points out that, viewed this way, the focus shifts away from blaming a person to organisational and institutional responsibility. In the field of healthcare, on which Reason concentrated, blaming the person leads to a failure to realise that the same set of circumstances could lead to similar errors, regardless of the people involved. Ultimately it thwarts the development of safer healthcare institutions.

'Active failures are like mosquitoes. They can be swatted one by one but they still keep coming. The best remedies are to create more effective defences and to drain the swamps in which they breed, the swamps (being) the ever-present latent conditions.' (Reason, 1990)

Reason emphasised the importance of a sound reporting culture in a system of risk management. 'Without a detailed analysis of mishaps, incidents, near-misses and free lessons, we have no way of uncovering recurrent error traps or of knowing where the edge is until we fall over it.' (Reason, 1990)

Exercise 1: Importance of controls

Required

Evaluate the importance of effective internal controls to different stakeholder groups for a large retail organisation such as M&S (a UK-based retailer of clothes and food).

Solution

1.3 Elements of internal control

1.3.1 The COSO cube

COSO (2013) uses a diagram, commonly referred to as the COSO 'cube', which details the features of an internal control framework. The integrated components set out in the COSO cube (shown below) complement those discussed in the 2017 COSO publication 'Enterprise Risk Management: Integrating with Strategy and Performance'.

The COSO cube illustrates how internal controls operate across three dimensions, making it very flexible:

(a)   Objectives in relation to operations, reporting and compliance

(b)   Components of internal control

(c)   Levels of the organisation (such as entity level or operating unit) where the internal control applies

Enterprise Risk Management (ERM): The system used to apply the COSO approach.

Key term

While the COSO cube is unlikely to be examined in detail, it does provide a framework for identifying and managing risk (already seen in Chapter 7) and how that informs an organisation's internal controls.

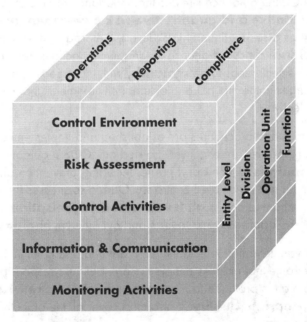

(Source: COSO Cube, 2013)

The COSO cube (2013) framework consists of a number of interrelated components.

Component	Explanation
Control Environment	This covers the tone of an organisation, and sets the basis for how risk is viewed and addressed by an organisation's people, including risk management philosophy and risk appetite, integrity and ethical values, and the environment in which they operate. The board's **attitude, participation and operating style** will be a key factor in determining the **strength** of the control environment. An unbalanced board, lacking appropriate technical knowledge and experience, diversity and strong, independent voices is unlikely to set the right tone. The example set by board members may be undermined by a failure of management in divisions or business units. Mechanisms to control line management may not be sufficient or may not be operated properly. Line managers may not be aware of their responsibilities or may fail to exercise them properly.
Risk Assessment	Risks are analysed considering likelihood and impact as a basis for determining how they should be managed. The analysis process should clearly determine which risks are controllable, and which risks are not controllable. The COSO guidance stresses the importance of employing a combination of **qualitative and quantitative risk assessment methodologies**. As well as assessing inherent risk levels, the organisation should also assess **residual risks** left after risk management actions have been taken. Risk assessment needs to be **dynamic**, with managers considering the effect of changes in the internal and external environments that may render controls ineffective.
Control Activities	Policies and procedures are established and implemented to help ensure the risk responses are effectively carried out. COSO guidance suggests that a **mix of controls** will be appropriate, including prevention and detection and manual and automated controls. COSO also stresses the need for controls to be performed across **all levels of the organisation**, at **different stages within business processes** and over the **technology environment**.
Information and Communication	Relevant information is identified, captured and communicated in a form and timeframe that enables people to carry out their responsibilities. The information provided to management needs to be **relevant and of appropriate quality**. It also must cover all the objectives shown on the top of the cube. Effective communication should be **broad** – flowing up, down and across the entity. There needs to be **communication with staff**. Communication of risk areas that are relevant to what staff do is an important means of strengthening the internal environment by embedding risk awareness in staff's thinking. There should also be effective communication with third parties such as shareholders and regulators.

Component	Explanation
Monitoring Activities	Risk control processes are monitored and modifications are made if necessary. Effective monitoring requires **active participation** by the board and senior management, and **strong information systems**, so the data senior managers need is fed to them.
	COSO has drawn a distinction between **regular review** (ongoing monitoring) and **periodic review** (separate evaluation). However, weaknesses are identified, the guidance stresses the importance of **feedback and action**. Weaknesses should be reported, assessed and their root causes corrected.

1.3.2 Financial Reporting Council's (FRC) Guidance on Risk Management, Internal Control and Related Financial and Business Reporting

The FRC follows a very similar approach to the COSO cube: 'A company's systems of risk management and internal control will include: risk assessment; management or mitigation of risks, including the use of control processes; information and communication systems; and processes for monitoring and reviewing their continuing effectiveness' (FRC, 2014).

Exam Focus Point

Question 3 of the Strategic Business Leader exam in September 2018 featured a task which asked candidates to assess the control weaknesses facing the featured organisation. The control weaknesses were set out in one of the exhibits. Candidates were expected to explain the consequences of the weaknesses identified and to provide recommendations for making improvements.

1.3.3 Advantages and disadvantages of internal control frameworks

There are a number of **advantages** of adopting an internal control framework. However, there have also been some **criticisms** made of models such as the COSO framework.

Advantages	Disadvantages
Alignment of risk appetite and strategy	Internal focus – ignores the external environment and the risks they pose
Link growth, risk and return	
Choose best risk response	Risk identification – prioritises sudden events over more gradual risks that evolve over time
Minimise surprises and losses	
Identify and manage risks across the organisation	Risk assessment – makes the process appear too simplistic and thus too easy
Provide responses to multiple risks	
Seize opportunities	Stakeholders' involvement in risk management often tends to get ignored
Rationalise capital	

BPP
LEARNING
MEDIA

Activity 1: Widmerpool

ACCA Professional skills focus

Scepticism: Challenge

You are a partner in an accountancy practice. One of your clients, Widmerpool, has expanded significantly over the last few years and is likely to seek a listing in a couple of years' time. You have been contacted by the Chief Executive, Mr Kenneth, for advice on areas relating to the control and risk management systems.

Up until recently, the main board has dealt with all significant issues relating to the company. In view of the current plans to seek a listing, Widmerpool has recently appointed three non-executive directors, and has used them to staff the audit committee that has just been established. Mr Kenneth is also wondering whether to set up a separate risk committee. Ideally he would like the audit committee's brief to be restricted to the accounting systems. There have recently been various incidents that appear to indicate problems with the ways Widmerpool's employees deal with risk.

In one incident a worker was trapped in a machine. A fellow worker tried to help and both were seriously injured. A subsequent investigation found that safety instructions appeared to be adequate and there was sufficient safety equipment available. However, staff had not been using the right equipment, appeared ignorant of safety issues and seemed unwilling or unable to comply with instructions.

In another instance one of Widmerpool's most significant suppliers, Stringham, with whom Widmerpool has been trying to develop much closer relations, supplied Widmerpool with confidential information concerning its operations. Two of Widmerpool's managers discussed these details in a local restaurant, but left the documentation relating to Stringham behind when they left the restaurant. Another customer removed this information and offered to sell it to one of Stringham's main competitors. The competitor declined the offer, and reported the situation to the police and Stringham. As a result Stringham has decided to terminate its relationship with Widmerpool. Widmerpool's organisational handbook stresses the need to keep sensitive business information confidential, but does not provide detailed guidance.

Widmerpool recently carried out a staff satisfaction survey. One of the comments made was that as the company has grown bigger, the board has become more distant from operations and seems primarily concerned with ensuring that profits increase each year. As a result, staff have become laxer in following internal procedures, as they believe that they are being judged solely on whether their department fulfils its financial targets.

Required

Draft the response to Mr Kenneth, explaining why Widmerpool's internal guidance and control procedures have failed to ensure that Widmerpool's employees deal carefully with business risks.

(8 marks)

Professional skills marks are available for demonstrating **scepticism** skills in challenging the current controls in place.

(2 marks)

(Total = 10 marks)

Solution

Exam Focus Point

The Strategic Business Leader specimen 2 exam featured a public sector rail company, Rail Co, which was responsible for providing rail services within the country of Beeland. The second question required candidates to act in the capacity of an assistant auditor, working for the National Audit Authority (NAA), the Beeland government's audit authority. The NAA was conducting an investigation into the performance of Rail Co following negative publicity relating to poor levels of service. Candidates were provided with a newspaper article which highlighted the deteriorating performance of Rail Co and a copy of Rail Co's latest board minutes which highlighted a number of operational issues. Part (b) of question 2 asked candidates to draft a letter to be sent to the Chair of the Rail Co Trust Board which reviewed 'the effectiveness of the internal controls at Rail Co using evidence from the minutes of the latest Rail Co board meeting and any other suitable source'. Candidates were also expected to provide a justification 'that the chief executive of Rail Co [was] failing in his fiduciary duties to the trustees [...]' (ACCA, 2017a).

This task was worth 8 technical marks and tested the ACCA Professional Skill of Scepticism. To produce a good answer candidates needed to make use of the specified exhibit information, as well as addressing the two distinct parts of the task ie the effectiveness of internal controls and to justify the view that the chief executive was failing in his fiduciary duties. To earn the two professional skills marks candidates needed to demonstrate scepticism by 'questioning the opinions and assertions made by the chief executive at the recent board meeting' (ACCA, 2017a).

1.4 Categories of control

1.4.1 Corporate, management, business process and transaction controls

This classification is based on the idea of a pyramid of controls, from corporate controls at the top of the organisation, to transaction controls over the day-to-day operations.

Corporate controls include general policy statements, the established core culture and values and overall monitoring procedures such as the audit committee

Management controls encompass planning and performance monitoring, the system of accountabilities to superiors and risk evaluation

Business process controls include authorisation limits, validation of input, and reconciliation of different sources of information

Transaction controls include complying with prescribed procedures and accuracy and completeness checks

1.4.2 Administrative and accounting controls

Administrative controls are concerned with achieving the objectives of the organisation and with implementing policies. The controls relate to the following aspects of control systems. • Establishing a suitable organisation structure • The division of managerial authority • Reporting responsibilities • Channels of communication	**Accounting controls** aim to provide accurate accounting records and to achieve accountability. They apply to the following. • The recording of transactions • Establishing responsibilities for records, transactions and assets

1.4.3 Prevent, detect, correct and direct controls

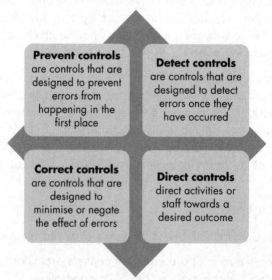

The existence of these types of controls are highly relevant in addressing issues relating to human error and issues of waste in the workplace.

Human error

Human error concerns an unintended action by an individual which has led to an undesirable outcome. Human error is often caused by carelessness, distraction or fatigue. A transposition error where two figures are erroneously switched around when entering invoices into an accounting computer system is an example of human error.

Waste

Wastage in the workplace is concerned with the loss of organisational resources. Waste in the workplace is often associated with the loss of physical materials and/or inventory in traditional manufacturing environments but can also extend to wastage in terms of lost employee time.

Real world example

The following real-world example illustrates how prevent, detect, correct and direct controls can be applied in different contexts in the workplace when addressing human error and waste.

Internal controls to reduce instances of human error might include:

Prevent

The finance manager in the finance department may conduct a review of the list of supplier payments prepared by the accounts clerk prior to authorisation. Such a review might involve checking the invoices received from individual suppliers against the goods received notes and against the list of supplier payments. This three-way match of documents should help to prevent payments being made for items not received.

Detect

The preparation of a regular bank reconciliation should help the organisation to detect whether there are any errors between the organisation's bank statements and underlying accounting records. This should help to identify any transposition errors in the accounting records.

Correct

To reduce the impact of an employee accidentally opening an email containing a virus which would corrupt the data held on the organisation's computer network, a daily back-up of all data held should be taken to reduce the level of disruption.

Direct

Machinery in a factory may be set up so that it will not operate without the operator using the required safety guards. Such a control should stop the operator from harming themselves by erroneously trying to use the machine.

Internal controls to reduce instances of waste might include:

Prevent:

Ensuring that inventory and resources coming into the organisation are counted in and are reviewed prior to use, to ensure that they are fit for purpose. This should help to prevent resources being used in production and throughout the organisation which will need to be scrapped later on. Such a control would also save the time of those workers that would have been lost in working with the inputs that had to be scrapped.

Detect

During a production run of a particular item a factory manager might compare the amount of raw material used to produce 100 units against the cost card information or budget to detect any variances in usage. Such a control may help the organisation to identify inefficiencies in its production processes.

Correct

A warehouse manager might conduct a regular review of all inventory held to identify any items nearing the point at which they become obsolete. Such a control helps to ensure that all items of inventory are being used in the correct order i.e. oldest inventory items are used in production before the newest. This allows for corrective steps to be taken by using all inventory up and helps to reduce inventory holding costs.

Direct

To ensure that a firm's lorry drivers are to work safely the organisation may require that all drivers have to undergo a sobriety or drugs test before every long-haul delivery they undertake. Such a control forces the organisation's drivers to comply and helps to reduce the scope for deliveries to turn up late and/or damaged.

Essential reading

See Chapter 8 section 1 of the Essential Reading, available in Appendix 2 of the digital edition of the Workbook, for more detail regarding controls.

1.4.4 Discretionary and non-discretionary controls

Discretionary controls are controls that, as their name suggests, are subject to human discretion. For example, a control that goods are not dispatched to a customer with an overdue account may be discretionary (the customer may have a good previous payment record or be too important to risk antagonising).	**Non-discretionary controls** are provided automatically by the system and cannot be bypassed, ignored or overridden. For example, checking the signature on a purchase order is discretionary, whereas inputting a PIN number when using a cash dispensing machine is a non-discretionary control.

1.4.5 Voluntary and mandated controls

These types of controls are split between those that are required and therefore have to be implemented and those that are not required but the organisation chooses to implement. Deciding on which to prioritise will be the challenge for organisations in such industries.

Voluntary controls
- Chosen by the organisation to support the management of the business.
- Authorisation controls, certain key transactions requiring approval by a senior manager, are voluntary controls.

Mandated controls
- Required by law and imposed by external authorities.
- A financial services organisation may be subject to the control that only people authorised by the financial services regulatory body may give investment advice.

1.4.6 General and application controls

These controls are used to reduce the risks associated with the computer environment.

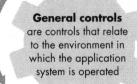

General controls are controls that relate to the environment in which the application system is operated

Application controls are controls that prevent, detect and correct errors and irregularities as transactions flow through the business system (basically inputs, processes and outputs)

1.4.7 Financial and non-financial controls

Financial controls focus on the key transaction areas, with the emphasis being on the **safeguarding of assets** and the **maintenance of proper accounting records** and **reliable financial information**. Financial controls need to ensure that: • Assets and transactions are recorded **completely** and **accurately** in the accounting records. • Entries are posted **correctly** within the accounting records • **Cut-off** is applied correctly, so that transactions are recorded in the correct year • The accounting system **can provide** the necessary data to prepare the annual report and accounts • The accounting system **does provide the data as required** – that the system is organised to supply on time and in a usable format the data that underpins the accounts and the other content of the annual report	Non-financial controls tend to concentrate on wider performance issues. • **Quantitative non-financial controls** include numeric techniques, such as performance indicators, the balanced scorecard and activity-based management. • **Qualitative non-financial controls** include many topics we have already discussed, such as organisational structures, rules and guidelines, strategic plans and human resource policies.

Syllabus links

In Chapter 9 further consideration is given to the types of internal controls which can be used by organisations to address instances of fraud.

1.5 Control procedures

Although we have seen the various categories of control that could be used by an organisation, each will rely on a number of procedures to operate effectively. Commonly used control procedures (or control activities) can be remembered using the 'APIPS' mnemonic.

BPP
LEARNING
MEDIA

Key terms

APIPS: The most common forms of control activity: **a**uthorisation; **p**erformance reviews; **i**nformation processing; **p**hysical controls; **s**egregation of duties.

Control procedures: The activities that make up any system of internal control (see 'APIPS' above).

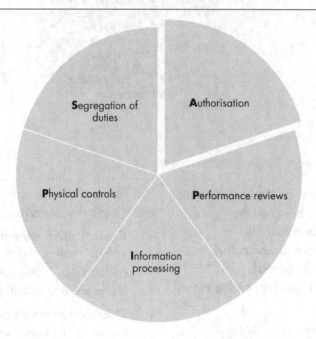

(Diagram: APIPS)

1.6 Controls over financial reporting

Controls over financial reporting need to be focused on **key financial reporting objectives**.

This should help managers carry out effective risk assessments and mean they only implement **appropriate controls**, rather than implementing 'standard' controls that are not useful for the business.

In particular robust controls need to be in place to ensure the quality of financial reporting – for example:

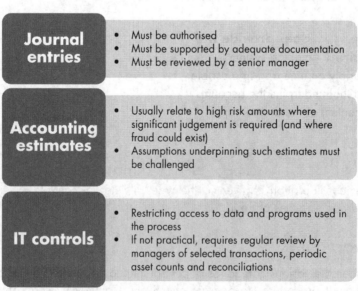

Journal entries
- Must be authorised
- Must be supported by adequate documentation
- Must be reviewed by a senior manager

Accounting estimates
- Usually relate to high risk amounts where significant judgement is required (and where fraud could exist)
- Assumptions underpinning such estimates must be challenged

IT controls
- Restricting access to data and programs used in the process
- If not practical, requires regular review by managers of selected transactions, periodic asset counts and reconciliations

Other particularly important controls to ensure the accuracy of financial reporting information include:

- **Full documentation** of assets, liabilities and transactions

- **Matching of source documents** and accounting records
- **Confirmation** of information by suppliers, customers and banks
- **Reconciliation of information** from different source documents and other sources
- **Completeness checks** over **documents** and **accounting entries**
- **Reperformance** of accounting calculations

Activity 2: PKG High School Governing Body

ACCA Professional skills focus

Evaluation: Assess & Communication: Persuade

PKG High School has 900 pupils, 40 teachers, 10 support staff and a budget of $3 million per annum, 85% of which represents salary and salary-related costs. PKG's local authority allocates government funding for education to schools based on the number of pupils. It ensures that the government-approved curriculum is taught in all schools in its area with the aim of achieving government targets. All schools, including PKG, are subject to an independent financial audit as well as a scrutiny of their education provision by the local authority, and reports of both are presented to the school governing body.

The number of pupils determines the approximate number of teachers, based on class sizes of approximately 30 pupils. The salary costs for teachers are determined nationally and pay scales mean that more experienced teachers receive higher salaries. In addition, some teachers receive school-specific responsibility allowances.

PKG is managed on a day-to-day basis by the headteacher. The governance of each school is carried out by a governing body comprising the headteacher, elected representatives of parents of pupils, and members appointed by the local authority. The principles of good corporate governance apply to school governing bodies, which are accountable to parents and the local authority for the performance of the school.

The governing body holds the headteacher accountable for day-to-day school management, but on certain matters, such as building maintenance, the headteacher will seek expert advice from the local authority.

The governing body meets quarterly and has as its main responsibilities budgetary management, appointment of staff and education standards. The main control mechanisms exercised by the governing body include scrutiny of a year-to-date financial report, a quarterly non-financial performance report, teacher recruitment and approval of all purchases over $1,000. The headteacher has expenditure authority below this level.

The financial report (which is updated monthly) is presented at each meeting of the governing body. It shows the local authority's budget allocation to the school for the year, the expenditure incurred for each month and the year to date, and any unspent balances. Although there is no external financial reporting requirement for the school, the local authority will not allow any school to overspend its budget allocation in any financial year.

PKG's budget allocation is only just sufficient to provide adequate educational facilities. Additional funds are always required for teaching resources, building maintenance, and to upgrade computer equipment. The only flexibility the school has in budget management is to limit responsibility allowances and delay teacher recruitment. This increases pupil-contact time for individual teachers, however, and forces teachers to undertake preparation, marking and administration after school hours.

Note. A local authority (or council) carries out services for the local community and levies local taxes (or council tax) to fund most of its operations.

Required

You are a consultant acting on behalf of the local authority and have been asked to write a report to the main education committee in which you:

Evaluate the effectiveness of the governing body's control over PKG High School.   **(8 marks)**

Professional skills marks are available for demonstrating **evaluation** skills in assessing the priority and impact associated with particular control weaknesses.   **(2 marks)**

Recommend ways in which it might be improved.   **(8 marks)**

Professional skills marks are available for demonstrating **communication** skills in persuading the committee of the changes that need to be made.   **(2 marks)**

(Total = 20 marks)

Solution

2 Monitoring

2.1 Information

2.1.1 Types of information

In order to fulfil their duties effectively the board of directors (and sub-committees) need a wide range of information, which is used for a number of different reasons and will ultimately help in the monitoring of effective risk management and sound systems of internal control:

External information about competitors, suppliers, impact of future economic and social trends

Financial information – important for internal purposes and to fulfil legal requirements for true and fair external reporting

Non-financial information such as quality reports, customer complaints, human resource data

2.1.2 Levels of information

Strategic information	Tactical information	Operational information
Used to plan the objectives of the organisation, and to assess whether the objectives are being met in practice	Used to decide how the resources of the business should be employed, and to monitor how they are being, and have been, employed	Used to ensure that specific operational tasks are planned and carried out as intended
<ul><li>Derived from both **internal and external** sources</li><li>**Summarised** at a high level</li><li>Relevant to the **long term**</li><li>Concerned with the **whole organisation**</li><li>Often prepared on an '**ad hoc**' basis</li><li>Both **quantitative and qualitative**</li><li>Often **uncertain**, as the future cannot be accurately predicted</li></ul>	<ul><li>Primarily **generated internally** (but may have a limited external component)</li><li>**Summarised at a lower level**</li><li>Relevant to the **short and medium term**</li><li>Concerned with **activities or departments**</li><li>Prepared **routinely and regularly**</li><li>Based on **quantitative** measures</li></ul>	<ul><li>Derived from **internal** sources such as transaction recording methods</li><li>**Detailed**, being the processing of raw data (for example transaction reports listing all transactions in a period)</li><li>Relevant to the **immediate term**</li><li>**Task-specific**</li><li>Prepared very **frequently**</li><li>Largely **quantitative**</li></ul>

2.1.3 Qualities of good information

Information should be characterised as ACCURATE using the following qualities:

Quality	Example
Accurate	Figures should add up, the degree of rounding should be appropriate, there should be no typos, items should be allocated to the correct category, and assumptions should be stated for uncertain information.
Complete	Information should include everything that it needs to include, for example external data if relevant, comparative information and qualitative information as well as quantitative. Sometimes managers or strategic planners will need to build on the available information to produce a forecast using assumptions or extrapolations.
Cost-beneficial	It should not cost more to obtain the information than the benefit derived from having it. Providers of information should be given efficient means of collecting and analysing it. Users should not waste time working out what it means.
User-targeted	The needs of the user should be borne in mind; for instance, senior managers need strategic summaries, and junior managers need detail.
Relevant	Information that is not needed for a decision should be omitted, no matter how 'interesting' it may be.
Authoritative	The source of the information should be a reliable one. However, subjective information (eg expert opinions) may be required in addition to objective facts.
Timely	The information should be available when it is needed. It should also cover relevant time periods and the future as well as the past.
Easy to use	Information should be clearly presented, not excessively long, and sent using the right medium and communication channel (email, telephone, hard-copy report).

2.1.4 Sources of good information

The information directors need to be able to monitor controls effectively comes from a wide variety of sources. Directors can obtain information partly through their own efforts. However, if information systems are to work effectively, it is vital that they identify particular people or departments who are responsible for providing particular information.

Controls must be built into the systems to ensure that those responsible provide that data. This is particularly important in the context of the information that supports the contents of the financial statements and is used by internal and external audit and the audit committee.

What sort of information is required for good decisions to be made by an organisation? The diagram shows some of the typical sources of good information and the haphazard nature of how they sometimes emerge.

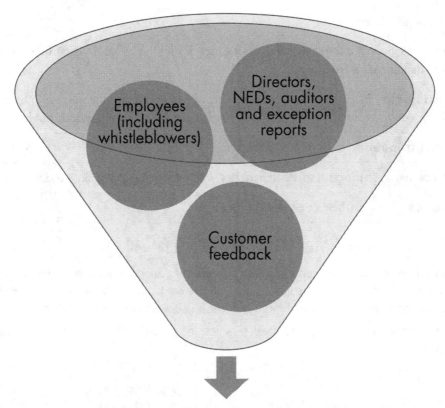

Information for good decision making

2.2 Reviewing internal controls

2.2.1 Internal control reports

In order to be able to carry out an effective review, boards or board committees should regularly receive and review reports and information on internal control, concentrating on:

(a) What the **risks** are and strategies for **identifying**, **evaluating** and **managing** them

(b) The **effectiveness** of the management and internal control systems in the management of risk, in particular how risks are **monitored** and **how** any **deficiencies** have been dealt with

(c) Whether **actions** are being taken to **reduce** the risks found

(d) Whether the results indicate that **internal control** should be **monitored more extensively**

> **Essential reading**
>
> See Chapter 8 section 2 of the Essential Reading, available in Appendix 2 of the digital edition of the Workbook, for more detail on how boards can review internal control reports.

2.2.2 Annual review of controls

The FRC's (2014) guidance sets out that the board should conduct an **annual review** of its internal control systems. This should involve reviewing the 'effectiveness of the systems to ensure that it has considered all significant aspects of risk management and internal control for the company for the year under review and up to the date of approval of the annual report and accounts. The board should define the processes to be adopted for this review, including drawing on the results of the board's on-going process such that it will obtain sound, appropriately documented evidence to support its statement in the company's annual report and accounts.' (FRC, 2014).

BPP
LEARNING
MEDIA

An annual review should cover:

The **changes** since the last **assessment** of **risks** faced, and the company's **ability** to **respond** to **changes** in its business environment
The **scope** and **quality** of management's monitoring of risk and internal control and of the work of internal audit, or consideration of the need for internal audit if the company does not have it
The **extent** and **frequency** of reports to the board
Significant controls, **failings** and **deficiencies** with material impacts on the accounts
The **effectiveness** of the **public reporting** processes

2.2.3 External reporting on risk management and internal controls

Stricter requirements on external reporting have been introduced because of the contribution of internal control failures to corporate scandals. The requirements have tried to address the concerns of shareholders and other stakeholders that management has exercised proper control.

The following factors can be considered best practice in respect of board review and reporting in most jurisdictions.

An acknowledgement that they are responsible for the company's system of internal control and reviewing its effectiveness

An explanation that such a system is designed to manage rather than eliminate the risk of failure to achieve business objectives, and can only provide reasonable and not absolute assurance against material misstatement or loss

Best practice on board review and reporting for most jurisdictions

A summary of the process that the directors have used to review the effectiveness of the system of internal control and consider the need for an internal audit function if the company does not have one; there should also be disclosure of the process the board has used to deal with material internal control aspects of any significant problems disclosed in the annual accounts

Information about those deficiencies in internal control that have resulted in material losses, contingencies or uncertainties which require disclosure in the financial statements or the auditor's report on the financial statements

The information provided must be meaningful, taking an overall, high-level view. It must also be reliable. The work of **internal audit** and the **audit committee** can help ensure reliability.

Exam Focus Point

The March/June 2019 exam released by ACCA featured a clothing retailer called SmartWear. In Task 3 candidates were required to draft a memo to SmartWear's buying and merchandising director, which evaluated the effectiveness of the internal control systems at the company, and which also recommended control improvements to rectify a number of areas of concern. The issues raised were set out in an internal audit report and included issues relating to the performance of the company's existing suppliers' and internal reporting provisions.

Professional skills marks were available for commercial acumen skills in respect of the recommendations made. The examining team noted that 'many good candidates used the common-sense structure: issue – outcome – recommendation, which tended to result in good [easy to mark] answers. [...] Weaker candidates just reiterated the various problems in the scenario and possibly the outcome, but did not provide useful and/or sensible solutions.' (ACCA, 2019a).

To earn the 4 professional skills marks on offer candidates had to use the information provided to evaluate the internal control problems and use professional judgement when providing sensible recommendations in respect of control improvements. The answer needed to be presented as a memo and be structured in such a way that it targeted the needs of the buying and merchandising director.

2.2.4 Sarbanes-Oxley

The requirements relating to companies under the Sarbanes-Oxley legislation are rather stricter than under the UK regime.

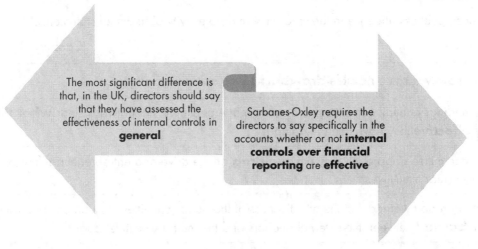

The most significant difference is that, in the UK, directors should say that they have assessed the effectiveness of internal controls in **general**

Sarbanes-Oxley requires the directors to say specifically in the accounts whether or not **internal controls over financial reporting** are **effective**

The directors cannot conclude that controls are effective if there are **material deficiencies** in controls: severe deficiencies that result in a more-than-remote likelihood that material misstatements in the financial statements won't be prevented or detected.

Under Sarbanes-Oxley, disclosures should include a **statement of management responsibility**, details of the **framework** used, disclosure of **material deficiencies** and also a **statement by the external auditors** on management's assessment of the effectiveness of internal control.

How much value reports give has been debated, particularly in America where some believe that the Sarbanes-Oxley legislation is too onerous. If reporting is compulsory, companies cannot apply a cost-benefit analysis to determine whether it is justified. It would certainly appear to be more beneficial for a larger company with elaborate control systems, where most of the shares are held by external shareholders.

2.3 Audit committees

2.3.1 Advantages and disadvantages

The Cadbury report (1992) summed up the benefits that an audit committee can bring to an organisation:

'If they operate effectively, audit committees can bring significant benefits. In particular, they have the potential to:

(a) Improve the quality of financial reporting, by reviewing the financial statements on behalf of the Board

(b) Create a climate of discipline and control which will reduce the opportunity for fraud

(c) Enable the non-executive directors to contribute an independent judgement and play a positive role

(d) Help the finance director, by providing a forum in which he can raise issues of concern, and which he can use to get things done which might otherwise be difficult

(e) Strengthen the position of the external auditor, by providing a channel of communication and forum for issues of concern

(f) Provide a framework within which the external auditor can assert his independence in the event of a dispute with management

(g) Strengthen the position of the internal audit function, by providing a greater degree of independence from management

(h) Increase public confidence in the credibility and objectivity of financial statements.'

(Cadbury, 1992: p.68)

There are, however, some possible **drawbacks** with an audit committee:

Since the findings of audit committees are rarely made public, it is not always clear **what they do or how effective** they have been in doing it
The audit committee's approach may act as a **drag** on the drive and entrepreneurial flair of the company's senior executives
The Cadbury report warned that the effectiveness of the audit committee may be compromised if it acts as a **'barrier'** between the external auditors and the main (executive) board
The Cadbury committee also suggested that the audit committee may be compromised if it allows the main board to **'abdicate its responsibilities** in the audit area', as this will weaken the board's responsibility for reviewing and approving the financial statements
The audit committee may function less effectively if it falls under the influence of a **dominant board member**, particularly if that board member is the only committee member with significant financial knowledge and experience

2.3.2 Who should be on the audit committee?

According to the UK Corporate Governance Code (2018), the board should establish an audit committee of at least three (two in the case of smaller companies) members, who should all be independent non-executive directors. The board may delegate some of its duties to the Audit Committee (and the Risk Committee).

The board should satisfy itself that at least one member of the audit committee has recent and relevant financial experience. (Under SOx having fulfilled the role of CEO is not sufficient experience to qualify as the financial expert on the audit committee.)

The audit committee should have written terms of reference. Under SOx this is referred to as the Audit Committee Charter.

2.3.3 Responsibilities of the audit committee

The responsibilities of the audit committee encompass:

Monitoring and Reviewing
- Financial statements
- Price-sensitive information
- Internal financial controls
- Independence of external auditors

Overseeing
- Effective internal audit
- Appointment of external auditors
- Remuneration of external auditors

Policy setting
- Non-audit service provided by external auditors (NB most are barred under SOx)

The audit committee also has other specific responsibilities:

Whistleblowers

Audit committees need to ensure there are adequate whistleblower procedures in place within the company. They have to ensure that any problems will be brought to their attention and cannot be intercepted by management.

Auditor requests

The audit committee must respond credibly to requests and enquiries from both internal or external auditors – this could relate to accessing sensitive information, visiting a representative cross-section of the organisation or responding to awkward questions.

Responses to auditors

As part of their overall remit for overseeing internal control and risk management, the audit committee will ensure that the organisation assesses the appropriateness of responses to auditors' recommendations (including taking actions when identified as necessary).

2.4 Internal audit

2.4.1 Role of internal audit

Internal audit is a form of control put in place by the board to help achieve the company's objectives.

Internal audit is an important part of the internal control system and it can therefore be regarded as having the same objectives as the rest of the internal control system: ie safeguarding assets; economy, efficiency and effectiveness of operations; reporting; compliance.

It is inevitable that internal audit will focus on **operational controls**. In some companies, however, the problem may be a failure of strategic level controls, due to management override of controls or poor strategic decision making. However, internal audit's role in relation to strategic controls will be limited, as most checking procedures have been followed at board level. The board must ultimately be responsible for the operation of strategic controls.

Essential reading

See Chapter 8 section 3 of the Essential Reading, available in Appendix 2 of the digital edition of the Workbook, for more detail on the type of work that the internal audit function conduct.

2.4.2 Assessing the quality of internal audit

The internal audit department reports to the audit committee who will carry out an **annual review** of the internal audit function using the following criteria:

Scope of work (how far-reaching their work is)

Authority (whether their terms of reference are sufficiently broad and whether their reports have been reviewed and action taken)

Independence (auditors should be independent of the activities they audit – see below)

Resources (in terms of hours, physical resources and appropriate knowledge, skills and experience)

Illustration 2

Pickett (2010) in the *Internal Auditing Handbook* suggests that the concept of independence involves a number of key qualities.

Objectivity	Judgements made in a state of detachment from the situation or decision
Impartiality	Not taking sides, in particular not being influenced by office politics in determining the work carried out and the reports given
Unbiased views	Avoiding the perception that internal audit is out to 'hit' certain individuals or departments
Valid opinion	The audit opinion should be based on all relevant factors, rather than being one that pleases everyone.
No spying for management	Again, internal audit should serve the whole organisation. Managers who want their staff targeted might be trying to cover up their own inadequacies.
No no-go areas	Being kept away from certain areas will fatally undermine the usefulness of internal audit and mean that aggressive (incompetent?) managers are not checked.
Sensitive areas audited	Internal audit must have the abilities and skills to audit complex areas effectively
Senior management audited	Internal audit must cover the management process and not just audit the detailed operational areas
No backing off	Audit objectives must be pursued fully in a professional manner and auditors must not allow aggressive managers to deflect them from doing necessary work and issuing valid opinions.

Independence of internal auditors can be achieved by the following.

- The department should report to the **board** or to a special **audit committee** and not to the finance director.

- Management should ensure staff recruited to internal audit internally **do not conduct audits** on departments in which they have worked.

- Where internal audit staff have also been involved in **designing** or **implementing new systems**, they should not **conduct post-implementation audits**.

- Internal auditors should have **appropriate scope** in carrying out their responsibilities, and unrestricted access to records, assets and personnel.

- **Rotation of staff** over specific departmental audits should be implemented.

2.4.3 Assessing the ongoing need for internal audit

As part of their role of monitoring internal audit, the audit committee should carry out a formal annual review of internal audit. If there is no internal audit function present, the audit committee should consider annually whether there is still no need for internal audit or if one might now be required.

Factors that will influence this decision are:

| Company size Company complexity | Unexpected risk events Problems in the internal control | Cost v benefit analysis |

Activity 3: PKG High School – Review and Audit of Controls

ACCA Professional skills focus

Communication: Persuade

PKG High School has 900 pupils, 40 teachers, 10 support staff and a budget of $3 million per annum, 85% of which represents salary and salary-related costs. PKG's local authority allocates government funding for education to schools based on the number of pupils. It ensures that the government-approved curriculum is taught in all schools in its area with the aim of achieving government targets. All schools, including PKG, are subject to an independent financial audit as well as a scrutiny of their education provision by the local authority, and reports of both are presented to the school governing body.

The number of pupils determines the approximate number of teachers, based on class sizes of approximately 30 pupils. The salary costs for teachers are determined nationally and pay scales mean that more experienced teachers receive higher salaries. In addition, some teachers receive school-specific responsibility allowances.

PKG is managed on a day-to-day basis by the headteacher. The governance of each school is carried out by a governing body comprising the headteacher, elected representatives of parents of pupils, and members appointed by the local authority. The principles of good corporate governance

BPP LEARNING MEDIA

apply to school governing bodies which are accountable to parents and the local authority for the performance of the school.

The governing body holds the headteacher accountable for day-to-day school management, but on certain matters, such as building maintenance, the headteacher will seek expert advice from the local authority.

The governing body meets quarterly and has as its main responsibilities budgetary management, appointment of staff and education standards. The main control mechanisms exercised by the governing body include scrutiny of a year-to-date financial report, a quarterly non-financial performance report, teacher recruitment and approval of all purchases over $1,000. The headteacher has expenditure authority below this level.

The financial report (which is updated monthly) is presented at each meeting of the governing body. It shows the local authority's budget allocation to the school for the year, the expenditure incurred for each month and the year to date, and any unspent balances. Although there is no external financial reporting requirement for the school, the local authority will not allow any school to overspend its budget allocation in any financial year.

PKG's budget allocation is only just sufficient to provide adequate educational facilities. Additional funds are always required for teaching resources, building maintenance, and to upgrade computer equipment. The only flexibility the school has in budget management is to limit responsibility allowances and delay teacher recruitment. This increases pupil-contact time for individual teachers, however, and forces teachers to undertake preparation, marking and administration after school hours.

Note. A local authority (or council) carries out services for the local community and levies local taxes (or council tax) to fund most of its operations.

Required

You are a consultant acting on behalf of the local authority and have been asked to explain why the review and audit of control systems is important for the governing body of a school such as PKG.

(5 marks)

Professional skills marks are available for demonstrating **communication** skills in persuading the local authority of the importance of a review and audit of control systems. **(2 marks)**

(Total = 7 marks)

Solution

Exam Focus Point

The Strategic Business Leader specimen 2 exam featured a public sector rail company, Rail Co, which was responsible for providing rail services within the country of Beeland. The fourth question required candidates to act as an internal auditor. Candidates were provided with a spreadsheet which had been prepared by Rail Co's financial controller. The spreadsheet analysed the ticket sales and rail usage on the Beeland rail network and also provided details of the estimated levels of fraud on the Rail Co network. Part (a) of question 4 asked candidates to 'analyse the information presented in the spreadsheet produced by the financial controller, questioning any assumptions he may have made, and [to] explain the implications of the findings for Rail Co' (ACCA, 2017a). This task was worth 8 technical marks and tested the ACCA Professional Skill of Scepticism. To produce a good answer candidates needed to adopt a questioning mind-set especially when considering the assumptions made by the financial controller. To earn the two professional skills marks candidates needed accurately analyse the information provided in the spreadsheet and to reflect on the impact of this in relation to Rail Co's revenues.

Part (b) of question 4 was closely connected to part (a) as candidates were asked to 'recommend to the audit and risk committee, with justifications, suitable measures or safeguards which could be implemented by Rail Co to reduce the levels of fraud occurring on the network' (ACCA, 2017a). This was worth 8 technical marks and tested the ACCA Professional Skill of Commercial Acumen. The focus on commercial acumen meant that any measures recommended to reduce fraud needed to be practical and capable of being implemented.

Internal control systems

Internal control

Definitions of internal control

Systems and attitudes

Objectives of internal control

- RORCS:
  - Risks
  - Operations
  - Reporting
  - Compliance
  - Safeguard assets
- Inherent limitations of internal control

Elements of internal control

- COSO cube
- Financial Reporting Council's (FRC) Guidance
- Advantages and disadvantages of using internal frameworks

Categories of control

- Corporate, management, business process and transaction
- Administration and accounting
- Prevent, detect, correct and direct
- Discretionary and non-discretionary
- Voluntary and mandated
- General and application
- Financial and non-financial

Control procedures

APIPS:

- Authorisation
- Performance review
- Information systems
- Physical controls
- Segregation of duties

Controls over financial reporting

- Journal entries
- Accounting estimates
- IT controls

Monitoring

Information

- Types of information
- Levels of information
- Qualities of good information
- Sources of good information

Reviewing internal controls

- Internal control reports
- Annual review of controls
- External reporting on risk management and internal controls
- Sarbanes-Oxley

Audit committees

- Advantages and disadvantages
- Who should be on the audit committee?
- Responsibilities of the audit committee

Internal audit

- Role of internal audit
- Assessing the quality of internal audit
  - Scope
  - Authority
  - Independence
  - Resources
- Assessing the ongoing need for internal audit

Knowledge diagnostic

1. Internal control is a process that needs to be appropriate to the organisation and its objectives

2. Although each system of internal controls is unique, there is always likely to be a control environment, control activities; and the same overall objectives of the system: reporting; operations; risks; compliance; and safeguarding assets (RORCS)

3. While there are many different categories of control, there are likely to be only five types of control procedure: authorisation; performance reviews; information processing; physical controls; and segregation of duties (APIPS)

4. Monitoring requires good information, supplied at the right level and obtained from the right sources

5. The process of monitoring, reviewing and reporting on internal controls is likely to be completed by the audit committee supported by an internal audit function if deemed necessary by the complexities of the organisation

BPP
LEARNING
MEDIA

Question practice

Now try the question below from the Further question practice bank (available in the digital edition of the Workbook):

Q8 *LMN*

Further reading

There are articles on the ACCA website written by members of the SBL examining team which are relevant to your studies and which would be useful to read:

Internal audit

This article explores the important role that internal audit plays in organisations.

COSO enterprise risk management framework

This article explores the key features of the COSO framework:

Approaching SBL overview

This article provides a one-page summary of the key features of the SBL exam.

Approaching SBL reading and planning

This article provides a one-page summary of how best to approach the SBL exam.

SBL – 10 things to learn from the September 2018 sitting

This article highlights some of the issues that ACCA identified in candidates' answers during the September 2018 SBL exam sitting. The article provides some useful advice for improving your chances of passing the SBL exam.

Strategic Business Leader – The importance of effective communication for SBL

This article provides some useful insights into the different formats which you will be expected to use when answering SBL exam tasks.

Own research

Reflect on your learning from both this chapter and Chapter 7 on risk management and see if you can start to fit the two elements together in the context of either your own organisation or one you are familiar with – if you were in a position of strategic leadership, what do you think you would need to do to ensure you were fulfilling your responsibilities (this assumes that you know what they are?)

Following this period of reflection, you may still have some questions about the way each of these various approaches works.

If so, try the following activities:

*   Select some famous UK companies and review the governance sections of their annual reports (for example M&S, BT or Barclays Bank)

    Look at how they approach their risk and control responsibilities: are they all the same?

*   Now have a look at some examples from the USA (for example Nike, Starbucks or Disney) – what's different about this process of disclosing internal controls in the US?

*   Finally, consider companies from elsewhere in the world (for example Adidas in Germany, PSA Groupe in France or ArcelorMittal in Luxembourg) – how do they present information about risks and controls?

Exercise answer

Exercise 1

(a) **Shareholders** want to ensure that their investment is protected. The benefit of internal controls for them is that the controls will reduce the incidence of fraud and error. Controls will also manage risks faced by the company, thus reducing the overall risk faced by investors. However, controls cost money to design, implement and monitor and this will reduce the value of the shareholders' investment. They therefore want an appropriate balance of controls, so more controls over high-risk areas and fewer over areas where they are less exposed.

(b) **Debt providers** want to protect the capital they have put into the company and to receive interest. They will want to make sure that controls are adequate to protect their investment. They will be less concerned with controls being costly unless the cost is so great as to put the whole company at risk and thereby expose any creditors to risk.

(c) **Employees** are concerned about job security so will want to see controls that are adequate to protect the future of the company. Employees were particularly badly affected by the Mirror Group corporate failure where Robert Maxwell misappropriated pension funds. Employees are therefore concerned to see adequate controls over their pension funds. They also have a stake in the reputation of the company and therefore in how reputation risk is managed. Employees have to operate controls and will therefore not want them to add an unnecessary burden to their work. They will want controls that protect them against any perceived threats.

(d) **Customers** will want their dealings with the company to be pleasant and hassle free. They will be unhappy about controls that are overly intrusive (M&S traditionally had a reputation for no quibbling over returns and gained Christmas sales from people buying presents that could be returned). On the other hand, customers will want to be assured of the safety (and recently the ethical provenance) of the products they are buying and will expect adequate controls in this area.

(e) **Government and regulators** will want to ensure that adequate controls exist to cover statutory compliance. They may audit this themselves (VAT and PAYE compliance) or respond when there is a breach (health and safety).

Applying ethical principles

9

Learning objectives

On completion of this chapter, you should be able to:

	Syllabus reference no.
Evaluate organisational decisions using the Tucker 5-question approach	A3(a)
Describe and critically evaluate the social responsibility of accountants acting in the public interest	A3(b)
Assess management behaviour against the codes of ethics relevant to accounting professionals including the IESBA (IFAC) or professional body codes	A3(c)
Analyse the reasons for and resolve conflicts of interest and ethical conflicts in organisations	A3(d)
Assess the nature and impacts of different ethical threats and recommend appropriate safeguards to prevent or mitigate such threats	A3(e)
Recommend best practice for reducing and combating fraud, bribery and corruption to create greater public confidence and trust in organisations	A3(f)

Business and exam context

The application of ethical principles demands an understanding of what those ethical principles are – you should have already met them earlier in your studies but we will revisit them in the context of three areas (fraud, bribery and corruption) where 'doing the wrong thing' is a realistic problem for many organisations due to the sometimes complex nature of how business is conducted.

We will counter this by remembering that as a professional, an accountant's primary duty is to behave in the public interest and so this chapter will also look at how you can ensure that you are always 'doing the right thing' including the application of techniques designed to help you arrive at the right decision, whatever the circumstances.

Ethics is a core part of the Strategic Business Leader syllabus so this content is crucial for you to fully understand how to approach the exam.

Chapter overview

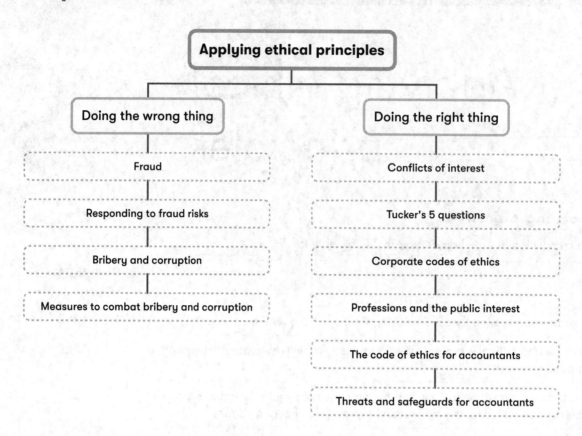

Applying ethical principles

Doing the wrong thing

- Fraud
- Responding to fraud risks
- Bribery and corruption
- Measures to combat bribery and corruption

Doing the right thing

- Conflicts of interest
- Tucker's 5 questions
- Corporate codes of ethics
- Professions and the public interest
- The code of ethics for accountants
- Threats and safeguards for accountants

1 Doing the wrong thing

1.1 Fraud

Key term

Fraud: The deliberate act of gaining an advantage by knowingly breaking the law.

An act or statement that creates an advantage but requires a false representation of the facts for it to be accepted. However, the key point that distinguishes **fraud** from an honest mistake is intent.

All organisations run the risk of loss through the fraudulent activities of employees, including management. Some common types of fraud are:

- Ghost employees – salaries or wages are collected for employees who don't exist
- Inflating expense claims – either individually or in collusion with other staff
- Stealing assets – either physically or virtually (for example online scams such as 'phishing')
- Manipulation of financial statements – for either personal or corporate gain

According to Cressey (1973) there are three factors that must all be present at the same time for an ordinary person to commit fraud:

Pressure
Motivation to commit fraud comes from a financial problem that cannot be solved by legitimate means (such as bills, drug or gambling addiction or even a social pressure to succeed)

Opportunity
Usually, fraud can be perpetrated because someone is able to, either because there is a low perceived risk of getting caught or the fraud can be easily concealed

Rationalisation
The fraudster must be able to justify the decision at the very least to themselves, usually because they perceive themselves to either have no choice or that they have been wronged in some way and deserve the proceeds of this particular crime

(Cressey's Fraud Triangle, 1973: p.30)

BPP
LEARNING
MEDIA

Real world examples

In September 2011, Kweku Adoboli, a trader at the Swiss bank UBS, was arrested after allegedly having lost the bank £1.5 billion. The frauds that Kweku Adoboli was charged with allegedly took place between October 2008 and September 2011 and allegedly involved reporting fictitious hedges against legitimate derivative transactions. Mr Adoboli worked for UBS's global synthetic equities division, buying and selling exchange traded funds which track different types of stocks or commodities such as precious metals. Mr Adoboli was convicted in November 2012 on charges of fraud.

In September 2011, UBS announced plans to scale back its investment banking activities to reduce its risks. Its chief executive, Oswald Gruebel, resigned.

A subsequent investigation by UBS revealed a failure of key controls in two areas:

- Failure to obtain bilateral confirmation with counterparties of certain trades within the bank's equities business

- Failure by those involved in inter-desk reconciliation processes to ensure transactions were valid and accurately recorded in the bank's records. Cancellations of, or amendments to, internal trades that should have been supervisor-reviewed were not checked.

There was also evidence that compliance systems did detect some unauthorised or unexplained activity, but this was not adequately investigated.

Exercise 1: Preventing fraud

You work as an internal auditor for an organisation in the construction industry. Contracts are frequently awarded for supplying many different products depending on what the organisation's projects require. However, you have been alerted by the Head of Internal Audit to three separate ongoing investigations into fraudulent activity in the award of contracts to suppliers. The Head of Internal Audit is keen to provide the audit committee with information that might help them understand the risks that this activity presents before a suitable fraud response plan can be implemented.

Required

Give examples of indicators of fraud in a procurement tendering process.

Solution

Essential reading

See Chapter 9 section 1 of the Essential Reading, available in Appendix 2 of the digital edition of the Workbook, for more detail about possible fraud risks.

1.2 Responding to fraud risks

Activity 1: Indicators of fraud

ACCA Professional skills focus

Scepticism: Probe

You are a consultant working at an organisation which has experienced a number of fraud problems:

- Ghost employees
- Inflating expense claims
- Stealing assets
- Manipulation of financial statements

Required

You have been asked to draw up a briefing note for the audit committee which recommends a series of improvements to the way the organisation deals with fraud, using the following terms of reference:

- Considering the conditions that are likely to be present for fraud to be committed, what should an organisation do to prevent the existence of such conditions?

- What specific controls could be introduced to reduce to acceptable levels the risk of the frauds mentioned above recurring?

Draft the briefing note required, using the terms of reference. **(7 marks)**

Professional skills marks are available for demonstrating **scepticism** skills in probing the reasons for fraud and the most suitable forms of response. **(2 marks)**

(Total = 9 marks)

Solution

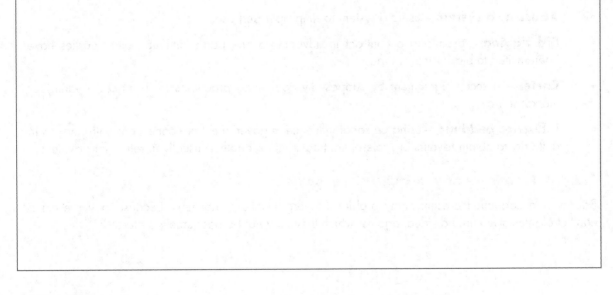

1.3 Bribery and corruption

1.3.1 Impact of bribery and corruption

Bribery: Influencing someone to behave inappropriately by means of money, goods or services.

Corruption: Deviation from prescribed behaviour, usually in conjunction with some other gain.

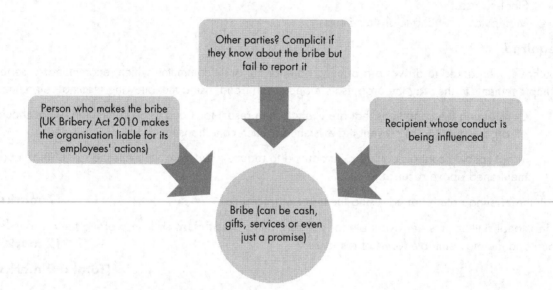

Other parties? Complicit if they know about the bribe but fail to report it

Person who makes the bribe (UK Bribery Act 2010 makes the organisation liable for its employees' actions)

Recipient whose conduct is being influenced

Bribe (can be cash, gifts, services or even just a promise)

1.3.2 Aspects of bribery

Bribery is an example of corruption. Other forms of corruption include the following.

- **Abuse of a system** – using a system for improper purposes

- **Bid rigging** – promising a contract in advance to one party, although other parties have been invited to bid for the contract

- **Cartel** – a secret agreement by supposedly competing producers to fix prices, quantity or market share

- **Influence peddling** – using personal influence in government or connections with persons in authority to obtain favours or preferential treatment for another, usually in return for payment

1.3.3 Why bribery and corruption are problems

Bribery and corruption present many problems to organisations, not least because they present a conflict of interests to an individual against which they may not be adequately protected.

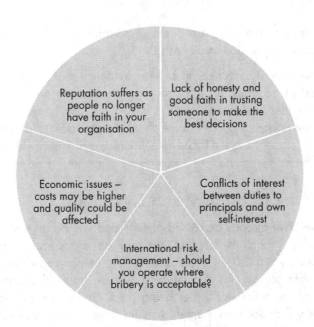

Essential reading

See Chapter 9 section 2 of the Essential Reading, available in Appendix 2 of the digital edition of the Workbook, for more detail about why bribery and corruption are problematic.

Real world examples

In April 2012 Barstow (2012) writing in *The New York Times* published details of an alleged bribery scandal at retail giant Walmart. The paper alleged that executives in Walmart's Mexican subsidiary had given payoffs to local officials in return for help getting permits to build new Walmart stores in Mexico. Top executives in Mexico had known about these payments but had concealed them from Walmart's main board.

In 2005 the main board was tipped off by a former executive in Mexico. An internal investigation allegedly revealed $24 million in suspected bribery payments. However, the original investigation team was accused of being too aggressive and was dropped from the case. Responsibility for the investigation was transferred to one of the Mexican executives alleged to have authorised bribes. This executive exonerated their fellow executives and Walmart's main board accepted this. Although a report was made at the time to the US Justice Department, Walmart played down the significance of the allegations. Executives in Mexico were not disciplined – one was promoted to vice chair.

At the time of the investigation in 2005 Walmart was facing pressure on its share price. The company's Mexican operations were its biggest success, highlighted to investors as a model of future growth. Barstow (2012) highlighted that there was evidence that main board directors were well aware of the devastating consequences the allegations could have if made public.

This was not the first time that there had been issues over corruption in Mexico. An investigation in 2003 revealed that Walmart de México had systematically increased sales by helping high-volume customers evade sales taxes. Executives had failed to enforce anti-corruption policies and ignored warnings from internal auditors. The company ultimately paid back-taxes of $34.3 million.

Walmart's shares fell by nearly 9% in the days after *The New York Times* published Barstow's (2012) allegations. The fall at Walmart also dragged down the whole Dow Jones Industrial Average. Walmart faced the possibility of massive legal liabilities under the US's Foreign Corrupt Practices Act. One of Walmart's institutional investors began action against executives and board members, and sought changes in the company's corporate governance. A group of New York City pension funds said they would vote against re-electing five Walmart directors. One of Walmart's managers started an online petition urging the company to undertake a thorough and independent

BPP
LEARNING
MEDIA

investigation. The manager claimed that most of the signatories were current and former employees fed up with the philosophy of expansion at all costs.

Even only a few days after the story broke, there was evidence that Walmart's strategic ambitions may have been damaged by scandals. Its attempts to open stores in new areas and other dealings appeared to be coming under increased scrutiny. It had recently been focusing on bigger cities where there was more bureaucracy to overcome than in suburban and rural areas. The bribery scandal appeared to have made it more difficult for Walmart to proceed with its expansion plans.

1.4 Measures to combat bribery and corruption

Many of the measures we have already discussed about fraud will be relevant to combating bribery. Recent legislation in certain countries has put pressure on organisations to introduce sufficient controls. Under the UK Bribery Act (2010), for example, if an employee or associate of a commercial organisation bribes another person, the organisation will be liable if it cannot show that it had adequate procedures in place to prevent bribes being paid. Under previous legislation, a company was only likely to be guilty if senior management was involved. Now, however, it must demonstrate that its anti-corruption procedures are sufficient to stop any employees, agents or other third parties acting on the company's behalf from committing bribery.

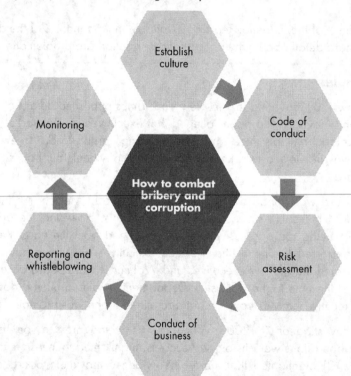

Essential reading

See Chapter 9 section 3 of the Essential Reading, available in Appendix 2 of the digital edition of the Workbook, for more detail about how to combat bribery and corruption.

Illustration 1

Guidance published by the UK Ministry of Justice (2011) on the Bribery Act suggests that what is seen as adequate will depend on the bribery risks faced by the organisation, and the nature, size and complexity of the organisation. The UK guidance is based on six principles:

(a) **Proportionate procedures**. Measures taken should be proportional to risks and nature, size and complexity.

(b) **Top-level commitment**. Top-level management should be committed to preventing bribery and promoting a culture where bribery is viewed as unacceptable.

(c) **Risk assessment**. Organisations should assess the nature and extent of their exposure to bribery internally and externally. Some activities, for example extraction, and some markets, for example countries where there is no anti-bribery legislation, may be at higher risk.

(d) **Due diligence**. The organisation should carry out due diligence procedures in relation to those who perform services for it, or on its behalf.

(e) **Communication**. Bribery prevention policies and procedures should be embedded and understood throughout the organisation through communication and training.

(f) **Monitoring and review**. The organisation should monitor and review anti-bribery procedures and improve them as required. The guidance emphasises that risks are dynamic, and procedures may need to change if risks alter.

2 Doing the right thing

2.1 Conflict of interest

A conflict of interest generally occurs in one of two ways:

- When one party is in a position to derive some form of benefit from actions or decisions taken made when acting in an official capacity, for example, a company director personally benefitting from a decision made at work.

- They can also arise when one party's actions or objectives are incompatible with the objectives of another party.

Disagreement is often a central feature of conflicts of interest. Such conflicts are not uncommon in a business context given the varied range of stakeholders that exist and the different interests that they hold. Common examples of conflicts of interest include:

- Employees may demand better pay and conditions, whereas the organisation's management want to maintain the employees pay and conditions at existing levels so that the organisation is able to achieve its profit targets. A similar situation may occur regarding suppliers to large organisations, as they want to sell goods at higher prices with the organisation's management pushing for lower prices.

- An organisation may wish to create new jobs by building a new factory on a piece of land, designated as being environmentally important, due to a shortage of available sites elsewhere. This may cause a conflict between the organisation and environmental protection groups. Local government authorities may also become involved in such situations as they need to balance job creation against protecting the local environment.

- Customers want to pay lower prices for the products and services provided by the organisation, whereas the organisation's management are likely to want to maximise profits by charging the highest prices they can. This may cause conflict especially where customers have limited choice from where to purchase products and services. Management may be incentivised to charge higher prices for products and services to trigger profit-related bonuses.

Conflicts of interest such as those illustrated above may also give rise to ethical conflicts. In your Strategic Business Leader exam, you need to be alert to the fact that the information provided may require you to not only consider commercial conflicts of interest that exist between stakeholder groups but to also identify the ethical conflicts that lie within them.

It is possible that requirements in the exam may require you to provide practical measures which the management at the featured organisation could take to address the ethical conflicts that you identify.

2.1.1 Ethical conflicts of interest in the exam

In the Strategic Business Leader exam, you may be presented with a scenario containing an array of detail of which much is potentially relevant. While it is not possible to identify definitively the types of ethical requirements that you may encounter, you may be faced with requirements which ask you to:

- Analyse the ethical implications of a proposed strategy or course of action set out in the exam information or Exhibit and;

- Make recommendations concerning how to address the ethical issues that you identify.

When faced with questions featuring ethical conflicts you may find it helpful to adopt the following approach:

- Read the relevant task information/ Exhibit

- Identify the ethical issues at stake e.g. proposed course of action/ strategy and the impact this may have on the stakeholder groups specified in the scenario i.e. employees / customers etc

- Make use of any appropriate ethical guidelines and/or draw upon the scenario information which may indicate whether the proposed course of action will give rise to a conflict of interest or contradict the featured entity's own published code of ethics and/or undermine its business model

- Make clear, logical and appropriate recommendations for action. It is important that any recommendations you make could be implemented in reality by the management at the featured entity. Making inconsistent/unrealistic recommendations will undermine the quality of your answer.

Justifying recommendations in practical business and ethical terms

As with all scenario-based questions there is likely to be more than one acceptable answer, and marks will depend on how well the case is argued, rather than for getting the 'right' answer. It is important to note that the guidance provided above is only intended to provide you with a start point for considering ethical conflicts of interest that may appear in your Strategic Business Leader exam. As such you will need to use your discretion when determining whether some or all of the points listed are relevant to attempting the question.

2.1.2 Resolving ethical conflicts

There is no single, universal best way of resolving ethical conflicts in business as no two situations are likely to be exactly the same. This is not helped by the fact that 'doing the right thing' is seldom clear cut and tends to be highly subjective. When analysing ethical conflicts, organisations may follow some of the steps highlighted in section 2.1.1 above. Ultimately, the approach taken by organisations to resolve ethical conflicts will be influenced by a range of factors including:

- The attitude of the leader (and board of directors) to ethical matters and the 'tone at the top' that they have set

- Management/ leadership style e.g. autocratic v participative

- The culture of the organisation and presence of an organisational code of ethics or code of conduct

- The presence of any laws or regulations governing conduct in certain matters

- The existence of guidelines governing the work performed by particular professions e.g. accountants

- The extent of the power and interest of the stakeholder groups in conflict, and the extent to which these can be viewed as legitimate

2.1.3 Frameworks for dealing with ethical conflicts and dilemmas

Although there is no single, universal best way of resolving ethical conflicts/ dilemmas, a number of different frameworks exist which leaders in organisations can look to use when dealing with ethical situations. One such framework is Tucker's 5 question model.

Exam Focus Point

It is important to note that Tucker's 5 question model is the only framework which is specifically mentioned in the Strategic Business Leader syllabus which can be used when evaluating ethical matters. Therefore, it is important that you are comfortable with the key features of this.

2.2 Tucker's 5 questions

Given the ethical issues we have already discussed, evaluating organisational decisions can present something of a challenge. **Tucker's 5 questions** (1990) are a benchmark against which to test the ethical credentials of a decision. Ask yourself, is the decision:

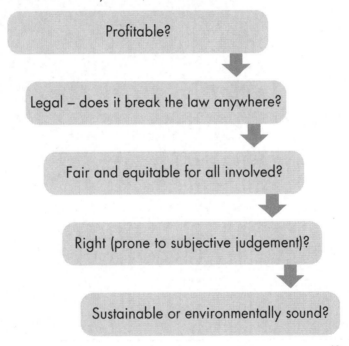

Profitable?

Legal – does it break the law anywhere?

Fair and equitable for all involved?

Right (prone to subjective judgement)?

Sustainable or environmentally sound?

(Source: Tucker, 1990)

Activity 2: Low tax payments

ACCA Professional skills focus

Scepticism: Question

GSA is a listed pharmaceutical company that operates across different countries but has its headquarters in a European country. In general terms it always complies with the law – financial statements are filed on time, employee and sales taxes are paid over to the local tax authority – but despite the parent company recording high operating profits, it recently paid a very low level of corporate tax due to apparent loopholes in the legislation (sometimes referred to as 'legal tax avoidance').

This low tax payment became a controversial news story and led to calls for a boycott of the company's products unless they voluntarily paid more corporate tax. GSA's Chief Executive Martyn Rice has agreed to respond to the media on behalf of the board but wishes to obtain the thoughts of the audit committee before proceeding any further.

Required

You are a non-executive director for GSA and tend to provide ethical advice to your colleagues on the audit committee.

Assess the proposal to make no voluntary payment of corporate tax by the organisation using a suitable ethical decision-making model. **(5 marks)**

Professional skills marks are available for demonstrating **scepticism** skills in questioning the facts of the case and seeking evidence. **(2 marks)**

(Total = 7 marks)

Solution

2.3 Corporate codes of ethics

Organisations have responded to wide and varied pressures from external stakeholders to be seen to act ethically by publishing ethical codes.

Ethical codes contain a series of statements setting out the organisation's core values and explaining how it sees its responsibilities towards its stakeholders. They cover specific areas such as gifts, anti-competitive behaviour and so on. However, often they do little more than describe current acceptable practices.

The typical features of an ethical code could be as follows:

> • Guidance on acceptable and unacceptable behaviour
> • Specific examples of company expectations
> • Links to the organisation's mission and objectives
> • Clear guidance on consequences and sanctions
> • Standards for the ethical treatment of suppliers, customers, employees

Exam Focus Point

Question 3 of the Strategic Business Leader exam in September 2018 featured a task which asked candidates to prepare a confidential memo to discuss the ethical and reputational concerns raised at an emergency management meeting. The meeting was called following an incident involving protestors at one of the sites operated by the organisation featured in the exam.

2.4 Professions and the public interest

The code of ethics of the International Ethics Standards Board for Accountants (IESBA, 2018) defines professionalism in terms of professional behaviour.

Key term

Professional behaviour: Imposes an obligation on professional accountants to 'comply with relevant laws and regulations and avoid any conduct that may bring discredit to the profession.' (IESBA, 2018: p.18)

Among the most important obligations for modern **professional accountants** is maintaining confidentiality and upholding ethical standards, including **acting in the public interest**.

The **public interest** is considered to be the collective wellbeing of the community of people and institutions the professional accountant serves, including clients, lenders, governments, employers, employees, investors, the business and financial community and others who rely on the work of professional accountants (IESBA, 2018).

Key term

The public interest: The collective wellbeing of the community of people and institutions the professional accountant serves.

2.4.1 Influence of the accountancy profession on organisations

The influence of the accountancy profession on business and society is potentially huge. It can be established simply by considering all the different involvements that accountants have:

(a) Financial accounting
(b) Audit
(c) Management accounting
(d) Consulting
(e) Taxation

It is obvious that if accountants also operate to combat fraud, bribery and corruption in organisations, the public's confidence and trust in such organisations will be increased and thus our own reputation will be enhanced.

BPP
LEARNING
MEDIA

The financial information included within accounts can have a number of uses:

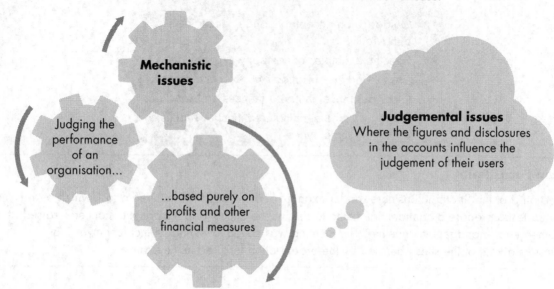

Critics of the accountancy profession emphasise that accountants' prime role is that of resource allocation, and thereby they act as agents of capitalism. They argue that accountancy regulations:

(a) Are too passive, allowing too great a variety of accounting treatments, and failing to impose meaningful responsibilities on auditors such as an explicit responsibility to detect and report fraud

(b) Emphasise the wrong principles, giving priority to client confidentiality over disclosure in the wider public interest

2.5 The code of ethics for accountants

2.5.1 Principles-based approach

The International Ethics Standards Board for Accountants (IESBA) (2018) *Code of Ethics* provides a good illustration of a principle-based approach:

(a) The code clarifies up-front acceptance by the accountancy profession of its responsibility to act in the public interest.

(b) The detailed guidance is preceded by the underlying fundamental principles of ethics.

(c) The guide supplies a conceptual framework that requires accountants to identify, evaluate and address threats to compliance, and applying safeguards to eliminate the threats or to reduce them to an acceptable level.

Advantages of a principles-based framework	Disadvantages of a principles-based framework
The onus is on the professional accountant to think about relevant issues in a given situation, rather than simply avoiding a checklist of unacceptable actions.	Ethical codes cannot include all circumstances and dilemmas, so accountants need a very good understanding of the underlying principles.
A framework prevents professionals interpreting legalistic requirements narrowly to get around the ethical requirements.	International codes cannot fully capture regional cultural variations in beliefs and practice.
It allows for variations, which is important as situations differ.	Principles-based codes can be difficult to enforce legally, unless the breach of the code is blatant. Most are therefore voluntary and perhaps, therefore, less effective.
It can accommodate a rapidly changing environment, such as the one in which accountants operate.	

2.5.2 The fundamental ethical principles

The ACCA's *Code of Ethics and Conduct for members* is published within its own Rulebook (2019) , which is broadly based on the same principles as the IESBA Code (2018). The table below details fundamental principles upon which the code is based. These can be easily remembered using the **PIPCO** mnemonic:

Fundamental principles	
Professional competence and due care	Members have a continuing duty 'to attain and maintain professional knowledge and skill at the level required to ensure that a client or employing organization receives competent professional service, based on current technical and professional standards and relevant legislation; and [to] act diligently and in accordance with applicable technical and professional standards.' (ACCA, 2019c: p.273)
Integrity	Members should 'be straightforward and honest in all business and professional relationships'. (ACCA, 2019c: p.273)
Professional behaviour	Members should 'comply with relevant laws and regulations and should avoid any conduct that the professional accountant knows or should know might discredit the profession''. (ACCA, 2019c: p.273)
Confidentiality	Members should 'respect the confidentiality of information acquired as a result of professional and business relationships'. (ACCA, 2019c: p.273).
Objectivity	Members should 'not compromise professional or business judgments because of bias, conflict of interest or undue influence of others.' (ACCA, 2019c: p.273)

Key terms

Professional competence and due care: The fundamental ethical principle associated with maintaining professional skills and carrying out your duties to the best of your ability.

Integrity: The fundamental ethical principle associated with honesty and truthful behaviour.

BPP
LEARNING
MEDIA

Professional behaviour: The fundamental ethical principle associated with acting in a manner that respects the accountancy profession.

Confidentiality: The fundamental ethical principle associated with respecting information and not abusing it.

Objectivity: The fundamental ethical principle associated with avoiding bias.

PER alert

Performance Objective 1 'Ethics and Professionalism' of the Practical Experience Requirement requires you to 'act with integrity, objectivity, professional competence and due care and confidentiality' (ACCA, 2019b). To help you generate examples of how you have demonstrated compliance with Performance Objective 1 you are strongly advised to read through the following sections.

Syllabus link

Ethics forms a key part of the Strategic Business Leader syllabus, and links closely to the Ethics and Professional Skills Module (EPSM) that you are required to complete on your journey towards full ACCA membership. One of the units that you will need to complete focuses on your knowledge of ethical and professional values and behaviours. You are therefore strongly advised to complete the EPSM before sitting your Strategic Business Leader exam as this will assist with your exam preparations.

Safeguards against breach of compliance with the IESBA (2018) and ACCA (2019) guidance include:

(a) Safeguards created by the profession, legislation or regulation (eg corporate governance)

(b) Safeguards within the client/the accountancy firm's own systems and procedures

(c) Educational training and experience requirements for entry into the profession, together with continuing professional development.

PER alert

A key part of Performance Objective 1 'Ethics and Professionalism' which we mentioned earlier highlights the importance of developing a commitment to both personal and professional knowledge and development. ACCA (2019b) note that this will require you to become 'a life-long learner and continuous improver'. To demonstrate your achievement of this Performance Objective you will need to give consideration to the steps that you have taken to maintain your professional competence.

2.6 Threats and safeguards for accountants

Threats to independence of action and conflicts of interest include:

- Advocacy
- Self-interest
- Intimidation
- Familiarity
- Self-review

They are sometimes referred to by the mnemonic 'AS IFS'.

Key terms

Advocacy: The ethical threat arising from representing a client in two different capacities.

Self-interest: The ethical threat arising from actions that benefit you and not your clients.

Intimidation: The ethical threat arising from being forced into a course of action against your will.

Familiarity: The ethical threat arising from having a personal connection with a client.

> **Self-review:** The ethical threat arising from reviewing your own work (in other words, a failure to be sufficiently sceptical).

2.6.1 Advocacy threat

An advocacy threat arises in certain situations where the audit firm assumes the client's part in a dispute or somehow acts as their advocate. The most obvious instance of this would be when a firm acts as an expert witness in a court case in support of its audit client.

Relevant safeguards might be:

(a)   Using different departments in the firm to carry out the work
(b)   Making full disclosure to the client's audit committee
(c)   Withdrawal from an engagement if the risk to independence is considered too great

2.6.2 Self-interest threat

The ACCA *Code of Ethics and Conduct* published in its Rulebook (2019) highlights a great number of areas in which a self-interest threat to independence might arise (frequently in the context of the external auditor, but generally applicable to all members).

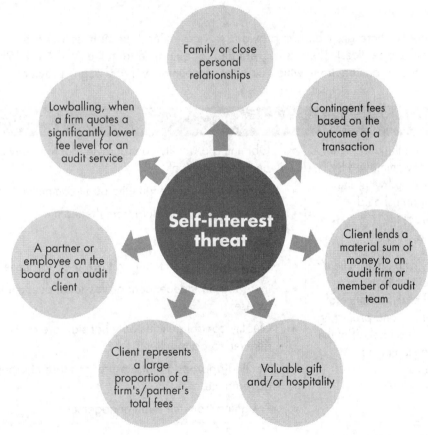

(Adapted from: ACCA, 2019c)

Safeguards in these situations might include:

(a)   Discussing the issues with the audit committee of the client

(b)   Taking steps to reduce the dependency on the client

(c)   Consulting an independent third party such as ACCA

(d)   Maintaining records such that the firm is able to demonstrate that appropriate staff and time are spent on the engagement

(e)   Compliance with all applicable audit standards, guidelines and quality control procedures

2.6.3 Intimidation threat

An intimidation threat arises when a professional accountant is deterred from acting objectively by threats, actual or perceived. Situations which might create intimidation threats include:

(a) Threats of dismissal
(b) Threats of litigation
(c) Pressure to reduce fees or the extent of work performed

Safeguards would include disclosure of such threats to the audit committee for their consideration, review of work for any evidence of bias and even the possibility of removing affected individuals from the area under threat.

2.6.4 Familiarity threat

Familiarity threat is where independence is jeopardised by the audit firm and its staff becoming over-familiar with the client and its staff. As a result they may become too sympathetic to their views and interests.

Safeguards usually include rotation of affected individuals away from the position creating the threat and a quality control review of anyone's work if there is a familiarity threat present.

2.6.5 Self-review threat

Self-review threat is where an audit firm provides services other than audit services to an audit client (ie providing multiple services). There is a great deal of guidance from the ACCA (2019) and IESBA (2018) about threats arising from which services accountancy firms might provide to their audit clients.

Threat	Safeguards
If an individual on the audit team had been recently employed by, or otherwise involved with, the client, the audit firm should consider the threat to independence arising	<ul><li>Obtaining a quality control review of the individual's work on the assignment</li><li>Discussing the issue with the audit committee</li><li>Removing the individual from the team</li></ul>
Having custody of an audit client's assets, supervising client employees in the performance of their normal duties, and preparing source documents on behalf of the client also pose significant self-review threats	<ul><li>Ensuring non-audit team staff are used for these roles</li><li>Involving an independent professional accountant to advise</li><li>Quality control policies on what staff are and are not allowed to do for clients</li><li>Making appropriate disclosures to those charged with governance</li><li>Resigning from the audit engagement</li></ul>

Threat	Safeguards
Preparing accounting records and financial statements, and then auditing them	• Using staff members other than audit team members to carry out work • Obtaining client approval for work undertaken
Providing valuation services where audited financial statements include figures generated by the valuation	• Using separate personnel for the valuation and the audit • Second partner review • Confirming that the client understands the valuation and the assumptions used • Ensuring the client acknowledges responsibility for the valuation
Provision of internal audit services to an external audit client is permitted in most jurisdictions, but not in the US under Sarbanes-Oxley	• The firm should ensure that the client acknowledges its responsibility for establishing, maintaining and monitoring the system of internal controls
Assuming management responsibility for an audit client. Management responsibilities might include, for example, making decisions relating to the use of the client's resources.	• Ensuring that the client's management team make all decisions relating to the management of the organisation.

Activity 3: Tax savings

 ACCA Professional skills focus

Scepticism: Challenge

GSA is a listed pharmaceutical company that operates across different countries but has its headquarters in a European country. You work as a consultant for a small professional firm which has been asked to act as advisers to GSA. The Finance Director of GSA studied with the engagement partner so is happy to give him the work, especially as he believes that the firm's experience in tax advice can help identify any future tax loopholes. The engagement is very high-profile for your firm, so it has been offered at a discount to the firm's normal fees, although you understand that the GSA board has indicated that it expects fees to stay low as it wants your firm to act as both internal and external auditors in order to improve efficiencies.

You are in the corridor about to attend a planning meeting between your firm and GSA when you overhear the end of a conversation between the engagement partner and the Finance Director in the meeting room: '...obviously, if the tax savings identified are sufficiently imaginative and creative, there will be a special bonus for you, although this will need to be hushed up to satisfy those who feel we should all now be acting in the public interest...'

Required

Critically evaluate what you have heard in the corridor by considering the following issues:

Identifying the ethical threats presented in the scenario. **(5 marks)**

Explaining what is meant by the public interest in this case. **(2 marks)**

 BPP LEARNING MEDIA

Describing the nature of the conversation that you have overheard, including any possible actions that you feel you may need to take. **(3 marks)**

Professional skills marks are available for demonstrating **scepticism** skills in challenging the views expressed in the scenario. **(2 marks)**

(Total = 12 marks)

Solution

Applying ethical principles

Doing the wrong thing

Fraud
- Intentional act to gain advantage by deception
  - Pressure
  - Opportunity
  - Rationalisation
  (Cressey's Fraud Triangle)

Responding to fraud risks
Suitable internal controls:
- Segregation of duties
- Authorisation
- Performance review

Bribery and corruption
- Impacts:
  - Bribery = influencing the actions of someone
  - Corruption = deviation from honest behaviour
- Aspects of bribery – can lead to the following problems:
  - Lack of honesty
  - Conflicts of interest
  - International risk management
  - Economic issues
  - Reputation

Measures to combat bribery and corruption
- Establish culture
- Code of conduct
- Risk assessment
- Business conduct
- Reporting
- Monitoring

Doing the right thing

Conflicts of interest
- Conflicts of interest in the exam
  - Read relevant task information
  - Identify ethical conflicts at stake
  - Use scenario information
  - Make recommendations
  - Justify recommendations
- Resolving ethical conflicts
  - No one best way to achieve
  - Resolving conflicts is influenced by a range of factors
- Frameworks for dealing with ethical conflicts and dilemmas
  - A number of frameworks exist

Tucker's 5 questions
Is the decision you are making:
- Profitable?
- Legal?
- Fair and equitable?
- Right?
- Sustainable?

Corporate codes of ethics
- Values and expected behaviours
- Consequences and sanctions

Professions and the public interest
- Influence of the accountancy profession on organisations
  - Mechanistic
  - Judgemental

The code of ethics for accountants
- Principles-based approach
- The fundamental ethical principles (ACCA, 2019):
  - Professional behaviour
  - Integrity
  - Professional competence and due care
  - Confidentiality
  - Objectivity

Threats and safeguards for accountants
- Advocacy threat
- Self-interest threat
- Intimidation threat
- Familiarity threat
- Self-review threat

Knowledge diagnostic

1. Fraud occurs if there is pressure to commit such an act, there is opportunity to go unnoticed and the perpetrator can rationalise the behaviour – it is an intentional act so cannot be seen as error

2. Bribery is about improper influence while corruption is about deviation from proper behaviour – however, it is not always straightforward when determining either of these in practice3.
    Tucker's 5 questions allow us to determine if a decision is right: is it profitable, legal, fair, right and sustainable?

4. Codes of ethics exist for organisations in general (corporate codes) and for accountants (the fundamental ethical principles known as 'PIPCO') (ACCA, 2019) who need to justify their actions in the public interest

5. Threats to acting in an ethical manner can be summarised by 'AS IFS' but they can be mitigated by suitable responses known as safeguards

Question practice

Now try the question below from the Further question practice bank (available in the digital edition of the Workbook):

Q9 *Pogles*

Further reading

There are articles on the ACCA website written by members of the SBL examining team which are relevant to your studies and which would be useful to read:

Ethical decision making

This article considers different approaches that can be taken when making ethical decisions.

Approaching SBL overview

This article provides a one-page summary of the key features of the SBL exam.

Approaching SBL reading and planning

This article provides a one-page summary of how best to approach the SBL exam.

SBL – 10 things to learn from the September 2018 sitting

This article highlights some of the issues that ACCA identified in candidates' answers during the September 2018 SBL exam sitting. The article provides some useful advice for improving your chances of passing the SBL exam.

Strategic Business Leader – The importance of effective communication for SBL

This article provides some useful insights into the different formats which you will be expected to use when answering SBL exam tasks.

Own research

Fraud is always a topical issue and by the time you read this chapter, a brand new story may have emerged, so try and stay alert to stories of companies or individuals who have committed, or are being investigated about fraud, bribery or corruption.

If you need some inspiration, you can research the following examples:

- **Fraud** – UK grocer Tesco in 2015 was investigated for manipulating its financial statements by recognising income items inappropriately

- **Bribery and corruption** – Arms manufacturer BAE has been under scrutiny for many years over deals made with Saudi Arabia for weapons – was it a bad thing to pay illegal bribes that would guarantee jobs in its factories?

Exercise answer

Exercise 1

As part of your remit to consider the possible risks of fraud in a procurement process, you could have identified a series of stages in the process – the list presented below is structured in a way that is more detailed than required for the marks on offer, but should still show you what areas you needed to cover.

(a) **Suppliers**

Examples include **disqualification of suitable suppliers**, a very **short list of alternatives** and **continual use** of the **same suppliers** or a single source. The organisation should also be alert for any signs of personal relationships between staff and suppliers.

(b) **Contract terms**

Possible signs here include **contract specifications** that do not make commercial sense and contracts that include special but unnecessary specifications that only one supplier can meet.

(c) **Bid and awarding process**

Signs of doubtful practice include **unclear evaluation criteria, acceptance of late bids** and **changes in the contract specification** after some bids have been made. Suspicions might be aroused if reasons for awarding the contract are unclear or the contract is awarded to a supplier with a **poor performance record** or who appears to **lack the resources** to carry out the contract.

(d) **After the contract is awarded**

Changes to the contract after it has been awarded should be considered carefully, along with a large number of **subsequent changes in contract specifications** or **liability limits**.

This is perhaps one of the risk areas over which the company can exert the greatest control, through a coherent corporate strategy set out in a fraud policy statement and the setting up of strict internal controls.

BPP
LEARNING
MEDIA

Assessing and managing risk and ethical issues

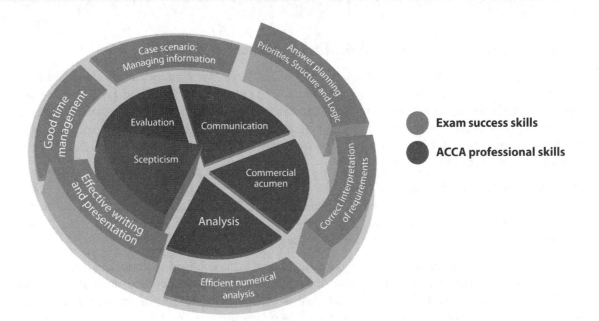

Introduction

In Stage 3 you have learned about the importance of assessing and managing risk and ethical issues.

However, only 80% of marks are awarded for the application of knowledge. The remaining marks are awarded for good demonstration of the specific ACCA Professional Skills outlined in the requirement.

You need to able to:

1. Identify the ACCA Professional Skill in the task requirement. Remember the five: Analysis, Communication, Commercial Acumen, Evaluation and Scepticism

2. Understand what the skill requires in the context of the question

3. Consider how to demonstrate the skill(s) as part of your answer planning

The ACCA Professional Skills are assessing your ability to present your answers to a standard which would be expected in the workplace. However, in order to do this effectively in the Strategic Business Leader Exam, you must develop a further series of Exam Success Skills, so you are able to produce your very best solution in the four-hour timeframe.

Therefore, success in Strategic Business Leader requires the simultaneous demonstration of syllabus knowledge, ACCA Professional Skills and Exam Success Skills. This Skills Checkpoint specifically targets the development of your skills as you progress through the syllabus. This should provide you with all of the tools that you will need during the Learning phase, so you can focus on these improving at the Revision Stage.

The five Skills Checkpoints focus each on one of the five ACCA Professional Skills and provide further guidance on how to develop certain Exam Success Skills, so you can effectively manage questions and meet the expected standard for both knowledge and skills.

Your role

Developing skills requires more than listening and reading, it requires you to try for yourself, use guidance and feedback to consider whether you have met the skills objective, then plan for further improvement. In Strategic Business Leader, you should include a focus on skills development in every question you attempt as part of your normal approach. The Skills Checkpoints will take you through a series of steps where you will attempt aspects of a question and review your progress from a skills perspective.

Focus on ACCA Professional Skill: Scepticism

There are three essential elements to scepticism that ACCA have identified for their professional skills. The first is the ability to probe deeply into the underlying reasons for issues and problems, beyond what is immediately apparent from the usual sources and opinions available. It seems sensible to consider scepticism as an enhanced form of professional curiosity where you do not simply take what you are told at face value but instead look beneath the obvious and consider what questions and queries you might have from a given situation.

The second is to question facts, opinions and assertions, by seeking justifications and obtaining sufficient evidence for their support and acceptance. Again, this seems logical once you have started to probe something more deeply: are you happy with what you have been told or does it need something else to satisfy you that all is as it should be?

The third and final approach to demonstrating scepticism is to challenge information presented or decisions made, where this is clearly justified, in a professional and courteous manner. Assuming you have asked questions and received insufficient or inappropriate responses, the next step for you is to push back and state that you are not satisfied with the response and that you need something else. The skill description continues to set this in context, in the wider professional, ethical, organisational or public interest which is critical when allied to the need for professional behaviour.

Demonstrating Exam Success Skills

For this question, we will focus on the following exam success skills:

- **Correct interpretation of requirements**. You will have heard the advice 'read the question' or 'RTQ' many times as part of your studies so far, and we are not going to change that now! However, some task requirements may prove difficult to understand due to long, complex sentences and multiple verbs, which indicate a series of tasks instead of just one. It is therefore critical that you can deconstruct the task requirement to isolate each verb and ensure you plan to supply a suitable response in each case.

- **Answer planning: Priorities, Structure and Logic**. Once you know what the task requirement is looking for, you can start to search for answers to the list of things you need to do. Reading the case with this list in mind will help you quickly isolate the important things and discount the rest. Note that for Roasta Bean Co which follows, we only have one case scenario, but in the real exam there will be the overview and a number of supporting exhibits, so this process is going to require some time (at least 10% of the time allocated to the question). At this stage, you will also aim to work out the number of marks available for each task requirement which should allow you to start considering the number of points a good answer should contain to score well.

- **Effective writing and presentation**. Once you have your answer plan, the structure of your answer should have started to take shape: judicious use of expanded bullet points with suitable sub-headings using appropriate language should act as a series of signposts that lead the reader through your answer.

Skills Activity

 Read the following task requirement for the question 'Roasta Bean Co', identifying the verbs and the professional skills being examined, and start to set up your answer plan. Remember your skills of 'Correct interpretation of the requirements' as there are two task requirements here and they are not straightforward to interpret!

Required

Recommend the control mechanisms that should be implemented to reduce the problems associated with the ethical risks. **(10 marks)**

Discuss the extent of the responsibilities of internal audit for ensuring that the ethical problems do not recur. **(6 marks)**

Professional skills marks are available for demonstrating **scepticism** skills in relation to your recommendations and discussion. **(2 marks)**

(Total = 18 marks)

- There are evidently problems within this organisation, so you need to isolate them first.

- You then need to consider the ethical issues associated with these risks – are they connected in any way?

- What should be done to try and reduce the impact of these risks for part (a) – again, are there any connected activities or suggestions here?

- How much can (and should) internal audit do to help for part (b)?

 You should now read the scenario, considering the ethical issues that may have led to the problems you find, how they can be addressed and how much the internal auditors can do to try and help. The scenario has been annotated to show what sort of things you should be looking for when performing this kind of 'active' reading.

Question – Roasta Bean Co (18 marks)

> It appears that the ethical issues have been identified already using these sub-headings – this is good news!

Roasta Bean Co ('RBC') is a chain of coffee shops that operates 75 shops in its home country. A number of ethical problems have recently arisen at RBC, and an emergency meeting of its board has been convened to discuss their implications.

Thefts from stores

> This is concerning – how have dishonest people been employed in the first place and how have they been able to get away with this in one of RBC's shops? Suggests poor recruitment and poor ethics

Three employees in one shop have been dismissed for thefts of both produce and cash. These thefts were only identified because one of the employees was foolish enough to steal, and then sell, the bags of coffee beans on the premises of the RBC coffee shop in which they worked. A customer reported the incident to the chief executive of RBC and an investigation of the shop revealed that two other employees had also been involved in the theft.

> Why did no employee spot this or report it? Again, poor example being set and no control in shops. Perhaps Internal Audit could monitor this?

Drug dealing

One of the coffee shop managers was reported by a customer, and subsequently arrested, for selling illegal Class A substances in their RBC coffee shop and allowing drugs to be taken on the site. Police investigations showed that this had been taking place for at least ten months.

Fair trade

A routine advertising campaign promoting RBC stated, *'RBC is aiming to have all its coffee supplied by Fair Trade suppliers'*. However, a former RBC Head Office employee recently stated in the national press that only around 60% of RBC coffee was procured from Fair Trade suppliers. An investigation revealed that the figure was in fact around 80% but the percentage bought from Fair Trade suppliers had fallen by 5% over the past year.

RBC's Chief Executive is very concerned about all these issues. He feels that they demonstrate that RBC has a poor ethical culture and could seriously damage the company's reputation. They wish to introduce measures to improve RBC's ethical culture and to use the company's recently appointed internal auditors to ensure that the measures are effective.

STEP 3 You are now in a position to create an answer plan.

Guidance in helping you develop your answer plan

As the question is worth 18 marks, using two minutes per mark as a guide equates to a total of 36 minutes to attempt the task requirement. Working on the basis that you will spend at least five minutes creating your answer plan this leaves 31 minutes to write up your answer.

Each point you make could score up to two marks, so for part (a) you are looking at five separate points, while part (b) for six marks would require three separate points.

Demonstrating scepticism would be necessary to earn the two professional marks and these seem to relate to probing more deeply into the reasons behind these ethical issues and considering just how much evidence the internal audit team can realistically create if, for example, a prosecution is required into drugs offences.

Having already annotated the scenario with the task requirements in mind, your answer plan may start to look something like this.

- How to stop the problems of theft, drug abuse and breaking company policy?
  - Recruitment of the right kind of people
  - Training in how to behave
  - Sanctions for those that do not behave
  - Better monitoring and support for employees who may know about these problems but not have an outlet for reporting them
  - Culture – is the 'tone from the top' appropriate to encourage suitable ethical behaviour?
- What can Internal Audit do about this?
  - As much as the board wants them to do
  - Greater involvement in systems testing in shops
  - Any other evidence that could be used to highlight problems (eg other KPIs such as customer complaints)
  - Mystery shopping or surprise visits?

STEP 4

Check the requirements

Before you start writing up your answer it is worthwhile reviewing the task requirement again to ensure that there is nothing that you have overlooked.

- Part (a) requires recommendations, so make them clear and specific, stating what actions should happen and how they would address each ethical issue

- Part (b) is a discussion of points that may not all be in harmony with each other, but must state the extent of Internal Audit's involvement to answer the question

 STEP 5

Complete your written answer

You can now bring your workings together to create a solution, making sure that you use logical headings and short punchy sentences. Drawing together the key points from the scenario with your recommendations and discussions will show the marker that you have dealt with both task requirements. A model answer is given below, with comment boxes illustrating where the answer is demonstrating good scepticism skills.

Suggested solution

(a) **Board example**

> This displays scepticism because you are demonstrating that you can probe into the reasons for poor ethical behaviour – in this case, the lack of ethical leadership by the board

The board should make clear when communicating with staff that they are committed to ethical behaviour and they expect staff to be committed as well. Appointing a board member as **ethics champion** emphasises board commitment as well as being a contact point for whistleblowing (discussed further below).

Code of conduct

A code of conduct could be used to **remind staff of RBC's objectives** of being an ethical business. Staff should be required to commit to the code when they join RBC. This would strengthen the basis for disciplinary action if they transgress.

Communication with employees

> This displays scepticism because you are demonstrating that you can probe into the reasons for poor ethical behaviour – in this case, the lack of clear policy on sourcing coffee beans

The board needs to ensure that specific **ethical objectives** are **communicated unambiguously** to staff. With RBC, although coffee was ideally meant to be sourced 100% from Fair Trade suppliers, it has been impossible recently to attain this target. There may therefore have been confusion, and local managers may have regarded it as acceptable to source from non-Fair Trade suppliers if there were significant cost advantages in doing so.

Central policies

One way of preventing problems with the use of non-Fair Trade suppliers would be to insist that shops only used suppliers on a **centrally approved list**. Alternatively, a **central purchasing function** could be responsible for making purchases for all shops.

Recruitment

One way of reducing the risk of dishonest acts by staff is to ensure that staff who are recruited do not have records of bad behaviour. References should be **required and confirmed for all staff**.

Appraisal

Staff should also be **regularly appraised** and the results of appraisals **communicated to senior management**. If appraisals indicate staff unhappiness, this may suggest that problems are more likely to occur.

Disciplinary procedures

There should be clear disciplinary sanctions against staff who are found guilty of dishonesty or unethical behaviour, including **dismissal from employment**. If necessary, staff accused of dishonesty should be suspended until the accusation is resolved.

Manager rotation

Staff may not have reported problems because of misplaced loyalty to, or fear of, management or colleagues. One way of preventing this would be to **rotate managers between shops on a regular basis**, to prevent a situation where managers allow problems to persist over a long time.

Whistleblowing

Both the drug dealing and the coffee beans sales were reported by customers and not staff. This suggests a lack of channels for staff to **report problems confidentially**, and therefore the board needs to make clear who staff should contact if they have concerns.

This displays scepticism because you are demonstrating that you can probe into the reasons for poor ethical behaviour – in this case, the lack of a suitable whistleblowing function at RBC

Monitoring procedures

Lastly the board should review evidence available from **information systems and internal audit work** and investigate signs of problems. The shops where there were ethical problems may have been underperforming in other areas.

(b) ### Extent of responsibilities

The **extent of internal auditors' responsibilities** are **defined by the board**. They can be given wide-ranging duties in relation to fraud, unlike external auditors whose responsibilities are concentrated on frauds that have a material impact on the financial statements.

Specific tests

Audit tests could be used as a matter of course to pick up certain problems. Here, for example, **reviewing shop purchase records** and checking whether suppliers used were, or could have been, Fair Trade would have identified that problem.

Consideration of other evidence

Internal audit should be alert for evidence that does not directly indicate fraud, but indicates the **general possibility of problems** at the shops. These include accounting results that are very much better or worse than other shops and high staff turnover. Inadequate records or unwillingness to respond to auditor enquiries should also put the auditors on alert. These are signs that the shop may be high risk and thus require greater audit work.

This displays scepticism because you are demonstrating awareness of the underlying reasons for these behaviours

Recommendations for improvements

Internal audit will be responsible for making recommendations to management for improvements in systems that could prevent problems occurring, or make it easier for management to detect them. These include **shortcomings in human resource procedures**, such as failure to check references properly. They could also include improvements in the **reports** provided by the information systems. Internal audit feedback could be a very useful source of information when changes in the information systems are being considered.

> This displays scepticism because you are demonstrating awareness of how to obtain sufficient evidence

Audit approach

Conducting audits solely by **pre-announced visits** may limit the assurance the audit gives, since staff at the shops may behave while the auditors are there and cover their tracks beforehand. **Surprise visits** may identify issues such as **shortages of cash or inventory**.

Lack of evidence

> This displays scepticism because you are challenging the assumption made by the Chief Executive of RBC that Internal Audit can solve every problem

However, internal audit can only reasonably be expected to detect frauds that impact in some way on the **business's systems**. It appears that the drug dealing manager took care to ensure that they covered their tracks, and did not leave any information for the internal auditors to detect. Internal auditors can also only be expected to work within their **own areas of expertise**. They are not trained members of the Police Drug Squad.

Prevention of problems

Internal audit should always have a **monitoring and detection role**. To preserve internal audit independence, it should not be responsible for implementing systems that prevent problems occurring. If these are fully effective, then there will be nothing for internal audit to detect.

 STEP 6 **Complete the exam success skills diagnostic**

Finally, use the diagnostic below to assess how effectively you demonstrated the exam success skills in answering the question.

Exam Success Skills	Your reflections/observations
Case scenario: Managing information	Did you extract the key points from the scenario? In this case, the ethical issues were specifically identified; however, not every question you do will highlight the problems in the same way, so be prepared to exercise your 'analysis' skills if required.
Correct interpretation of requirements	Did you identify that the task requirement consisted of two verbs, 'recommend' and 'discuss'? Did you appreciate the importance of displaying your scepticism skills?
Answer planning: Priorities, Structure and Logic	Did you adopt a systematic approach to planning, understanding the task requirements first, then working through the scenario to extract relevant information?
Efficient numerical analysis	Not applicable in this question.
Effective writing and presentation	Have you used headings to structure your answer, with short sentences and paragraphs? Are your points made clearly and succinctly?
Time management	Did you allocate sufficient time to attempt both parts of the task requirement?
Most important action points to apply to your next question	

Summary

Answering exam questions is like any other skill – the more you practise, the better you will get! But, after attempting a question, make sure you take time to reflect and debrief how well you managed it, whether you followed the key steps and whether you demonstrated professional skills. Carry forward your learning points to the next question you attempt, and over the course of your studies you will see significant improvements.

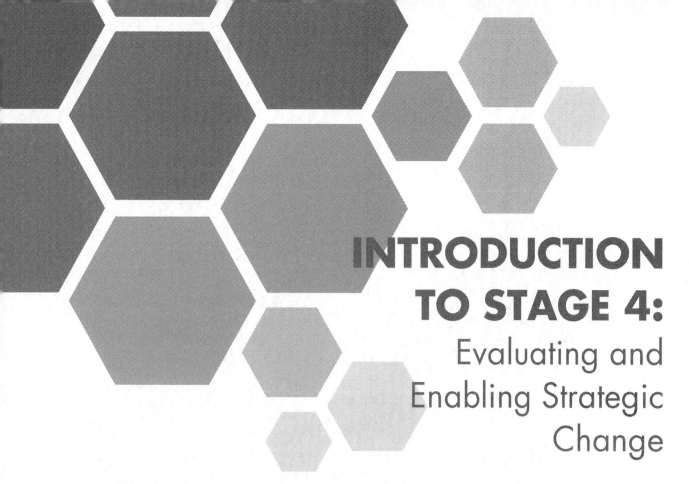

INTRODUCTION TO STAGE 4:
Evaluating and Enabling Strategic Change

Evaluating and Enabling Strategic Change

In 1999, a former English teacher called Jack Ma started a company with some friends called Alibaba.com. Mr Ma had been introduced to the internet on a recent visit to the US and was convinced that it was being under-exploited in his native China. The site was designed to enable business-to-business e-commerce, letting exporters post product listings and buyers browse. By exploiting technology to enable and be part of China's export boom, the business grew rapidly. In 2003 it founded Taobao, a consumer-to-consumer online shopping platform, and has since acquired and developed a number of technology and media-related businesses.

In 2014, Alibaba listed on the New York Stock Exchange and raised $25bn, making it the largest IPO ever, anywhere in the world. In 2016 sales made over its platforms were greater than the revenues of Walmart, one of the world's largest retailers. The company has faced periodic controversy over fraudulent sellers and sales of counterfeit goods but has generally managed to retain the strong reputation essential for people to trade on it with confidence.

As Alibaba illustrates, technology opens up opportunities for new business ventures at the same time as threatening existing ones. A successful business exploits technology to meet a real need, but also ensures that it has a strong business model, which will generate strong financial returns. The main site, Alibaba, earns most of its revenues from fees paid by merchants for privileges, while the main revenues from Taobao are earned from advertising. Unlike companies such as Amazon, Alibaba does not supply any goods itself, acting simply as an intermediary between buyer and seller.

In this section, we will review some of the developments in technology shaping business and how they can be applied. We will also look at the tools of financial analysis that can be used to evaluate opportunities and determine whether they are financially beneficial or not.

Financial analysis 10

Learning objectives

On completion of this chapter, you should be able to:

	Syllabus reference no.
Explain the relationship between an organisation's financial objectives and its business strategy	G1(a)
Discuss how advances in information technology have transformed the finance function and the role of the finance professional	G1(b)
Evaluate alternative structures for the finance function using business partnering, outsourcing and shared or global business services	G1(c)
Determine the overall investment requirements of the organisation	G2(a)
Assess the suitability, feasibility and acceptability of alternative sources of short and long-term finance, including initial coin offerings (ICO), available to the organisation to support strategy and operations	G2(b)
Review and justify decisions to select or abandon competing investments or projects applying suitable investment appraisal techniques	G2(c)
Justify strategic and operational decisions taking into account risk and uncertainty	G2(d)
Assess the broad financial reporting and tax implications of taking alternative strategic or investment decisions	G2(e)
Assess organisation performance and position using appropriate performance management techniques, key performance indicators (KPIs) and ratios	G2(f)
Discuss, from a strategic perspective, the continuing need for effective cost management and control systems within organisations	G3(a)
Evaluate methods of forecasting, budgeting, standard costing and variance analysis in support of strategic planning and decision making	G3(b)
Evaluate strategic options using marginal and relevant costing techniques	G3(c)

Business and exam context

Like other business functions, finance is in the process of being transformed by technology. Routine transactions are being automated and new possibilities are being opened up, such as outsourcing and shared service centres. This means that, in turn, accountants are expected to spend less time in producing reports and processing transactions, instead focusing on being true business partners, adding value to their organisation and helping them to run more effectively. This includes being able to understand and interpret information in a wide range of formats, including published accounts, budget reports, key performance indicators and investment appraisal. Accountants are expected to understand the links between different types of information, how they link to the wider context and the implications for the organisation. They also need to be able to use management accounting techniques in support of decision making, recognising that the financial issues are only one part of the picture, and non-financial issues are important as well.

It is important to stress that your finance knowledge from Applied Skills exams is assumed knowledge in SBL. However, the detailed techniques will not be tested in this exam. Instead, you will be expected to be able to analyse quantitative and qualitative information and draw appropriate conclusions to help solve organisational problems.

Chapter overview

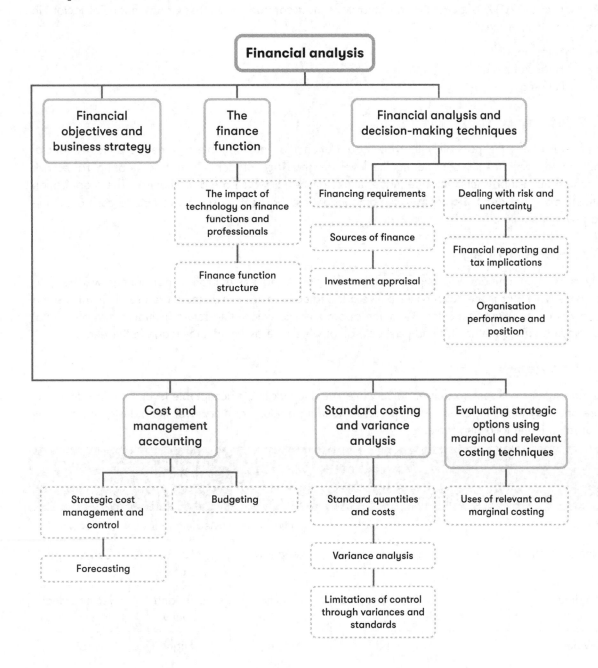

1 Financial objectives and business strategy

Johnson *et al* (2017) suggest that organisations must consider a number of key financial factors in assessing their strategy.

- Financial risk
- Financial return
- Funding

1.1 Financial risk

Financial risk is the possibility that an organisation may not be able to meet its critical financial obligations. This means considering the level of **gearing**, or debt. Increased gearing raises risk because interest payments must be made, unlike dividends which are discretionary. The organisation should also consider its **liquidity** – the amount of cash or assets easily convertible to cash available to pay immediate bills.

1.2 Financial return

Investors in a company will expect a financial return, and not-for-profit organisations will need to consider value for money of services delivered. Strategic decisions will therefore usually involve some analysis of the returns expected. Common approaches to calculating return include return on capital employed, NPV analysis, IRR and payback, all of which are assumed knowledge in this exam.

1.3 Funding

Organisations will seek to deliver value while keeping risk to an acceptable level. Funding decisions are one way to manage risk. An appropriate funding model may vary over the industry life cycle as illustrated in the following table:

	Launch (Question mark)	Growth (Star)	Maturity (Cash Cow)	Decline (Dog)
Business risk	Very high	High	Medium to low	Low
Financial risk, therefore	Keep very low	Keep low	May be increased	Can be high
Funding	Venture capital	Equity	Debt and equity	Secured debt
Dividends	Nil	Nominal, if any	High	Total

(Adapted from: Ward, 1993)

Real world examples

In theory, the overriding financial goal of commercial organisations is to maximise profit, and this requirement is imposed on them by shareholders. However, a detailed study of 12 large US companies published in Harvard Business Review (Donaldson, 1985) challenged this view, arguing instead that:

- Companies have no absolute financial priorities – they change over time
- Goals are prioritised based on the relative power of stakeholders
- Goals are inevitably limited by the environment
- Financial goals are unstable due to shift in power and influence in the company
- Reconciling demand for, and supply of, funds means that all goals are interdependent
- Managers have difficulty committing to all the financial goals

This means that financial goals may not always be well-aligned with business strategy and more care should be taken to ensure that financial goals are consistent with each other, the environment and the business strategy. The role of politics and power struggles within organisations should also be recognised.

2 The finance function

Like most other business functions, the finance function and the role of those who work in it have been transformed in recent years by technology and other changes in the business environment. This has led to the development of new models for organising the finance function.

2.1 Impact of technology on finance functions and professionals

A number of specific developments in technology are having an impact on finance functions, including:

- **Big Data** – modern technology gives the ability to analyse large amounts data very quickly and deliver results in real time. This may include financial and non-financial data. Organisations are increasingly requiring this from their finance functions.

- **Cloud computing** – traditionally, finance systems have been hosted by the organisations but software vendors are now providing cloud-based solutions. These can reduce costs by eliminating the need for in-house hardware and maintenance staff and offer benefits such as a more intuitive interface, mobile access and built-in analytics.

- **Predictive analytics** – specialist software can use data to assess probable future trends. This might include sales, inventory or cashflow.

In addition, finance functions are increasingly being affected by **FinTech**, a general term covering a range of technologies including secure payment and Blockchain.

In order to benefit from these tools, finance professionals need to ensure they understand relevant technology and are willing to embrace the changes it brings. The overall effect is to reduce the time spent in processing transactions and reconciling information, and more on generating and interpreting reports.

Syllabus link

The general impact of these tools and others is explored in Chapters 11 and 12.

2.2 Finance function structure

Illustration 1

These changes have implications for the way a finance function is structured. Many organisations adopt a **business partner** approach. This means that some finance professionals are fully embedded in the operational divisions, bringing their financial expertise to the management process. They will be expected to gain a good understanding of the business and be commercial in their approach.

A complementary approach is to **outsource** aspects of routine processing to an external provider. This can bring benefits of economies of scale, efficiency and investment in technology, but may bring issues of control. An organisation will need to ensure that its provider has strong controls in place over areas such as fraud and misstatement and may be required to confirm this for regulatory purposes. Professional firms can assist by reviewing a provider's controls and providing some assurance that they are effective.

An alternative approach, which keeps some of the benefits of outsourcing while mitigating some of the risks, is to set up **shared or global business services**. This is an in-house function which provides finance support to all functions within the business, even if they are separate subsidiaries or based in different countries.

Key term

Business partner: Means finance (or other support) professionals being fully embedded in the operations of the business.

Syllabus link

We introduced the concept of internal partnering in Chapter 6, this is again considered in Chapter 13. The general concepts of outsourcing and shared services will be explored further in Chapter 13.

Real world example

NHS Shared Business Services (NHS SBS) provides finance and accounting support to much of the UK's National Health Service, along with payroll, employee benefits and procurement. It is a joint venture between the UK government's Department of Health and a private consulting firm, Sopra Steria. Services include managing general ledger processing, compliance reporting, invoicing and payment collection as well as generating management reports. The NHS SBS (2018) website highlights that over 35% of NHS organisations use them, and that to date it has delivered audited savings of £400m to its clients.

Take some time to research NHS SBS, or an equivalent shared service centre. You may find it easier to research organisations in the public sector rather than private sector as they tend to make more information public. How does it operate and how are cost savings and efficiencies achieved?

Activity 1: Syngen plc

ACCA Professional skills focus

Evaluation: Appraise

You are the group financial controller at Syngen, a multinational company which has grown steadily and has ambitions to expand further in the next few years. Most finance staff work in one of several regional 'hubs' that support a number of countries in that region. There are an increasing number of complaints from the business about the support provided by the finance function, and now the Operations Director has emailed the Finance Director, your manager, setting out his dissatisfaction. Your manager has asked you to consider whether outsourcing or a shared or global business service approach would help to address these issues, and send her an email with your thoughts. She would also like you to identify the key practical issues to consider if they do move ahead with one of these solutions.

Required

Prepare a draft response to the Finance Director. **(12 marks)**

Professional skills are available for demonstrating **evaluation** skills in **appraising** whether these solutions would address the concerns specified. **(2 marks)**

(Total = 14 marks)

Exhibit 1 – Email from Operations Director

To: Finance Director
From: Operations Director

As you know, I have previously expressed concerns about the support the business receives from the finance function and wanted to set them out in writing for your consideration. Every year, the costs we are allocated for the finance function increase and yet the support we receive gets worse. What is more, the support really varies according to when we ask for it. At the beginning of each month, we keep getting told they can't help because they are dealing with month-end close, and then at year end everything else seems to shut down for a month. The business doesn't stop at that time and we still need reports and analysis.

I also have real concerns about the amount of time some of our processes are taking. In this day and age, why are invoices being signed off in person? Some of our key suppliers are complaining about the delays in payment this causes. In some countries, we have electronic approval so clearly it can be done. Why not everywhere?

This is something I want to raise at a board meeting so wanted to give you some time to consider how to address it. We are happy to co-operate with any solution that will improve these issues.

Regards

Solution

3 Financial analysis and decision-making techniques

3.1 Financing requirements

There are three types of decision relevant to the financial requirements of the business:

1   **Investment** decisions – identify investment opportunities and decide which ones should be accepted

2   **Financing** decision – how should the organisation be financed in the short and long term?

3   **Dividend** decisions – how much to pay out as dividends to shareholders

These are very much interrelated. The investment decisions determine the amount of finance needed and dividend decisions affect the amount of cash available for re-investment.

Organisations will need to prepare cash forecasts to understand what funding will be required in the future. It is much easier to raise funding if time is available, rather than do so in an emergency. The organisation may consider including **sensitivity analysis** in their forecast to understand the impact of changes in certain variables, such as demand or inflation, on their future cash needs.

Any forecast deficiency will need to be funded by borrowing, selling investments or delaying payments to suppliers and pulling in payments from customers (sometimes known as **leading and lagging**).

Key terms

Sensitivity analysis: Means calculating the effect of changes in certain variables such as demand or inflation on a forecast.

Leading and lagging: Means raising cash by delaying payments to suppliers and accelerating receipts from customers.

3.2 Sources of finance

A number of sources of finance are available to organisations, although this will vary. For example, a not-for-profit organisation cannot raise equity finance and may not wish to borrow, so will have to finance itself from operating cashflows. As with other key strategic decisions, sources of finance can be evaluated using the SAF model:

- **Suitability** – is the method of finance appropriate for the use we want to make of it? For example, a long-term asset can be financed by long-term debt but it would be inadvisable to finance working capital this way.

- **Acceptability** – will the method be acceptable to stakeholders, including current providers of finance? For example, risk-averse shareholders might not want a company to take on additional debt.

- **Feasibility** – can the additional finance be raised? Are the banks prepared to lend, or shareholders to invest more money?

A summary of the most common sources of finance is set out below:

Method	Advantages	Disadvantages
Retained profits/Operating cashflows	Simple, no change in ownership	Restricts dividend payouts, may not be sufficient for growth
Issue shares	Long-term capital	May dilute existing control
Bank loan	Repayments are known and can be budgeted, flexible, quick, no dilution of control	Increases gearing and financial risk, interest must be paid, may be restrictive covenants and/or security required
Bank overdraft	Flexible, only pay interest on amount owing, does not count towards gearing as short-term debt	Repayable on demand so less reliable, often more expensive
Loan capital	Similar to bank loan, may not have restrictive covenants	Slower to put in place than bank loan, more public, will carry issue costs

Method	Advantages	Disadvantages
Initial coin offering (ICO) (ICOs are discussed in greater detail in section 3.2.1)	Simple, no change in ownership, enable start-up and smaller companies to attract international investors	Failure to raise the amount of funding required means the company has to return any funds raised to investors ICOs tend to be unregulated and have become associated with fraud

3.2.1 Initial coin offering (ICO)

Key term

Initial coin offering (ICO): Involves the creation of virtual 'tokens' which are sold to raise funds for business projects.

An initial coin offering (ICO) is a relatively recent development that is increasingly being used by companies seeking funding for their operations. ICOs involve raising funds for business projects through the use of internet technologies and cryptocurrencies. Cryptocurrencies are digital currencies which are increasingly being used to facilitate transactions made online, well-known examples include Bitcoin and Ethereum currencies. Cryptocurrencies are discussed in more detail in Chapter 12.

ICOs tend to be used by start-up and smaller companies that do not have access to traditional methods of finance. ICOs allow companies to raise funds to support business projects that they wish to undertake. Common projects include plans to develop and launch new products and services. Companies wishing to raise funds for their business project aim to attract potential investors by publishing a 'whitepaper' which details the aims of the project. A whitepaper might include the details of the new product/service to be developed, the required level of funding needed to support the project, the length of time that the ICO remains open, and the types of currency that investors can use to support the project ie cryptocurrencies or real currencies.

In the event that the target level of funding is not reached during the offer period, any funds raised up until to this point are returned to investors. Where the required level of funding is achieved, investors receive a virtual 'token' in exchange for their investment. It is important to note that tokens do not provide investors with an equity stake in the company. ICOs only benefit the investor when the business project that they helped to fund is successful. Successful business projects increase the value of the token, thereby allowing the investor to realise a profit when they sell their 'token' investment to other interested parties.

ICOs are currently unregulated in many parts of the world as regulators attempt to establish rules to control how they are used. As such ICOs tend to be regarded as high risk, particularly for investors, due to the volume of fraudulent schemes associated with their operation. In recent times a growing number of fraudulent ICO schemes have been reported, which operate with the intention of stealing the funds invested by unsuspecting investors.

PER alert

Performance Objective 9 'Evaluate investment and financing decisions' of the Practical Experience Requirement requires you to 'advise on the appropriateness and cost of different sources of finance' (ACCA, 2019b). It is therefore important that you take the time to ensure that you understand the implications for organisations when choosing between different sources of finance.

3.3 Investment appraisal

You have previously learned about the investment appraisal techniques return on capital employed, payback, net present value and internal rate of return. These are assumed knowledge in this exam. You will not be required to prepare these analyses but may well be required to review them and use them to decide whether a particular investment opportunity should be selected or abandoned.

Key terms

Return on capital employed: Is also known as accounting rate of return or return on investment. It can be used for projects as well as organisations.

Payback: Is a calculation of how long it will take an investment to pay itself back, ignoring the time value of money.

Net present value: Is a calculation of all cash flows relating to an investment, allowing for the time value of money.

Internal rate of return: Is the discount rate that will bring the net present value to zero for a given set of cash flows.

Essential reading

See Chapter 10 sections 1 to 6 of the Essential Reading, available in Appendix 2 of the digital edition of the Workbook, for more detail about the types of investment appraisal techniques that exist.

Activity 2: Investment appraisal

ACCA Professional skills focus

Scepticism: Challenge

You are a management accountant providing support to an operational division. The manager of the division has shown you an NPV analysis and made some comments on the approach used. This is given below as Exhibit 1.

Required

Critically evaluate the manager's comments on the investment appraisal approach used to evaluate internal projects. **(10 marks)**

Professional skills marks are available for demonstrating **scepticism** skills in challenging the comments made. **(2 marks)**

(Total = 12 marks)

Exhibit 1 – Meeting notes

The company uses the Net Present Value (NPV) technique as a way of choosing which projects should be undertaken. Figure 1 shows an example comparison of two computer system applications that had been under consideration. Project One was selected because its Net Present Value (NPV) was higher ($25,015) than Project Two ($2,090).

In discussing this, the manager of the division said to you. 'In the end, Project One was a disaster. Looking back, we should have gone with Project Two, not Project One. We should have used simple payback, as I am certain that Project Two, even on the initial figures, paid back much sooner than Project One. That approach would have suited our mentality at the time – quick wins. Whoever chose a discount rate of 8% should be fired – inflation has been well below this for the last five years. We should have used 3% or 4%. Also, calculating the IRR would have been useful, as I am sure that Project Two would have shown a better IRR than Project One.'

		Year 0 $'000	Year 1 $'000	Year 2 $'000	Year 3 $'000	Year 4 $'000
Project 1						
Costs	Hardware costs	50	0	0	0	0
	Software costs	50	0	0	0	0
	Maintenance costs	10	10	10	10	10
	Total	110	10	10	10	10
Benefits	Staff savings	0	40	5	0	0
	Contractor savings	0	20	10	10	10
	Maintenance savings	0	0	10	40	60
	Total	0	60	25	50	70
	Cash flows	−110	50	15	40	60
	Discount factor at 8%	1.000	0.926	0.857	0.794	0.735
	Discounted CF	−110.000	46.300	12.855	31.760	44.100
Project 2						
Costs	Hardware costs	50	0	0	0	0
	Software costs	30	10	10	0	0
	Maintenance costs	10	10	10	10	10
	Total	90	20	20	10	10
Benefits	Staff savings	0	30	10	5	0
	Contractor savings	0	30	15	15	15
	Maintenance savings	0	0	10	20	20
	Total	0	60	35	40	35
	Cash flows	−90	40	15	30	25
	Discount factor at 8%	1.000	0.926	0.857	0.794	0.735
	Discounted CF	−90.000	37.040	12.855	23.820	18.375

Figure 1: NPV calculation for two projects (with a discount rate of 8%)

Solution

3.4 Dealing with risk and uncertainty

Decisions frequently need to be made under conditions of risk and uncertainty. A number of techniques have been developed to help make these decisions and are assumed knowledge from your previous studies. We will here particularly focus on decision trees and expected values.

Key terms

Risk: Involves situations or events which may or may not occur, but whose probability of occurrence can be calculated statistically and the frequency predicted.

Uncertainty: Involves situations or events whose outcome cannot be predicted with statistical confidence.

Expected value (or **EV**): Is a weighted average value, based on probabilities.

The expected value for a single event can offer a helpful guide for management decisions.

If the probability of an outcome of an event is p, then the expected number of times that this outcome will occur in n events (the expected value) is equal to n × p. The higher the EV, the better the project.

However, evaluating decisions by using expected values has a number of limitations.

(a)   The **probabilities** used when calculating expected values are likely to be estimates. They may therefore be **unreliable** or **inaccurate**.

(b)   Expected values are **long-term averages** and may not be suitable for use in situations involving one-off decisions. They may therefore be useful as a **guide** to decision making.

(c)   Expected values do not consider the **attitudes to risk** of the people involved in the decision-making process. They do not, therefore, take into account all of the factors involved in the decision.

(d)   The time value of money may not be taken into account: $100 now is worth more than $100 in ten years' time.

Probabilities and expected values can be represented diagrammatically using **decisions trees** in order to aid decision making.

Key term

A decision tree: Is a diagram which illustrates choices and the possible outcomes of decisions. It shows both the probability and the value of expected outcomes.

To help with decision making, we work from right to left and calculate the expected value (EV) at each outcome point. This may be used to calculate revenues, cost, contribution or profit.

For example, below is a decision tree for a new product which has been developed. The company is trying to decide whether to test-market it or abandon it.

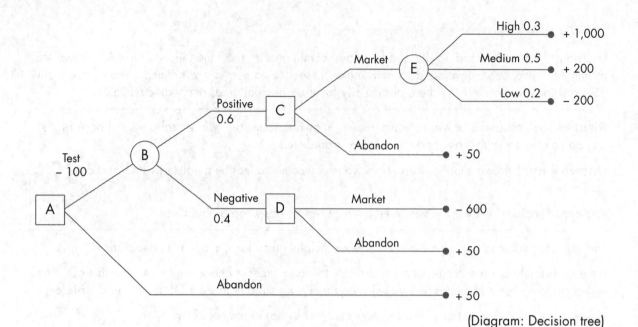

(Diagram: Decision tree)

Working right to left, we can use this to help our decision as follows:

(a)   At point E, the EV is 360 ([0.3 × 1,000] + [0.5 × 200] + [0.2 × –200]).

(b)   At point C we therefore have a choice of marketing the product with an EV of 360 or abandoning it with an EV of 50. We will choose to market the product so the EV at point C is 360.

(c)   At point D we can market the product with an EV of –600 or abandon it with an EV of 50. We will abandon it, so the EV at point D is 50.

(d)   At point B, we have a 0.6 probability of C with an EV of 360 and a 0.4 probability of D with an EV of 50. Our EV at point B is therefore 236 ([0.6 × 360] + [0.4 × 50]).

(e)   At point A we can test-market the product which gives EV of 136 (EV at B minus marketing costs of 100). Alternatively, we can abandon the product, which gives a value of 50. **In the absence of other factors, we will choose to test-market the product because it gives higher EV.**

Evaluating decisions by using a decision tree has a number of limitations:

- The time value of money may not be taken into account.

- Decision trees are not suitable for use in complex situations.

- The outcome with the highest EV may have the greatest risks attached to it. Managers may be reluctant to take risks which may lead to losses.

- The probabilities associated with different branches of the tree are likely to be estimates, and possibly unreliable or inaccurate.

3.5 Financial reporting and tax implications

When making strategic and investment decisions, it is important to take all relevant information into account, and this include relevant financial reporting and tax implications. In the SBL exam, you may need to take significant tax and FR implications into account when evaluating or choosing between alternative strategies and this should be given in the scenario or relevant exhibit.

This will not involve detailed consideration of tax and reporting issues. For example, you may be required to consider significant differences in tax rates or other types of fiscal burden on an organisation in different jurisdictions of a multinational corporation. If considering raising equity or debt or whether to purchase or lease a major asset, there may be particular tax or FR implications.

However, it will deal with strategic level implications that a business leader, not necessarily a tax or FR expert, would need to be aware of.

Real world example

In 2016 the European Commission ruled that tax arrangements between the US technology company Apple and the government of Ireland amounted to state aid and were illegal under European law. Most of Apple's foreign profits are earned by Irish subsidiaries, who hold the rights to their intellectual property but, under a deal agreed by the Irish government, those entities were not tax resident anywhere and therefore paid little tax. Apple contested the ruling, saying that their arrangements were not special and open to any company. Nonetheless, such a high-profile company may be concerned about the reputational damage resulting from the controversy, and the appearance that they have developed their corporate structure with the main aim of minimising tax paid.

3.6 Organisation performance and position

It is likely that in your exam you will be required to analyse data and draw conclusions about an organisation's performance over a time period and its current position. This may well involve analysing a wide range of data including financial ratios, non-financial key performance indicators and qualitative data. Your previous studies covering financial ratios and performance management are assumed knowledge here, but the emphasis will be on high-level analysis, not on preparing information.

It is vital that your analysis draws links between the different performance indicators and any background information you have. This will be a test of your commercial awareness and ability to 'think on your feet'.

Essential reading

See Chapter 10 section 7 of the Essential Reading, available in Appendix 2 of the digital edition of the Workbook, for more detail about the calculation of key financial ratios.

Activity 3: Performance evaluation

ACCA Professional skills focus

Analysis: Enquire

You are a consultant who is reviewing data about a client, ALPHA plc. As a first step in the engagement, you have been asked to assess their current performance against budget. An analysis of this is given below as Exhibit 1.

Required

Using the information below, prepare an appraisal of the performance of ALPHA compared to budget for 20X0 covering non-financial and financial indicators. **(16 marks)**

Professional skills marks are available for demonstrating **analysis** skills in enquiring, by analysing appropriate data sources **(4 marks)**

(Total = 20 marks)

Exhibit 1 – ALPHA performance data

The current date is December 20X1.

ALPHA is a large manufacturing company that specialises in the design and manufacture of internet-enabled televisions. It was formed a number of years ago, following the merger of two rival companies, and is now one of the three largest TV manufacturers in Asia. ALPHA employs over 2,000 staff at its head office and four manufacturing plants, which are all in the same Asian country, Jurania. ALPHA is listed on the Juranian stock exchange. In recent years, it has particularly built its reputation on the basis of being a low-cost supplier.

The following is a summary of the performance of ALPHA last year (20X0). ALPHA reports its performance in the currency of its home country, the Juranian dollar (J$).

20X0

Financial performance	Actual	Budget
	J$ millions	J$ millions
Sales revenue	1,793	1,941
Gross (Factory) profit	1,177	1,320
Pre-tax profit	652	790
Capital employed (average)	2,835	2,550
Cash (closing)	179	485
Finished goods inventory (average)	38.2	20.0
Raw material inventory (average)	11.4	9.5
Work in process (average)	0.8	0.3

20X0

Other performance indicators	Actual	Budget
Share price (closing) (J$)	334.50	400.00
Earnings per share (J$)	46.00	50.00
Number of employees (average)	2,259	2,128
Sales (million units)	2.35	2.40
Number of finished units re-worked	54,000	29,375*
Percentage of purchases from suppliers rejected (by value)	4.25%	3.00%
Average production cost of sales per unit (J$)	262	259
Average sales price per unit (J$)	763	809
New product lines developed	12	10
New product lines successfully launched	1	4
Products returned from customers as faulty (per 1,000 units sold)	28	20
Warranty claims (per 1,000 units sold)	56	30
Number of working employee days lost to industrial disputes	2,500	3,200
Finished goods inventory days	22.6	11.8
Work in progress days	0.47	0.18
Raw material days	6.75	5.58
Net margin	36.4%	40.7%
ROCE	23%	31%

* Flexed for actual production levels

Solution

 Exam Focus Point

The Strategic Business Leader specimen 2 exam featured a public sector rail company, Rail Co, which was responsible for providing rail services within the country of Beeland. The second question required candidates to act in the capacity of an assistant auditor, working for the National Audit Authority (NAA), the Beeland government's audit authority. The NAA was conducting an investigation into the performance of Rail Co following negative publicity relating to poor levels of service. Candidates were provided with spreadsheet information which included a variety of data relating to the results of a recent passenger survey, and other performance information. Part (a) of question 2 asked candidates to prepare a report for the Rail Co Trust Board which evaluated 'the implications of the findings of the passenger survey results' and reviewed 'the actual and relative performance of Rail Co over the last three years' (ACCA, 2017a).

This task was worth 12 technical marks and tested the ACCA Professional Skill of Analysis. To produce a good answer candidates needed to address the two parts of the task ie the implications of the findings and review of performance. To earn the two professional skills marks candidates needed to support their answer by including a 'wide range of relevant calculations on both customer survey results of Rail Co and its relative performance' (ACCA, 2017a). Candidates were also expected to reflect upon the results of the data and calculations performed.

4 Cost and management accounting

4.1 Strategic cost management and control

Any organisation needs to manage its costs in order to achieve its strategic objectives. A cost leader will seek to minimise costs so that they can reduce prices and compete effectively, and a differentiator will aim to manage costs so as to improve its margins. A not-for-profit organisation will aim to manage costs in order to make the best use of its resources.

PER alert

Performance Objective 12 'Evaluate management accounting systems' of the Practical Experience Requirement requires you to 'evaluate management accounting techniques and approaches in an organisation' (ACCA, 2019b). To help you identify the types of management accounting techniques that you may have encountered in the workplace you are advised to take the time to read through the remaining sections of this chapter.

There are various techniques of overhead apportionment which are used to measure costs including overhead absorption and activity-based costing. These allow assessment of the full cost of a product or service.

Key term

Full cost: Is the total amount sacrificed to achieve a particular objective, including all related costs.

Full costing supports decision making in a number of areas including:

- Pricing and output – how many should be made and what price charged to the customer?

- Exercising control – by comparing actual and budgeted performance and addressing discrepancies

- Assessing efficiency – current processes can be compared with different locations, or alternative methods of working, to determine the current efficiency.

- Assessing performance – revenue generated by a product or service can be compared to its full cost.

Strategic cost management means not just measuring costs and performance against budget but focusing on what is driving costs, whether they can be reduced, and whether resources are being allocated in the best possible way to support the achievement of the organisation's strategy.

4.2 Forecasting

Exam Focus Point

Question 1 of the Strategic Business Leader exam in September 2018 featured a task which asked candidates to analyse the financial and non-financial issues involved in deciding whether or not to accept a contract. Candidates were expected to make use of the financial forecast information that had been provided in one of the exhibits.

Forecasting can help with planning and decision making by making predictions about the future. They can be **qualitative** and based on judgement. Techniques for doing this include:

(a) The **Delphi technique** involves selecting a panel of experts, each of whom is asked to produce an independent forecast. These forecasts are shared, and each then goes on to produce a revised forecast. The process continues until they are in agreement and a definitive forecast is produced.

(b) **Sales force opinions** involve a sales manager gathering input from the sales team and collating their opinions into an aggregate forecast.

(c) **Executive opinions** arise from meetings of high level managers during which they develop forecasts based on their knowledge of their own individual areas of responsibility.

BPP
LEARNING MEDIA

(d) **Market research** involves the use of customer surveys to evaluate potential demand.

Organisations can also use **quantitative** techniques, which are based on the use of historical data to predict the future. They involve the identification of patterns and variations between variables, including linear regression and time series analysis.

You have seen these techniques in your previous studies. In SBL, you will not be required to perform detailed calculations. The emphasis will be on reviewing analysis and evaluating it in support of strategic planning and decision making for the scenario organisation.

4.2.1 Linear regression

Linear regression measures the relationship between two variables:

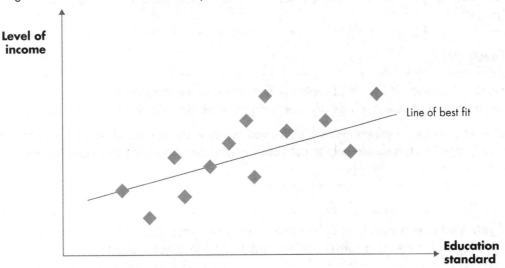

(Diagram: Linear regression)

The strength of the relationship is measured by **correlation coefficient** (often shown as 'r') which can range from +1 (exact positive relationship) through 0 (no relationship) to –1 (exact negative relationship).

The **coefficient of determination** is calculated as r^2 and explains the proportion of variation in one variable that is explained by variation in the other. For example, if r = 0.992, then r^2 is 0.984, suggesting that 98.4% of the variation in y can be explained by variation in x.

There are a number of issues with using linear regression:

(a) It can establish a relationship between two variables, but this does not mean that a change in one variable **causes** a change in the other. The relationship may be coincidence, or caused by other variables.

(b) It depends on having enough data, and the data being reliable.

(c) When used for forecasting, it assumes that the past is a reliable guide to the future, which may not be correct.

4.2.2 Time series analysis

Time series analysis aims to separate seasonal and cyclical fluctuations from long-term underlying trends. It is therefore a form of regression analysis where one variable represents time.

Advantages	Disadvantages
It takes account of seasonal patterns, which most organisations experience.	It ignores factors other than time that cause change.
It is widely understood and fairly straightforward.	It does not take account of how old data is.

Advantages	Disadvantages
Past data may not be reliable.	As with all regression, it assumes that the future will show the same trend as the past.

Key terms

Linear regression: Is the numerical relationship between two variables.

The coefficient of determination: Explains the proportion of variation in one variable that is explained by variation in the other.

Time series analysis: Aims to separate seasonal and cyclical fluctuations from long-term underlying trends.

4.3 Budgeting

PER alert

Performance Objective 13 'Plan and control performance' of the Practical Experience Requirement requires you to 'co-ordinate, prepare and use budgets, selecting suitable models' (ACCA, 2019b).

To help you achieve this Performance Objective you are strongly advised to read through this short section on budgeting as it should help to put your experiences of budgeting at work into the wider context of the strategic planning process.

Key term

A budget: Is a business plan for the short term, usually one year. It is likely to be expressed in financial terms and its role is to convert the strategic plans into specific targets.

It therefore fits into the strategic planning process as follows.

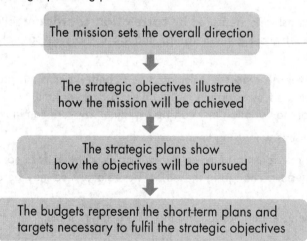

The mission sets the overall direction

The strategic objectives illustrate how the mission will be achieved

The strategic plans show how the objectives will be pursued

The budgets represent the short-term plans and targets necessary to fulfil the strategic objectives

These budgets will then have to be **controlled** to ensure the planned events actually occur. This is as much a part of the budgeting process as actually setting the budget.

4.3.1 Benefits and limitations of budgets

There are five main benefits of budgets.

1   **Promotes forward thinking**. Potential problems are identified early, therefore giving managers time enough to consider the best way to overcome that problem.

2   **Helps to co-ordinate the various aspects of the organisation**. The activities of the various departments and sections of an organisation must be linked so that the activities complement each other.

3   **Motivates performance**. Having a defined target can motivate managers and staff in their performance. Managers should be able to relate their own role back to the organisational objectives, seeing as the budgets are based on these objectives.

4   **Provides a basis for a system of control**. Budgets provide a yardstick for measuring performance by comparing actual against planned performance.

5   **Provides a system of authorisation**. Allows managers to spend up to a certain limit. Activities are allocated a fixed amount of funds at the discretion of senior management, thereby providing the authority to spend.

However, budgets also have their limitations.

1   Employees may be **demotivated** if they believe the budget to be unattainable.

2   **Slack** may be built in by managers to make the budget more achievable.

3   Focuses on the **short-term results** rather than the underlying causes.

4   Unrealistic budgets may cause managers to make decisions that are **detrimental** to the company.

4.3.2 Successful budgeting

Successful budgetary control systems tend to share the same common features.

- **Senior management** take the system seriously. They pay attention to, and base decisions on, the monthly variance report. This attitude cascades down through the organisation.

- **Accountability**. There are **clear responsibilities** stating which manager is responsible for each business area.

- **Targets** are **challenging but achievable**. Targets set too high, or too low, would have a demotivating effect.

- **Targeted reporting**. Managers receive specific, rather than general purpose, reports so that they do not have to wade through information to find the relevant sections.

- **Short reporting periods**, usually a month, so that things can't go too wrong before they are picked up.

- **Timely reporting**. Variance reports should be provided to managers as soon as possible after the end of the reporting period. This is so they can take action to prevent the same problems occurring in the next reporting period.

- **Provokes action**. Simply reporting variances does not cause change. Managers have to act on the report to create change.

5 Standard costing and variance analysis

A standard: Is a carefully predetermined quantity target which can be achieved in certain conditions.

Key term

It is often used as the basis for budgeting and for control purposes, by comparing the standard against actual results. It may also be used as a basis for valuing inventory.

5.1 Standard quantities and costs

Key terms

> **A standard cost:** Is an estimated unit cost.
>
> **Standard costing:** Involves the establishment of predetermined estimates of the costs of products or services, the collection of actual costs and the comparison of the actual costs with the predetermined estimates. The predetermined costs are known as standard costs and the difference between the standard and the actual cost is known as a **variance**. The process by which the total difference between standard and actual results is analysed is known as **variance analysis**.

Standard costs are of most benefit for repetitive processes. Standard costing is therefore most suited to mass production and repetitive assembly work and less suited to organisations which produce to customer demand and requirements.

Standards are useful in providing data for income measurement and pricing decisions and can help to improve the efficiency of an organisation. However, standards set too highly can have a demotivating effect if they are not perceived to be achievable.

5.2 Variance analysis

When actual performance is compared to standards and budgeted amounts, there will inevitably be **variances**. They may be favourable or adverse, depending on whether they result in an increase to, or a decrease from, the budgeted profit figure. At this level, you will not be expected to calculate variance but may be required to interpret or criticise a variance report.

Variances may occur for a number of reasons. One possible reason is that the budget itself was not realistic. However, there are many other reasons why variances may arise, including poor staff performance, changes in market conditions or process inefficiencies.

> **Essential reading**
>
> See Chapter 10 section 8 of the Essential Reading, available in Appendix 2 of the digital edition of the Workbook, for more detail about variances and their meaning.

5.3 Limitations of control through variances and standards

Standards and variances are useful for decision making but they have limited application. For example, where spending is discretionary, such as for advertising or human resource development, there is no direct link between inputs and outputs. There are also potential problems when applying standard costing techniques.

(a) Standards can quickly become **out of date**. Regularly monitoring and updating standards can be costly and time consuming.

(b) Variances for which a manager is held accountable can be influenced by factors that are **out of the control** of that manager.

(c) **Lines of responsibility** between managers can be difficult to define.

(d) Once a standard has been met, there is **no incentive to improve**.

(e) May encourage undesirable behaviour, such as encouraging managers to build up excess inventories, leading to significant storage and financing costs. This could happen if managers exploit opportunities for bulk purchase discounts to attain a favourable direct materials price variance.

6 Evaluating strategic options using marginal and relevant costing techniques

When an organisation is trying to decide between two or more possible courses of action, only **costs that vary with the decision** should be included in the decision analysis, ie it should only consider **relevant costs**.

Key term

> **Relevant costs:** Are those costs that are relevant to a particular decision. All fixed costs are irrelevant to the decision because they will be the same whatever decision is made. Similarly, any costs which do not represent cash, or have already been incurred, are not considered relevant.

As fixed costs are ignored, **marginal cost** (the cost of producing one additional unit) usually equals the variable cost per unit. This will be true unless there is a step in the fixed costs, in which case that step, or increment, will be included as well as the variable costs.

6.1 Uses of relevant and marginal costing

Marginal analysis is particularly useful in four key areas of decision making:

1   Marginal analysis can be used to decide **whether or not a special contract should be accepted** by determining the contribution (revenue less cost) that the price offered would yield. Positive contributions suggest the organisation would be better off accepting, rather than rejecting, the special contract. However, there will also be other factors that are difficult, or impossible, to quantify which will also have to be considered before a final decision is made. For example, the contract itself may have a negative contribution, but it may lead to further more lucrative contracts, or help the organisation enter a new market.

2   Usually output is restricted by level of demand, rather than by the organisation's ability to produce. However, sometimes there is a **limit to the amount that can be produced due to a scarce (limiting) factor**, such as labour, space or machinery. The most profitable combination of products will occur where the contribution per unit of the scarce factor is maximised.

3   A common decision faced by businesses is whether to **produce the product or service they sell themselves or whether to buy it from another business**. Marginal costing can help with this by identifying the contribution of both options, as with accepting or rejecting contract decisions. However, there will be other factors that the organisation will have to take into account when making this decision. These other factors include loss of control of quality, potential unreliability of supply, and access to expertise and specialisation.

4   Many organisations produce separate financial statements for each department or section in order to attempt to assess the relative effectiveness of each one. By using these to look at the variable costs, the **contribution for each can be determined**. This means the organisation can determine the contribution to the overall organisation that the individual departments make. Departments that make a positive contribution should not be closed even if individually they make a loss. This is because the fixed costs would still be incurred and the organisation would be worse off without it.

Activity 4: DynoCars

ACCA Professional skills focus

Evaluation: Estimate

You are a management accountant working for DynoCars, a niche car manufacturer. You have been asked to assist in evaluating the financial case for outsourcing the manufacture of one of their car models.

Required

Evaluate the financial case for and against the outsourcing option. **(8 marks)**

Professional skills marks are available for demonstrating **evaluation** skills in estimating the impact of your calculations on the decision facing the organisation. **(2 marks)**

(Total = 10 marks)

Exhibit 1 – Background information

DynoCars manufactures three car models: the Family, the Luxury, and the Small.

The company is suffering from capacity constraints and, to address this, is considering outsourcing the manufacture of the Small model to an overseas company. Information relevant to this decision is presented in Figure 1. The potential manufacturer has quoted a production price of $3,500 per car.

There are 112 production hours available in total per week at DynoCars' manufacturing site (seven days per week, two eight-hour shifts) which can be used for a combination of the three product lines.

The weekly overhead costs are $35,000 per week at the site. If the production of the Small model is outsourced, it is forecast that overhead costs will fall by $1,250 per week. The transportation cost is estimated at $250 for each outsourced Small model produced.

	Family	Luxury	Small
Selling price per car ($)	9,999	12,999	6,999
Variable cost per car ($)	7,000	10,000	4,500
Weekly demand (cars)	6	5	6
Production time per car (hrs)	9	10	8

Figure 1: Information relevant to the outsourcing decision

Solution

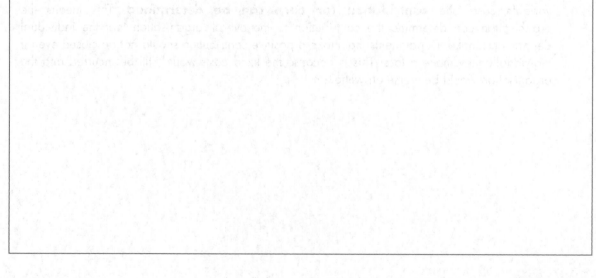

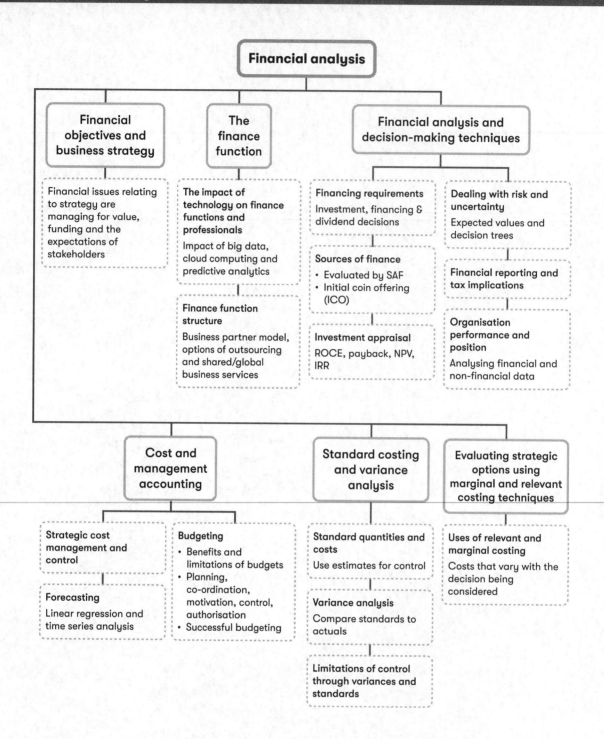

Financial analysis

Financial objectives and business strategy

Financial issues relating to strategy are managing for value, funding and the expectations of stakeholders

The finance function

The impact of technology on finance functions and professionals

Impact of big data, cloud computing and predictive analytics

Finance function structure

Business partner model, options of outsourcing and shared/global business services

Financial analysis and decision-making techniques

Financing requirements

Investment, financing & dividend decisions

Sources of finance
• Evaluated by SAF
• Initial coin offering (ICO)

Investment appraisal

ROCE, payback, NPV, IRR

Dealing with risk and uncertainty

Expected values and decision trees

Financial reporting and tax implications

Organisation performance and position

Analysing financial and non-financial data

Cost and management accounting

Strategic cost management and control

Forecasting

Linear regression and time series analysis

Budgeting
• Benefits and limitations of budgets
• Planning, co-ordination, motivation, control, authorisation
• Successful budgeting

Standard costing and variance analysis

Standard quantities and costs

Use estimates for control

Variance analysis

Compare standards to actuals

Limitations of control through variances and standards

Evaluating strategic options using marginal and relevant costing techniques

Uses of relevant and marginal costing

Costs that vary with the decision being considered

Knowledge diagnostic

1. Johnson *et al* (2017) suggested that key financial issues in evaluating strategy include financial risk, financial return and funding.

2. A study by Donaldson (1985) emphasised that financial goals are changeable and influenced by the environment, internal constraints and the politics of the organisation.

3. The role of the finance function, and the people who work in it, is being transformed by a number of developments in technology including big data, cloud computing and predictive analytics.

4. Finance functions are responding by moving to a 'business partner' model, and considering whether to outsource certain activities, or move them into a shared or global business service centre.

5. Businesses need to make three types of financial decision – investment, financing and dividend.

6. Common sources of finance include retained cashflows, shares, loans, overdrafts, loan capital and initial coin offerings (ICO). They should be evaluated using the criteria of suitability, acceptability and feasibility.

7. Key investment appraisal techniques include return on capital employed, payback, net present value and internal rate of return. At this level, you need to be able to interpret the results of these analyses.

8. Many decisions are made under conditions of risk and uncertainty. Expected values and decision trees are two techniques that can help with this.

9. You may need to consider high-level financial reporting and tax implications of strategic decisions, but do not need to consider them in detail.

10. You need to be able to evaluate the performance and position of an organisation, drawing together financial and non-financial information to give a coherent picture.

11. A strategic approach to cost management means not just measuring costs but using the information to improve business control and performance, ensuring that resources are being used effectively to support the strategy.

12. Forecasting can involve qualitative techniques, based on judgement, or quantitative techniques such as linear regression and time series analysis.

13. The budget is a short-term business plan translated into financial terms. It has a number of benefits but can also cause problems such as demotivation and focus on the short term at the expense of the long term.

14. A standard cost is a predetermined cost which is used for control and possibly inventory valuation.

15. Variance analysis compares performance to actual results in order to highlight organisational issues which may need addressing.

16. Decision making generally involves considering relevant costs, those which are directly affected by the decision. This will exclude fixed costs, non-cash items and costs already incurred.

Question practice

Now try the question below from the Further question practice bank (available in the digital edition of the Workbook):

Q10 *Hammond Shoes*

Further reading

There are articles on the ACCA website written by members of the SBL examining team which are relevant to your studies and which would be useful to read:

Performance appraisal

This article explores how to interpret information in the context of performance appraisal.

Performance indicators

This article focuses on the interaction between objectives, critical success factors, and key performance indicators.

Approaching SBL overview

This article provides a one-page summary of the key features of the SBL exam.

Approaching SBL reading and planning

This article provides a one-page summary of how best to approach the SBL exam.

SBL – 10 things to learn from the September 2018 sitting

This article highlights some of the issues that ACCA identified in candidates' answers during the September 2018 SBL exam sitting. The article provides some useful advice for improving your chances of passing the SBL exam.

Strategic Business Leader – The importance of effective communication for SBL

This article provides some useful insights into the different formats which you will be expected to use when answering SBL exam tasks.

Own research

It is important to link the topics covered in this chapter to a practical, real-world context. As such, we have suggested some areas for you to investigate further:

- Find out about the main performance indicators used in your organisation or department (or another organisation with which you are familiar), both financial and non-financial. How were these indicators chosen? What follow-up action is taken when they are reported?

- What is the approach to budgeting in this organisation? Can you identify any benefits and problems?

- See if you can find an example in your organisation of a business decision which has been justified in financial terms. If you can't, try to find information about one online (hint: you may have more luck looking at public sector organisations than private sector ones, as they tend to disclose more information). What decision-making techniques were used? How were these chosen?

Applications of IT   11

Learning objectives

On completion of this chapter, you should be able to:

	Syllabus reference no.
Discuss from a strategic perspective the need to explore opportunities for adopting new technologies such as cloud and mobile technology within an organisation	E1(a)
Discuss key benefits and risks of cloud and mobile computing	E1(b)
Assess and advise on using the cloud as an alternative to owned hardware and software technology to support organisation information system needs	E1(c)
Discuss how information technology and data analysis can effectively be used to inform and implement organisation strategy	E2(a)
Describe big data and discuss the opportunities and threats big data presents to organisations	E2(b)
Identify and analyse relevant data for decisions about new product developments, marketing and pricing	E2(c)
Discuss from a strategic perspective the continuing need for effective information systems control within an organisation	E4(a)
Assess and advise on the adequacy of information technology and systems security controls for an organisation	E4(b)
Evaluate and recommend ways to promote cyber security	E4(c)
Evaluate, and if necessary, recommend improvements or changes to controls over the safeguard of information technology assets, to ensure the organisation's ability to meet business objectives	E4(d)

Business and exam context

In this chapter we explore the increasingly important role that information technology and information systems play in the operation of most organisations. We begin our discussion by considering the growing need for organisations to embrace new technologies. Technological advances in mobile technology and cloud computing have led to fundamental changes in how organisations operate and arrange their activities.

We then move on to consider the impact that the so-called 'internet of things' is having, and how the growing amount of data now available is helping organisations to inform and implement their strategies. These developments have led to the creation of the term 'big data'. As we shall see the term big data covers structured data such as sales figures which can be neatly stored in organisational databases, as well increasingly unstructured data sets such as photos or social media posts. The rise of big data presents organisations with both opportunities but also a significant number of challenges.

The final sections of the chapter are devoted to the need for increased cybersecurity and IT/IS controls. Data is becoming increasingly sought by criminal groups, including hackers, as they seek to exploit the value placed upon it by senior managers in organisations. Organisations need to implement appropriate controls to safeguard the value of their data and information assets.

Chapter overview

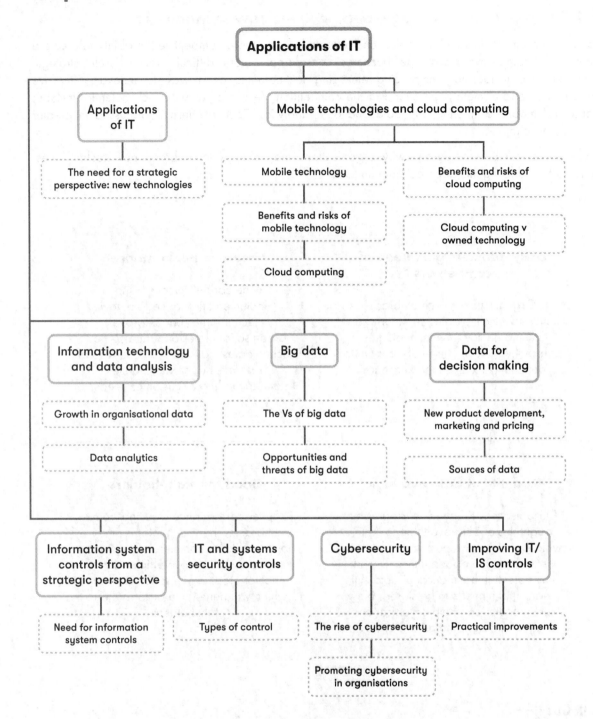

1 Applications of IT

1.1 The need for a strategic perspective: new technologies

As the environments in which organisations operate become more competitive the ability to create a sustainable competitive advantage becomes considerably more difficult. As a result, strategic managers are increasingly embracing emerging technologies as a way to innovate, improve performance and ultimately get ahead of the competition. Technologies with such potential include: cloud and mobile computing, big data and data analytics. Each of these is discussed in greater detail in this chapter.

There are a number of reasons why organisations may choose to embrace new technologies. Reasons for adopting this approach may include:

Early adopters get ahead of competitors

Organisations which embrace innovative technologies can learn how best to deploy new technologies before their rivals. This enables them to potentially increase market share.

Improve performance

The careful selection and implementation of certain new technologies can improve organisational performance eg new technologies may lead to better use of resources or create a better understanding of customer needs.

Quantity of data available

Organisations today have far greater quantities of data available to them which, unlike in the past, they can now use to exploit to opportunities. Despite this potential, having lots of data still means that it needs to be stored. New technologies can help organisations analyse and store the data they have.

Good for stakeholders

Better performance resulting from embracing new technologies may boost profits for commercial entities, or reduce costs/improve efficiencies for not-for-profit organisations. All of which will benefit the organisation's stakeholders.

Syllabus link

The pace of technological change has led to a number of new terms appearing in the business press in recent years. Terms such as FinTech and Blockchain are two such examples. Consideration is given to both terms in Chapter 12 when we explore e-business. The so-called 'internet of things' is another popular term, consideration of this is given later in this chapter when we discuss data analytics.

2 Mobile technologies and cloud computing

Mobile technologies and cloud computing have become increasingly important to most types of organisations in recent years.

2.1 Mobile technology

Key term

> **Mobile technology:** Is concerned with technology that is portable. Mobile technology devices include: laptops, tablet computers, smartphones, GPS technologies. Such devices enable users to communicate with one another in different ways, some of which may make use of the internet. Communicative features of mobile technologies include: Wi-Fi connectivity, Bluetooth and 4G technologies.

As the definition above illustrates, the widespread use of mobile technology has enabled those working within organisations to improve the ways in which they interact with one another, as well as with external stakeholder groups such as customers, suppliers and users of the organisation's services in the case of not-for-profit entities. The use of mobile technology has been instrumental in the sharing of information around the world. The rise in the amount of data generated and transferred between parties using mobile technologies does however heighten the need for improved data protection.

2.2 Benefits and risks of mobile technology

As with all technological advances, mobile technology offers a range of benefits and risks, some of which are discussed below:

Benefits of using mobile technologies	Risks of using mobile technologies
Allows access to organisational information and data when away from the workplace	The **purchase costs** of the latest devices (computers and phones) can be expensive and may be prohibitive in the case of smaller organisations. Furthermore, the increasing speed at which new mobile technologies are released increases the rate at which such devices become **obsolete**.
Makes it easier for organisational stakeholders to interact with the organisation; for example, customers can use mobile technologies to pay for goods without having to physically visit the organisation as payments can be made over the internet	The greater use of mobile technology devices increases the number of entry points for **unauthorised individuals** to gain access to organisational data, ie hackers may steal data or create viruses. To mitigate such risks robust measures are needed to **protect data**. These might take the form of firewalls, passwords and the provision of training in using mobile internet networks.

2.3 Cloud computing

Cloud computing technologies have changed the ways in which organisations store and manage their data. An increasing amount of organisational data is now held in servers operated by cloud-based service providers.

Key term

> **Cloud computing:** Is a model for enabling ubiquitous, convenient, on-demand network access to a shared pool of configurable computing resources (eg networks, servers, storage, applications and services) that can be rapidly provisioned and released with minimal management effort or service provider interaction (National Institute of Standards and Technology, 2011).

2.4 Benefits and risks of cloud computing

Cloud computing may provide an organisation with a number of benefits; however, these need to be considered against the risks:

Benefits	Risks
Using cloud computing services may be more **cost effective** than operating in-house technology.	The organisation has to **give up control** of its data to an external party being the cloud-based service provider. Such providers may be in remote locations and as a result this increases the risk should the provider suffer some form of **disaster event**.
Cloud computing offers **greater flexibility** to organisations as there are lots of service providers around to choose from. Furthermore, establishing a cloud-based approach to data storage and management can be done **faster** than establishing the technology in-house.	Data held by the service provider may be **stolen**, **lost** or **corrupted**.
Storing organisational data on the cloud means that it is **accessible anywhere around the world** where there is internet connectivity.	Increased danger that the service provider's own staff may **interfere with data** stored on its servers.
Cloud computing is **available** to both very large organisations and smaller entities.	**Failure to keep up payments** to the service provider to store data on the organisation's behalf may **lead to a loss of access or even the deletion of data**.

2.5 Cloud computing v owned technology

Building upon the benefits and risks outlined above in this section we explore the dilemma currently facing the senior management within many organisations: should the organisation pursue a cloud-based approach to data management or instead manage data using owned hardware and software in-house?

Answering this question will depend on a number of factors. Organisations with IT staff that possess the required levels of expertise to manage IT/IS systems may prefer to retain data storage and data management in-house. Complex data compliance requirements and a risk-averse attitude among senior management about allowing external parties to control organisational data make in-house retention more likely.

For some organisations, particularly small and medium-sized entities which need a global presence but lack the necessary IT expertise and resources to manage data in-house, a cloud-based approach offers a viable alternative.

 Real world examples

A report published by IT solutions firm, GFI Software™ (n.d) compared some of the main considerations when choosing between in-house IT data storage solutions and adopting a cloud-based approach. Some of the key findings have been summarised below. The final column in the table outlines the most appropriate outcome following the comparison of the two options:

Topic	In-house	Cloud	Outcome
Expertise	Employing top IT staff with niche skills can be very expensive	Cloud-based service providers provide staff with the expertise	Cloud
Support	Employing staff to monitor IT/IS infrastructures 24 hours a day is expensive	Cloud-based service providers monitor 24/7, however they may not monitor the data regarded as being most important to the organisation	In-house
Customisation	Data held internally can be customised to fit the organisation's needs	Although cloud-based service providers offer lots of choices around how data is configured and held, this will be limited	In-house
Service level agreements (SLAs)	When there is an outage it is the responsibility of the in-house IT team to get the IT/IS infrastructure operational again	SLAs put the onus on cloud-based service providers to restore systems. The organisation may benefit from financial penalty payments for any downtime.	Cloud

The level of significance given to each area of consideration outlined above will vary from organisation to organisation and will therefore influence the end decision.

Real world examples

An article by Bown (2016) highlighted the key findings from research conducted by Temenos, a software company based in Switzerland, which suggested that approximately 9 out of every 10 financial institutions now make some use of business applications which are operated in the cloud. Both Amazon and Google now offer cloud-based computing services. As Bown (2016) highlighted, the increased use of cloud-based applications is now creating new financial technology companies. Norwegian technology firm, Auka, created 'the first mobile payments platform run entirely on Google Cloud' (Bown, 2016).

3 Information technology and data analysis

The widespread use of information technology and data analysis tools is having a significant effect on how organisations inform and implement their strategies.

3.1 Growth in organisational data

Organisations today have more transactional data than they have ever had before – about their customers, suppliers and their operations. The ability to capture and store all of this data has been

BPP
LEARNING
MEDIA

made possible by advances in information technology. The growth of the internet, multimedia, wireless networks, smartphones, social media, sensors and other digital technology are all helping to fuel a data revolution. In the so-called 'Internet of Things', sensors embedded in physical objects such as mobile phones, motor vehicles, smart energy meters, RFID tags and tracking devices all create and communicate data which is shared across wired and wireless networks that function in a similar way to the internet. The timing and location of cash withdrawals from ATM machines could also be a potential source of data. Consumers using social media, smartphones, laptops and tablets to browse the internet, to search for items, to make purchases and to share information with other users also all create trails of data. Similarly, internet search indexes (such as Google Trends) can be sources of data for analysis.

Key term

The 'Internet of Things': This relates to sensors embedded in physical objects which are capable of creating, communicating and sharing data across wired and wireless networks that function in a similar way to the internet.

3.2 Data analytics

It is important to note however, that data on its own is usefulness unless it can be analysed in some way. SAS (2016) highlight that data analytics refers to the ability to analyse and reveal insights in data which had previously been too difficult or costly to analyse, due to the volume and variability of the data involved. The aim of data analytics software is to extract insights from unstructured data or from large volumes of data.

Being able to extract insights from data is of crucial importance. For example, data may help organisations to understand the complexity of the environment in which they are operating, and to respond swiftly to the opportunities and threats presented by it; or to develop new insights and understanding into what customers need or want.

Illustration 1

The following illustration shows how insurance companies have combined the power of information technology and data analytics to inform and implement their strategy.

Annual rises in car insurance premiums have made this a contentious issue for motorists around the world. For a number of years car insurance companies have set premiums with reference to a range of factors. Metrics such as age and gender are regarded as key measures when assessing the risks posed by drivers, with younger males being collectively viewed as representing a higher risk than older drivers. As a result, younger male drivers tend to be charged correspondingly higher car insurance premiums. Although it is easier for insurers to view all young males in this way, it overlooks the fact that they are not all dangerous when out on the road.

In recognition of this insurers have started to change their strategies to assessing risk, in the hope that this will make them more competitive. In recent years a number of car insurance companies have started using apps installed on the mobile phones of the drivers they insure as a way of measuring how safely they drive. Drivers are incentivised to download the insurer's app on the basis that it may save them money on their insurance premiums. Car insurance apps work by tracking the driver when in their car through the use of GPS technologies. Drivers receive a score based on the way in which they drive. Those drivers deemed to be safe behind the wheel are eligible to pay reduced premiums on the grounds that they represent a lower risk than unsafe drivers. In addition to tracking how drivers behave, most car insurance apps provide users with useful tips concerning how they can improve their driving.

The use of insurance apps has enabled insurers to improve their image among motorists by making them more responsive to concerns over rising premiums and has helped them to take a more individualistic approach to assessing the risks posed by the drivers they insure.

4 Big data

Big data: 'Is a popular term used to describe the exponential growth and availability of data, both structured and unstructured.' (SAS, 2016)

Exam Focus Point

Question 4 of the Strategic Business Leader exam in September 2018 required candidates to prepare presentation slides and supporting notes which discussed the benefits and costs (to the featured entity) of investing in big data analytics. You are strongly advised to take the time to carefully read through the following section on big data.

4.1 The Vs of big data

SAS (2016) cite the work of Laney (2000), who suggested that big data can be defined by considering the three Vs: volume, velocity and variety. The three Vs have now been extended to include veracity. It is important to note that other authors may refer to other terms when discussing big data, however in this section we shall focus solely on the four Vs.

Volume
The vast volume of data generated is a key feature of big data

Variety (or variability)
A common theme in relation to big data is the diversity of source data, with a lot of the data being unstructured (ie not in a database)

Veracity
This concerns the truthfulness of captured data

Velocity
This refers to the speed at which 'real time' data is being streamed into the organisation, and with which it is processed within the organisation

(Adapted from: SAS, 2016)

Activity 1: Retail World

ACCA Professional skills focus

Communication: Inform

Assume that it is late 20X6.

You are a finance professional working for Retail World (RW). You report to the newly appointed finance director. The new finance director, whose background is in a non-retail environment, is keen to understand the sales trends of the organisation, as well trends in the industry overall, in order to help develop a strategy which can take advantage of these trends in the future. As a result he asked you to attend a conference for professionals working in the retail sector. One of the sessions you attended at the conference focused on the increasing role that big data is playing in business. Interested to learn more, the finance director has asked you to investigate the ways RW could use big data, and to highlight the benefits that the company could obtain from its use.

Required

Using the information provided in Exhibit 1, **discuss** how the volume, veracity, velocity and variety Vs of big data could be used to enhance strategic development within RW. **(10 marks)**

Professional skills marks are available for demonstrating **communication** skills when informing the finance director about the uses of big data in relation to strategic development at RW. **(2 marks)**

(Total = 12 marks)

Exhibit 1 – Retail World

Retail World (RW) is a major international retail chain, selling groceries, clothing, electronic items, toiletries and homeware items. It has grown rapidly across a number of different countries, offering a broad product range to suit a wide range of customer segments. Growth has been through the expansion of existing stores, in addition to the opening of new stores.

The company's IT systems are fully integrated and associated controls are rigorous, allowing the data to be manipulated in many ways. The number of stores has grown annually and RW's CEO believes that this is the best indicator of expected future revenue. The average number of stores expected to be in operation in 20X7 is 3,700 rising to 4,000 in 20X8.

Solution

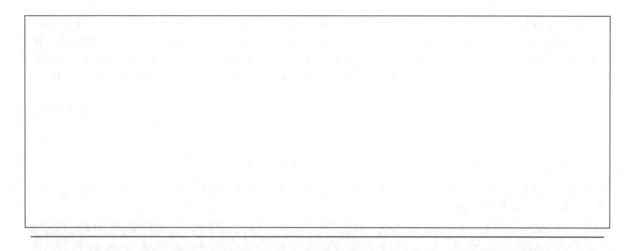

 Real world examples

In March 2014, Wall (2014) reported on the growing emphasis that big business is now placing on the role of big data.

It's not big, it's just bigger

Wall (2014) notes the word of Laurie Miles, Head of Analytics for big data specialist SAS, who explains that 'the term big data has been around for decades, and we've been doing analytics all this time. It's not big, it's just bigger.' Miles highlights that, for many years, organisations held traditional structured data, which could be neatly stored and organised in databases. However, over the last 20 years, the rise of the internet has led to a 'proliferation of so-called unstructured data, generated by all our digital interactions, from email to online shopping, text messages to tweets, Facebook updates to YouTube videos'. This has resulted in increasingly large and complex data sets, which have become harder to analyse. It is predicted that 90% of all the data in existence today has been created in the past few years. (Wall, 2014).

The big challenge

Wall (2014) highlights that the challenge for big business has been to capture and analyse these vast quantities of data, which may be of use in a commercial context. Miles notes 'data is only as good as the intelligence we can glean from it, and that entails effective data analytics and a whole lot of computing power to cope with the exponential increase in volume'.

Wall (2014) reports that a significant number of large entities have already turned to big data analytics with the aim of gaining a competitive advantage over their rivals. Proponents of big data analytics argue that the insights gained may lead to improvements throughout the entire organisation.

'Practically, anyone who makes, grows and sells anything can use big data analytics to make their manufacturing and production processes more efficient and their marketing more targeted and cost-effective.' (Wall, 2014).

Wall (2014) draws an important distinction between the role of big data analytics compared to historic data analysis. Big data is not just about understanding historic business intelligence, but instead combines several 'real time' data sets, which make it increasingly useful to big businesses.

The big questions

Wall (2014) notes that the rise of big data has had its implications. Organisations looking to exploit the opportunities presented have encountered a significant shortage of individuals with the required skills in the job market to analyse the data. Wall (2014) highlights the words of Duncan Ross, Director of Science at Teradata, who notes: 'big data needs new skills, but the business and academic worlds are playing catch up. The job of the data scientist didn't exist ten years ago.'

BPP
LEARNING
MEDIA

Questions have also been raised over who ultimately owns the data that organisations hold and who is responsible for keeping such data safe from hackers. Does it belong to the individual or customer, the company, the service provider hosting the data or the national jurisdiction where the data is held? (Wall, 2014) Such questions are unlikely to go away in the short term, as Miles highlights; it is a 'legal minefield'.

4.2 Opportunities and threats of big data

Big data presents organisations with significant opportunities, but these need to be matched against the threats posed by its use.

Opportunities offered by big data to organisations	Threats associated with big data
Processing greater quantities of data should allow organisations to **identify new trends and patterns** relevant to the organisation's success. Patterns may give deeper understanding of customer requirements. Data can be captured from both internal and external sources to reveal insights not previously known. For example, as more customers use the internet, smartphones and social media in their everyday lives, these can now also be sources of data for organisations alongside any data they may capture internally – for example, from customer loyalty cards or the transactions recorded in EPOS tills.	Capturing and storing greater quantities of data increases the scope for things to go wrong. Attempts by **hackers** to access organisational data sets are on the increase as such groups look to exploit the value of the data held. The widespread use of IT infrastructures in capturing and storing data in digital form presents a challenge in keeping it safe from the threats posed by computer **viruses**. This is a significant threat for those organisations whose business model is heavily dependent on transferring data over the internet, such as an online retailer. Viruses which **corrupt** organisational data may potentially have a devastating impact. The threats posed by hackers and viruses raise legal considerations especially if stolen or corrupted data relates to individual consumers. The organisation may **face legal action** if it is found that its measures for protecting data were not deemed sufficient.
The ability to process large data sets in real time allows organisations to **respond to changing conditions faster**. For example, online retailers are able to compile records of each click and interaction a customer makes while visiting a website, rather than simply recording the final sale at the end of a customer transaction. Moreover, retailers who are able to utilise information about customer clicks and interactions quickly – for example, by recommending additional purchases – can use this speed to generate **competitive advantage**.	The use of big data increases the danger that an organisation's management spend longer trying to determine the value and patterns within the vast amounts of data they have captured, instead of concentrating on running the organisation. The possession of lots of data **does not guarantee** that its analysis will identify any trends or patterns of any commercial use. Furthermore, there is a focus on finding correlations between data sets and **less of an emphasis on causation**. Critics suggest that it is easier to identify correlations between two variables than to determine what is actually causing the correlation.

Opportunities offered by big data to organisations	Threats associated with big data
Organisations increasingly have access to more diverse types of data. Historically data has tended to be in structured form (ie can be stored in databases), however there has been a growth in **unstructured data** (ie not in a database) which organisations have access to. For example, keywords from conversations people have on Facebook or Twitter, and content they share through media files (tagged photographs, or online video postings) could be sources of unstructured data. Such data provides organisations with a range of **new opportunities**, including: understanding what customers are saying about the organisation's products and services, and monitoring consumer reactions to competitor's products.	The diverse types of data available present a challenge to organisations as they need to find ways of capturing, storing and processing the data. If data is too big, moves too fast, or doesn't fit within an organisation's existing information systems, then in order to gain value from it, an organisation needs to find an alternative way to process that data. As a result, organisations may feel compelled to invest in upgrading their IT infrastructures to capture and store more data even if **the benefits of such an approach have not been fully considered**. The **technical and financial costs** imposed by regularly upgrading the organisation's hardware may be prohibitive for smaller organisations. Furthermore, just because an organisation is able to invest in the IT systems to analyse big data does not mean that the **skills in the job market** exist which will enable it to extract meaning from captured data.
Big data can provide organisations with an increasing amount of **accurate and detailed performance data** – in real or almost real time. By analysing the variability in performance – and the causes of that variability – organisations then can manage performance to higher levels.	For that data to be beneficial for decision making it needs to be reliable and truthful. If the data is **not truthful** (for example, due to bias or inconsistencies within it) this will reduce the value of any decisions which are informed by it. Moreover, **hidden biases** in the data could present significant risks to an organisation – for example, if the organisation develops a new product believing there is sufficient customer demand to make the product viable, when in fact that demand does not exist.

Real world examples

The following real-world example provides an interesting insight into how retailer Sainsbury's has been able to improve the performance of its monitoring of its suppliers as it strives to meet its sustainability commitments.

The *Accounting for Sustainability* website included a blog written by Sainsbury's Brand Director, Judith Batchelar, in which she explains how big data technologies are helping the retailer to achieve its aim of sourcing sustainable wild fish. 'Farmed fish is easier for us to manage, as we know where the farms are and we know how the fish are being managed, including the impact we are having on the local environment. Wild fish is not so easy. Much of it is caught thousands of miles away, in the middle of large oceans, where it is difficult to see what's really going on, let alone manage it. We have to rely on the certification process for the fish, but the paper-based system only starts when the fish is landed. We want to know what is happening at sea.' (Batchelar, 2017)

The big challenge for retailers concerns the fact that about 25% of the fish caught around the world is caught illegally. Working with technology firm, Satellite Catapult, Sainsbury's is able to view, in real time the vessels which are fishing on its behalf. Batchelar (2017) notes that 'earth observation satellites photograph fishing vessels around the world using that vessel's automatic location communicator (they can even see when vessels have switched this signal off). The satellites then collate this data with other data sets which can tell them the vessel's home port, its licence and quota, and the method of fishing it is meant to use. They take this information and, by using complex algorithms, can tell whether the vessel is behaving as would be expected, given everything we know about that vessel… so now we really can "measure what matters" when it comes to illegal, unreported and unregulated fishing. Protecting "Life below water" becomes a real possibility.'

5 Data for decision making

As we discussed in the previous section on big data, in order for an organisation's senior management to make informed decisions they need good quality data.

5.1 New product development, marketing and pricing

When making decisions about new product development, marketing and pricing strategies, senior management will want relevant data which will help them to answer the following key questions.

5.1.1 New product development decisions

- What are the potential costs of launching new products?
- What are the potential benefits of launching new products?
- Will new product development help the organisation achieve its objectives?
- Can the organisation develop existing products or is a totally new product required?
- Does the organisation have the required skills and competences needed?
- Should the organisation launch the product?

5.1.2 Marketing decisions

- How should new and existing products/services be promoted?

- Through which channels should the product/service be delivered?

- What features does the product/service need to have to meet customer needs?

- How important will the organisation's people be in developing/delivering the product/service to customers?

- Will organisational processes need to be updated to produce/sell the product/service?

- How might competitors respond to an initiative to the introduction of new products/services?

- What might the impact of the competitor response be?

- Which customers are most important/profitable to us?

- Why are some groups of customers more profitable than others?

5.1.3 Pricing decisions

- How is customer demand for a product/service likely to vary at different prices?

- How will this affect profits and cash flows?

- How does the proposed price fit with the organisation's overall generic strategy?

- How does it compare to competitors' prices?

- How do competitors' costs compare with ours?
- Are competitors vulnerable because of their cost structure or their product/service portfolio (or are we vulnerable because of our cost structure or our product/service portfolio)?

5.2 Sources of data

In order to determine answers to the above, an organisation will need to undertake some form of research. Market research might take the form of desk research (secondary research). Sources of desk research might include: reviewing competitor annual reports, databases, production records, records from the finance department, talking to the R&D team, customer complaints and customer loyalty schemes. Field research (primary research) involves getting information directly from respondents to gauge their opinions on a number of matters and might include getting feedback from customers on the organisation's latest marketing campaign or product release. Primary research methods include: asking customers to undertake questionnaires, getting feedback from focus groups, undertaking customer interviews.

Although a significant degree of traditional market research is still undertaken, organisations are now increasingly capturing this data about customer opinions from social media channels and through the technologies which make up the 'internet of things'.

Activity 2: Holiday Company

ACCA Professional skills focus
Commercial acumen: Demonstrate awareness

Assume the date is mid 20X6.

You are Boris Day, a management consultant; you are currently undertaking a consultancy assignment at the Holiday Company (HC). HC currently offers travel agency services by giving travel advice and making travel bookings for customers who physically visit the offices located in most major towns in the country. However, it is progressively reducing this part of the business while simultaneously trying to achieve a greater proportion of its revenue online. To help meet this objective, HC is in the process of forming a new business unit to market and sell luxury holidays. You have been engaged to provide advice to the HC board on establishing the new business unit. During your initial meetings with the managing director and director of marketing of the new business unit you have made some notes (Exhibit 1) which detail their future plans.

Required

Using the information and data provided in Exhibit 1, **describe** a strategic approach to establishing prices in the context of Inspirations. You should recognise both economic and non-economic factors in your approach. **(10 marks)**

Professional skills marks are available for **commercial acumen** in demonstrating awareness skills in the context of pricing at Inspirations. **(2 marks)**

(Total = 12 marks)

Exhibit 1 – Inspirations

The holiday product range marketed by HC's new business unit will be named Inspirations. It is intended that Inspirations will provide a high quality, bespoke holiday service for discerning clients. HC has decided that this new business unit will have its own mission statement of 'delivering a high-quality service for discerning travellers'. The new managing director of Inspirations has stated that it has an objective of achieving annual revenue of $100m by 20X8. This would be approximately 25% of the total forecast revenue for HC that year, but it is expected to represent only about 5% of the total number of holidays sold by HC. The type of holidays offered by Inspirations is already provided by some of HC's competitors.

BPP
LEARNING
MEDIA

Dilip Kharel, the new director of marketing of Inspirations, has stated that the internet should be increasingly used as the main source of marketing and selling the holidays, as 'the days are almost gone when families visit a 'high street' travel agency to plan their holiday; it's all done now from the comfort of the home'. He believes that potential customers of Inspirations will not want to visit high street travel agencies.

Inspirations will offer holidays in a wide variety of locations, including the Caribbean, Africa and Asia, and plan to offer 'themed' trips, such as gourmet food holidays and heritage trips. Different countries may have different requirements for visiting tourists, such as visa regulations. Inspirations does not own hotels or aircraft and therefore the majority of holidays offered will be provided by third-party suppliers, such as hotel and airline companies. This means that Inspirations can lack control over some elements such as passenger taxes. Inspirations will have representatives on site in all resorts to meet guests at airports and to address any issues they have with the holiday. However, the hotels and excursions will not be solely or exclusively offered to Inspirations' guests. For example, there will be other guests at a hotel who have not booked through Inspirations.

Dilip is concerned about this. He feels that the company needs to be able to differentiate itself, either in the overall holiday experience itself or in the marketing of it, so that customers are more likely to book such holidays through Inspirations, rather than through a competitor, or indeed through booking with the hotel directly. He also recognises the importance of adopting an appropriate pricing strategy which meets the needs of the organisation (HC and Inspirations) and customers alike.

Solution

Exam Focus Point

The March/June 2019 exam released by ACCA featured a clothing retailer called SmartWear. Task 4(a) required candidates to write a report on behalf SmartWear's sales and marketing director, for presentation to the board, which described the benefits of introducing a customer database management system (CDMS), including a loyalty scheme for SmartWear. Professional skills marks were available for demonstrating commercial acumen in respect of the wider external factors impacting on the decision to implement the system. The examining team noted that 'candidates appeared to do well, with most earning very high marks for this question by correctly discussing the many benefits of a CDMS. Most of the answers noticed the more obvious benefits, e.g. analysis of trends, targeted marketing, predict future trends, inform future product lines and so on. However, other benefits, such as cost saving, accuracy of data, shared access, remote access and so on were, in the majority of cases, missed. The biggest mistakes related to getting carried away with part of a relevant syllabus area, then taking it way too far. One common example was a strong focus on the 6 I's of e-marketing – by doing this in a very generic, unapplied manner – and getting carried away with listing and detailing all the many different types of promotion that the company may choose to offer its loyalty card customers. These candidates rarely answered the question that they had been asked.' (ACCA, 2019a).

To earn the 2 professional skills marks candidates had to strongly describe the benefits of introducing the CDMS at SmartWear in light of the case information provided. This needed to consider the issues from the perspective of the sales and marketing director and be presented in a report format.

6 Information system controls from a strategic perspective

Key terms

An information system: Consists of the systems, processes and procedures involved in collecting, storing, processing and distributing information.

The information systems (IS) strategy: Is the long-term plan for systems to exploit information in order to support organisational strategies or create new strategic options.

In order to manage the performance of their organisations effectively, managers need relevant and reliable performance information. However, while information systems themselves are important to an organisation, the information which they provide is perhaps even more important. As a result information systems need to be controlled if the output they provide to an organisation's strategic managers is to be meaningful. It is important to recognise that an organisation's information systems are made up of more than just the technological aspects (ie computers, databases etc); it is concerned with how information flows around the organisation.

Ultimately, strategic managers need information for decision making and control, and the role of the systems is to provide that information. An underlying consideration of an information strategy is that an organisation's information systems should provide the appropriate type and amount of information which management need to select, implement and control its chosen organisational strategy. However, this also means that the information strategy needs to be aligned to the overarching organisational strategy, in terms of the type of information available. For example, if an organisation is pursuing a differentiation strategy based on the high quality of its products, then information about aspects of product quality will be required in order to measure and manage performance.

As we explored earlier when we considered the increasing use of data, the way an organisation manages and uses information could, in itself, become a source of competitive advantage – for example, if the organisation is able to respond to market trends or opportunities more quickly than its rivals on the basis of the information it gathered about those opportunities.

BPP
LEARNING
MEDIA

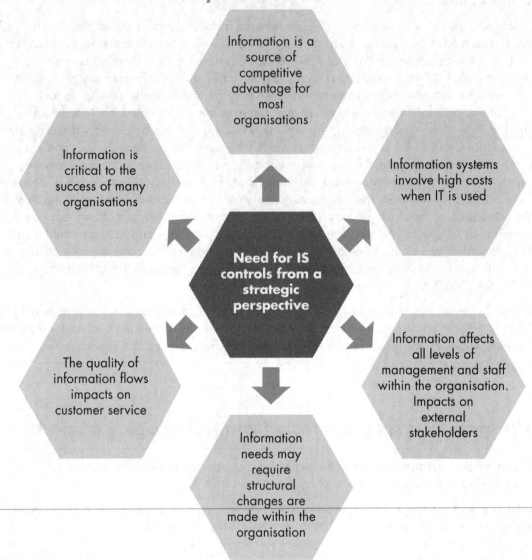

Information is a source of competitive advantage for most organisations

Information is critical to the success of many organisations

Information systems involve high costs when IT is used

Need for IS controls from a strategic perspective

The quality of information flows impacts on customer service

Information affects all levels of management and staff within the organisation. Impacts on external stakeholders

Information needs may require structural changes are made within the organisation

7 IT and systems security controls

For an organisation's IT assets and systems to operate effectively, it is critical that adequate control measures are in place to help prevent theft, fraud and human error.

Real world examples

In 2015, the details of over 37 million accounts were stolen from Canadian based extramarital affairs website Ashley Madison and posted on the internet. The company's tagline – 'life is short, have an affair' – encouraged users to set up an online account with a view to meeting married individuals or people in committed relationships (Thielman, 2015).

Thielman (2015) suggested that Canadian police were investigating the connection between the website's hack and the suicides of two people believed to have had active Ashley Madison accounts. Shortly after the hack, the company's CEO Noel Biderman resigned his position after leaked emails showed that he had had extramarital affairs himself having previously denied the accusations. Subsequent investigations into the hacked data showed that the company had failed to adequately encrypt user details making it easy for hackers to access and publish account details.

IT and systems security controls are often classified in one of two ways, as either general or application controls. General controls relate to the wider computer environment and may include organisational policies relating to the use of hardware, or the procurement of hardware. Application controls relate specific pieces of software and often cover controls over the processing of transactions.

BPP LEARNING MEDIA

Exercise 1: Controls

Although there are a number of threats to the security of organisational IT/IS infrastructures, some of the most common threats come from the following sources:

(1)   Hacking
(2)   Viruses
(3)   Input error

Required:

For each of the three threats listed above, briefly explain the threat to data security, and what can be done to prevent them.

Solution:

7.1 Types of control

When assessing the adequacy of existing IT/IS controls, an organisation should compare them against four types of control (see table below). The four types of control can be classified as being either general or application controls.

Controls over physical access	Logical access controls
Controls over physical access are predominantly directed toward preventing unauthorised individuals gaining access to an organisation's IT and IS assets. Controls are aimed at stopping damage to the IT infrastructure which may occur as a result of natural hazards, eg a fire. Controls can be **simple** or advanced. **Simple controls** might include ensuring that doors leading to an organisation's IT systems remain locked when not in use. Locks can be combined with: keypad systems or card entry systems. Other controls may focus on the use of personnel. Ensuring that receptionists and security guards are on duty outside of working hours may help control human access. This can be supplemented by the use of intruder alarms. **Advanced controls** are those that recognise individuals immediately, without the need for personnel or cards. However, biometric machines which can identify a person's fingerprints or scan the pattern of a retina are expensive, so are used only in highly sensitive industries, like defence.	Logical access controls are aimed at ensuring that only authorised users of IT systems are provided with access to those systems. Such measures are directed towards identifying and confirming the authenticity of the user. A common mechanism in protecting computerised data is through the use of **passwords**. Keeping track of failed attempts can alert managers to repeated efforts to break into the system. In these cases, the culprits might be caught, particularly if there is an apparent pattern to their efforts.
Operational controls	**Controls over data input**
Operational controls are aimed at ensuring that an organisation's day-to-day activities run effectively. Most organisations establish operational controls aimed at influencing an individual's behaviour. **Segregation of duties** Strong internal company policies often stop situations arising which lead to one individual having too much power over a particular function. This is often achieved through ensuring a segregation of duties. For example, the person dealing with processing the monthly payroll should not have responsibility for adding new employees to the payroll or authorising the monthly payment of salaries from the organisation's bank. **Audit trail** In the context of IT systems and controls, an audit trail is a record showing who has accessed a computer system and what operations that individual has performed. Audit trails are useful,	Input controls should ensure the accuracy, completeness and validity of data input into a computer system. Such controls are integrated into the software used. Controls are likely to focus on: **Data verification**: This involves ensuring data entered matches source documents. **Data validation**: This involves ensuring that data entered is not incomplete, unreasonable or duplicated, eg a system should flag and reject invoice numbers which have been duplicated when input. There are a number of general checks that can be used, depending on the data type. **Check digits**. A digit calculated by the program and added to the code being checked to validate it. **Control totals**. For example, a batch total totalling the entries in the batch.

Operational controls	Controls over data input
both for maintaining security and for recovering lost transactions. Accounting systems include an audit trail component that is able to be output as a report.	**Range checks**. Used to check the value entered against a sensible range, eg the parameters for an organisation's nominal ledger coding may require that statement of financial position codes must be between 5000 and 9999; for example, account code 6200 may relate to inventory.
	Limit checks. Similar to a range check, but usually based on an upper limit. For example, must be less than $999,999.99. The aim is that the software should identify unreasonable input values. In the case of a small company, posting a sales invoice for $1.3m to the account's software should be rejected.
	Compatibility checks. Ensure that two entries to the system are compatible. The value of a sales invoice posting should be compatible to the sales tax posting.
	Format check. Only accepts postings to the system which are in the correct format; otherwise be rejected. For example, dates must be posted in a particular format, dd/mm/yy.

Syllabus link

Issues around IT/IS controls are relevant to our discussions in Chapter 8 about internal control systems.

Essential reading

See Chapter 11 section 1 of the Essential Reading, available in Appendix 2 of the digital edition of the Workbook, for more detail on organisational controls specific to computerised accounting processes.

8 Cybersecurity

8.1 The rise of cybersecurity

Key terms

Cybersecurity: Is concerned with the protection of systems, networks and data in cyberspace.

Cyberspace: Is the term used to describe the environment in which communication over IT networks takes place.

The frequency of 'cyber attacks' on the IT systems used by organisations is continuing to rise at an alarming rate and has highlighted the need for improved cybersecurity. The increased emphasis on cybersecurity requires organisations to change their approach to protecting data, and the steps intended to be taken in the event that their data is breached. For many organisations, data security has predominantly focused on maintaining adequate internal controls, designed to protect the data from threats within the organisation. However, cybersecurity measures increasingly need to take account of the external threats:

- Threats now emerge from different parts of the world, and often involve criminal groups, corporate espionage and hackers.

- The heavy dependence on IT systems in modern business has proliferated the need for organisations to link their IT systems together throughout their supply chains. The growing number of servers, mobile devices and cloud computing applications used increases the number of ways in which hackers can gain access to data.

- Security failures can have far wider implications than only affecting the organisation's IT systems, and may include reputation damage, loss of intellectual property and disruption to operations.

8.2 Promoting cybersecurity in organisations

To address the challenges presented by such threats senior management are having to do more to promote an awareness of cybersecurity throughout the organisation. This may involve:

- Making cybersecurity issues for those not working in the organisation's IT department **easier to understand**. All too often the language used among IT professionals is of a technical nature, which makes it harder for other employees to understand. Communicating the need for all employees to play their part in combating cyber risks is crucial.

- Employing a **Chief Information Security Officer** to help communicate the threats posed by cyber risks should help other employees understand their role when using the organisation's IT/IS infrastructure.

- **Reorganising roles and responsibilities** to ensure that there is accountability for cybersecurity matters within the organisation. This should help ensure that in the event of a cyber-attack there is a team of individuals with the required responsibility to address the matter.

- **Determining accountability for cyber risks at the strategic apex**. A member of the board should be assigned responsibility for heading up cybersecurity matters. Having a member of the board in this role should help promote 'buy in' among all employees that the senior management take the issue seriously. This should help to create a cybersecurity conscious **culture**.

- **Learning from past security breaches**. Following a security breach, senior management should use this as an opportunity to promote the importance of cybersecurity throughout the organisation and should look to put in place measures to address the weaknesses that permitted security breaches to occur in the past.

- **Determining the organisation's tolerance to the cyber risks** is an important step in designing management strategies. Such an exercise may lead to the conclusion that additional funding is required to enhance the cybersecurity features of the organisation's IT/IS infrastructure.

- Ensuring that **non-executive board members play an active role in promoting cybersecurity** during their interactions with the board. This may involve keeping their knowledge about the evolving nature of cyber risks up to date and challenging the executive directors about the need for following best practice in cybersecurity.

It is important to note that the ability of organisations to implement the approaches to promoting cybersecurity outlined above will vary from organisation to organisation. In the case of smaller organisations addressing the matter of cybersecurity is likely to prove particularly challenging.

9 Improving IT/IS controls

9.1 Practical improvements

Earlier in the chapter we introduced the different types of IT/IS controls that exist; in this section we explore some of the practical measures that senior management can take to improve and enhance the organisation's existing IT/IS controls so that the organisation is able to meet its objectives.

Practical measures are might include:

Continuity planning. Organisations should have in place measures to address failures of IT/IS infrastructures to ensure the organisation can continue to function. This may consist of a plan which details the contact details for crisis management staff, customers, suppliers, the location of offsite data back-up storage media.

Systems development and maintenance. Organisations need security controls to protect the data held in IT/IS infrastructures. This requires regular updating of software and hardware, and to ensure that the controls remain fit for purpose.

Personnel security measures. Organisations need suitable processes for ensuring that only trustworthy employees are recruited to use IT/IS infrastructures. All employees should receive adequate training on using the organisation's IT/IS infrastructures. Training should be undertaken as regularly as needed to keep skills up to date.

Asset classification and control. Assigning an 'owner' to manage certain pieces of information held within IT/IS infrastructures is important as information/data is an asset to the organisation. Making certain individuals accountable for ensuring that key pieces of information are up-to-date and protected should improve security.

Compliance measures. Organisations need to ensure that organisational policies relating to the use of IT/IS infrastructures and data exist and are enforced. Policies should also conform to the law where appropriate ie data protection.

It is important to note that the measures provided above are not exhaustive and any improvements needed to enhance existing IT/IS controls will be driven by the situation facing the organisation.

Applications of IT

Applications of IT

The need for a strategic perspective: new technologies

Strategic managers are increasingly embracing emerging technologies as a way to innovate, improve performance and ultimately get ahead of the competition

Mobile technologies and cloud computing

Mobile technology
- Mobile technology is concerned with technology that is portable
- Mobile technology devices include: laptops, tablet computers, smartphones, GPS technologies

Benefits and risks of mobile technology
- Benefits: greater access to information/data, stakeholder interaction
- Risks: costs/obsolescence/ hackers

Cloud computing

Growing amounts of organisational data is now held in servers operated by cloud-based service providers

Benefits and risks of cloud computing
- Benefits of cloud computing include: cost effectiveness, flexibility, accessibility of data.
- Risks include: loss of control, data might be stolen, lost or corrupted

Cloud computing v owned technology

Organisations need to determine whether to pursue a cloud-based approach to data management or to manage data using owned hardware and software in-house

Information technology and data analysis

Growth in organisational data

Has been caused by the 'Internet of things'

Data analytics

Analyse and reveal insights in data

Big data

The Vs of big data

Volume, velocity, variety and veracity

Opportunities and threats of big data
- Opportunities include: new trends and patterns, improve responsiveness
- Threats include: hackers, viruses, focus on correlation not causation

Data for decision making

New product development, marketing and pricing
- Senior management need quality data
- New product development decisions
- Marketing decisions
- Pricing decisions

Sources of data

Information system controls from a strategic perspective

Need for information system controls

Information systems need to be controlled if the output they provide to an organisation's strategic managers is to be meaningful

IT and systems security controls

Types of control

Controls over physical access, logical access controls, operational controls and controls over data input

Cybersecurity

The rise of cybersecurity

Cybersecurity is concerned with the protection of systems, networks and data in cyberspace

Promoting cybersecurity in organisations

Cybersecurity can be promoted through a range of activities

Improving IT/ IS controls

Practical improvements

Establishing continuity plans, regularly maintaining systems, introduce organisational IT/IS policies, employ trustworthy staff, and assign information 'owners'

BPP
LEARNING
MEDIA

1. As the environment in which organisations operate becomes more competitive, the ability to create a sustainable competitive advantage becomes considerably more difficult. Strategic managers are increasingly embracing emerging technologies as a way to innovate, improve performance and ultimately get ahead of the competition.

2. Mobile technology is concerned with technology that is portable. Mobile technology devices include: laptops, tablet computers, smartphones, GPS technologies. Such devices enable users to communicate with one another in different ways, some of which may make use of the internet. Communicative features of mobile technologies include: Wi-Fi connectivity, Bluetooth, and 4G technologies.

3. Mobile technology allows greater access to organisational information and data, and makes it easier to interact with organisational stakeholders. The purchase costs, the speed of obsolescence and the threat of unauthorised individuals gaining access are risks.

4. Cloud computing is a model for enabling ubiquitous, convenient, on-demand network access to a shared pool of configurable computing resources (eg networks, servers, storage, applications and services) that can be rapidly provisioned and released with minimal management effort or service provider interaction (National Institute of Standards and Technology, 2011).

5. Benefits of cloud computing include: cost effectiveness, flexibility, accessibility of data. Risks include: loss of control, data might be stolen, lost or corrupted.

6. Organisations need to determine whether to pursue a cloud-based approach to data management or to manage data using owned hardware and software in-house.

7. Harnessing the insights presented by the data organisations which have available to them through the use of information technology tools is having an effect on how they inform and implement their strategies.

8. In the so-called 'Internet of Things', sensors embedded in physical objects such as mobile phones, motor vehicles, smart energy meters, RFID tags and tracking devices create and communicate data which is shared across wired and wireless networks.

9. Data analytics refers to the ability to analyse and reveal insights in data which had previously been too difficult or costly to analyse, due to the volume and variability of the data involved.

10. 'Big data is a popular term used to describe the exponential growth and availability of data, both structured and unstructured' (SAS, 2016).

11. Volume, velocity, variety and veracity make up the Vs of big data.

12. Big data offers opportunities including: the identification of new trends and patterns in data, making organisations more responsive. Threats associated with big data include: hackers, viruses, focus on correlation not causation.

13. To make informed decisions senior management need quality data. When making decisions about new product development, marketing and pricing strategies, senior management will want relevant data on a range of issues.

14. An information system consists of the systems, processes and procedures involved in collecting, storing, processing and distributing information.

15. Information systems need to be controlled if the output they provide to an organisation's strategic managers is to be meaningful.

16. General controls relate to the wider computer environment, and may include organisational policies relating to the use of hardware, or the procurement of hardware. Application controls to relate specific pieces of software and often cover controls over the processing of transactions.

17. The types of controls which exist include: controls over physical access, logical access controls, operational controls and controls over data input.

18. Cybersecurity is concerned with the protection of systems, networks and data in cyberspace.

19. Cybersecurity can be promoted through a range of activities including: reducing the amount of technical jargon associated with cybersecurity, employing a Chief Information Security Officer, reorganising roles and responsibilities, and determining accountability for cyber risks.

20. There are a range of practical measures that senior management can take to improve existing IT/IS controls, including: establishing continuity plans, regularly maintaining systems, introduce organisational IT/IS policies, employ trustworthy staff, and assign information 'owners'.

BPP
LEARNING
MEDIA

Question practice

Now try the question below from the Further question practice bank (available in the digital edition of the Workbook):

Q11 *Shop Reviewers Online*

Further reading

There are articles on the ACCA website written by members of the SBL examining team which are relevant to your studies and which would be useful to read:

Applying big data and data analytics in Strategic Business Leader

This article explores the concept of big data and considers how it can be used to inform and implement business strategy.

Approaching SBL overview

This article provides a one-page summary of the key features of the SBL exam.

Approaching SBL reading and planning

This article provides a one-page summary of how best to approach the SBL exam.

SBL – 10 things to learn from the September 2018 sitting

This article highlights some of the issues that ACCA identified in candidates' answers during the September 2018 SBL exam sitting. The article provides some useful advice for improving your chances of passing the SBL exam.

Strategic Business Leader – The importance of effective communication for SBL

This article provides some useful insights into the different formats which you will be expected to use when answering SBL exam tasks.

Own research

It is important to link the topics covered in this chapter to a practical, real-world context. As such, we have suggested some areas for you to investigate further. Research a well-known organisation (if you struggle to find an organisation to consider you may find it helpful to choose a well- known business listed on a recognised stock exchange such as the FTSE 100), and consider the following:

- Consider the extent to which your chosen organisation is dependent on technology. Would the organisation be able to compete without the technology it uses in its day-to-day operations?
- How has the organisation been positively or negatively affected by advances in technology?
- How does the organisation use the data it has at its disposal?
- Has the organisation been affected by cyber-attacks in the past? If so, what did the organisation do to address this matter? If not, why do you think this was?

Exercise answer

Exercise 1

(1) **Hacking** is unauthorised access into an IT system.

Controls might include: usernames, passwords, install firewalls.

(2) A **virus** is a software program which causes damage to an IT system by making unauthorised amendments to program and data files and sometimes damages the hardware of the system.

Controls might include: anti-virus software, messages within the software may be displayed which warn the user about downloading a file or programs from the internet.

(3) **Input errors** are mistakes by users when inputting data into an IT system. It arises from human error, for example pressing the wrong keys on a keyboard, or copying a data item incorrectly.

Controls might include: staff training on how to input data accurately, and through the use of validation checks on the data input into the system.

E-business

Learning objectives

On completion of this chapter, you should be able to:

	Syllabus reference no.
Discuss and evaluate the main organisation and market models for delivering e-business	E3(a)
Assess and advise on the potential application of information technology to support e-business	E3(b)
Explore the characteristics of the media of e-marketing using the 6 Is of interactivity, intelligence, individualisation, integration, industry structure and independence of location	E3(c)
Assess the importance of online branding in e-marketing and compare it with traditional branding	E3(d)
Explore different methods of acquiring and managing suppliers and customers through exploiting e-business technologies	E3(e)
Identify and assess the potential impact of disruptive technologies such as Fintech, including cryptocurrencies and blockchain	H2(a)
Assess the impact of new product, process and service developments and innovation in supporting organisation strategy	H2(b)

Business and exam context

Internet technologies are now integral to almost every organisation, taking the form of email, collaboration tools, selling online, use of social media, web-based applications and many other tools. Running a successful organisation requires an awareness of the potential and pitfalls of technology, and judgement about the best way to respond. Technology is often, though not always a key driver of innovation, as it opens up new possibilities in products or services to be provided, or in how processes are carried out. One influential idea in this field is that of disruptive innovation, innovation which offers products or services in a way that will not appeal to existing customers. Research suggests that established companies, focusing on their existing customer relationships, then become vulnerable to failure.

In the exam, you are not expected to show detailed knowledge of the internet-based technologies themselves, but you are expected to appreciate the impact they have on organisations, and ways in which leaders can respond. Creativity and innovation are critical characteristics of modern professional accountants and you will be expected to demonstrate these in your solutions.

Chapter overview

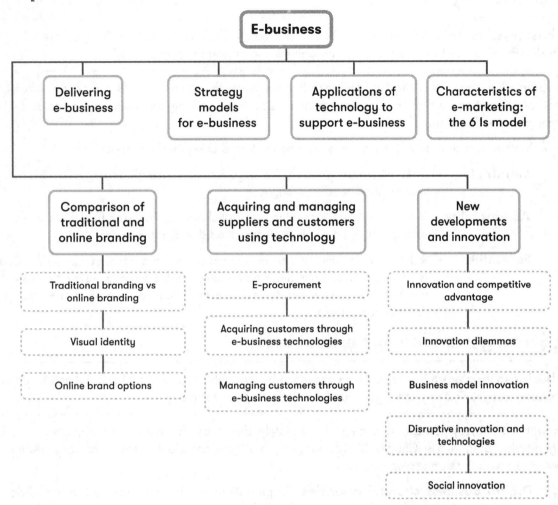

1 Delivering e-business

Key term

> **E-business:** Has been defined by IBM (1997) as cited by Chaffey and Smith (2013) as 'the transformation of key business processes through the use of internet technologies'.

An alternative term used is **digital business** but this means the same thing. As internet technologies are now a routine part of life for many people, e-business and digital business are increasingly synonymous with business.

As with other aspects of strategy, e-business can be evaluated using the SAF model:

- **Suitability** – does e-business support the organisation's overall strategy, or does the strategy itself need to change?

- **Acceptability** – is a new strategy acceptable to stakeholders? For example, if we move to selling online, how will our established distributors react?

- **Feasibility** – technology investments can be expensive and require specialist skills. Can we acquire these skills and finance and will the benefits justify the cost? A frequent issue with e-business is establishing a pricing model that is commercially viable.

2 Strategy models for e-business

Key term

> **E-business strategy:** Is defined as the approach by which the application of internal and external electronic communications can support and influence corporate strategy.

As with all strategy, e-business strategy is ultimately driven by the vision and objectives of the organisation as a whole. Chaffey (2015) suggests that there are eight areas where organisations should review and select strategic options.

1. **Digital business channel priorities**. Organisations need to consider their mix of 'bricks and clicks' and how far they want to sell goods or services online, rather than in physical outlets or via call centres. They will also need to consider how to allocate resources across digital channels. How much should be invested in desktop vs. mobile platforms? Should the company invest in social media platforms and if so which ones?

2. **Market and product development strategies**. Which products and services should be delivered online and to which target markets? Ansoff's matrix can be helpful here (see Chapter 6). A company can use e-business to target particular groups, for example they may provide special offers online for their most profitable customers.

3. **Positioning and differentiation strategies**. How will the company position its online offering relative to competitors in relation to product quality, service quality, price and fulfilment time? This has similarities to the marketing mix (see Chapter 6).

4. **Business, service and revenue models**. E-business provides an opportunity to innovate in these areas. For example, holiday companies and retailers often display customer reviews of products on their websites. Amazon sells products from other retailers alongside and in competition with its own. We examine business models in more detail later in this chapter.

5. **Marketplace restructuring**. Technology can change market structures themselves and organisation can take advantage of this. This may take the form of **disintermediation** (removal of intermediaries such as distributors or brokers), **reintermediation** (creation of new intermediaries such as search engines and comparison sites) and **countermediation** (established companies setting up their own intermediaries).

6. **Supply chain management capabilities**. Companies can use technology to integrate more closely with their suppliers, or participate in online marketplaces. This is e-procurement, which is examined later in this chapter.

7. **Internal knowledge management capabilities**. As we saw in Chapter 5, knowledge management can be a key source of competitive advantage. Organisations should consider whether technology can help in the creation and dissemination of knowledge.

8. **Organisational resourcing and capabilities**. Adopting these strategies will require organisational change, which may include the following:

   - Strategy process and performance improvement – the process for selecting, implementing and reviewing digital business initiatives;

   - Structure – where will these capabilities sit within the organisation?

   - Senior management buy-in – this is essential for the strategies to be successful;

   - Marketing integration – different channels of communication to customers need to be integrated with each other, requiring marketing and technology staff to work closely together;

   - Online marketing focus – initiatives are needed to exploit the potential of online marketing. This is covered in more detail later in the chapter;

Partnering with other organisations – some activities will be delivered best by other companies. We look at **outsourcing** in more detail in Chapter 13. A number of 'stage models' have been developed to assess how advanced a company is in its adoption of e-business. Chaffey (2015) synthesises these models as follows:

	1. Web presence	2. E-commerce	3. Integrated e-commerce	4. Digital business
Services available	Interaction with product catalogues and customer service	Transactional e-commerce	E-commerce integrated with other systems and personalisation of services	Full integration between all internal processes and elements of the value network
Organisational scope	Isolated departments	Cross-organisational	Cross-organisational	Across the enterprise and beyond
Transformation	Technological infrastructure	Technology and e-commerce responsibilities	Internal business process and structure	Change to digital business culture and processes linked to partners'
Strategy	Limited	Sell-side e-commerce strategy	E-commerce strategy integrated with business strategy	Digital business strategy is fully part of business strategy

Exercise 1: Identifying stages

Required

Consider the organisation you work for, or another organisation with which you are familiar. What stage are they at in the model above? What would moving to the next stage look like?

Solution

3 Application of technology to support e-business

A good way to consider the impact of technology is to use **value chain analysis** and identify processes within the value chain where it can be used to add value. Some examples are given below.

Syllabus link

You covered value chain analysis in Chapter 5.

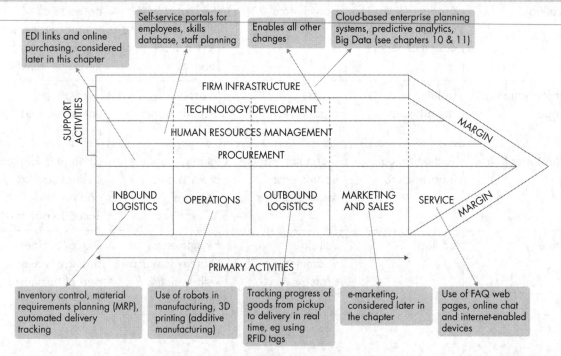

Having identified areas that could be more efficient or effective from the value chain analysis, the IS/IT strategy can be used to try and determine how those activities and, in particular, the competitively significant activities, can be improved.

(a) Can **linkages** between the different activities be improved by the use of IT? For example, information from support activities may be made available to primary activities on a more timely basis.

(b) Can IS/IT improve the **information flow** through the primary activities? For example, linking sales and marketing with operations or outbound logistics using a central database to provide sales and marketing with online details of products being produced.

(c) Can more effective **links** be formed with external entities? For example, can inbound logistics be improved by using EDI?

(d) Can IS/IT be used to **decrease the cost** of any activity? For example, is there room for more automation or transformation of activities, or even re-engineering using currently available IT tools and techniques?

As well as making incremental changes to the value chain, technology can enable organisations to transform their operations by use of disruptive technology and product, process or service innovation. We consider these areas later in the chapter.

4 Characteristics of e-marketing: the 6 Is model

The 6 Is of marketing, developed by McDonald and Wilson (2011), summarise the ways in which the internet can add customer value and hence improve the organisation's marketing effectiveness.

The 6 Is highlight the characteristics of e-marketing from both a practical and strategic perspective

Interactivity	Customers tend to initiate contact, a company can gather and store responses, and these can be used to tailor future interactions.
	Traditional media are mainly 'push' media – the marketing message is broadcast from company to customer – with limited interaction. On the internet, it is usually a customer who seeks information on a website – it is a 'pull' mechanism.
	Interaction between organisations and their customers can include email, recommendations, community sites, blogs and photographs.
Intelligence	The internet can be used as a low-cost method of collecting marketing information about customer perceptions of products and services. Web analytics show which pages are being visited, where users were referred from, where they are, and what users click on when they are there. This information can be used to make the website more attractive and encourage purchasing, or other interaction.
Individualisation	Communications can be tailored to the individual, unlike traditional media where the same message is broadcast to everyone. This can be based on intelligence previously gathered about the customer.
Integration	E-marketing can be integrated with other marketing channels. This may apply to communications from organisation to customer, for example customers may receive a voucher when making a purchase and can claim a reward via the organisation's website. It also may apply to communications from the customer to the organisation, for example using a web form to request a phone callback.

BPP LEARNING MEDIA

Industry structure	e-marketing can bring about changes to the entire structure of industries. As discussed above, this may take the form of **disintermediation** or **reintermediation**.
Independence of location	It may be possible to sell into international markets with no local sales force or customer service team, or very small teams, thus opening up new sales opportunities. This tends to be simpler when products are virtual, such as software or digital content, than when products are physical.

Activity 1: Accounting Education Consortium

ACCA Professional skills focus

Commercial acumen: demonstrate awareness

You are a consultant reviewing the marketing of your client, Accounting Education Consortium. Assume it is now mid-20X8.

Required

Using the information provided, explain, in the context of AEC, how the marketing characteristics of electronic media (such as the internet) differ from those of traditional marketing media such as advertising and direct mail. **(10 marks)**

Professional skills marks are available for demonstrating **commercial acumen** in demonstrating awareness of the value drivers at AEC, and how e-marketing can help them to be successful.

(2 marks)

(Total = 12 marks)

Exhibit 1 – Background information on the Accounting Education Consortium

The Accounting Education Consortium (AEC) offers professional accountancy education and training courses. It currently runs classroom-based training courses preparing candidates for professional examinations in eight worldwide centres. Three of these centres are also used for delivering continuing professional development (CPD) courses to qualified accountants. However, only about 30% of the advertised CPD courses and seminars actually run. The rest are cancelled through not having enough participants to make them economically viable.

AEC has developed a comprehensive set of course manuals to support the preparation of its candidates for professional examinations. There is a course manual for every examination paper in the professional examination scheme. As well as being used on its classroom-based courses, these course manuals are also available for purchase over the internet. The complete set of manuals for a professional examinations scheme costs $180.00 and the website has a secure payment facility which allows this to be paid by credit card. Once purchased, the manuals may be downloaded or they may be sent on a CD to the home address of the purchaser. It is only possible to purchase the complete set of manuals for the scheme, not individual manuals for particular examinations. To help the student decide if they wish to buy the complete manual set, the website has extracts from a sample course manual. This sample may be accessed, viewed and printed once a student has registered their email address, name and address on the website.

AEC has recently won a contract to supply professional accountancy training to a global accounting company. All students working for this company will now be trained by AEC at one of its worldwide centres.

Website

The AEC website has the following functionality:

Who we are: A short description of the company and its products and services.

Professional education courses: Course dates, locations and standard fees for professional examination courses. This schedule of courses is printable.

Continuing professional development: Course dates, locations and standard fees for CPD courses and seminars. This schedule is also printable.

CPD catalogue: Detailed course and seminar descriptions for CPD courses and seminars.

Downloadable study material: Extracts from a sample course manual. Visitors to the site wishing to access this material must register their email address, name and address. 5,500 people registered last year to download study material.

Purchase study material: Secure purchase of a complete manual set for the professional scheme. Payment is by credit card. On completion of successful payment, the visitor is able to download the manuals or to request them to be shipped to a certain address on a CD. At present, 10% of the people who view downloadable study material proceed to purchase.

Who to contact: Who to contact for booking professional training courses or CPD courses and seminars. It provides the name, email address, fax number, telephone number and address of a contact at each of the eight worldwide centres.

Marketing strategy

The marketing manager of AEC has traditionally used magazines, newspapers and direct mail to promote its courses and products. Direct mail is primarily used for sending printed course catalogues to potential customers for CPD courses and seminars. However, she is now keen to develop the potential of the internet and to increase investment in this medium at the expense of the traditional marketing media. Table 1 shows the percentage allocation of her budget for 20X8, compared with 20X7. The actual budget has only been increased by 3% in 20X8.

Table 1

Percentage allocation of marketing budget (20X7–20X8)

	20X8	20X7
Advertising	30%	40%
Direct mail	10%	30%
Sponsorship	10%	10%
Internet	50%	20%

Solution

---

5 Comparison of traditional and online branding

> **A brand:** Is a name, symbol, term, mark or design that enables customers to identify and distinguish the products of one supplier from those offered by competitors (Pride and Ferrell, 2014).

Brands convey a message of confidence, quality and reliability to their target market, which is particularly important in e-commerce where there are often concerns over privacy and security. For online retailers, it will include home or welcome page design, navigation and online support.

5.1 Traditional branding vs online branding

Online branding (sometimes referred to as e-branding and digital branding) concerns the use of the internet as a means of promoting the organisations brand. The approach followed by many organisations when creating a brand in the traditional sense would make use of traditional methods of marketing communications. Traditional branding is associated with the mediums of TV/ radio and newspaper, magazine and print advertising. Despite many similarities, online branding differs in important ways from traditional branding and must be approached differently. A company's entire character, identity, products and services can be communicated in seconds on the web and customers make judgements just as fast.

BPP
LEARNING
MEDIA

5.1.1 Traditional branding

Although, traditional approaches to branding enable organisations to reach a large audience of potential customers, in reality only a small proportion of those in receipt of the marketing message will be interested in making a purchase. Traditional branding has its weaknesses:

- The process of creating a brand which will appeal to a mass audience is extremely expensive. The traditional approach often involves the use of marketing ad agencies which charge large fees for their services.

- It has historically proven difficult for organisations to know whether their brand messaging has been successful beyond correlating brand promotions with increases or decreases in sales.

- Once a brand and the marketing messaging around the brand have been published in print or advertised on TV it is not easy for organisations to quickly update the message should an error be identified, or a change be needed.

- Amending a poorly received change to an organisations brand image may not only take a long time but will most likely incur significant costs. For example, a bad reaction among customers to a change in the brand logo of a clothing retailer will force the retailer to incur significant costs in undertaking a re-branding exercise to reduce any damage caused.

5.1.2 Online branding

In contrast to traditional branding, online branding allows smaller organisations to create a brand more easily, at very little cost which can very quickly be used to attract potential customers. This has been facilitated by the rapid growth in the use of the internet over the last thirty years. The growth in the use of social media platforms like Facebook and Instagram among younger consumers has enabled organisations to more clearly target the products and services they offer to these groups. It has also made it easier for organisations to create a 'buzz' around the products and services they sell. The creation of a 'buzz' can be achieved by making use of social media to promote the organisation's latest offerings and permits the organisation to enter into two-way communications with those groups most likely to be interested in making a purchase. The use of buzz scores have become increasingly important in online brand management. A buzz score assigns a buzz ranking to those brands that the public are most aware of at particular points in time. Those brands deemed to have achieved better recognition have the highest rankings.

Online branding is consistent with the increasing number of people that use the internet to search for product and service reviews before deciding whether to make a purchase or not. By promoting brands in those online spaces, where people are searching for reviews, improves brand visibility and increases the likelihood of future purchases. The use of online branding has made it possible for 'real time' changes to be made to any brand messaging published online to reflect changing trends and tastes.

Online branding has also made it easier for organisations to measure the success of brand marketing campaigns. This is evident as many large organisations today make use of tools like Google Trends to monitor the number of people that have run searches for their brands. Some entities have taken to tracking conversations left on social media about the organisation's brands as this enables them to better understand what people are actually saying and thinking about their brands.

It is important to recognise that despite the benefits that online branding brings it is likely that, for the foreseeable future, traditional branding and its online variant will continue to co-exist.

5.2 Visual identity

An effective visual identity, also known as 'look and feel' is important online, as is a memorable **domain name**. Unfortunately, there are a limited number of names available, and each name has been given to the first applicant. Every company still wants .com since this is where the customers look first.

BPP
LEARNING
MEDIA

5.3 Online brand options

Migrate traditional brand online – this can make sense if the brand is well known and has a strong reputation eg Marks & Spencer or Disney. However, there is a risk of jeopardising the brand's good name if the new venture is not successful.

Extend traditional brand – a variant. This involves altering the brand image to suit online audiences.

Partner with existing digital brands – co-branding occurs when two businesses put their brand names on the same product as a joint initiative, one of which can be an established digital brand.

Create a new digital brand – because a good name is extremely important, some factors to consider when selecting a new brand name are that it should suggest something about the product, be short and memorable, be easy to spell, translate well into other languages and have an available domain name.

6 Acquiring and managing suppliers and customers using technology

6.1 E-procurement

Key term

E-procurement: Is the purchase of supplies and services through the internet and other information and networking systems, such as Electronic Data Interchange (EDI).

Typically, e-procurement websites allow authorised and registered users to log in using a password. The supplying organisation will set up its website so that it recognises the purchaser, once logged in, and presents a list of items that the purchaser regularly buys. This saves searching for the items required and also avoids the need to key in name, address and delivery details. Depending on the approach, buyers or sellers may specify prices or invite bids. Transactions can be initiated and completed. Once the purchases are made, the organisation will periodically be billed by the supplier. Ongoing purchases may qualify customers for volume discounts or special offers.

Options for implementing e-procurement include:

Model	How it works	Examples
Public web	Individual buyers find individual suppliers on the web and make a purchase. There is no structural relation between buyer and supplier.	Webshops like Amazon
Exchange	Suppliers and buyers trade through a third party open marketplace. They have no structural relationship even though they may regularly deal with each other.	Autobytel
Supplier-centric	An individual supplier gives access to buying organisations for a pre-negotiated product range. Buyer and supplier have a contractual relationship.	Dell
Buyer-centric	Individual companies have contracts with a number of different suppliers. The catalogue and ordering system are maintained within the buying organisation. The system is fully integrated into corporate financial control and reporting systems.	Many software suppliers

Model	How it works	Examples
B2B marketplace	An independent third party has agreements with a number of buying and supplying organisations. Buyers and suppliers deal with each other through a marketplace. Both are bound by agreements with the marketplace.	Alibaba

Essential reading

See Chapter 12 section 1 of the Essential Reading, available in Appendix 2 of the digital edition of the Workbook, for detail about the benefits and risks of using e-procurement.

6.2 Acquiring customers through e-business technologies

Techniques to achieve acquisition include:

(a) **Search engine optimisation** – skilled website design can put a supplier high up among search results.

(b) **Newsgroups and forums** providing expert opinion and useful help are a way for businesses to communicate with their peers and customers in an informal environment.

(c) **Newsletters** allow an organisation to send news about the company, new products or services and any new information that has been posted on the website via email.

(d) **Link building and partnership campaigns** can greatly benefit a business, significantly boosting its online presence. Reciprocal links are an exchange of links between two site owners. Affiliate networks are based on paying commission on sales referred from other sites.

(e) **Viral marketing** is about creating a buzz about products or services. Viral marketing relies on word of mouth or, in the online sense, getting people to share the online application with others.

(f) **Banner advertising** is similar to advertisements seen in newspapers and magazines. They are the graphical strips commonly seen across the top of website pages.

(g) **Social media** marketing interactions enable organisations to promote their products and services directly to prospective customers that use social media platforms.

6.3 Managing customers through e-business technologies

Trying to attract 'sticky customers' (customers who will bring repeat business) is a crucial goal for many online businesses.

Marketers aim to do this by offering **promotions** of various kinds. These promotions range from discounts and sweepstakes to loyalty programs and higher concept approaches such as thank-you notes and birthday cards.

Extranets offer secure tunnels to remote databases, which let users access inventory data, examine special discounts, view delivery status, research products, place and fulfil orders, and collaborate via a secure internet connection.

An **online community** is a multi-way online environment where members encourage each other to contribute content and interact. These may be hosted on social media, or on the company's own systems.

Baxter (n.d.) highlights the existence of the following **types of community**:

Types of online community

Communities of practice where members share a vocation or profession	**Communities of circumstance** where members share a personal situation

Communities of purpose
where members share
a common objective

Communities of interest where members share a hobby or interest	**Communities of geography** where members live in the same area

Opt-in emails are promotional emails that have been requested by the individual receiving them. Unlike promotional emails that get sent out to large lists of recipients without regard to whether or not they want the information, opt-in emails are only sent to people who specifically request them.

Data mining is a set of statistical techniques that are used to identify trends, patterns and relationships in data. Data mining is closely linked to big data, which we explored in Chapter 11.

Most data mining models are one of two types:

(a) **Predictive**: using known observations to predict future events (for example, predicting the probability that a recipient will opt out of an email list)

(b) **Descriptive**: interrogating the database to identify patterns and relationships (for example, profiling the audience of a particular advertising campaign)

Real world example

Data mining at Netflix

Netflix was founded in the US 1997 as a DVD sales and rental company. It has developed significantly over the years and now specialises in online video-on-demand. In 2013 it moved into content production with the release of *House of Cards*. It was reported that in August 2019 Netflix had 158 million subscribers worldwide.

Netflix makes extensive used of data mining techniques, employing about 800 developers to write algorithms that analyse their subscribers' viewing habits. This allows them to recommend shows their viewers might like and informs their purchase and commissioning of new films and series. These are multi-million dollar decisions, but the data reduces the risk of failure. By analysing customer life-cycles, they also enhance their customer acquisition and retention strategy.

(Adapted from: Xu *et al*, 2016)

Cookies are a technology that allows a website to remember individual visitors' surfing and/or purchase history and preferences. This information is placed on the visitor's hard disk and when they revisit the site, it references the cookie and is able to show the visitor product selections and recommendations, and offer personalised welcomes and streamlined ordering (through remembering names, addresses and credit card details).

Activity 2: Moor Farm

ACCA Professional skills focus

Communication: clarify

Moor Farm is a large estate in the rural district of Cornaille. The estate covers a large area of forest, upland and farmland. It also includes two villages, and although many of the properties in these villages have been sold off to private homeowners, the estate still owns properties which it rents out. The estate also has a large mansion house set inside a landscape garden designed in the 19th century by James Kent. The garden, although now overgrown and neglected, is the only surviving example of his work in the district. The estate was left as a gift to a charitable trust ten years ago. The trust is based at the estate. A condition of the gift to the trust was that the upland and forest should be freely accessible to visitors.

The estate has appointed a new manager who is due to take over the estate when the current manager retires. She is working alongside the current manager so that she understands her responsibilities and how the estate works. As a one-off project, she has commissioned a stakeholder survey which has requested information on the visitor experience to help with a planned re-design of the estate's website. The website is generally thought to be well structured and presented, but it receives fewer visitors than might reasonably be expected. It provides mainly static information about the estate and forthcoming events but currently users cannot interact with the site in any way. You are a consultant assisting the new manager in identifying potential improvements.

Required

Write a brief report to the manager discussing how the website could be further developed to address some of the issues highlighted in the survey. **(10 marks)**

Professional skills marks are available for demonstrating **communication** skills in clarifying the advice to be given to the manager. **(2 marks)**

(Total = 12 marks)

Exhibit 1 – Extracts from the survey:

'We had a good day, but the weather was awful. If we had known it was going to rain all day, then we probably would have postponed the visit until a fine day. It spoilt a family day out.' **Visitor with small family**

'We were very disappointed, on arrival, to find that the family fun day was fully booked.' **Visitor who had travelled 100 km with two small children to visit a special event**

'We all love it here, but we didn't know you had a website!! We almost had to type in the complete website address before we found it! I am sure more people would come if they could only find the website!' **Visitor aged mid-20s**

'As usual, we had a great time here and took great photos. It would have been nice to be able to share our pleasure with other people. We would recommend it to anyone who loves the outdoors.' **Visitor – family with teenage children**

'We met the volunteers who were excavating the buildings in the landscape garden. They were so helpful and knowledgeable. They turned something that looked like a series of small walls into something so much more tangible.' **Visitor – elderly couple**

'We are regular visitors and we really want to know what is going on! There are many of us who would like to really be involved with the estate and help it thrive. We need more than just occasional questionnaires.' **Visitor – hiking group**

Solution

---

7 New developments and innovation

Key term

Innovation: Involves the conversion of new knowledge into a new product, process or service and the putting of this new product, process or service into actual use (Johnson *et al*, 2017).

7.1 Innovation and competitive advantage

Johnson *et al* (2017) highlight that for many organisations, product innovation and being the **first mover** may be a major source of competitive advantage.

(a)   First movers can establish scale ahead of competitors, and thereby gain **economies of scale**.

(b)   Customers may find they are locked in to innovative suppliers by unacceptable **costs of switching** to competitors, particularly if the first mover can establish **technological standards**.

(c)   The **learning** (or experience) **curve** effect may bring cost advantages.

(d)   A first mover may gain easier **access to scarce resources** than followers, such as raw materials or skilled labour.

(e)   It can lead to an enhanced **reputation**, particularly if a dominant brand can be established.

However, late-movers may benefit in two ways:

- Imitate technological and other innovation, which is much less expensive than being a pioneer
- Late-movers can learn from the mistakes of the innovators, and avoid them

7.2 Innovation dilemmas

Johnson *et al* (2017) suggest that there are a number of choices relating to innovation which managers must resolve, including:

Driver	**Technology push** – innovation comes from new knowledge created by researchers, which is then developed and sold. This emphasises the importance of investment in research & development (R&D)	**Market pull** – users, not producers are the source of innovation. These in turn can be subdivided: **Lead users**, are the most demanding users of a product or service, such as top sportspeople or hobby fanatics. Innovation arises from understanding their needs and ideas, then translating them into products and services. **Frugal innovation**, is driven by the needs of poor consumers, often in emerging markets for products that are cheap, simple and robust. Prahalad (2013) argued for this approach, saying that companies should recognise 'the fortune at the bottom of the pyramid'.
Focus	**Product innovation** relates to the final product or service to be sold, introducing a new one or adding new features.	**Process innovation** relates to the way in which the product is produced and distributed, especially gains in costs or reliability.
Involving those outside the organisation	**Closed** innovation relies on the organisation's internal resources and maintains secrecy to protect competitive advantage.	**Open innovation** involves exchanging ideas with those outside the organisation. This may include collaboration with other companies or universities, or **crowdsourcing**, broadcasting a specific problem and awarding prizes for the best solutions.

7.3 Business model innovation

Key term

A business model: Describes a value proposition for customers and other participants, an arrangement of activities that produces this value, and associated revenue and cost structures (Johnson *et al*, 2017).

A business model involves three elements:

- **Value creation** – this particularly focuses on the target customers and how their needs are being met, but also value for any other participants.

- **Value configuration** – the way resources and activities in the value chain are combined. This includes what activities are performed, who performs them and how they are linked.

- **Value capture** – the cost structure of resources and activities and the revenue stream from customers and any other relevant parties. This includes how value will be apportioned between various participants,

Once established in an industry, business models tend to be taken for granted and rarely questioned. This means there can be significant competitive advantage for those who develop innovative business models, whether new entrants (for example Airbnb challenging the business model of hotels) or established companies (such as Nestlé with Nespresso – see below).

Real world example

Nespresso

Based in Switzerland, Nestlé SA is one of the largest food and drink companies in the world, with a wide variety of products. Since 2000, one of its most successful business units has been Nespresso, which supplies coffee capsules which are turned into coffee using specialist machines. By supplying individual portions of many different types of coffee, it delivers customisation and convenience. Manufacturing household appliances is not Nestlé's core competence, so they partnered with specialists to design and manufacture the devices. The design was protected by 1,700 patent applications.

Nespresso represents two major innovations in the business model:

1)   Instead of distributing the capsules through retailers, they are sold directly online, and in a few exclusive boutiques. This gives them direct contact with the customer and higher margins.

2)   No money is made on the sale of the machines – profit is earned on the sale of the capsules, where gross margins are estimated to be 85% compared with 40–50% for regular drip-coffee brands.

The idea of selling coffee in capsules is not new but Nestlé has successfully created a new business model and it would be very hard for a competitor to copy the entire system.

(Adapted from: Matzler et al, 2013)

Essential reading

See Chapter 12 section 2 of the Essential Reading, available in Appendix 2 of the digital edition of the Workbook, for further discussion about the emergence of ecosystems in business. The idea that business environments are becoming more akin to ecosystems was introduced in the essential reading for chapter 2, where we considered the emergence of such environments in relation to stakeholders. The essential reading for chapter 12 further considers the role that digital business platforms play in ecosystem environments. Although, the concept of ecosystems is not specified in the Strategic Business Leader syllabus, this content is highly topical as it represents a recent development in the broad subject of e-business.

7.4 Disruptive innovation and technologies

Key term

Disruptive innovation: Describes a process by which a product or service takes root initially in simple applications at the bottom of a market and then relentlessly moves up market, eventually displacing established competitors.

The term **disruptive innovation** was coined by Christensen (1997). Based on a detailed study of the computer disk drive industry, he argued that most innovation was **sustaining innovation**, improvements to existing products or services which companies could sell to their existing customers. Well-run companies are good at exploiting these innovations, and the established industry leaders tend to be the first to exploit them.

However, periodically there was an innovation which shrank the size of disks. The smaller disks initially had lower performance than the larger ones and were of no interest to most current customers. However, they were lighter and cheaper and appealed to manufacturers of smaller computers. Over time, the smaller disks improved and displaced the larger ones. Industry leaders often failed to respond until it was too late because they were focused on the needs of their current customers. A new set of industry leaders took their place as the whole market shifted to demanding smaller disk drives.

Christensen argued this was a general pattern — firms do not respond to brand new technologies focused on different markets, because they are attached to their current business model as well as their relationships with existing customers. They are reluctant to 'cannibalise' their existing businesses by introducing something different. Two ways in which companies can try to protect themselves from disruption are:

1. Develop a portfolio of real options (McGrath & MacMillan, 2000). These are limited investments that keep options open, enabling them to respond quickly to opportunities.

2. Develop new venture units. These are internal units to develop new ideas which are kept separate from the core business, often located in a different place physically, so that they do not get 'stifled' by the organisation.

Real world example

FinTech

Financial technology, or FinTech, is having a major impact on the world of finance and is growing fast, with many predictions that it will mean extensive disruption to established businesses in this area. Examples of FinTech include:

*   Peer-to-peer lenders replacing banks for lending and saving

*   Peer-to-peer money transfer services replacing banks for money transmission and foreign exchange

*   Firms providing payment security and verification

*   Financial advice driven by algorithms, offered at much lower cost than traditional advisors

*   App-based insurance companies

*   Digital-only start-up banks, with no legacy of branch networks, call centres or complex systems

Start-up businesses in these areas will face intense competition from established banks, who are determined that they will survive and are investing heavily in this area.

(Adapted from "FinTech – transforming finance", ACCA, 2016a)

Blockchain and cryptocurrencies are predicted to have a disruptive effect on a number of global business practices.

BPP LEARNING MEDIA

7.4.1 Blockchain

Key term

> **Blockchain:** Is a public form of bookkeeping that uses a digital ledger to allow individuals to share a record of transactions.

Blockchain is a type of incorruptible distributed ledger that allows information to be recorded and shared with a network of individuals. In essence, Blockchain is a public form of bookkeeping which makes use of internet technologies to instantly verify and record the transactions that take place between individuals. The public nature of blockchain means that every individual can view the transactions made by participants in that network. This means that participants can view the date, time, value of transactions, and the individuals involved, thereby creating a shared record of events.

It is anticipated that blockchain will have a disruptive impact on a wide range of industries as it increases the levels of transparency over transactions. Greater use of blockchain should allow organisations including firms of accountants and auditors to more easily verify the transactions undertaken by clients when preparing (and auditing) financial statements. The use of blockchain should also make it easier for accountants to verify the background and transactional history of prospective new clients, especially when undertaking money laundering procedures. Blockchain will also be beneficial to providers of finance as they will be able to make more informed decisions about which prospective clients they should lend to.

7.4.2 Cryptocurrencies

Key term

> **Cryptocurrency:** Is a digital currency, which uses internet technologies to facilitate transactions made online. Cryptography is a key feature of cryptocurrency.

Cryptocurrencies are a form of digital currency which do not exist in physical form, Bitcoin and Ethereum are two of the best known cryptocurrencies. A key feature of cryptocurrency is that it makes use of the science of cryptography. Cryptography involves encrypting the code behind digital currencies so that they cannot be counterfeited by criminals. Cryptocurrencies have had a disruptive effect on traditional banking systems as they are not controlled by a central bank in the same way as conventional currencies. This lack of control has led to dramatic fluctuations in the value of cryptocurrencies as they are traded and exchanged around the world. Cryptocurrencies work in a similar way to conventional currencies in as much that they can be used to pay for (and to receive payments for) goods and services purchased online. Transactions made using cryptocurrencies make use of blockchain technology, which as discussed above helps to ensure that all transactions made between participants are verified and recorded on the distributed ledger.

Cryptocurrencies are having a disruptive effect on traditional payment methods as an increasing number of companies have started to accept Bitcoin payments on certain purchases. As the use of cryptocurrencies gradually becomes commonplace it is predicted that this will have a disruptive effect on organisations as they are forced to develop their IT infrastructures to be capable of accepting cryptocurrency payments.

7.5 Social innovation

Key term

> **Social innovation:** Describes 'a broad range of organisational and inter-organisational activity that is ostensibly designed to address the most deep-rooted "problems" of society, such as poverty, inequality and environmental degradation.' (Tracey & Stott, 2016)

Societies have always innovated but there has been increasing recent interest in studying innovation that is aimed primarily at benefitting society rather than creating and capturing economic value. This can take many forms, but Tracey & Stott (2016) suggest it can be divided into three categories:

- **Social enterprise** – creating new organisations, whether for-profit or not-for-profit, whose primary goal is to address social challenges. An example would be Fairphone, a Dutch company which manufactures and sells 'ethical' smartphones.

- **Social intrapreneurship** – addressing social challenges from inside established organisations. For example, engineering firm Arup has set up a non-profit venture, Arup International Development, to provide a range of socially beneficial services.

- **Social extrapreneurship** – Establishing platforms that can co-ordinate effort towards social goals. An example would be the Ellen Macarthur Foundation, which works with a range of organisations in many sectors and countries to promote the idea of the 'circular economy', emphasising re-use and regeneration of materials rather than a linear 'take, make, dispose' model.

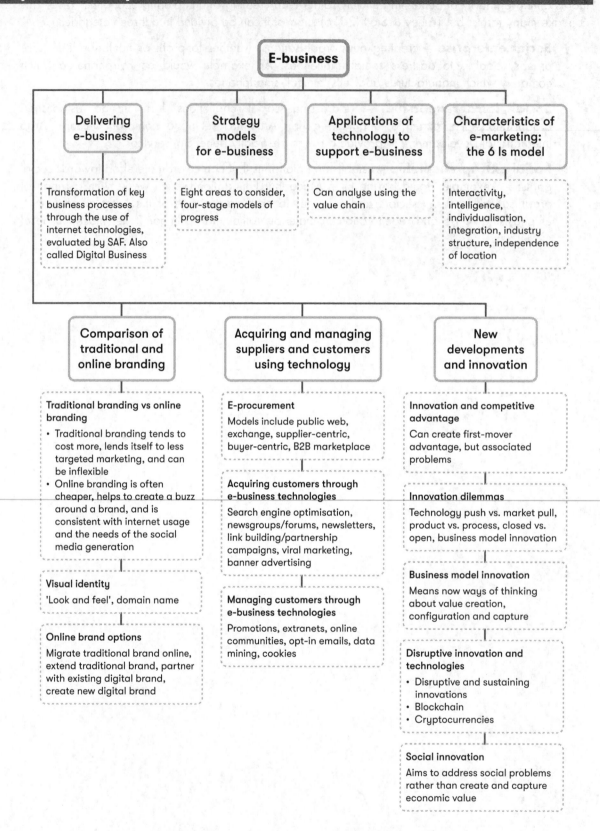

E-business

Delivering e-business

Transformation of key business processes through the use of internet technologies, evaluated by SAF. Also called Digital Business

Strategy models for e-business

Eight areas to consider, four-stage models of progress

Applications of technology to support e-business

Can analyse using the value chain

Characteristics of e-marketing: the 6 Is model

Interactivity, intelligence, individualisation, integration, industry structure, independence of location

Comparison of traditional and online branding

Traditional branding vs online branding
- Traditional branding tends to cost more, lends itself to less targeted marketing, and can be inflexible
- Online branding is often cheaper, helps to create a buzz around a brand, and is consistent with internet usage and the needs of the social media generation

Visual identity
'Look and feel', domain name

Online brand options
Migrate traditional brand online, extend traditional brand, partner with existing digital brand, create new digital brand

Acquiring and managing suppliers and customers using technology

E-procurement
Models include public web, exchange, supplier-centric, buyer-centric, B2B marketplace

Acquiring customers through e-business technologies
Search engine optimisation, newsgroups/forums, newsletters, link building/partnership campaigns, viral marketing, banner advertising

Managing customers through e-business technologies
Promotions, extranets, online communities, opt-in emails, data mining, cookies

New developments and innovation

Innovation and competitive advantage
Can create first-mover advantage, but associated problems

Innovation dilemmas
Technology push vs. market pull, product vs. process, closed vs. open, business model innovation

Business model innovation
Means now ways of thinking about value creation, configuration and capture

Disruptive innovation and technologies
- Disruptive and sustaining innovations
- Blockchain
- Cryptocurrencies

Social innovation
Aims to address social problems rather than create and capture economic value

Knowledge diagnostic

1. E-business is 'the transformation of key business processes through the use of internet technologies', also known as digital business. It can be evaluated using the SAF model.

2. E-business strategy involves considering channel priorities, market and product development strategies, positioning and differentiation strategies, business, service and revenue models, marketplace restructuring, supply chain management capabilities and internal knowledge management capabilities.

3. The stages organisations go through in adopting e-business can be described as web presence, e-commerce, integrated e-commerce and digital business.

4. The impact of technology on an organisation can be analysed using the value chain.

5. The 6 Is model (McDonald & Wilson, 2011) describes characteristics of e-marketing as interactivity, intelligence, individualisation, integration, industry structure and independence of location.

6. Online branding increases dependence on an effective visual identity, including the domain name. Brands have a number of options when migrating online.

7. E-procurement is using internet technologies to simplify purchasing decisions and processes. It can be used via public web, exchange, supplier-centric, buyer-centric and B2B marketplace.

8. E-business technologies offer scope to win new customers by techniques such as search engine registration, newsgroups and forums, newsletters, link building and partnership campaigns, viral marketing and banner advertising.

9. E-business technologies can be used to manage customers and encourage repeat business by techniques such as promotions, extranets, online communities, opt-in emails, using data and placing cookies on machines.

10. Innovation can be a source of competitive advantage but also brings risks.

11. Managing innovation means dealing with a number of dilemmas – technology push vs. market pull, product vs. process innovation and closed vs. open innovation.

12. Innovation can relate to the business model – value creation, configuration and capture.

13. Disruptive innovation means brand new technologies focused on new markets. Firms often fail to respond to this due to their relationships with established customers.

14. Blockchain and cryptocurrencies are predicted to have a disruptive effect on a number of global business practices.

15. Social innovation means innovation to address social problems rather than create and capture economic value. It can take the form of social enterprise, social intrapreneurship or social extrapreneurship.

BPP
LEARNING
MEDIA

Question practice

Now try the question below from the Further question practice bank (available in the digital edition of the Workbook):

Q12 *Jayne Cox Direct*

Further reading

There are articles on the ACCA website written by members of the SBL examining team which are relevant to your studies and which would be useful to read:

E-commerce

This article explores the role of e-commerce in business.

Approaching SBL overview

This article provides a one-page summary of the key features of the SBL exam.

Approaching SBL reading and planning

This article provides a one-page summary of how best to approach the SBL exam.

SBL – 10 things to learn from the September 2018 sitting

This article highlights some of the issues that ACCA identified in candidates' answers during the September 2018 SBL exam sitting. The article provides some useful advice for improving your chances of passing the SBL exam.

Strategic Business Leader – The importance of effective communication for SBL

This article provides some useful insights into the different formats which you will be expected to use when answering SBL exam tasks.

Own research

The business press is always full of stories about innovative companies and structural changes to industries that result. The music and news media industries are often cited as examples, where established organisations have struggled to keep pace with changing technology, and new competitors are taking their place. Entire new business models have been created, such as subscription-based music streaming and digital newspaper subscriptions.

Choose one of these industries, or another one undergoing rapid change, and find out about one of the major industry organisations.

- How are they adapting to change?
- Are they leading it or following?
- How successful have they been so far?

Exercise answer

Exercise 1

The answer to this exercise will be dependent on the organisation that you chose to consider.

Evaluating and enabling strategic change

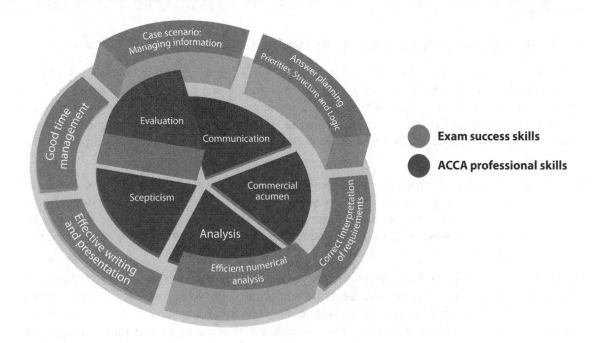

Exam success skills

ACCA professional skills

Introduction

In Stage 4 you have learned about financial analysis, application of technology and e-business.

However, only 80% of marks are awarded for the application of knowledge. The remaining marks are awarded for good demonstration of the specific ACCA Professional Skills outlined in the task requirement.

You need to able to:

1. Identify the ACCA Professional Skill in the task requirement. Remember the five: Analysis, Communication, Commercial Acumen, Evaluation and Scepticism

2. Understand what the skill requires in the context of the question

3. Consider how to demonstrate the skill(s) as part of your answer planning

The ACCA Professional Skills are assessing your ability to present your answers to a standard which would be expected in the workplace. However, in order to do this effectively in the Strategic Business Leader Exam, you must develop a further series of Exam Success Skills, so you are able to produce your very best solution in the four-hour timeframe.

Therefore, success in Strategic Business Leader requires the simultaneous demonstration of syllabus knowledge, ACCA Professional Skills and Exam Success Skills. This Skills Checkpoint specifically targets the development of your skills as you progress through the syllabus. This should provide you with all of the tools that you will need during the Learning phase, so you can focus on these improving at the Revision Stage.

The five Skills Checkpoints each focus on one of the five ACCA Professional Skills and provide further guidance on how to develop certain Exam Success Skills, so you can effectively manage questions and meet the expected standard for both knowledge and skills.

Your role

Developing skills requires more than listening and reading, it requires you to try for yourself, use guidance and feedback to consider whether you have met the skills objective, then plan for further improvement. In Strategic Business Leader, you should include a focus on skills development in every question you attempt as part of your normal approach. The Skills Checkpoints will take you through a series of **steps** where you will attempt aspects of a question and review your progress from a skills perspective.

Focus on ACCA Professional Skill: Evaluation

There are three essential elements to evaluation that ACCA have identified for their professional skills. The first is the ability to assess and use professional judgement when considering organisational issues, problems, or when making decisions; taking into account the implications of such decisions on the organisation and those affected. This includes determining the importance of a problem, weighing up advantages and disadvantages, and the potential impact of a decision on key stakeholders.

The second is to estimate trends or make reasoned forecasts of the implications of external and internal factors on the organisation, or of the outcomes of decisions available to the organisation. You need to be able to present and justify forecasts and estimates, possibly relating to developments in the environment and their impact on the organisation, or the possible impact of decisions on an organisation's performance.

The third and final approach to evaluation is to appraise facts, opinions and findings objectively, with a view to balancing the costs, risks, benefits and opportunities, before making or recommending solutions or decisions. This can include presenting the arguments for and against a proposal, and making recommendations that follow on from the balance of advantages and disadvantages. The ability to weigh up evidence in this manner and present a reasoned recommendation is one of the key hallmarks of a professional.

Demonstrating Exam Success Skills

For this question, we will focus on the following exam success skills:

- **Case scenario: Managing information** . You will be given a lot of information in the exam and it will be easy to feel overwhelmed. You need to develop the skill of assimilating the information you are provided with and identifying which pieces are most important to you in putting together your answer. Remember that your answers need to relate directly to the scenario given and not be vague or generic. By the time you are attempting full cases, it is recommended that you are spending at least 40 minutes on reading and interpreting the information provided. This is a shorter question, but you need to make sure you have understood the key information before starting your answer.

- **Answer planning: Priorities, Structure and Logic**. Before you start writing, or attempting calculations, it is vital that you stop and think about what you need to do, and, in some form, draft notes on the key points you are going to make. This will give your answer more focus, logic and structure. Use the marks available as a guide to the depth required in your answer, as well as how much time to spend on it and plan your calculations to ensure you are doing the important ones. The aim is that, by the time you start writing, you have a clear idea of what calculations need doing and, as far as possible, what you want to say.

- **Efficient numerical analysis.** Whatever format you use to lay out your calculations, it needs to be very clear to the marker what you have calculated and why it is relevant to the question. You need to show your workings so that, if you have made an error in your calculation, you will still get credit for attempting it, and you will not lose marks for any follow-on errors. Reference your workings clearly to the main part of your answer. Do not spend too long on a particular calculation, as any one calculation will not carry many marks. If you are struggling with it, make an assumption and move on to the rest of your answer.

Skills Activity

 Read the following task requirement for the question 'Housham Garden', identifying the verbs and the professional skills being examined, and start to set up your answer plan. Use your answer planning skills to identify what you need to do.

You are a business analyst who undertakes voluntary work for Housham Garden Trust ('HGT'). You have been asked to suggest immediate short-term changes, proposals which can be implemented immediately or within three months and will generate quantifiable income or savings.

Required

Using the data provided, show why HGT is losing money and recommend immediate and other short-term (within three months) changes for HGT, quantifying the increased income or cost savings that these changes should bring. **(15 marks)**

Professional skills marks are available for demonstrating **evaluation** skills in relation to your calculations and recommendations. **(2 marks)**

(Total = 17 marks)

- You are told that HGT is losing money so need to identify why. At its simplest, you are looking out for data on revenues and costs, which are leading to a loss.

- You then need to use your commercial judgement to make recommendations about how to address this – increasing revenues or reducing costs.

- You need to do some calculations about your recommendations to show their impact.

 You should now read the scenario, looking out for data on revenues and costs, and clues as to improvements that could be made. The scenario has been annotated to show what sort of things you should be looking for when performing this kind of 'active' reading.

Question – Housham Gardens (17 marks)

Housham Garden is a large garden in the country of Euphorbia, where gardening and visiting gardens is a popular pastime. For many years the garden was neglected, until bought by the Popper family who painstakingly restored the garden and four years ago opened it to the public. The garden is now owned and operated by a charitable trust set up by the Popper family – the Housham Garden Trust (HGT) – with initial funding provided by a legacy from the late Clive Popper.

> The level of fixed costs is an important data point in calculating why HGT is running at a loss

However, HGT is finding it difficult to meet its costs and it is gradually spending the legacy. It is estimated that fixed costs are currently $60,000 per annum. The price of entry into the garden is $5 per visit. At present, there are approximately 1,000 visits per month and the garden is open for eight months a year. It is closed for a period when the weather is usually much colder and few plants are flowering.

> This gives you the data to work out current revenue.

> There may be potential to open the gardens in the winter, but this is not a short-term change so outside the scope of the question

There is a café in the garden and it is estimated that 60% of visitors visit the café and buy drinks and food. However, each purchase is relatively modest. The current trust administrator estimates that the average contribution is $1.25 per visitor using the café.

A survey undertaken by a local university revealed that most consumers felt that the admission price for a garden such as Housham was too high. It revealed that the average consumer would be willing to pay an entry fee of $3.25, and indeed similar gardens in Euphorbia charge about this amount.

HGT currently advertises the garden in the monthly magazine *Heritage Gardens*. Each display advertisement costs $500 per issue. Adverts have been booked for the next six months, but it is possible to cancel the last three of these without incurring cancellation charges.

Respondents were critical of the food offered by the café. One respondent commented that quality 'had gone down since the café was moved into the garden. Really, there is very little choice, and I could not find anything substantial enough for lunch'. Her reference to the relocation of the café into the garden refers to the fact that the café used to be in the gatehouse of the garden. At this time, many people just visited Housham to use the café and did not pay for admission into the garden. It was decided that moving the café inside the garden would encourage people to pay for garden entry. However, this has not occurred. It is estimated that the café has lost about 500 visits per month and this has had an adverse effect on staff morale and food quality. The gatehouse area where the café was originally situated is still empty.

In the recent consumer survey, 20% of the respondents said that they would buy an annual (calendar year) ticket giving access to the garden for eight months if it were offered for $9. The customer survey also asked visitors where they had heard of the garden. Table 1 summarises their responses. The 200 respondents were only allowed to make one choice for how they heard about Housham Gardens.

How did you hear of Housham Gardens?	Number of respondents
Personal recommendation from a friend	110
Recent articles in the local newspaper	50
Internet	10
Heritage Gardens magazine	10
Other	20

Table 1: How visitors heard about the gardens: one day survey on 13 March 20X2

The reference in Table 1 to recent articles in the local newspaper concerns a series of articles written by the HGT administrator outlining the problems of the trust and the fact that short-term cash flow problems might cause the garden's temporary closure. One visitor commented that 'we had never heard of Housham Gardens until then, and we only live four kilometres away'.

 STEP 3 You are now in a position to create an answer plan.

Guidance in helping you develop your answer plan

As the question is worth 17 marks, using two minutes per mark as a guide equates to a total of 34 minutes to attempt the task requirement. Working on the basis that you will spend at least five minutes creating your answer plan, this leaves 29 minutes to write up your answer. Of the 15 technical marks available, nine were for calculations, so it was absolutely vital that you did not overlook these.

Demonstrating evaluation would be necessary to earn the two professional marks. These would be earned by making reasonable estimates of the impact of changes proposed, and their implications for stakeholders. Where you did not have specific data, you could make a reasonable assumption for the purposes of your illustration.

Having already annotated the scenario with the task requirements in mind, your answer plan may start to look something like this.

- Calculate revenue and costs to show loss
- Potential improvements

    - Reduce entry price – breakeven calc?
    - Annual ticket – potential take-up?
    - Improve café – estimate impact
    - Relocate café – estimate impact
    - Evaluate advertising spend – recommend change?

 Check the requirements

Before you start writing up your answer it is worthwhile reviewing the task requirement again to ensure that there is nothing that you have overlooked. The key point to re-emphasise is that you need to quantify the impact of your recommendations, so some kind of calculation is essential for each point.

 Complete your written answer

You can now bring your workings together to create a solution, making sure that you use logical headings and short punchy sentences. You can present your calculations either in a data table or individually, in your discussion of the recommendation. Either way is fine as long as it is clear – the latter approach has been adopted for this solution. A model answer is given below, with comment boxes illustrating where the answer is demonstrating good evaluation skills.

Suggested solution

Analysis of why HGT is running at a loss

HGT is currently making an annual loss of $14,000. This is illustrated by the following:

> This is the critical calculation required and so has been prioritised here.

	$
Revenue ($5 per visit × 1,000 visits per month × 8 months)	40,000
Contribution from café ($1.25 per visitor × 1,000 visits per month × 8 months × 60%)	6,000
Fixed costs	(60,000)
Annual shortfall	(14,000)

Immediate action HGT could take

Reduce entry price

The recent survey conducted by the local university indicates that consumers regard the current entry fee of $5 to be too expensive. Many visitors have stated that they are only prepared to pay an entry

fee of $3.25 on average. If HGT lowers the admission fee, this will result in a breakeven visitor volume of 15,000 visitors per annum (see Working).

The workings below are based on the assumption that 60% of visitors continue to use the café, and the average contribution generated per café sale remains at $1.25.

Working

$3.25 (revised admission fee) + 60% × $1.25 (café contribution) = $4

Fixed costs $60,000/$4 = 15,000 visitors per annum

Implications of change in visitor numbers

The proposed reduction in the admission fee may increase the visitor numbers by almost 90% of current levels. The trust will need to give consideration to the potential implications of increasing the number of visits by 7,000 per annum. Monitoring visitor satisfaction levels to ensure that any significant increase in numbers does not detract from the experience of visiting the gardens is likely to be key.

The decision is also complicated by the uncertainty of whether a reduction in the admission fee will translate to an increase in anticipated visitor numbers. A revised $3.25 admission fee may actually reduce the contribution to fixed costs.

Implications of introducing an annual ticket

The recent consumer survey conducted by the trust suggested that 20% of respondents would be prepared to purchase an annual ticket to gain admission to the gardens for a fee of $9 per annum. Such a move would prove beneficial as this would improve HGT's cash position, through a one-off inflow of money.

At present the gardens receive 8,000 visits per annum, however the number of actual visitors remains unknown. On the assumption that 5,000 visitors visit per annum and 20% of these individuals take up the annual pass ticket this would result in a cash inflow of $9,000 (5,000 visitors × 20% × $9). In evaluating the viability of this option the trust would need to consider the likely loss of repeat income from those visitors who currently pay $5 per visit, but will no longer pay when they visit because they hold an annual ticket.

Short-term changes

Improve the café

The trust should consider enhancing the existing visitor experience when using the café. Recent visitors have been particularly critical of the food offered. Improvements to the menu, with an increased emphasis on quality, should help to address the current situation.

As it stands, only 60% of visitors buy food in the café, and the average contribution ($1.25) per visitor is also low.

If the quality of food was improved, this could lead to an increase in the usage rate and contribution per visitor. If, for example, average contribution increased to $1.75, coupled with 75% usage rate, this would result in additional contribution of $4,500 over the 8-month season ($1.75 × 8,000 visits per annum × 75% – $6,000).

However, before making any changes, HGT should carry out a feasibility assessment. The lack of visitor support for the decision to move the café from the gatehouse site suggests a potential weakness in the trust's strategic approach to understanding what its visitors want.

Re-locate the café

HGT should also consider moving the café back to the gatehouse area. The recent visitor survey suggests that visitors have been deterred from visiting the café due to its relocation from outside the grounds to within the gardens. This has resulted in the café losing 500 visits per month, which in turn has impacted negatively on morale and food quality, as well as revenue.

Financially, moving the café into the garden has resulted in the loss of $625 worth of contribution per month or $5,000 per annum ($1.25 average contribution × 500 visits per month). As visitors now have to pay to gain access to the café this may also contribute to a greater expectation in terms of the quality of experience when they visit. Repositioning the café in the more popular gatehouse location may serve to address the issues identified. Furthermore, it is likely this could be achieved relatively quickly as the gatehouse area is still empty.

> Evaluation here means developing a reasonable hypothesis that might explain the data we have.

Advertising spend

The trust may also consider reducing its current advertising spend. Only ten respondents from 200 (5%) claimed to have heard of Housham Gardens via through the advertisements placed in the 'Heritage Gardens' magazine. This issue was further compounded by the fact that a recent visitor commented on having not heard of the gardens, despite only living four kilometres away. Cancelling three months of the adverts currently booked will result in a saving of $1,500 and avoid incurring the associated cancellation charges should the decision to cancel be made later. The income generated each month by the advert stands at $287.50 (see Working) compared to expense of $500 a month to place the advertisement. The trust may decide to access the target market using a more appropriate medium, eg regional newspaper advertising.

> Again, this shows good skills in working out how to compare the costs and benefits of the current approach to advertising. The recommendation leads on from the analysis.

Working:

(1,000 visits per month × 5% = 50 visits × $5 admission fee = $250) + (50 café visits × 60% × $1.25 = $37.50)

 Complete the exam success skills diagnostic

Finally, use the diagnostic below to assess how effectively you demonstrated the exam success skills in answering the question.

Exam Success Skills	Your reflections/observations
Case scenario: Managing information	Did you extract the key points from the scenario? This included the numerical data, but also the hints in the text about the problems being faced.
Correct interpretation of requirements	Did you pick up on the need to quantify the impact of the suggestions you made? Not doing so would mean losing a lot of marks. Were you clear that the task requirement only related to immediate and short-term changes?
Answer planning: Priorities, Structure and Logic	Did you adopt a systematic approach to planning, understanding the task requirements first, then working through the scenario to extract relevant information?
Efficient numerical analysis	In your planning stage, did you identify the calculations that would be needed to evaluate your recommendations? This required some thought, so needed to be built in to your planning time. Carrying out irrelevant calculations would not have earned credit.

Exam Success Skills	Your reflections/observations
Effective writing and presentation	Have you used headings to structure your answer, with short sentences and paragraphs? Are your points made clearly and succinctly? Are your calculations clearly linked to the relevant part of your answer?
Time management	Did you allocate sufficient time to discuss a range of proposals, and carry out supporting calculations for each?
Most important action points to apply to your next question	

Summary

Answering exam questions is like any other skill – the more you practise, the better you will get! But, after attempting a question, make sure you take time to reflect and debrief how well you managed it, whether you followed the key steps and whether you demonstrated professional skills. Carry forward your learning points to the next question you attempt, and over the course of your studies you will see significant improvements.

INTRODUCTION TO STAGE 5:
Implementing Strategic Change

Implementing Strategic Change

IBM is a US-based company with a global reach which was incorporated in 1911 by the amalgamation of four companies. One of these, the Tabulating Machine Company, had been set up to exploit the patented technology of punched card data processing equipment, created to tabulate the 1890 US census. The company grew and introduced countless technology innovations, earning the nickname 'Big Blue'. By the 1960s, the company dominated the market for business computers, prompting an antitrust investigation which continued until 1982 before being dropped. As the personal computer market developed in the 1980s, IBM tried to replicate its dominance in the corporate market, but found itself struggling against new, more focused competitors.

In 1993, facing the possibility of bankruptcy, the company appointed an outsider as its Chief Executive for the first time since 1914. Lou Gerstner was a former McKinsey consultant with no experience in the technology industry, but he was committed to a transformation of the company. Gradually, IBM moved away from low-margin hardware to higher-margin software and services. Gerstner retired in 2002, later writing a book about his experiences called *Who Says Elephants Can't Dance?* IBM continued its transformation, selling off its personal computer business to Lenovo in 2005, and acquiring a number of consulting and design businesses. Over time, the core of the business completely transformed from selling physical items to being knowledge-based. This change has been highly successful. In 2019 it earned revenue of $77bn, with net income of $7.7bn, employing approximately 350,000 people worldwide.

Not all organisations go through changes as dramatic as IBM, but all organisations need to be agile and able to adapt to new conditions, taking into account the context in which they are operating. A great deal of change is of a small scale, consisting of refining or redesigning processes, automating systems or outsourcing. Big-picture goals need to be combined with attention to detail, as change programmes break down into individual projects that need to be carefully managed if their proposed benefits are to be realised. This is how transformations can happen, no matter how big they need to be.

Enabling success and strategic change

13

Learning objectives

On completion of this chapter, you should be able to:

	Syllabus reference no.
Advise on how an organisation's structure and internal relationships can be re-organised to deliver a selected strategy	H1(a)
Advise on the implications of collaborative working and partnering, such as franchising, organisation process outsourcing, shared services and global business services	H1(b)
Discuss how talent management can contribute to supporting organisation strategy	H3(a)
Assess the value of the four view (POPIT – people, organisation, processes and information technology) model to the successful implementation of organisation change	H3(b)
Apply the Baldrige model for world class organisations to achieve and maintain business performance excellence	H4(a)
Assess and advise on how an organisation can be empowered to reach its strategic goals, improve its results and be more competitive	H4(b)
Apply and explore different types of strategic change and their implications	H5(a)
Analyse the culture of an organisation using Balogun and Hope Hailey's contextual features	H5(b)
Manage change in the organisation using Lewin's three-stage model	H5(c)

Business and exam context

This is the first of the final three chapters in which our focus turns to the practicalities associated with implementing the organisation's chosen strategy. This chapter is effectively formed of three related issues: organisational structures and internal relationships, improving performance, and strategic change. The chapter starts by considering the different types of organisational structure that can be adopted. For many years the static pyramidal hierarchy has formed the basis of ideas about organisational structure. However, the challenges of the modern business environment have led not only to new structural designs, but also to a complete re-evaluation of basic assumptions about organisation structure and the internal relationships which exist.

It is important to realise that in recent years there has been a move towards collaborative working within organisations, and between organisations and external parties. Building relationships with suppliers, competitors and customers increases the flexibility to respond to change. Our discussion then moves on to consider some key concepts relating to improving organisational performance: the Baldrige model, empowerment and talent management. When an organisation develops a new strategy it is inevitable that the process of implementing the strategy will lead to some form of change. In the final sections we explore some of the key issues associated with strategic change. Strategic change is closely connected to process redesign and project management, which are considered in Chapters 14 and 15 respectively.

Chapter overview

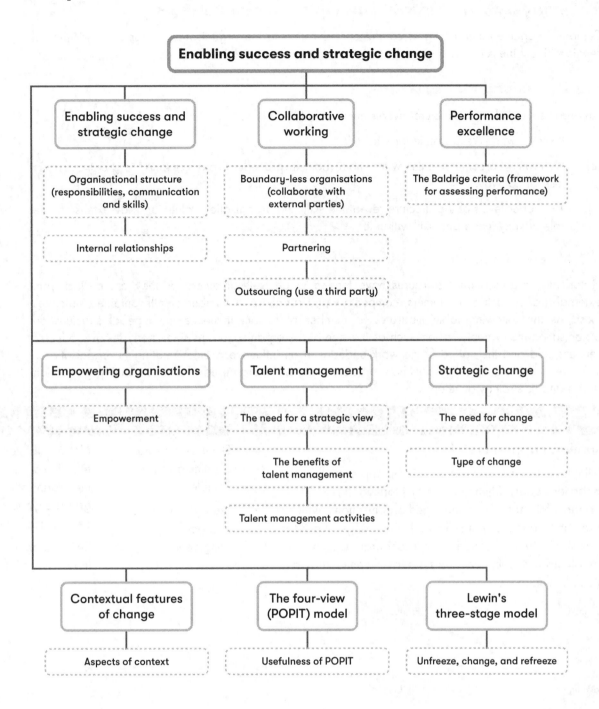

1 Enabling success and strategic change

1.1 Organisational structure and internal relationships

Senior management need to give careful consideration to the organisation's structure and internal relationships if the selected strategy is to be implemented successfully.

1.2 Organisational structure

An organisation's formal structure reveals much about it.

(a) It shows who is responsible for what.

(b) It shows who communicates with whom, both in procedural practice and, to great extent, in less formal ways.

(c) The upper levels of the structure reveal the skills the organisation values and, by extension, the role of knowledge and skill within it.

1.2.1 Types of structure

Historically, organisational structures have tended to be 'self-contained' as they are distinct from external groups such as customers, competitors and suppliers. A number of self-contained structures exist. As the following table illustrates, a number of factors influence the type of structure an organisation may adopt. Factors such as the age of the organisation, its size, the types of products/services sold and the nature of the work undertaken all influence choices relating to organisational structure. The table also highlights how structures may be re-organised over time as the organisation grows and its strategy develops.

Types of organisational structure	Advantages	Disadvantages
1 Simple/Entrepreneurial The simple/entrepreneurial structure is the approach that most organisations adopt when they are first formed. It is appropriate for small owner-managed organisations, which tend to pursue a strategy of selling a limited range of products or service. Commonly found in sole trader organisations where all organisational decisions are taken centrally by a single individual. Finance Production Marketing Distribution	• Decision making is quick and flexible • Strong control and goal congruence	• Not possible or effective once the organisation grows beyond a certain size • Reliance on leader

Types of organisational structure	Advantages	Disadvantages
2 Functional As organisations start to grow and their strategies become more complex the ability of the owner to make all managerial decisions becomes impossible as the need for specialist skills in a number of areas increases. The simple structure develops into a functional structure were people are organised according to the type of work they do. **Functional departmentation** Managing director Production director — Marketing director — Financial director — Engineering director — Personnel director etc ... etc ... etc Sales manager — Marketing director ... Management accountant — Financial accountant Sales manager — Marketing manager (Adapted from: Johnson *et al*, 2017)	• Work is based on specialism • Gives economies of scale in operations • Offers clear career progression	• Can lead to co-ordination and communication problems • Leads to 'silos' where people do not understand how the whole business works
3 Divisional The divisional structure, and holding company structure mentioned below, are commonly found in larger organisations which pursue a diverse range of strategies. The divisional structure sees the organisation divided into semi-autonomous units, based on geography, product or market. **Simple divisionalisation** Organisation's head office Division A — Division B — Division C Functions ... Functions ... Functions	• Specialism on basis of divisionalisation • Provides clear performance measurement and accountability for divisional managers • Gives authority to divisional managers and prepares them for senior management	• Divisions may duplicate each other's functions, leading to waste • Divisions can become more bureaucratic than they would be as independent organisations, owing to the performance measures imposed by the strategic apex
4 Holding company structure In a holding company structure, these divisions are separate legal entities. Holding company Subsidiary A — Subsidiary B — Subsidiary C Sub-subsidiary D — Sub-subsidiary E ... Sub-subsidiary F		• Complexity of management and reporting — having head office or a holding company imposes additional costs

Types of organisational structure	Advantages	Disadvantages
5 Transnational structure Combines some independence for national units, with certain functions that are run globally. For instance a specialised R&D function may be based in one country but used by all territories.	• Improves responsiveness to local conditions • Can lead to major economies of scale	• Can create complex relationships within the organisation • Complexity of structure can create difficulties of control
6 Matrix The matrix structure (matrix management) can operate as a structure in its own right or can be set up as a sub structure within most of the organisational structures already discussed (with the exception of the simple/entrepreneurial structure). Matrix structures are often appropriate for organisations which purse strategies involving lots of project work. Matrix type structures maintain co-ordination by co-working across functions, addressing some of the disadvantages of functional structures. This usually means some form of dual authority that can be complex and confusing and may make control more difficult. (Adapted from: Mullins, 2002: p.551)	• Allows for flexible deployment of staff as requirements change • Improved communication and co-operation	• Increased potential conflict between managers • Complex to run and can lead to slow decision making

---

Essential reading

See Chapter 13 section 1 of the Essential Reading, available in Appendix 2 of the digital edition of the Workbook, for more detail about team based and project based structures.

1.3 Internal relationships

Internal relationships concerning responsibility and authority for decision making are particularly important. There are two important issues in internal relationships:

- The degree of centralisation

- The way the centre relates to the strategic business units in the case of conglomerate organisations. Conglomerate organisations were introduced in Chapter 6.

1.3.1 Centralisation

Centralisation refers to the level in the organisation's structure at which decisions are taken. For example, an organisation which operates a divisional structure may require individual divisions to follow the strategy determined by head office. As a result centralisation offers control and standardisation. By contrast decentralisation utilises talent and local knowledge at lower levels within the organisation, for example at a divisional level.

Key terms

Centralisation: Means a greater degree of central control.

Decentralisation: Means a greater degree of delegated authority to regions or sub-units.

1.3.2 Advantages of centralisation

Advantage	Comment
Control	Senior management can exercise greater control over the activities of the organisation and co-ordinate their subordinates or sub-units more easily.
Standardisation	Procedures can be standardised throughout the organisation.
Corporate view	Senior managers can make decisions from the point of view of the organisation as a whole, whereas subordinates would tend to make decisions from the point of view of their own department or division.
Balance of power	Centralised control enables an organisation to maintain a balance between different functions or divisions.
Experience counts	Senior managers ought to be more experienced and skilful in making decisions.
Lower overheads	When authority is delegated, there is often a duplication of management effort (and a corresponding increase in staff numbers) at lower levels of hierarchy.
Leadership	In times of crisis, the organisation may need strong leadership by a central group of senior managers.

1.3.3 Advantages of decentralisation

Advantage	Comment
Workload	It reduces the stress and burdens of senior management.
Job	It provides subordinates with greater job satisfaction by giving them more say in making decisions which affect their work.
Local knowledge	Subordinates may have a better knowledge than senior management of 'local' conditions affecting their area of work.
Flexibility and speed	Delegation should allow greater flexibility and a quicker response to changing conditions. If problems do not have to be referred up the chain of command to senior managers for a decision, decision making will be quicker.
Training	Management at middle and junior levels are groomed for eventual senior management positions.
Control	By establishing appropriate sub-units or profit centres to which authority is delegated, the system of control within the organisation might be improved.

1.3.4 Strategic management relationships

In Chapter 6 we introduced the concept of the conglomerate type of organisation, which consists of a portfolio of different businesses. A vital feature of the relationship between the corporate centre

BPP
LEARNING
MEDIA

(head office) and its divisions/business units is how responsibility for strategic decisions is divided between them.

There are three generally accepted possible roles for the centre:

- Determination of overall strategy and the allocation of resources
- Controlling divisional performance
- Provision of central services

Goold and Campbell (1987) identified three major approaches to running divisionalised conglomerates:

Strategic planning style

The centre establishes extensive planning processes through which it works with divisional managers to make substantial contributions to strategic thinking, often with a unifying overall corporate strategy. Performance targets are set in broad terms, with an emphasis on longer-term strategic objectives.

Strategic control style

This style involves a fairly low degree of planning influence but uses tight strategic control. The centre prefers to leave the planning initiative to divisional managers, though it will review their plans for acceptability. Firm targets are set for a range of performance indicators and performance is judged against them.

Financial control style

Each division is controlled by the imposition of strict financial targets. Divisional managers are appraised on their ability to generate sufficient performance, but are free to decide upon how this is achieved, giving them high levels of autonomy.

2 Collaborative working

Traditionally, external commercial relationships have been, to a greater or lesser extent, **adversarial**, in that each organisation has attempted to obtain for itself as much as possible of the value created overall in the value network. While this is still characteristic of most external relationships, many new ones have been created that focus more on **co-operation** than rivalry. These new structures are known as boundary-less organisations.

2.1 Boundary-less organisations

Key term

Boundary-less organisations: Are those which have structured their operations to allow for collaboration with external parties.

Building relationships with suppliers, competitors and customers should increase the organisations' flexibility to respond to change. There are various forms of boundary-less organisation, these include hollow, modular, network and virtual organisation structures.

2.1.1 Hollow structure

In a hollow structure the majority of the company's non-core processes are outsourced to specialist providers, leaving the company free to concentrate on its value-adding activities. Value-adding activities often relate to R&D, marketing and manufacturing. The outsourcing of certain functions effectively makes the organisation a 'hollowed out' entity, allowing it to reduce its workforce and cut costs. The remaining staff are then free to manage the relationships created with the third party outsourcer.

2.1.2 Modular structure

The modular structure involves outsourcing certain production processes to specialist outsourcers. The core company will then assemble the outsourced components in-house to produce a final product. This type of structure is commonly used in hi-tech industries, such as aircraft manufacture. For example, an outsource partner will provide the engines which the aircraft manufacturer can then bolt onto the finished plane.

2.1.3 Networks

Networks are groups of organisations or individuals who co-operate to deliver services to customers. For example, a building contractor might deliver a building project by managing a range of other specialist contractors, rather than carry out the work themselves. Such a loose, fluid approach is often used to achieve innovative response to changing circumstances.

2.1.4 Virtual structures

A virtual organisation appears as a single entity from outside to its customers, but is in fact a network of different organisational nodes (individuals, teams or even entire organisations) often linked through technology.

Essential reading

See Chapter 13 section 2 of the Essential Reading, available in Appendix 2 of the digital edition of the Workbook, for more detail on collaborative working practices between organisations and customers.

Syllabus links

In Chapter 6 we introduced the concept of external and internal partnering. In Chapter 6 we considered partnering from the context of how it can help organisations to achieve business growth. In the following section we explore the implications for organisations when adopting a partnering approach.

2.2 Partnering

In Chapter 6 we introduced the concept of partnering and how this is being used by organisations to achieve business growth. In this section we consider the implications for organisations when adopting a partnering approach.

2.2.1 Internal partnering

As highlighted in Chapter 6, internal partnering is concerned with increasing the levels of co-operation and collaboration between the various functions and departments that exist within organisations. A key aim of internal partnering is to enhance the efficiency of internal operations by addressing the issues that often arise when departments fail to work together. An example of this type of failing would include a situation where a company's marketing department announce the launch date of a new product to customers, without realising that the production department are working towards a later launch date. As this example illustrates instances such as this may cause the company some embarrassment and in a worst case scenario may even lead to lost sales if customers choose to purchase a competitor's product instead.

For internal partnering to be successful managers need to understand better how the activities of their respective departments interact with and impact upon other parts of the organisation. This requires breaking down the barriers that exist between departments by improving the methods of communication between teams. This helps to create greater understanding of the different challenges facing other parts of the business. Effective internal partnering involves viewing problems as shared challenges, so that a problem facing a particular department is viewed as a challenge that workers and managers in the wider business can help to overcome. Internal partnering often requires cultural change as people need to be encouraged to work more collaboratively with others in different departments. To help achieve this change organisations need to avoid to setting departmental measures which only focus on the performance of the activities undertaken by that department. Organisational performance should also include measures for assessing interdepartmental co-operation and measures which assess the outcome of interdepartmental projects.

2.2.2 External partnering

External partnering arrangements have implications for the way in which businesses are organised. In Chapter 6, we highlighted that external partnering can take many forms, one of the most common is franchising. Franchising arrangements place legal obligations on both the franchiser and franchisee. Establishing a franchise arrangement requires the franchiser to organise its operations in such a way as it is able to maintain control over its franchised partners. Control issues here tend to relate to the franchisees use of franchised intellectual property, the approaches used by the franchisee to market and sell franchised goods and services, and issues associated with upholding the franchiser's quality standards.

Franchisers will develop performance measures and reporting systems to ensure that the franchisee complies with the terms of the franchise agreement. As franchising arrangements are collaborative by nature, franchisers are also required to provide support to franchisees. Support here may include providing customer service training to franchisees so that there is consistency between owned and franchised operations, and may also include support with marketing and advertising. Many franchisers have set up dedicated teams, which are distinct from their non-franchised operations, to provide this support.

2.3 Outsourcing

The concept of the boundary-less organisation has become increasingly possible due to the emergence of organisational process outsourcing.

Outsourcing: Involves an organisation contracting out certain internal business functions to a third party.

Key term

Organisations very often outsource those functions which are considered to be non-critical, such as payroll processing.

Activity 1: Ergo City

ACCA Professional skills focus

Communication: Clarify

You are Johnathan Edwards, a management consultant working on an assignment at Ergo City Authority (ECA). ECA administers environmental, social care, housing and cultural services to the city of Ergo. Recently the authority was approached by Pro-Tech, an IT service company which proposed changing ECA's existing approach to managing its IT department. You were appointed to provide advice on this matter. The CEO was particularly keen to get an external consultant involved as there had been a lot of confusion among the ECA board about the potential benefits that the Pro-Tech proposal might bring. Having conducted a review of the current issues facing ECA (Exhibit 1), and the proposal from Pro-Tech (Exhibit 2), you are now preparing a slide which will form part of a presentation that you are due to give to the CEO and the board.

Required

Using the information provided in the two Exhibits, prepare ONE presentation slide, with supporting notes which evaluates the potential benefits to ECA of outsourcing its IT function to Pro-Tech Public.
(10 marks)

Professional skills marks are available for demonstrating **communication** skills in clarifying the potential benefits to the authority of outsourcing its IT.
(2 marks)

(Total = 12 marks)

Exhibit 1 – Ergo City Authority

The city itself has many social problems and a recent report from the local government auditor criticised the Chief Executive Officer (CEO) for not spending enough time and money addressing the pressing housing problems of the city. ECA has had its own internal Information Technology (IT) department for many years. However, there has been increasing criticism of the cost and performance of this department. Some employees are lost through natural wastage, but there have never been any redundancies in IT and the labour laws of the nation, and strong trade unions within ECA, make it difficult to make staff redundant. As a result the IT department has steadily grown in size.

In the last few years there has been an on-going dispute between managers in the IT department and managers in the finance function. The dispute started due to claims about the falsification of expenses but has since escalated into a personal battle between the director of IT and the finance director. The CEO has had to intervene personally in this dispute and has spent many hours trying to reconcile the two sides. However, issues still remain and there is still tension between the managers of the two departments.

A recent internal human resources (HR) survey of the IT department found that, despite acknowledging that they received above average pay, employees were not very satisfied. The main complaints were about poor management, the ingratitude of user departments, ('we are always being told that we are overheads, and are not core to the business of ECA') and the absence of promotion opportunities within the department. The ingratitude of users is despite the IT department running a relatively flexible approach to fulfilling users' needs. The director of IT is also critical of the staffing constraints imposed on him. He has recently tried to recruit specialists in web services and 'cloud computing' without any success. He also says that 'there are probably other technologies that I have not even heard of that we should be exploring and exploiting'.

Exhibit 2 – Pro-Tech proposal

The CEO has been approached by a large established IT service company, Pro-Tech, to form a new company Pro-Tech-Public that combines the public sector IT expertise of ECA with the commercial and IT knowledge of Pro-Tech. The joint company will be a private limited company owned 51% by Pro-Tech and 49% by ECA. All existing employees in the IT department of ECA will be transferred to Pro-Tech who will then enter into a 10-year outsourcing arrangement to provide IT services with ECA. The CEO is very keen on the idea and he sees many other authorities following this route.

Solution

The benefits and implications of outsourcing are considered in the following table.

Advantages of outsourcing	Disadvantages and implications of outsourcing
Removes uncertainty about cost, as there is often a long-term contract where services are specified in advance for a fixed price. It may also result in achieving economies of scale.	An organisation may have highly confidential information and to let outsiders handle it could be seen as risky in commercial and/or legal terms.
Outsource arrangements can be established so that they last for many years. This encourages future planning.	An organisation may find itself locked in to an unsatisfactory contract.
Specialist outsourcers possess greater skills and knowledge. A specialist outsourcer can share staff with specific expertise between several clients.	The use of an outsourcer organisation does not encourage awareness of the potential costs and benefits of conducting certain processes within the organisation.
It offers flexibility (contract permitting). Resources may be able to be scaled up or down depending on demand.	If at a future date the decision is made to bring a process back in-house there are no guarantees that the required skills (eg IT experts) will be readily available in the job market.

As the above table illustrates, trust is an important element between the organisation and the outsource provider. To address concerns around the quality of the outsourced processes being provided it is common practice for service level agreements (SLAs) to be used.

2.3.1 Offshoring

Key term

Offshoring: Is a form of outsourcing that involves an external entity based in a different country providing an organisation with a particular product or process which had previously been provided in-house.

Real world example

Offshoring became particularly popular in the late 1990s when a number of well-known global financial institutions (banks and insurance companies) decided to set up customer call centre operations in countries such as India. The principal rationale for this shift concerned the vast pool of graduate labour which could be utilised at a lower cost than available in home markets. This shift saw a number of new call centres being established and operated by external third parties which provided the required staff and facilities.

In recent years the trend towards offshoring appears to be shifting once more. An article by Davies in 2016 reported that the mobile phone group, EE, had announced plans to create 600 jobs in the UK. The announcement followed the arrival of EE's new CEO, Marc Allera, who pledged to improve customer satisfaction following growing numbers of customer complaints about poor levels of service offered by EE's offshore call centres. The proposal led to EE abandoning its call centre operations in India, South Africa and the Philippines. The company set itself a target of ensuring that at least 80% of all customer service calls were answered by EE staff in the UK by the end of 2016. In January 2017 it was reported that EE had delivered on its pledge and had in fact created 1,000 customer service operator jobs in the UK and Ireland (The Register, 2017).

2.3.2 Shared servicing

Key term

Shared servicing: Is an alternative to outsourcing, where shared service centres (SSC) consolidate the transaction-processing activities of many operations within an organisation.

Shared service centres aim to achieve significant cost reductions while improving service levels through the use of standardised technology and processes. Many large organisations have moved to centralise their IT support functions. It is common now for one IT helpdesk to serve the entire organisation, as opposed to individual divisions or departments having their own designated IT support.

Advantages of shared services	Disadvantages and implications of shared services
Reduced headcount due to economies of scale, resulting from bringing operations to a single location.	**Loss of business-specific knowledge**. For example, creating a consolidated finance function which broadly handles financial matters for the entire organisation may lack an understanding of specific finance issues affecting individual departments or business units.
Associated **reduction** in premises and other overhead **costs**.	**Removed from decision making**. Building on from the point above, an SSC finance function is unlikely to be able to provide meaningful financial information for decision making if finance personnel are removed from the day-to-day realities facing a particular department or business unit.
Knowledge sharing should lead to an **improvement in quality** of the service provided.	**Weakened relationships**. Geographical distance between the site of the SSC and the respective areas it serves may weaken the relationships between the two.
Allows standard approaches to be adopted across the organisation, leading to more consistent management of organisational data.	

2.3.3 Global business services

Global business services are a relatively new development which are being used by large, global organisations.

A **global business service:** Effectively brings together existing shared service and outsourcing arrangements together to form an integrated, collaborative framework which helps to co-ordinate and support the global operations of the organisation in areas including finance, HR, IT and procurement.

3 Performance excellence

Having considered issues relating to structure and internal relationships we now move onto explore how organisations can ensure high levels of performance.

3.1 The Baldrige Criteria

The Baldrige Criteria™ for Performance Excellence (National Institute of Standards and Technology) provide a framework for assessing performance, with a view to improving performance. The underlying purpose of the Baldrige model is to help organisations improve, and achieve excellence.

The framework doesn't prescribe how an organisation should behave or operate. Instead, it is used to assess an organisation's performance, helping the organisation identify its own strengths, and opportunities for improvement, as well as prioritising the areas where improvement is needed to attain organisational sustainability.

This lack of prescription means that Baldrige can be used by not-for-profit organisations (eg education; health care providers) as well as commercial manufacturing and service companies.

The framework is based on the idea that the following beliefs and behaviours (referred to as core values and concepts) are found in high-performing organisations (and underpin organisational success):

- Visionary leadership
- Focus on success
- Ethics and transparency
- Societal responsibility
- Organisational learning and agility
- Valuing people
- Customer-focussed excellence
- Delivering value and results
- Management by fact: an emphasis on feedback, and a fact-based, knowledge-driven system for improving performance and competitiveness

Organisations can use the core values and concepts outlined above as a criteria against which they can assess their performance in relation to the seven categories outlined in the diagram below.

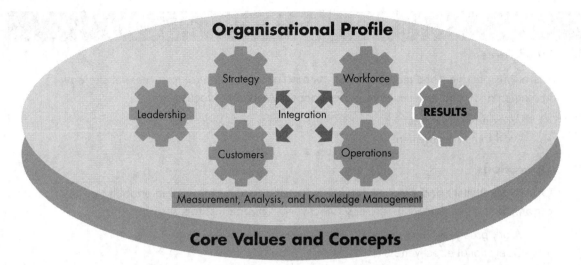

(Diagram: The Baldrige Excellence Framework, (National Institute of Standards and Technology, n.d))

3.1.1 Elements of the Baldrige assessment

Organisational profile: The organisation describes what is important to it – its operating environment, competitive environment, key relationships.

Criteria questions assess how well an organisation accomplishes the things which are important to it. The basic principle of the Baldrige model is that six key criteria shape an organisation's ability to achieve the seventh criteria (consistently delivering excellent results).

	Criteria
1	**Leadership** Leaders must set the direction for their organisation and establish clear performance expectations for it. 'Leadership' focuses on: • The role of senior leadership • Governance and social responsibilities
2	**Strategy** Strategic plans are then developed, and the strategies and goals needed for the organisation to achieve its performance expectations are defined. 'Strategy' focuses on: • Strategy development • Strategy implementation
3	**Customers** (or 'beneficiaries' for not-for-profit organisations – eg students or patients). To be successful, the strategies must enable the organisation to meet the needs of its **customers** effectively. (For a commercial organisation, this means meeting the needs of its customers better than competitors within the markets it serves.) 'Customers' focuses on: • Listening to the voice of the customer • Customer engagement
4	**Measurement, Analysis and Knowledge Management** The organisation needs appropriate systems to provide feedback (**measurement**) to strategic leaders about the performance **results** achieved. The focus here is on: • Measurement, analysis and improvement of organisational performance • Knowledge, management, information and information technology (IT)

	Criteria
5	**Workforce** The efforts of skilled and motivated staff (**workforce**) are central to successful strategy implementation and excellence in performance. 'Workforce' focuses on: • Working environment • Workforce engagement
6	**Operations** Operating efficient and effective processes (**operations**) – are vital in enabling an organisation to implement its strategy effectively. 'Operations' focuses on: • Work processes • Operational effectiveness
7	**Results** (compared to other organisations, and over time) In addition to assessing each of the criteria individually, the framework also highlights the importance of **integration** between strategy, customers, workforce and operations in delivering results. As such, the Baldrige Criteria seek to promote excellence across an entire organisation, rather than focusing on individual pockets of excellence within an organisation. 'Results' focuses on: • Products/processes • Customers • Workforce • Leadership and governance • Financial and market

Organisations that have received the Baldrige Award (demonstrating that they applied the Baldrige Criteria) report improved performance across a range of areas: better financial results; satisfied, loyal customers; improved products and services; and an engaged workforce.

3.1.2 Analysing performance

Criteria 1-6 in the framework are evaluated in relation to four dimensions:

Approach	How does the organisation accomplish its work? How effective are its key approaches?
Deployment	How consistently are key processes used in relevant parts of the organisation?
Learning	How well has the organisation evaluated and improved its key approaches? How well have improvements been shared within the organisation? What is the potential for innovation within the organisation?
Integration	How well are the organisation's approaches aligned to its current and future needs? How well are processes and operations, and any associated targets and performance measures, harmonised across the organisation?

Similarly, 'results' are also evaluated against four dimensions (albeit different ones to the dimensions for the other criteria):

Levels	What is the organisation's current performance level?
Trends	Are results in this aspect of performance improving, staying the same, or getting worse?

Comparisons	How does the organisation's performance compare with that of other organisations, or against benchmarks/targets?
Integration	Does the organisation track the results that are important to it, and which consider the needs and expectations of key stakeholders? Does the organisation use the results of its performance tracking in decision making?

Remember, the underlying purpose of the framework is to help organisations improve. So, while it could be a concern for an organisation if the analysis identifies gaps or weaknesses, what is potentially more important is what the organisation does to address its weaknesses, to close the gaps, and to take advantage of opportunities available to it.

4 Empowering organisations

During our discussion of the Baldrige model we highlighted the important role that the organisation's workforce play in improving performance; in this section we explore the concept of empowerment and how workers can contribute to the success of the organisation.

In the widest sense the process of empowering an organisation involves identifying and removing those constraints which prohibit the attainment of the organisation's strategic goals and the improvement of performance. As highlighted by the Baldrige model the process of enhancing an organisation's performance requires that consideration is given to a range of factors which may present weaknesses in need of improvement. Overcoming such weaknesses may require that a number of actions be taken including: investing in new technologies, enhancing existing processes, and the development of new strategies.

However, as we shall explore most contemporary writing on the subject of empowerment relates to the important role played by the organisation's workforce.

4.1 Empowerment

Key term

Empowerment: Is the term for making workers (and particularly work teams) responsible for achieving, and even setting, work targets, with the freedom to make decisions about how they are to be achieved.

Empowerment includes two key aspects:

(a) Allowing workers to have the freedom to decide how to do the necessary work, using the skills they possess and acquiring new skills as necessary to be an effective team member.

(b) Making workers responsible for achieving production targets and for quality control.

The drive to empower workers was caused by a realisation that all too often it is the individuals working lower down the organisation that have the knowledge and understanding of what is going wrong with a process. The problem is that these individuals do not have the required power to change how the process works, as this rests with the management who lack the understanding needed to make the necessary changes. This highlights the need to amend organisational cultures so that employees are given the freedom to challenge existing ways of working.

Empowerment goes hand in hand with:

(a) **Delayering**. Delayering involves the reduction of the number of management levels from bottom to top. The responsibility previously held by middle managers is, in effect, being given to operational workers

(b) **Flexibility**, since giving responsibility to the people closest to the product and customer encourages responsiveness – and cutting out layers of communication, decision making and reporting speeds up the process

(c) **New technology**, since there are more 'knowledge workers' in the new organisation. Such people need less supervision, being better able to identify and control the means to clearly understood ends. Better information systems also remove the mystique and power of managers as possessors of knowledge and information in the organisation.

4.1.1 Achieving empowerment

Empowering workers requires the organisation to adopt an approach to human resource management which views employees as being an important strategic asset, which is capable of providing a source of competitive advantage. In this case the role of the manager becomes one of supporting staff to find solutions to better meet the objectives of the organisation, as opposed to simply ensuring compliance with organisational rules. The change in structure and culture as a result of empowerment is illustrated in the following diagram.

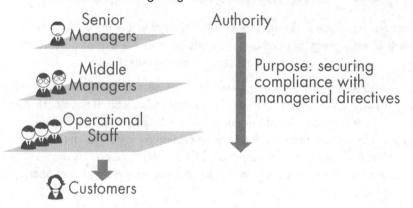

Empowerment structure: supporting workers in serving the customer

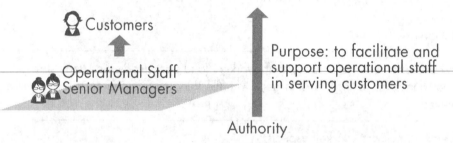

(Diagram: Hierarchical and empowerment structures)

5 Talent management

Key term

Talent management: Is principally concerned with initially attracting and subsequently identifying, developing and retaining individuals within the organisation who are considered to be important to the future success of the organisation.

5.1 The need for a strategic view

The human resource departments (HR) in many organisations are increasingly taking a strategic view of their workforce, with the need to identify and manage talented individuals being deemed critical to the creation of a competitive advantage. Skills shortages in the job market coupled with increasingly competitive conditions have driven the increasing focus on talent management. There has been a drive among larger organisations to identify those workers capable of enabling the organisation to achieve its strategic objectives in both the short and longer term.

5.2 The benefits of talent management

A successful talent management strategy should be closely aligned to the organisation's strategy. Benefits associated with adopting a talent management approach include:

- The creation of a learning organisation where workers are encouraged to challenge assumptions and to search for improvements to existing processes to help achieve organisational objectives

- Attracting new talent to the organisation to help develop new products/services to make the organisation more competitive

- Supporting succession planning as workers are prepared for future role leadership roles

Essential reading

See Chapter 13 section 3 of the Essential Reading, available in Appendix 2 of the digital edition of the Workbook, for more detail on the topic of succession planning. Succession planning is closely linked to the topic of talent management.

5.3 Talent management activities

Organisational talent management programmes aim to develop the potential offered by talented individuals. The remit of talent management has evolved to include individual development, performance enhancement, workforce planning and succession planning. Activities undertaken as part of a talent management programme might include:

Activity 2: Blue Cherry Mobile

ACCA Professional skills focus

Communication: Persuade

You are Alisha Kemp; you are a business professional working for Blue Cherry Mobile (BCM). Working as a business analyst you provide support services to all areas of the business including the human resources (HR) department.

BCM is a global manufacturer of mobile phones; in recent times the company has seen a significant deterioration in its performance with sales falling dramatically. Following the announcement last month of BCM's quarterly results the company's CEO has resigned. BCM's nomination committee are due to begin the process of finding a replacement soon. In light of the company's performance the BCM board undertook a review of the company's expenditure on a range of activities including its graduate recruitment programme. At the last board meeting a number of directors raised concerns about the associated costs and apparent failures of BCM's graduate recruitment programme, with one director proposing that the scheme be shut down before the next intake.

You have been approached by BCM's Chair; he agrees that improvements are needed to BCM's graduate recruitment programme, but is very keen to ensure that it is maintained. As a result he would like to present some counter-arguments to address the concerns raised by the other directors.

Required

Using the information provided in Exhibit 1, prepare a brief note which suggests some of the ways in which BCM's graduate recruitment programme could be developed to be more consistent with the principles of talent management. **(8 marks)**

Professional skills marks are available for demonstrating **communication** skills in displaying persuasiveness in the suggestions made.

(2 marks)

(Total = 10 marks)

Exhibit 1 – BCM's struggles

Up until a couple of years ago Blue Cherry Mobile (BCM) was the leading manufacturer of mobile phone handsets in all of the major global markets it competed in. Since this time the company has seen its share of the mobile phone handset market fall significantly as new competitors have entered the market; as a result BCM's financial performance has deteriorated.

One competitor in particular, Kiwi Phones, has been very successful in eroding BCM's global market share, as the company has introduced a series of phones with significantly more advanced features than those offered by BCM's best-selling devices. Kiwi's latest model, the Ki2000, is capable of projecting images onto a surface, such as a whiteboard, and is increasingly used by business professionals when giving work-related presentations.

BCM has for a number of years recruited graduates from some of the world's top science and technology universities as part of its graduate recruitment programme. Graduates are recruited to work in BCM's R&D department. Over the last year, a number of these recruits have been poached by Kiwi. A significant proportion of those recruits who have left BCM over the last year have cited a reluctance to incorporate new technological features into BCM's latest models as their reason for leaving. One leaver commented 'I need to leave BCM in order to further my career, I have lots of good ideas it is just a shame that I cannot seem to get anyone in management to listen to them'. Another commented 'I have been at BCM for three years, I completed the graduate programme six months ago. Since this time I have been working in an admin role as I was told that there was no longer any space for me in the R&D department as this would be needed for the next intake of graduates'.

Solution

Exam Focus Point

The Strategic Business Leader specimen 2 exam featured a public sector rail company, Rail Co, which was responsible for providing rail services within the country of Beeland. The third question required candidates to act in the capacity of the non-executive chairperson of a sub-committee. Following the removal of the previous chief executive the role had been advertised and two individuals had been shortlisted for a final interview. Part (b) of question 3 asked candidates to prepare two presentation slides, with accompanying notes, which explained 'to the NCG [nominations and corporate governance committee], the contribution which the chief executive should be expected to make in terms of talent management, to support the necessary change programme required at Rail Co' (ACCA, 2017a). This task was worth 6 technical marks and tested the ACCA Professional Skill of Communication. To produce a good answer candidates needed to focus on talent management and the role that it plays in helping organisations, and to also consider how the new chief executive could support talent management. To earn the two professional skills marks candidates needed to convey relevant information in an appropriate tone. Presenting the answer in the prescribed format (presentation slides with notes) was of critical importance.

Essential reading

See Chapter 13 section 4 of the Essential Reading, available in Appendix 2 of the digital edition of the Workbook, which considers how organisations can develop the skills of their workforce to embrace the changes being brought about by advances in digital technologies. This content is highly topical to the wider discussion of the impact that organisational change has on individuals in the work environment.

BPP
LEARNING
MEDIA

6 Strategic change

6.1 The need for change

As we explored in earlier chapters, the need for change may arise from a number of sources including changes in the environment, a review of strategic capability or a decision to implement a new strategy.

Syllabus links

We will consider the impact of change in relation to the redesign of internal processes in Chapter 14. Projects result in some form of change. Consideration of how to manage such projects is discussed in Chapter 15, when we explore the subject of project management.

Change can be analysed in terms of:

(a)   The type of change required
(b)   The wider context of the change
(c)   Forces facilitating and blocking change

6.2 Type of change

Johnson *et al* (2017), quoting Balogun and Hope Hailey (2008), analyse change on two axes: these are its scope and its nature.

The **scope** of change is its extent: the measure of scope is whether or not the methods and assumptions of the existing paradigm must be replaced. The paradigm represents the common, basic assumptions and beliefs held by those within the organisation.

The **nature** of change may be incremental and built on existing methods and approaches, or it may require a 'big bang' approach if rapid response is required, as in times of crisis.

Types of change

Scope of change

		Realignment	Transformation
Incremental		Adaptation	Evolution
Nature of change			
'Big bang'		Reconstruction	Revolution

(Adapted from: Balogun and Hope Hailey, 2008: p.21)

Balogun and Hope Hailey's (2008) four types of change can be summarised as follows:

(a)   **Adaptation** is the most common type of change. It does not require the development of a new paradigm and proceeds step by step. The majority of change falls into this category.

(b)   **Reconstruction** can also be undertaken within an existing paradigm but requires rapid and extensive action. It is a common response to a long-term decline in performance. An example would be cost cutting in response to falling profits.

(c)   **Evolution** is an incremental process that leads to a new paradigm. It may arise from careful analysis and planning or may be the result of learning processes. Its transformational nature may not be obvious while it is taking place.

(d)   **Revolution** is rapid and wide-ranging response to extreme pressures for change. A long period of strategic drift may lead to a crisis that can only be dealt with in this way. Revolution will be very obvious and is likely to affect most aspects of both what the organisation does and how it does them.

Illustration 1

The following illustration provides examples of Balogun and Hope Hailey's four types of change and their implications in relation to a supermarket chain.

Adaptation

The decision by a supermarket chain to introduce a home delivery service to customers in a selected region. This change is a form of adaptation, as the company is simply attempting to move with the times as competing supermarkets already offer this service. The fundamental nature of the supermarket chain's business model has not changed, as it is still operating as a supermarket.

Reconstruction

The supermarket's home market is suffering from a prolonged recession. The supermarket chain could be forced to undertake a rapid form of reconstruction. The impact of a significant fall in customer demand for the produce offered by the supermarket may lead to the closure of the most unprofitable outlets. Making staff redundant in the affected stores would cause upheaval throughout the organisation but would not ultimately change the supermarket's culture or business model.

Evolution

The decision to introduce the home delivery service (mentioned above) may be part of a long-term plan to close down all of the supermarket's physical stores over a number of years, with the view of becoming an online retailer only. Such an evolutionary change would lead to a change in the chain's culture and business model.

Revolution

Revolutionary change at the supermarket would be driven by extreme pressures. An example would be the decision by the owners of the chain to sell off its investment to a new owner. A new parent company may move to instill its own culture throughout the supermarket chain. Changes could result in the closure of existing stores or changes to the supermarket's existing supply chain.

7 Contextual features of change

The context of change is provided by the organisational setting; this has many aspects and can therefore be very complex. Organisational change can be considered under eight general headings proposed by Balogun and Hope Hailey (2008). One of the eight headings is 'scope': this has already been discussed.

The headings represent a wide range of influences, the impact of each will vary from organisation to organisation. Perhaps one of the most complex and problematic aspects of introducing any form of organisational change concerns the management of cultural considerations. As we shall see all of the contextual features can assist when analysing the culture of an organisation.

7.1 Aspects of context

(a) The **time available** may vary dramatically, but can often be quite limited when responding to competitive or regulatory pressure. The amount of time available will also be influenced by cultural considerations, as the attitudes and perceptions of those within the organisation will largely determine whether they regard the amount of time available to achieve a change as acceptable or not.

(b) The **preservation** of some organisational characteristics and resources may be required. Changes to cultural 'status' symbols such as office locations and job titles may cause resistance to the change programme if not carefully managed.

(c) **Diversity** of general experience, opinion and practice is likely to ease the change process: homogeneity in these factors is unlikely to do so. An organisational culture where the sharing of ideas and challenging of existing ways of working is common practice may prove useful when implementing a change programme. Especially if it helps others within the organisation to understand the reason for the change.

(d) The **capability** to manage and implement change is obviously important. To a great extent, this depends on past experience of change projects, both among managers and among lower-level staff. Stories told by those within the organisation about successful or unsuccessful change programmes provide a useful insight into how future change proposals will be treated by staff.

(e) **Capacity** to undertake change depends on the availability of resources, particularly finance, and IS/IT, and management time and skill, but it is important to note that unrealisable or out-dated systems could become a blockage in the change process.

Capacity from a cultural perspective is particularly important in relation to change projects as it is those operational workers within the organisation who are likely to have the best understanding of whether or not a change can be successfully implemented. A lack of belief among those within the organisation about the resources and skills needed to successfully introduce a change will create resistance.

(f) The degree of workforce **readiness** for change will affect its success. Readiness may be contrasted with **resistance** to change, which can exist at varying levels of intensity and may be widespread or confined to pockets. The workforce of an organisation with a positive attitude to change is likely to display features of readiness. Readiness and resistance may be influenced by the tone at the top of the organisation and the stories told about historical change projects.

(g) The **power** to effect change may not be sufficient to overcome determined resistance among important stakeholder groups. This can apply even at the strategic apex, where, for example, major shareholders, trustees or government ministers may constrain managers' freedom of action. Overcoming such cultural resistance to change will require senior management to adopt an appropriate leadership style to create buy-in to the change.

8 The four-view (POPIT) model

The POPIT model, also known as the four-view model (Paul *et al*, 2010), focuses on four interrelated aspects when analysing opportunities for organisational improvement. It considers the following aspects: people, organisation, processes, and IT.

Application of the POPIT model helps organisational leaders to understand where problems lie within each of the four aspects, this in turn helps identify where improvements to existing ways of working can be achieved.

Some analysts argue that the leaders and teams responsible for introducing organisational change focus too much on the process and technological aspects and ignore the impact change has on people and the organisation. The POPIT model helps to ensure that a holistic view is taken and that the relationships between the four aspects are considered. The POPIT model is not designed to be a burden for the change process, but should instead be viewed as a simple and quick approach when understanding an organisation's position and its operating environment so as to create a baseline from which change can evolve.

Syllabus links

The POPIT model is very closely connected to the subjects of process redesign and project management which are discussed in Chapters 14 and 15 respectively. You may find it useful to revisit this section when you have reviewed the next two chapters.

The POPIT (four-view model)

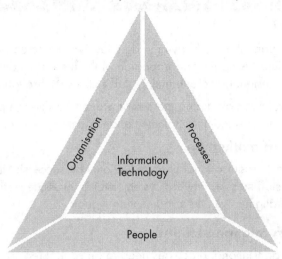

(Adapted from: Paul *et al*, 2010: p.9)

8.1 Usefulness of POPIT

As mentioned above the application of the Paul *et al* (2010) POPIT model forces project teams to take a far more holistic view during the implementation of change, identifying those issues which may hinder an organisational change project.

The table below sets out the four views of the POPIT model (Paul *et al*, 2010) and the consideration each is likely to require.

POPIT heading	Areas for consideration
Processes	**IT support** The level of IT support within an organisation should be assessed. Organisations with poor IT support in place are likely to need to address such weaknesses as part of process improvement. **Manual processes & system workarounds** Existing processes which require physical documents and paperwork to be passed around the organisation should be identified as part of the design stage of process change, as there may be scope to eliminate these.
Organisational context	**Management support** The project team should assess the level of management support for organisational change. A lack of understanding relating to the proposed introduction of new processes or technology in the workplace may be met by resistance among employees. **Cross-functional working** In order for processes to work effectively, it is critical that departments co-operate beyond functional boundaries. Therefore, the project team need to consider how departments interact with one another. **Jobs and responsibilities** Consideration will need to be given to the job roles and responsibilities of existing employees. Organisational change projects should ensure that all staff affected have clear, well-defined job roles and associated responsibilities

POPIT heading	Areas for consideration
People	**Skills** Ensuring that staff have the right level of skill to carry out a given change is critical. A significant proportion of the time spent designing a change may be designated to enhancing staff skill levels through the use of training. Involving staff during the design stage of a change project may help to ensure a smoother implementation phase. **Staff motivation** Most organisational change will only be successful if consideration is given to staff morale. Reward systems which influence staff motivation may need to be aligned with the organisation's goals.
Information Technology	**Information systems** Organisational processes need to be configured so that they help facilitate the flow of critical information.

9 Lewin's three-stage model

We now consider the key stages involved in successfully implementing an organisational change.

9.1 Unfreeze, change and refreeze

Although the essence of change is that it enables a person, department or organisation to move from a current state to a future state, Lewin (1958) suggested that organisational changes actually have three steps (stages): 'unfreeze', 'change' (or 'move') and 'freeze' or 'refreeze'.

Organisational change involves 're-learning': not merely learning something new, but trying to unlearn what is already known and practised in an organisation. This is a key part of the 'unfreeze' stage.

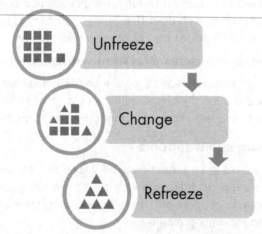

(Diagram: Unfreeze-change-refreeze model)

9.1.1 Unfreeze

This first step involves unfreezing the current state of affairs, and creating the motivation to change. This means defining the current state of an organisation, highlighting the forces driving change and those resisting it and picturing a desired end state.

Crucially, the unfreeze stage involves making people within an organisation ready to change: making them aware of the need (trigger) for change, and creating a readiness to change among the workforce.

A key part of this stage is weakening the restraining forces that are resisting change, and strengthening the driving forces that are promoting change.

Approaches to the unfreeze stage include:

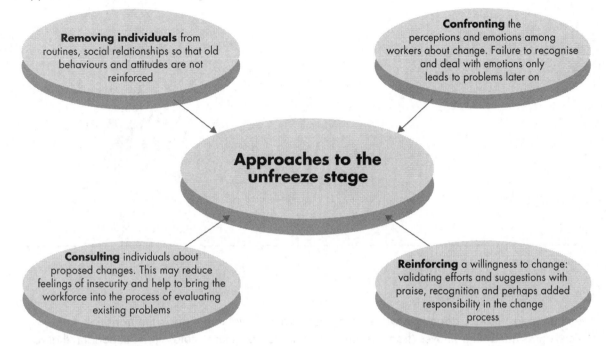

Removing individuals from routines, social relationships so that old behaviours and attitudes are not reinforced

Confronting the perceptions and emotions among workers about change. Failure to recognise and deal with emotions only leads to problems later on

Approaches to the unfreeze stage

Consulting individuals about proposed changes. This may reduce feelings of insecurity and help to bring the workforce into the process of evaluating existing problems

Reinforcing a willingness to change: validating efforts and suggestions with praise, recognition and perhaps added responsibility in the change process

Effective communication, explaining the need for change, is essential for the unfreeze process to work successfully. 'Unfreezing' an organisation may sound simple enough in theory but, in practice, it can be very difficult because it involves making people ready to change.

Rational argument will not necessarily be sufficient to convince individuals of the need to change, particularly if they stand to lose out from the change, or will have to make significant personal changes as a result of the change. Sometimes the need for change may be obvious to all employees – for example, the arrival of a new competitor in the market leading to a dramatic reduction in market share.

However, if the need for change is less obvious, then the 'unfreezing' process may need to be 'managed' in some way, to make staff appreciate the need for change.

Exercise 1: ABC Air

ABC Air is an airline based in the country of Arcadia. ABC Air has just completed the research, design and planning phase of a project designed to streamline its procurement and inventory management operations. The agreed solution involves the merger of these departments into a single 'inventory management' department to be located in a foreign country. This change has been facilitated by the emergence of a new integrated software program allowing these activities to be seamlessly managed by a single entity.

The main driver behind the choice of location was cost, which is much lower in the foreign country due to cheaper labour and land costs, along with a more flexible employment framework. Implementing these plans will necessitate the closure of the existing facility in Arcadia, resulting in hundreds of compulsory redundancies.

Required

Identify why staff within ABC Air will be resistant to change and advise the management on how to lessen this resistance.

BPP
LEARNING
MEDIA

Solution

9.1.2 Change (or 'move')

The change (or 'move') stage involves learning new ways of working. This is the transition stage, by which an organisation moves from its current state to its future state. It is important that an organisation encourages the participation and involvement of its staff in this phase so that they do not feel alienated by the change process.

This phase is mainly concerned with identifying the new, desirable behaviours or norms; communicating them clearly and positively; and encouraging individuals and groups to 'buy into' or 'own' the new values and behaviours. Johnson *et al* (2017) suggest five styles of change management which leaders can adopt during the change stage:

Education and communication is an approach based on persuasion: the reasons for change and the means by which it will be achieved are explained in detail to those affected by it. It is appropriate when change is incremental.

Collaboration, or **participation**, brings those affected by strategic change into the change management process by getting them involved in the creation of new routines during the implementation of a change.

Intervention tends to be undertaken by a change agent (often an outsider such as a management consultant) who delegates some aspects of the change process to teams or individuals, while providing guidance and retaining overall control.

Direction is a top-down style in which managerial authority is used to establish and implement a change programme based on a clear future strategy. It is thus suited to transformational change.

Coercion is an extreme form of direction, being based on the use of power to impose change. It is likely to provoke opposition but may be the best approach in times of confusion or crisis.

9.1.3 Refreeze

The refreeze stage involves stabilising (refreezing) the new state of affairs, by setting policies to embed new behaviours, and establishing new standards. It is crucial that the changes are embedded throughout an organisation to ensure that staff do not lapse back into old patterns of behaviour.

Once new behaviours have been adopted, the refreeze stage is required to consolidate and reinforce them, so that they become integrated into the individual's habits, attitudes and relationship patterns.

- Habituation effects (getting accustomed to the new situation) may be achieved over time, through practice, application and repetition.

- Positive reinforcement can be used to reward and validate successful change. For example, an element of a staff bonus scheme could be dependent on staff members adopting the new methodology.

Activity 3: Auto Direct

ACCA Professional skills focus

Commercial acumen: Show insight

You have recently started work as a finance professional at Auto Direct. Auto Direct is based in the country of Ambion. At last week's board meeting Mark Howe, the Managing Director of Auto Direct, asked each of the company's directors to provide him with some suggestions relating to a proposal to expand the business. Due to other work commitments the finance director has asked you to prepare this work on his behalf. To assist you he has prepared some background information relating to Auto Direct and the proposal (Exhibit 1).

Required

Using the information provided in Exhibit 1, identify the type of change being proposed by Mark Howe and briefly suggest practical approaches for managing the proposed change at Auto Direct.

(8 marks)

Professional skills marks are available for **commercial acumen** in showing insight when suggesting approaches for managing the proposed change. **(2 marks)**

(Total = 10 marks)

Exhibit 1 – Proposed restructuring

Auto Direct created an innovative way of selling cars to the public which takes advantage of the greater freedom given to independent car distributors to market cars more aggressively within the country of Ambion. This reduces the traditional control and interference of the automobile manufacturers, some of which own their distributors. Mark Howe has opened a number of showrooms since he first set up the business 10 years ago. Today Auto Direct has 20 outlets in and around Capital City.

Auto Direct's business model is deceptively simple; Mark buys cars from wherever he can source them most cheaply and has access to all of the leading volume car models. He then concentrates on selling the cars to the public, leaving servicing and repair work to other specialist garages. This provides a classic high-volume/low-margin business model.

Mark now wants to expand the business nationally. His immediate plans are to grow the number of outlets by 50% each year for the next three years. Such growth will place considerable strain on the existing organisation and staff. Each showroom has its own management team, sales personnel and administration. Currently the 20 showrooms are grouped into a Northern and Southern Sales Division with a small head office team for each division. Auto Direct now employs 250 people, the majority of which belong to the Ambion Auto Union (AAU). To deliver the proposed change Mark envisages that a number of existing staff members will be required to relocate in the short term to help establish the new outlets throughout Ambion.

Solution

Chapter summary

Enabling success and strategic change

Enabling success and strategic change

Organisational structure and internal relationships

Organisational structure (responsibilities, communication and skills)

Types of structure (simple, functional, divisional, holding company, transnational and matrix)

Internal relationships

- Centralisation (degree of central control)
- Advantages of centralisation (control, standardisation)
- Advantages of decentralisation (local knowledge, flexibility)
- Strategic management relationships (strategic planning, strategic control, financial control)

Collaborative working

Boundary-less organisations (collaborate with external parties)

- Hollow structure (non-core processes outsourced)
- Modular structure (production processes outsourced)
- Networks (groups of organisations co-operate to deliver service)
- Virtual structures (network of organisations linked via technology)

Partnering

- Internal partnering (co-operation and collaboration)
- External partnering (takes many forms including franchising)

Outsourcing (use a third party)

- Offshoring (outsourcing in a different country)
- Shared servicing (consolidate transaction-processing activities)
- Global business services (global approach to shared servicing and outsourcing)

Performance excellence

The Baldrige criteria (framework for assessing performance)

- Elements of the Baldrige assessment (leadership, strategy, customers, measurement, workforce, operations, results)
- Analysing performance

BPP
LEARNING
MEDIA

Empowering organisations

Empowerment
- Workers responsible for setting and achieving work targets
- Achieving empowerment (give workers freedom, may need to change culture and approach to HR)

Talent management

The need for a strategic view
People source competitive advantage

The benefits of talent management
Create a learning organisation, attract new talent, succession planning

Talent management activities
Activities (coaching, networking, communication and involvement with the board and key customers)

Strategic change

The need for change
Balogun and Hope Hailey's scope and nature of change

Type of change
Adaptation, reconstruction, evolution and revolution

Contextual features of change

Aspects of context
Time, preservation, diversity, capability, capacity, readiness, power and scope

The four-view (POPIT) model

Usefulness of POPIT
Organisation, processes, people and IT

Lewin's three-stage model

Unfreeze, change, and refreeze
- Unfreeze (weaken resistance)
- Change (or 'move') (transition stage)
- Refreeze (stabilise new state)

Knowledge diagnostic

1. Senior management need to give careful consideration to the organisation's structure and internal relationships if the selected strategy is to be implemented successfully.

2. An organisation's formal structure reveals: who is responsible for what, it shows communication patterns, the skills the organisation values.

3. Historically, organisational structures have tended to be 'self-contained' as they are distinct from external groups.

4. Factors such as the age of the organisation, its size, the types of products/services sold and the nature of the work undertaken all influence choices related to organisational structure.

5. There are a number of structural types: simple, functional, divisional, holding company, transnational and matrix.

6. Internal relationships concerning responsibility and authority for decision making are particularly important. There are two important issues in internal relationships: the degree of centralisation and the way the centre relates to the strategic business units.

7. Goold and Campbell (1987) identified three major approaches to running divisionalised conglomerates: strategic planning, strategic control and financial control.

8. Traditionally, external commercial relationships have been, to a greater or lesser extent, adversarial. While this is still characteristic of most external relationships, many new ones have been created that focus more on co-operation than rivalry.

9. Boundary-less organisations are those which have structured their operations to allow for collaboration with external parties. There are various forms of boundary-less organisation, these include hollow, modular, virtual and network organisation structures.

10. Internal partnering is concerned with increasing levels of co-operation and collaboration between departments in the same organisation. External partnering involves collaborating with external third parties, it also has implications for the way in which organisations are organised.

11. Outsourcing involves an organisation contracting out certain internal business functions to a third party.

12. Offshoring is a form of outsourcing that involves an external entity based in a different country providing an organisation with a particular product or process which had previously been provided in-house.

13. An alternative to outsourcing is shared servicing, where shared service centres (SSC) consolidate the transaction-processing activities of many operations within an organisation.

14. A global business service effectively brings together existing shared service and outsourcing arrangements together to form an integrated, collaborative framework.

15. The Baldrige Criteria™ for Performance Excellence provide a framework for assessing performance, with a view to improving performance. The underlying purpose of the Baldrige model is to help organisations improve, and achieve excellence.

16. In the widest sense the process of empowering an organisation involves identifying and removing those constraints which prohibit the attainment of the organisation's strategic goals and the improvement of performance.

17. Empowerment is the term for making workers (and particularly work teams) responsible for achieving, and even setting, work targets, with the freedom to make decisions about how they are to be achieved.

BPP
LEARNING
MEDIA

18. Talent management is principally concerned with initially attracting and subsequently identifying, developing and retaining individuals within the organisation who are considered to be important to the future success of the organisation.

19. The need for change may arise from a number of sources including changes in the environment, a review of strategic capability or a decision to implement a new strategy. Johnson *et al* (2017), quoting Balogun and Hope Hailey (2008), analyse change on two axes: these are its scope and its nature.

20. Balogun and Hope Hailey's (2008) four types of change are: adaptation, reconstruction, evolution and revolution.

21. Organisational change can be considered under eight general headings proposed by Balogun and Hope Hailey (2008): time, preservation, diversity, capability, capacity, readiness, power and scope.

22. The POPIT model, also known as the four-view model (Paul *et al*, 2010), focuses on four interrelated areas when undertaking organisational change: organisation, processes, people and IT.

23. The essence of change is that it enables a person, department or organisation to move from a current state to a future state. Lewin (1958) suggested that organisational changes actually have three steps (stages): 'unfreeze', 'change' (or 'move') and 'freeze' or 'refreeze'.

Further study guidance

Question practice

Now try the question below from the Further question practice bank (available in the digital edition of the Workbook):

Q13 *8-Hats*

Further reading

There are articles on the ACCA website written by members of the SBL examining team which are relevant to your studies and which would be useful to read:

Approaching SBL overview

This article provides a one-page summary of the key features of the SBL exam.

Approaching SBL reading and planning

This article provides a one-page summary of how best to approach the SBL exam.

SBL – 10 things to learn from the September 2018 sitting

This article highlights some of the issues that ACCA identified in candidates' answers during the September 2018 SBL exam sitting. The article provides some useful advice for improving your chances of passing the SBL exam.

Strategic Business Leader – The importance of effective communication for SBL

This article provides some useful insights into the different formats which you will be expected to use when answering SBL exam tasks.

Own research

It is important to link the topics covered in this chapter to a practical, real-world context. As such, we have suggested some areas for you to investigate further research a well-known organisation and consider the following:

- How has the organisation's structure changed over the years?

- Which type of structure does the organisation have now?

- Has the organisation embraced new collaborative approaches to working? If so, what are the features of this?

- Has the organisation made changes to its processes, systems or business model? If so, how did the organisation manage resistance when implementing the change?

- Why is Lewin's three stages of change model still in use today despite having been devised in 1958? There are a number of interesting articles available on the internet which provide useful critiques of Lewin's work in relation to change management, you are strongly advised to review these.

Exercise 1

Reasons for resistance:

1 Inertia, staff generally do not like change as a function of human nature
2 Fear of losing jobs
3 If staff are unionised this will galvanise and focus resistance
4 Jealousy on behalf of Arcadian staff seeing jobs transferred to the foreign country
5 Changes will feel like a criticism of existing performance

Lessening resistance:

1 Consult with staff, try to take on board their ideas
2 Work with unions to reduce the threat of strike action
3 Communicate clearly the need and rationale behind the changes
4 Take legal advice to ensure redundancies are handled fairly
5 Provide money for redundant staff to retrain or re-skill

Process redesign 14

Learning objectives

On completion of this chapter, you should be able to:

	Syllabus reference no.
Evaluate the effectiveness of current organisational processes	H6(a)
Establish an appropriate scope and focus for organisation process change using Harmon's process-strategy matrix	H6 (b)
Establish possible redesign options for improving the current processes of an organisation	H6 (c)
Assess the feasibility of possible redesign options	H6 (d)
Recommend an organisation process redesign methodology for an organisation	H6 (e)

Business and exam context

Strategies are, to some extent at least, delivered by means of processes. We have already seen how processes fit with structures and relationships and we have examined control processes in some detail. In this chapter, we go on to examine processes in the wider sense, the contribution they make to organisations and strategy and, overall, how processes may be improved and made more effective. The topic of process redesign is intimately linked to project management which we consider in the next chapter.

Chapter overview

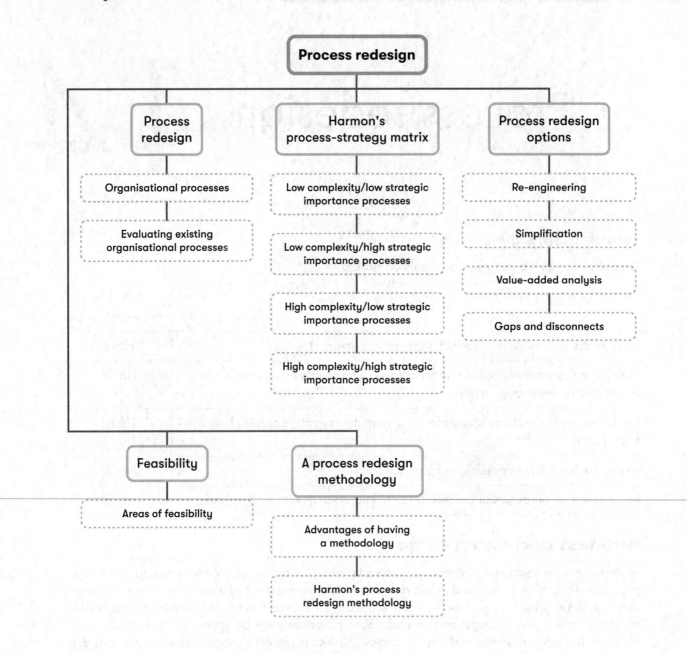

1 Process redesign

1.1 Organisational processes

Organisational processes of all kinds have been subject to efforts towards their improvement for many years. As we discussed in Chapter 5, the value chain analyses the organisation as a collection of activities, but these activities are also joined together in processes.

A process: 'Is a bounded set of activities that are undertaken, in response to some event, in order to generate an output'. (Harmon, 2014)

1.1.1 Drivers of process redesign

As the environment changes, an organisation's management need to consider the potential impact external developments may have on the internal capabilities (including processes) of the organisation. From time to time, organisations may be required to align (or re-align) their goals with the environment. External regulation, or developments by competitors, will often require organisations to makes changes to existing organisational processes in order to respond effectively.

Organisations may seek to improve their processes in order to:

- Reduce costs, particularly during an economic downturn
- Provide a scaleable platform for expanding production, or entering new markets
- Offer better products or services in order to be more competitive
- Exploit opportunities offered by technology (eg cheaper communication)
- Execute a new strategic direction

Illustration 1

This illustration highlights how changes in the external environment can lead to process redesign.

Competition among supermarket chains is fierce, price wars and innovation in retailing are common. Busier lifestyles have led customers to demand greater flexibility in how they shop. Competitors in the supermarket sector have been driven to modify their offering to help attract customers. This is evident as, over the last 20 years, a number of supermarket chains have redesigned the processes associated with shopping for groceries. The ability for customers to order their groceries over the internet and to have them delivered to their home address at a time to suit represented a major process redesign. This development required supermarkets to invest heavily in the IT infrastructures needed to operate websites with the functionality to accept orders and to develop the processes associated with operating a fleet of delivery vans.

Furthermore, growing demand from customers to spend less time queuing at the checkout when visiting a supermarket store has led most major chains to redesign the checkout process that customers encounter when paying for their groceries. The development of self-service checkouts, where customers scan and process the payment for goods themselves has enabled supermarket chains to become more responsive to the needs of their customers, as shoppers are able to spend less time at the checkout. It also allowed the supermarkets to save on the associated costs and floor space of having fewer conventional manned checkouts.

Not all proposals to redesign organisational processes come directly from the external environment. Paul *et al* (2010) note that operational staff in an organisation may also push for changes to existing business processes in order to deliver short-term improvements.

1.2 Evaluating existing organisational processes

1.2.1 Gap analysis

Once the need for process redesign has been established, management need to consider the practicalities of defining the improvement required. This will lead to the establishment of a formal project team designated to explore and evaluate the available options to achieve the desired change. This evaluation will often involve a 'gap analysis' where the project team assess the organisation's current position and processes. Manwani (2008) highlights that 'gaps' between the current position and targeted end state are then revealed. The gap analysis should help to provide the project team with an idea of the work required to implement a successful change.

The 'gaps' identified will help to determine the type of process redesign required. For example, a process redesign project to upgrade an organisation's existing website is likely to result in a relatively basic change, whereas changes of a more complex nature will require a fundamental rethinking of existing processes. Gap analysis gives particular consideration to the organisation's core resources, including its people and IT infrastructure. The project team may conduct face-to-face interviews with users of existing processes and may even observe staff while they work to better understand the improvements needed.

1.2.2 Need for a holistic view

Manwani (2008) highlights the importance of taking a holistic view of proposed process redesign projects. This is particularly important in helping the project team gain an understanding of how different activities and resources interact. Most process redesign programmes will affect more than one area of the organisation.

For example, the decision to introduce a new corporate website is likely to require a focus on both the human and technical elements. Understanding how these elements interrelate helps to raise questions that the project team will need to consider. These could include:

- Are those affected by the change likely to need training to use the website effectively?

- Will customers want to use it?

- Will it affect what our customers purchase from us?

- Will the introduction of a new website require improvements to the existing site or a complete upgrade of the existing IT infrastructure?

- Will the change be supported by the use of in-house technical support or be provided by a third party?

1.2.3 Business case and benefits

Proposals for a process change are drawn together to produce a business case. This sets out supporting recommendations to help management decide the most appropriate process redesign project to undertake. The business case will include the associated costs of the change options identified. The project team will set out the improvement objectives that the desired change will achieve. For example, a new call management system at a call centre should lead to improved call response times, which will lower the number of customer complaints and boost sales.

Syllabus links

We will look at the activities involved in undertaking a project in greater detail in Chapter 15 when we consider the subject of project management. As we will see in Chapter 15 the business case and benefits management are key elements in project management.

2 Harmon's process-strategy matrix

When an organisation's senior management have decided that a process needs to be redesigned, careful consideration needs to be given how best to achieve the change. Harmon's (2014) process-strategy matrix uses two criteria to categorise processes, and the best approach to improving them:

Process complexity and dynamics	Strategic importance: Low	Strategic importance: High
High	Outsource	Improve
Low	Automate/ Outsource	Automate

(Adapted from: Harmon, 2014)

The degree of **process complexity and dynamics** is plotted on the vertical axis; the horizontal axis shows the degree of **strategic importance of the process**. Process 'dynamics' means the extent to which the process is subject to adjustment in response to external stimuli. The effect of this analysis is to create four classes of processes, each of which can be used in relation to a particular improvement strategy (Harmon, 2014).

2.1 Low complexity/low strategic importance processes

Low complexity/low strategic importance processes need to be carried out as efficiently as possible as there is little scope for improving them. These processes should be **automated** as far as possible using technology and standard off-the-shelf software. In some cases such processes may be **outsourced**, eg payroll processing.

2.2 Low complexity/high strategic importance processes

Low complexity/high strategic importance processes are key to the organisation's success. **Automation** should be used to reduce costs and gain efficiency. The organisation's management should aim to improve the efficiency of such processes, eg product assembly.

2.3 High complexity/low strategic importance processes

High complexity/low strategic importance. These processes will cause problems if they are not performed, however they do not add much value. As these processes are complex, they may be hard to automate. Organisations may decide to **outsource** these processes to a specialist outsource partner, eg large-scale logistics and distribution.

2.4 High complexity/high strategic importance processes

High complexity/high strategic importance. These are critical and involve a lot of human expertise. These processes will be a priority for major **improvements**, eg negotiating partnerships, new product development.

Activity 1: Dollar and Dime Bank

> **ACCA Professional skills focus**
>
> Commercial acumen: Use judgement

You are a finance professional working for Dollar and Dime Bank (DD). In addition to your duties in the finance department you are also a member of a newly formed process change project team. The team consists of employees from across a number of functional departments within DD; the team has been put together to help DD undertake three process initiatives. The three process initiatives relate to processes involving DD's use of Information Technology. During the most recent project meeting you made some notes on the three process initiatives (Exhibit 1).

Required

Using the information provided in Exhibit 1, recommend and justify a solution option for each of the three process initiatives. **(6 marks)**

Professional skills marks are available for demonstrating **commercial acumen** in displaying judgement when providing justified recommendations for each process initiative. **(2 marks)**

(Total = 8 marks)

Exhibit 1: Potential process initiatives

The three process initiatives under consideration are as follows:

- The first process initiative relates to DD's recent acquisition of rival bank, Fortunes Bank. DD would like to integrate the two bespoke payroll systems currently being operated by the two banks into one consolidated payroll system. This will save the cost of updating and maintaining two separate systems.

- Updating of all personal desktop computer hardware and software used throughout DD. This update is intended to reflect contemporary technologies and the subsequent maintenance of that hardware. This will allow the desktop to be standardised and will bring staff efficiency savings.

- The senior management at DD recently identified the need for a private personal banking service for wealthy customers. Processes, systems and software will have to be developed to support this new service. High net worth customers have been identified by the DD as an important growth area.

The project manager of the process initiatives has indicated that DD's senior management will consider three solution options for each initiative. These are outsourcing, the purchase of a standard, off-the-shelf software package solution or the development of bespoke systems.

Solution

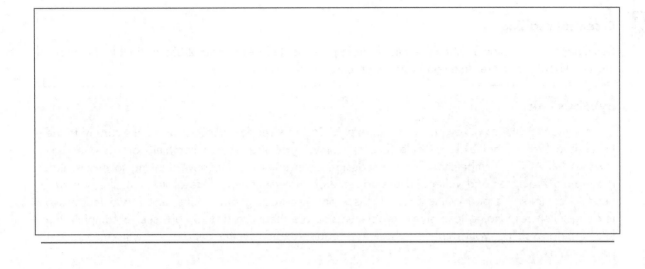

3 Process redesign options

In this section, we will look more closely at the techniques that are available for use in the redesign activity itself. Harmon (2014) calls these techniques **redesign patterns**.

Key term

A process redesign pattern: Is a general approach to redesigning processes for their improvement.

Syllabus links

The focus of process redesign is upon improving existing ways of working, sometimes this may involve undertaking a radical programme of change to significantly improve the performance of existing processes. This topic ties in closely to our earlier discussion of the types of change which we considered in Chapter 13.

PER alert

Performance Objective 5 'Leadership and Management' of the Practical Experience Requirement requires you to 'work with others to recognise, assess and improve business performance. You use different techniques and appropriate technologies to support business improvement' (ACCA, 2019b). You could illustrate your achievement of this Performance Objective by drawing upon any experience of process redesign projects that you have been involved with in the workplace.

Harmon (2014) describes four **basic redesign patterns**:

3.1 Re-engineering

Key term

Re-engineering: Starts with a clean sheet of paper.

Re-engineering is also known as business process re-engineering (BPR).

Key term

Business process re-engineering: 'Is the fundamental rethinking and radical redesign of business processes to achieve dramatic improvements in critical contemporary measures of performance, such as cost, quality, service and speed.' (Hammer and Champy, 2001: p.50)

The BPR approach is used when large-scale change is to be introduced. The aim is to achieve major efficiency improvements. This pattern is hardly **redesign** at all, since its philosophy is to question all assumptions and start from scratch. Harmon (2014) says that re-engineering can achieve **very large-scale improvements**, but it is inevitably **highly disruptive** and has a **high risk of dramatic failure**.

Essential reading

See Chapter 14 section 1 of the Essential Reading, available in Appendix 2 of the digital edition of the Workbook, for more detail on business process re-engineering (BPR).

Syllabus link

Process redesign forms a key part of the Strategic Business Leader syllabus, and links closely to the Ethics and Professional Skills Module (EPSM) that you are required to complete on your journey towards full ACCA membership. Process redesign often involves innovative thinking to ensure that redesigned processes add value and are capable of implementation. One of the units that you will need to complete as part of the EPSM focuses on encouraging open mindedness and innovative thinking when responding to business problems. You are therefore strongly advised to complete the EPSM before sitting your Strategic Business Leader exam as this will assist with your exam preparations.

Activity 2: Super-Food Supermarkets

ACCA Professional skills focus

Commercial acumen: demonstrating awareness

You have recently started working in the finance department of Super-Food Supermarkets (SFS). SFS is a chain of 20 supermarkets. You report to the finance director. The CEO at SFS has challenged each director to suggest ways in which the company could operate more efficiently. The finance director has been charged with considering how business process re-engineering (BPR) could be used to improve SFS's supply chain processes, and she has asked for your assistance. She has provided you with some notes about SFS's supply chain operations (Exhibit 1).

Required

Briefly explain how adopting the principles of BPR could help SFS to improve its supply chain operations. You should also mention any implications for SFS of adopting BPR.   **(6 marks)**

Professional skills marks are available for **commercial acumen** in demonstrating awareness of BPR and how it could be used at SFS in relation to its supply chain.   **(2 marks)**

(Total = 8 marks)

Exhibit 1 – SFS supply chain operations

When inventory items reach their re-order level in one of SFS's supermarket stores, the in-store computerised inventory system informs the inventory clerk. The clerk then raises a request daily to the SFS central warehouse for replenishment of inventory via email. If the local warehouse has available inventory, it is forwarded to the supermarket within 24 hours of receiving the request. If the local warehouse cannot replenish the items from its inventory holding, it raises a purchase order to one of its suppliers. The supplier delivers the inventory to the warehouse and the warehouse then delivers the required inventory to the supermarkets within the area. The SFS area warehouse staff conduct all business communication with suppliers.

Solution

3.2 Simplification

Key term

Simplification: Eliminates redundant process elements.

Harmon (2014) says that simplification is a far less radical pattern of redesign. It starts on the assumption that most established organisational processes are likely to have developed **elements of duplication or redundancy**. This assumption is probably most valid in relation to large-scale processes that cut across departmental or functional boundaries.

Harmon (2014) highlights that the simplification approach commences with **identification and modelling** of all the systems, activities and sub-processes involved in the organisational process under investigation. Each element is then subject to challenge and may illustrate a number of issues with existing processes:

- It may not actually be necessary
- It may provide information that is available elsewhere
- It may be a bottleneck
- It may repeat something done in another place

Whenever possible, activities are removed from the process so that duplication and unnecessary complexity are gradually eliminated. This pattern is likely to produce **improvements**. Harmon (2014) suggests that **judgement and flexibility** are needed to use this approach, since apparently similar activities may incorporate subtle differences that are important in one departmental context but not in another.

Exercise 1: Process improvement

PS is a company which supplies and maintains heating systems for commercial customers with large premises. Customers who need emergency servicing or repairs ring a helpline and describe the problem to customer services staff. The engineer will then raise a request to the warehouse for any spares and equipment they believe will be necessary and visit the customer. However, there are increasing customer complaints that the engineer often brings the wrong items and needs to make a repeat visit, delaying the repairs and costing the company money.

Required

Suggest possible reasons for this problem and potential solutions.

Solution

Potential reasons	Solutions

3.3 Value-added analysis

> **Value-added analysis:** Eliminates activities that do not add value. This has parallels with the concept of 'lean' production.

> **Essential reading**
>
> See Chapter 14 section 2 of the Essential Reading, available in Appendix 2 of the digital edition of the Workbook, for detail on the concept of 'lean' production. Close parallels exist between value-added analysis and lean production.

Harmon (2014) notes that the aim of value-added analysis is to eliminate processes that do not add value. Value-added analysis approaches processes from the point of view of the customer. Here, 'customer' means whoever receives the output of the process, so internal customers are included.

Harmon (2014) highlights that **value-adding activities** satisfy three conditions:

- The customer is willing to pay for the output
- The process changes the output in some way
- The process is performed correctly at the first attempt

Four categories of activity are defined by Harmon (2014) as **non-value-adding**:

- Preparation and set-up activities
- Control and inspection activities
- Movement of a product
- Activities that result from delay or failure of any kind

There is a third category: **value-enabling activities**. Harmon (2014) suggests that these are essential preliminaries to value-adding activities. If you think about this for a moment, you will see that, just as with the simplification approach, judgement is required here: an obvious instance lies in the area of preparation and set-up. We have defined such activities as non-value-adding, but, surely, they are essential preliminaries?

Bearing in mind that the overall intention is to eliminate non-value-adding activities, we may thus suggest that where preparation and set-up are concerned, we should aim to ensure that they qualify as value-enabling activities by making them as simple and cost effective as possible.

Value-added analysis commences with **identification and modelling** of all the systems, activities and sub-processes involved in the organisational process under investigation. Each element is then **categorised** according to the criteria discussed above. Harmon (2014) suggests that, typically, only 20% of the activities making up a process are identifiable as value-adding, with most of the remainder falling into the value-enabling category. When all the clearly value-adding and value-enabling activities have been identified, the remainder may be examined in detail. Careful consideration can lead to the development of new methods that eliminate much non-value-adding work in preliminary activities.

Illustration 2

This illustration shows how the removal of non-value-adding activities can be achieved following a value-added analysis:

- Physical movement of products can be minimised by careful **workplace layout.**

- **Workflow systems** eliminate transit time for documents by scanning all documents to produce electronic copies which are transferred at the click of a mouse.

Essential reading

See Chapter 14 section 3 of the Essential Reading, available in Appendix 2 of the digital edition of the Workbook, for more detail on workflow systems.

3.4 Gaps and disconnects

Gaps and disconnects: Target problems at departmental boundaries.

Key term

A major problem with many processes is likely to be due to failures of communication between organisational departments and functions. These failures can produce continuing **gaps and disconnects,** both in the processes themselves and in the management of those processes.

Harmon (2014) notes that this approach commences in the usual way, with **identification and modelling** of the selected process, but its focus is on occasions when information or materials pass from one department or function to another, since this is where gaps and disconnects are to be found.

Rummler and Brache (1995) identify that gaps and disconnects can occur at three levels:

(a) The organisation as a whole
(b) The process
(c) The job or performance level

It is only at the second and third of these levels that problems relating to actual **workflow** and **activities** appear. At the organisational level, they are entirely concerned with the **design of processes** and the **monitoring** and **control** of **process outcomes**. These are clearly **management activities**.

Activity 3: The Institute of Information Systems Architects

> **ACCA Professional skills focus**
>
> Evaluation: appraise

You are a consultant working for a management consultancy firm, based in the country of Gaulle. You are currently undertaking an assignment at the Institute of Information Systems Architects (IISA). The Head of the IISA approached your firm as he would like some advice on redesigning the script handling process that the IISA operates. One of your colleagues has prepared some background information about the IISA (Exhibit 1) and the current script handling process (Exhibit 2).

Required

Using the information in the Exhibits, suggest two options for the redesign of the current script handling process at the IISA. Explain the advantages and disadvantages of each option.

(10 marks)

Professional skills marks are available for **evaluation** skills in appraising the current situation and suggesting two options for the redesign. **(2 marks)**

(Total = 12 marks)

Exhibit 1 – IISA background information

The Institute of Information Systems Architects (IISA) was founded a number of years ago by representatives of a number of organisations who felt that systems architecture should have its own qualification. The Institute has its own Board which reports to a Council of 13 members. Policy is made by the Board and ratified by Council. The IISA is registered as a private limited company.

All the examinations are open book, one-hour examinations, preceded by 15 minutes' reading time. At a recent meeting, the IISA Board rejected the concept of computer-based assessment. They felt that competence in this area was best assessed by written examination answers. The IISA is based in Capital City where it employs staff to administer its examination scheme and provide services to its members. It also employs two chief examiners on a full-time basis. These examiners are responsible for setting the IISA certificate examinations which take place monthly in training and conference centres around the country of Gaulle. At present no examinations are currently held outside of Gaulle, although this is something the IISA Board are keen to explore. The nature of the Board and its relationship with the Council make it a very conservative organisation. It is notably risk averse and is only confident about its expertise within fairly restricted bounds of information systems architecture. In recent years the IISA Board has become concerned about falling candidate numbers, with fewer candidates attempting the IISA's exams. The Board has concluded that this drop reflects the maturing marketplace in Gaulle.

Exhibit 2 – The script handling process

The examinations are held in conference centres and training rooms around the country. The open-book nature of the examination means that many of the security measures surrounding closed-book examinations are no longer required. However, examinations are invigilated by an external invigilator employed by the IISA on a contract basis. The invigilator hands out the examination scripts at the start of the examination and collects them at the end. They then take them home and arrange for a secure designated courier to collect the scripts and take them to the IISA headquarters in Capital City. When they arrive in Capital City, administrative employees identify the appropriate and available markers and send the scripts, by secure designated courier, to these markers. The markers then mark the scripts and return them (again by secure courier) to the IISA headquarters. In recent times the IISA has struggled to find markers of sufficient experience to mark the scripts; this is an ongoing issue. The administrative employees then review the need to audit selected scripts. All scripts with a mark between 45 and 55 are sent to an auditor for second marking. The auditor (like the marker and the invigilator) is employed by the IISA on a contract basis. Once audited, the scripts are returned with a recommended mark. Again, transport between the auditor and the headquarters is only through secure, designated couriers. If the candidate has scored less than 45 or greater than 55 their results are published straight away. The candidate is notified by email or by post of their actual mark. Candidates whose scripts were audited are sent their marks after the audit has been completed.

It has been suggested that changes in the script handling process should be made before the organisation attempts to expand overseas. A process diagram of the current script handling process is presented below.

Script handling system

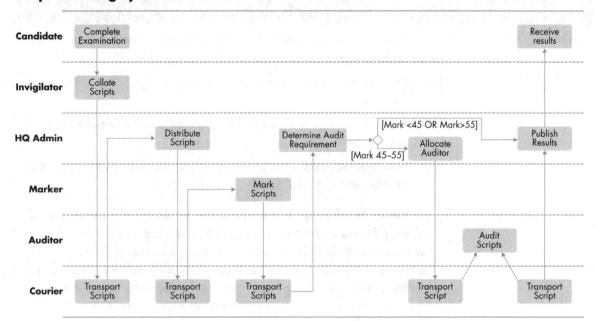

Solution

4 Feasibility

The feasibility of any proposed redesign pattern must be considered. The feasibility study is the mechanism by which the organisation filters out proposals that would cost too much, cause too much disruption, make excessive demands on human and other resources or have side effects whose undesirability outweighs their advantages.

4.1 Areas of feasibility

The assessment of feasibility can be broken down into a number of areas.

Area of feasibility	Detail
Technical feasibility	The assessment of technical feasibility will **depend on the nature of the technology involved**. • Does all the necessary technology exist or is significant **innovation** required? • Is the technology mature enough to use or is further **development** likely to be required? • How **specialised** is the required technology and is **the expertise** to make use of it available?
Social feasibility	The **social feasibility of a project depends on the nature and extent of those effects**. There are obvious human resource management implications to most projects, in the area of forming, leading and motivating the project team. The progress and outcome of a process improvement project may also have important consequences for employees outside the team, eg staff redundancies, training and changed work patterns.
Environmental concerns	Consideration of a project in environmental terms is usually not so much about feasibility as about **acceptability**. Several different stakeholder groups are likely to have environmental concerns and their opinions and reactions may affect both the progress of a project itself and the desired characteristics of its deliverables.
Financial feasibility	It is appropriate to submit proposed process changes to **cost-benefit analysis**, though this can be very difficult when the benefits are largely in intangible form. Part of the difficulty lies in identifying the benefits and part in assigning monetary values to them. Dealing with intangible or qualitative benefits is likely to be particularly important in the public and voluntary sectors, where objectives such as improved road safety or education are common.

5 A process redesign methodology

Once a process has been selected for significant improvement, it is helpful for organisations to follow a structured methodology. Process redesign methodologies are similar to the approaches we cover in the next chapter when we discuss the role of project management.

5.1 Advantages of having a methodology

Following a process redesign methodology provides the organisation's management with certain advantages:

- A methodology is effectively a plan which provides **discipline** for the overall redesign process and helps to prevent it from losing focus.

- Successful implementation depends on **acceptance by staff and managers** who will have to operate the new process: the methodology emphasises the need for obtaining support at all appropriate stages.

5.2 Harmon's process redesign methodology

Harmon (2014) proposes a **process redesign** methodology which consists of five phases:

Phase 1   **Planning**

Goals are set, project scope is defined, project team members and other roles are identified and the overall schedule is developed.

Phase 2   **Analysis**

Current workflow is documented, problems identified and a general approach to a redesign plan is established.

Phase 3   **Redesign**

Possible solutions are considered and the best chosen; objectives for the next phase are defined.

Phase 4   **Development**

All functional implications are followed through, aspects are improved, including management and information systems.

Phase 5   **Transition**

The redesigned process is implemented; modifications are undertaken as required.

Each of the five phases is considered in greater detail in the following sections.

5.2.1 Planning

Harmon (2014) highlights that a process redesign plan is needed by the redesign team so that the scope of their work is clearly defined. Ideally, a high-level plan will have been defined by the senior management within the organisation. Such a plan should include an account of how the process they design supports the organisation's overall strategy and goals and how it relates to other processes and stakeholders.

The planning phase ends with the agreement of a **detailed project plan**, including **time and cost budgets**, at the senior management/executive committee level. Planning documentation at this stage will state the project's assumptions, goals, constraints, scope and success measures. It is particularly important that resource and systems constraints are considered in detail.

At the same time, the members of the **process redesign team** must be identified.

5.2.2 Analysing the existing process

This phase results in the preparation of **full documentation** of the existing processes and sub-processes concerned. This involves the use of process diagrams and organisation charts. Process diagrams provide a useful way of summarising the activities involved in an organisational process; they can also identify potential areas of improvement in the process. The diagram in the last activity (Activity 3) was a process diagram.

BPP
LEARNING
MEDIA

Goals, activities, inputs and outputs are identified, named and described in detail. Known problems with the system are noted, as are descriptions of past attempts to improve them. It is also necessary to consider **how the process is managed**, what personal managerial responsibilities are involved and whether improvements to the management system are required. In particular, **performance measures and incentives** should be examined.

Once the analysis is complete, the **project goals and assumptions** should be re-examined and revised as necessary.

5.2.3 Designing the new process

Design of the new process itself is only part of this phase: there are other important aspects. Harmon (2014) notes:

(a) Design of **supporting management roles and responsibilities** is required, as are the supporting performance measures.

(b) Rationalisation of **reporting responsibilities** may be possible and desirable. A new organisation structure may result.

(c) Where very complex processes are concerned, it may be appropriate to **run simulations and prepare cost estimates** on two or more possible new designs. This is likely to require the use of software tools.

(d) The new design must be **fully documented**.

The final essential output from this phase is, once again, approval from senior management. To achieve this, it will be necessary to explain the new process in detail.

5.2.4 Development

This phase of the process follows the design through into all of its **functional and resource implications**. New Information System (IS) resources of hardware and software are specified and designed; job descriptions are created and staff training provided; other necessary resources are acquired.

At this stage, the implications of organising by processes, rather than by functions, become apparent. The new process is more likely to be effective if it, and the staff and resources committed to it, are managed by a process manager rather than by a group of separate functional managers. The development phase ends when all the new arrangements have been tested and found satisfactory and the new process is ready for installation.

5.2.5 Transition

Harmon (2014) notes that the success of the transition phase depends on successful **change management**: it can be harmed or even prevented by opposition or passive resistance by employees or users of the new process. There must be support from senior management and close liaison with the managers who have to make the new process work. This may lead to revisions to the process. Eventually, this phase merges into routine monitoring of the process for efficiency and potential further improvements.

Chapter summary

Process redesign

Process redesign

Organisational processes
- Drivers of process redesign
- Internal and external developments

Evaluating existing organisational processes
- Gap analysis
  - Current v desired position
- Need for a holistic view
  - Need to consider how activities and resources interact
- Business case and benefits
  - Helps management decide which projects to undertake

Harmon's process-strategy matrix

Low complexity/low strategic importance processes
Automate/outsource

Low complexity/high strategic importance processes
Automate

High complexity/low strategic importance processes
Outsource

High complexity/high strategic importance processes
Improve

Process redesign options

Re-engineering
Starts with a clean sheet of paper

Simplification
Eliminates redundant process elements

Value-added analysis
Eliminates activities that do not add value

Gaps and disconnects
Target problems at departmental boundaries

Feasibility

Areas of feasibility
Technical, social, environmental, financial

A process redesign methodology

Advantages of having a methodology
Discipline and acceptance

Harmon's process redesign methodology
- Planning
  - Goals set, scope defined
- Analysing the existing process
  - Workflow documented, problems identified, redesign plan established
- Designing the new process
  - Possible solutions considered
- Development
  - Functional implications followed through
- Transition
  - Redesigned process is implemented

BPP
LEARNING
MEDIA

1. Organisational processes of all kinds have been subject to efforts towards their improvement for many years.

2. 'A process is a bounded set of activities that are undertaken, in response to some event, in order to generate an output.' (Harmon, 2014)

3. From time to time, organisations may be required to align (or re-align) their goals and processes in response to external changes.

4. Some changes are driven from within the organisation as operational staff may push for changes to existing organisational processes in order to deliver short-term improvements.

5. Evaluating existing processes may involve 'gap analysis'. This is where the project team assess the organisation's current position and processes and compare these to a targeted end state. The 'gaps' identified will help to determine the type of process redesign required.

6. A holistic view is needed as most process redesign programmes will affect more than one area of the organisation.

7. Proposals for a process change are drawn together to produce a business case. This sets out supporting recommendations to help management decide the most appropriate process redesign project to undertake.

8. Harmon's (2014) process-strategy matrix uses two criteria to categorise processes, and the best approach to improving them: process complexity and dynamics, and strategic importance of the process.

9. Low complexity/low strategic importance processes should be automated or outsourced.

10. Low complexity/high strategic importance processes should be automated.

11. High complexity/low strategic importance should be outsourced.

12. High complexity/high strategic importance should be improved.

13. A process redesign pattern is a general approach to redesigning processes for their improvement.

14. Harmon (2014) describes four basic redesign patterns. Re-engineering starts with a clean sheet of paper. Simplification eliminates redundant process elements. Value-added analysis eliminates activities that do not add value. Gaps and disconnects target problems at departmental boundaries.

15. The feasibility of any proposed redesign pattern must be considered. The assessment of feasibility can be broken down into a number of areas: technical, social, environmental and financial.

16. Once a process has been selected for significant improvement, it is helpful for organisations to follow a structured methodology

17. A methodology is effectively a plan which provides discipline for the overall redesign process and helps to prevent it from losing focus. Successful implementation depends on acceptance by staff and managers, therefore following a plan which achieves this is of critical importance.

18. Harmon (2014) proposes a process redesign methodology which consists of five phases: planning, analysis, redesign, development, and transition.

Further study guidance

Question practice

Now try the question below from the Further question practice bank (available in the digital edition of the Workbook):

Q14 *Hooper University*

Further reading

There are articles on the ACCA website written by members of the SBL examining team which are relevant to your studies and which would be useful to read:

Job design

This article gives further consideration to the concept of business process re-engineering.

Approaching SBL overview

This article provides a one-page summary of the key features of the SBL exam.

Approaching SBL reading and planning

This article provides a one-page summary of how best to approach the SBL exam.

SBL – 10 things to learn from the September 2018 sitting

This article highlights some of the issues that ACCA identified in candidates' answers during the September 2018 SBL exam sitting. The article provides some useful advice for improving your chances of passing the SBL exam.

Strategic Business Leader – The importance of effective communication for SBL

This article provides some useful insights into the different formats which you will be expected to use when answering SBL exam tasks.

Own research

It is important to link the topics covered in this chapter to a practical, real world context. As such, we have suggested some areas for you to investigate further. Research a well-known organisation, and/or think about the organisation for which you work and consider the following:

- Identify a number of processes that your chosen organisation undertakes.

- Using Harmon's process-strategy matrix, categorise the processes identified.

- Do the recommendations per Harmon's process-strategy matrix seem appropriate in light of your knowledge of the organisation's processes?

Exercise 1

Potential reasons	Solutions
Information collected from the customer is incorrect or insufficient to diagnose the equipment needed	Improved training in understanding the products for customer services staff Customer speaks directly to a trained engineer about their problem
Information is correct but the engineer wrongly predicts the parts required	Improved training for engineers in product and customer knowledge Increased specialisation of engineers in certain products
The customer's system has been modified in a way that is not in PS's records	Customer contract term to inform PS of any modifications Regular checking/inspection of customer systems
The wrong part has been issued to the engineer by the warehouse	Parts to be checked by the engineer before they leave for the customer Review sub-process of issuing parts that have been ordered to identify errors Wholly automated feed-through from engineer's order to issuing parts
The relevant part is out of stock	Improved stock control and re-ordering

Project management

15

Learning objectives

On completion of this chapter, you should be able to:

	Syllabus reference no.
Determine the distinguishing features of projects and the constraints they operate in	H7(a)
Discuss the implications of the triple constraint of scope, time and cost	H7 (b)
Prepare a business case document and project initiation document	H7 (c)
Analyse, assess and classify the costs and benefits of a project investment	H7 (d)
Establish the role and responsibilities of the project manager and the project sponsor	H7 (e)
Assess the importance of developing a project plan and its key elements	H7 (f)
Monitor and formulate responses for dealing with project risks, issues, slippage and changes	H7 (g)
Discuss the benefits of a post-implementation and a post-project review	H7 (h)

Business and exam context

Project management is an important aspect of putting strategy into action. In the first place, for many organisations their activities consist largely of projects: civil engineering contractors and film studios are two obvious examples. Secondly, even where operations are more or less continuous, the need for continuing strategic innovation and improvement in the way things are done brings project management to the forefront of attention. Finally, even relatively low-level, one-off projects must be managed with a view to their potential strategic implications.

As we saw in Chapter 14, project management is also very closely linked to process redesign and information technology issues. For example, major changes in technology are usually implemented through projects and project management.

Chapter overview

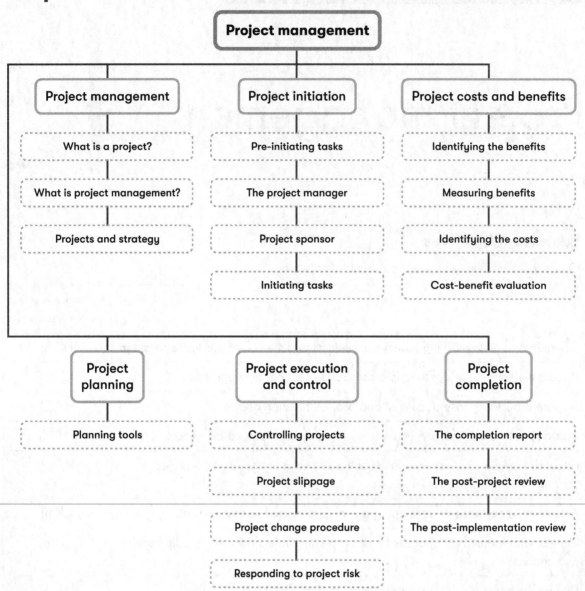

1 Project management

1.1 What is a project?

To understand project management, it is necessary to first define what a project is.

Key terms

> **A project:** Is 'an undertaking that has a beginning and an end and is carried out to meet established goals within cost, schedule and quality objectives' (Haynes, 1997: p.3).
>
> **Resources:** Are the money, facilities, supplies, services and people allocated to the project.

In general, the work which organisations undertake involves either **operations** or **projects**. Operations and projects are planned, controlled and executed. So how are projects distinguished from 'ordinary work'?

Projects	Operations
Have a defined beginning and end	Ongoing
Have resources allocated specifically to them, although often on a shared basis	Resources used 'full time'
Are intended to be done only once	A mixture of many recurring tasks
Follow a plan towards a clear intended end result	Goals and deadlines are more general
Often cut across organisational and functional lines	Usually follows the organisation or functional structure

An activity that meets the first four criteria above can be classified as a project, and therefore falls within the **scope of project management**. Whether an activity is classified as a project is important, as projects should be managed using **project management techniques**.

Common examples of projects include:

- Producing a new product, service or object
- Changing the structure of an organisation
- Developing or modifying a new information system
- Implementing a new procedure or process

1.2 What is project management?

Project management is the combination of systems, techniques and people used to control and monitor activities undertaken within the project.

Key term

> **Project management:** 'Integration of all aspects of a project, ensuring that the proper knowledge and resources are available when and where needed, and above all to ensure that the expected outcome is produced in a timely, cost-effective manner. The primary function of a project manager is to manage the trade-offs between performance, timeliness and cost' (CIMA, 2005).

1.2.1 The triple constraint

Projects are generally considered successful if they meet three specified objectives in terms of the following (the 'triple constraint'):

(a) **Scope** – this relates to all of the work that needs to be done and all of the deliverables that constitute the project's success. Scope is closely connected to the issue of quality.

(b) **Time** – this concerns the agreed date for the delivery of the project.

(c) **Cost** – this relates to authorised spend on the project.

All three objectives are important: an organisation's management want their projects to finish on time, within budget **and** to produce the required deliverable. The relative importance of each objective may depend partly on the type of project being undertaken. Where a project is aiming to beat a competitor to market, or has a non-negotiable deadline (eg organising the launch of a new product that has been advertised for a particular date) time will be a priority. In the case of a project with a limited budget, cost is a priority: once resources run out, the project ceases – complete or not! In a safety-critical project (such as building or aircraft construction) ensuring the quality of all project deliverables is a priority.

Later in this chapter we explore some of the ways in which project managers can respond to the challenges presented by the triple constraint.

Activity 1: ABC Co

ACCA Professional skills focus

Analysis: Consider

The current date is March 20X5. You are a finance professional working for ABC Co in the country of Ecuria. ABC specialises in the development and manufacture of cutting edge technological innovations which it sells to the general public.

Required

Using the information provided in Exhibit 1, discuss the implications of the principle of the triple constraint in relation to the launch of the T4i. **(6 marks)**

Professional skills marks are available for demonstrating **analysis** skills when considering the implications of the triple constraint in relation to the T4i project. **(2 marks)**

(Total = 8 marks)

Exhibit 1 – The T4i project

Last year a small team of engineers at the company undertook a project to develop a prototype of the world's first flying car, the T4i. The T4i's design is based on the technology used by aviation enthusiasts that fly radio-controlled drones. The T4i can take the weight of two adults, who are then able to fly the device using on-board controls. Last month a team of independent experts acting on behalf of the Ecurian government advised that the T4i was safe to fly; in turn the Ecurian government granted ABC provisional consent to develop the T4i further with a view to manufacturing and selling it to the general public.

The consent given by the government is provisional on a number of modifications being made to the existing T4i model; these include the installation of landing lights and sound alarms to alert those on the ground when the device is coming into land. Keen to get the T4i to market as soon as possible the board at ABC have booked a launch party to unveil the T4i. The directors have charged the company's engineers with making the required modifications before the official launch. If the modifications are not made by the time of the launch, government restrictions mean that ABC will be unable to accept customer orders for the T4i.

The T4i is due to be launched on 1 May 20X5. The launch has been heavily publicised, a prestigious private airport venue has been booked and over 400 attendees are expected. ABC Co have arranged for many newspaper journalists to attend. The modifications to the T4i are, however, not quite finished, so although orders are intended to be taken at the launch this will depend on the engineers' progress.

Solution

A high-level overview of the main stages involved in the project management process is summarised in the figure below.

Step 1   The project process begins with a plan detailing the work to be performed ie a plan to build a house.

Step 2   Once a plan has been determined the project team will undertake the tasks involved in the project ie start constructing the house.

Step 3   The progress of the project has to be recorded ie the extent of the build that is complete by a set point in time.

Step 4   The progress needs to be compared to the plan in Step 1.

Step 5   Following the findings of Step 4, in the event that the progress of the project is not as far as originally intended then action to improve this situation is needed, this might involve adding extra resources to the project ie more builders etc.

The project management process

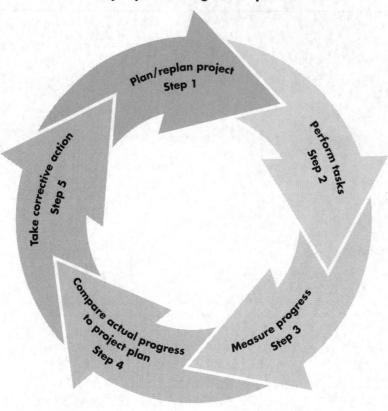

(Diagram: The project management process)

1.2.2 Project challenges

The nature of project work often presents project managers with a number of common challenges. Some of these are outlined in the table below:

Challenge	Comment
Teambuilding	The work is carried out by a team of people, often from varied work and social backgrounds. The team must 'gel' quickly and be able to communicate effectively with each other.
Expected problems	Expected problems should be avoided by careful design and planning prior to commencement of work.
Unexpected problems	There should be mechanisms within the project to enable these problems to be resolved quickly and efficiently.
Delayed benefit	There is normally no benefit until the work is finished. The lead-in time to this can cause a strain on the eventual recipient who is also faced with increasing expenditure for no immediate benefit.
Specialists	Contributions made by specialists are of differing importance at each stage.
Potential for conflict	Projects often involve several parties with different interests. This may lead to conflict.

1.3 Projects and strategy

Project management in its widest sense is fundamental to much strategy. This is because very few organisations are able to do the same things, in the same ways, year after year. Continuing **environmental change** forces many organisations to include extensive processes of **adaptation** to their strategies. Circumstances change and new conditions must be met with new responses or initiatives. Each possible new development effectively constitutes a project.

Project management can be a **core strategic competence** for organisations working in such industries as consulting and construction. Such organisations must ensure that they maintain and improve their project management abilities if they are to continue to be commercially successful. The very nature of project work means that organisations need to develop appropriate approaches when managing the ethical implications of implementing a change programme. Very often projects are initiated to bring about improvements in organisational performance and as such may lead to changes in working practices which affect project stakeholders, for example, a project may require that certain staff members are made redundant in order to achieve required strategic objectives. Therefore those tasked with project management need to develop communication and negotiation skills as these are likely to be particularly important when managing the concerns of key project stakeholders. Such skills are likely to be just as important as the technical skills required when undertaking a project.

Syllabus links

Projects may link to many topics in the syllabus as follows:

- Some organisations' **operations** largely consist of projects, eg building contractors. Such organisations will need to make project management a **core competence**.

- **Changes** in **strategy** may require projects to be undertaken, eg launching a new product or integrating an acquisition

- Organisations looking to change their **structure** may manage this as a project

- All projects need to be **consistent** with an organisation's **strategy**

- Significant **changes in processes** are likely to require projects, including new **technology** implementation

1.3.1 Project selection

Organisations have limited resources and therefore need to be selective about which projects they decide to carry out. As with strategies, projects can be assessed using the Johnson *et al* (2017) criteria of suitability, acceptability and feasibility.

2 Project initiation

When a project has been approved in general terms, it should be the subject of a number of management processes and tasks before the actual project work begins. Schwalbe (2015) highlights that such tasks can be broken down into pre-initiating tasks and initiating tasks. The pre-initiating tasks follow on directly from the formal project selection process.

2.1 Pre-initiating tasks

Pre-initiating tasks are the responsibility of the senior managers who decide that the project should be undertaken.

(a) **Determination of project objectives** and **constraints**. This involves setting the project scope, but also identifying time or cost constraints. (This was discussed in the previous section)

(b) Selection of the **project manager**

(c) Identification of the **project sponsor**

2.2 The project manager

The project manager: Takes responsibility for ensuring the desired result is achieved on time and within budget.

Some project managers have only one major responsibility: a specific project. However, anyone responsible for a project, large or small, is a project manager. As a result, many project managers will have routine work responsibilities outside their project goals, which may lead to conflicting demands on their time.

2.2.1 The role of the project manager

The role a project manager performs is, in many ways, similar to those performed by other managers. There are, however, some important differences, as shown in the table which follows.

Project managers	Operations managers
Are often **generalists** with wide-ranging backgrounds and experience levels	Usually **specialists** in the areas managed
Oversee work in **many functional areas**	Relate closely to **technical tasks** in their area
Facilitate, rather than supervise, team members	Have **direct technical supervision** responsibilities

The process of selecting a project manager will largely be driven by the perceived importance of the project being undertaken and the skills that the organisation's senior management believe are needed to deliver the project successfully.

2.2.2 The responsibilities of a project manager

The overall issue for all project managers is understanding how to balance the factors of scope, resources, time and risk.

However, a project manager also has responsibilities both to management and also to the project team.

Responsibilities to management

- Ensure resources are used efficiently – strike a balance between cost, time and results

- Keep management informed with timely and accurate communications

- Manage the project to the best of their ability

- Behave ethically, and adhere to the organisation's policies

- Maintain a customer orientation (whether the project is geared towards an internal or external customer) – customer satisfaction is a key indicator of project success

Responsibilities to the project and the project team

- Take action to keep the project on target for successful completion

- Ensure the project team has the resources required to perform tasks assigned

- Help new team members integrate into the team

- Provide any professional support required when members leave the team, either during the project or on completion. Professional support may involve helping project team members to settle back into functional roles following their involvement in a completed project, or when they are required to adjust to a new role when undertaking future projects.

2.2.3 Duties of a project manager

The project manager's responsibilities give rise to a number of fairly standard duties and managerial activities.

Duty	Comment
Detailed planning	Budgeting, resource requirements, activity scheduling
Obtain necessary resources	Resources may already exist within the organisation or may have to be bought in; resource requirements unforeseen at the planning stage will have to be authorised separately by the project board or project sponsor
Team building	Build cohesion and team spirit in the project team
Communication	Keep all stakeholders suitably informed and ensure that members of the project team are properly briefed; manage expectations
Co-ordinating project activities	Co-ordination will be required between the project team, external suppliers, the project owner and end users
Monitoring and control	Monitor progress against the plan, and take corrective measures where needed
Problem resolution	Even with the best planning, unforeseen problems may arise
Quality control	Understand and manage quality procedures; agree and manage any appropriate trade-off of functionality against achieving deadlines

PER alert

Performance Objective 5 'Leadership and Management' of the Practical Experience Requirement requires you to 'manage resources – including teams – to deliver your objectives to agreed deadlines. You motivate other people and you're actively involved in helping them to develop' (ACCA, 2019b). You could illustrate your achievement of this Performance Objective by drawing upon any experience that you have of managing projects in the work place.

2.3 Project sponsor

Key term

The project sponsor: Provides and is accountable for the resources invested into the project and is responsible for the achievement of the project's objectives.

It is common to refer to the person or group providing the resources to a project (and project manager) as the **project sponsor**. The project sponsor may, in fact, be the senior management at the top of the organisation, or may be a person or committee at a lower level; the essential feature is that the project sponsor has the budgetary capability to authorise the project.

The project sponsor will not be involved in the management of the project and may not have the capacity to provide effective supervision for the project manager. Under these circumstances, the project sponsor may appoint a **project owner**, whose role will be to review project plans and progress at regular intervals and to arbitrate on any conflicts that may arise between project and line management. Of course, in smaller organisations, the roles of project sponsor and project owner may be combined.

BPP
LEARNING MEDIA

2.4 Initiating tasks

Initiating tasks are carried out by the project manager. Two of the most important tasks carried out at this stage concern the preparation of a business case for the project and the drafting of the project initiation document.

2.4.1 Preparation of a business case

Key term

> **A business case:** Is a key document for a project. It is used to propose a course of action to senior management for their consideration.

When the project selection process is complete and a project selected for action, there is likely to be a great deal of information available to justify the decision to proceed. However, it is unlikely that a full account of the project has been prepared. A **business case** is a reasoned account of **why** the project is needed, **what** it will achieve and **how** it will proceed.

An important use of the business case in any project is to maintain **focus** and to ensure that the project remains on track. It is possible that final approval for a large project will depend upon the preparation of a satisfactory business case. A business case is not, of course, something that is confined to commercial organisations: the principles are equally applicable to any organisation undertaking a project.

A typical business case will include:

- Description of **current information/issues** (the problem or problems to be solved)

- Analysis of **costs and benefits**, including any **assumptions** and consideration of **intangible** costs and benefits. We consider costs and benefits in more detail in the next section

- Any **impact** of the project on the organisation in addition to the cost, such as changes in structure or recruitment of staff

- Key **risks**, including an assessment of their **significance** and any action to be taken to **mitigate** them

- **Recommendations**

Essential reading

See Chapter 15 section 1 of the Essential Reading, available in Appendix 2 of the digital edition of the Workbook, for more detail about building the business case.

2.4.2 The project initiation document

Key term

> **The project initiation document (also known as the project charter):** Complements the business case: while the business case explains the need for work on the project to start, the charter gives authorisation for work to be done and resources used.

The **project initiation document** (also known as the project charter) complements the business case: while the business case explains the **need** for work on the project to start, the project initiation document gives **authorisation** for work to be done and resources used. The project initiation document also has an important role in internal communication within the organisation, since it can be given wide distribution in order to keep staff informed of what is happening. The exact content of a project initiation document will vary from organisation to organisation and from project to project, but some elements are likely to be present, including:

- Project title
- Project purpose and objectives

- Project start date and expected finish date
- Details of the project sponsor and project
- Authorisation by the main stakeholders

Other elements of information may be included.

- Outline schedule of work
- Budget information
- Outline of project scope and work sequence
- Further details of roles and responsibilities

Exam Focus Point

The Strategic Business Leader specimen 2 exam featured a public sector rail company, Rail Co, which was responsible for providing rail services within the country of Beeland. The final question required candidates to act in the capacity of a project manager working for Rail Co. The director of Projects and Infrastructure at Rail Co had recently proposed that the company invest in an online ticket sales system. The intention was that the project would be completed within 12 months, with the development of the system being undertaken by an external firm. Part (a) of the question asked candidates to prepare a business case for the board which justified 'why the investment in online ticket sales could assist Rail Co in producing detailed and timely customer data to assist in customer relationship management' (ACCA, 2017a). This task was worth 8 technical marks and tested the ACCA Professional Skill of Evaluation.

To produce a good answer candidates needed to set out their answer using a business case format which evaluated the benefits that the proposed new system could bring in terms of generating customer data. To earn the two professional skills marks candidates needed to display 'professional judgement in assessing the impact of the system on timely customer data and CRM [...and to also demonstrate] 'a clear ability to assess the impact of the new system on the stakeholders of Rail Co' (ACCA, 2017a). Part (b) of the question asked candidates to 'produce a project initiation document (PID) which could be used by Rail Co to assist in planning the implementation of an online ticket sales system' (ACCA, 2017a). This was also worth 8 technical marks and tested the ACCA Professional Skill of Communication. To earn the two professional skills marks candidates needed to ensure that their PID would help with the implementation of the project.

Exam Focus Point

Question 2 of the Strategic Business Leader exam in September 2018 featured a task which asked candidates to prepare a memo which critically evaluated the outline contents of a project initiation document (PID) that had been prepared by a junior member of a project team. Candidates were also expected to recommend improvements to the PID provided.

3 Project costs and benefits

In the previous section we introduced the important role that the business case plays in project management. A key section of the business case is devoted to consideration of the associated costs and benefits of undertaking the project.

This section should provide the benefits first, followed by the costs. This is to help the reader appreciate the benefits before they are faced with the costs in achieving them.

3.1 Identifying the benefits

Many organisations have adopted a benefits management approach to identify benefits. Benefits management is made up of five key stages as shown by the following diagram:

Stages of benefits management

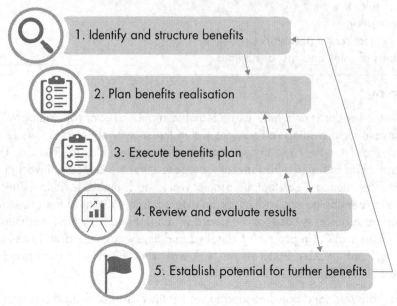

1. Identify and structure benefits
2. Plan benefits realisation
3. Execute benefits plan
4. Review and evaluate results
5. Establish potential for further benefits

(Adapted from: Ward and Daniel, 2006: p.105)

The first stage of the diagram, **identifying and structuring benefits**, is important for inclusion in the business case. The point of the business case is to secure funding by demonstrating the benefits for the organisation that the project will bring.

Ward and Daniel (2006) note that the purpose of identifying and structuring benefits is to:

- Establish agreed objectives for the investment
- Identify all the potential benefits that may arise if the objectives of the investment are met (including where in the organisation it will occur)
- Understand how those benefits could be realised
- Determine ownership of the benefits
- Determine how the benefits can be measured to prove they have occurred
- Identify any issues that could delay the project or cause it to fail
- Produce an outline business case to decide whether to proceed with the project or stop investment at this stage

Notice that as part of this process, it is important to determine who **owns** the benefit and how it will be **measured**. If a perceived benefit cannot be measured, or no one owns it, then that benefit does not really exist.

3.2 Measuring benefits

As well as identifying benefits, it is important to establish how they will be **measured**. Ward and Daniel (2006) note that benefits can be classified as **observable**, **measurable**, **quantifiable** and **financial**.

Key terms

Observable: Benefits are those which are measured by experience or judgement. 'Soft' benefits such as staff morale fall into this category.

Measurable: Benefits relate to an area of performance that could be (or already is being) measured, but it is not possible to quantify how much performance will increase as a result of the change.

Quantifiable: Benefits are those where the level of benefit that will result from the change can be reliably forecast based on the evidence in place.

Financial: Benefits are quantified benefits that have had a financial formula (such as cost or price) applied to them to produce a financial value for the benefits.

Financial benefits are most useful for establishing a business case, with observable benefits much less useful (but should not be ignored).

Essential reading

See Chapter 15 section 2 of the Essential Reading, available in Appendix 2 of the digital edition of the Workbook, for more detail about project benefits.

Activity 2: Freshco supermarkets

ACCA Professional skills focus

Commercial acumen: Use judgement

You are a senior finance manager working for Freshco supermarkets. You report to the finance director.

Freshco operates a number of supermarkets across the country; it has always prided itself on the service it provides to its customers. At last week's board meeting, Freshco's customer service director highlighted his concerns over a recent spike in the number of customer complaints his team have received. A common theme in the complaints received relates to increasing queuing times that customers are experiencing at the checkout. The customer service director has proposed a project to address the current issue. The finance director has provided you with some notes (Exhibit 1) from the meeting; he has had a meeting with the customer service director and has asked if the finance department could assist him in correctly classifying the benefits associated with undertaking the project so that his proposal can be approved by the board at the next meeting.

Required

Using the information provided in the exhibit, identify and classify the benefits that are likely to result from the proposed project. **(6 marks)**

Professional skills marks are available for demonstrating **commercial acumen** in using judgement when classifying the benefits presented by the project. **(2 marks)**

(Total = 8 marks)

Exhibit 1

Every Freshco supermarket has 20 checkout points and most of the time not all are manned, but at peak times all are manned and there are significant queues, prompting customer complaints. The number of complaints is tracked, but beyond this Freshco does not otherwise measure customer feedback. As a result Freshco is considering improving the scanning technology at its tills. Based on the experience of other users of the technology, this will cut the average time taken to process a customer's shopping from 4 minutes to 20 seconds.

Solution

3.3 Identifying the costs

As we have seen with project benefits, predicting costs can also be difficult – particularly as some may not be recorded. Ward and Daniel (2006) highlight the types of costs that should be included as part of the project cost assessment:

- **Purchase costs** such as hardware, software, consultancy and materials

- **Internal systems development costs** such as developing/purchasing software

- **Infrastructure costs**. These are costs that are incurred exclusively for the new system.

- **Costs of carrying out the changes** should be included to provide a complete financial view of the investment. This includes costs such as training, recruitment, redundancy, refitting buildings and so on.

- **Ongoing costs**. These are the permanent costs involved in the new ways of working. They should be either explicitly stated as additional costs or netted off against the benefits.

We can see from this that a project will include both **capital** and **operational** costs.

Key terms

Capital expenditure: Acquires or produces an asset whose value continues to be used (or consumed) over several financial years.

Operating costs: Refer to any expenditure on things whose value is used up within the same financial year.

The majority of capital expenditure is likely to occur at the start of the project and prior to implementation. This could involve expenditure on items such as building new facilities, refits and refurbishment, new technology and systems and so on.

Operating expenditure can be non-recurrent, such as consultancy fees, or can be recurrent, such as staff salaries. Recurrent operating expenditure could continue long after the project has been completed and the finished solution implemented.

Recurrent operating costs are as relevant to the business case as the capital and non-recurrent operating costs incurred during the project itself. However, it is easy to overlook such costs as part of 'business as usual'. If such costs would not be incurred if the project did not go ahead, then those costs must be built into the business case if it is to be a true representation of the worth of the project.

3.4 Cost-benefit evaluation

Once the costs and benefits have been quantified and assumptions verified, an investment appraisal can be undertaken. Techniques commonly used here include:

*   **Accounting rate of return** takes the average profit that the investment will generate and expresses it as a percentage of the average investment made over the life of the project.

*   **Payback period** is the length of time it takes for the initial investment to be repaid out of the net cash inflows from the project.

*   **Net present value** is the sum of the discounted value of the net cash flows from the investment.

*   **Internal rate of return** is the discount rate that, when applied to its future cash flows, will produce an NPV of zero.

You should be familiar with these techniques from your earlier ACCA studies.

4 Project planning

The unique nature of each project means that careful planning is an essential component of project management. Many project failures can be traced to failures of planning.

4.1 Planning tools

The project plan is used as a reference tool for managing the project. The plan is used to guide both project execution and project control. It outlines how the project will be planned, monitored and implemented. There are a number of tools which project managers can use when planning the delivery of a project.

4.1.1 Work breakdown structure

Key term

Work breakdown structure (WBS): Is the analysis of the work required to complete the project, broken down into manageable components.

Work breakdown structure (WBS) is fundamental to traditional project planning and control. Its essence is the **analysis** of the work required to complete the project broken down into **manageable components**.

WBS allows the project manager to consider the **outputs** (or **deliverables**) the project is required to produce. This can then be analysed into physical and intangible components, which can in turn be further analysed down to whatever level of simplicity is required. Working backwards in this way helps to **avoid preconceived ideas** of the work the project will involve and the processes that must be undertaken.

The WBS can allow for several levels of analysis, starting with major project phases and gradually breaking them down into major activities, more detailed sub-activities and individual tasks that will last only a very short time. The delivery phase of many projects will break down into significant stages or sub-phases. These are very useful for control purposes, as the completion of each stage is an obvious point for reviewing the whole plan before starting the next one.

4.1.2 The project budget

Project budget: The amount and distribution of resources allocated to a project.

Key term

Building a project budget should be an orderly process that attempts to establish a realistic estimate of the cost of the project. There are two main methods for establishing the project budget: **top-down** and **bottom-up**.

Top-down budgeting describes the situation where the budget is imposed **from above**. Project managers are allocated a budget for the project based on an estimate made by senior management. The figure may prove realistic, especially if similar projects have been undertaken recently. However, the technique is often used simply because it is quick, or because only a certain level of funding is available.

In **bottom-up budgeting** the project manager consults the project team, and others, to calculate a budget based on the tasks that make up the project. WBS is a useful tool in this process.

4.1.3 Gantt charts

A Gantt chart: Shows the deployment of resources over time.

Key term

A **Gantt chart**, named after the engineer Henry Gantt who pioneered the procedure in the early 1900s, is a horizontal bar chart used to plan the **time scale** for a project and to estimate the **resources** required. Maylor (2010) notes that the Gantt chart displays the time relationships between tasks in a project. Two lines are usually used to show the time allocated for each task, and the actual time taken.

A simple Gantt chart, illustrating some of the activities involved in a network server installation project, follows.

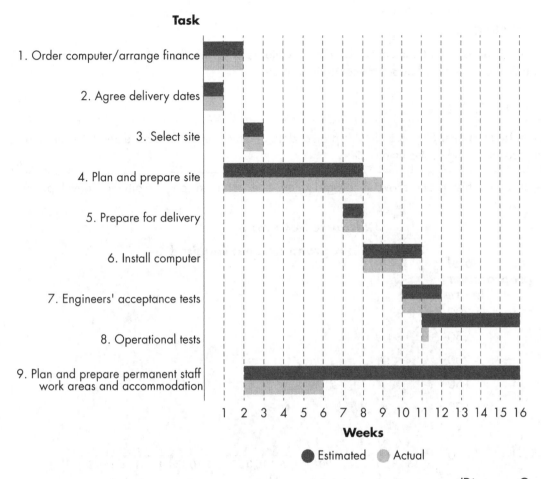

(Diagram: Gantt chart)

The chart shows that at the end of the tenth week, Activity 9 is running behind schedule. More resources may have to be allocated to this activity if the staff accommodation is to be ready in time for the changeover to the new system.

Activity 4 has not been completed on time, although it appears that this has not had an impact on subsequent activities. Activity 6 appears to have completed ahead of time.

A Gantt chart does not show the interrelationship between the various activities in the project as clearly as a **network analysis diagram** (described below). A combination of Gantt charts and network analysis will often be used for project planning and resource allocation.

4.1.4 Network analysis (or critical path analysis)

Critical path analysis (CPA): Aims to ensure the progress of a project, so the project is completed in the minimum amount of time.

Key term

Maylor (2010) highlights the use of **network analysis,** also known as **critical path analysis** (CPA), as a useful technique to help with planning and controlling large projects, such as construction projects, research and development projects, and the computerisation of systems.

CPA aims to ensure the progress of a project, so the project is completed in the **minimum amount of time**. It pinpoints the tasks **on the critical path**, which is the longest duration sequence of tasks in the project; a delay to any of these tasks would **delay the completion** of the project as a whole. The technique can also be used to assist in **allocating resources** such as labour and equipment.

Essential reading

See Chapter 15 section 3 of the Essential Reading, available in Appendix 2 of the digital edition of the Workbook, for more detail about critical path analysis.

4.1.5 Resource histogram

Key term

A resource histogram: Shows a view of project data in which resource requirements, usage and availability are shown against a time scale.

A simple resource histogram showing programmer time required on a software development program follows:

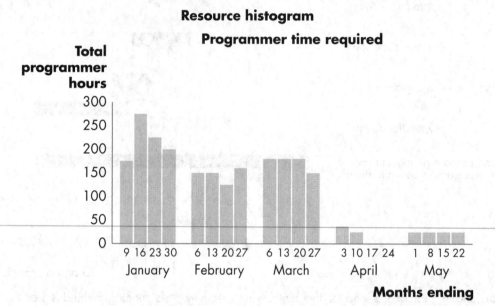

(Diagram: Resource histogram)

Some organisations add another bar (or a separate line) to the chart showing resource availability. The chart then shows any instances when the required resource hours exceed the available hours. Plans should then be made to either obtain further resource for these peak times, or to reschedule the work plan. Alternately, the chart may show times when the available resource is excessive, and should be redeployed elsewhere. An example follows:

Resource histogram showing resource availability

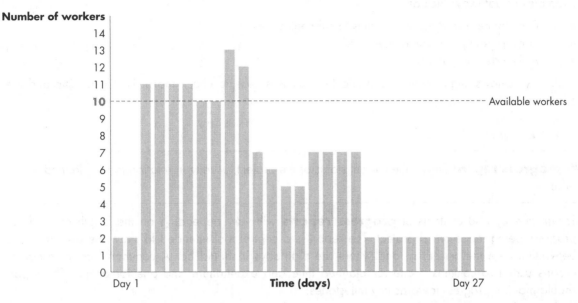

(Diagram: Resource histogram)

The number of workers required on the ninth day is 13. Using this information the project manager can then consider whether any of the non-critical activities can be re-scheduled to reduce the requirement to the available level of 10 workers.

Essential reading

See Chapter 15 section 4 of the Essential Reading, available in Appendix 2 of the digital edition of the Workbook, for a discussion of the importance of data visualisation in project management.

5 Project execution and control

The process of delivering the project is often referred to as project execution. Project execution and the processes involved in controlling the project are in essence two separate stages but they tend to happen at the same time. Projects need to be monitored closely to ensure that benefits are being realised and costs kept under control.

5.1 Controlling projects

There are a number of techniques which can be used by the project manager to help control project activity.

5.1.1 Gateways

Key term

A gateway: Is a project review point at which certain criteria must be met before the project can pass through the gateway and proceed to the next stage.

A project **gateway** is a predetermined point where the project will be reviewed. This may include a review by independent experts. It aims to ensure that benefits are being realised, key issues have been resolved, risks dealt with and that the project should go on to the next stage.

It aims to prevent **'scope creep'** whereby the scope of the project becomes expanded without proper consideration.

Scope creep: Relates to uncontrolled changes in the scope of a project.

Examples of gateways include:

- Prior to the awarding of contracts to subcontractors
- Prior to going live with a new system
- At key decision points

Gateway reviews might involve revisiting the business case to check that it is still realistic and the assumptions remain valid.

5.1.2 Progress reports

A progress report: Shows the current status of the project, usually in relation to the planned status.

The frequency and contents of **progress reports** will vary depending on the length of, and the progress being made on, a project. The report is a control tool intended to show the discrepancies between where the project is, and where the plan says it should be. A common form of progress reports uses two columns – one for planned time and expenditure and one for actual. The report should monitor progress towards key milestones.

A milestone: 'Is a significant event in the life of the project, usually completion of a major deliverable.' (Greer, 2002: p.11)

5.2 Project slippage

Slippage: Occurs when a project is running behind schedule.

5.2.1 Addressing slippage

Exercise 1: IT project

Required

A project to develop and implement a new IT system has fallen three weeks behind schedule. So far, the money spent is in line with the budget. What options are available to the project manager to deal with this?

Solution

When a project has slipped behind schedule, there are a range of options open to the project manager. Some of these options are summarised in the following table.

Action	Comment
Do nothing	After considering all options it may be decided that things should be allowed to continue as they are.
Add resources	If capable staff are available, and it is practicable to add more people to certain tasks, it may be possible to recover some lost ground. Are extra funds available to hire more staff? Could some work be subcontracted?
Work smarter	Consider whether the methods currently being used are the most suitable – for example, would prototyping be more effective at eliciting requirements?
Replan	If the assumptions that the original plan was based on have been proved invalid, a more realistic plan should be devised.
Reschedule	A complete replan may not be necessary – it may be possible to recover some time by changing the phasing of certain deliverables.
Introduce incentives	If the main problem is team performance, incentives such as bonus payments could be linked to work deadlines and quality. This is a positive incentive. In some cases, poor team performance may need to be addressed through more negative responses, for example, disciplinary action if staff are not working to the level required of them.
Briefings and motivation	If the project is long, it may be beneficial for the manager to hold update briefings with the team to renew their energy and enthusiasm and thereby increase productivity.
Change the specification	If the original objectives of the project are unrealistic, given the time and money available, it may be necessary to negotiate a change in the specification. This change could either be to reduce the **number of activities** included in the scope, or to reduce the level of **quality** required in each activity.

There are also two specific courses of action a project manager should consider if a project starts to slip dramatically, but has a fixed deadline and so cannot be delayed. These are **fast-tracking** and **crashing**.

5.2.2 Fast-tracking

Fast-tracking involves taking activities that are normally done in sequence, and doing them in parallel instead (for example, starting construction alongside the design phase, instead of waiting for the design phase to be completed before beginning construction).

5.2.3 Crashing

Crashing involves assigning additional resources to the critical path. For example, if one person was working on a 12-day activity on the critical path, and it was essential to reduce the path length to eight days, a second person could be added to work on the activity.

Crashing usually leads to an increase in the cost of the project, but this may be considered an acceptable trade-off for getting the project back on schedule.

BPP
LEARNING
MEDIA

5.3 Project change procedure

Some of the reactions to slippage discussed above would involve changes that would significantly affect the overall project. Other possible causes of changes to the original project plan include:

- The availability of new technology
- Changes in personnel
- A realisation that user requirements were misunderstood
- Changes in the environment
- New legislation, eg data protection

The earlier a change is made, the less expensive it should prove. However, changes will cost time and money and should not be undertaken lightly. When considering a change the project manager should conduct an investigation to discover:

(a) The **consequences of not implementing** the proposed change
(b) The **impact of the change** on time, cost and quality
(c) The expected **costs and benefits** of the change
(d) The **risks** associated with the change, and with the status quo

The process of ensuring that proper consideration is given to the impact of proposed changes is known as **change control**. Changes will need to be implemented into the project plan and communicated to all stakeholders.

5.4 Responding to project risk

Projects carry an element of **risk**, for example the risk of an inappropriate system being developed and implemented. Risk management is concerned with identifying such risks and putting in place policies to eliminate or reduce these risks. The identification of risks involves an overview of the project to establish what could go wrong, and the consequences. Risk management may be viewed as a six-stage process:

Stage 1   **Plan the risk-management approach**

Determine the degree of risk aversion that the project sponsor is prepared to tolerate.

Stage 2   **Identify and record risks**

Identified risks should be recorded in a risk register. This will include details such as: a description of the risk, the probability of the risk occurring, and the potential impact on the project should it occur.

Stage 3   **Assess the risks**

There are two aspects to the assessment of risk.

- The probability/likelihood that the risk event will actually take place.
- The consequences of the risk event if it does occur.

The likelihood and consequences of risks may be plotted on a matrix so that those high impact, high likelihood risks are identified.

Stage 4	**Plan and record risk responses**

Schwalbe (2015) highlights that there are four strategies when dealing with risk.

Avoidance: activities that could carry risk are not performed or are removed from a project. For example, an acquisition is rejected because of the potential legal liabilities attached to the potential acquisition target.

Reduction or mitigation: the potential for the risk cannot be removed, but mitigation can reduce the severity of any loss or the likelihood of the loss occurring, for example, by entering into an escrow agreement alongside the purchase of a bespoke software solution.

Transference: the risk is passed on to someone else, perhaps by means of insurance, or possibly by building it into a supplier contract.

Absorption or acceptance: the potential risk is accepted in the hope or expectation that the incidence and consequences can be coped with if necessary.

Stage 5	**Implement risk-management strategies**
Stage 6	**Review the risk-management approach and actions for adequacy**

Risk management is a continuous process. Procedures are necessary to regularly review and reassess the risks documented in the risk register.

Activity 3: The Knowledge Partnership

ACCA Professional skills focus

Commercial acumen: Show insight

It is 4 December 20X4 and today is your first day in your new job. You were recently appointed as a senior finance manager working for The Knowledge Partnership LLP (TKP). The Knowledge Partnership LLP (TKP) offers project and software consultancy work for clients based in Zeeland. As you wait in reception for your new line manager to come and take you to the finance department you start reading through the latest edition of TKP's internal newsletter (Exhibit 1). The newsletter is dated 2 November 20X4 and describes one of the projects currently being undertaken by the partnership.

Required

Using the information provided in the exhibit analyse how TKP itself and the iProjector project demonstrate the principles of effective risk management. **(12 marks)**

Professional skills marks are available for demonstrating **commercial acumen** by displaying insight into how TKP and the iProjector project exhibit the characteristics of effective risk management. **(2 marks)**

(Total = 14 marks)

Exhibit 1 – The iProjector project

The project client is the developer of the iProjector, a tiny phone-size projector which is portable, easy to use and offers high definition projection. The client was concerned that their product is completely dependent on a specialist image-enhancing chip designed and produced by a small start-up technology company. They asked TKP to investigate this company. We confirmed their fears. The company has been trading for less than three years and it has a very inexperienced management team. We suggested that the client should establish an escrow agreement for design details of the chip and suggested a suitable third party to hold this agreement. We also suggested that significant inventory of the chip should be maintained. The client also asked TKP to look at establishing patents for the iProjector throughout the world. Again, using our customer contacts, we put them in touch with a company which specialises in this. We are currently engaged with the client in examining the risk that a major telephone producer will launch a competitive product with functionality and features similar to the iProjector.

Further information:

TKP only undertakes projects in the business culture which it understands and where it feels comfortable. Consequently, it does not undertake assignments outside Zeeland.

TKP has $10,000,000 of consultant's liability insurance underwritten by Zeeland Insurance Group (ZIG).

Solution

6 Project completion

6.1 The completion report

The completion report: Summarises the results of the project, and includes client sign-off.

On completion of the project the project manager should produce a report which details:

- The outcomes of the project compared to the objectives
- The final cost of the project compared to the budget
- The time taken to complete the work compared to the schedule

The main purpose of the completion report is to document (and gain sign-off for) the end of the project.

6.2 The post-project review

Key term

> **The post-project review:** Is a formal review of the project that examines the lessons that may be learned and used for the benefit of future projects.

The review is intended to be beneficial to the organisation as it considers the success of the project by asking the following.

(a)   Was the project achieved on time and within budget?

(b)   Was the management of the project as successful as it might have been, or were there bottlenecks or problems? This review covers:

(i)   Problems that might occur on future projects with similar characteristics.

(ii)   The performance of the team individually and as a group.

In other words, any project is an **opportunity to learn how to manage future projects more effectively**.

Real world examples

In 2008, the BBC (British Broadcasting Corporation) launched the Digital Media Initiative (DMI) project. The project aimed to modernise the BBC's existing production operations, moving the corporation away from the use of video tape towards digital production.

In 2013, the project was abandoned after years of technical problems in getting the technology to work and delays in reporting on the project's progress. The BBC (2014b) reported that the estimated project cost was £125.9m.

Hewlett (2014) highlighting the findings of a National Audit Office inquiry, reported that the deteriorating fortunes of DMI were not adequately reported, either within management or, critically, to the BBC Trust. 'A 'code red' warning of the imminent project failure for example, from the BBC's own internal project management office from February 2012, wasn't reported to the Trust until July that year.

Hewlett (2014) noted that the BBC Director General (the most senior executive officer at the organisation) at the time had believed that the technology was being used on programmes including the early evening 'One Show'.

A later report by the National Audit Office reported that 'the BBC had hoped to save £98m by introducing the new system. However, the final estimate of the benefits it brought to the BBC was zero. The report blamed the project's failure on confusion, a lack of planning and insufficient scrutiny' (BBC, 2014b).

Commenting on the National Audit Office report, Margaret Hodge MP of the Public Accounts Committee (the body which overseas UK government spending) wrote, 'this report reads like a catalogue of how not to run a major programme. The BBC needs to learn from the mistakes it made and ensure that it never again spends such a huge amount of licence fee payer's money with almost nothing to show for it' (BBC, 2014b).

The BBC responded, saying it had adopted new procedures for managing big projects in the light of the problems with the DMI project (BBC, 2014b).

In 2016 a report by the National Audit Office titled the *Management of the BBC's critical projects*, highlighted the findings of a review into the BBC's oversight of its critical projects portfolio. The report highlighted that the BBC had strengthened its oversight process of major projects. In response to the report's findings the BBC Trust highlighted the improvements it had made to the way in which the BBC's project management team now operated:

*   Experienced staff now 'review and challenge submissions from project teams prior to reporting this information upwards. This process provides additional assurance that projects will deliver their expected benefits on time and on budget' (National Audit Office, 2016).

BPP
LEARNING
MEDIA

- The 'speed of project reporting to the Executive Board and the BBC Trust had improved', with reporting now taking 'less than half the amount of time that it took three years ago. As a result, problems are raised and dealt with much quicker, reducing the risk of project failure' (National Audit Office, 2016).

- The BBC has introduced new project assurance arrangements in recent years, including 'increased frequency of project reporting to the Executive Board, a single point of accountability for each project, and the introduction of integrated approvals and reviews' (National Audit Office, 2016).

6.3 The post-implementation review

Key term

> **Post-implementation reviews:** Are assessments of the completed working solution.

The post-implementation review focuses more specifically on the output that was produced by the project. It is carried out for three main reasons.

- To determine how well the project met its objectives, delivered the expected benefits and addressed the requirements that were originally defined

- To consider the working solution to see if further improvements could be made to optimise the benefit delivered

- To identify lessons that can be learned and fed back into the **output production process**; this could involve improving processes such as research and development, and operational processes as well as making changes to who is involved in certain processes and the timings at which individual processes are carried out

In order to do this, work will centre around determining the current situation, identifying the benefits actually being delivered in comparison to those originally defined by the project, and identifying any further improvements that could be made and the learning points for the future.

Chapter summary

Project management

Project management

What is a project?
A project has a beginning and an end and is carried out to meet established goals within cost, schedule and quality objectives

What is project management?
- The combination of systems, techniques, and people used to control and monitor activities undertaken within the project
- The triple constraint (scope, cost and time)
- Project challenges

Projects and strategy
Project selection (suitability, acceptability and feasibility)

Project initiation

Pre-initiating tasks
Set objectives, select project manager, identify the project sponsor

The project manager
- The role of the project manager is to take responsibility for ensuring the desired result is achieved on time and within budget
- The responsibilities of a project manager
- Duties of a project manager

Project sponsor
Provides and is accountable for the resources invested into the project and is responsible for the achievement of the project's objectives

Initiating tasks
- Preparation of a business case (This a key document for a project. It is used to propose a course of action to senior management for their consideration)
- The project initiation document (Gives authorisation for work to be done and resources used)

Project costs and benefits

Identifying the benefits

Measuring benefits
Observable, measurable, quantifiable and financial

Identifying the costs
Capital expenditure and operating costs

Cost-benefit evaluation
Accounting rate of return, payback period, NPV and IRR

Project planning

Planning tools
- Work breakdown structure
  (The project is broken down
  into manageable components)
- The project budget
  (The amount and distribution
  of resources allocated to a
  project)
- Gantt charts
  (Shows the deployment of
  resources over time)
- Network analysis (or critical
  path analysis)
  (CPA aims to ensure the
  progress of a project, so the
  project is completed in the
  minimum amount of time)
- Resource histogram
  (Shows a view of project data
  in which resource
  requirements, usage, and
  availability are shown against
  a time scale)

Project execution and control

Controlling projects
- Gateways are project review
  points
- It is at this point that certain
  criteria must be met before the
  project can pass through the
  gateway and proceed to the
  next stage
- Progress tests show the current
  status of the project, usually in
  relation to the planned status

Project slippage
- Slippage occurs when a project
  is running behind schedule
- Addressing slippage
- Fast-tracking
- Crashing

Project change procedure

Responding to project risk
Avoidance, reduction,
transference, and acceptance

Project completion

The completion report
Summarises the results of the
project, and includes client
sign-off

The post-project review
Is a formal review of the project
that examines the lessons that
may be learned and used for the
benefit of future projects

The post-implementation review
Are assessments of the
completed working solution

Knowledge diagnostic

1. A project is 'an undertaking that has a beginning and an end and is carried out to meet established goals within cost, schedule and quality objectives' (Haynes, 1997: p.3).

2. Project management is the combination of systems, techniques, and people used to control and monitor activities undertaken within the project.

3. Projects are generally considered successful if they meet three specified objectives in terms of the following (the 'triple constraint'): scope, time, and cost.

4. Projects and strategy are closely connected. Circumstances change and new conditions must be met with new responses or initiatives. Each possible new development effectively constitutes a project.

5. Project management can be a core strategic competence for organisations working in such industries as consulting and construction.

6. As with strategies, projects can be assessed using the Johnson *et al* (2017) criteria of suitability, acceptability and feasibility.

7. Some project managers have only one major responsibility: a specific project. However, many project managers, will have routine work responsibilities outside their project goals.

8. The project sponsor provides and is accountable for the resources invested into the project and is responsible for the achievement of the project's objectives.

9. A business case is a key document for a project. It is used to propose a course of action to senior management for their consideration. A business case is a reasoned account of why the project is needed, what it will achieve and how it will proceed.

10. The project initiation document (also known as the project charter) complements the business case: while the business case explains the need for work on the project to start, the charter gives authorisation for work to be done and resources used.

11. Measuring project benefits involves classifying them as observable, measurable, quantifiable and financial.

12. Once the costs and benefits have been quantified and assumptions verified, an investment appraisal can be undertaken. Techniques commonly used here include: accounting rate of return, payback period, NPV and IRR.

13. The project plan is used as a reference tool for managing the project. The plan is used to guide both project execution and project control. It outlines how the project will be planned, monitored and implemented.

14. Projects need to be monitored closely to ensure that benefits are being realised and costs kept under control. Gateways and progress reports are key methods of control.

15. Slippage occurs when a project is running behind schedule. Slippage can be addressed in a number of ways including through fast-tracking and crashing.

16. Project completion involves a number of activities including the preparation of a completion report, a post-project and post-implementation review.

Question practice

Now try the question below from the Further question practice bank (available in the digital edition of the Workbook):

Q15 *LDB*

Further reading

There are articles on the ACCA website written by members of the SBL examining team which are relevant to your studies and which would be useful to read:

Approaching SBL overview

This article provides a one-page summary of the key features of the SBL exam.

Approaching SBL reading and planning

This article provides a one-page summary of how best to approach the SBL exam.

SBL – 10 things to learn from the September 2018 sitting

This article highlights some of the issues that ACCA identified in candidates' answers during the September 2018 SBL exam sitting. The article provides some useful advice for improving your chances of passing the SBL exam.

Strategic Business Leader – The importance of effective communication for SBL

This article provides some useful insights into the different formats which you will be expected to use when answering SBL exam tasks.

Own research

It is important to link the topics covered in this chapter to a practical, real-world context. As such, we have suggested some areas for you to investigate further. Research a well-known project with which you are familiar. There are often stories in the media about large IT projects, and large scale construction projects such as the building of sports stadia and ships. Then consider the following:

- Was the project a success or a failure?
- Which factors contributed to the project's success or failure?
- How did the project team manage the issues which arose during the execution phase of the project?
- What lessons could the project team learn having undertaken the project?

Exercise answer

Exercise 1

- Do nothing – it may not be feasible to make up the time

- Add resources by hiring extra staff, but this will mean additional cost

- Consider whether there are any ways of working more efficiently to speed things up

- Develop a revised plan with a later deadline, especially if it seems that, with hindsight, the original plan was unrealistic. This may need negotiating with the project client, internal or external

- Aim to improve team performance with incentives for meeting deadlines and/or sanctions if staff do not meet them. Performance may also be improved by better communication

- Change the specification of the project, for example narrow the scope in order to meet the deadline

BPP
LEARNING
MEDIA

SKILLS CHECKPOINT 5

Implementing strategic change

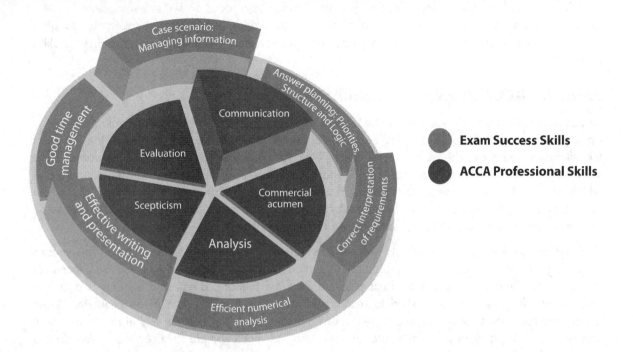

Exam Success Skills

ACCA Professional Skills

Introduction

In Stage 5 you have learned about the importance of Implementing Strategic Change.

However, only 80% of marks are awarded for the application of knowledge. The remaining marks are awarded for good demonstration of the specific ACCA Professional Skills outlined in the task requirement.

You need to able to:

1. Identify the ACCA Professional Skill in the task requirement. Remember the five: Analysis, Communication, Commercial Acumen, Evaluation and Scepticism

2. Understand what the skill requires in the context of the question

3. Consider how to demonstrate the skill(s) as part of your answer planning

The ACCA Professional Skills are assessing your ability to present your answers to a standard which would be expected in the workplace. However, in order to do this effectively in the Strategic Business Leader Exam, you must develop a further series of Exam Success Skills, so you are able to produce your very best solution in the four-hour timeframe.

Therefore, success in Strategic Business Leader requires the simultaneous demonstration of syllabus knowledge, ACCA Professional Skills and Exam Success Skills. This Skills Checkpoint specifically targets the development of your skills as you progress through the syllabus. This should provide you with all of the tools that you will need during the Learning phase, so you can focus on these improving at the Revision Stage.

The five Skills Checkpoints each focus on one of the five ACCA Professional Skills and provide further guidance on how to develop certain Exam Success Skills, so you can effectively manage questions and meet the expected standard for both knowledge and skills.

Your role

Developing skills requires more than listening and reading, it requires you to try for yourself, use guidance and feedback to consider whether you have met the skills objective, then plan for further improvement. In Strategic Business Leader, you should include a focus on skills development in every question you attempt as part of your normal approach. The Skills Checkpoints will take you through a series of **steps** where you will attempt aspects of a question and review your progress from a skills perspective.

Focus on ACCA Professional Skill: Communication

To communicate effectively you need to be able to express yourself clearly and convincingly using an appropriate medium. Displaying good communication also involves being sensitive to the needs of the intended audience. The name of the exam 'Strategic Business Leader' should provide a clear steer that you will have to prepare responses to task requirements which are of a strategic nature and which will be of interest to senior officers within an organisation. Individuals such as the CEO, Chair or a director on the board will not be interested in lots of operational detail; they will however be concerned about the main strategic issues facing the organisation.

Communicating with such individuals will require you to adopt a professional tone. This means preparing answers which avoid ambiguity, repetition and unnecessary detail such as technical jargon. Supporting your work using facts gleaned from the scenario detail and exhibits is a critical skill, especially when you are asked to recommend solutions to address a given problem. When attempting such tasks, using the word 'because' in your answer is a useful technique to use as it ensures that you justify any recommendations you provide. For example, 'I recommend you do this because...'

Presenting your work in the format specified in the task requirement is a key part of demonstrating your communication skills. If you are asked to present your work using a report format it is important that you do so. Task requirements in the exam may specify the use of a format which you have not come across before in your earlier ACCA studies; you may be asked to prepare a presentation slide accompanied with supporting notes. In such cases it is perfectly acceptable to use bullet points in communicating the key issues from your answer on the presentation slide.

Demonstrating Exam Success Skills

For this question, we will focus on the following exam success skills:

- **Case scenario: Managing information.** This question contains quite a lot of detail as you are provided with some background information about the featured organisation, detail about one of the organisation's internal processes and a diagram which shows in a visual form the different stages involved in the featured process. To avoid being overloaded by all of the information it is important that you take a moment to think carefully about how this detail links to the task requirement. Therefore, a good starting point is to read the task requirement. Understanding what is expected of you should help to keep you focused and may reduce feelings associated with information overload. This is especially important as you have a lot of information to take in, in a relatively short amount of time. Starting with the task requirement should also help you to identify which elements of the scenario information will be of the most use when formulating your answer.

- **Correct interpretation of requirements**. This is closely connected to the points raised above. To avoid a situation where you answer a different question to the one actually asked, it is important that you carefully read the task requirement a couple of times. Here you need to be looking out for the verb(s) used; in some task requirements you may find that more than one verb is used, and therefore that you are being expected to do more than one thing when answering the question. Once you have done this you should read through the scenario detail as you should now have an idea of what you are looking out for. You should annotate any relevant points that you pick out from the scenario while bearing in mind the verbs specified in the task requirements. These points will form part of your answer plan. This approach is particularly useful when you have more than one verb to consider, as it ensures that you are generating sufficient points for use in answering the question.

- **Effective writing and presentation**. You should always use sub-headings in your answer, as this helps to keep your answer on track, especially if there are more than two verbs in the task requirement. Headings can be used as a checklist as they allow you to ensure that all of the main points are included in your answer. Unless told otherwise, such as being asked for a bullet-pointed slide, it is important that you write your answer using short, punchy sentences. You need to make it as easy as possible for the marker to award your work the marks on offer; avoiding lots of detail in your answer will help with this.

Skill Activity

 Read the task requirement for the following question, identify the verbs and the professional skills being examined, and set up your answer plan.

In this case you are expected to consider two verbs: 'analyse' and 'recommend'. When you are asked to analyse something you are being asked to give reasons for a situation having occurred or to provide an explanation of what has happened. In this case you are effectively being asked to identify the weaknesses (faults) in WET's current membership renewal process that have given rise to the problems listed by the CEO (the low response to payment requests, the despatch of renewal reminders for people who have already paid, and the failure to send renewal invoices to some members). The inclusion of the three problems listed by the CEO above the task requirement is intended to direct you to the weaknesses which have caused them.

The second verb, recommend, requires you to advise appropriate actions that the recipient will be able to understand. In the context of the scenario you are therefore required to put forward actions which would resolve the weaknesses/faults that you identify from your analysis. When you are asked to provide recommendations it is important that any suggestions you make are realistic and could be implemented in light of the situation outlined in the scenario.

One thing you should have noticed is that there is no specific mention of any particular theory in the task requirement, and therefore using the scenario and drawing upon your knowledge of organisational processes to make sensible points in your answer would be perfectly acceptable.

Under the task requirement you should have picked up on the fact that it is your 'communication' skills which are being tested. This professional skill requires you to 'inform', 'clarify' and 'persuade'. To earn these professional marks you will need to produce an answer which concisely informs WET's CEO of the current faults in the membership process. Your ability to clarify and simplify the issues you identify is particularly important in light of the amount of detail provided in the scenario. Any recommendations you make will need to be sufficiently persuasive if the CEO is to act upon them.

Although the task requirement does not specify any given format when presenting your answer, you would still need to be mindful of the fact that you are preparing a response to the CEO, and would therefore need to adopt a professional tone.

 You should now briefly read the scenario. Remember your 'managing information' skills, as the aim here is to pick out the key pieces of scenario detail which are going to help you answer the question. You may find it helpful to have the process diagram to hand as you go through the narrative detail.

Question – The Wetland Trust (17 marks)

The Wetland Trust (WET), is a charity formed a number of years ago with the aim of preserving, restoring and managing wetlands in the country of Arcadia. The wetlands of Arcadia are areas of natural habitat made up of land that is saturated with moisture, such as swamp, marsh or bog.

Since its formation, the Trust has acquired the four remaining wetland sites left in the country. The Trust's work is funded through the receipt of membership fees. Membership is through an annual subscription which gives members the right to visit the wetlands. Each wetland is managed by volunteers who provide access and guidance to members. Administrative costs have risen at a faster rate than subscriptions. Administrative staff are all full-time paid employees of the charity.

> Suggests WET is potentially losing out on membership fee income. Again this is a weakness.

However, despite an increase in staff numbers, there is a substantial backlog of cleared applications in the Membership Department which have not yet been entered into the membership computer system. The membership computer system is one of the systems used to support administration. However, the functionality of this software is relatively restricted and cumbersome and there have been complaints about its accuracy. For example, **members claim that renewal reminders are often sent out to people who have already paid** and that **members who should have received renewal invoices have never received them**. As a result the CEO commented that 'we seem to be wasting money and losing members'.

> This is a weakness as it is embarrassing to chase members for renewals if they already have paid.

WET's CEO is keen to improve the technology that supports the charity. **WET's current website is very rudimentary**, but she sees 'email and website technology as facilitating the acquisition, retention and satisfaction of our member's needs.'

> Might have implications for recommendations to improve the current membership renewal process.

Membership renewal process

> This may possibly be an area in need of improvement as cheque payments are slow.

One month before the date of membership renewal, the computer system (Membership System) sends a renewal invoice to a current (not lapsed) member giving subscription details and asking for payment. A copy of this invoice is sent to the Membership Department who file it away. Approximately 80% of members decide to renew and send their payment (either by providing credit card details (60%) or as a **cheque (40%)**) to WET. The Membership Department matches the payment with the renewal invoice copy. The invoice copy (stamped paid) is sent to **Sales and Marketing who use it to produce a membership card and send this card, together with a Guide to Sites booklet, to the member**. The Membership Department passes the payment to the Finance Department.

> This is a weakness as people are receiving their membership details and their payment hasn't necessarily cleared yet.

> The Membership Department have to handle the original renewal invoice and payment, and then receive confirmation later on that they can update the membership system to record that the payment has been made. This seems long-winded.

Finance now submits payments to the bank. It currently takes the Finance Department an average of **five days from the receipt of renewal to notifying the Membership Department of the cleared payment**. Once cleared, Finance notifies the Membership Department by email and they update the **Membership System to record that the payment has been made**. As mentioned before, there is a backlog in entering these details into the computer system. **Some cheques do not clear, often because they are filled in incorrectly** (for example, they are unsigned or wrongly dated). In these circumstances, Finance raises a payment request and sends it to the member. Once the member re-submits a replacement cheque, it again goes through the clearing process.

> Seems like a long time.

> Weakness of accepting cheque payments.

> Weakness with accepting credit card payments.

Credit card payments are cleared instantly, but again there may be problems with the details. For example, **incorrect numbers and incorrect expiry dates will lead to the transaction not being authorised** and so, in these circumstances, **Finance again raises a payment request**. The

> If a member has received their membership card but the payment has not been accepted by WET, members might be inclined to ignore a payment request.

Extra work for the finance department

members' response to payment requests is very low (about 5%). The finance manager has described this as scandalous and 'an unethical response from supposedly ethical people'. Also, not shown on the diagram: **one week before renewal, the Membership System produces a renewal reminder and sends it to the member. Some members pay as a result of this reminder.** If payment is not received then the member details are recorded as 'lapsed'.

If a member has received their membership card but the payment has not been accepted by WET, members might be inclined to ignore a payment request.

Figure: Membership renewal process

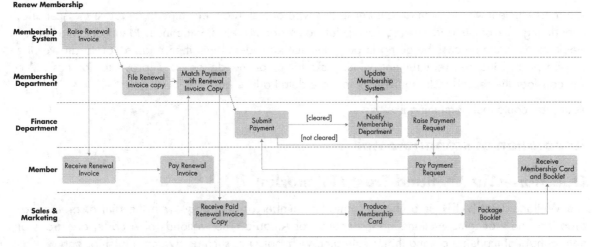

Required

WET's CEO has identified a number of problems with the current membership renewal process including:

- the low response to payment requests
- the despatch of renewal reminders for people who have already paid
- the failure to send renewal invoices to some members

Analyse faults in the current membership renewal process that caused the problems identified above and **recommend** solutions that would remedy these faults. **(15 marks)**

Professional skills marks are available for demonstrating **communication** skills when highlighting the faults in the current process and for suggesting practical solutions in addressing these faults.

(2 marks)

(Total = 17 marks)

A brief review of the scenario shows the following:

- The organisation is a charity. The fact that the charity only receives funding from the membership fees that it earns means that its members are key stakeholders.

- This therefore tells us that any problems related to the membership renewal process are likely to be very important to the organisation.

- The fact that administrative costs are rising at a faster pace than the fees received from memberships suggests that at some point the charity may well run into financial difficulties if this trend continues.

- There is a back log of uncleared applications. Again this is not good, given that the charity receives all of its funding from the memberships it sells.

- The existing IT infrastructure is regarded as being rudimentary.

- The inclusion of the diagram provides a visual aid which complements the narrative detail about the membership process.

STEP 3 You are in a position from which you can create an answer plan. A good starting point here is to focus on the weaknesses and disconnects that you identify in the current process. Any recommendations you think of will come from the faults that you identify.

Guidance in help you develop your Answer plan

As the question is worth 17 marks, using two minutes per mark as a guide equates to a total of 34 minutes to attempt the task requirement. Working on the basis that you will spend at least five minutes creating your answer plan, this leaves 29 minutes to write up your answer.

The most efficient way to plan an answer to this type of task requirement is to annotate the scenario, underlining key points and making very brief notes about their significance. Identifying the faults/weaknesses in the process by going through the scenario detail will then enable you to answer the second part of the task requirement, which asks for recommendations to improve the process. We will consider the second task requirement in more detail a little later on.

Your plan could look something like this:

Annotation of scenario detail

Question – The Wetland Trust (17 marks)

The Wetland Trust (WET), is a charity formed a number of years ago with the aim of preserving, restoring and managing wetlands in the country of Arcadia. The wetlands of Arcadia are areas of natural habitat made up of land that is saturated with moisture, such as swamp, marsh or bog.

Since its formation, the Trust has acquired the four remaining wetland sites left in the country. The Trust's work is funded through the receipt of membership fees. Membership is through an annual subscription which gives members the right to visit the wetlands. Each wetland is managed by volunteers who provide access and guidance to members. Administrative costs have risen at a faster rate than subscriptions. Administrative staff are all full-time paid employees of the charity.

> *This is not good given WET's dependence on its members.*

> *Suggests WET is potentially losing out on membership fee income. Again, this is a weakness.*

However, **despite an increase in staff numbers, there is a substantial backlog of cleared applications** in the Membership Department which have not yet been entered into the membership computer system. The membership computer system is one of the systems used to support administration. However, the functionality of this software is relatively restricted and cumbersome and there have been complaints about its accuracy. For example, **members claim that renewal reminders are often sent out to people who have already paid** and that **members who should have received renewal invoices have never received them**. As a result the CEO commented that 'we seem to be wasting money and losing members'.

> *This is a weakness as it is embarrassing to chase members for renewals if they already have paid.*

WET's CEO is keen to improve the technology that supports the charity. WET's current website is very rudimentary, but she sees 'email and website technology as facilitating the acquisition, retention and satisfaction of our member's needs'.

470

Membership renewal process

One month before the date of membership renewal, the computer system (Membership System) sends a renewal invoice to a current (not lapsed) member giving subscription details and asking for payment. A copy of this invoice is sent to the Membership Department who file it away. Approximately 80% of members decide to renew and send their payment (either by providing credit card details (60%) or as a **cheque (40%)**) to WET. The Membership Department matches the payment with the renewal invoice copy. The invoice copy (stamped 'paid') is sent to **Sales and Marketing who use it to produce a membership card and send this card, together with a Guide to Sites booklet, to the member**. The Membership Department passes the payment to the Finance Department.

Finance now submits payments to the bank. It currently takes the Finance Department an average of five days from the receipt of renewal to notifying the Membership Department of the cleared payment. Once cleared, Finance notifies the Membership Department by email and they update the Membership System to record that the payment has been made. As mentioned before, there is a backlog in entering these details into the computer system. Some cheques do not clear, often because they are filled in incorrectly (for example, they are unsigned or wrongly dated). In these circumstances, Finance raises a payment request and sends it to the member. Once the member re-submits a replacement cheque, it again goes through the clearing process.

Credit card payments are cleared instantly, but again there may be problems with the details. For example, incorrect numbers and incorrect expiry dates will lead to the transaction not being authorised and so, in these circumstances, Finance again raises a payment request. The **members' response to payment requests is very low (about 5%)**. The finance manager has described this as scandalous and 'an unethical response from supposedly ethical people'. Also, not shown on the diagram: **one week before renewal, the Membership System produces a renewal reminder and sends it to the member. Some members pay as a result of this reminder**. If payment is not received then the member details are recorded as 'lapsed'.

Figure: Membership renewal process

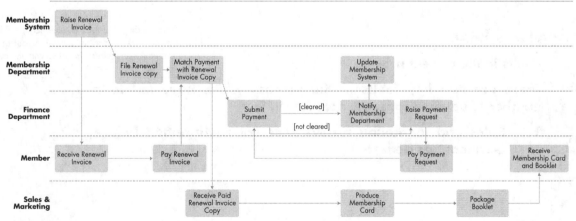

To ensure that you receive the professional skills marks it is important that you communicate a response to both parts of the question by not only identifying the faults in the process but are able to generate a range of solutions. You may find it helpful to set out your answer plan using a two-column table, one half of which outlines the faults in the process, while the other outlines some recommendations. Below is an example of two of the faults we identified and how these could be addressed:

Faults in current membership renewal process	Recommended solutions
The sales and marketing department currently receive renewal confirmation before the member's payment has cleared. Therefore membership cards are issued prior to WET receiving the payment.	The process needs to be changed so that the sales and marketing department only issue membership cards once receipt of the payment has been confirmed by the finance department.
The five days taken by the finance department to notify the membership department about those payments which have cleared is too long.	The process could be improved by introducing online payments through WET's website. WET would receive payments quicker. WET's website would need improving though as this has been described as rudimentary.

As the table above illustrates it is important that any solutions you recommend are realistic, and could be implemented by WET's CEO if considered appropriate.

 Check the requirements

Before you start writing up your answer it is worthwhile reviewing the task requirement again to ensure that there is nothing that you have overlooked. In this case ensuring the following will be important:

- Have you focused on the faults in the current process which were outlined by the CEO?

- Have you generated a sufficient number of faults and recommendations to ensure that you have produced a well-balanced answer which will earn the communication skills marks?

 Complete your written answer

You can now bring your workings together to create a solution, making sure that you use logical headings and short punchy sentences. Drawing together the key points from the scenario with your recommendations will show the marker that you have dealt with both task requirements. A model answer is given below, with comment boxes illustrating where the answer is demonstrating good communication skills.

Suggest Solution

> This sentence displays good communication skills as it is informing the reader that following your analysis there are effectively two main issues with the current process.

> Good use of headings. This makes it easier for the marker to identify the points raised, especially if the same terms are used from the task requirement, ie 'Faults'

Faults in the current process

There are two key faults in the process which have led to a number of adverse consequences for WET:

1. **Sales and marketing receive renewal confirmation before payment has cleared**

This has led to the sending out of membership cards and booklets to members prior to their payment clearing. Once this is received, the member would conclude that their payment had cleared and therefore would not respond to any request for payment. **This may be why there is a low rate of response to payment requests**.

Where these membership details are sent to members whose payments may have not cleared, those members may accidently receive a year's free membership.

These members, however, would be recorded in the system as 'lapsed' and would not be requested to renew the following year. It is likely that this is why some members are not receiving renewal notices.

2. **Reminder notice is sent out one week before renewal, irrespective of whether the renewal is actually 'in progress'.**

    This has led to renewal reminders being sent out to those members whose payments are awaiting clearance. This means that reminders are received by members whose payment will clear, or possibly already has. Those whose payments do not clear will also receive this letter; however, as mentioned above, given that they have already received their membership pack, they will assume it did clear and ignore the renewal.

From receipt of the payment, it takes Finance five days to notify the membership department that payment has cleared, and there is a backlog of cleared notifications awaiting entry to the computer systems. This means renewal reminders may also be sent in error to members whose details have not yet been updated by the membership department.

Members received their card and booklet before payment has cleared and these people will also receive a renewal letter.

The people receiving these un-needed renewal letters may view this as wasteful and inefficient. This may cause the members to leave WET in favour of another charity that they perceive to be more efficient, one that will put their donation to maximum use.

Recommended solutions

Notification to sales and marketing department

Finance should only send notification of a membership renewal to the sales and marketing department after payment has cleared, to ensure only fully paid members receive the membership card and booklet.

Review reminder letter process

Renewal reminders should be only sent to individuals that have not responded to the renewal notice. This can be done by updating the membership system when a payment is received to show that it is being processed. This will reduce wastage and improve customer perceptions of WET.

However, this will involve a change to the computer system and add more work to the already pressurised membership department (there is already a backlog of cleared payments). It will also involve a further handoff between the finance and membership departments which increases the risk of error and further delays.

The problems can also be reduced by employing more staff in the membership department, however, this will increase administration costs.

Handoff reduction

The current system involves many handoffs which increase the time taken to carry out processes as well as increasing the risk of error and cost of the process. Reducing the number of handoffs between departments would improve the process.

One way this could be achieved would be by the finance department entering membership details of cleared payments into the system themselves rather than notifying the membership department that the payment has cleared. However, the finance department would require access to the system, appropriate training and sufficient resource to deal with the backlog.

Bring payment validation forward in the process

Payment validation should be part of the primary activity, rather than a separate activity as it is currently.

Early validation could be achieved by offering the member the option of making their payment online using credit/debit cards. This would eliminate the problem of errors in the details provided, as the details would be immediately validated by the card provider. This would mean that WET would receive the money quicker and would reduce the number of finance requests, therefore also reducing costs and possibly headcount in the finance departments.

To do this the internet site will have to be developed to be capable of taking secure payments. This will involve both initial costs and transaction fees from the provider of the financial solution.

Direct debits

Members should be encouraged to set up direct debits for their membership; an incentive such as a small reduction in annual membership may encourage members to choose this option. Direct debits then allow for automatic renewals to take place which do not require any action from the members. The members would have to opt out of membership rather than opt in as they do under the current process, therefore action is only required if they chose not to renew their membership. This should both improve member retention and reduce administration as those memberships can be quickly and easily processed with no need to send out reminder letters, therefore easing the pressure on the membership department and reducing administrative costs.

In order for this to happen changes will need to be made to the membership computer system.

 STEP 6 **Complete the exam success skills diagnostic**

Finally, use the diagnostic below to assess how effectively you demonstrated the exam success skills in answering the question.

Exam Success Skills	Your reflections/observations
Case scenario: Managing information	Did you extract the key points from the scenario and diagram? In this case, you should have seen that the organisation was a not-for-profit and therefore reference to shareholder wealth and similar concepts would be inappropriate. The fact that the charity was totally dependent on the membership fees to support its operations made the issue of addressing any weaknesses in the membership renewal process of critical importance.
Correct interpretation of requirements	Did you identify that the task requirement consisted of two verbs, 'analyse' and 'recommend'? Did you appreciate the importance of displaying your communication skills?
Answer planning: Priorities, structure and logic	Did you adopt a systematic approach to planning, understanding the task requirements first, then working through the scenario to extract relevant information? Did you stop to consider the diagram provided, in addition to the narrative detail?
Efficient numerical analysis	Not applicable in this question.
Effective writing and presentation	Have you used headings to structure your answer, with short sentences and paragraphs? Are your points made clearly and succinctly?
Time management	Did you allocate sufficient time to attempt both parts of the task?
Most important action points to apply to your next question	

Summary

Answering exam questions is like any other skill – the more you practise the better you will get! But, after attempting a question, make sure you take time to reflect and debrief how well you managed it, whether you followed the key steps and whether you demonstrated professional skills. Carry forward your learning points to the next question you attempt, and over the course of your studies you will see significant improvements.

Chapter 1 Strategy, leadership and culture

Activity 1: Academic Recycling Company

Tackling the question

Lots of information is given to you in the case and many marks can be gained simply by pulling out the relevant points. You can apply the theory in this chapter about differing leadership approaches to identify the changes in style, and why they might have gone wrong.

How to earn the professional skills marks

You are being assessed on your ability to analyse this situation and form an opinion about why things went wrong for Sully. Consequently, it is your ability to investigate and consider various elements that will show how well you understand the problems faced by Sully and his leadership style.

However, don't forget that as well as analysing Sully's leadership style before and after the training course, you also have to explain why the change in style was unsuccessful. For example, as well as the appropriateness of the different styles in relation to the workforce, how did the speed with which Sully tried to make the change affect its effectiveness?

Suggested solution

From: A Consultant

To: Sully Truin

Subject: Analysis of leadership issues at Academic Recycling Company – CONFIDENTIAL

Hi Sully – as discussed, here is my analysis of your changing leadership style and some reasons for the problems that you have been experiencing.

Prior to attending the course

Your original management style was autocratic and focused on tight control. This was because you believed that employees wished to avoid work and responsibility and therefore needed detailed direction and close control. The jobs of the employees therefore increasingly began to consist of simple, repetitive tasks which were carried out in accordance with well-defined procedures. Other matters, even trivial ones, were escalated up to you for you to resolve. The escalation of these simple issues seems to have further reinforced your opinion of the inadequacies of your employees and the need for tight controls in order to ensure their work got done. You were displaying a largely autocratic style of leadership.

After attending the course

The course promoted a more democratic style of leadership which evidently has caused you to question your approach to management. You attempted to implement a style in which subordinates are involved in task planning and where leadership responsibilities are shared.

Why the change of leadership was unsuccessful

There are a number of reasons why the change in your leadership style was not successful. First, the **speed of change** was such that you radically changed your approach overnight. This will have been confusing for employees and will have made it very hard for them to understand what was expected of them under this new approach.

BPP
LEARNING
MEDIA

In addition, the **employees were uncomfortable** with your new style. The original approach was a fairly good match between the leader, the subordinates and the tasks. Employees who had not liked your tough-minded management approach will have previously left the organisation. The **remaining staff are the ones who prefer to have their work clearly specified and tightly controlled**. This style may also have influenced choices when appointing new members of staff, selecting those that will fit in with your views and the culture of the organisation. The views of the staff can be seen in their suggestions that you revert back to the original style.

The original approach would also appear to have been **well suited to the tasks** carried out by the employees for which you have developed a 'tight administration process' and have 'closely defined what needs to be done for each contract and how it should be monitored'. The processes are straightforward, but when quick decisions are required they are escalated up to you. You are experienced in making fast decisions and have sufficient authority to do so. When this decision-making responsibility was moved to subordinates, they felt they **lacked both the experience and the authority**. They therefore consulted colleagues and the decision-making process took much longer.

However, although reverting to the old style might be preferred by the employees, it **does not solve the original problems** faced by you: being heavily relied upon to the point that it is damaging to your health and preventing the company from expanding.

Many theorists have suggested that there is **no one best way of leadership** and that the style which is appropriate in any given context will depend on the nature of the work and the people involved. No management style is likely to fit all situations and the **approach required will vary** at different times depending on business needs. In order to resolve problems or get things done a democratic manager may, at some point, need to adopt an authoritarian approach and vice versa.

I hope this makes sense and is constructive – please contact me should you wish to discuss this further.

Kind regards,

A. Consultant

Activity 2: iCompute

Tackling the question

Using the Cultural Web as a framework is a good approach, as this will help you structure your answer and help you identify the relevant information provided to you in the scenario. Note that although the cultural web has been used in this model answer, the question did not ask for any specific model or framework to be used (as in the real exam). You might, therefore, have taken an alternative approach to answering this question. There are a number of frameworks and perspectives through which the culture of an organisation can be assessed and you will still be awarded marks if you have chosen a different approach.

How to earn the professional skills marks

To score highly you should make sure that, as well as picking out the relevant points via your analysis skills (investigate and consider) you state what effect this is currently having on iCompute and the long-term effect this might have should the behaviour continue.

Suggested solution

The cultural web model can assist in understanding the culture at iCompute as follows.

Stories

Stories circulate between the employees of an organisation and often relate to the history of the organisation and can be very indicative of the issues that exist.

Stories at iCompute revolve around the weakness of the current management which is presented in comparison with the management of the past.

Symbols

Logos, language and terminology, offices, cars and titles used commonly within an organisation are all symbols which give clues towards the culture of an organisation.

At iCompute the main language and symbols are dominated by technology. Possessing gadgets such as the most up-to-date mobile telephone is not only considered to be important but is also seen as a reflection of the individual's technical competence.

Playing computer games is referred to as a typical after-work activity. Combined with the culture of long working hours this could be potentially viewed as divisive.

There appears to be a constant distraction caused by technological objectives and new alternatives seem to cause doubt and delay. This was referred to by one of the managers as a 'state of constant technical paralysis'.

Another manager suggests that customers are viewed as either incompetent or lazy due to their need to make calls to the support team, indicating a need to refocus managers towards customers.

Routines and rituals

Routines and rituals relate to 'the way we do things around here'.

At iCompute, there is a culture of long working hours and male-oriented after-work activities such as playing football and playing computer games. This culture would quickly alienate any member of staff who may prefer to go home to undertake family commitments, or who do not have interest in taking part in such activities.

Such a male-focused culture is likely to contribute to the company's difficulty in recruiting females and also to its high first-year labour turnover. The culture therefore is contributing to the need to incur high recruitment and training costs.

Control systems

In contrast to the technical focus of iCompute, there is a limit to how far technical expertise is rewarded. In order to be promoted, it is necessary for the technical staff to move into management and the evidence given in the scenario suggests that this is not always successful. There is the general view that the managers are technically out of date and any technical work they produce is generally viewed with contempt and quickly replaced.

The management of iCompute have recognised that there is a lack of measurement systems to permit adequate control; however, the recent attempts to introduce a system that would improve time recording has been met with anger from the software developers.

Paradigm and conclusion

When iCompute was first established, it was an entrepreneurial organisation with a strong work ethic focused around innovation and aggressive management. The organisation now appears to have superficially matured, but the analysis of the culture within the organisation would suggest that this is not actually the case.

Managers appear to avoid problems by failing to negotiate with customers, outsourcing problematic functions such as software support, and attempting to gain control by installing formal computer systems.

The culture has directly impacted on the ability of the organisation to attract and retain female staff and has created high levels of staff turnover as only a particular 'type' of employee will be suited to an organisational culture such as this.

In order for iCompute to move forwards and recruit a more balanced and stable workforce, the culture of the organisation must change. The focus must move away from the technology-centric attitudes towards a more business-focused approach.

Chapter 2 Stakeholders and social responsibility

Activity 1: Stakeholders

Tackling the question

The list of possible answers to the question of 'who or what is a stakeholder' is theoretically endless, especially as you are not given much detail in the scenario – however, you can infer plenty from the details that you have been given and develop your answer from there. The mark scheme of 6 + 2 = 8 marks means that you need at least six stakeholders and then their claims need to have been considered fully enough to merit the two professional marks.

How to earn the professional skills marks

Acting with commercial acumen requires you to demonstrate an awareness of wider external factors and to act with perception and insight into a situation. Some of the stakeholders here are obvious (employees, suppliers, customers etc) while others (such as involuntary stakeholders from the natural world) may not be quite so obvious. Coupled with the need to identify stakeholder claims as well, this is not an easy task but could be asked for in virtually any situation.

Suggested solution

The list of stakeholders is likely to include the following (with their claims in brackets)

- **Shareholders** who require a return on their investment – (this is a direct claim because they are in contact with the organisation already)

- **Lenders** who require their loans to be serviced in full and on time (also direct)

- **Customers** who require good quality projects to be completed (also direct)

- **Suppliers** who require being paid on time (also direct)

- **Employees** who require good working conditions and being paid on time (also direct)

- **The general public** who require no adverse effects from the organisation and its projects (such as safe housing, reliable infrastructure)(direct/indirect)

- **The government** which requires tax to be paid on corporate profits and other expenses, plus the ideal of maximising employment levels in the economy (probably also direct)

- **Professional bodies** which require the organisation's accreditation process to be robust to maintain their reputation (also direct)

- **Flora and fauna** whose natural environment is affected by civil engineering projects being built – (they require a clean, unspoilt environment to live in, but their claims are indirect because they did not ask to be affected by the organisation's projects)

- **People living near a construction project** (whether housing or some other kind) who require a quiet, clean and safe environment in which to live but who may be adversely affected by either the construction process or the finished asset (again, likely to be indirect)

Activity 2: Goaway Hotels

Tackling the question

Remember that we are talking about one specific decision so we need to focus on that decision and how each of the identified stakeholders will affect the process of changing terms and conditions.

How to earn the professional skills marks

Assessing means using professional judgement when considering issues. In this case, you will show that judgement by carefully considering the different stakeholders and the potential impact of the hotel's decisions on them.

Suggested solution

Taking each stakeholder in turn:

The board of directors – need to be kept informed about the decision to change working conditions

Power: Low, surprisingly perhaps. However, the new employment legislation appears to limit significantly directors' freedom to reduce labour costs by changing contractual terms. The directors also have little say over the decision of shareholders to sell shares. (This demonstrates that you cannot take anyone's role for granted.)

Level of interest: High, as this is a major decision, integral to the directors' plans for the future of the Goaway hotel chain. It may also have a significant effect on their remuneration.

Shareholders – they need to be kept satisfied due to their role in any decisions taken

Power: High, because the shareholders are currently in a position to sell their shares if they feel that they have received a good offer. If they do, unions and employees may find that the international company is able to take a much tougher approach.

Level of interest: Low, as none of them participates actively in Goaway's decision making. Their main concern is whether to continue to take dividends or realise a capital gain from their investment.

Trade unions – they are key players and will need to be managed closely when the decision is made

Power: High. This is because they have the economic power to take legal action to prevent Goaway from changing their members' employment terms.

Level of interest: High. This is because they wish to protect their members.

Migrant workers – minimal effort should be deployed as they do not have much effect on the decision

Power: Low. This is because replacement workers can be recruited easily from the home country.

Level of interest: Low. The migrant workers seem quite happy with their current employment terms, even though these are not as favourable as the home country's workers.

Each stakeholder group would be plotted on Mendelow's matrix as follows:

Level of interest

	Low	High
Power **Low**	A Migrant workers	B Directors
High	C Shareholders	D Trade unions

Activity 3: Corporate social responsibility

Tackling the question

Balance is the key to answering this question as the slide requires both viewpoints to help inform the board. You would probably need at least three points on each side to have a good chance of scoring the marks on offer here.

How to earn the professional skills marks

Inform means to communicate concisely, objectively and unambiguously, using appropriate media. It is essential that you use the slide format as requested, but do not overload your slides with too much detail. The detail should be contained within the presenter's notes.

Suggested solution

The slide could look like this:

Business case for CSR	Business case against CSR
• Builds reputation	• Does not support shareholders
• Attracts investors/employees/customers	• Cost vs benefit?
• Competitive advantage	• Time-consuming
• Branding	• Credible?
• Unregulated	

Presenter's notes

For

- Reputation (eg focusing on health and safety for employees pre-empts the need for legislation to be imposed by outside regulators)

- Attraction of individuals or organisations who support good CSR and see the company as being a good place to work

- CSR can create competitive advantage (especially as the wider construction industry has a reputation for poor health and safety)

- Can tie into our branding to reinforce 'responsible' credentials

- Unregulated = easy to incorporate (because there's no 'wrong' answer, so you will always be right whatever you do)

Against

- Organisations are responsible to shareholders ∴ CSR is 'stealing' their funds

- Benefits do not outweigh costs (no tangible evidence to support CSR)

- Time-consuming to implement across a business

- Seen as PR only (most stakeholders in construction will think it's only done for this reason) so is it going to be seen as credible or merely cynical?

Activity 4: CSR and tax

Tackling the question

This solution has been framed around the Gray, Owen and Adams model but any similar approach could have been used as long as four different perspectives were adopted. For example, taking Carroll's model – GSA could have considered the following responses:

- **Economic** – why pay more tax if it reduces our profits (regardless of what the law says)? Note that this perspective ignores the law, a position that most organisations cannot take.

- **Legal** – why pay more taxes if the law says we have paid enough already? We already pay more than we want to because we want to obey the law.

- **Ethical** – maybe we should acknowledge that paying more corporate tax than we need to is the right thing to do and presents a view of us being more socially responsible.

- **Philanthropic** – we will rearrange our tax strategy to pay what we think is right and start to fill in some of the social and economic gaps left behind by government policy via targeted donations and other benevolent initiatives.

How to earn the professional skills marks

Part of demonstrating commercial acumen is the ability to show insight and perception in understanding work-related and organisational issues, including the management of conflict, demonstrating acumen in arriving at appropriate solutions or outcomes. This is a classic example of such a conflict where there is probably no right answer – however, the depth of your analysis is what you are being asked to show here, along with good awareness of the external factors the company must deal with.

Suggested solution

Taking Gray, Owen and Adams as an example, GSA could reach a number of different perspectives regarding the decision to pay more tax on a voluntary basis.

- **Pristine capitalist** – the company should not pay any more tax than is legally due as that would erode shareholder wealth.

- **Expedient** – the company could pay tax to present the impression that it wishes to empathise with its customers, thus reducing the threat of further adverse reputational damage and sales boycotts (it may even attempt to calculate the point at which marginal extra tax paid equals marginal sales restored).

- **Social contract** – the company should pay a fair amount of tax as society expects it to play its part.

- **Social ecologist** – all companies should pay as much tax as possible in order to support society and those who need assistance.

- **Socialist** – the company should definitely pay more tax just like the workforce has to (employing expensive tax advisors that employees cannot afford is unfair).

- **Radical feminist** – the company should pay tax in order to empathise with society and the pain it feels from punitive taxation.

- **Deep ecologist** – the company should donate money to an environmental pressure group (eg Greenpeace) and consider whether it is operating with enough of a social and environmental mandate to continue trading (as a pharmaceutical company, this is debatable).

Chapter 3 Impact of corporate governance on strategy

Activity 1: Rules for corporate governance

Tackling the question

The key to any set of briefing notes is to try and consider as many of the alternatives as possible so the person you are briefing is as prepared as they can be for their meeting. The marks scheme is suggesting six marks so to maintain balance you would have needed to consider at least three points for each side to score well here.

How to earn the professional skills marks

Communication skills are critical for this exam and to earn these marks your answer needs to show that you can clarify the points you are making in a way that simplifies complex issues and can be easily understood.

Suggested solution

The benefits of having international codes of corporate governance include the following.

(a) It provides a standardised approach which helps multi-national companies to enforce consistent codes across their operations.

(b) It gives investors the understanding and therefore confidence to invest in global capital markets.

(c) It makes it easier for countries to implement corporate governance codes since they are not having to produce their own codes from scratch.

(d) It ensures a minimum level of corporate governance.

However, a number of problems have been identified with international codes of corporate governance.

(a) International principles represent a lowest common denominator of general, fairly banal and meaningless principles.

(b) Any attempt to strengthen the principles will be extremely difficult because of global differences in legal structures, financial systems and structures of corporate ownership, cultural and other economic factors.

(c) As international guidance has to be based on best practice in a number of regimes, development will always lag behind changes in the most advanced regimes, who will always feel theirs is the best one to start with.

(d) The codes will have no legislative power if they differ from local laws and regulations.

Activity 2: Chair and chief executive

Tackling the question

Clearly there are more points here than you might expect to see in a traditional set of FAQs – however, there are a number of angles that you could have taken. Take the USA for example where the role of Executive Chair is more commonplace than in the UK: you could have explained this in your answer to try and show balance.

How to earn the professional skills marks

Commercial acumen skills require you to demonstrate judgement in identifying the key points as to why these two roles are best kept separate. However, as the previous points explain, should you have concluded that these roles could easily be combined, professional skills marks would still be awarded if you drafted the solutions to your FAQs in line with what's most appropriate for the organisation and prioritising the key points.

Suggested solution

Frequently asked questions

Separating the roles of Chair and Chief Executive (CEO)

Separating the roles ensures that there is not a single individual with unfettered power. The principle that the roles should be separated was established following the frauds carried out by Robert Maxwell at Mirror Group Newspapers in the early 1990s.

The CEO can then run the company, while the chair can run the board. Separation of the roles allows them both to be given suitable focus. The chair should be looking to the interests of the shareholders; the CEO is concerned with implementing the board's strategy.

It reflects the reality that both jobs are demanding roles. In particular in large companies (eg FTSE100 companies) it would be too demanding for one person to carry out both functions.

Having two different people in the role brings two different perspectives, two sets of experience and skills and therefore improves decision making.

The separation of roles avoids the risk of conflicts of interest. The CEO's remuneration will contain performance-related bonuses. They may be inclined to take unacceptable risks to make sure that they earn their bonus.

Accountability to shareholders

The board cannot make the CEO truly accountable for management if it is led by the CEO.

Separation of the roles means that the board is more able to express its concerns effectively by providing a joint channel of reporting (the chair) for the non-executive directors.

Note. The UK Corporate Governance Code (2018) suggests that the CEO should not go on to become chair of the same company. If a CEO did become chair, the main risk is that they will interfere in matters that are the responsibility of the new CEO and thus exercise undue influence over them.

Activity 3: Non-executive directors

Tackling the question

Starting with the marks scheme, eight marks are awarded here for a task with three components – what should the split of marks be in this case? There are probably more advantages than disadvantages (hence the reason for the widespread use of NEDs!) so you should be favouring these in your answer: assuming one mark for each point, you could go with four advantages, two disadvantages and two ways of overcoming these and this would nicely provide the eight marks on offer.

How to earn the professional skills marks

The professional skill in this activity is commercial acumen, specifically using judgement in identifying key issues and demonstrating how to resolve problems by recommending suitable solutions. Provided that your answer covers all this, you should score well.

Suggested solution

The main **advantages** of bringing NEDs onto our board are as follows:

- They bring external expertise and experience, which helps the board view matters from a much wider perspective

- NEDs bring an independent and objective view, without being clouded by ego or reward

- NEDs demonstrate compliance with virtually all corporate governance codes throughout the world

- The use of NEDs will provide assurance to, and confidence for, our many stakeholders (such as lenders, suppliers, regulators, employees)

BPP
LEARNING
MEDIA

The key **disadvantages** with NEDs tend to centre around two issues:

- Lack of independence – this comes from a variety of factors: as their length of service increases, they become more closely aligned with an organisation; this is exacerbated by cross-directorships (NEDs sharing executive and NED roles across two different companies); reward schemes can create conflicts of interest too (such as inflated pay or the inappropriate use of share options)

- Lack of effectiveness – this comes from not having the right calibre (either in terms of quality or experience – unfortunately, the organisations that most need NEDs are unlikely to be able to offer the same lucrative remuneration as other organisations that need them far less) or having insufficient numbers of NEDs (or those without enough authority to make a difference).

How to **overcome** these disadvantages:

- Independence issues could be addressed by offering service contracts that stick to best practice in terms of length of service

- Full disclosure of NEDs and their remuneration helps to reduce conflicts of interest appearing 'under the radar'

- Training and induction to the organisation will help with effectiveness issues

- Market rates of pay can help with both independence (making them reasonable) and effectiveness (attracting the right calibre)

Activity 4: Remuneration packages

Tackling the question

There are nine marks on offer for explaining the six separate elements of a remuneration package – to score one and a half marks in each case, you will not only need to explain each component but also illustrate something about the role that is played by human nature (allied to the professional skills marks).

How to earn the professional skills marks

Commercial acumen marks are awarded here for displaying perception of, and insight into, a work-related issue, specifically one which manages personal conflicts of interest.

Suggested solution

Basic salary will be in accordance with the terms of each director's contract of employment, and is not related to the performance of the company or the director. Instead it is determined by the experience of the director and what other companies might be prepared to pay (the market rate). There are elements of both recruitment and retention when agreeing a basic salary – however, it is unlikely to be the only part of an executive's remuneration (see next point).

Performance-related pay (often as a cash bonus) is paid for good performance (usually hitting a specific financial target). To guard against excessive payouts, some companies impose limits on bonus plans as a fixed percentage of salary or pay. Transaction bonuses tend to be much more controversial. Some chief executives get bonuses for acquisitions, regardless of subsequent performance, possibly indeed further bonuses for spinning off acquisitions that have not worked out.

Basic and bonus are often the majority of an executive director's remuneration package, but the proportion each makes up of the whole package needs to tread a fine line:

- Too much basic and not enough bonus means the director is unlikely to try that hard – where's the incentive?

- Too much bonus and not enough basic however could lead to excessive risk-taking by the director so should be set at an ambitious but not dangerous level.

Benefits could include transport, such as a company car, health insurance provision, life assurance, holidays, expenses and loans. The remuneration committee should consider the benefit to the director and the cost to the company of the complete package. Also the committee should consider how the directors' package relates to the package for employees; ideally perhaps the package offered to the directors should be an extension of the package applied to the employees.

Pensions Many companies may pay pension contributions for directors and staff. In some cases, however, there may be separate schemes available for directors at higher rates than for employees. The UK Corporate Governance Code (2018) states that, as a general rule, only basic salary should be pensionable. The Code emphasises that the remuneration committee should consider the pension consequences and associated costs to the company of basic salary increases and any other changes in pensionable remuneration, especially for directors close to retirement.

Directors may be awarded **shares** in the company (aligning their interests with those of shareholders) with time limits on when they can be sold in return for good performance: to encourage long-term performance improvement, it is expected to be a number of years before shares can be sold. Some shareholders may acquire a speculative shareholding simply to earn a short-term gain, which is perceived to go against corporate strategy best practice, so setting time limits reduces the risk of this occurring.

Share options give directors the right to purchase shares at a specified exercise price over a specified time period in the future. If the price of the shares rises so that it exceeds the exercise price by the time the options can be exercised, the directors will be able to purchase shares at lower than their market value – this also aligns directors' and shareholders' interests to focus on longer-term performance. [The UK Corporate Governance Code (2018) states that non-executive directors' remuneration should not include share options or other performance-related elements, as this may impact upon their independence.]

Chapter 4 The external environment

Activity 1: Organic fruit farm

Tackling the question

Although in the exam you would be expected to present your answer to a requirement like this, we have used a 'two-column' format here to emphasis the 'analysis' element of the answer.

Analysis involves investigating relevant information, and then **reflecting on its implications**.

So, in this activity, you first need to identify (from the scenario) the factors which could affect the farm, and then consider **how** they affect it, and **what their impact could be**.

Remember, the way external factors affect an organisation is by presenting opportunities or threats. So, you need to think how any of the factors in the scenario could present an opportunity or a threat to the farm (and what that opportunity or threat is).

The 'two-column' approach we have used as a template provides a structure in which to do this:

- Identifying the factors (in the left-hand column); and then
- Considering their impact (in the right-hand column).

How to earn the professional skills marks

In effect, the analysis in the right-hand column explains **how** or **why** the factors in the left-hand column will affect the farm. These points – explaining 'how' or 'why' – are the ones which will help you to score the **professional skills marks** available, because they demonstrate that you have considered the information available, and reflected on its implications for the organisation in the scenario.

BPP
LEARNING
MEDIA

Suggested solution

Environmental factor	Impact of the factors
Social – consumers' attitudes to organic food are changing because of concerns about health and the environment. Organic food is perceived as more socially responsible than non-organic alternatives. [**Note.** You could also have included these points in relation to the **'Environmental/Ecological'** aspect of the PESTEL model – because a key factor in the growth of the organic farming industry has been the drive for more environmentally friendly products.]	These changing consumer attitudes will increase industry demand from organic farms. However, farmers' accountability – and compliance with organic certification – is necessary to maintain consumer confidence in buying organic produce.
Technological – the industry needs to use technology (such as sophisticated weather management systems and atmospherically controlled tunnels) to avoid using fertilisers and pesticides.	Technological developments will increase yields, and also reduce problems of seasonality and perishability by extending the life of the product through storage. This will benefit farmers' cash flows. Further technological advances may enable the industry to reduce costs further in future. If the price of organic produce can also be reduced, this could make the products accessible to more consumers. (At the moment, organic products are typically more expensive than non-organic ones.)
Legal (regulatory) – there is significant regulation in the food industry generally, and particularly in relation to organic produce. Organic farms need to obtain the relevant certification before they can start selling produce as organic; and then they need to comply with all the appropriate regulations regarding production, packaging and labelling.	There are severe sanctions for breaching regulations. As a result, compliance is very important, and the associated costs of compliance are likely to be high. Any changes in regulations or standards in the future could lead to additional compliance costs. However, the existence of strict regulations should help to ensure consumer confidence in the industry.

Activity 2: Happy Days theme parks

Tackling the question

Although the requirement doesn't specifically mention Porter's five forces, the fact that you are asked to analyse the industry and to investigate the impact of environmental forces on 'the profitability of the industry' should have been clear indicators that the five forces was the most appropriate framework to use here.

A sensible approach to the question would be to use each force as a heading and then think how the information provided in the scenario could affect each force.

How to earn the professional skills marks

Once you have identified the factors in the scenario that could affect each force, you need to think about the impact they have on the industry and its profitability.

For example, the scenario tells us that 'significant capital and technology [are] required to develop … new rides.' But what is the significance of that? The capital and technology requirements are barriers to entry, and so reduce the threat of new entrants.

Identifying relevant points in the scenario (such as capital and technology requirements) can help you earn technical marks, but to earn the professional marks, you need to identify the implications of the information in the scenario. How do the factors affect the strength of the forces, and therefore in turn how do they affect the level of profit which can be sustained in the industry?

Suggested solution

Threat of new entrants – Low

The barriers to entry to the theme park industry in Western Europe are high due to difficulty and cost of acquiring sites, and the high capital cost of building rides.

The maturity of the market, and strong market position (and brand name) of the existing multi-national entertainment corporations will also act as a barrier to potential entrants.

In the short term, the economic climate may also act as a barrier to entry since consumer spending is falling, making potential parks less profitable.

Competitive rivalry – High

The mature market in Western Europe means competition is intense, and opportunities for growth are limited. Companies have to spend large amounts of money maintaining state-of-the-art rides in order to attract, and retain, customers.

The current economic climate means competition will be intensified further, as parks try to attract customers against a backdrop of reduced consumer spending.

The multinational operators are likely to be better placed to withstand competition than smaller, local parks because they have access to greater resources. This might lead to multinational operators acquiring regional or local parks. However, industry consolidation in this way is likely to increase competitive rivalry even more.

Threat of substitutes – High

There is a wide variety of other tourist attractions, cultural and entertainment offerings, all competing for a share of household leisure spend. Therefore the threat of substitutes, offering an alternative 'day out', is quite high.

However there is an element of thrill/risk associated with theme parks which may mean these other leisure pursuits are not perfect substitutes.

Bargaining power of consumers – Relatively high

As well as having a choice between visiting a theme park or a substitute 'day out', customers also have a choice of different theme parks to attend.

Therefore, although individual consumers will have little bargaining power, consumers collectively are likely to have a relatively high degree of power. This is reflected in the fact that 'price' is seen as one of the key success factors for a park.

Conclusion

The competitive forces suggest that the theme park industry in Western Europe is fiercely competitive, which is likely to restrict the level of profit it can sustain in the long run.

BPP
LEARNING
MEDIA

Activity 3: Scenario plans

Tackling the question

Note that the requirement isn't asking about the process NESTA should go through to produce a scenario plan, but rather how it might use the scenarios as part of the decision-making process around whether or not to expand into Eurobia.

Exhibit 1 suggests a number of areas of uncertainty, which should have been a clue that NESTA could use scenarios to think about how different outcomes from these uncertainties could affect its decision.

How to earn the professional skills marks

The underlying issue NESTA's managers are trying to resolve is how attractive is the market in Eurobia for them to enter. Simply telling them how to construct a scenario plan, or the stages involved in doing so, will not provide them with any insight into Eurobia's attractiveness.

By contrast, exploring how key elements of the market might change in future could have much more practical benefit to them. As such, to score the professional skills marks, you need to focus on the areas of uncertainty, and how these could be used in the scenarios, rather than simply describing the process of scenario planning in general terms.

Suggested solution:

Scenarios help managers to envisage alternative futures in highly uncertain business environments.

A scenario is a detailed and consistent view of how the business environment of an organisation might develop in the future. Scenarios are built with reference to key influences and change drivers in the environment. They inevitably deal with conditions of high uncertainty, so they are not forecasts: instead, they are internally consistent views of potential future conditions.

For the scenarios to be most use, the influencing factors should be:

- Limited to a few significant ones

- Largely out of the control of the organisation. Macroeconomic forces are usually outside the control of the organisation and it can only react to, not influence, them.

Factors which could be used to develop scenarios in NESTA could be:

- **Change to the economic climate**. The success of the dollar shops seems to have been built on the economic recession being experienced in Eurobia. An improvement in the economy may lead to a loss of customers, as branded products and more upmarket suppliers are sought out. Scenarios should be prepared for the economic situation improving, declining and remaining constant.

- **Competitor response**. It is not easy to predict how the existing competitors will react to NESTA's entry to the marketplace. Therefore, scenarios should consider the possibility of an aggressive response, a muted response and no response.

- **Conventional supermarket approach**. The conventional supermarkets have not currently adopted a fixed-price discount approach. However, they may decide to establish outlet style stores to allow them to do so. They could also acquire one of the established dollar stores (competitors) and enter the market this way.

- **Internet shopping**. Many customers are now choosing to shop online rather than visit physical shops and the effect of this has been significant in many areas of retail. The implications of this trend could be considered within the scenarios.

These factors would then be combined into scenarios. The attractiveness of the Eurobia market would then be assessed for each scenario along with tactics for entering the market under those circumstances.

Chapter 5 Strategic capability

Activity 1: Carriages

Tackling the question

To produce a good answer you need to present your work in accordance with the instructions set out in the question detail. In this case you are told that you are 'keen to impress the client's management team and want to make your slide interesting and attention grabbing'. The need to only produce the one slide and supporting notes, coupled with the limited number of marks indicate that lots of detail is not required, the mention of 'attention grabbing' should be a clue that the inclusion of a diagram would be appropriate if it helps you to answer the question. In this case using the detail from the exhibit to plot out the main points on the value chain diagram would be a good approach to follow as you can then use this to construct some brief notes to support your answer; this is the approach used in the suggested solution.

How to earn the professional skills marks.

As the 'inform' skill is a communication skill, you need to ensure that you express yourself in a clear and concise manner using the appropriate medium. In this case as you are instructed to prepare one slide to be used in a presentation with some supporting notes it is important that you do not provide too much detail. As the requirement asked for the inclusion of supporting notes it was important that you included these.

Suggested solution

Slide: Value-adding activities at Carriages restaurant

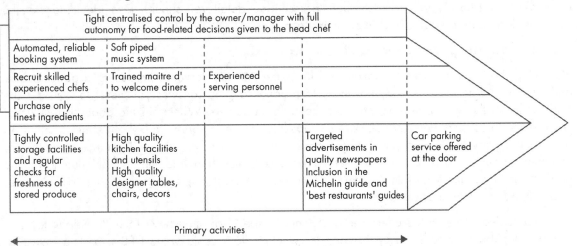

Primary activities

Supporting notes:

Value adding activities

Firm infrastructure is characterised by the tight control which Carriages owner has over the business. This is evident as all hiring decisions are decided by the owner. This level of control is crucial in ensuring only the very best staff are employed. The autonomy provided to the Head Chef is key in ensuring that only best ingredients are purchased and most creative dishes made.

Inbound logistics are characterised by the role that the reliable automated booking system plays, as in this sense diners are viewed as an input into the restaurant. The skills provided by appointing only experienced chefs adds value as only the highest quality dishes are prepared. The focus on only ordering the finest ingredients, supported by regular freshness checks help to add value as all food served is guaranteed to be as fresh as possible.

Operations relate to the running of the kitchen, and the restaurant environment which diners are exposed to such as the service provided by the large numbers of attentive waiting staff and the ambience created by the use of classical music. These activities help to create an enjoyable dining experience.

Outbound logistics at Carriages relate to the physical delivery of dishes from the kitchen to the diners. The use of experienced waiting staff helps to create a sense of occasion while at the restaurant.

Marketing and sales activities help to reinforce the quality of the experience. Inclusion in the Michelin guide over the last 20 years has helped to distinguish the dining experience at Carriages from a standard restaurant. This ultimately adds value to the diners.

Service activities in this case relate to the activity of parking the diner's cars and then retrieving them at the end of the meal. This helps to support the entire dining experience, and crucially is something which cannot be matched by other local restaurants.

Activity 2: DRB Electronic Services

Tackling the question

It is important to note that the question did not specify the use of a particular model when answering the question. As the requirement asked you to 'analyse the activities of DRB' this should have given you a sufficient hint that Porter's value chain was an appropriate model to use.

A good approach to use when structuring your answer was to use the main sections from the model as headings around which you could build your answer. To produce a good answer it was absolutely essential that you used the detail provided in the Exhibit to highlight the key activities undertaken by DRB. As you read through the scenario detail you should have identified that the activities described all related to DRB's primary activities.

How to earn the professional skills marks

Identifying the key activities undertaken by DRB is the first step towards producing a good answer and earning the technical marks, however, to produce a great answer you need to consider the significance of these activities and the value they offer customers. When thinking about 'significance' you needed to consider whether each activity was likely to be important to DRB in terms of achieving a competitive advantage. Is re-packaging a product without modifying the performance of a piece of equipment going to give DRB's customers a better product than had they simply purchased the product directly from SK Co? In this case the answer is clearly no, such activity therefore provides DRB with no competitive advantage.

When considering the 'value offered to customers' aspect you may have found it helpful to have taken a step back from the detail to consider whether you would value DRB's existing activities. Would you be more or less inclined to purchase from DRB as a result of the activities they undertake?

Breaking the requirement down in this manner will help you to earn those valuable professional skills marks.

Suggested solution

Inbound logistics

Inbound logistics at DRB consist of handling and storing fully configured inbound equipment imported from SK. Once the equipment arrives DRB staff conduct quality inspections to ensure that they are fit for purpose prior to being re-branded. Ensuring that equipment received passes the quality assurance inspection is a critical activity for DRB. Quality assurance is essential for pre-configured equipment where customers have high expectations of reliability. In turn high quality reduces **service costs**, and contributes to **customer satisfaction**.

Operations

The process of re-branding and re-packaging the products form the main part of DRB's operations activities. The process of storing the re-branded equipment for resale and returning those products which failed the inspection would also constitute operations activities. Given that DRB does not enhance the features of the imported equipment it can be argued that the process of re-branding and re-packaging does **not add any value to the customer**. Re-branding and re-packaging will not enhance the performance of the equipment once in use by customers. Furthermore, these activities are being undertaken **in a relatively high-cost country**, despite the fact that they add little value.

Outbound logistics

Domestic customers collect their products from DRB, whereas business customers generally prefer DRB to deliver and install the equipment on their behalf. Customer feedback indicates that the installation **service is particularly valued by customers**. However, DRB's market is segmented into domestic and business customers, and the installation service only applies to the smaller (business) market. Nonetheless, most of DRB's larger competitors cannot offer an equivalent service so this is currently a **source of competitive advantage** for DRB. However, if DRB increases the amount it supplies outside its home region then it is likely this **level of service will be uneconomic to maintain**.

Marketing and sales

DRB's marketing and sales activities consist of advertising its products in local and regional newspapers. This is supplemented by a website which enables potential customers to enquire about the availability of products via an email facility. At present sales and marketing are currently only minor activities at DRB. They **will have to be developed** if the company is to achieve its growth targets. Furthermore, the **limited functionality of the website** offers very little value to customers or potential customers.

Service

The provision of on-site technical support and a 'back-to-base' facility for customers with equipment out of warranty are service activities. Customer feedback indicates that after-sales **service is particularly valued by customers**. Most of DRB's large competitors only offer an impersonal, off-shore call centre service, so DRB's personal service is currently a **source of competitive advantage**. However, if DRB increases the geographic area which it supplies then it is likely this level of service will be **uneconomic to maintain**.

Activity 3: The Marlow Fashion Group

Tackling the question

When attempting this question it was important that you recognised that you were not asked to provide a full SWOT analysis on the operations of the Marlow Fashion Group. Including an assessment of the external opportunities and threats facing the group would earn you no credit and only waste your time if you were attempting this requirement under exam conditions. To produce a good answer it was important to remember that strengths and weaknesses are internal factors. Note also the requirement is to identify and explain; so for each strength or weakness you identify you must explain its strategic significance.

How to earn the professional skills marks

The professional skills marks available in this question tested your communication skills, and specifically your ability to inform. In order to illustrate your communication skills you need to be able to express yourself clearly and convincingly using an appropriate medium while being sensitive to the needs of the intended audience. To earn these marks it was important that you presented your answer in the required format, ie laid out as a report headed up in the correct report style including

BPP
LEARNING
MEDIA

the use of section headings in the body of your answer. As a short report was requested it was important not to provide too much detail.

Adopting an appropriate tone was also very important as this work was being undertake as part of a professional engagement. You should have also noted that at the current time Susan Grant has not yet decided whether to join the Marlow Fashion Group as a director; as a result it is highly likely that the assessment you provide will be used by her in making her decision. Therefore, producing an informative and well-reasoned account of the strengths and weaknesses identified was crucial.

Suggested solution

To: Susan Grant
From: A consultant

Strategic strengths and weaknesses in Marlow Fashion Group

This report looks at the strengths which are helping Marlow Fashion Group (Marlow) achieve its commercial success, and the weakness that are hindering it. It is also important to note that features of a company that have historically been **strengths can shift to become weaknesses as the competitive environment changes** over time, meaning that the company needs a strategic turnaround in order to survive. This appears to be the case with Marlow.

Strengths

Market position and reputation. Marlow has successfully developed a niche market for its products, based around traditional style and elegance. This enabled it to expand successfully, and developed Marlow as a worldwide brand with a reputation for design excellence and quality.

Premium prices. Marlow's reputation for quality has enabled it to charge premium prices for its clothes. The ability to sustain a high price premium is important in retaining the profitability of the company.

Supplier relationships. Marlow has built up a strong relationship with its suppliers. This relationship with the suppliers is important in maintaining the quality of the clothes produced, and so has facilitated the brand's reputation and global expansion of the group.

Loyal network of franchise partners. Marlow has created a strong family atmosphere among its network of retail partners around the world. As with the strong supplier relationships, this network has also helped facilitate the global expansion of the group.

Weaknesses

Outdated business model. The business model which has served Marlow well in the past is no longer appropriate to the fashion world in which they are now competing.

Lack of outsourcing, and high cost base. The competitive environment in which Marlow operates is becoming increasingly competitive. Therefore clothing retailers are increasingly looking to outsource the manufacture of their clothes. However, the approach pursued by Marlow prevents this, and means that the company's **cost base is higher** than it should be, because the company is failing to benefit from any economies of scale which outsourced providers enjoy. Consequently, Marlow's costs are also likely to be higher than its competitors, reducing its profitability.

Unclear strategy. One of Marlow's strengths was the niche position and brand reputation it established for itself. However, the changes in its environment have now led to some uncertainty as to whether Marlow Fashion is a brand, a manufacturer, a retailer or an integrated fashion company. It is likely that to be successful in the future, Marlow will need to **identify its core competences** and focus only on its core activities.

Outdated styles. Women's tastes in clothing have also changed and Marlow's emphasis on soft, feminine styles has become outdated. Consequently, demand for the clothes they sell has declined, and this has prompted a **significant fall in Marlow's sales and profits**.

Narrow product range. Although Marlow produces a comprehensive range of women's clothing, it is all built round the theme of traditional style and elegance. This means that Marlow's products are **over-concentrated** in one style, and therefore extremely vulnerable to a fall in demand as styles change.

Resistance to change. The tight control which Rodney and Betty Marlow exerted over product design has **prevented recognition of the changes in consumer tastes**, meaning the company has continued to produce the type of designs that served it well in the past, rather than the designs which consumers now want.

This resistance to change can also be seen in the management team's reluctance to accept that the significant fall in sales and profits reflects the shift in demand for women's clothing.

Lack of awareness of competitive environment. It is possible that the failure to adapt product design and manufacturing processes to keep pace with current trends may be as much due to Rodney and Betty Marlow not being aware of the current trends as them resisting change. Either way, the failure to produce clothes which current tastes demand is causing a significant fall in sales.

Rapid turnover of CEOs. Marlow has had a new Chief Executive Officer every year. A succession of CEOs of this nature is indicative of a company which is performing poorly – with each new CEO being brought in to try to turn around its fortunes.

Conclusion

The changes in the market for women's wear have caused Marlow to move from a strategically sound position to one where it now needs a swift strategic turnaround. Its products and markets have changed, and its value chain no longer delivers any distinctive value to its customers. These issues need addressing urgently to try to reverse the decline in the company's sales and profitability.

Chapter 6 Competitive advantage and strategic choice

Activity 1: Shoal plc

Tackling the question

Although the requirement does not specifically mention the BCG matrix, the fact that you are asked to 'analyse the position of the three companies in Shoal plc's portfolio' provided a hint that you needed to use the matrix when formulating your answer. The inclusion of the sales turnover figures in respect of the whole market and for each company was a clue that you needed to determine each company's relative market share and the level of market growth, both of which are the axes on the BCG matrix.

How to earn the professional skills marks

To demonstrate your 'judgement' skills you needed to ensure that you only focused on the key points in your presentation slide. Being able to prioritise the key issues in this case related to simply stating the position and recommended actions that the Shoal plc board take. Including lots of detail on the presentation slide would not be appropriate as this is intended to be a visual aid to back up the detailed analysis contained in the supporting notes. Furthermore, it was important that the recommended actions that you included in your slide could in fact be implemented in reality by the board at Shoal plc. This is particularly important especially as the firm for which you work has been specifically appointed by Shoal plc to provide them with professional management consultancy advice.

BPP
LEARNING
MEDIA

Suggested solution

Slide: Position and contribution

Position:	Action:
ShoalFish – Dog	Potentially retain or lease out
ShoalPro – Cash Cow	Retain
ShoalFarm – Question Mark	Invest/divest

Notes

ShoalFish

Using the BCG matrix, in 20X2 ShoalFish has the characteristics of a dog. It has a small (11.3%) market share and the market itself is declining (5% over two years). However, despite being an apparent dog, disposing of the company may not be in Shoal plc's interest as it perceives there are synergies between ShoalFish and the other companies in the Shoal plc portfolio; it provides 40% of the fish used by ShoalPro, and it could directly supply the Captain Haddock restaurants post-acquisition, therefore keeping the cost of raw materials down.

Shoal Plc must determine whether it can tolerate the declining performance of ShoalFish for the sake of the supply chain to the other companies in the group. If this is not feasible, a possible alternative may be to lease or sell their boats to individual owners with the guarantee of sales to Shoal plc companies. Given that owner-skippered boats account for almost half of the boats in the western oceans the leasing option could be a viable alternative.

ShoalPro

ShoalPro is a mature organisation that is still expanding (market growth of +2% from 20X0 to 20X2). It has a market share of just over 40% and so is likely to be the market leader. Although a significant percentage of its fish is provided by ShoalFish it is increasingly processing fish for other companies.

These characteristics (high relative market share; slow growth) in the BCG matrix suggest ShoalPro is a cash cow. ShoalPro is a key part of Shoal plc and should be retained and maintained.

ShoalFarm

ShoalFarm is a fairly recent addition to the Shoal plc group and has a low market share (9.3%) of a growing market. ShoalFarm is growing at a slower rate (+12% from 20X0 to 20X2) than the market as a whole (+20% over same period). ShoalFarm has the potential to be a significant provider to both ShoalPro and the Captain Haddock restaurants, and could replace fish supplies from ShoalFish if the latter continues to decline.

ShoalFarm could be classified as a question mark in the BCG matrix as it requires further investment to allow it to become a key player in a significant market place. If Shoal plc is happy to provide this investment, then ShoalFarm should be expanded and developed. If it does not wish to take this risk, then it may be better to divest itself of this company.

The three companies are closely linked in the value chain, however there are conflicting forces that both reduce the dependency between the companies and encourage the synergies of a vertically integrated group. The proposed acquisition of Captain Haddock could lead to additional synergies, but only if the correct relationships are set up between the companies.

Activity 2: Elite Fabrics

Tackling the question

As we have seen before in other activity questions the requirement here did not mention the use of any particular model(s); as a result it was perfectly acceptable to adopt a free-form approach when structuring your answer. You needed to read the requirement carefully as this was made up of two separate parts. Firstly, you needed to 'evaluate' the consequences of the proposed move into retailing, and secondly to 'assess' the change in competences required by the expanded business. Failure to fully read the requirement increased the likelihood that you would produce a solution which only answers part of the question. Clearly, in order to determine the consequences of the proposal and the required change in EF's competences you would have needed to draw upon your knowledge of strategic capability. This was covered in Chapter 5.

How to earn the professional skills marks

In order to earn the 'assess' skills marks you needed to determine the advantages and disadvantages associated with EF's proposed move into retailing. There was a clue immediately above the requirement as to what you needed to do in respect of answering this element of the question as it mentioned the advantages and disadvantages to EF of expanding into retailing. This is the approach used in the suggested solution.

Suggested solution

Forward vertical integration into retail outlets

EF is proposing changing its business model further so that it has exclusive outlets for its own products. The intention is to earn more of the value in the value system.

Advantages

- EF would have **total control over production, pricing and marketing**. It could develop a precise marketing strategy that further differentiates the product, enabling an even more targeted focus on its desired customer base. Moreover, it will have more freedom to develop marketing messages and integrate its marketing strategy.

- EF will also be able to ensure that its products are available and visible, and are not competing in the same clothes racks as other competitors – thereby **avoiding price comparisons**. In other words, EF will not depend on retailers' professional buyers to order or display its products.

EF will **become fully informed of its target market**. It may be able to make clothes to order, if customer measurements can be transmitted electronically to the factory: this would be an example of **mass customisation**.

Drawbacks

- EF will acquire a range of high street properties, with management problems of their own. **Debt service** will eat into any extra profits that are made on clothing sales.

- **Higher risk**. If EF's clothes go out of fashion, the stores will become an expensive liability. Owning a chain of retail outlets involves a much higher proportion of fixed costs than cloth and clothing manufacture. Much depends on the location of the shops.

- If EF products are exclusively sold in its own shops, **EF may forgo the sales it would have made at the department stores**.

- EF will need to produce a **wide-enough range** of products to encourage customers to enter. EF may have to supplement its own wares with others by other suppliers – will it be able to do so cost-effectively?

Required changes to EF's competences

- As EF is acquiring the chain, it will inherit the many competences needed, providing both that it can keep the staff and that EF's managers integrate the acquisition in a sensitive way.

- Inventory management for many small retail stores may prove to be quite complicated. EF may well inherit the inventory systems currently employed in the acquired company. If not, new systems will need to be purchased and staff training undertaken to enable them to be used in EF's shops.

- EF needs to understand high street retailing, display and merchandising (ensuring a suitable range of clothes is available in the right volumes and at the right time).

- EF needs a more responsive distribution system.

- EF is now running three different types of business. To benefit from economies of scale it may need a performance monitoring system for each business.

Chapter 7 Assessing and managing risk

Activity 1: Risk awareness

Tackling the question

This is a test of how you can explain the various ways that the board's views of risk are shared by staff (and vice versa if there is concern that staff are not being listened to about risks in the organisation's manufacturing sites).

How to earn the professional skills marks

These are communication (inform) marks, and the response is in the form of an IM for the purpose of placating some potentially difficult questions, so concise, objective and sensitive responses are going to be rewarded here.

Suggested solution

Embedding risk awareness:

- Good leadership from the board down – risk is always on the board's monthly agenda
- Communication of values that support the achievement of risk management in line with stakeholder views of risk – intranet; meetings; appraisal objectives and targets
- Compliance/risk management department to connect the board and the workforce
- Build risk identification into job descriptions
- Create risk register
- Training of staff in risk awareness in manufacturing sites
- Workshops to share best practice/eliminate poor practice
- Monitoring (eg by Internal Audit)
- Shadowing employees (especially as part of induction)
- Ethical codes with sticks and carrots

Activity 2: Risk committee

Tackling the question

Obviously there is no right answer to the overall question of who should be on a risk committee, as it will always depend on the organisation in question. However, in practice, the best mix of risk committee membership is probably a mixture of both types of director. Your answer must not lead the board to either type of director – instead it should provide balance, so for the six marks on offer you need to structure your points 50:50.

How to earn the professional skills marks

Although a presentation slide is usually going to require strong communication skills, the activity asks you to demonstrate evaluation skills here – this is to appraise a series of facts and work towards a balanced view that the board can then use to make decisions. Your slide must have this balance to secure the marks.

Suggested solution

Risk committee:

Executive directors

- Sound knowledge of the organisation and its products, employees and customers
- Risk is a key concern in our industry so needs the highest level of attention
- Remuneration can be linked to risk management for directors
- Supports strategic plan of imminent listing

Non-executive directors (NEDs)

- Recent appointment of NEDs brings independence and objectivity ('a fresh pair of eyes')
- External experience can add to the board's existing skill set
- NEDs will have no 'baggage' from any previously disputed decisions
- No incentive to pursue risk unnecessarily as NEDs are paid a flat fee

Activity 3: Risk appetite

Tackling the question

This is not straightforward, as you are almost contradicting yourself to some extent – in the first part of your answer, you need to alert the board to the risks they face so they don't ignore them, but in the second part, you need to justify why more risk may need to be embraced. It is difficult at this stage to go into too much detail, as the rest of the process for managing risks is covered later in this chapter, but an overall awareness of why you can't ignore risks but why seeking risk (eg entering new markets or acting as a disrupter in existing markets) is not always a bad thing.

How to earn the professional marks

The commercial acumen skills in this activity require you to show some insight into why more risk may be asked for (remember that no organisation stands still and cannot operate in a vacuum).

Suggested solution

Why is risk always present for our organisation?

- Although we are growing, we cannot ignore the changing business environment – so PESTEL factors (such as changing consumer tastes) or Porter's five forces (such as competition) cannot be ignored

- We have a number of individual employees at all levels who are making decisions about products and services for customers that relate to inherently risky activities

- Due to our growing nature, control failures are inevitable and some controls may be bypassed in pursuit of maintaining growth

- Every sector operates with unexpected hazards on a daily basis (such as faulty equipment, user error or freak accidents)

BPP
LEARNING
MEDIA

Why might we wish to embrace more risk?

- Despite these inherent risks, we may still be subject to greater demands from our stakeholders (customers, suppliers, lenders and eventually shareholders) all of whom might expect us to increase risk in some way (eg pursuing greater growth to meet the level of investment offered)

- The market environment will become more competitive and we may need to innovate to stay ahead – this may require more risk to be embraced (such as investing in new products and services or changing some of our existing services)

Activity 4: Airline risks

Tackling the question

This is a slightly artificial activity as it is essentially asking you to carry out some research (either on British Airways (BA) or a similar airline with which you are familiar) so the process is of greater importance than the end product. Obviously, if five risks were asked for, you needed to supply at least five risks! Remember that this activity is designed to help you develop the right skills, rather than be indicative of the type of task you will get in the real SBL exam.

Hopefully, you will have investigated the various elements of BA's operations to identify some key risks – as they are so high profile, it is likely that any risks they face have been the subject of media interest.

How to earn the professional skills marks

Commercial acumen skills are awarded here for demonstrating awareness of organisational and wider external factors which contribute to the wider organisational objectives. The list would have needed to be specific to BA or your chosen airline to secure these marks.

Suggested solution

Numerous risks could be identified for British Airways (BA) or indeed any airline. Some of the key ones may include the following.

- Demand falls due to economic factors (customers can no longer afford to travel)

- Competition from low-cost airlines

- Rise in oil prices making fuel more expensive

- Industrial action from cabin crew as BA attempts to manage its staff

- Crew availability (such as the recent problems experienced by RyanAir and other companies)

- Poor service, whether from baggage handling, standards of in-flight care or customer complaints handling

- Fleet replacement – are planes able to continue flying safely and efficiently? Is cabin, check-in and online technology fit for purpose?

- Bad weather disrupting flights – snow, storms etc

- Concerns about climate change leading people to fly less

- Safety – injury to passengers and/or staff from terrorism or accidents

Activity 5: Categorising airline risks

Tackling the question

This builds on your answer for Activity 4 so to score well, you need to show how you have matched the risks you created with suitable categories. As there is no 'correct' list of categories, the choices you make are always going to be arbitrary, but must still display some logic to be considered sufficient to score marks.

How to earn the professional marks

The professional skill being tested here is evaluation, so to score the marks, you need to demonstrate that you can assess each risk and show the necessary judgement required to allocate risks to suitable categories, prior to suitable assessment later in the risk management process.

Suggested solution

The risks identified could be categorised as follows (again using British Airways as an example):

*   Demand falls due to recession – **ECONOMIC** (an aspect of environmental/PESTEL risk)

*   Competition – **BUSINESS** (could be environmental/PESTEL or Stakeholder)

*   Rise in oil prices – **FINANCIAL**

*   Industrial action – **OPERATIONAL**

*   Crew availability – **OPERATIONAL**

*   Poor service – again, likely to be **OPERATIONAL**

*   Fleet replacement – **INVESTMENT**

*   Bad weather disrupting flights – snow, storms etc – **EVENT**

*   Concerns about climate change leads people to fly less – **SOCIAL/ENVIRONMENT** (an aspect of environmental/PESTEL risk)

*   Safety – injury to passengers and/or staff (perhaps due to terrorism?) – **HEALTH AND SAFETY**

Additional categories that would apply to British Airways would also be:

*   Foreign exchange (**FINANCIAL**)
*   Changes in regulations or tax (**POLITICAL**)
*   Fines or reputational damage due to breaches of laws or regulations (**COMPLIANCE**)

Activity 6: TARA

Tackling the question

It is unlikely in the real exam that you will be given the TARA framework, so you need to remember how it is constructed. Similarly, the real exam may not choose to follow the model closely by providing you with one risk for each of the four quadrants. However, once you have allocated the risks, a suitable response should appear, although the tutor notes below show how complex this process can be!

How to earn the professional skills marks

The skill here is analysis, which requires you to consider information so their implications can be considered appropriately and ensure that your conclusions follow on from the information used.

Suggested solution

	Impact	
	Low	**High**
High	'Shoplifting in a supermarket: this happens quite often but items stolen tend to be of low value' This suggests high likelihood and low impact, so the TARA model would recommend **reducing** this risk – probably using controls such as CCTV and store detectives.	'Loss of human life as part of drilling for oil on an oil rig' This is not straightforward – it is certainly possible that lives could be lost on an oil rig and this represents a significant impact – will this mean that an oil exploration company **avoids** such activity though?
Low	'A courier company experiencing minor, infrequent delays due to 'rush hour' traffic' This appears to happen occasionally with little impact to achieving goals – rather than investing in controls to avoid travelling at these times, it is probably easier to just **accept** these risks.	'Repairing significant property damage arising from unexpected flooding' This is suggesting a high impact event that is unlikely to occur frequently enough to deploy controls such as flood defences – it is therefore a risk that will be **transferred** (usually via insurance).

(Left axis label: **Likelihood**)

Tutor note. In some cases, risk may be assessed as being so great that **risk avoidance** is the only possible response (for example, the risk to foreign workers based in a politically volatile country would lead to immediate termination of operations and the evacuation of staff).

However, risk avoidance may not always be recommended when a risk is assessed as high impact and high likelihood because in some cases, controls could be deployed rather than just avoid the risk altogether.

For example, consider the idea of an economic downturn affecting consumer confidence – such economic events are cyclical and can therefore be predicted with some certainty, making them likely and their impact significant. However, no retailer would avoid trading simply because of this risk – they would find ways of off-setting this risk somehow using a combination of other response methods. The idea of managing risks in a more pragmatic manner will be discussed later in this section.

Tutor note. Transferring risk is often referred to as the 'insurance' option but can every situation assessed as high impact and low likelihood be insured? Certainly, the more likely such a risk becomes, the higher the insurance premium would be until something is deemed 'uninsurable' (such as the damage to a company's reputation).

Let's also think about **outsourcing** as a way of transferring risk – is it the same as insurance where you pay someone else to deal with a particular problem? Companies choose outsourcing as a way of addressing a specific risk: over-spending, running out of production capacity or even the risk of poor service delivery. Are these risks eliminated by the use of an outsourcing provider? It all depends on who bears the ultimate risk – poor quality products may be the fault of the outsourced manufacturer but if your reputation suffers from using them to save costs, you have not really transferred this risk. If, however, the outsourced manufacturer is liable for any damage to your reputation, then perhaps this is an insurance arrangement after all.

Chapter 8 Internal control systems

Activity 1: Widmerpool

Tackling the question

This is a good example of why you need to read scenarios carefully and highlight all relevant data. Every point our answer makes is supported by relevant information from the scenario. The eight marks on offer and the use of the verb 'explain' suggest that up to two marks could be awarded for each area of control failure.

How to earn the professional skills marks

You are being asked to advise a client on their own weaknesses, which requires tact and diplomacy in challenging the client's current practices. Remember that all points must be factual and backed up by evidence.

Suggested solution

There could be up to four main areas where control systems need to be reviewed.

Lack of detail in guidance

The problems over the suppliers' data may indicate that some of the organisational guidance is written too much in terms of **general principles**, without enough examples of detailed application. It would appear that the guidance needs to spell out that confidential information should not be removed from the office, and staff should not talk about business matters outside work.

Lack of awareness of risks

The accident with the machine indicates that **staff did not understand the risks** involved, despite the health and safety documentation. This could be because they failed to read the documentation or they read it but failed to understand it. This also suggests that **training**, on-the-job or in formal courses, was **non-existent or ineffective**.

Poor culture

The problems over Stringham's information and the difficulties over the machine indicate that a **culture of carelessness** is prevalent at Widmerpool. Managers, in positions of responsibility, should naturally be careful with confidential information. The comments in the staff survey also seem to suggest the culture is poor, that the board is seen as **not caring** about internal controls and procedures.

Lack of enforcement

The staff comments underline what happened over the machine, that the company's internal procedures are not being **enforced by managers**. The survey comments suggest that, while the board is receiving sufficient financial information about the profitability of operations, it is not getting the non-financial data it needs to obtain assurance that **control systems are operating effectively**.

Activity 2: PKG High School Governing Body

Tackling the question

It is very easy to stray from the subject and talk too generally about controls – the question asks you to evaluate (often, as it is here, concentrating on the deficiencies), and recommend what the governing body should be doing. Our answer is based around the structure of:

- How the governing body is constituted and how it operates
- The data it gets (financial/non-financial, internal/external)
- The decisions it takes and the monitoring it carries out

BPP
LEARNING
MEDIA

This is a useful way of analysing how any governing body works.

You may have felt that the question could have given more detail about what the governing body is doing and the information it receives. It is valid to assume that if you're not told anything about key aspects of governance, such as a committee system, then they aren't being operated when they should be.

It's also easy to fail to consider whether financial and other resources are being used to maximum efficiency. Spending limits often mean that expenditure is made to the limits set down, with little consideration of whether value for money has been obtained.

Note that this was set in a public sector context which is entirely possible for the real exam. Note also that our answer has amalgamated deficiencies and improvements for each category – had you followed the structure of the answer and shown parts (a) and (b) separately (or perhaps in a two-column approach matching each of (a) and (b) on a line-by-line basis), this would have been perfectly acceptable.

How to earn the professional marks

Part (a) focuses on evaluation skills and in particular assessing the control weaknesses. You will earn the skills marks for showing that you can exercise judgement in prioritising which issues are most significant.

Part (b) is likely to be a sensitive topic as you are discussing potential weaknesses in the governance of the school, so the focus here is on your communication skills. The skill of 'persuade' means using compelling and logical arguments, so you need to make sure that your reasoning is clear, and backed up with evidence. You also need to ensure you are explaining why something is an issue, or should be improved.

Suggested solution

(i) **Structure and workings of governing body**

Membership

The governing body includes representatives of the key stakeholder group of parents and the local authority.

However, it may be a **more effective monitor** if it includes representation from key internal stakeholders. Certainly it should include staff representatives and might include pupil representatives as well.

Committee system

Having the full governing body consider all relevant items at every meeting may not be the most efficient way of operating, and it may mean that some **key risk areas receive insufficient attention**.

Although committees may be difficult to staff, a **committee system** with each committee concentrating on certain key aspects of running the school may be the best way to conduct decision making, with committees reporting into the main governing body. Certainly it may provide a good mechanism for parent representatives to use their particular expertise.

1 **Audit committee**

An **audit committee**, including members with financial expertise, could be responsible for detailed scrutiny of expenditure and liaising with auditors. Its remit could also cover **compliance with legislation** and the **operation of internal controls**. This would leave the main governing body to concentrate on the split of expenditure and the overall review of control systems.

2   **Staff recruitment committee**

Because of the significance of staffing, the board should establish a separate recruitment committee. The committee should be involved in specific recruitment decisions, and should also proactively consider **staffing needs**. For example, are there **sufficient experienced members** of staff and does the staff body as a whole have an **appropriate range of skills** in key areas such as IT? The committee must consider how **staffing headcount needs** can be **reconciled with planned staff expenditure**.

The committee should also consider the **balance between teachers and other support staff**, whether support staff, with specific skills, need to be recruited or whether their numbers could be reduced and more teachers recruited. It should also be involved in **internal promotion decisions** and consider the effectiveness of the **system of responsibility allowances**.

Induction of governing body members

There appear to be **no induction procedures** for new governing body members that would enhance their knowledge of what the school does and the requirements the governing body has to meet.

Certainly parent governors will need this understanding if they are to be **effective governors** (hopefully the local authority will have selected suitably qualified and knowledgeable members).

(ii) **Information received by governing body**

Financial information

It is unclear whether the financial information is sufficiently detailed. The governing body needs to ensure that it receives **sufficient information about expenditure**, particularly because of the wide discretion the headteacher has and the lack of **segregation of duties**.

Expenditure should be **classified** into **different categories** depending on its materiality and the ways it is controlled. The information should include **what has been spent**, **expenditure commitments** and **phasing of expenditure during the year**; not all expenditure will be made in even amounts over the year. The governing body also needs to ensure that the **reliability** of the monthly financial report is reviewed because of its importance for decision making. As the external auditors may not spend time on this, this review should perhaps be carried out by members of the audit committee.

Financial variances

Although the governors receive information about variances from budgeted expenditure, there is nothing mentioned about how they are, as they should be, informed of action planned if an overspend appears likely.

They should have input into what should be done.

Non-financial information

There appears to be a lack of non-financial information that the governors need in order to **ensure that educational standards** are being **maintained**. An **annual inspection by the local education authority** would not be frequent enough.

Governors should be supplied with the results of internal methods of assessing the effectiveness of teaching such as **termly exams** and **internal quality reviews** of teaching programmes. Since staffing is both a major element of expenditure and vital in ensuring standards, governors should be receiving details about staff such as **results of appraisals** and **staff development programmes**. Having parent, staff and pupil representatives on the governing body will help measure the **satisfaction levels** of these key stakeholder groups; the governors ought to consider other methods such as regular staff and parent surveys.

BPP
LEARNING
MEDIA

External information

No mention has been made of whether the governing body is receiving the external information which it will need for longer-term decision making.

The governing body should be receiving details of population trends in the area and the impact of changes in schools provision. It should also be considering specific information about other schools in the area that it can use for **benchmarking purposes**, such as pupil numbers, disposition of staff, facilities and exam results.

(iii) **Actions taken by governing body**

Strategic decision making

The governing body's time horizon appears to be limited to a year, and it does not appear to be considering longer-term issues; there seems to be **no strategic plan**.

Better information should help it **modify** its strategy in response to local issues such as changes in pupil numbers, the opening of new schools, particularly specialist schools or government-promoted schools (such as UK academies) and changes in educational practice (such as increased use of information technology).

Flexibility of decision making

The governing body needs to consider whether its decision making is too constricted; the governors may have the flexibility to take decisions that ensure **better use of resources** and **better risk management**.

For example it may consider whether class sizes can be increased in the lower age ranges, to allow smaller class sizes and greater preparation time for more advanced teaching. It should also consider whether to include a **contingency fund** for urgent items of additional expenditure on staff, buildings and IT.

Review of small items of expenditure

The governing body does not appear to take any interest in expenditure under $1,000. There may be scope for the headteacher to abuse this by **spreading significant expenditure** out so that individual items are below $1,000, but the total sum is quite substantial.

The governors should **review all expenditure** below $1,000, even if they don't approve it in advance. There may be scope for raising the limit on certain types of expenditure, so that the governing body does not spend time considering what is essentially non-discretionary expenditure.

Communication

The governing body needs to consider how its **work should be communicated**; there is **no evidence** of how this is happening at present.

Clearly the headteacher will have prime responsibility for communicating and what the governing body publishes should be consistent with what the headteacher is saying. However, **communication of what the governing body is doing** and the **issues it is considering** should prove to staff, pupils and current and prospective parents that the school is **well run**. It should also aid **future recruitment** onto the governing body.

Activity 3: PKG High School – Review and Audit of Controls

Tackling the question

Remember that the stakeholders are different to those of a company, but they still need the assurance provided by an objective review. Benchmarking is likely to be a particularly important aspect of the audit, given that the governing body is responsible for educational standards.

How to earn the professional marks

The communication skills of being able to persuade are most important here as you are attempting to educate the local authority with the benefit of your knowledge, so you need to present your findings in an authoritative manner to score well.

Suggested solution

Independent and objective assurance

Having an external review carried out should provide an **unbiased view** of how the school is performing. In particular this provides **reassurance to stakeholders such as parents and the local authority** that the school is providing education of sufficient quality and expenditure is being properly controlled.

Aid to monitoring

Like the board of directors in a listed company, the governors are responsible for establishing and maintaining a sound system of internal control and risk management. The review should provide **feedback** to the headteacher and governing body to enable them to set priorities for systems improvements, based on the areas of **greatest risk**. It should also highlight where the headteacher and governors should **focus their own monitoring activity**.

Expert opinion

The external reviewers can make recommendations based on their **knowledge of best practice in other schools**. This can provide the school with **benchmarks** that it can incorporate into financial and non-financial performance indicators.

Chapter 9 Applying ethical principles

Activity 1: Indicators of fraud

Tackling the question

The reasons for fraud could be many and varied – we have chosen to use those suggested by Cressey due to the absence of any further detail in the scenario – however, how you deal with each condition must be clear and specific so the audit committee members understand how to stop these conditions from flourishing.

You have more structure to work with in the second part as each of the areas of recommendation relates to specific fraud risks.

Make sure that you justify the award of up to one mark in each case by making what you say specific enough to not need any further explanation but remember that the requirement is to produce briefing notes, so they do not need to be comprehensive.

How to earn the professional skills marks

You have been asked to consider the use of the professional skill 'scepticism' as part of this activity, meaning that you need to have attempted to **probe**, **question** and **challenge** as part of the briefing note. You are an independent consultant so can be objective and ambitious in your recommendations without fear of creating any conflicts of interest.

BPP
LEARNING
MEDIA

Conditions for fraud to occur

Pressure

- Reward staff satisfactorily to reduce the need for them to consider fraud as a solution to their problems

- Adopt suitable sympathetic HR policies that are sensitive to employee problems (and can identify problems such as a gambling addiction)

Opportunity

- Remove temptation by making any fraud more likely to be spotted

- Introduce or improve controls and segregation of duties to reduce the likelihood of fraud occurring

Rationalisation

- Ensure good examples are set by senior staff to discourage fraud as a viable option
- Obtain good references for staff to isolate those with previous criminal backgrounds
- Discipline offenders visibly to reinforce the message that such behaviour will not be tolerated

Recommended controls

Ghost employees

- Head count reconciliations to establishment listings should be performed (eg surprise visits by internal audit)

Inflating expense claims

- Back-up receipts must be obtained for expenses to be reimbursed
- Consider reducing authorisation levels to allow a greater proportion of costs to be reviewed
- Good remuneration policies
- Consider data analytics to identify patterns that may indicate a greater risk of fraud

Stealing assets

- Asset registers should be regularly maintained and reviewed, with assets periodically inspected

- Tracking systems should be considered for items above a certain value (eg RFIDs)

Manipulation of financial statements

- Audit (both internal and external) to challenge the assumptions underpinning performance and position

- Introduce a whistle-blower policy to allow staff to feed back any questionable behaviour without fear of retribution by senior staff

Activity 2: Low tax payments

Tackling the question

As is expected for this exam, the requirement does not specifically ask for any one model to be used; however, you can infer from the fact that it is the only ethical decision-making model you know and that the requirement is worth five marks so you should probably be using the Tucker model!

In each case, ask the question 'is the decision to not voluntarily pay more tax....' and consider the bigger picture as you are acting in the role of non-executive director.

How to earn the professional skills marks

Scepticism requires the use of three types of skill: the ability to probe, challenge and question, so your answer needs to display evidence of these being used – for example, considering what the impact of paying it would be from a series of different angles.

Suggested solution

Using the Tucker 5-question model, the company's decision to not voluntarily pay more tax is assessed below.

- **Profitable?** – Initially yes, as shareholders' funds have not been diverted to pay a voluntary sum (however, paying tax voluntarily would reduce the threat of a sales boycott which may offset any payment made so there may be a trade-off here).

- **Legal?** – Yes – in either case (paying or not paying tax) GSA is operating within the law.

- **Fair?** – GSA may establish how widespread the use of such tax avoidance really is – if others in the same industry have also adopted this policy, it will probably continue to feel there is 'safety in numbers' (however, this will inevitably attract criticism that as GSA can afford the best tax experts to interpret the law, such advice is too expensive for others, leading to inequity in tax advice).

- **Right?** – Very difficult to call – as there is such resistance from the public, the continuing defence of these actions as legal tax avoidance appears unsustainable (see below).

- **Sustainable?** – There are no environmental issues but this may affect profits in the longer term, leading to questions over how economically sustainable such a policy really is. We must consider our reputation in the eyes of our stakeholders when making this decision.

Activity 3: Tax savings

Tackling the question

You have been given plenty of scope here, so can consider the facts as presented and use your knowledge of the syllabus to structure a suitable answer: ASIFS in part (a) and theory in part (b). Part (c) requires a bit more application but you must be prepared for this in the real exam.

How to earn the professional skills marks

Acting with scepticism does not necessarily mean always assuming the worst in people, but given the situation as presented in the scenario, that's where you should be aiming to start! Be critical and consider what seems to be happening here and what it means for you in your role.

(a) **Identify the ethical threats presented in the scenario:**

Advocacy – acting as tax advisers at the same time as being independent external auditors (there is some self-review threat here too)

Self-interest – low fees; compromised ethics in order to retain the engagement

Intimidation – pressure to reduce fees; could a small firm stand up to a large multinational if they disagreed on a proposed accounting treatment or modification to the auditor's opinion?

Familiarity – the partner is friends with the FD which could lead to a lack of objectivity and independence in certain judgements during the audit

Self-review – internal audit services will need to be relied upon for external audit opinion

BPP LEARNING MEDIA

(b) **Explain what is meant by the public interest in this case:**

The public interest relates to public **confidence** in professions, who act for the collective well-being of the **community** of people that they serve (including clients, lenders, governments, employers, employees, investors, the business and financial community and others who rely on the work of those professions).

In this case, the public interest is those who feel the company should be **paying its fair share of taxes to support the national economy**, and those who feel that the accountancy firm **should not assist the company to this aim**, as it **owes a duty to society as well as to its clients**. Any conflicts of interest should be identified as such by awareness of the various threats mentioned above and may lead the firm to either adopt certain **safeguards** before they can act or **decline** to act in certain cases.

(c) **Describe the nature of the conversation that you have overheard, including any possible actions that you feel you may need to take:**

The conversation appears to have been discussing **further tax avoidance** and possibly even **illegal tax evasion** and the payment of a bonus to the firm for securing such savings on behalf of the company. This sounds like a situation where **bribery and corruption** are being discussed – you are now placed in a **difficult position** as you need to consider your **responsibilities as an employee** (albeit in a retained consultant capacity) but also your **responsibilities as a professional to act in the public interest**, which should be **above** those owed to your employer if illegal or unethical activity is being considered.

To address this conflict of interests, you may wish to **consult** an independent partner (such as an ethics partner) within the firm – however, given the **size of the firm** here, this may not be **practical** and no such role may exist. It may be **illegal** if you are aware of **possible criminal activity** but **do not disclose it**, so in the absence of any **formal mechanism** within the firm you may wish to present your concerns to a **third party** – this process is known as '**whistleblowing**' which satisfies your duty to act in the public interest but would probably lead to your **departure** from the firm.

The **threat** of such retaliation from an employer (such as legal action, disciplinary procedures, redundancy and poor employment references) can be significant, especially as your reputation is so crucial, and so presents a difficult choice for any whistle-blower.

Chapter 10 Financial analysis

Activity 1: Syngen plc

Tackling the question

To do well in this requirement, you will need to use the information in the email and link it to the potential benefits of outsourcing or shared/global business services. It is best to work through the information provided line-by-line, ensuring you have picked out and responded to the relevant pieces of information. The second part of the question is idea generation, thinking about what would practically be involved.

How to earn the professional skills marks

To demonstrate your 'appraise' skills you needed to show that you have carefully considered the information and clearly demonstrated how the proposed solution will address the situation. In this case, it is likely that the problems identified can be addressed by the proposed solutions, but this needs to be argued not simply asserted.

Suggested solution

To: Finance Director
From: Financial Controller

Reviewing the email from the Operations Director, it does seem likely that the issues raised could be assisted by part of our finance function being either outsourced or moved into a shared or global business service centre.

Cost

It is usually possible to make cost savings by these means. This is partly because a shared service centre can achieve economies of scale by processing a larger volume of transactions, so concentrating our regional hubs into one service centre would help with this. An outsourced provider who processes transactions on behalf of a large number of clients would have higher volumes still, and even more scope to benefit from this.

There may also be opportunities to reduce cost by locating some of our functions, particularly to do with processing, in a low-cost location.

Variable support

Currently, our staff are fully committed during month-end and year-end close and are not available to support the business. A shared service model may help to some extent – the shared service centre could deal with processing and that would free up other staff to take on more of a business partner role and focus on supporting the business.

However, it seems that the issue may be that we simply need more processing staff at certain times of year than others. An outsourced provider could help us manage this – by taking on responsibility for managing resource and having flexibility across a number of different clients, they could reduce the pressure.

Processing times

By bringing together our processing functions, it will be easier to invest in modern technology that will assist with processing times. For example, it will be easier to introduce online authorisation for payments across the whole country. An outsource provider is also likely to maintain their investment in the latest technology, as they can recover the cost of that investment across a number of clients.

Practical issues to consider

Moving to a shared service model would be a major undertaking and outsourcing a larger one still. We may want to consider whether a shared service centre would be a good 'first step' before we consider full outsourcing. Other considerations would include:

- Clarifying the drivers for the move, and the benefits we expect to see

- Choosing a partner if we outsource. This will be a critical decision.

- Deciding on a location, balancing cost considerations with the need for a good supply of appropriately skilled labour, and also considering compatibility of time zones with ours

- Identifying those activities which are suitable to move into the new model. These will tend to be the less strategically important and most routine activities.

- Setting up a project team to evaluate and manage the transition. We may not have this expertise in-house and it might be helpful to bring in support from external consultants.

- Managing the impact on existing staff, whose jobs may be transferred or eliminated

These issues should not be under-estimated and we should manage expectations of the Operations Director. Moving to a different finance function model will not be a 'quick fix' or a simple process.

BPP
LEARNING
MEDIA

Activity 2: Investment appraisal

Tackling the question

The requirement is to 'critically evaluate' remarks using scepticism, so there is a clear hint that the manager's assertions should not necessarily be taken at face value. When you receive information, it is important to consider whether it is reliable, and that will depend on the nature of the information, the source, its plausibility and so on.

How to earn the professional skills marks.

In order to earn the 'challenge' skills marks you needed to demonstrate that you were systematically working through the assertions to see if they were supported by the available evidence. Where they were not, you needed to point this out.

Suggested solution

Payback rate

Project 1

All figures in $'000

C/F	0	-110	-60	-45	-5
	Year 0	Year 1	Year 2	Year 3	Year 4
Total costs	110	10	10	10	10
Total savings	0	60	25	50	70
Cumulative	-110	-60	-45	-5	55

Project 2

All figures in $'000

C/F	0	-90	-50	-30	-5
	Year 0	Year 1	Year 2	Year 3	Year 4
Total costs	90	20	20	10	10
Total savings	0	60	35	40	35
Cumulative	-90	-50	-30	-5	20

The calculations above show that both Projects would have had a payback period of 4 years, however, Project 1 ($55) would pay back more than Project 2 ($20) therefore Project 1 would still have been preferable and so selected.

Payback ignores any cashflows that would be received in the years after payback. With hindsight, we know Project 1 was a disaster, and it is possible Project 2 may have generated more revenue subsequent to payback.

However, had the payback method been used, any such future cashflows would not have been considered at the time of appraisal and so Project 1 would still have been selected over Project 2. The manager's assertion that this method would have led to the selection of Project 2 is therefore incorrect.

The discount rate

The discount rate is not the same as the inflation rate. Although inflation may be taken into account, other factors such as interest forgone (the opportunity cost of investing elsewhere), the cost of capital (the cost of borrowing to fund the investment) and risk are influential in determining the discount rate. The discount rate used will include a risk allowance which determines the required rate of return for a project to be considered to be viable.

To determine the appropriate discount rate to use, it would be useful to have further information about risk-free interest rates, the risk profile of the company and the company's cost of capital.

However, note that even if the discount rate was changed to 3% or 4%, this would make no difference as to which project was selected. It would in fact increase the attractiveness of Project 1 as there would be less discounting of the cash flows in Years 3 and 4. This would actually increase the gap in the NPV between Projects 1 and 2.

The internal rate of return (IRR)

The IRR is the discount rate that would give an NPV of zero for the net cash flows of each project, and the two Projects are of a similar scale. Therefore, in this case the project with the greater NPV will produce the higher IRR, and so the result under IRR will the same as that selected under NPV (ie Project 1 would still have been selected).

IRR may have been important, however, if the company has to achieve an internal hurdle rate, or when different scales of investment are being compared. Neither of these situations exist here.

Activity 3: Performance appraisal

Tackling the question

There is a lot of data here, of different types, so it is important to focus first on the key indicators and then what could be driving its changes. For a quoted company, the share price is a critical performance measure, which is driven by changes in profit, and expectations of future profit. The company is in a fast-moving, competitive manufacturing business so we can expect quality and innovation to be critical, measured respectively by data on faults and new product lines. Avoid saying simply 'x is below budget by y%'. You will need to comment meaningfully on the figures in order to score well at this level.

How to earn the professional skills marks

In order to earn the 'enquire' skills marks you needed to demonstrate that you were analysing your data sources to come to appropriate conclusions. You would also show that you were not just commenting on the numbers, but seeing if they could shed light on the reasons for ALPHA's financial underperformance.

Suggested solution

Non-financial indicators

We budgeted for the launch of ten new product lines; we actually launched 12, but of these only one was successful compared to a budget of four. This requires further investigation, since these figures may indicate a **degree of over-optimism** both about the volume of R&D we are able to undertake and about the overall competence of our R&D organisation. There is a risk that ALPHA is developing new product lines for which there is no demand. Alternatively, the marketing aspects of new product development may require attention if new lines are not being promoted effectively.

Output quality seems to have been much worse than expected, with rework, customer returns and warranty claims all much higher than budget.

The actual number of units rejected and sent for **rework** was 54,000 against a flexed budget of 29,375; this represents an adverse variance of 84%.

BPP
LEARNING
MEDIA

Warranty claims and other returns amount to 8.4% of all units sold. This is a very high figure, especially when we consider the number of units which also had to be reworked. This suggests there are serious problems in ALPHA's quality control procedures. Eighty-four warranty claims and returns per '000 units equates to 197,400 dissatisfied customers in the year. We must not overlook the effect of the high rate of returns on our reputation and brand values.

The average selling price is almost 6% below budget; which in the light of quality issues suggests ALPHA may be having to discount prices to generate sales. This, combined with the returns problem and the 50,000 unit shortfall on the sales budget, indicates a degree of customer dissatisfaction that should be of concern.

Financial indicators

ALPHA is a listed company and **EPS** is a key market indicator; its shortfall on budget of 8% is reflected in its **share price**, which, at J$334.5, is over 16% lower than forecast. Not surprisingly, the company's poor performance is translating into a loss of value for its shareholders.

The main reasons for the shortfall in EPS are clear: **turnover** shows 7.6% adverse variance and **gross margin** of 65.6% is lower than the planned 68%: together these effects produce a gross profit shortfall on budget of 10.8%. These figures should be a serious cause for concern. Sales are below budget (possibly due to quality issues damaging the company's brand – see below) yet at the same time direct costs (%) are over budget. Some of the overspend may reflect the high labour costs associated with the level of re-working currently being required, but there should be wider concerns that costs are not being controlled tightly enough.

Net margin, at 36.4%, is similarly disappointing when compared with the 40.7% budgeted and indicates that indirect costs are also higher than expected. It has already been remarked that headcount is significantly above budget; and this will have an impact on the level of direct costs. However, ALPHA needs to review its level of overheads critically in the light of below-budgeted sales.

Average capital employed was J$2,835m, which is 11.2% higher than expected. Taken together with this, the fall in turnover and the evident increase in costs of all types produce a **return on capital employed** of 23%, against a budget of 31%. Again, this is an indicator that the company is not currently generating the level of value that it should be.

The closing **cash balance** of J$179m is much lower than the J$485m budgeted. We note that pre-tax profit at J$652m is J$138m lower than budget, which may account for some of the J$306m shortfall. We have no figures that would indicate any specific cash shortfall, though we note that average inventories are J$20.6m above budget. It is not really appropriate to use these average figures to discuss the year-end cash position, but their magnitude compared with the budget variance seems to suggest that significant demands have been made on cash during the year, and may suggest that there are **weaknesses in the business's working capital management**.

Inventories themselves deserve comment because they have run significantly above budget in all categories, and total almost 30 days cost of sales.

Finished goods inventory is particularly noticeable, having averaged J$38.2m against a budget of J$20m, an adverse variance of 91%. This represents 22.6 days rather than the 11.8 days budgeted. There could well be a link here to the significant overall sales variance, but it also looks like controls over the level of finished goods held could be improved.

WIP, at 0.47 days, is significantly higher than the 0.18 days budgeted, which should raise concerns over the efficiency of the production process – especially if ALPHA is operating a JIT manufacturing system.

Raw material inventories, at 6.75 days, also seem high for a routine mass production operation; the budget, at 5.58 days seems to indicate an acceptance that this is normal. Greater attention to delivery scheduling may be fruitful.

Headcount averaged 2,259, against 2,128 budgeted, an increase of 6.16%. Unfortunately, there does not seem to have been a corresponding increase in worthwhile activity. Sales were significantly down on budget (2.35 million units against 2.40, an adverse variance of 2.1%; J$1,793m value against J$1,941m, an adverse variance of 7.6%; sales per employee J$793,714 against J$912,124, an adverse variance of 13%). The increased headcount alongside lower than budgeted sales means that sales per employee have fallen from 1,128 (budget) to 1,040 (actual). This indicates that efficiency is falling, although this could be in part due to ALPHA's products becoming less desirable in the market place.

The adverse variance in unit production cost of sales (J$262 against J$259) is also likely to reflect this increase in headcount. There may also be a link between the employment of new, inexperienced staff and the clear indications of deteriorating quality.

Summary

ALPHA's performance is disappointing compared to budget expectations. Important features are significant quality problems and failure to control costs of all kinds.

Workings

Sales per employee

Budget J$1,941m/2,128 = J$912,124

Actual J$1,793m/2,259 = J$793,714

Variance **(912,124 – 793,714)/912,124 × 100% = 12.98%**

Activity 4: DynoCars

Tackling the question

This question involves using management accounting techniques from your previous studies but, unlike the lower level exams, you will not be specifically directed as to what calculations to make or what techniques to use. You need to carefully consider the specific information given. There is a clue in the mention of capacity constraints, which suggests that production capacity is a limiting factor and it would be worth analysing whether the current mix of production utilises this resource well.

How to earn the professional skills marks

In order to earn the 'estimate' skills marks you needed to identify that the issue is not quite as simple as it first appears. Rather than just comparing the direct cost of manufacturing in-house with outsourcing, you need to think about the organisation as a whole. This would lead you to consider limiting factor analysis, which provides this perspective. You then need to draw clear implications of your analysis for the decision the organisation needs to make.

Case for outsourcing

If we consider the Small model in isolation from the other DynoCar products we can see the main benefits that would be achieved by outsourcing its production. The relevant supporting information is shown in Figure 1 below.

	Small
Selling price per car ($)	6,999
Variable cost per car ($)	4,500
Weekly demand (cars)	6
Production time per car (machine hours)	8
Contribution (6,999 – 4,500)	2,499
Contribution per machine hour (2,499/8)	312
Production time (6 × 8)	48

Figure 1: Information relating to the in-house production of Small

The cost of manufacture quoted by the potential outsource provider is $3,500 which is cheaper than the $4,500 variable cost of manufacturing this car at the existing site, therefore saving DynoCars $1,000 per car. There is also a transport cost of $250 per car associated with the outsourcing option which reduces this saving to $750, however this still suggests that outsourcing the production of the Small is more attractive than retaining production in house.

Even the most profitable combination generates only a relatively small profit margin. Figure 2 shows more information about the entire range.

	Family	Luxury	Small
Selling price per car ($)	9,999	12,999	6,999
Variable cost per car ($)	7,000	10,000	4,500
Weekly demand (cars)	6	5	6
Production time per car (machine hours)	9	10	8
Contribution	2,999	2,999	2,499
Contribution per machine hour	333	300	312
Production time	54	50	48

Figure 2: Information relating to the current production of the DynoCar range

The case for outsourcing is further supported by the fact that DynoCar is unable to meet the demand for its products using its current facilities. The production capacity at its site is 112 hours, which is 40 hours short of the 152 (54 + 50 + 48) hours of demand. This demand could be met and profits could be increased if the outsourcing option is taken.

In addition, the scenario suggests this option would save overheads of $1,250 per week.

Case against outsourcing

The most profitable combination of products produced using the current system is as follows:

	Cars produced	Hours of production	Contribution
Family	6	54	$17,994 (6 × $2,999)
Luxury	1	10	$2,999 (1 × 2,999)
Small	6	48	$14,994 (6 × $2,449)
		112	$35,987

If the Small is outsourced, the most profitable combination would be as follows:

	Cars produced	Hours of production	Contribution
Family	6	54	$17,994 (6 × $2,999)
Luxury	5	50	$14,995 (5 × 2,999)
		104	$32,989

This combination gives a total contribution of $32,989 which is less than the forecast $33,750 weekly overhead cost and utilises only 104 production hours, leaving 8 production hours unused. This may mean that the production site may no longer be viable in the future once Small is outsourced.

It may be possible to address this by changing to a three-shift pattern to increase production capacity to 168 hours (7 days, 3 shifts of 8 hours each) per week. This would mean that demand (152 hours) is met leaving 16 hours (168 – 152) available for maintenance. DynoCar would have to determine whether or not this is feasible and if they consider the 16 hours of maintenance time to be sufficient.

Conclusion

Overall, outsourcing would be more financially viable than producing Small in house, but it would leave the factory in a loss-making position. DynoCar may want to revisit their business model and evaluate the outsourcing of all manufacturing. On the other hand, they may have different reasons for maintaining the factory (eg brand, social responsibility) which would apply even if it does not make a profit.

Chapter 11 Applications of IT

Activity 1: Retail World

Tackling the question

A good approach to structuring your work was to use the four Vs (volume, veracity, velocity and variety) as a framework around which to develop your answer. You might have found it useful to set the scene to your answer by briefly explaining what each of the Vs represents and to explain the implications of each in modern business. However, to achieve good marks it was crucial that you applied your knowledge of big data to RW and its approach to strategic development. For example, when considering the V of volume, possessing greater quantities and types of customer data would clearly be useful to RW. Such data should allow RW to identify trends in customer purchasing behaviour and could help the company to plan which products it offers more of to customers, or in which locations it should potentially open up more stores.

How to earn the professional skills marks

The professional skills marks in the question were on offer for demonstrating your communication skills with a particular focus on your ability to inform. To earn these marks you needed to ensure that you presented your answer in a clear and concise manner, which took into account the fact that the intended recipient of your work was RW's finance director.

Suggested solution

Four Vs of big data

Big data is a generic term used to describe the exponential growth of data, provided from numerous sources, available to organisations. The data is not useful in itself; it is the analysis of such data which provides valuable insights to an organisation. The use of big data can lead to an in-depth insight into trends and the driving forces behind those trends.

The four Vs of big data, volume, veracity, velocity and variety, can be examined to determine their contribution towards strategic development.

Volume can enhance the understanding of customer requirements and behaviour. The more data available, the greater the reliability of the trends and relationships discovered. The use of big data would allow RW to use multivariate analysis over a greater time period or a greater number of shorter time periods to understand purchasing patterns better. This could help RW to create better strategies to capitalise on discovered trends.

Veracity refers to the truthfulness of data once captured. Given that RW is a major international retailer and is continuing to expand at a rapid pace, it is of crucial importance that the data used to base decisions on where to open new stores is not flawed and does not contain errors. Bad data will lead to poor decisions when determining strategy. In the case of RW it would appear likely that the data held will of a good quality as the company operates rigorous controls over its IT system.

Velocity refers to the speed of use of real-time data. As the majority of business transactions are now carried out using technology, these transactions can be captured and processed in real time if sufficient processing capacity is available. This ensures that strategies can be continually updated, in order to deliver competitive advantage. For example, as a new product is trending on social media, RW may then ensure they stock this product and aggressively market it in order to capture greater market share. Similarly, when customers are shopping online, RW could analyse their transactions in real time and use current and historic customer information to make recommendations for further purchases.

Variety refers to the different sources from which data is provided. As sources take different forms and include those not in RW's control, this is a challenging aspect of big data. However, if managed

BPP
LEARNING
MEDIA

correctly, the variety provides the most detailed understanding of the market place, segmentation and individual customers. This could include competitor and industry information, sourced through key words online, to hashtags on social media and discussion forums.

Benefits

There are many potential benefits which could be obtained through the analysis of big data. RW could use the results to reliably determine where to locate their new stores. By accessing customers' shopping habits from credit and debit card records, they could determine which competing stores are used, and in which locations. This could help in the strategic planning of store locations, especially as RW is intending to continue to grow store numbers, at least over the next two years. This could help maximise the additional revenue to be gained from new stores.

The use of big data will allow RW to identify trends in shopping habits and could lead to the discovery of previously unsuspected trends, allowing RW to capitalise on these before its industry competitors have even recognised the trend.

Further revenue streams are also available through the selling of data. Given the industry RW is in, there will be a number of branded items on offer to customers. Manufacturers of these brands are keen to carry out their own analysis and will pay for information to help with this. RW could capitalise on this new revenue stream.

Overall therefore, RW may well find itself at a competitive disadvantage if it fails to explore the use of big data. However, as with all decisions, the cost-benefit implications would need to be considered before implementation.

Activity 2: Holiday Company

Tackling the question

Although, the focus of this question was upon pricing, it also incorporates elements of both new product development and marketing. Consideration was given to these three issues earlier in this chapter. To produce a good answer it was crucial that you considered the fact that the holiday packages to be offered by Inspirations were intended to be marketed at the luxury end of the market, and therefore the pricing approach adopted would need to support this.

In essence the requirement was asking you to describe the economic (financial) and non-economic (non-financial) factors that would impact on the pricing approach used by Inspirations. The trick to producing a good answer was to draw upon the scenario detail. When considering economic influences it was interesting to note that there was very little in the way of financial detail in the scenario; however, you were told that the new managing director of Inspirations had set an objective of 'achieving annual revenue of $100m by 20X8. This would be approximately 25% of the total forecast revenue for HC that year, but it is expected to represent only about 5% of the total number of holidays sold by HC'. This little snippet of information provided the basis for one of the key economic influences on the pricing approach, in this case the amount of revenue to be generated.

You should have been able to identify a range of non-economic factors relatively easily by posing the question: If you wanted to sell a product or service what factors would you want to consider when setting the price? Hopefully, you would have considered factors such as competitors' prices, customer affordability, the associated costs of offering the product/service, and type of image/perception intended on being projected by the product/service. You could then use these points as the basis of your answer in relation to Inspirations' pricing strategy.

How to earn the professional skills marks

'Demonstrating awareness' requires you to consider the specific context of a scenario in relation to a particular issue; in this case the scenario detailed HC's establishment of a new business unit to sell luxury holidays and required consideration of setting an appropriate pricing strategy. To earn the professional skills marks it was important that you pitched your work at a strategic level. The fact that you have been appointed to provide advice to the board of directors, and in light of the requirement which asked for a description of a 'strategic approach' to establishing prices should have provided a clear indication that you needed to take a high level view of the situation at Inspirations. Considering strategic level matters such as the new business unit's objectives and mission, and its competitors, in relation to its approach to pricing were what was needed.

Suggested solution

There are a number of influences which must be considered when determining a pricing strategy which will deliver the business and corporate objectives of an organisation.

Mission and objectives

Clearly, the objectives which are to be achieved should form a key element when determining the pricing strategy. HC's new business unit has the mission of 'delivering a high quality service for discerning travellers', and aims to 'achieve revenue of $100m by 20X8'. If the business unit is aiming for high quality, then its pricing strategy should be in line with this, in order that customer perception is in line with what the company hopes to deliver. This may lead to a premium pricing strategy for Inspirations to maintain the suggestion of a difference between the standard holidays offered and the new range of holidays. Prices should be higher to reflect the quality offered. HC must also consider the desired revenue, 25% of total company revenue but only 5% of volume; this suggests that the pricing must be set at a higher level than current offerings in order to achieve this. Price is a key element in differentiating its product.

While organisations may use discounting as an aid to getting market share, a clear objective of HC, the use of discounting, in this market segment, would contradict the desired message of premium quality.

Cost

If a price fails to take cost into consideration, then the organisation may not be profitable and difficulties may arise in the long term. Although organisations have been known to sell products as a loss leader in order to attract other purchases, it does not seem as if this would be an appropriate strategy for Inspirations. It must cover its costs when deciding its prices.

The premium holidays offered will make use of the best hotels, with high ratings and quality features, and intend to use premium airlines and seat options only. These will be costly to the company and should be incorporated into the price. Inspirations could choose to price each individual option on a 'cost plus margin' basis, or simply ensure that the overall cost is covered when deciding the final price using some other basis.

Competition

There are a number of competitors already operating in the luxury holiday market, and Inspirations must consider what it is charging for equivalent services. Given the transparency of information available over the internet, customers may be able to compare holidays and prices online, however, this transparency may be reduced to an extent given the bespoke nature of the holidays to be offered. Inspirations does not own the hotels it intends to use for the holidays offered, and will not have exclusive use of them. Therefore, the price should either match those offered by similar competitors, or they should differentiate in some way and therefore be able to charge a justifiably higher price.

Customers

Customers will have a limit regarding what they are prepared to pay for a particular offering. Inspirations must ensure that its pricing is within that limit for its target customer group. Given that these are luxury holidays, Inspirations is targeting higher income customers. While price competition may not be the main focus for these customers, they will still want perceived value for money. This will determine the upper price they are prepared to pay.

Controls

There are a number of external influences affecting the travel industry. Although it is often the airline or the hotel company which is subjected to these influences, such as local passenger taxes and visa requirements, the holiday company must consider these when determining its pricing strategy. For example, should these be incorporated into the price of the holiday or shown separately? Also, can the airline or hotel companies impose controls on the holiday company, such as a legal requirement not to discount their prices in any way?

Chapter 12 E-business

Activity 1: Accounting Education Consortium

Tackling the question

The requirement did not specifically mention the 6 Is but it is the best way of answering the question. You can generate ideas by looking at each in turn. You do need to make sure that everything is being related back to the organisation in the scenario.

How to earn the professional skills marks

To demonstrate your 'demonstrate awareness' skills you needed to show that you have understood the key drivers of success at AEC. They need to identify the potential customers for their services and then approach them in the best way to encourage them to buy. This needed to be the focus of your response.

Suggested solution

In traditional marketing media, such as advertising and direct mail, the marketing message is initiated by the **supplier sending out a message** to potential customers. However, there is limited interaction with the customer. In electronic media, **the customer plays a much more active role**, for example visiting a website to find out information about a course or seminar.

Interactivity – interactivity is a key feature of electronic media, creating a dialogue between supplier and customer. Usually this dialogue is through email exchanges. For example, AEC could use emails to provide customers with information about courses which may be of interest to them.

However, in order to do this AEC **needs to know the email address** of potential customers, and the courses they could be interested in. At the moment, AEC only collects personal information about people who wish to download study material; there isn't a facility on the website for **potential customers to register their interest** in a particular course, so that AEC can then send them further details about the course, and any special deals available to encourage them to book on the course.

In this respect, the functionality of AEC's website is more characteristic of traditional media (that is, sending out generic messages) rather than encouraging the interactivity which is characteristic of electronic media.

Individualisation – another characteristic of electronic media is that they allow marketing messages to be **tailored to specific market segments**, whereas with traditional media a single message is sent to all market segments.

For example, some of AEC's courses are for non-qualified candidates preparing for their professional exams while others are for qualified accountants fulfilling their CPD requirements. At the moment, AEC has a single website for all students. However, students could be asked to indicate which courses they are interested in (professional exams, or CPD) when they first visit the website, and then the **information could be filtered** so that only parts relevant to them are displayed on the screen, or they are taken to different screens depending on their interest.

The interactivity noted above also promotes individualisation. Once students have registered an interest in a particular course, or for a course in a particular location, subsequently emails individually relevant to them can be sent out advertising courses for related subjects in the nearest centre to them.

Intelligence – because advertisers using traditional media do not engage in any dialogue with potential customers, they cannot use their marketing to find out anything about customers' requirements, and also which products or services are meeting them most effectively.

However, website software allows web owners to **record information every time a user clicks on a page**. For AEC, this would be useful to see which pages on its website (ie which courses) potential customers view most frequently. It would also be useful for AEC to see how the number of visitors to a web page translates into them signing up for a course of study material.

If the **conversion rate from hits (visits) to sales** is low for particular products it suggests there is either a problem with the web page promoting that product (for example, it is not clear to follow), or with the underlying product itself (for example, potential customers are put off by the price of a course).

AEC could possibly even get more customer intelligence by including a **short survey on its website** asking visitors to the site for their feedback, on either the site itself, or the products AEC is offering.

Integration – advertisers can use the intelligence which they gather from customers to add value to their products or services, by sharing the intelligence with other people across their company.

For example, at the moment only 10% of people who view AEC's downloadable study material proceed to purchase it. The online marketing team should discuss this low conversion rate with other areas of the business to assess whether there is anything that could be done to make the material more attractive to potential customers. These discussions could be with the authors of the material to discuss if it could be made more student-friendly, or with the finance department to see if any discounts or incentives could be offered to make the price more attractive.

Independence of location – by its nature, internet marketing has a global reach and so allows advertisers to access potential customers who were outside the reach of traditional media. Moreover, the internet is also accessible 24 hours a day, 7 days a week, so it allows potential customers to find information about a company's products and services outside normal office hours.

The ability to communicate globally may be more useful to AEC for selling study material than selling courses. Although AEC has eight worldwide centres, it is only likely to be practical for students to attend these centres if they live relatively close to them. However, study materials can be sent to students wherever they live.

There are some practical considerations here though. The procedures for booking courses do not support the 'global' aspect of the electronic media, for example, because customers cannot book a course online.

Activity 2: Moor Farm

Tackling the question

This is a very practical, applied question that involves taking account of the feedback you are given and considering specific ways in which the website could help to address these. A good approach would be to work through the comments one by one, then offering advice on how to address the issue.

How to earn the professional skills marks

You will earn the professional skills marks by communicating in a way appropriate to your audience – the manager of the farm. She does not want discussion of theoretical models or vague comments. She is looking for specific, actionable ideas that will help address her issues. You also need to ensure that you use a report format of some sort as that has been specifically requested.

BPP
LEARNING
MEDIA

Suggested solution

Report

To: Manager, Moor Farm

From: A. Consultant

Date: XX/XX/XX

There are a number of ways in which the website could be further developed to address some of the issues highlighted in the survey.

Search engine optimisation

A key problem noted with the website is the difficulty in finding it: 'We didn't know you had a website. We almost had to type in the complete website address before we found it!' If people cannot find the website, it doesn't matter how good it is, it will not do its job. Moor Farm needs to determine what terms are most directly relevant, for example 'moor farm', 'walking' 'hiking' 'rural' and 'Cornaille' are possibilities, and ensure they are included in such a way as to optimise search engine listings. There is conflicting advice as to the best way to achieve this. Sponsored links could be a good approach for a charity organisation such as this estate.

Weather feed

Some visitors have commented that the weather spoilt a good day out. A live weather feed on the home page of the website may help prevent this from happening, so that visitors who require better weather can plan their visit to suit their needs and gain more enjoyment from their day at the estate. Webcams placed at a number of points around the estate would allow visitors to view the estate 'live' and make an informed decision on conditions. The pictures from the webcam could also be supplemented by photos and videos of the estate 'at its best' in good weather conditions, perhaps encouraging people to visit the estate.

Online booking

The estate occasionally holds events, the details of which are provided on the website. However, the stakeholder survey highlighted the disappointment of a family that had travelled 100km to the estate, only to find that the event was sold out. Improving the interactivity of the website to allow online booking and payment would allow families to secure their tickets before setting out. They would also prevent a wasted trip in the situation of the event being fully sold out.

Introducing online booking would also allow the estate to predict demand prior to the event allowing it to adjust the scale and make any alterations as necessary. Cash flow will also be improved as payment will be received in advance.

Feedback

There does not appear to be the facility on the existing website for customers to post comments, photos or recommendations. Such feedback both helps to attract new customers to the estate, and also helps the estate to understand where improvements can be made to better meet customer demand.

The knowledge and enthusiasm of the volunteers could also be captured in the form of a blog describing what they are doing and what is currently going on at the estate. Social networking sites such as Twitter could be linked to this.

Online community

The stakeholder survey highlighted that there are a number of regular visitors to the estate who are keen to know what is going on. However, it would seem they are not getting this information at present. This could be solved via the website by setting up a community which can be joined online. The members will then be sent e-newsletters, regular updates and special offers. A section of the website could be dedicated to this community, and members can access it by logging in to their account.

In addition to meeting the demands of the regular visitors, establishing an online community would provide the estate with the opportunity to build a marketing profile of likely visitors and better understand what different visitors want from the estate.

Conclusion

Development of the website does offer scope to address the issues raised in the visitor survey, and thus contribute to the success and financial sustainability of Moor Farm going forward.

Chapter 13 Enabling success and strategic change

Activity 1: Ergo City

Tackling the question

Reading the question requirement carefully was particularly important as you were not asked to evaluate the drawbacks of the outsourcing arrangement, but were instead only expected to comment on the benefits. Discussing the drawbacks would earn you no marks and would waste your time if you were attempting the question under exam conditions. It was important that you made active use of the two exhibits (especially Exhibit 1), as this provided lots of detail about the issues facing ECA. Understanding the issues at ECA should have helped to make it easier to generate a range of benefits that outsourcing might bring. It was important that you kept your answer at a high level especially as the ECA board is unlikely to have lots of time to listen to a highly detailed presentation. Identifying and commenting on the key benefits associated with the proposal would have been sufficient.

How to earn professional skills marks

The professional skills marks were available for clarifying the benefits on offer to ECA of outsourcing its IT function. Your ability to provide clarity when discussing a given issue is a key communication skill. In this case clarity was needed as there was some confusion among the ECA board when discussing the benefits offered by the Pro-Tech proposal. You could have earned the professional skills marks by focusing on the key points (in this case the benefits) and by keeping the level of detail in your answer to a minimum. The fact that you needed to produce a single presentation slide and some supporting notes should have helped contain the length of your answer.

Suggested solution

Slide: potential benefits of outsourcing IT to Pro-Tech-Public

- Reduction in staffing costs
- Resolve internal conflicts (IT and Finance Department)
- Allow ECA to focus on core business activities
- Gain access to new technological opportunities
- Improve staff morale/offer employees opportunities
- Stake in a new company/opportunities to provide IT to other authorities

Note. Outsourcing could be beneficial to ECA for a number of reasons:

Reduction in staffing costs

ECA has well documented problems in shedding labour as the IT department has steadily grown in size. Therefore staff costs are likely to be too high. Outsourcing would allow demand to be matched to supply and so IT staff costs would only be incurred when needed.

Internal conflicts

Outsourcing could potentially resolve the ongoing conflict between the finance and IT department or, if resolution is impossible, it would at least be passed on to the outsource provider. This would free up the CEO's time.

BPP
LEARNING
MEDIA

Core business activities

ECA has been criticised for not addressing the housing problems of the city. Outsourcing a non-core activity, such as IT, would allow ECA to focus more on core business activities.

Technological opportunities

The outsourced IT provider should be at the leading edge of technology and have highly skilled and knowledgeable staff. This should allow ECA access to the new technological opportunities that the director of IT wishes to explore and exploit.

Staff morale

There is low staff morale in the current IT department at ECA which is partly influenced by the ingratitude of users. In the outsourced company, IT would be the core business function and so it is likely the staff will feel more highly valued and their morale might improve. The outsourced company may provide employees with better promotion and development opportunities.

Stake in new company

ECA will hold a significant stake in the new company and the CEO has observed that is it likely that other authorities will follow the outsourcing route in the future. ECA's stake in the new company may help Pro-Tech-Public to gain contracts with those authorities due to its extensive public sector experience. In addition the new company may bring in income to ECA.

Activity 2: Blue Cherry Mobile

Tackling the question

Clearly to make a reasonable attempt at answering this question you would need to have an understanding of the principles of talent management. As this requirement is effectively asking you to come up with suggestions to improve the graduate recruitment programme to bring it in line with the principles of talent management it is important that any suggestions you make are realistic in light of the situation outlined in the scenario detail.

How to earn the professional skills marks

To demonstrate your 'persuade' skills you need to be able to construct a well-reasoned, counter-argument to a stated point of view. In this case you are told that the Chair of the board wishes to put forward a counter-argument to address the concerns of those directors unhappy with the performance of the graduate recruitment programme. It was important to remember that the Chair's argument is not simply that the programme be maintained but instead how the current scheme could be developed and improved by acting upon your suggestions to bring the current scheme in line with the principles of talent management. To do this it was therefore important that you were able highlight the benefits of the current graduate recruitment programme and to suggest ways in which BCM could get more out of the scheme if the principles of talent management were adopted. This required supporting your argument with facts outlined in the Exhibit.

Suggested solution

BCM's management need to take a strategic view of human resource management. This involves not only recruiting talented individuals to develop new products in the short term but to also provide opportunities for the graduates to develop into the long term. This could be achieved by allowing graduates to make more meaningful contributions to the work of the R&D department. This is illustrated by the leaver who commented that 'I have lots of good ideas, it is just a shame that I cannot seem to get anyone in management to listen to them.'

Developing a strategic view of human resources will require BCM's **management to listen** more proactively to the suggestions of the graduates. This may involve assigning them special projects which are distinct from the main workings of the R&D department so that they can test out new ideas and innovations that they may have. In light of the fact that BCM's graduates are recruited from top universities increases the potential for break-through innovations to be discovered which could be integrated into future phone designs. Addressing this issue is of critical strategic importance for BCM especially as Kiwi Phones is eroding the company's market share through releasing increasingly advanced devices.

Appointing a CEO with a strong background and/or interest in talent management is needed. This is an important step as it helps to ensure that BCM's talent management strategy is led and supported from the top.

The graduate programme needs to be developed so that those individuals who complete the scheme are put to work in more meaningful ways, as at present graduates appear to being placed in unsuitable administrative roles. BCM should look to use these individuals in **coaching roles** so that they can support the new graduate recruits. This would provide them with the opportunity to develop their managerial skills.

Activity 3: Auto Direct

Tackling the question

When attempting the question it is important to recognise that the requirement is effectively formed of two parts. The first part requires you to draw upon your knowledge of Balogun and Hope Hailey (2008), as you need to consider which of the four types of change relates to the situation at Auto Direct. The second part did not require the use of any specific theory, as you were asked to 'briefly' suggest practical approaches for managing the proposed change. Picking up on the use of the word 'briefly' here was crucial as there were potentially a number of different points you could have made. Writing too much can be as damaging as writing too little.

How to earn the professional skills marks

When asked to 'show insight' you need to remember that this is effectively your opportunity to display your understanding of real-world issues that organisations face, such as change management considerations when undertaking a new strategy. To earn the professional skills marks you needed to ensure that your suggestions of approaches for managing the change were indeed practical, and could feasibly be implemented. Considering whether or not your suggestions would be accepted by key stakeholders (in this case Auto Direct's workforce) is a good way of assessing their viability.

Suggested solution

Type of change

The change that has been proposed, while extensive, is incremental and does not involve the transformation of the organisation. It therefore falls into the category of adaptation, which implies that a step-by-step approach which leaves Auto Direct's existing business model and approach unchanged would be appropriate. Therefore, any change strategies need to be consistent with this type of change.

Approaches for managing the proposed change

While good project management of a programme of change is very important, it is the human aspects of the change management process that are crucial. This is because change will not happen unless people make it happen. A number of strategies are proposed for dealing with this aspect of change management.

Participation

Participation in decision making is sometimes recommended as a way of improving motivation generally and may be useful in the context of the change at Auto Direct. It would be advantageous to involve staff in the decisions which will affect them, their conditions and their work processes. Participation is likely to be particularly important as some of Auto Direct's existing staff are expected to have to relocate to the new outlets when established. Allowing staff to participate in some way, for example by being allowed to state their preferences in terms of the new outlet they would be

BPP
LEARNING
MEDIA

prepared to relocate to, may help to reduce feelings of uncertainty and cynicism about the change among the workforce.

Communication and education

Communication with Auto Direct's workforce about the proposed change will be critical to the successful implementation of the change. In the event that the decision is made to proceed, information outlining the change should be made available to all staff as early as possible. Such communication should detail why the change is necessary and the course that will be followed during its implementation. Although the change proposal does not include any scope for redundancies, there is likely to be anxiety among the workforce, particularly around the issue of job security. Concern is common during periods of change, and a programme of communication and education can go a long way to allay it.

Negotiation

Sometimes neither participation nor communication can resolve all problems and some degree of negotiation may be required between Auto Direct's workforce and the management. This is often the case when the labour force is strongly organised. Given that the majority of Auto Direct's workforce are members of the AAU, this suggests that any aspects of the change proposal which the workforce disapprove of may have to be worked out by going through formal channels with the trade union.

Chapter 14 Process redesign

Activity 1: Dollar and Dime Bank

Tackling the question

As the requirement asks you to recommend and justify a solution for each of the three process initiatives, this is a clue that you would need to address each in turn. The suggested solution below deals with each initiative individually. Given that there were three process initiatives and three solution options specified it would be reasonable to assume that each initiative could be matched to one of the solutions mentioned in the scenario. Although no specific theory was mentioned in the requirement you should have realised that referring to the axes on Harmon's process-strategy matrix would be an appropriate way to structure your answer. Using the theory in this way provides a neat framework through which the three initiatives can be considered.

How to earn the professional skills marks

Displaying your judgement requires you to identify the key issues in the information provided and to recommend solutions to resolve a particular matter. In this case, to earn the professional skills marks you need to consider the three process initiatives detailed in the exhibit and then justify which of the three solution options outlined by the project manager would be most appropriate. Simply stating that purchasing a software solution in respect of the integration of the two bespoke payroll systems would not be sufficient. You need to explain why purchasing the software solution would be appropriate.

Suggested solution

The integration of the two bespoke payroll systems

Operating payroll systems is likely to be regarded as being of low strategic importance. Despite this, payroll is a necessary process, even though it does not add any significant value to the end customer. Payroll systems are likely to be viewed as being of relatively low complexity as they tend to be simple and straightforward to operate. As a result payroll can be automated to some extent.

Recommendation

DD should purchase a standard, off-the-shelf software package solution and transfer data from both existing systems to the new one. Any possible issues with transferring the data will have to be taken into consideration.

Updating of all personal desktop computer hardware and software

The process of updating all personal desktop computer hardware and software is likely to be of low strategic importance, particularly as this process is unlikely to form part of the core competences of the bank. Despite this the process is likely to be of high complexity, as DD will need to deploy individuals with the required expertise to update the computers. The need for expertise makes the process too complex to automate. It is unclear from the scenario detail whether DD has employees with the required expertise in-house or not to carry out the update.

Recommendation

In light of the above analysis, DD should look to outsource this work to a specialist technology company.

Development of processes, systems and software to support the new private personal banking service

The development of processes, systems and software needed to support the new private banking service can certainly be regarded as being of high strategic importance. This is due to the fact that DD has identified high net worth customers as an important growth area. As a result this process could potentially be a source of competitive advantage. In addition, as DD intends for this to be a personalised service which requires human interaction and judgement, this makes this a high complexity process.

Recommendation

It is therefore recommended that DD pursue a bespoke in-house development approach to this initiative. The potential for this process to deliver high future profits suggests that it should be given high priority and resources should be focused on this area.

Activity 2: Super-Food Supermarkets

Tackling the question

The use of the words 'briefly explain' coupled to the limited amount of detail provided in the exhibit should make it sufficiently clear that a long answer is not required. Clearly, to produce a good answer you would need to have an understanding of the principles of BPR. The suggested solution below begins with the definition of BPR as offered by Hammer and Champy. Setting out the answer in this way is useful as some of the key themes of BPR can then be picked out in relation to the situation at SFS. Despite this it is important not to overlook the second element of the requirement which asks you to mention the implications of SFS adopting BPR.

How to earn the professional skills marks

In order to demonstrate awareness skills you need to display an appreciation of a 'real world' concept, in this case BPR and how this could be used in relation to SFS's supply chain. In light of the requirement which asked you to consider how BPR could 'improve' SFS's supply chain as well as to consider the 'implications' it is crucial that you are able to apply both aspects in a practical setting, in this case to the scenario detail.

Suggested solution

Business Process Re-engineering (BPR) 'is the fundamental rethinking and radical design of business processes to achieve dramatic improvements in critical contemporary measures of performance, such as cost, quality, service and speed' (Hammer and Champy, 2001: p.50).

BPP
LEARNING
MEDIA

In other words, BPR involves significant change in the business rather than simply making minimal or incremental changes to processes. This is essentially different from procedures such as automation where existing processes are simply computerised. Although some improvements in speed may be obtained, the processes are essentially the same. For example, the local warehouse could use EDI to send an order to the supplier, which may be quicker than email. However, the process of sending the order and receiving the goods to the warehouse is the same.

Using BPR, the actual reasons for the business processes being used are queried, and where necessary replaced with more efficient processes. For example, rather than inventory being ordered from the store via the central warehouse, the supplier could monitor inventory in each store using an extranet. When goods reach the re-order level, the supplier would already be aware of this and could send the goods directly to the store. Not only does this provide inventory replenishment much more quickly, it is also more cost effective for SFS as the central warehouse effectively becomes redundant.

Key features of BPR involve the willingness of the organisation to accept change and the ability to use new technologies to achieve those changes. As a result SFS would have to clearly explain the benefits to staff from using the new systems, to ensure that they are accepted. SFS may also need to obtain additional skills in IT and the ability to implement and use those systems. New hardware and software will also certainly be required. The aim of BPR is to provide radical improvements in efficiency and cost savings. Amending the supply chain as noted above will help to achieve these benefits.

Activity 3: The Institute of Information Systems Architects

Tackling the question

There are a range of options which you could mention to improve the script handling process. However, the IISA's decision to continue with open book written examinations, and not to adopt computer-based assessment, should be noted and reflected in your answer. It is also important to include a reference to the falling number of candidates attempting the IISA's exams and the risk-averse nature of the organisation. Including such points shows that you have made use of the detail in the exhibits. A good way of structuring your answer is to suggest each appropriate redesign option in turn; this will help to ensure that your answer gives sufficient consideration of two distinct options. It is important not to be put off by the inclusion of the process diagram in the exhibit. This is included to supplement the narrative detail provided. You may find that by taking a moment to read the detail while reviewing the visual aid helps you to better understand the stages involved in the process.

To produce a good answer you need to explain how the options you suggest would address a problem with the current script handling process. Ensuring that you consider the advantages and disadvantages associated with each is of critical importance, as the requirement explicitly asks for this.

How to earn the professional skills marks

To demonstrate your ability to 'appraise', you need to consider the facts of a situation, in this case the current process for handling scripts at the IISA, before making appropriate recommendations on how to improve the process. As the detail outlined below the requirement asks you to provide a balanced appraisal of the two options you suggest, it is important that you consider the advantages and disadvantages of these. Clearly, an answer which only discusses the merits of a given suggestion would fail to show sufficient 'appraisal' skills.

Suggested solution

Option 1: Remove the need for couriers

The first option is to essentially remove the dependency on couriers. This could be achieved through the use of a workflow system which would treat the examination scripts as an electronic document. At present all scripts are currently moved three times by couriers, and audited scripts have two further movements, to and from the auditors. Each movement incurs cost and delays, and increases the risk of losing the physical script. If the script was scanned into a computer system (either by the invigilator at the examination centre or by HQ Admin after one courier movement) then the script could be distributed electronically. Scanning by the invigilator appears to offer the best solution, but the technical feasibility of providing high quality portable scanners to invigilators would have to be investigated. Markers and auditors would work with electronic copies of the script, either marking the script on screen or by physically marking a script they had chosen to print out. However, all marks would be entered into the workflow system and so even if markers and auditors print out copies of the script they would not physically distribute it. Markers would have to be provided with appropriate technology for downloading and printing out examination scripts. However, these technical requirements are not particularly onerous. It can be reasonably assumed that markers and auditors already have access to the internet.

Interestingly, because the cost of data transmission is not related to physical location, the IISA could consider employing markers and auditors overseas and this would allow them to address the marker shortage alluded to in the case study scenario. The workflow solution also provides them with a scaleable process which would cope with the planned expansion of the scheme. However, the IISA is noted as a risk-averse organisation and they may not wish to use, or pay the cost of, such a technology-dependent solution. The transmission of scripts across the internet may also raise security issues which would have to be addressed.

Option 2: Relocate markers and auditors to reduce HQ admin

The second option is to retain the physical scripts but to reduce their movement by relocating markers or auditors or reducing the direct involvement of HQ Admin. For example, scripts may be sent directly from the invigilator to the marker and from the marker to the auditor. This would remove one transport of scripts (for scripts not requiring audit) and a further movement for scripts requiring audit. However, such time and cost savings may not be too attractive given the problems of maintaining marker and auditor addresses and availability. It could be argued that removing HQ Admin from this process is very risky as it removes important controls performed by full-time employees of the IISA. Markers and auditors are sub-contracted resources. An alternative to reducing the involvement of HQ Admin is to move the physical location of marking or auditing. For example, the role of marker and invigilator might be combined so that people who have invigilated the examination are also paid to mark the scripts and to submit them to HQ Admin. The process may be further streamlined by inviting auditors to HQ to perform their auditing. These two changes would reduce the physical movement of scripts to one move (invigilator/marker to HQ Admin). Furthermore, this movement would take place **after** the scripts were marked and so markers/invigilators could be asked to physically record their marks before sending the scripts. Hence, there is a fail-safe system if the scripts are lost. The script scanning option does not offer this (unless scripts are scanned by the invigilator at the examination centre). This second option is technically less risky and expensive than the script scanning option and so might be a more appropriate solution in an organisation which is noted as being risk averse.

Chapter 15 Project management

Activity 1: ABC Co

Tackling the question

As the requirement asks you to discuss the 'triple constraint' in relation to the launch of the T4i it is of crucial importance that you explore each of these in your answer. You could potentially use each of the constraints (scope, time and cost) as headings when structuring your answer. However, it is equally valid to adopt a free-form approach as illustrated by the suggested solution below. In order to produce a really good answer you should look to highlight which of the three constraints is the most important in light of the scenario detail.

How to earn the professional skills marks

The 'consider' skill requires you to use the information provided in the scenario in order to reflect upon its implications. In this case, this means considering the implications of the triple constraint on the launch of the T4i. Therefore it is important that you relate the issues of scope, time and cost back to the ability of ABC to launch the T4i, and don't just provide a description of the three constraints.

Suggested solution

The launch date of the T4i has been announced and this therefore means that the project deadline is fixed. This indicates that time is the key constraint. The directors at ABC have heavily promoted the launch and have even gone to the lengths of booking a prestigious private airport venue to host 400 attendees at the product's launch party. Although the T4i will be formally launched on 1 May 20X5, ABC's ability to accept orders for the product is totally dependent on the engineers having made the requirement modifications.

This raises some interesting considerations around the scope of the T4i project as the product at the current time (March 20X5) is not quite finished. Due to the short time frame it is possible that the T4i displayed at the launch party may not quite be the finished item. Clearly, such quality issues will need to be explained to those individuals attending the launch in order to avoid an embarrassing situation where those in attendance are unable to place an order for the product due to the government's restrictions.

To ensure such a situation does not arise, it is important that the landing lights and alarm modifications are made to the T4i prior to the launch party. This will enable ABC to showcase T4i and highlight these new safety features. In order to ensure a successful launch of the T4i, ABC should make sufficient funds available to address any technical deficiencies as soon as possible as time, and not cost, is the key constraint.

Activity 2: Freshco supermarkets

Tackling the question

As the requirement tells you to use the exhibit in order to 'identify and classify the benefits' from the proposed project this should be a clue that you need to carefully read through the information provided in order to pick out those potential benefits which you could then discuss. Drawing on your knowledge of how project benefits are classified (observable, measurable, quantifiable and financial) is crucial as this gives you a framework around which to construct an answer. This is the approach illustrated in the suggested solution, with every benefit considered under each heading.

How to earn the professional skills marks

The skill of using your judgement requires you to identify the key issues in a scenario and to make points which help to resolve the issue at hand. In this case you need to ensure that you are able to identify the different types of benefit from the limited detail provided in the exhibit and are then able to illustrate why you have classified the benefits as you have. In answering this question you need to be mindful of the fact that your classification will form the basis of the customer service director's argument for getting the project agreed at the next board meeting, therefore your answer needs to support this.

Suggested solution

Observable benefits

Are those which are measured by experience or judgement. Subjective benefits such as staff opinions fall into this category. In relation to the situation at Freshco, observable benefits are likely to include improved staff morale due to shorter queues, less stress and fewer complaints at peak times.

Measurable benefits

Relate to an area of performance that could be (or already is being) measured, but it is not possible to quantify how much performance will increase as a result of the change. In relation to Freshco customer satisfaction is likely to improve due to less queuing time but it is not possible to say by how much as this is not being tracked at present. Increased revenue might also fall into this category – more customers may choose to shop at Freshco, but it would be very hard to estimate how many, or how much they might spend.

Quantifiable benefits

Are those where the level of benefit that will result from the change can be reliably forecast based on the evidence in place. At Freshco the improvement in processing time is a benefit that can seemingly be estimated reliably.

Financial benefits

Are quantified benefits that have had a financial formula (such as cost or price) applied to them to produce a financial value for the benefits. Improved checkout technology will lead to faster processing. Faster processing will presumably mean fewer checkout staff are required at non-peak times. It should be possible to estimate the impact of this fairly accurately and so the reduction in staff costs.

Activity 3: The Knowledge Partnership

Tackling the question

A good approach to adopt before starting the question is to consider what constitutes effective risk management. Risk management involves a series of stages (including identifying and assessing risks, and taking steps to eliminate them). You could have looked to use these stages in structuring your answer. However, if you were unable to remember them, it would have been just as effective to think about what you would need to do to manage a given risk. Ultimately, risk management is concerned with identifying the risks associated with undertaking a particular project or activity, and putting in place policies to eliminate or reduce them.

How to earn the professional skills marks

To earn the professional skills marks you need to demonstrate your ability to 'show insight'. Showing insight requires you to use your knowledge of best practice in risk management and to illustrate how TKP and the iProjector project display these characteristics. Central to this is having an appreciation of the wider business environment and the actions that real-life organisations can take to address the risks they face. Simply explaining the term 'risk management' with no application to the commercial detail set out in the scenario would be insufficient to score the professional skills marks.

Suggested solution

Risk assessment

Effective risk management involves a series of stages, some of which are considered here in relation to TKP and the iProjector project. Initial risk management involves the identification and assessment of risk. Risk assessment is largely focused on determining the probability that a risk event will occur and the consequences that may arise as a result.

Risk-management strategies

Once risks have been identified and assessed appropriate risk-management strategies can be deployed. Dealing with risk involves four strategies: avoidance, reduction, transference and acceptance.

Avoidance

A risk-avoidance strategy involves avoiding those activities that carry risk. It is evident that TKP is pursuing a risk-avoidance approach as it only undertakes 'projects in the business culture which it understands'. As a result TKP does not undertake assignments outside of Zeeland. There is no evidence of a risk-avoidance strategy being followed in respect of the iProjector project.

Transference

Risk transference involves passing risk on to another party. This is often achieved through the use of insurance. TKP itself has taken out a consultant's liability insurance policy to protect the firm from claims up to the value of $10,000,000 for issuing poor advice. Due to the inability to assess the likely impact of potential future claims, the pursuit of a risk-transference strategy using an insurance company seems highly appropriate. Although TKP is liable to pay the insurance premiums when they fall due, these costs are clearly outweighed by the benefit and peace of mind that such insurance policies offer the firm's management.

It is also evident that TKP transferred risk in respect of the iProjector project. The developer of the iProjector sought TKP's advice on establishing a worldwide patent on the device to reduce the risk that competitors will copy the product. Due to a lack of specialism in this area TKP referred the client to a company with expertise in patent protection, thereby transferring the provision of the advice to a third party.

Reduction (mitigation)

Risk reduction is appropriate in cases where a risk cannot be removed but the likelihood of the loss occurring can be reduced in some way. In the iProjector project, TKP has identified that the manufacturer of the chip used in the client's iProjector product has been trading for less than three years and has a very inexperienced management team. To avoid future problems resulting from this TKP has suggested that an escrow agreement be established between the client and the chip manufacturer. This is an example of a risk-reduction strategy, as an escrow agreement would require the chip manufacturer to place the design details of the chip with a suitable third party. In the event that the chip manufacturer ceased trading, TKP's client would still be able to gain access to the chip used in producing the iProjector. The nature of this risk to TKP's client is likely to be high as failure of the supplier could critically damage production of the iProjector.

As a short-term risk-management strategy TKP has also suggested to the client that significant quantities of the chip be held in inventory to alleviate concerns over the company's supply chain.

Acceptance

A risk-acceptance strategy is where a potential risk is accepted in the hope or expectation that the incidence and consequences can be coped with if necessary. Risk acceptance is usually appropriate where the likelihood of a risk occurring is deemed low or the consequences of it happening are insignificant or if it is not possible to mitigate/transfer the risk. In the case of the iProjector project, the client is 'concerned that a major telephone producer will launch a competitive product with functionality and features similar to the iProjector'. Although this risk is of justifiable concern to the client, in reality there is very little that can be done to stop a competitor producing a similar product to the iProjector. In such cases the only realistic option here is to accept the risk.

Bibliography

AA1000 AccountAbility Principles Standard (2008). [Online]. Available from: http://www.accountability.org/standards/ [Accessed 4 July 2017].

AA1000 AccountAbility Principles Standard (2018). [Online]. Available from: https://www.accountability.org/wp-content/uploads/2018/05/ AA1000_ACCOUNTABILITY_PRINCIPLES_2018_Single_Pages.pdf [Accessed 14 October 2019].

ACCA (2016a) *FinTech Transforming finance* [Online]. Available from: https://www.accaglobal.com/an/en/technical-activities/technical-resources-search/2016/september/fintech–transforming-finance.html [Accessed 16 October 2019].

ACCA (2017a) *ACCA Strategic Business Leader Specimen Exam 2* [Online]. Available from: https://www.accaglobal.com/content/dam/acca/global/PDF-students/acca/SBL/ S18_SBL_Specimen_Paper_2_Clean_Proof_110319.pdf [Accessed 16 October 2019].

ACCA (2019a) *Examiner's report Strategic Business Leader (SBL) March 2019* [Online]. Available from: https://www.accaglobal.com/content/dam/acca/global/PDF-students/acca/SBL/sbl-examreport-m19.pdf [Accessed 10 October 2019].

ACCA (2019b) *Achieve Performance Objectives* [Online]. Available from: https://www.accaglobal.com/content/dam/ACCA_Global/Students/per/PER-Performance-objectives-achieve.pdf [Accessed 10 October 2019].

ACCA (2019c) *Rulebook* [Online]. Available from: https://www.accaglobal.com/content/dam/ACCA_Global/Members/Doc/rule/2019-Rulebook-effective-1-January-2019).pdf [Accessed 15 October 2019].

Adair, J. (1979) *Action-Centre Leadership*. Gower Publishing Ltd.

Airbnb, (2019), *About Us*. [Online]. Available from: https://news.airbnb.com/about-us/ [Accessed 14 October 2019].

Ansoff, H. I. (1987) *Corporate Strategy* (2nd edition). London, Penguin.

Anzolin, E. (2014) *Nutella maker Ferrero buys Turkish hazelnut company.* [Online]. Available from: http://www.reuters.com/article/us-ferrero-hazelnuts-turkey-idUSKBN0FL2CY20140716 [Accessed 16 October 2019].

Balogun, J., and Hope Hailey, V. (2008) *Exploring Strategic Change* 3rd edition. Harlow, Pearson Education Limited.

Barstow, D. (21 April 2012) Wal-Mart Hushed Up a Vast Mexican Bribery Case. *The New York Times*. [Online]. Available from: https://www.nytimes.com/2012/04/22/business/at-wal-mart-in-mexico-a-bribe-inquiry-silenced.html [Accessed 16 October 2019].

Batchelar, J. (2017) Big data: *A smart catch for consumers at Sainsbury's.* [Online]. Available from: https://www.accountingforsustainability.org/en/knowledge-hub/blogs/big-data-fishing-sainsburys.html [Accessed 16 October 2019].

Baxter, H. (n.d.), *An Introduction to Online Communities* [Online]. Available from: http://www.providersedge.com/docs/km_articles/An_Introduction_to_Online_Communities.pdf.

BBC (2014a) *Fear of failure stalked Royal Mail sale* [Online]. Available from: https://www.bbc.co.uk/news/28263467 [Accessed 16 October 2019].

BBC (2014b) *Mark Thompson apologises over project failure at BBC* [Online]. Available from: http://www.bbc.co.uk/news/entertainment-arts-26016820 [Accessed 16October 2019].

BBC (2014c) *Network Rail boss Mark Carne will not take bonus* [Online]. Available from: https://www.bbc.co.uk/news/uk-30633231 [Accessed 8 December 2019].

BBC (2017) *Executive pay: 'Fat Cat Wednesday' highlighted* [Online]. Available from: http://www.bbc.co.uk/news/business-38498003 [Accessed 16 October 2019].

Blake, R.R., and Mouton, J.S. (1985) *The Managerial Grid III*, Gulf Publishing Company.

Booms, B.H., and Bitner, M.J. (1981) Marketing strategies and organisation structures for service firms. In Donnelly, J.H and George, W.R. (eds). *Marketing of Services*, American Marketing Association. Chicago, Illinois. pp.47–51.

Bown, J. (2016) *Fast cash: The high-speed world of cloud-based finance.* [Online]. Available from: http://www.bbc.co.uk/news/business-36129408 [Accessed 16 October 2019].

Bradshaw, T. and Mishkin, S. (25 August 2014) Amazon buys Twitch to woo gamers. *The Financial Times.* [Online]. Available from: https://www.ft.com/content/82c24782-2c98-11e4-ada0-00144feabdc0 [Accessed 14 October 2019].

Bratton, J. (1992) *Japanization at Work.* London, The MacMillan Press Ltd.

Bratton, J., and Gold, J. (2012) *Human Resource Management.* 5th edition. Palgrave MacMillan Press Ltd.

British Airlines (2019) *Company information* [Online]. Available from: https://www.britishairways.com/en-gb/information/about-ba/company-information/head-office [Accessed 16 October 2019].

Buchanan, D.A. and Huczynski, A.A. (2010) *Organisational Behaviour.* 7th edition. Harlow, Pearson Education Limited.

Cadbury Committee, (1992), Report of the Committee on the Financial aspects of Corporate Governance, London, Gee.

Campbell, A., and Yeung, S. (1991) Sense of Mission, *Long Range Planning,* 24 (4), 13.

Carroll, A. B. (1991) The Pyramid of Corporate Social Responsibility: Toward the Moral Management of Organizational Stakeholders. *Business Horizons* 34:39–48.

Chaffey, D. (2015) *Digital Business and E-Commerce Management.* 6th edition. Harlow, Pearson Education.

Chaffey, D., and P.R, Smith (2013) *E-marketing Excellence.* 4th edition. Oxford, Routledge.

Christensen, C (1997) *The Innovator's Dilemma,* Harvard Business Review Press.

CIMA (2005) *CIMA Official Terminology.* Oxford, CIMA Publishing.

Cleaver, L. Interviewed by: Lazarus, L. *IBM.* (22 November 2016) IBM website.

Committee of Sponsoring Organisations of the Treadway Commission, (2013) Internal Control – Integrated Framework Executive Summary [Online]: Available from https://www.coso.org/Documents/990025P-Executive-Summary-final-may20.pdf [Accessed 16 October 2019].

COSO (2017) *Enterprise Risk Management: Integrating with Strategy and Performance* [Online]. Available from: https://www.coso.org/Documents/2017-COSO-ERM-Integrating-with-Strategy-and-Performance-Executive-Summary.pdf [Accessed 14 October 2019].

Cressey, D. R. (1973). *Other People's Money.* Montclair: Patterson Smith.

Davidson, S., Harmer, M. and Marshall, A. (2014) *The new age of ecosystems: Redefining partnering in an ecosystem environment.* [Online]. Available from: https://www-01.ibm.com/common/ssi/cgi-bin/ssialias?htmlfid=GBE03617USEN [Accessed 22 November 2018].

Davies, E. (24 April 2016) EE ditches foreign call centres – as new boss looks to create 600 jobs and put customers first. *This is Money.* [Online]. Available from: www.thisismoney.co.uk [Accessed 16 October 2019].

Donaldson, G (1985) Financial Goals & Strategic Consequences, *Harvard Business Review*, May issue.

Drucker, P. (1989) *The Practice of Management*. Oxford, Butterworth-Heinemann.

Eco-Management and Audit Scheme, (2019) *How does it work?* [Online]. Available from: http://ec.europa.eu/environment/emas/index_en.htm [Accessed 14 October2019].

Facebook, (2019), *FAQs.* [Online]. Available from: https://investor.fb.com/resources/default.aspx [Accessed 14 October 2019].

Fiedler, F.E. (1967) A Theory of Leadership Effectiveness. London, McGraw-Hill.

Financial Reporting Council (FRC). (2014) *Guidance on Risk Management, Internal Control and Related Financial and Business Reporting* [Online]. Available from: https://www.frc.org.uk/getattachment/d672c107-b1fb-4051-84b0-f5b83a1b93f6/Guidance-on-Risk-Management-Internal-Control-and-Related-Reporting.pdf [Accessed 15 October 2019].

Financial Reporting Council (FRC). (2018) *UK Corporate Governance Code.* [Online]. Available from: https://www.frc.org.uk/getattachment/88bd8c45-50ea-4841-95b0-d2f4f48069a2/2018-UK-Corporate-Governance-Code-FINAL.PDF [Accessed 16 October 2019].

French, W.L., and Bell, C.H. (1998) *Organization Development: Behavioral Science Interventions for Organization Improvement.* 6th edition. Pearson.

GFI Software™ (n.d). *On-premise vs cloud-based solutions* [Online]. Available from: https://www.gfi.com/whitepapers/Hybrid_Technology.pdf [Accessed 11 July 2017].

Global Food Safety Initiative. (2019). *What is GFSI?* [Online]. Available from: https://www.mygfsi.com/about-us/about-gfsi/what-is-gfsi.html [Accessed 16 October 2019].

Global Reporting Initiative, (2016) Consolidated set of GRI Sustainability Reporting Standards. [Online]. Available from: https://www.globalreporting.org/standards/?g=a79fcbfc-99be-47a2-bcb9-400f23a017cd [Accessed 16 October 2019].

Goold, M and Campbell, A. (1987) *Strategies and Styles.* Oxford, Blackwell.

Gray, R., Owen, D. and Adams, C. (1996) *Accounting and Accountability; Changes and Challenges in Corporate Social and Environmental Reporting,* Harlow: Prentice Hall Europe.

Greenbury Committee, (1995), 'Directors' Remuneration – Report of a Study Group', chaired by Sir Richard Greenbury.

Greer, M. (2002) *The Project Manager's Partner,* 2nd edition. United States of America, American Management Association.

Hammer, M. and Champy, J. (2001) *Reengineering the corporation.* New York, Nicholas Brealey Publishing.

Hampel Committee, (1998), Committee on Corporate Governance – Final Report, London, Gee.

Harmon, P. (2014*) Business Process Change.* 3rd edition. Amsterdam, Morgan Kaufman.

Hax, A.C. and Wilde II, D.L. (1999) The Delta Model, *Sloan Management Review*, 40 (2), 11–28.

Haynes, M. (1997) *Project Management.* Fifty-Minute Series Book. Crisp Publications.

Henderson, B. (1970) *The Product Portfolio.* [Online]. Available from: https://www.bcgperspectives.com/content/classics/strategy_the_product_portfolio/ [Accessed 16 October 2019].

Hersey, P. and Blanchard, K.H. (1993) *Management of Organizational Behaviour: Utilizing Human Resources.* 6th edition. Upper Saddle River, NJ, Prentice-Hall.

Hewlett, S. (3 February 2014) BBC's Media Initiative failed because of more than poor oversight. *The Guardian* [Online]. Available from: https://www.theguardian.com/media/media-blog/2014/feb/03/bbc-digital-media-initiative-failed-mark-thompson [Accessed 16 October 2019].

Higgs (2003), 'Review of the Role and Effectiveness of Non-executive Directors' International Corporate Governance Network (2005). [Online]. Available from: https://www.icgn.org/ [Accessed 29 June 2017].

Hsu, J. (2016) *Twitch could be a $20 billion company inside Amazon.* [Online]. Available from: https://www.wired.com/2016/08/twitch-could-be-a-20-billion-company-inside-amazon/ [Accessed 16 October 2019].

IBM (2016) *Jam events.* [Online]. Available from: https://www.collaborationjam.com/IBMJam/ [Accessed 16 October 2019].

IBM (2017) *In or out? Succeeding in the ecosystem economy.* IBM.

IESBA (2018) *Handbook of the International Code of Ethics for Professional Accountants.* [Online]. Available from: https://www.ifac.org/system/files/publications/files/IESBA-Handbook-Code-of-Ethics-2018.pdf [Accessed 16 October 2019].

Institute of Directors in Southern Africa (IoDSA). (2016). *King IV Report on Corporate Governance for South Africa 2016.* [Online]. Available from: https://www.adams.africa/wp-content/uploads/2016/11/King-IV-Report.pdf [Accessed 15 October 2019].

International Corporate Governance Network (ICGN) (2017) *Global Governance Principles* [Online]. Available from: http://icgn.flpbks.com/icgn_global_governance_principles/ICGN_Global_Governance_Principles.pdf [Accessed 11 October 2019].

International Integrated Reporting Council (2018) [Online]. Available from: http://integratedreporting.org/wp-content/uploads/2015/03/13-12-08-THE-INTERNATIONAL-IR-FRAMEWORK-2-1.pdf [Accessed 16 October 2019].

International Organisation for Standardization (2015) *ISO 14000 family – Environmental management* [Online]. Available from: https://www.iso.org/iso-14001-environmental-management.html [Accessed 16 October 2019].

International Integrated Reporting Council (2019) *What is integrated thinking!* [Online]. Available from: https://integratedreporting.org/faqs/#what-is-integrated-thinking [Accessed 11 October 2019].

International Organisation for Standardization (2019) *ISO 14005: 2019 has now been published!* [Online]. Available from: https://committee.iso.org/sites/tc207sc1/home/news/content-left-area/news-and-updates/iso-140052019-has-now-been-publi.html [Accessed 14 October 2019].

Jensen, M.C., and Meckling, W.H. Theory of the Firm: Managerial Behavior, Agency Costs and Ownership Structure. *Journal of Financial Economics* (October 1976).

Johnson, G. (1992) Managing strategic change: strategy, culture and action', *Long Range Planning*, vol. 25, no. 1, pp. 28–36.

Johnson, G., Scholes, K., and Whittington, R. (2017) *Exploring Strategy.* 11th edition. Harlow, Pearson Education Limited.

Kelly, E. (2015) *Introduction:Business ecosystems come of age.* [Online]. Available from:https://www2.deloitte.com/insights/us/en/focus/business-trends/2015/business-ecosystemscome-of-age-business-trends.html [Accessed 22 November 2018].

Kotler, P., and Armstrong, G. (2010) *Principles of Marketing.* 13th edition. Upper Saddle River, NJ, Pearson Prentice Hall.

KPMG. (2016) *King IV™ Summary Guide*. [Online]. Available from: https://home.kpmg.com/za/en/home/insights/2016/10/king-iv-summary-guide.html [Accessed 15 October 2019].

Lewin, K. (1958) Group decision and social change. In Maccoby, E.E., Newcomb, T. and Hartley, E. (eds.) *Readings in Social Psychology*. Holt, Reinhart and Winston. Pp.197–211.

Lush (2019) *Is Lush an Ethical Company*. [Online]. Available from: https://uk.lush.com/article/lush-ethical-company [Accessed 14 October 2019].

Management Today (2013) *Words-worth: going plural*. [Online]. Available from: http://www.managementtoday.co.uk/words-worth-going-plural/article/1037901 [Accessed 16 October 2019].

Manwani, S. (2008) *IT Enabled Business Change*. Swindon, The British Computer Society.

Matten, D., and Crane, A. Corporate Citizenship: Toward an Extended Theoretical Conceptualization *Academy of Management Review* (2005), Vol. 30, No. 1, 166–179.

Matzler, K., Bailom, F., von den Eichen, S. & Kohler, T. (2013) "Business model innovation: coffee triumphs for Nespresso", *Journal of Business Strategy*, vol. 34 no. 2.

Maylor, H. (2010) *Project Management*. 4th edition. London. Financial Times Prentice Hall.

McCarthy, E.J. (1960) *Basic Marketing: A Managerial Approach*. R.D. Irwin.

McDonald, M. and Wilson, H. (2011) *Marketing Plans*. 7th edition. United Kingdom, Wiley.

McGrath, R. & MacMillan, I. (2000) *The Entrepreneurial Mindset*, Harvard Business School Press.

McGregor, D. (1987) *The Human Side of Enterprise*. London, Penguin Books Ltd.

Mendelow, A. (1991) Proceedings of the 2nd International Conference on Information Systems. Cambridge, MA.

Mitchell et al (1997) "Toward a Theory of Stakeholder Identification and Salience: Defining the Principle of Who and What Really Counts", Academy of Management Review, vol. 22, no. 4, pp. 853–886.2.

Monetary Authority of Singapore (2018) *Code of Corporate Governance* [Online]. Available at: http://www.mas.gov.sg/~/media/MAS/Regulations%20and%20Financial%20Stability/Regulatory%20and%20Supervisory%20Framework/Corporate%20Governance%20of%20Listed%20Companies/Code%20of%20Corporate%20Governance%206%20Aug%202018.pdf [Accessed 16 October 2019].

Montanari, J.R. and Bracker, J.S. (1986) The Strategic Management Process at the Public Planning Unit Level. *Strategic Management Journal*, 7, 251–265.

Morse, A. (2016) *Management of the BBC's critical projects*. National Audit Office.

Mullins, L. (2002) *Management and Organisational Behaviour*. Harlow, Prentice Hall.

National Institute of Standards and Technology (2011). Final Version of NIST Cloud Computing Definition [Online]. Available from: https://www.nist.gov/news-events/news/2011/10/final-version-nist-cloud-computing-definition-published [Accessed 16 October 2019].

National Institute of Standards and Technology (n.d). *Baldrige Performance Excellence Program*. [Online]. Available from: https://www.nist.gov/baldrige/how-baldrige-works [Accessed 16 October 2019].

NHS Shared Business Services (2018) *About Us*. [Online]. Available from: https://www.sbs.nhs.uk/nhs-sbs-about-us [Accessed 16 October 2019].

Nike (2017) *Mission statement*. [Online]. Available from: https://about.nike.com/ [Accessed 14 October 2019].

Nonaka, I. and Takeuchi, H. (1995) *The Knowledge-Creating Company*. Oxford, Oxford University Press.

Organisation for Economic Co-operation and Development (2004). [Online]. *OECD Principles of Corporate Governance*. Available from: http://www.oecd.org/daf/ca/corporategovernanceprinciples/31557724.pdf [Accessed 16 October 2019].

Organisation for Economic Co-operation and Development (2015) *G20/OECD Principles of Corporate Governance*. [Online]. Available from: https://www.oecdilibrary. org/docserver/9789264236882en.pdf?expires=1547220731&id=id&accname=guest&check sum=899ABDB29EE10ACC4FCE8EB60C6AFDB0 [Accessed 11 October 2019].

Paul, D., Yeates, D. and Cadle, J. (2010) *Business Analysis*. 2nd edition. Swindon, British Informatics Society Limited.

Perlmutter, V.H. (1969) Tortous Evolution of Multinational Enterprises. *Columbia Journal of World Business,* 1, 9–18.

Peters, T. and Waterman, R. (1982) *In Search of Excellence*. New York, Harper and Row.

Pickett, K.H. (2010) *The Internal Auditing Handbook*. United Kingdom, John Wiley and Sons Ltd.

Porter, M. (1980) *Competitive Strategy*. New York, Free Press.

Porter, M. (1985) *Competitive Advantage: Creating and Sustaining Superior Performance.* New York, Free Press.

Porter, M. (1990) *The Competitive Advantage of Nations*. New York, Palgrave Macmillan.

Prahald, C.K. (2013) *The Fortune at the Bottom of the Pyramid*. Upper Saddle River, Prentice Hall.

Pride, W.M. and Ferrell, O.C. (2014) *Marketing*. 17th edition. United States of America, South-Western Cengage Learning.

PWC, (2019) *King IV: Steering point*. [Online]. Available from: https://www.pwc.co.za/en/publications/king4.html [Accessed 15 October 2019].

Reason, J. (1990) The Contribution of Latent Human Failures to the Breakdown of Complex System. *Royal Society*, 327 (1241) 475–484.

Rummler, G.A., and Brache, A.P. (1995) *Improving performance: How to Manage the White Space on the Organization Chart*. 2nd edition. San Francisco, Jossey-Bass Inc.

Sarbanes-Oxley Act 2002 [Online]. Available at: https://www.sec.gov/about/laws/soa2002.pdf [Accessed 16 October 2019].

SAS, (2016) *Big Data: What it is and why it matters*. [Online]. Available from: http://www.sas.com/en_us/insights/big-data/what-is-big-data.html#dmimportance [Accessed 16 October 2019].

Schein, E. (1985) *Organisational Culture and Leadership*. San Francisco, Jossey-Bass.

Schwalbe, K. (2015) Information Technology Project Management. 8th edition. Cengage Learning.

Smartsheet (2019), *Top Project Management Excel Templates*. [Online]. Available from: https://www.smartsheet.com/top-project-management-excel-templates [Accessed 16 October 2019].

Smith Committee (2008), Consultation on Proposed Changes to Guidance on Audit Committees, (The Smith Guidance).

Tannenbaum, R., and Schmidt, W.H. (1973) How to Choose a Leadership Pattern. Harvard Business Review. 162–175m 178–180.

The Bribery Act 2010. London, TSO.
Attribution statement: http://www.nationalarchives.gov.uk/doc/open-government-licence/version/3/.

The Bribery Act 2010 – *Quick start guide* (2011). London, TSO.
Attribution statement: http://www.nationalarchives.gov.uk/doc/open-government-licence/version/3/.

The Register. (13 January 2017) EE brings 1,000 call centre jobs to UK and Ireland. *The Register*. [Online]. Available from: https://www.theregister.co.uk/2017/01/13/ee_brings_1000_call_centre_staff_back_to_blighty_and_ireland/ [Accessed 16 October 2019].

Thielman, S. (28 August 2015) Ashley Madison CEO Noel Biderman resigns after third leak of emails. *The Guardian*. [Online]. Available from: https://www.theguardian.com/technology/2015/aug/28/ashleymadison-neil-biderman-stepping-down [Accessed 30 November 2016].

Tracey, P. & Stott, N. (2016) Social innovation: a window on alternative ways of organizing and innovating. *Innovation: Management, Policy & Practice*, DOI: 10.1080/14479338.2016.1268924.

Tucker, G. Ethical Analysis for Environmental Problem Solving. Agenda for Action Conference Proceedings. Canadian Centre for Ethics and Corporate Policy. 1990, 53–57.

Tufte, E.R. (2001) *The Visual Display of Quantitative Information*. 2nd Edition. Cheshire, CT, United States of America, Graphics Press.

Turnbull Committee, (1998), Combined Code – Principles of Good Governance and Code of Best Practice.

Turner, A. (2009) *The Turner Review: A regulatory response to the global banking crisis*. [Online]. Available from: http://www.fsa.gov.uk/pubs/other/turner_review.pdf [Accessed 4 October 2018].

Visser, W. (2011) *The Age of Responsibility: CSR 2.0 and the New DNA of Business*. London, Wiley.

Wall, M. (2014) *Big data: Are you ready for blast-off?* [Online]. Available from: http://www.bbc.co.uk/news/business-26383058 [Accessed 16 October 2019].

Ward, J., and Daniel, E. (2006) *Benefits Management: Delivering Value from IS & IT Investments*. England, John Wiley and Sons Ltd.

Ward, K. (1993) *Corporate Financial Strategy*, Oxford, Butterworth-Heinemann.

Weihrich, H. (1982) The TOWS Matrix: A Tool for Situational Analysis, *Long Range Planning* 15 (2), 54–66.

Wind, Y. Douglas, P.S., Perlmutter, V.H. (1973) Guidelines for Developing International Marketing Strategies. *Journal of Marketing*.

World Economic Forum. (2016) Digital Enterprise: how to survive disruption and thrive in the digital age. [Online]. Available from: http://reports.weforum.org/digital-transformation/digitalenterprises-established-players-must-reinvent-themselves/ [Accessed 19 December 2018].

World Economic Forum. (2017) *Digital Transformation Initiative*. [Online]. Available from: http://reports.weforum.org/digital-transformation/wpcontent/blogs.dir/94/mp/files/pages/files/wef-platform-report-final-3-26-17.pdf [Accessed 7 May 2019].

Xu, Z., Frankwick, G. & Ramirez, E. (2016) Effects of big data analytics and traditional marketing analytics on new product success: A knowledge-fusion perspective. *Journal of business Research*, vol. 69, iss. 5, pp. 1562–1566.

Yueh, L. (2013) *Alibaba*. [Online]. Available from: http://www.bbc.co.uk/news/business-22996410 [Accessed 16 October 2019].

Yukl, G. (2013) *Leadership in Organizations,* Harlow, Pearson Education.

Index